CYBELE, ATTIS
AND RELATED CULTS

RELIGIONS IN
THE GRAECO-ROMAN WORLD

EDITORS

R. VAN DEN BROEK   H.J.W. DRIJVERS
H.S. VERSNEL

VOLUME 131

CYBELE, ATTIS
AND RELATED CULTS

Essays in Memory of
M.J. Vermaseren

EDITED BY

EUGENE N. LANE

E.J. BRILL
LEIDEN · NEW YORK · KÖLN
1996

BL
820
.C8
C83
1996

This series Religions in the Graeco-Roman World presents a forum for studies in the social and cultural function of religions in the Greek and the Roman world, dealing with pagan religions both in their own right and in their interaction with and influence on Christianity and Judaism during a lengthy period of fundamental change. Special attention will be given to the religious history of regions and cities which illustrate the practical workings of these processes.
Enquiries regarding the submission of works for publication in the series may be directed to Professor H.J.W. Drijvers, Faculty of Letters, University of Groningen, 9712 EK Groningen, The Netherlands.

The paper in this book meets the guidelines for permanence and durability of the Committee on Production Guidelines for Book Longevity of the Council on Library Resources.

Library of Congress Cataloging-in-Publication Data

Cybele, Attis and related cults : essays in memory of M.J. Vermaseren
 / edited by Eugene N. Lane.
    p.   cm. — (Religions in the Graeco-Roman world ; v. 131)
 Includes bibliographical references and index.
 ISBN 9004101969 (alk. paper)
    1. Cybele (Goddess)—Cult.   2. Attis (God)—Cult.   3. Rome–
 –Religion.   4. Vermaseren, M.J. (Maarten Jozef) I. Vermaseren, M.
 J. (Maarten Jozef)   II. Lane, Eugene, 1936-   .   III. Series.
 BL820.C8C83   1996
 292.2'114—dc20   95-50321
                                                                         CIP

Die Deutsche Bibliothek - CIP-Einheitsaufnahme

Cybele, Attis and related cults : essays in memory of M.J.
Vermaseren / ed. by Eugene N. Lane. – Leiden ; New York ;
Köln : Brill, 1996
    (Religions in the Graeco-Roman world ; Vol. 131)
    ISBN 90–04–10196–9
 NE: Lane, Eugene, N. [Hrsg.]; GT

ISSN 0927-7633
ISBN 90 04 10196 9

CONTENTS

Eugene Lane
Introduction vii

Rose Lou Bengisu
Lydian Mount Karios 1

A.T. Fear
Cybele and Christ 37

Giulia Sfameni Gasparro
Per la storia del culto di Cibele in Occidente:
il santuario rupestre di Akrai 51

Tamara Green
The Presence of the Goddess in Harran 87

Patricia A. Johnston
Cybele and Her Companions on the Northern Littoral
of the Black Sea 101

Eugene N. Lane
The Name of Cybele's Priests the "Galloi" 117

Elpis Metropoulou
The Goddess Cybele in Funerary Banquets
and with an Equestrian Hero 135

Friederike Naumann-Steckner
Privater Dank – Silbervotive aus Nordafrika 167

Panayotis Pachis
"Γαλλαῖον Κυβέλης ὀλόλυγμα" (Anthol.Palat.VI,173)
L'élément orgiastique dans le culte de Cybèle 193

Mary Jane Rein
Phrygian Matar: Emergence of an Iconographic Type 223

NOEL ROBERTSON
The Ancient Mother of the Gods
A Missing Chapter in the History of Greek Religion 239

LYNN ROLLER
Reflections of the Mother of the Gods in Attic Tragedy 305

JAMES O. SMITH
The High Priests of the Temple of Artemis at Ephesus 323

KIRK SUMMERS
Lucretius' Roman Cybele 337

SAROLTA A. TAKÁCS
Magna Deum Mater Idaea, Cybele, and Catullus' *Attis* 367

ROBERT TURCAN
Attis Platonicus 387

J.F. UBIÑA
Magna Mater, Cybele and Attis in Roman Spain 405

Index 435

INTRODUCTION

Eugene Lane

It gives me great pleasure to present to students of ancient religion this volume of essays on Cybele, Attis, and related cults, in memory of Maarten J. Vermaseren.

As we are all aware, the last scholarly undertaking of the late master was his massive collection of evidence for the cult of the Mother of the Gods and her consort throughout the Mediterranean world, *Corpus Cultus Cybelae Attidisque (CCCA)*. He never lived to see conclusions based on his gathering of evidence, although he had in a way anticipated this in his book, *Cybele and Attis*, published in 1977 just as the *CCCA* series was beginning. The present volume endeavors in some way to rectify this situation. But it also gives scholars the opportunity to pursue new avenues of thought concerning this multifarious divinity. It is becoming increasingly evident, that, so far from being a monolithic, unchanging "Oriental" or "Anatolian" cult, as it has frequently been presented, the worship of the Great Mother changed and developed, absorbing ever new components and characteristics as it moved from East to West, from one civilization to another, as well as developing diachronically.

There is as a result a remarkable geographical spread among the topics covered by these articles—the majority of which, significantly, are by women, who seem more interested in this cult than their male counterparts. Tamara Green starts us the farthest east with her consideration of female divinities in Harran, the fabled city of the Mood God. Mary Jane Rein brings us squarely into the reputed homeland of Cybele-worship, Phrygia, but adds a new hypothesis in seeing Miletus as a center for the diffusion of this cult. On the other hand, Rose Lou Bengisu departs somewhat from the narrow focus on the Mother Goddess to discuss related cults of the Kel Dağ near Sardis, and James O. Smith discusses an aspect of the cult of Artemis at Ephesus, a cult in many ways similar to that of Cybele. My own contribution, while retaining the emphasis on Asia Minor, shifts to Cybele's priests the Galli, and introduces the possibility of a significant Celtic contribution to the cult as we later know it. Panayotis Pachis also deals with Cybele's clergy, but this time with a priestess, and is unique among the contributors to this volume in stressing the subjective side of the Mother's worship. A geographical diversion, before we pass on to Greece, is furnished by Patricia Johnston, who takes us to the north shore of the Black Sea, so that we may trace the cult's vicissitudes in that area.

As we come now to Greece, we find that the article by Elpis Metropoulou, while geographically wide-ranging, is centered in that country as she analyzes previously neglected iconographic types of Cybele (and claims for the Great Mother some Anatolian monuments previously thought to be gravestones). But the Greek element is squarely in the forefront of Noel Robertson's revisionist and thought-provoking essay, probably the most revolutionary in this volume, on the Greek Mother of the Gods, as it is in Lynn Roller's discussion of our goddess in Attic tragedy, her affinities with Demeter, and the like—an article which carries on Prof. Roller's distinguished record of publication on this subject.

As we head west, we find Giulia Sfameni Gasparro's article firmly integrating the Hellenistic rock-cut sanctuary at Akrai into the diffusion of the international Mother-cult, not representing an aberrant local religious phenomenon, as some have thought, and showing how this cult paved the way for the well-known adoption of Cybele into Rome in 204 B.C. That introduction serves as starting place for Sarolta Takács' essay on the cult in Rome, with emphasis on Catullus' well-known poem on Attis. Another renowned Latin literary treatment of our goddess is that by Lucretius, and this forms the subject of Kirk Summers' essay, in which he strives to show the Romanness of Lucretius' description. After Friederike Naumann-Steckner takes us on a detour into Roman North Africa, J.F. Ubiña leads us into the far west of the Roman world as he investigates and presents the form which the cult took on in present-day Spain and Portugal.

Two more articles are not so much geographical as temporal in their extension of the survey of this cult: Andy Fear investigates the interrelationship of Cybele-worship and Christianity, and Robert Turcan—while maintaining a more traditional view of the cult, and not adhering to some of the more revisionist theses put forward by Robertson, Roller, and myself—expounds the Neo-Platonic interpretation of the figure of Attis.

All in all, I feel, we have here an interesting variety of approaches to the cult of "Cybele," the Great Mother. In conversation with nonspecialist friends, I always liken the study of this religion to the story of the blind men and the elephant: the one who feels the leg finds the elephant like a tree; he who feels the tail finds the elephant like a rope, etc. Yet if enough blind men feel enough of the elephant, we will end up with a pretty accurate composite picture of the beast. Something of the sort I hope this volume has accomplished with the cult of the Mediterranean Great Mother.

LYDIAN MOUNT KARIOS

Rose Lou Bengisu

Foreword

The religious attitudes of Lydian culture reflect a dualism of plain and mountain, of agriculture and pastoralism. Recent discoveries in the Lydian region of Mount Tmolus have shed new light on the local manifestations of these religious attitudes. These finds offer deeper insight into the local history of the surrounding region when they are examined in the context of their regional setting in antiquity.

The following account of such latest findings is offered with gratitude to the memory of the late M.J. Vermaseren whose dedicated scholarship continues to chart the way for scholars through the vast fields of Anatolian, Greek and Roman civilizations.

I. *Geography of the region: physical and ancient*

South of the city of Sardis, the capital of ancient Lydia, lies the broad mountain range of Tmolus. It stretches for more than a hundred kilometers across southern Lydia from the upper Cogamus in the east to the pass of the Karabel in the west.

The overall topography of this region can be described as a complex, densely contracted mass of high mountains separated by numerous and fertile highland valleys. The Tmolus range separates these valleys by a barrier, twenty or forty kilometers deep, bounded on the north by the alluvial plains of the Hermus and Caicus and on the south by the Cayster and Meander.[1]

* I wish to express my sincere thanks to Professor Eugene N. Lane, University of Missouri, who has generously assisted with his encouragement in the preparation of this work. I am especially grateful to Hasan Dedeoğlu, Director of the Manisa Museum, for permission to publish the sculpture in that museum. In addition, special thanks go to Mr. Wayne Furman, Office of Special Collections, New York Public Library, for permission to use the Wertheim Study and to Uğur Bengisu, who has kindly prepared the illustrations for this article.

[1] Comprehensive review of the history and historical geography of the Tmolus region appears in C. Foss "Explorations in Mount Tmolus" in *History and Archaeology*

The massive range of Tmolus rises to its highest peak at Mount Tmolus proper south east of the city of Sardis, today called Boz Dağ, the "Grey Mountain", and reaches an altitude of 2,152 meters. The Tmolus range has long been associated with the early legends and mythology of ancient Lydia. It was believed to have been the reputed birthplace of the gods Zeus and Dionysus.[2]

New discoveries in the Tmolus region substantiate descriptions by ancient sources. The account by the geographer Strabo specifically describes Mount Tmolus as a *blest* mountain with an "*exhedra*" on its summit, a work of the Persians, whence there is a view particularly of the Cayster plain.[3] Strabo does not mention which summit he is referring to. Until recently, literal translation of Strabo's text gave rise to confusion and speculation among scholars. Notably, interpretation of the word *exhedra* combined with the phrase τὰ κύκλῳ πεδία, which was generally understood to refer to the plains of the Cayster and Hermus, promoted the prevalent misconception that the *exhedra* functioned as an observation-post or watchtower intended for viewing the surrounding plains.[4]

Since the seventeenth century, repeated attempts have been made to locate the remains of the *exhedra*.[5] Recent discovery and confirmation of its location at the very summit of the Kel Dağ ("Bald Mountain") by this writer and Uğur Bengisu now allows a more precise

---

of Byzantine Asia Minor (Hampshire 1990) 21–51 [reprinted from *CSCA* 2 (Berkeley 1979)]; for the asymmetrical formation of the Tmolus range see D. Sullivan *Human Induced Vegetation Change in Western Turkey* unpublished dissertation Univ. of Calif. at Berkeley (1989) 60–62.

[2] Tmolus as the birthplace of Zeus (*infra*); Tmolus as the birthplace of Dionysus, see Euripides (*Bacchae* 461–64) and W. Quandt *De Baccho in Asia Minore culto* Diss. Phil. Hall (Halle 1912) 175–77; the legends of Mount Tmolus are surveyed in Preisendanz' article in Roscher's *Lexikon* (1922), s.v. *Tmolus*.

[3] Strabo 13.4.5. (Loeb) transl. H.L. Jones:

ὑπέρκειται δὲ τῶν Σάρδεων ὁ Τμῶλος, εὔδαιμον ὄρος, ἐν τῇ ἀκρωρείᾳ σκοπὴν ἔχον, ἐξέδραν λευκοῦ λίθου, Περσῶν ἔργον, ἀφ' οὗ κατοπτεύεται τὰ κύκλῳ πεδία, καὶ μάλιστα τὸ Καϋστριανόν· περιοικοῦσι δὲ Λυδοὶ καὶ Μυσοὶ καὶ Μακεδόνες

Above Sardeis is situated Mt. Tmolus, a blest mountain, with a look-out on its summit, an arcade of white marble, a work of the Persians, whence there is a view of the plains all around, particularly the Caÿster Plain. And round it dwell Lydians and Mysians and Macedonians.

[4] This subject will be treated in a forthcoming archaeological survey report by Stephen F. Sachs.

[5] See C. Texier *Asie Mineure* (Paris 1862) 246, cf. 250; E. Chishull *Travels in Turkey* (London 1747) 18; G. Weber "Hypaepa, le kaleh d'Aïasourat" in *REG* 5 (1892) 14 f.; however, most recently C. Foss (*supra* n. 1) 45 f.

reinterpretation of Strabo's text.[6] Analysis of this text in the expanded context of related regional findings, advances the identification of modern-day Kel Dağ as the ancient Lydian mount called Karios, so named after the Carian Zeus.

II. *The cultic connection between Lydia and Caria*

In an earlier study of the region, this author presented archaeological and textual evidence of the presence of the Lydians in the remote, mountainous region of the Tmolus south of the city of Sardis, which surrounds the modern-day lake of Gölcük, with the ancient Torrhebia.[7] The earlier study reconfirmed identification of the region surrounding Gölcük with the ancient Torrhebia and, therefore, the presence on this territory of the ancient Lydian mount called Karios and the temple of Karios who was the son of the Carian Zeus and the nymph Torrhebia.[8]

The definitive description of the region of Torrhebia was given by Nicolaus of Damascus, *apud* Stephanus of Byzantium, quoting the ancient Lydian historian, Xanthus, who states:

Ἐν δὲ τῇ Τορρηβίδι ἐστὶν ὄρος Κάριος καλεόμενον καὶ τὸ ἱερὸν τοῦ Καρίου ἐκεῖ. Κάριος δὲ Διὸς παῖς καὶ Τορρηβίας, ὡς Νικόλαος τετάρτῳ, ὃς πλαζόμενος περί τινα λίμνην, ἥ τις ἀπ' αὐτοῦ Τορρηβία ἐκλήθη, φθογγῆς Νυμφῶν ἀκούσας, ἃς καὶ Μούσας Λυδοὶ καλοῦσι, καὶ μουσικὴν ἐδιδάχθη καὶ αὐτὸς τοὺς Λυδοὺς ἐδίδαξε καὶ τὰ μέλη διὰ τοῦτο Τορρήβια ἐκαλεῖτο.

In the region of Torrhebia there is the mount called Karios and there is the temple of Karios. Karios, the child of Zeus and Torrhebia, as Nicolaus in his fourth book states, wandered by a nearby lake which

---

[6] Confirmation of its discovery appears in C. Foss (*supra* n. 1) *History and Archaeology* 49, Supp. Notes 3 "Mount Tmolus" and *AJA* 97 (April 1993) 318 "New Discoveries". For the *exhedra* identified as the rock-cut throne of Zeus, see Sachs (*supra* n. 4).

[7] See J. and L. Robert's identification of the lake in *Villes d'Asie Mineure*[2], 314–15; *Doc.d'Asie Mineure* (Paris 1987) 308–10; see Robert's last discussion regarding the two series of oracles in Hierapolis in relationship to Kareios and Karios in "Les Dieux des Motaleis en Phrygie" *JSav* (Paris 1983) 59–61, in which he states "dans cette région de la Lydie, Τορρηβίς, il y a une montagne appelée Karios et un sanctuaire de Karios". However, for select review with new regional findings, see R.L. Bengisu "Torrhebia Limne" in *Ege Universitesi Edebiyat Fakültesi Yayınları. Arkloloji Dergisi* 2, ed. H. Malay (Izmir 1994) 33–43, pls. 1–4.

[8] For the remains of Archaic styled egg-and-dart fragments with substantial traces of rockcut foundations at a hilltop site in Ovacık Yaylası overlooking Kel Dağ and the Cayster valley, see Bengisu (*supra* n. 7) 42, pl. 2 and Stephen F. Sachs (forthcoming).

was to be called after him Torrhebia, heard the voices of the nymphs
which Lydians also called Muses and thus he learned music and taught
it to the Lydians, and because of this the melodies were called Tor-
rhebian.[9]

This account, in addition to providing us with important topographic
information delineating the landscape of the surrounding region, identifies an early cultic connection between Lydia and Caria which is
indicated by the Lydian genealogy of Zeus-Torrhebia-Karios-Manes-
Atys-Torrhebus.[10]

An account of a cultic connection between Lydia and Caria is
given by Herodotus. It enforces Xanthus' account of Zeus Karios
whose sanctuary was also at Mylasa and who was a federal god of
the Carians, Mysians and Lydians.[11] According to Herodotus, only
Carians and their traditional kinsmen, Lydians and Mysians, were
admitted to the ancient sanctuary at Mylasa.[12]

Strabo reconfirms Herodotus' claim regarding a cultic connection
by stating ". . . but there is a third temple, that of the Carian Zeus,
which is a common possession of all Carians and in which as brothers, both Lydians and Mysians have a share."[13]

A further cultic connection between Lydia and Zeus Stratios is
offered by Plutarch with a legend of the *labrys*. This relates that it
was a part of the Lydian *regalia* introduced into Caria during the
time of Gyges (716–678 B.C.) and placed into the hands of Zeus,
which can be further substantiated by the coin types of Lydia and
Caria."[14]

---

[9] F. Jacoby *FGrH* (Berlin 1926) 11A,90, fr. 15; my translation.

[10] C. Talamo *La Lidia arcaica: tradizioni geneologiche ed evoluzione istituzionale* (Bologna 1979) 15 f. Prof. R. Gusmani has informed me by letter dated April 1994, "the personal name Torrebos looks like a derivation from indigenous linguistic material . . ."

[11] Herodotus 1.17.

[12] In same letter (April 1994) R. Gusmani mentions ". . . the name of Karios in Lydia could refer to such a religious relationship and to the origin of the cult" . . .
"It seems there is no positive evidence that the personal name Karos has anything to do with Karios, although this possibility cannot be excluded." W. Burkert *The Orientalizing Revolution* (Cambridge 1992) 88 proposes "Once the historical link, the fact of transmission has been established, then further connections, including linguistic borrowings, becomes more likely, even if those alone do not suffice to carry the burden of proof."

[13] Strabo 14.2.23 (Loeb) transl. H.L. Jones.

[14] Plutarch *Quaestiones Graecae* 45. For a general review of the coins, see A.B. Cook *Zeus: A Study in Ancient Religion* 2.1, 561–77, which also indicates the Lydians brought the *labrys* into connection with a goddess who appears on the coins of Mostene and Nysa; cf. T. Ritti "Apollo Kareios" in *Hierapolis 1: Fonte letterarie ed epigrafiche* (Roma

In a discussion of the antiquity of the Artemision in Ephesus, Pausanias mentions that the sanctuary was populated by Carians, Lydians and Amazon women. This may well reflect an early religious kinship between Lydians and Carians.[15]

The continuity of earlier traditions in Sardis becomes apparent in the cult of the Lydian Zeus called *Levs*. He was believed to have been worshiped at an unknown location from Archaic through Persian times.[16] The Lydian form of his name appears on a dedicatory sherd of the sixth century B.C., and on inscriptions from the necropolis in Sardis and from the Cayster valley in the vicinity of Tire.[17]

Local attestations furthermore refer to Persian Zeus Baradates, an aspect of Ahura Mazda, whose statue, temple and cult were introduced to Lydia in 367 B.C. by Artaxerxes II,[18] as well as to Zeus Polieus and Zeus Olympius, to whom Alexander the Great reportedly built a temple.[19]

The possible presence of the Carian Zeus in Sardis, as evidenced by a marble Antonine copy of Zeus found in excavations near the vicinity of the gymnasium, is proposed by G.P.R. Métraux who remarks ". . . the presence of a local Carian god in the Lydian capital needs explanation."[20]

1985) 135, Tav.24b; for the "déesse au nom inconnu" see Robert (*supra* n. 7) "Les Dieux" 60–61.

[15] Pausanias 7.2.1.

[16] G.M.A. Hanfmann *Sardis from Prehistoric to Roman Times* (Cambridge, Mass. 1983) 131.

[17] In G.M.A. Hanfmann "The Seventh Campaign at Sardis" *BASOR* 177 (February 1965) 13, fig. 13; R. Gusmani *Sardis* M3 (1975) 38–39, A 111 2, figs. 32–33; R. Gusmani *Lydisches Wörterbuch* (Heidelberg 1964) 160, nos. 3, 50, s.v. *lev-/lef-*. For the attested Lydian history of modern-day Tire in connection with Gyges, founder of the Mermnad dynasty, see G. Radet *La Lydie dans le monde grèc au temps des Mermnades* (687–546) BEFAR 63:1 16–17; however, see esp. R. Meriç, *et al. Die Inschriften von Ephesos* 7.1, Inschriften griechischer Städte aus Kleinasien 17.1 (Bonn 1981) 213–16, s.v. *Thyaria*.

[18] Hanfmann (*supra* n. 16) 93, 104; L. Robert "Uncle nouvelle inscription grecque de Sardes: Règlement d'l'autorité perse relatif á un cult de Zeus" *CRAI* (April–June 1975) 306–330, esp. 315, which states "Des iranisants ont relevé dans la religion de l'epoque achéménide l'existence d'autels, des temples, d'images." See esp. J. Duchesne-Guillemin *The Religion of Ancient Iran* (Bombay 1973) 6–7; M. Boyce "On the Zoroastrian Temple Cult of Fire" *Journal of the American Oriental Society* 95.3 (1975) 456 f.

[19] Arrian *Anabasis* 1.17,5–6; Hanfmann (*supra* n. 16) 45–46 mentions the discovery of three terracing walls on the Acropolis which ". . . may have been in some way altered to Alexander's temple to Zeus Olympios."

[20] G.P.R. Métraux *AJA* 75,155–59, esp. 157, pls. 35–36; see also G.M.A. Hanfmann, Nancy H. Ramage *Sculpture from Sardis: The Finds Through 1975. Sardis* R2, 106, figs. 231–32.

In 1983 Prof. G.M.A. Hanfmann concluded: " there was undoubtedly a sanctuary on top of Mount Tmolus . . ." and ". . . it seems
preferable to assume that there was an early fifth century B.C. statue
associated with an altar (or series of altars) for the offering of fiery
sacrifices in an open-air precinct either in the city or on Mt. Tmolus."[21]

From among the cults of Zeus local to Sardis, the testimony by
one of the earliest Greek poets, Eumelus of Corinth, who may have
lived during the eighth century B.C., is most significant. According
to Eumelus, Zeus was born in Lydia, *west* of Sardis on top of Mount
Tmolus at a place called Γοναὶ Διὸς Ὑετίου, subsequently called
Deusion.[22] Identification with Xanthus' ancient description of the surrounding region is strengthened by comparison with the textual fragment of Joannes Lydus who quotes Eumelus as saying:

> Εὔμηλος δὲ ὁ Κορίνθιος τὸν Δία ἐν τῇ καθ' ἡμᾶς Λυδίᾳ τεχθῆναι βούλεται,
> καὶ μᾶλλον ἀληθεύει ὅσον ἐν ἱστορίᾳ· ἔτι γὰρ καὶ νῦν πρὸς τῷ δυτικῷ τῆς
> Σαρδιανῶν πόλεως μέρει ἐπ' ἀκρωρείας τοῦ Τμώλου τόπος ἐστίν, ὃς πάλαι μὲν
> Γοναὶ Διὸς ὑετίου, νῦν δὲ παρατραπείσης τῷ χρόνῳ τῆς λέξεως Δεύσιον
> προσαγορεύεται.

> Eumelus the Corinthian says that Zeus was born in what today we call
> Lydia, and he is as reliable as anyone: for still today on the western
> side of the city of Sardis, on the mountain ridge of Tmolus, there is
> place which used to be called the Birth of Rain-bringing Zeus, and
> now with language altered by time is known as Deusion.[23]

Recent archaeological findings shed new light to confirm Eumelus'
account of the cult of Zeus as a rain god on the Tmolus. These findings also demonstrate the accuracy of Strabo's and Xanthus' texts. A
synthesis of the archeological, textual and related numismatic evidence
offers new light on the significance of the Tmolus region in antiquity.

---

[21] Hanfmann (*supra* n. 16) 93, 132. For the coin types which suggest the sanctuary was open-air see T.V. Buttrey *et al. Sardis* M7, (Cambridge, Mass. 1981) 10–11.
See esp. B. Trell, "Prehellenic Sanctuaries on the Greco-Roman Coins of Anatolia"
in *Proceedings of the Tenth International Congress of Classical Archaeology* (Ankara 1978) 119–
20, pls. 37–38.

[22] Joannes Lydus *De mensibus* 4.71 quoting Eumelus. For an interpretation by Prof.
Hanfmann of unusual evidence from Sardis of a second-to-third-century A.D. marble
gatepost found in the Hermus plain, which may refer to the birth of Zeus at Gonai-
Deusion in the Tmolus, see Hanfmann and Ramage (*supra* n. 20) 147, figs. 373–
375; cf. with a coin of Maionia in A.B. Cook *Zeus* 1,152, fig. 125. For the coin of
Sardis which may refer to the birthplace of Zeus on the Tmolus, see Cook *op. cit.*,
151, fig. 118; *BMC* Lydia, 261, pls. 27,6.

[23] Transl. J.G. Pedley *Ancient Literary Sources on Sardis. Sardis* M2 (Cambridge, Mass.
1972) n. 14; cf. A.B. Cook *Zeus* 2.2,957.

III. *Description of new archaeological findings*

Recent discoveries by this writer and Uğur Bengisu on the summit of the Kel Dağ, south *west* of the city of Sardis, on a ridge of the Tmolus range, provide new substantiation of earlier claims.[24] The summit, which rises to an altitude or 1,372 meters, surrounded by a range of foothills and abundant pine forests, is comprised of two peaks connected by an adjoining ridge. It affords a spectacular view overlooking much of the Cayster valley as far as the vicinity of Ephesus (fig. 1). The outline of the summit is dramatically visible from the Cayster valley as well as from the Hermus valley in the proximity of the Gygaean lake. New findings have revealed substantial traces of large, cut-marble foundation blocks belonging to a series of open-air terraces (figs. 2–5). The blocks come from the nearby ancient quarries we discovered on the sides of the steep slopes surrounding the south peak (fig. 6). The course of this previously unexplored *extension* of the ancient road over the Tmolus can be understood in terms of its strategic value.[25] However, it must be particularly regarded as a *key link* in providing direct, easy connection between the temple of Artemis Sardiane in Sardis with Kel Dağ and the temple of Artemis Ephesia in Ephesus (figs. 7–8).

The ancient road starts five minutes south of the Artemis temple in Sardis and leads directly up to Metallon, Lübbey Yaylası, Manastır Yeri, the south peak of the Kel Dağ, from whence it joins Lydo/Persian Hypaepa, Tire and Ephesus.[26]

The double peaks are prominent, bare, and whitish in appearance. They are connected by an adjoining ridge which suggests the appropriateness of this location as a sacred precinct, the form of double peaks being a well-known attribute of peak sanctuaries in the ancient world.[27]

---

[24] Foss (*supra* n. 6). For localization of Kel Dağ, see A. Philippson *Topographisch Karte des Westlichen Kleinasien* (Gotha 1913) where it appears as Gyr Dağ, a variant of the Turkish toponym Kır Dağ, which means "Bare Mountain."

[25] C.H. Greenewalt, Jr. (forthcoming). For earlier exploration of the roads over the Tmolus, see Foss (*supra* n. 1) "Explorations" 27 f. and *Byzantine and Turkish Sardis. Sardis* M4 (Cambridge, Mass. 1976) 115, sources 18–19, which refer to a late antique inscription in Sardis indicating the construction of an avenue with colonnades (ἔμβολος) which led from the *embolos* of Hypaepa until the tetrapyle, therefore indicating the *embolos* of Hypaepa should direct to the gate where the road started for Hypaepa; cf. L. Robert "Types Monetaire á Hypaepa de Lydie" *RN* 19 (1976) 35.

[26] For the nearby Hellenistic structure in Üçtepeler and the important sites of Metallon and Lübbey Yaylası see (*supra* n. 1) "Explorations" 30 f.

[27] E. Akurgal *The Art of the Hittites* (New York 1962) 77; B. Rutkowski *The Cult*

The scattered but abundant presence of Lydian, Hellenistic, Roman pottery and Roman roof tiles in addition to the open-air platforms which span the summit suggest a form of ritualistic activity at this location in antiquity. This archaeological evidence points to the identification of this site as an outdoor, sacred precinct (figs. 9–10).

Further archaeological investigations will determine what the precise functions of the now collapsed remains of adjoining walls had been. The construction is of mortarless, fieldstone masonry and can be viewed below the surface levels of the north peak facing Sardis. The remains suggest a separation in continuity with the nearby open-air terraces which stand in defined relationship to one another (fig. 11).

A select concentration of Roman roof tiles, numerous clay spindle whorls and a mixed assortment of Lydian, Hellenistic and Roman pottery viewed at the surface of the adjoining ridge between the peaks provide concrete, archaeological evidence indicating a form of habitation and perhaps ritualistic use of this location in antiquity.

Conveniently situated along the course of the ancient road leading up to the south peak, an L-shaped cave is referred to by the local villagers as Allah Evi ("God's House") (fig. 12). The inside of the cave is partially lit by daylight as a result of a natural fissure in the rock above. Local stories of various clay finds abound, although there are presently no sherds visible inside the cave. Future investigations may bear out the importance of this cave in relationship to a sanctuary.[28]

Our additional related findings include the intact remains of a white marble sculpture in the archaistic style (figs. 13–14)[29] and a white marble stele viewed together *in situ* at a raised hillside site below the south peak of the Kel Dağ near the village of Dikenli Köy ("Thorny Village") (fig. 15).[30] Subject to further archaeological investigation, the present evidence which consists of various marble architectural fragments surrounded by a concentration of pottery, indicates the probability of a structure, perhaps a rural shrine, having stood at this location in antiquity.

Places of the Aegean (New Haven 1986) 73–78; V. Scully *The Earth, The Temples and the Gods* (New Haven-London 1962) 9–24, 80 f.

[28] The cave as sanctuary, see A.B. Cook *Zeus* 2,1,836 f.; 2.1,249, n. 2; 2.2,971, n. 2; for the cave above Claros, see G. Bean *Aegean Turkey* (London 1979) 158; cf. W. Burkert *Greek Religion* (Cambridge 1985) 24–28; Rutkowski (*supra* n. 27) 46–71.

[29] Manisa Museum (article forthcoming by this author).

[30] For the stele identified as a *pillar* or *omphalos* from which flows the source of the Water of Life, see A.B. Cook *Zeus* 3.2,978–83 s.v. *Ambrosiai Petrai*.

Additional finds viewed in the village of Dikenli include a white marble door sill (fig. 16), white marble sarcophagus cover (fig. 17) and two marble column drums which were found lying on the pine forest floor above this site (figs. 18–19).

The remaining traces of an ancient waterway in nearby Su Çıktı ("The Water Came Out") which is constructed of mortarless field-stone masonry, extend at least fifty meters up to the solid bedrock of the mountain (fig. 20). This ancient enclosure provides a proper course for the cold, clear spring water which continues to flow down to the adjacent fields and villages below. Present-day Kel Dağ still provides water from among numerous spring sources in the mountain.

The importance of this spring within the proximity of three ancient cemeteries and four ancient marble quarries, in addition to the aforementioned findings point to the significance of this water source during antiquity. Rivers and springs were considered the basis of fertility in dry climates and must have been held sacred.

IV. *The cultic significance of water*

The sacred significance of water is well-known to the historian of ancient religions. C. Vermeule mentions "the sanctuary of the particular local form of Zeus was often near a spring or other water source." The combination of Zeus in connection with votive terracottas turns up "at a number of sites from Assos in the Troad south along the Ionian cost to Caria," which portray local forms of Zeus in connection with rituals concerning water.[31]

The cultic use of water, often in the form of a sacred spring, was associated with the cult of Anatolian Apollo[32] as well as with the god, Mên, who was repeatedly connected with water sources in the Lydian region.[33]

As protectress of water sources, lakes and marshes, the local forms

---

[31] C. Vermeule "Large and small sculptures in the Museum of Fine Arts, Boston" in *The Classical Journal* 63.2 (Chicago 1967) 57–60.

[32] For the sacred springs at Claros, Didyma and Smintheion, see H.W. Parke *The Oracles of Apollo in Asia Minor* (London 1985) 2 f., 129 f., 177. Recent discussion of the functions of springs in the context of oracles appears in W. Burkert "Olbia and Apollo of Didyma: A New Oracle Text" in *Apollo Origins and Influences* ed. J. Solomon (Tucson 1994) 49–60; Apollo as an Anatolian god, see Hanfmann (*supra* n. 16) 94 s.v. *Pldans/Qldans-Apollo*.

[33] For Mên's association with rivers in Lydia, see E.N. Lane in *Corpus Monumentorum Religionis Dei Menis* 3 (Leiden 1976) 107.

of Artemis were known in Lydian and Persian times as Artemis Ephesia (*ibśimsis*),[34] Artemis Sardiane (*sfardak*)[35] and Artemis Koloēnē (*kulumsis*). Her sanctuary stood on the Gygaean lake and is mentioned by Strabo as a place of great sanctity.[36]

At Hypaepa, five kilometers south east of Kel Dağ, connected by the ancient road, there existed in antiquity the sanctuary of the Iranian goddess Anaeitis, the Persian Artemis.[37] The essence of her fluvial nature is "rooted in the conception of her as the Heavenly River who feeds, so to speak, all the other rivers of the world." Traditionally viewed in connection with lofty (= celestial), pure water sources, her name Ardwī Sūrā Anāhitā "The Moist Strong Untainted," is grecised as ᾿Ανάειτις.[38]

The deeply religious aspect of the countryside surrounding Kel Dağ in antiquity most assuredly promotes the importance of pure, abundant water sources.

V. *The connection to other cults*

The road over the Tmolus provides a direct link between the temple of Artemis Ephesia, the summit of Kel Dağ and the temple of Artemis Sardiane. This may be viewed in connection with the "Sacrilege Inscription" (340–320 B.C.?) discovered in Ephesus, which reveals

---

[34] For the dual cult of Artemis and Kybele ". . . eventually consolidated to the worship of a single goddess, Artemis Ephesia", see M.J. Rein *The Cult and Iconography of Lydian Kybele* Diss. Ph.D. Harvard University (1993) 47–63. The importance of the rites of "lavatio" in connection with Artemis Ephesia is discussed by Ch. Picard *Ephèse et Claros* BEFAR 123 (Paris 1922) 316–18, 378.

[35] As a "branch" of the Ephesian cult in Sardis, her association with water is certain. In an effort to determine the earliest period of occupation at the Artemis temple precinct, G.M.A. Hanfmann (*supra* n. 16) 49, interestingly reports "Three sondages terminated in a sterile stratum of river-laid deposits, indicating that the precinct had originally been a torrent bed."

[36] Strabo 13.4.5. Hanfmann (*supra* n. 16) 91, 250 n. 13; "Lydiaka" *HSCP* 63 (1958) 73–6 presented the theory that the original Artemis was a goddess connected with a fish cult; J. Keil "Die Kulte Lydiens" in *Anatolian Studies Presented to Sir William Mitchell Ramsay* (Manchester 1923) 252. For the importance of lakes in accordance with fertility rites and myths of early Lydia, see L. Robert *BCH* 106 (1982) 334–52, esp. *BCH* 107 (1983) 484 (= *Doc.d'Asie Mineure* [1987] 296–314 and 342); see also A.B. Cook *Zeus* 3.2,988 f.

[37] The cult of Artemis-Anahita Anaeitis is surveyed by Robert (*supra* n. 25) 25–48, pls. 1–2.

[38] W. Malandra *Introduction to Ancient Iranian Religion* (Minneapolis 1983) 117 f.; cf. Robert (*supra* n. 25) 44–6 who states "Anahita est une déesse de la nature, et d'abord, de façon éclatante, des eaux: "Ardvî Sûra Anâhita, l'Humide, la Forte, la Sans Tache", elle est la Déesse Rivière."

there was an annual procession in which the worshipers of Ephesian Artemis marched from Ephesus to the branch of the Ephesian cult at Sardis.[39] The use of the ancient road which starts five minutes south of the Artemis temple in Sardis can be connected with such local mountain processions as it offers the most convenient route between these two cities as well as an appropriate mountain setting for such processions and rituals.[40]

The Tmolus region is associated with the goddess Artemis, revered as *Tmolia*, whose attested temple was located in the Tmolus range.[41]

This region significantly offers the appropriate mountain setting for the Lydian goddess, Kybele (*Kuvava*), who was worshiped at Sardis by mountain processions and rituals.[42]

The Persians, according to Herodotus, offered sacrifices to Zeus by going up to the *highest* mountains and calling the whole circle of the heaven Zeus.[43] The dramatic, lofty summit of Kel Dağ, as mentioned earlier, is connected to Hypaepa by the ancient road, and can, therefore, be considered as an accessible location *par excellence* for such local rituals.

Prof. L. Robert discusses the continuity of religious attitudes by indicating Hellenistic Zeus Polieus was either absorbed by, or amalgamated with Persian Zeus Baradates. He persuasively argues that a sacred precinct was *shared* by Zeus and Artemis, stating ". . . ce Zeus iranien, dont le sanctuaire était en tout cas voisin de celui d'Artemis, est le même qui fut appelè Μέγιστος Πολιεὺς Ζεύς ou Zeus Polieus".[44]

A conjunction of Zeus with Artemis may be discerned on the basis of the preserved colossal head of Zeus discovered in the cella of the Artemis temple in Sardis, which suggests from *c.* 220 B.C. on, Zeus was associated with Artemis in her temple and precinct.[45]

---

[39] Rein (*supra* n. 34) 73. See G.M.A. Hanfmann "The Sacrilege Inscription: The Ethnic, Linguistic, Social and Religious Situation at Sardis at the End of the Persian Era" in *Bull. of the Asia Institute* 1 (Detroit 1987) 1–8; esp. see "to the Chitons" as a locality in J. and L. Robert "Bulletin épigraphique" on *REG* 78 (1965) 155 no. 342.

[40] For earlier research which suggests the Karabel pass as the most direct and easily passable route between Ephesus and Sardis, see Rein (*supra* n. 34) 73; cf. J.K. Anderson "The Battle of Sardis in 395 B.C. in *CSCA* 7 (Berkeley 1974) 27–53.

[41] Athenaeus 14.636; Ps-Plutarch *De Fluviis* 7 (Pactolus) 5.

[42] See Rein (*supra* n. 34) 72 f. for discussion of these rituals in the context of the Kybele naiskos from Sardis; Euripides *Bacchae* 55,65 for association of these rituals with the Tmolus range.

[43] Herodotus 1.131.

[44] Robert (*supra* n. 18) 321, n. 52.

[45] Hanfmann (*supra* n. 16) 93.

A symbiosis problem, however, arises from an inscription of the Persian era found in the Artemis precinct which indicates Artemis shared a temple not with Lydian Zeus but with *Qldans*, considered by some as Apollo and others as "Lord", "Ruler", "King".[46]

A location in the city of Sardis in tentatively indicated in the "Fountains Inscription" of *c.* A.D. 200, in which a fountain flows from the mystery hall of Attis εἰς τὸ Διός—"to the (sanctuary) of Zeus."[47] Given the wealth of new findings in the nearby Tmolus region this inscription may well be construed as referring to a *rural* sanctuary of Zeus on the nearby Tmolus range.

The new evidence that has come to light points to the existence of an important cult location at the summit and surrounding slopes of the Kel Dağ. Its suitability and accessibility project the positive identification of Kel Dağ as a focal point for the regional cults of Mount Tmolus.

VI. *Conclusions*

The cultic connection between Lydia and Caria can be interpreted in terms of the Lydian history surrounding the modern-day region of Gölcük and Kel Dağ. It advances the localization and identification of Kel Dağ as the ancient Lydian mount called Karios, so named after the Carian Zeus.

Lydian identification with the cult of Zeus Karios provides a broad base for further inquiry regarding the origin of the cult in Lydia and its applied relationship to the local cults of Zeus, Kybele, Artemis, Apollo and Mên. In addition, it intriguingly promotes an unknown, local mythology connected with the Carian Zeus and the nymph Torrhebia, for whom the surrounding Lydian region of Tmolus is named.[48]

---

[46] Gusmani (*supra* n. 17) *LW*, 188, no. 23, line 1, *Qldans with Artimuλ.* "King" is Gusmani's preference. For Lydian Apollo Karios, whose appelative is "King of the Immortals" see Robert (*supra* n. 7) *JSav* "Les Dieux" 61.

[47] Hanfmann (*supra* n. 16) 132, 34. *Sardis* VII.1 (1932) no. 17, 11.6–7: κρήνη μυστηρίῳ ῎Αττει ἐναντία, ἀπόρρυτος εἰς τὸ Διός.

[48] Regarding the disappearance of indigenous names during the Hellenization of Lydia, L. Robert *Noms indigénes dans l'Asie Mineure gréco-romaine* (Paris 1963) 322 states "Les cultes y sont pour tout l'essential des cultes traditionels, vieilles divinités local . . ." and "Reliefs votifs et cultes d'Anatolie" in *Anatolia* 3 (Ankara 1958) 119 " . . . la chose est courant dans toutes les regions de l'Asie Mineure, où quelque antique divinité local, dieu or déesse, est resté le dieu topique."

By virtue of Strabo's testimony which implies the *exhedra* was a work of the Persians, one may accept the context of the Persian Zeus Baradates and Artemis in connection with the open-air precinct at the summit of the Kel Dağ. However, recent archaeological evidence suggests the continuance of an earlier tradition.

The accessibility of the summit of Kel Dağ as an open-air, sacred precinct de-emphasizes the suitability of the inaccessible summit of Boz Dağ, Mount Tmolus proper, which, in addition to being noticeably isolated from ancient roads, is far too remote for practical use.

The summit of Kel Dağ, which allows an unusually broad survey of the Cayster valley as well as an outstanding bird's eye view of the central Tmolus range, was undoubtedly useful for strategic purposes as well as a suitable form of refuge in times of imminent danger to its nearby populace. However, the heretofore held misconception of the *exhedra* having functioned primarily as a watchtower must be reconsidered with respect to its primary function as an outdoor, sacred precinct.

As a key link between the major cult centers of Ephesus and Sardis, further speculation regarding the ritualistic use of the summit in antiquity seems appropriate. Visible from both the Cayster and Hermus, the mountain is *dramatically* visible from nearby Hypaepa as well as from the nearby plateau of Ovacık Yaylası in the vicinity of Gölcük, the Lydian region of Torrhebia.

The localism of Anatolian religion has been well noted by scholars of Anatolian history. Although a decline of the Anatolian element is discerned as having occurred in the city of Sardis during the Hellenistic era, such localisms lived on in the countryside throughout Roman times.[49]

Present-day use of Kel Dağ by the surrounding villages in connection with rain-bringing rites amply reflects the continuance of an established historical tradition. Ongoing inquiry into these local traditions offers the fresh promise of further illustration of a dim past, rarely glimpsed until recently.

---

[49] Hanfmann (*supra* n. 16) 98; L. Robert *Nouvelles inscriptions de Sardes* 1 (Paris 1964) 35, 36, pl. 3.1.

SELECTED REFERENCES AND ABBREVIATIONS

Akurgal, E.	1962	*The Art of the Hittites*. New York
Anderson, J.K.	1974	"The Battle of Sardis in 395 B.C." in *California Studies in Classical Antiquity* 7, Berkeley.
BCH	1982–1983	L. Robert, articles in *Bulletin de correspondance hellénique*, Paris, reprinted *Documents d'Asie Mineure* in Bibliothèque des écoles françaises d'Athènes et de Rome, Paris 1987.
BE	1967	J. and L. Robert, 1967 installment of "Bulletin épigraphique" published annually in *Revue des études grecques*, Paris 1939–.
Bean, G.	1979	*Aegean Turkey*, London.
Bengisu, R.L.	1994	"Torrhebia Limne" in *Ege Universitesi Edebiyat Fakültesi Yayınları. Arkeoloji Dergisi* 2 ed. H. Malay. Izmir.
BMC	1901	B.V. Head. *Catalogue of the Greek Coins of Lydia in the British Museum*. London.
Burkert, W.	1982	*The Orientalizing Revolution*. Cambridge.
	1985	*Greek Religion*. Cambridge.
	1994	"Olbia and Apollo of Didyma: A New Oracle Text" in *Apollo Origins and Influences*. ed. J. Solomon. Tucson.
Butler, H.C.	1932	*Sardis, Publications of the American Society for the Excavation of Sardis*. VII.I. Cambridge, Mass.
Buttrey, T.V.	1981	T.V. Buttrey, A. Johnston, R. MacKenzie and M. Bates, *Greek, Roman, and Islamic Coins from Sardis*. Sardis Monograph 7. Cambridge, Mass.
Chisull, E.	1747	*Travels in Turkey*. London.
Cook, A.B.	1964–65	*Zeus: A Study in Ancient Religion*. Cambridge. (Reprint).
Foss, C.	1976	*Byzantine and Turkish Sardis*, Sardis Monograph 4. Cambridge, Mass.
	1978	"Explorations in Mount Tmolus" *California Studies in Classical Antiquity* 2. Berkeley. Reprinted in *History and Archaeology of Byzantine Asia Minor*. 1990.
	1993	"New Discoveries on Mount Tmolus" in *American Journal of Archaeology* 97.
Gusmani, R.	1964	*Lydisches Wörterbuch*. Heidelberg.
	1975	*Neue Epichorische Schriftzeugnisse aus Sardis* (1958–1971). Sardis Monograph 3. Cambridge, Mass.
Hanfmann, G.M.A.	1958	"Lydiaka" in *Harvard Studies in Classical Philology* 63. Cambridge, Mass.
	1965	"The Seventh Campaign at Sardis" in *Bulletin of the American Schools of Oriental Research*. 177. Jerusalem—Baghdad.
	1983	*Sardis from Prehistoric to Roman Times*. Cambridge, Mass.
	1987	"The Sacrilege Inscription: The Ethnic,

		Linguistic, Social and Religious Situation at Sardis at the End of the Persian Era" in *Bulletin of the Asia Institute 1* Detroit.
Hanfmann, G.M.A. and Nancy H. Ramage	1975	*Sculpture From Sardis: The Finds Through* 1975. Sardis Report 2. Cambridge, Mass.
Keil, J.	1923	"Die Kulte Lydians" in *Anatolian Studies Presented to Sir William Mitchell Ramsay*. Manchester.
Lane, E.N.	1976	*Corpus Monumentorum Religionis Dei Menis 3*. Leiden.
Meriç, R.	1981	Recep Meriç, Reinhold Merkelbach, Johannes Nollé and Sencer Sahin, *Die Inschriften von Ephesos* 7.1 in Inschriften griechischer Städte aus Kleinasien 17.1. Bonn.
Métraux, G.P.R.	1971	"A New Head of Zeus from Sardis" in *American Journal of Archaeology* 75.
Pedley, J.G.	1972	*Ancient Literary Sources on Sardis*. Sardis Monograph 2. Cambridge, Mass.
Philippson, A.	1913	*Topographische Karte des westlichen Kleinasien*. Gotha.
Picard, Ch.	1922	*Ephèse et Claros* in Bibliothèque des écoles française d'Athènes et de Rome 123. Paris.
Preisendanz, K.	1922	"Tmolus" in W.H. Roscher *Ausführliches Lexikon der griechischen und römischen Mythologie*. Leipzig.
Quandt, W.	1912	*De Baccho in Asia Minore culto*. Dissertationes Philogicae Hallenses 24. Halle.
Radet, G.	1967	*La Lydie dans le monde grec au temps des Mermnades* in Bibliothèque des écoles françaises d'Athènes et de Rome 63:1. Rome (Reprint of Paris 1893 edition).
Rein, M.J.	1993	*The Cult and Iconography of Lydian Kybele*. Dissertation Ph.D Harvard University. Cambridge, Mass.
Ritti, T.	1985	"Apollo Kareios" in *Hierapolis 1. Fonte letteraire ad epigrafiche*. Roma.
Robert, R.	1958	"Reliefs votifs et cultes d'Anatolia" in *Anatolia* (Dil ve Tarih Coğrafya Fakültesi) 3. Ankara.
	1962	*Villes d'Asie Mineure²*. Paris.
	1963	*Noms indigènes dans l'Asie Mineure gréco-romaine 1*. Paris.
	1964	*Nouvelles inscriptions de Sardes 1*. Paris.
	1975	"Un nouvelle inscription grecque de Sardes: Règlement de l'authorité perse relatif à un culte de Zeus." in *Comptes rendus des séances de l'Académie des inscriptions et belles-lettres*. Paris.
	1976	"Types Monétaires à Hypaepa de Lydie" in *Revue numismatique* 19. Paris.
	1983	"Les Dieux des Motaleis en Phrygie" in *Journal des savants*. Paris.
Rutkowski, B.	1986	*The Cult Places of the Aegean*. New Haven.

Scully, V.	1962	*The Earth, The Temples and the Gods*. New Haven.
Talamo, C.	1979	*La Lidia arcaica: tradizione geneologische ed evoluzione istituzionale*. Bologna.
Texier, C.	1862	*Asie Mineure*. Paris.
Trell, B.	1978	"Prehellenic Sanctuaries on the Greco-Roman Coins of Anatolia" in *Proceedings of the Tenth International Congress of Classical Archaeology*. Ankara.
Vermeule, C.	1967	"Large and small sculptures in the Museum of Fine Arts, Boston." in *The Classical Journal* 63.2 Chicago.
Weber, G.	1892	"Hypaepa, le kaleh d'Aïasourat" in *Revue des études grecques* 5. Paris.

Figure 1. View of north peak facing Sardis

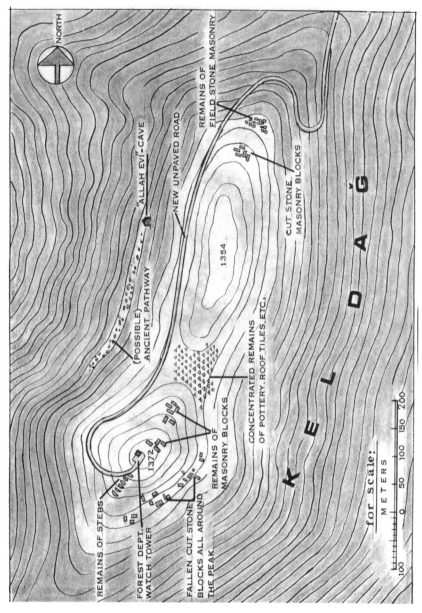

Figure 2. Map of the summit

Figure 3. Reconstructed bird's-eye view of Kel Dağ in antiquity

ROSE LOU BENGISU

Figure 4. Reconstructed view of the terraces at the north side of the main peak in antiquity

Figure 5. Marble blocks at the north, upper terrace

Figure 6. View of the main quarry below the summit with author seated

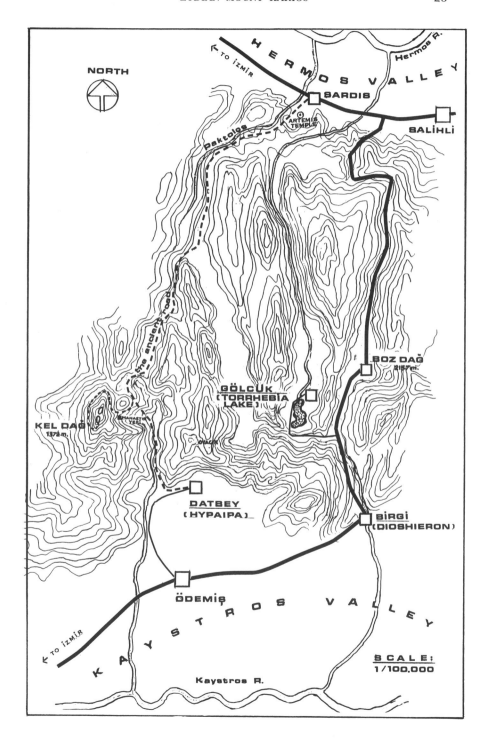

Figure 7. Map of the Central Tmolus, Kel Dağ and the ancient road

Figure 8. Ancient, paved road leading to the summit

Figure 9. Selection of Lydian, Hellenistic and Roman sherds from the summit

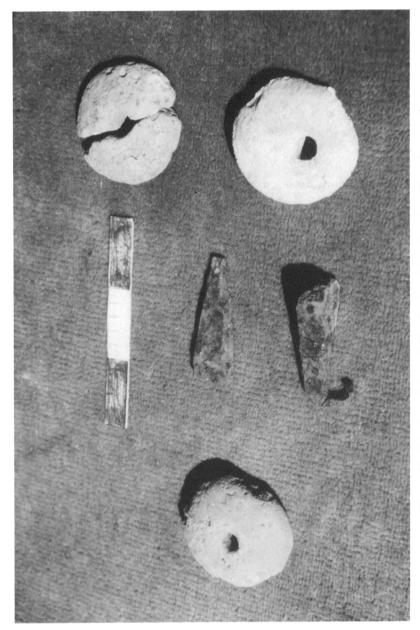

Figure 10. Selection of clay spindle whorls and metal anchors from the summit

Figure 11. Fieldstone masonry remains at north, lower terrace

Figure 12. Entrance to the cave below the summit

Figure 13. Frontal view of the marble sculpture in Dikenli

Figure 14. Rear view of the same sculpture

Figure 15. Marble stele in Dikenli

Figure 16. Marble door sill in Dikenli

Figure 17. Marble sarcophagus cover in Dikenli

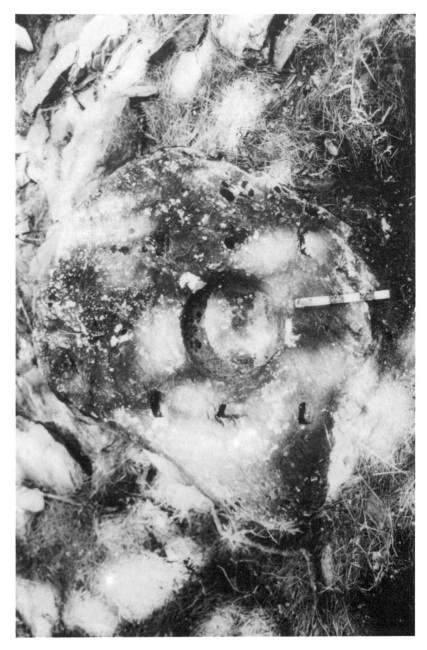

Figure 18. Marble column drum in situ above Dikenli

Figure 19. Marble column drum in situ above Dikenli

Figure 20. Entrance to the ancient waterway in Su Çıktı

CYBELE AND CHRIST

A.T. Fear

"Et ipse pileatus christianus est": thus a priest of Attis to St. Augustine in defence of his religion.[1] St. Augustine's reaction to this rather curious remark was one of disgust and contempt, but also of alarm: "it is only this way they can seduce Christians". Nor was he alone in his dislike of the metroac cult. Firmicus Maternus after writing an expose of the rites of Attis and Cybele concluded darkly "therefore the devil too has his christs"[2] and St. Jerome promptly reversed Cybele's cult title of *Mater Deorum* into that of *Mater Daemoniorum*.[3]

Both sides in this dispute could be seen as doing nothing more than engaging in a skirmish in the long battle fought out between paganism and Christianity in late antiquity. The priest's plea could have been that of the syncretist in general—arguing that both Christ and Attis are merely different manifestations of the same principle. While such an attitude is alien to a monotheist religious climate, it would have been more than familiar in late antiquity. A fourth-century account of Alexander Severus, for example, saw nothing incongruous in portraying the emperor venerating Jesus in his private chapel alongside Moses, Orpheus, Apollonius of Tyana, and his ancestors.[4] St. Augustine himself tells us of another pagan, Marius Victorinus, who could not see why espousing Christianity necessarily meant abandoning his other objects of worship.[5] On the other hand, the Christian authors cited above could be seen as simply re-iterating the Christian claim that pagan gods were in fact nothing but demons.

However the strength of the Christian attack on the metroac cult might suggest that more was at stake here. Mystery religions in general were not a focus of Christian polemic; Attis and Cybele on the other hand appear to have been a favourite target for the invective of Christian writers. Some have seen the attack going back to the

---

[1] *In Ioh.evang.* tract.7.6. Is there an insulting pun on Pilatus here?
[2] "habet ergo diabolus christos suos", *De Errore prof.rel.*22.3.
[3] *Adv.Iovinian.* II.17; *in Hoseam* I.4.14.
[4] *S.H.A. Alexander Severus* 29.
[5] St. Augustine, *Confessions* 8.2.3–5.

earliest days of Christianity interpreting the Whore of Babylon of Revelation 17.3–6 as a veiled depiction of Cybele.[6]

One approach for explaining why we find such a concentrated attack on the metroac cult would be to seek the answer in the structure of early Christian polemic. One of the standard sources used by Christian apologists to ridicule the beliefs of their opponents was the work of earlier pagan mythographers. St. Augustine's extensive use of Varro is a good example of this technique. The practices attacked are frequently those of early rather than contemporary paganism.[7] Unlike most mystery religions the metroac cult had arrived in Rome early in her history. It could be argued that this early arrival in Rome meant that archaic material on the cult was available for Christian polemicists in a way in which it was not for other sects. Were this the case the number of attacks on Cybele and Attis could be seen as a product of the sorts of source material available to Christian writers rather than any especially marked antipathy on their part towards the metroac cult. However this solution, while superficially attractive, is flawed. Early Roman antiquarian writers such as Varro were interested in early Italian religious practice, not all religious observances performed by their ancestors. As such it is extremely unlikely that they would have provided copious materials for later writers on the subject of Cybele. Christian antipathy to Cybele therefore cannot be explained as an accident of history.

If this literary explanation is unsatisfactory what others are available? Pragmatic considerations need to be examined. Clearly a popular pagan cult, which the metroac cult indubitably was, would be more likely to suffer denunciation than a smaller obscure one as it would have been seen as a more serious rival. However this in itself will not explain the venom and persistence of the attacks. One solution which immediately presents itself is the possibility that the metroac cult was seen as more threatening to Christianity than other pagan religions. Both St. Augustine and Firmicus Maternus dwell on the seductive nature of the cult and the danger they perceive is the nearness of its rituals to those of the Christian church.

St. Augustine's worries may have been justified. The cluster of heresies known normally referred to as "Montanist" in modern writ-

---

[6] P. Touilleux, *L'Apocalypse et des cultes de Domitien et de Cybèle* (Paris, 1935).

[7] See also Arnobius who frequently attacks early Roman religious belief rather than the paganism of his own day, e.g. *Adv.Nat.*5.1.

ing, but standardly called "Cataphrygian" in antiquity were possibly influenced by the cult of Cybele. St. Jerome accused Montanus of being a eunuch like the priests of Attis.[8] Such an accusation of course could simply be an insult based on the fact that the cult of Cybele originated from the same area as the heresy. Nevertheless it is interesting that Tertullian in his Montanist period angrily denies the accusation, made by orthodox Christians, that the fasting of the sect is a borrowing from the rites of Cybele.[9]

What were these perceived similarities? Like Christianity, the cult of Cybele promised immortality and resurrection. In both cases this promise came as a result of an act of sacrifice and death. For the Christian this was Christ's offering himself as the sacrificial Lamb at Calvary; in the case of acolytes of Cybele redemption came through the blood shed in the *taurobolium* ritual, and through the figure of the shepherd god Attis who became an increasingly prominent part of the cult in later antiquity.[10]

The youthful Attis after his murder was miraculously brought to life again three days after his demise. The celebration of this cycle of death and renewal was one of the major festivals of the metroac cult. Attis therefore represented a promise of reborn life and as such it is not surprising that we find representations of the so-called mourning Attis as a common tomb motif in the ancient world.[11]

The parallelism, albeit at a superficial level, between this myth and the account of the resurrection of Christ is clear.[12] Moreover Attis as a shepherd occupies a favourite Christian image of Christ as the good shepherd.[13] Further parallels also seem to have existed: the pine tree of Attis, for example, was seen as a parallel to the cross of Christ.[14]

---

[8] St. Jerome, *Ep*.41 "abscisum et semivirum . . . Montanum"; cf. W.H.C. Frend, *The Rise of Christianity* (London, 1984) 253 for the hypothesis that Montanus was "perhaps a one-time priest of Cybele".

[9] Tertullian, *De Ieiunio* 2.4,16.7.

[10] Cybele too had always held out some sort of promise against death, see *CIL* 2.57* from Idanha a Velha, Portugal.

[11] Two examples which spring to mind are the Attis figures found on the so-called Torre de los Escipiones near Tarragona in Catalonia.

[12] Echoes of it exist in our own times. See G. Seferis, "often when I go to the Good Friday service it is difficult for me to decide whether the god being buried is Attis or Christ", *Dokimes* B.14.

[13] See the depiction of Christ as the Good Shepherd on a fresco in the Crypt of Lucina, the Catacomb of St. Callixtus dating to the early third century A.D. and on the mosaics from the early fourth century mausoleum at Centcelles.

[14] Firmicus Maternus, *De Errore prof.rel*.27.1, cf. Arnobius, *Adv.Nat*.5.17. For St. Martin's possible encounter with a pine belonging to the metroac cult see Sulpicius

Beyond Attis himself, Cybele too offered a challenge to Christian divine nomenclature. Cybele was regarded as a virgin goddess and as such could be seen as a rival to the Virgin Mary.[15] By the fourth century the title Mother of God, theotokos, was commonly given to Mary by Christians;[16] Cybele as the mother of the Gods, *mater Deum*, here again presented a starkly pagan parallel to the Christian Mother of God.

There was rivalry too in ritual. The climax of the celebration of Attis' resurrection, the *Hilaria*, fell on the 25th March, the date that the early church had settled on as the day of Christ's death.[17] Once again the closeness of the dates and the fact that the metroac festival of resurrection would fall on the date of Christ's execution both threw down a psychological challenge in itself and may well have undercut the Christian celebration of the resurrection of Christ in the public mind.

Other metroac rituals can be seen to parallel Christianity in form as well as symbolic meaning. The *taurobolium* which involved the aspersion of the initiate in the blood of the sacrificed bull was seen as a counterpart to the Christian baptism by immersion in water.[18] A ritual meal also seems to have been regular feature of the cult.[19] A further parallel appears to have been fasting, which, as the accusations made against the Montanists mentioned above show, was both a controversial issue in early Christianity and an aspect of the metroac devotions. Proclus in the course of his worship of Cybele underwent a monthly fast.[20]

The exact relationship of the parallels between the two groups is highly problematic. One strand in the history of religion has sought to see Christian ritual as simply a variation on the theme of pagan mystery cults: in other words to see Christianity as just another mystery cult, albeit one which through imperial patronage eclipsed in the course of time all others. Such a view however becomes untenable when examined closely; the two groups have strikingly different agendas.[21]

Severus, *Vit.Martini* 13. For the "tree" of Christ see *Galatians* 3.13 and *1 Peter* 3.24.

[15] See Julian, *Hymn to the Mother of the Gods*, 166b; St. Augustine, *Civitas Dei* 2.26.

[16] Julian, *Against the Galilaeans* 262D.

[17] Computus pseudocyprianus (ed. Lersch) *Chronologie* 2.61.

[18] Firmicus Maternus, *De Errore prof.rel.*27.8.

[19] Clement of Alexandria, *Protr.*2.15; Firmicus Maternus, *De Errore prof.rel.*18.1.

[20] Marinus, *Vit.Procli* 19.

[21] For a casual assumption that Christianity was a mystery cult see H. Trevor-

Precisely the opposite position was held by early Christian writers such as St. Augustine: they believed that it was pagan ritual that had based itself upon Christian practice. The hand of the devil was frequently detected being the inspiration for such imitation.[22]

Were the early Christians any more justified in making these allegations than those who assert Christianity was derivative of paganism? Vermaseren believes that much of what was perceived was merely in the eye of the Christian beholder (which is not of course to question the sincerity of the belief), and notes that our knowledge of metroac ritual is mainly derived from early Christian sources which inevitably discuss the conflict in terminology supportive of their position.[23] The frequency of attacks on the cult are explained by seeing it as offering a particularly easy target, especially in the case of Attis, for a triumphant Christianity on the offensive against paganism.[24]

However in favour of St. Augustine's position is the fact that the metroac cult did modify itself in significant ways with the passing of the years. The *taurobolium* appears as a late feature of the cult, being introduced into the rites of Cybele only in c. A.D. 160.[25] Moreover, at first far from being the redemptive ceremony graphically described by Prudentius,[26] it appears to have been a normal sacrifice of a bull for the well-being initially of the emperor and then for the provider of the sacrificial animal. It was only in c. A.D. 300, a time when the conflict between Christianity and paganism was reaching a head, that the term was used to describe a ceremony involving a baptism of blood.[27] Attis too with his strong emphasis on resurrection seems to be a late-comer to the cult;[28] the stress on the *Hilaria* as celebrating

---

Roper, *The Rise of Christian Europe* (London, 1965) 58. A scathing and cogent denunciation of this approach is found in B. Metzger, "Considerations of methodology in the study of the mystery religions and early Christianity", HTR 48 (1955) 1–20.

[22] Tertullian, *De ieiunio* 16 "quam diabolus divinorum aemulator imitatur".

[23] M. Vermaseren, *Cybele and Attis* (London, 1977) 180 "All the same many scholars have attempted to draw a parallel with Christianity, especially with respect to the March ceremonies. This is chiefly due to the early-Christian writers themselves". For a stronger denial which asserts the primitive church borrowed from pagan mysteries see A. Loisy, *Les mystères païens et le mystère chrétien* (Paris, 1930).

[24] M. Vermaseren, *op. cit.,* 180.

[25] For an in-depth study of this aspect of the metroac cult see R. Duthoy, *The Taurobolium* (Leiden, 1969).

[26] *Peristephanon Martyrorum* 10.1006–1050.

[27] e.g. *CIL* 14.42 from Ostia dating A.D. 251–3.

[28] Dionysius of Halicarnassus (*Roman Antiquities* 2.19) found no trace of the cult of Attis in Rome in his day. For a general discussion of Attis' relationship with the cult of Cybele see G. Showerman, "Was Attis at Rome under the Republic?", *Transactions*

the resurrection of Attis also appears to increase at the beginning of
the fourth century A.D.: the same time as the change in the *taurobolium*
towards being a rite of personal redemption occurred.[29]

While these changes could simply be the mutation of a religion
over time, and it is important to remember that here we are discussing a period of centuries not merely of years, they do seem to have
been provoked by a need to respond to the challenge of Christianity.
This is not in itself however enough to demonstrate that such change
was intentional; religions change to meet contemporary needs and
the alterations in the rituals accorded to Cybele could have been a
phenomenon of this sort. However was this process a gradual and
unconscious one? One factor which suggests that this might not have
been the case is the highly prominent place that the cult came to
occupy in the self-conscious intellectual defence of paganism in late
antiquity.

Polybius in the second century B.C. had asked his audience rhetorically who could be intellectually so idle as not to want to discover how Rome had risen to dominate the world.[30] A similar sort
of question with regard to Christianity must have haunted the minds
of many pagans in the fourth century. Their answer to this problem
seems to have been that Christianity had fundamentally changed the
religious agenda of their society and that this change had to be
confronted on its own ground. The defence of paganism consequently
mounted appears, in part, to have been an attempt to create an
"anti-christianity"—a systematised pagan theology which would counter
Christian doctrine (which, however crude it was said to be by pagans,[31] was clearly shaping the pattern of religious thought at the
time) in those areas where it seemed to have most attraction.

Although the notion of a "created" religion seems odd to modern
eyes, it was not unknown in antiquity. The recent work of Ulansey
has attempted to demonstrate how another mystery cult, that of
Mithras, may well have been such an intellectual construct which
used an old form of Near Eastern religion for new purposes.[32] Ptolemy
I's creation of the popular cult of Serapis provides another example

of the American Philological Society 31 (1900) 46–59, H. Hepding, *Attis, seine Mythen und
sein Kult* (Giessen, 1903) 143 ff. and H. Graillot, *Le Culte de Cybèle* (Paris, 1912) 71 ff.
[29] M. Vermaseren, *Cybele and Attis* (London, 1977) 123.
[30] Polybius, 1.1.
[31] See Origen, *Contra Celsum* 6.1–2.
[32] D. Ulansey, "Mithraic Studies: a paradigm shift?", *Religious Studies Review* 13

of this process. The modern period provides countless examples of cults developed out of Christianity and other major religions, though perhaps a closer parallel to the suggested process here would be the late renaissance construct of "speculative" freemasonry from the initiation ceremonies of "operative" stone masons.

It is easy to see how an adaptation of the Cybele cult would have been attractive to pagan intellectuals. Fertility cults were widespread in antiquity; this would give a rejuvenated metroac cult both a broad-based appeal via syncretism while retaining a form of unity with which to counter Christian worship.[33] Allegorical readings of metroac mythology allowed the cult to be integrated into the popular cult of *Sol Invictus*. Attis became emblematic of the sun god, and Cybele of mother earth.[34]

Cybele also had several other potential advantages in the battle against Christ. Unlike Christianity, the metroac cult was indubitably old, venerability being much valued as mark of validity in antiquity. Moreover, Christianity also laboured under the problem of being "new" and was seen as the product of a rootless group who had repudiated their *mores maiorum*.[35] Cybele on the other hand had possessed an official cult at Rome since the Second Punic War and, given her Phrygian origins, could be connected to Troy, the legendary cradle of the Roman people.[36] Therefore the cult could appeal both to those who were attracted by the esoteric and "mystical" while at the same time preserving a sense of being Roman, something that would have been impossible for rival cults such as that of the Egyptian goddess Isis.

Religious "over-achievement" in the form of sexual and other forms of continence, again a popular and at times troublesome aspect of primitive Christianity, could also find a place within the cult.[37] The former could be suggested via an allegorical reading of the version

---

(1987) 17–45; *The origins of the Mithraic mysteries: cosmology and salvation in the ancient world* (Oxford, 1989); "The Mithraic mysteries", *Scientific American*, December 1989.

[33] See Varro, *apud* St. Augustine, *Civitas Dei* 7.24.

[34] See Macrobius, *Saturnalia* 1.21.7–11.

[35] See the accusations of Celsus *apud* Origen, *contra Celsum* 2.1 ff.; cf. Tertullian *ad Nat*.1.10, Lactantius *De M.P.34*.

[36] See E. Gruen, "The advent of the Magna Mater" in his *Studies in Greek Culture and Roman Policy* (Leiden, 1990) for an account of the adoption of the cult at Rome. c.f. Virgil, *Aeneid* 10.252 ff.

[37] For a discussion of this aspect of Primitive Christianity see R. Lane-Fox, *Pagans and Christians* (London, 1986) ch. 7 "Living Like Angels".

of the legend where Attis castrated himself. As has been seen, severe fasting was also a feature of the cult.

Leading pagan intellectuals such as Symmachus enrolled themselves in the cult in large numbers.[38] More importantly perhaps Julian the Apostate made the cult of Cybele one of the centre pieces in his attempt to organise classical paganism into a coherent religious alternative to the Christian faith. This alone would probably have been enough to mark it out for especial dislike by Christians. The emperor probably underwent the *taurobolium* ritual[39] and his metroac "Hymn to the Mother of Gods" is still extant. Julian's espousal of the cult may well have been a case of the Emperor simply following the intellectual current of the paganism of his day rather than the creation of a new policy himself. Certainly some of his contemporaries also used metroac beliefs in a similar way. Sallustius Philosophicus, for example, when discussing "theological" myth used precisely the story of Attis to show how myth embodied neo-Platonic truths.[40] Nor did Cybele's role in such projects lapse with the death of Julian. In the following century the neo-Platonist Proclus wrote a Cybeline "bible" in which, with divine assistance, he revealed the theology of the cult.[41] Once again the reactionary nature of this activity is clear: before the impact of Christianity there had been no need for pagan cults to produce doctrinaire scriptures.

We can see therefore how the changes in the metroac cult might not have been merely mutations which took place unconsciously over time to ensure the cult's survival in the religious marketplace of antique polytheism, but could rather have been a deliberate attempt to produce a rival to Christianity. This rival, born as a reaction to the Christian agenda, used the symbolism and ethos of the Christian church while claiming them firmly for paganism. Cybele as the stan-

---

[38] Symmachus *Ep.*2.34; Prudentius, *Contra Symm.*1.624–630. Other devotees included the senator Vettius Agorius Praetextatus and his wife Paulina *CIL* 6.1779, and Ceionius Rufius Volusianus, *A.E.* 1945, 55 & *A.E.* 1955, 180 = the Lampadius of Ammianus Marcellinus 27.3.5. Ceionius was the praetorian prefect of Italy in A.D. 355 and Praefectus Urbi in A.D. 365. According to Ammianus, he prided himself on being the best spitter in Rome.

[39] St. Gregory of Nazianzus, *Or.c.Iul.*10.52, "with impious blood he washed away the waters of baptism."

[40] Sallustius Philosophicus 4. For an extended discussion see the commentary of A.D. Nock, *Sallustius* (Cambridge, 1926)

[41] Marinus, *Vit.Procli* 33. The work is sadly lost. Cf. ch. 19 of Marinus' biography where Proclus is said to have observed the commandments of the cult.

dard bearer of the new paganism therefore was set on an inevitable collision course with Christ.

This would explain the violent reaction of Christian writers to Cybele. Not only would her cult be seen as a direct challenge to the faith, but its rituals would be regarded as a deliberate blasphemous parody of Christian religious practice aimed at tempting the faithful away from the truth. Cybele and Attis became a target for Christian polemic not because they presented easy pickings, but because they had been posted at the fore-front of the battle.

Nevertheless the war was lost. Ironically the changes made in the cult were in many ways the reason for its downfall.

The *taurobolium* as an act of redemption may have seemed a useful counter to Christian notions of baptism and redemption, but it had one severe drawback: it was much more expensive. Although the sacrifice of a bull would have presented no hardship to the likes of Symmachus and his friends, even the cheaper *criobolium* would have been out of reach for many of the poor. Therefore by centering on this rite and insisting on its personal nature the metroac cult effectively disqualified itself from competing with Christianity at a popular level.[42] Moreover the increased expense was not offset by a promise of higher efficacy. The *taurobolium* unlike Christian baptism, which lasted for ever, seems only to have conferred its benefits for twenty years.[43] Such mundane points though often overlooked ought to be given due consideration when looking at the outcome of the conflict of religions in antiquity.

If the expense of the cult was a drawback so were the divinities worshipped. If the metroac cult was to perform its task it needed to present a myth of individual salvation—in the context of its mythology the figure used in this regard was Attis. Unfortunately Attis was a far less acceptable figure to Rome than Cybele. Not only was he

---

[42] Accusations of elitism formed part of Christian anti-pagan rhetoric, see Origen, *Contra Celsum* 7.60.

[43] *Carmen contra Paganos* 62 & *CIL* 6.512. Although we do have one attestation of the an initiate being *in aeternum renatus*, *CIL* 6.510, from undergoing the ritual, this appears to be the exception rather than the rule. Moore (C.H. Moore, "The duration of the efficacy of the Taurobolium" *Cl.Phil.*19 (1924) 363–365) suggests that the phrase should be read as expressing the overenthusiastic hopes of an individual believer rather than as a statement of metroac doctrine. A further alternative is that we should read *in aeternum* as a description of the state into which the initiate is being reborn, not as a description of the future duration of his rebirth; this would reconcile the stone with the rest of our corpus.

clearly foreign coming from outside the confines of the classical world,[44] but also deeply suspicious. Effeminate at best and self-castrator at worst he was an easy target for polemic. Attis' castration in myth and that of his devotees, the *Galli,* in reality, particularly raised problems for the cult's acceptance. Nothing could have seemed more characteristically oriental and alien to the Roman mind than the *Galli.* A slave of Q. Servilius Caepio who emasculated himself in devotion to Cybele was promptly deported from Italy and forbidden to return. The ritual purification of the city which followed serves to show the horror felt at these practices at the beginning of the first century BC was not merely personal but thought to be a matter of importance to the state.[45] Nor did this feeling dissipate over time. St. Augustine slyly speculated on why Varro did not discuss this subject in his account of the worship of the Mother of Gods, knowing full well that his readership would immediately assume that the omission was from dislike of or embarrassment at the practices concerned.[46] Augustine's rhetorical ploy is clear, he notes that even Varro, whom elsewhere he treats as a sophisticated defender of pagan ritual, wishes to disown Attis with the clear implication that to feel disgust towards Attis is not merely a Christian foible but an emotion shared by all civilised men, pagan and Christian alike.

The exotic nature of the cult and self-castration provided an ideal subject for Catullus' neotericism.[47] Tacitus informs his readership that eunuchs are not despised among barbarians (here dealing with the Parthians) but in fact that among them this is an avenue to power.[48] For Tacitus, and he believes for his readership, this fact is a clear marker of the "other". Juvenal's straightforward hostility to the cult is centred on the act of self-castration.[49] Julian in his *Hymn to the Mother of Gods* spends a great deal of time in allegorising away this aspect of the cult's mythology, referring to it as "much talked about amongst the rabble". Both the length of Julian's apology here and this reference show the unpopularity of the concept to its contemporary audience.[50]

---

[44] For common prejudices against such gods see Origen's comments on Celsus' assertion that Christianity was a barbarian religion, *Contra Celsum* 1.2. cf. Plato, *Epinomis* 987e.
[45] Julius Obsequens 44a.
[46] *Civitas Dei* 7.25.
[47] Catullus 63.
[48] *Annals* 6.31.
[49] Satire 2.110 ff., 6.513 ff.
[50] Julian, *Hymn to the mother of the gods* 168d.

The foreign nature of the cult was further emphasised by the fact that Roman citizens had been banned from the ranks of the *Galli* until Claudius allowed a citizen *archigallus* to be created with the proviso that he was not to be castrated, although the nicety of this distinction does not seem to have been understood by the generality of the population.[51] Additional laws against castration passed by the emperor Domitian would have further cut off the *Gallus* from the Roman citizen body.[52]

Not that this divide was one that many would wish to cross. Apart from a physical aversion, there was the fact that eunuchs had a poor reputation in the Roman world, being associated with sexual perversion and decadence generally.[53] A scholiast on Juvenal captures the general feeling of the Roman world when he likens the castrated archigalli to sodomites.[54] This low opinion was embedded in Roman law itself: the Galli were enrolled for the *tributum capitis* in the same category as prostitutes.[55]

A particularly unfortunate aspect of this problem was the rise to prominence in ancient religious thought of the Holy Man. Such devotees were expected to pursue ascetic lives of religious over-achievement in terms of abstinence and continence. Christianity could provide examples of such men in large numbers and religious dogma to support their endeavours. All the cult of Cybele could offer by way of a counter were attempts to allegorise away the account of Attis' castration and the all too real *Galli* who had exactly the opposite of the required reputation.

Nor was Cybele herself immune from this form of attack. Despite the mythological Phrygian connection to Rome, it was much easier to portray her as a bizarre oriental interloper rather than a genuine Roman.[56] Juvenal had no doubt that this was the case; to the satirist

---

[51] See for example, Servius, *Ad Aen.*9.115 "Mater magna . . . effecit ut cultores sui viriles sibi partes amputarent qui *archigalli* appellantur". Such confusion should not surprise us. Most Englishmen would be hard put to describe the differences between a vicar, a rector, and a priest.

[52] Suetonius, *Vit.Dom.*7. The alien nature of the *Galli* is dwelt upon by St. Augustine, *In Hos.*1.4.14.

[53] See the scathing denunciations of eunuchs made by Ammianus Marcellinus e.g. 18.4.

[54] Ad Juvenal 2.116 "Archigalli *cinaedi* quem magulum conspectum urcatum dicimus qui publica impudicitiam professus est". Once again the confusion between the *archigallus* and the *Gallus* is in evidence.

[55] Hephaestius Grammaticus, *Scholia* 1.94 (ed. R. Westphal).

[56] For Phrygia as a barbarian land see Cicero, *Pro Flacco* 27.65.

the *Mater Deum* becomes *turpis Cybele.* The goddess' foreign name rather than her Latin title is used deliberately to mark her out as a foreigner. For Juvenal, having established the foreign nature of the goddess, the epithet follows naturally and serves as a reinforcement.[57] "The Mother of Gods came from Pessinus wherever that is" remarked St. Augustine coyly and in a similar vein.[58]

As has been seen, there was a strong non-Christian tradition of hostility to the cult for Christian apologists to build upon. The most obvious example of this is found in Juvenal.[59] However such attacks were not just found at this populist level. Philosophers too denounced the cult. Seneca launched a fierce attack in his *De Superstitionibus,*[60] and Celsus in his anti-Christian work, *The True Logos,* likened Christianity to the metroac cult: a comparison that was not meant to be complimentary.[61] Ironically it is precisely Celsus' style of argument which was used by later Christian polemicists against the metroac cult. Belief in Cybele and Attis is presented as irrational and dependent on fantastic myths unlike the accepted truths of Christianity.[62] While earlier Christian apologists, such as Tertullian, had already used this line of attack on pagan belief, the dependence of later pagans on non-classical divinities allowed such an approach to be combined effectively with the arguments designed to show the alien nature of the cult outlined above. The self-same rhetoric that had been deployed against the Christian faith was now deployed in its defence: Christianity could pose as the defender of Roman values against those of the debauched orient. St. Augustine is quick both to praise the heroes of the early republic as exemplars of virtue and to show that the introduction of Cybele into the city brought with it nothing but eunuchs and decadence.[63]

A twist to this rhetoric of presenting Cybele as a foreign and dangerous interloper at Rome is provided by St. Augustine who talks of

---

[57] Juvenal, *Sat.*2.111.

[58] St. Augustine, *Civitas Dei* 3.12.

[59] For a general discussion see L. Richard, "Juvenal et les galles de Cybèle", *Revue de l'Histoire des Religions* 169.1 (1966) 51–67.

[60] *Apud* St. Augustine *CD* 6.10.

[61] Origen, *contra Celsum* 1.9,3.16.

[62] The anonymous author of the *Carmen contra Paganos* for example makes great play on the physical unpleasantness of the *taurobolium* and the fact that initiates kept their bloodstained robes to wear on special occasions, *Carmen contra paganos* (*Poetae Minores Latini* 3 (ed. Baehrens) 60–61. See also Arnobius, *Adv.Nat.*5.42.

[63] For the praise of early Roman heroes see *Civitas Dei* 5.18, for eunuchs *ibid.*, 7.26.

the ensnarement of the noble Scipio Nasica by Cybele which allowed her to be brought to Rome.[64] Roman history was full of such
potential threatening women and an educated Roman reading the
Civitas Dei would immediately have thought of Aeneas and Dido or
Antony and Cleopatra.

Another standard weapon in the attack on Christianity had been
the alleged obscenity of its rituals. However accurate the prurient
modern-day conception of Roman private life, the image which
Romans themselves wished to preserve was that of the moral peas-
ant farmer. Cults which indulged in dubious sexual practices at night
were frowned upon. Once again this rhetoric was turned round onto
the metroac cult with good effect. Its orgiastic rites did not fail to
draw comment. Decadence was something that in the popular mind
came from the East and Cybele's origins and the nature of her cult
provided ample ammunition on this score. Unlike Christian ritual,
there was no disguising the fact that Cybeline rites were orgiastic in
nature and some were secretive. Moreover the prime movers in such
things were the *Galli*, a group which, as has been seen, was regarded
with extreme suspicion.

"How can we think any good of rites which are shrouded in darkness, when such abominations (i.e. enactments of the myth of Cybele and Attis on stage) are produced in the light of day? Certainly
the practices performed in secret by those castrated perverts is their
affair. But it has not been possible to keep out of sight those unfor-
tunates so foully emasculated and corrupted". St. Augustine's language mirrors almost exactly the denunciation of Christian ritual by
earlier pagan authors.[65]

For St. Augustine Cybele was *dea meretrix*, the harlot goddess.[66]
Unfortunately for devotees of the cult there was a plausible base
upon which to build this accusation. This comprised not only the
rituals of the cult but its very foundation myths. Despite the allegorical interpretations of the Attis and Cybele legend its original form
told of a shepherd lusted after and consequently killed out of jeal-
ousy by the goddess. The nature of enactments of this legend on the
stage was more than enough to make refined ladies blush according
to St. Augustine.[67] It is interesting in this regard to find precisely

---

[64] *Civitas Dei* 2.5.
[65] *Civitas Dei* 6.7.
[66] *in Hoseam*, 1.4.14.
[67] *Civitas Dei* 2.4, 2.26.

such ladies of high degree enrolled in the cult.[68] Is Augustine making a more barbed attack here than is often assumed?

Cybele and Attis perished not with a bang but a whimper. The metroac cult slowly petered out in the face of growing hostility—the last attested *taurobolium* being recorded in A.D. 390.[69]

Attempts have been made to trace Cybeline influence in the Christian church in later generations but by and large these do not convince.[70]

Such a decline was of course inevitable given the political triumph of Christianity culminating in Theodosius the Great's outlawing of paganism in A.D. 391. However the "philosophising" metroac cult of late antiquity was in some regards not merely a casualty of power politics, but also a victim of its own devising. By adopting a more Eastern version of the cult than had been previously current at Rome in order to challenge Christianity, it laid itself open to a counter-attack by Christian writers on precisely the traditionalist Roman grounds its adherents believed themselves to be defending in the first place. The very nature of the cult opened up for Christian apologists to marshal for their cause all the arguments that had previously been used against them, and against a more plausible target. Secondary ammunition could be found in arguments used by pagan Roman authors against the self-same cult. They were not slow to take up the challenge and did so to good effect.

The pagan resistance to Christianity has often been divided into Roman "traditionalists" and "orientalists". In the end the adoption of "oriental" gods proved to be a mistake. These failed to cut the ground from under Christianity's feet and at the same time exposed their supporters to a devastating counter-attack based on the very principles they claimed to defend. Perhaps in the end the East did contribute significantly to the fall of pagan Rome, but not in the way that many of its old opponents such as the Elder Cato would have imagined.

---

[68] *CIL* 6.508, Serapias *h*(*onesta*) femina and *CIL* 6.502, an anonymous *c*(*larissima*) *f*(*emina*).

[69] *CIL* 6.512 = *ILS* 4154.

[70] Perhaps the most interesting of these is M.P. Carroll, *The Cult of the Virgin Mary* (Princeton, 1988). Carroll, a psychologist, argues that the same masochistic tendencies found among the *Galli* can be found in modern male devotees of the virgin Mary. However psychological similarities cannot prove historic continuity and Carroll fails to provide firm evidence for a link between the two groups.

PER LA STORIA DEL CULTO DI CIBELE IN OCCIDENTE: IL SANTUARIO RUPESTRE DI AKRAI

Giulia Sfameni Gasparro

"Ma almeno voglio invocare la Madre, la dea augusta, che spesso le fanciulle vengono a cantare con Pan, sulla soglia della mia porta, durante la notte".[1]

Nonostante i numerosi problemi esegetici e storici posti da questi versi pindarici,[2] si può legittimamente dedurre dall'evocazione della *Meter* nel contesto dell'ode dedicata a Ierone I di Siracusa la conoscenza da parte di quest'ultimo e del suo ambiente della figura e del culto di quella "dea augusta" invocata ad auspicio di guarigione per il tiranno siceliota. Né si può dubitare che la Madre divina, oggetto di cori femminili notturni con l'intervento di quel personaggio dalle nette connotazioni agresti e montane che lo stesso poeta definisce altrove "compagno della Gran Madre",[3] suo "innumerabile cane",[4] sia la *Kybela mater theon* che secondo la testimonianza di Filodemo Pindaro aveva fatto oggetto di un'ode, invocandola quale *despoina*.[5]

E' noto che proprio in questo primo quarto del V sec.a.C. emergono le prime sicure testimonianze della presenza in Grecia della dea frigia Cibele,[6] essendo appunto Pindaro il più antico testimone

---

[1] Pindaro, *Pyth*.III,77–79 ed. A. Puech p. 58.

[2] Sulla controversa datazione dell'Ode, attribuita da alcuni studiosi al periodo anteriore al viaggio del poeta a Siracusa da altri invece ad epoca posteriore, oltre U. von Wilamowitz-Moellendorf, *Pindaros*, Berlin 1922, pp. 224–232; 280–285; A. Puech, *Pindare*, vol. II, *Pythiques* (Coll.Budé), Paris 1922, p. 51 ss. si veda L. Lehnus, *L'Inno a Pan di Pindaro*, Milano 1979, pp. 5–55.

[3] *Parth*.3 ed. Puech p. 178.

[4] *Parth*.4 ed. Puech p. 178.

[5] Frag. 80 Bergk = Puech, *Adela* frag. 15 p. 208 da Philod., *perì eusebeias* 19,14. Per la ricostruzione del testo si veda A. Henrichs, "Toward a New Edition of Philodemus' Treatise On Piety", *GRBS* 13 (1972), pp. 67–98. Sul significato dell'appellativo della dea cfr., dello stesso A., "Despoina Kybele: ein Beitrag zur religiösen Namenkunde", *HSCPh* 80 (1976), pp. 235–286.

[6] Sul nome della dea quale interviene nelle più antiche iscrizioni rupestri frigie dell'inizio del VI sec.a.C. nella forma MATAR KYBILE o KYBILEIA cfr. C. Brixhe, "Le nom de Cybèle", *Die Sprache* 25 (1979), pp. 40–45; L. Zgusta, "Weiteres zum Namen der Kybele", *Die Sprache* 28 (1982), pp. 171–172. *Kybaba/Kybebe* è denominata la dea in Lidia come risulta da Ipponatte fr. 125 Degani (H. Degani, *Hipponactis Testimonia et Fragmenta*, Stuttgart—Lipsia 1991, p. 127) che pure conosce il parallelo

di un culto dalle tipiche connotazioni mistico-orgiastiche,[7] mentre il complesso documentario relativo all'introduzione del culto ad Atene e alla fondazione del *Metroon* che sarebbe stato distrutto durante l'invasione persiana del 480 a.C. per la qualità disparata delle fonti non permette conclusioni storico-religiose del tutto sicure[8] e comunque non consente di risalire oltre gli inizi del V sec.a.C.[9]

Alcune piccole terrecotte di figurine femminili sedute con un leoncello sui ginocchi rinvenute sull'Acropoli ateniese sono state datate nella seconda metà del VI sec.a.C.;[10] tali esemplari non sarebbero opere di importazione ionica bensì "eine freie Gestaltung des ionischen Kybelebildes mit attischen Stilmerkmalen".[11] Esse potrebbero dunque essere più recenti e la stessa F. Naumann propone la datazione indicata solo come verisimile.

Incerta è l'identificazione della dea frigia in una statuetta marmorea di personaggio femminile che forse recava sui ginocchi un animale (leone?).[12] Parimenti aperto a dubbi e a riserve ci sembra il tentativo

---

nome frigio *Kybelìs* (frag. 167 Degani p. 156). Erodoto (V,102) definisce *Kybaba* dea *epikorios* di Sardi: cfr. G.M.A. Hanfmann, "On the Gods of Lydian Sardis" in R.M. Boehmer-H. Hauptmann (edd.), *Beiträge zur Altertumskunde Kleinasiens, Festschrift für Kurt Bittel*, Mainz am Rhein 1983, pp. 219–321. Sul problema si veda anche M.R. Gusmani, "Der lydische Name des Kybele", *Kadmos* 8 (1969), 158–161.

[7] Per un'analisi delle più antiche fonti sul culto metroaco in Grecia e la definizione del suo peculiare carattere "mistico" ci sia permesso rimandare al nostro *Soteriology and Mystic Aspects in the Cult of Cybele and Attis* (EPRO 103), Leiden 1985.

[8] Una raccolta di tali documenti in R.E. Wycherly, *The Athenian Agora*, vol. II, *Literary and Epigraphical Testimonia*, Princeton 1957, pp. 150–159. Cfr. M.J. Vermaseren, *Corpus Cultus Cibelae Attidisque (CCCA)* (EPRO 50), vol. II, *Greciae atque Insulae*, Leiden 1982, 1–79. Tra il ricco materiale rinvenuto nell' *Agora* ateniese, che scende fino all'età imperiale romana, i documenti epigrafici e monumentali più antichi sono datati nel IV sec.a.C. Sul problema oltre le opere generali sul culto metroaco, fra le quali basti qui ricordare la più recente messa a punto di M.J. Vermaseren, *Cybele and Attis. The Myth and the Cult*, London 1977, pp. 32–35, cfr. N. Frapiccini, "L'arrivo di Cibele in Attica", *PP* 232 (1987), pp. 12–26.

[9] A parere di M.P. Nilsson, peraltro, la penetrazione in Grecia della dea anatolica, identificabile alla Madre degli dei nota alle fonti del V sec.a.C., sarebbe avvenuta "al più tardi alla fine del periodo arcaico" (*Geschichte der griechischen Religion*, vol. I, Munchen 1961, pp. 725–727). Sulle diverse posizioni degli studiosi in merito all'identità della *Meter theon* della più antica documentazione si veda il nostro contributo *Connotazioni metroache di Demetra nel coro dell' "Elena"* (vv. 1301–1365) in M.B. de Boer-T.A. Edridge (edd.), *Hommages à Maarten J. Vermaseren* (EPRO 68), vol. III, Leiden 1978, pp. 1153–1158.

[10] Cfr. J. de la Genière, "De la Phrygie à Locres épizéphyrienne: les chemins de Cybèle", *MEFRA* 97 (1985), p. 696 con rinvio a F. Winter, *Die Typen der figürlichen Terrakotten*, vol. I, Berlin—Stuttgart 1903, 43 n. 4; 50 n. 2a, b, c, e 3.

[11] F. Naumann, *Die Ikonographie der Kybele in der phrygischen und der griechischen Kunst*, Istanbuler Mitteilungen, Beiheft 28, Tübingen 1983, p. 146.

[12] J. de la Genière, *art. cit.*, p. 696 e n. 15. Cfr. F. Naumann, *op. cit.*, p. 145; p. 308 Cat.111, Taf.19,3.

di J. de La Genière di fare arretrare al VI sec.a.C. le attestazioni della presenza della dea sul suolo greco, sulla base di alcune statue di figure femminili in trono rinvenute in Laconia.[13] Di fatto, gli elementi iconografici (trono con supporti desinenti in zampe di leone in un caso, tracce di un animale nell'altro), non forniscono parametri inconfutabili per l'identificazione del personaggio ivi rappresentato. La presenza di Cibele nel VI sec.a.C. in area spartana, pertanto, pur probabile anche in considerazione dei rapporti con Samo attestati nel medesimo secolo, non può ritenersi del tutto certa.

E' noto infine che la lettura del nome—Themis—della dea che nel notissimo fregio del Tesoro dei Sifni a Delfi guida il cocchio cui sono aggiogati i leoni,[14] ha sottratto alla documentazione relativa alla presenza di Cibele nella Grecia continentale un importante punto di riferimento cronologicamente sicuro (c. 530/525 a.C.).

La sola indubbia attestazione di una conoscenza della dea frigia in Occidente agli inizi del VI sec.a.C. o addirittura negli ultimi anni del VII sec. rimane allora il grafito su un coccio fittile rinvenuto a Locri Epizefiri, in località Centocamere nell'area di un santuario di Afrodite.[15]

Tra le ipotesi formulate per spiegare la presenza della dea anatolica nella sua *facies* frigia in un'epoca così alta nella colonia magnogreca dalla ricca e variegata esperienza religiosa,[16] riteniamo più probabile quella che la connette, piuttosto che ad una regione della Grecia già conquistata da quel culto[17]—di cui come si è detto non permangono sicure attestazioni—all'ambiente della grecità microasiatica, sia direttamente[18] sia, con maggior probabilità, per la mediazione della vicina Siris, colonia di Colofone.[19]

---

[13] J. de la Genière, *art. cit.*, pp. 693–718; Ead., "Le culte de la Mère des dieux dans le Péloponnèse", *CRAI* 1986, pp. 29–48.

[14] V. Brinkmann, "Die aufgemalten Namensbeischriften an Nord- und Ostfries des Siphnierschatzhauses", *BCH* 109 (1985), N 17 p. 101 e pp. 123–126. Cfr. *CCCA* II,441 pl. CXXXI; F. Naumann, *op. cit.*, p. 309 Cat.121.

[15] M. Guarducci, "Cibele in un'epigrafe arcaica di Locri Epizefiri", *Klio* 52 (1970), pp. 133–138 = Ead., *Scritti scelti sulla religione greca e romana e sul cristianesimo* (EPRO 98), Leiden 1983, pp. 20–25; "Il culto di Cibele a Locri", *Almanacco Calabrese* 1972–1973, pp. 25–29. Cfr. *CCCA* IV,128.

[16] Un quadro della *facies* religiosa della città nei contributi ai due volumi degli *Atti del Sedicesimo Convegno di Studi sulla Magna Grecia. Taranto, 3–8 ottobre 1976* dedicato appunto a *Locri Epizefirii*, Napoli 1977.

[17] Così J. de la Genière nei due interventi sopra citati e in particolare *De la Phrygie*, p. 69: da Sparta.

[18] M. Torelli, *I culti di Locri* in *Locri Epizefirii*, *cit.*, p. 149 s.

[19] M. Guarducci, *loc. cit.*

Una rete di intensi rapporti commerciali e artistici con il mondo
ionico, di fatto, riflettono i ricchi materiali venuti alla luce nell'area
dell'antica colonia di Siris e in particolare nell'ambito del santuario
demetriaco la cui vita cultuale si prolunga, con vivace intensità, nel
centro di Eraclea, succeduto sul territorio alla distrutta Siris.[20] La
coroplastica in particolare attesta tali connessioni, nella serie delle
statuette del VI sec.a.C raffiguranti una dea spesso con *polos*, seduta
su un trono cui la figura stessa talora sembra fondersi, e che in qualche
caso mostra i piedi desinenti con zampe leonine.[21]

Non si identificherà certo la dea frigia in siffatta rappresentazione,
una volta che il motivo evocato rientra nel novero degli elementi decorativi né può essere ritenuto sostitutivo dell'animale che, sui ginocchi della dea o in posizione araldica al suo fianco, costituisce già in
quest'epoca uno dei segni distintivi inequivocabili dell'iconografia
metroaca.[22]

Tale è piuttosto il caso dei numerosi *naiskoi* in pietra da Marsi-
glia[23] e di quelli di Velia[24] e di Metaponto[25] che rivelano una diffusione
verso Occidente della figura della dea anatolica promanante dai centri
ionici d'Asia Minore, e delle due terrecotte siceliote già pubblicate
nel nostro volume su *I culti orientali in Sicilia*.[26]

Senza insistere ora su quanto già a suo tempo notato, ricordiamo
soltanto che l'esemplare gelese della dea con grande leoncello sui
ginocchi è databile con sicurezza, sulla base dei dati archeologici, in
epoca non posteriore al decennio 550–540 a.C. L'esemplare selinun-
tino, di identica fattura, può essere attribuito al medesimo periodo.

---

[20] Si vedano in proposito i contributi al XX Convegno di Studi sulla Magna
Grecia, Taranto 12–17 ottobre 1980 pubblicati negli Atti dal titolo *Siris e l'influenza
ionica in Occidente*, Taranto 1981.

[21] B. Neutsch, "Documenti artistici del santuario di Demetra a Policoro" in *Siris*,
cit., p. 106 e Tav.XXVI,4; XXVII,3–4; XXVIII,4.

[22] Sulla costituzione del tipo di Cibele in trono, spesso all'interno di un *naiskos*,
con leoncello sui ginocchi o ritto al suo fianco cfr. E. Will, "Aspects du culte et de
la légende de la Grande Mère dans le monde grec" in *Eléments orientaux dans la
religion grecque ancienne*, Colloque de Strasbourg 22–24 mai 1958, Paris 1960, pp. 95–
111. Si veda ora la dettagliata analisi di F. Naumann (*supra* n. 11).

[23] F. Naumann, *op. cit.*, pp. 303–307, nn. 69–108 Taf.19,1–2; *CCCA* V, Leiden
1986, 276–313 pl. CII–CXI.

[24] F. Naumann, *op. cit.*, p. 307 n. 109. Cfr. W. Johannowsky, "Un naiskos eleate
con dea seduta", *Klearkos* 12 (1961), pp. 118–128.

[25] F. Naumann, *op. cit.*, p. 307 n. 110: 480–460 a.C.

[26] G. Sfameni Gasparro, *I culti orientali in Sicilia* (EPRO 31), Leiden 1973, pp.
115–119; p. 276 s. Cat.330–330 bis, Tav.CV,146. Ora anche in *CCCA* IV, Leiden
1978, 166–167 pl. LXIV.

Le due statuette costituiscono pertanto una testimonianza irrefutabile della presenza della dea frigia in Sicilia in rapporto alle vivaci correnti commerciali e ai contatti culturali e religiosi tra i grandi centri sicelioti di età arcaica e le regioni greche micro-asiatiche, in particolare quelle di matrice ionica.

Anche Siracusa è interessata a tali movimenti, come dimostrano i numerosi e varii materiali di fabbrica ionica rinvenuti nell'area cittadina, che non è possibile ricordare in questa sede. Ai nostri fini è piuttosto utile notare la presenza di numerosi esemplari di statuette fittili di dea seduta in trono, di tipo ionico, soprattutto nelle necropoli.[27] Un esemplare, proveniente dalla Necropoli dell'Ospedale civile,[28] in tutto analogo alla Cibele di Gela e di Selinunte, purtroppo risulta mancante dell'oggetto che, come appare dai segni residui di attacco, doveva poggiare sulle ginocchia della dea. Se, come il confronto con i tipi noti fa sospettare, si trattava di un leoncello, avremmo la testimonianza di una presenza metroaca in età arcaica nella metropoli siceliota che comunque in età ieroniana, in quanto interlocutrice di Pindaro, doveva percepire il significato religioso dell'invocazione rivolta dal poeta alla Madre divina per la guarigione del tiranno siracusano.

Tuttavia solo un *naiskos* in marmo pentelico, databile nel IV sec.a.C., del tutto conforme al diffuso schema della dea in trono con il leone ritto al suo fianco e i due *propoloi* (fanciulla dadofora e giovinetto con *oinochoe*) raffigurati sulle ante del tempietto,[29] costituisce testimonianza di un culto, verisimilmente privato come in tanti analoghi casi,[30] nella Siracusa di tarda età classica o della prima età ellenistica. A tale monumento si può affiancare un rilievo, purtroppo molto rovinato, scolpito sulla roccia del colle Temenite, che tuttavia non può essere datato con certezza a causa delle sue pessime condizioni di conservazione.[31]

---

[27] Basti ricordare soltanto una statuetta di dea in trono con alta spalliera dalla Necropoli del Fusco (tomba 518) che P. Orsi propone di datare intorno alla metà del VI sec.a.C. (*NSc* 1897, p. 473: ora nel Museo archeologico di Siracusa inv. n. 16876).

[28] Tomba 43: Museo archeologico di Siracusa inv. n. 66577.

[29] *I culti*, pp. 119–121; p. 264 Cat.305 e Tav.LXI,99 con la relativa documentazione bibliografica. Cfr. *CCCA* IV,149 pl. L; F. Naumann, *op. cit.*, p. 331 n. 306.

[30] Si possono addurre a confronto soprattutto i numerosi esemplari ateniesi, in buona parte provenienti da dimore private. Cfr. *I culti*, pp. 119–121.

[31] *I culti*, p. 122; p. 265 s. Cat.306, Tav.LXII,100; *CCCA* IV,148 pl. XLIX; F. Naumann, *op. cit.*, p. 345 n. 440. La studiosa a p. 207 erroneamente attribuisce al monumento la provenienza dalla via dei Sepolcri e lo descrive come contemplante una scena complessa con le figure dei Dioscuri. Di fatto è stata operata una

L'indizio probante ma solo indiretto costituito dall'Ode pindarica
per Ierone I e i due monumenti di fine età classica o inizi di quella
ellenistica, il secondo dei quali si colloca in un contesto indubbia-
mente pubblico nella sua qualità di scultura adornante il pendio del
Colle Temenite, sono comunque insufficienti a spiegare l'esplosione
di religiosità metroaca che risulta invece inequivocabile dal grandioso
santuario rupestre della colonia siracusana di Akrai. Di fatto, per
valutare a pieno il significato storico di questo monumento singolare,
un *unicum* nella *facies* cultuale metroaca in Occidente, non è possibile
prescindere dai legami politici e culturali che, fin dalla sua fondazione
(*c.* 664–663 a.C.) hanno intimamente connesso la colonia acrense
alla madrepatria siracusana che, con l'occupazione del sito sul ver-
tice del grande altopiano che si erge alle sue spalle, compì un passo
decisivo nella realizzazione della propria politica espansionistica verso l'entroterra.[32]

Senza procedere ad un'analisi dettagliata del monumento, quale—
dopo l'opera fondamentale di L. Bernabò Brea—abbiamo già con-
dotto nel quadro della rassegna de *I culti orientali in Sicilia*,[33] e che é
stata riproposta nel prezioso *Corpus Cultus Cybelae Attidisque*[34] del Ma-
estro cui, con devozione e nel ricordo di un profondo sentimento di
amicizia, è dedicato questo contributo, intendiamo piuttosto cercare
di cogliere, dalla generale struttura e dai temi iconografici ancora leg-
gibili, i tratti distintivi della *facies* religiosa soggiacente all'intero
complesso sacro. Per questa via sarà possibile individuare i parametri
di riferimento iconografici e ideologici del monumento siceliota, nel
più ampio contesto del mondo mediterraneo nel periodo alto-ellenistico
in cui, con ogni verisimiglianza, esso si colloca. Sarà dato in tal modo
di misurare anche il grado di originalità della visione religiosa espressa
nel santuario acrense e il suo significato storico nel quadro del movimento di espansione del culto della Grande dea frigia in Occidente
in tale epoca.

Di fatto, dopo i primi sporadici episodi di età arcaica e oltre la
grande fase di età classica di acclimatazione sul suolo greco conti-

---

confusione con uno dei rilievi votivi a carattere funerario di quella zona siracusana.
Ciò ha indotto in errore J. de la Genière che annovera il monumento tra quelli che
attestano la triade della dea con i Dioscuri (*Le culte de la Mère des dieux*, p. 42 s.).

[32] Per una sintesi delle vicende storiche della cittadina si veda L. Bernabò Brea,
Akrai, Catania 1956, pp. 17–20.

[33] *I culti*, pp. 126–149; 267–276, Tavv.LXVI–CIV.

[34] *CCCA* IV,152–164 pl. LII–LXIII. Cfr. F. Naumann, *op. cit.*, pp. 202–208 e
Taf.30,2.

nentale con il parallelo profondo processo di ellenizzazione della personalità divina che ne è il fulcro e delle sue modalità rituali, la diffusione di tale culto riceve in età ellenistica una radicale accelerazione anche in rapporto all'introduzione ufficiale della Madre frigia nella Roma repubblicana, quale dea nazionale, protettrice della stirpe troiana di cui, per il tramite di Enea, la nuova potenza ormai prepotentemente attiva sullo scenario politico del Mediterraneo si proclama erede.[35]

In questa prospettiva il monumento acrense assume un particolare rilievo, posta la forte presenza romana in Sicilia nel corso del III sec.a.C., nel quadro movimentato delle note vicende politico-militari che, nello scontro decisivo con il nemico cartaginese, vedono compiersi proprio sul suolo siciliano il vittorioso destino della Repubblica romana e la sua prima affermazione come potenza di statura internazionale. Lo storico infatti non può fare a meno di chiedersi se e fino a che punto i contatti intensi e prolungati con la Sicilia e in particolare con il regno siracusano di Ierone II, nella cui orbita gravita il piccolo ma fiorente centro di *Akrai*, poterono familiarizzare i Romani, soldati e commercianti ma anche autorità politiche e militari, con un personaggio come la Gran madre anatolica, già pienamente naturalizzata in veste greca in quella terra ellenica che era la Sicilia, ma pur sempre legata alla sue radici asiatiche.[36]

Se dalla siciliana Erice lo stato repubblicano aveva ufficialmente

---

[35] Sul tema, dopo S. Aurigemma ("La protezione speciale della gran Madre Idea per la nobiltà romana e le leggende dell'origine troiana di Roma", *BCR*, 1900, pp. 31–65), si veda P. Lambrechts, "Cybèle, divinité étrangère ou nationale", *Bull.Soc.Anthrop.Préhist.*62 (1952), pp. 44–60. La tesi di J. Perret sul carattere piuttosto tardo della tradizione delle origini troiane di Roma (*Les origines de la légende troyenne de Rome*, Paris 1942) è stata rifiutata da P. Boyancé con buoni argomenti ("Les origines de la légende troyenne de Rome, *REA* 45, 1943, pp. 275–290 rist. in Id., *Etudes sur la religion romaine*, Roma 1972, pp. 153–170) Per le vicende complesse relative all'introduzione del culto metroaco nell'Urbe, dopo l'opera "classica" di H. Graillot, *Le culte de Cybèle Mère des dieux à Rome et dans l'Empire romain*, Paris 1912, pp. 25–69, cfr. T. Köves, "Zum Empfang der Magna Mater in Rom", *Historia* 12 (1963), pp. 321–347; F. Bömer, "Kybele in Rom. Die Geschichte ihres Kults als politisches Phänomen", *RM* 71 (1964), pp. 130–151.

[36] P. Lambrechts, che pure cita rapidamente il monumento acrense, non ne ha percepito la rilevanza storico-religiosa e, in considerazione della scarsa documentazione del culto metroaco in Sicilia e in Italia meridionale, ritiene di poter concludere sull'assoluta ininfluenza di queste regioni nel fenomeno dell'introduzione di esso a Roma ("Le culte métroaque en Sicile et en Italie méridionale", *BABesch* 39, 1964, pp. 162–166). Sulle presenze di italici e romani in Sicilia fra il III e il II sec.a.C. basti qui rimandare a A.J.N. Wilson, *Emigration from Italy in the Republican Age of Rome*, New York 1966, pp. 19–22; 55–64 e *passim*.

ricevuto nel 217 a.C. il culto di quella *Venus* madre di Enea che si configurava come protettrice dell' Urbe,[37] nel medesimo quadro dell'antica tradizione delle sue origini "troiane", esso poteva essere proclive a riconoscere nella dea sovrana dell'Ida troiano, acclimatata ormai sul suolo siceliota, una nuova efficace garante dei suoi destini imperialistici. E ciò nonostante che, nel momento della "chiamata" ufficiale del personaggio all'interno delle proprie strutture cultuali, la classe dirigente che decise le modalità dell'evento preferì, per evidenti motivazioni politiche oltre che di prestigio religioso, appellare direttamente alla patria anatolica della *Mater Magna deorum* per il tramite dell'utile alleato Attalo di Pergamo.

Comunque, al di là di tale questione aperta alle ipotesi e alle interpretazioni più diverse nell'assenza di prove documentarie che non siano quelle "indiziarie" offerte dalla generale situazione storica dai tratti sopra evocati, rimane intera tutta la carica storico-religiosa del problema posto dall'esistenza nel piccolo centro siceliota di un santuario metroaco dalle singolari connotazioni strutturali e iconografiche, spie di un'altrettanto specifica *facies* ideologica e cultuale per la quale—come vedremo—unici parametri di riferimento possono individuarsi nel quadro di una grecità orientale, delle isole egee e soprattutto delle regioni micro-asiatiche, le quali nel periodo ellenistico—nell'ormai piena maturazione dei legami antichi e intensi con la cultura e la religiosità locali—assistono ad una diffusa fioritura del culto metroaco.

L'omogeneità di una vera e propria sede cultuale di tipo rupestre è il primo elemento caratterizzante l'area dei rilievi acrensi scolpiti sulle pendici meridionali del Colle Orbo, detti localmente Santoni. Senz'altro da rifiutare è l'interpretazione del monumento come complesso di sculture votive, a carattere episodico e fortuito, pur affer-

---

[37] Cfr. R. Schilling, *La religion romaine de Vénus, depuis les origines jusqu'aux temps d'Auguste*, Paris 1954 (2a ed. Paris 1982), pp. 233–266; Id., "La place de la Sicile dans la religion romaine", *Kokalos* X–XI (1964–1965), pp. 275–279; D. Kienast, "Rom und die Venus von Eryx", *Hermes* 93 (1965), pp. 478–489. Per il rapporto fra le due dee "eneadi" sul Palatino si veda già A. Bartoli, "Il culto della Mater deum Magna Idaea e di Venere Genitrice sul Palatino", *Mem.Pont.Acc.Rom.Arch.*6 (1942), pp. 229–239. Per le varie fasi costruttive e cultuali del santuario metroaco del Palatino, dopo gli scavi di P. Romanelli ("Lo scavo al Tempio della Magna Mater sul Palatino e nelle sue adiacenze", *MAL* 46, 1962, cols. 201–330), si vedano i risultati delle più recenti ricognizioni archeologiche in P. Pensabene, "Nuove indagini nell'area del tempio di Cibele sul Palatino" in U. Bianchi-M.J. Vermaseren (edd.), *La soteriologia dei culti orientali nell'Impero romano. Atti del Colloquio internazionale Roma 24–28 Settembre 1979* (EPRO 92), Leiden 1982, pp. 68–108, Tavv.I–X.

mata a suo tempo da uno studioso attento di storia siciliana come
B. Pace.[38] Riconosciuta l'indubbia consistenza metroaca delle rappresentazioni, già accolta da autorevoli interpreti del passato e ormai acquisita stabilmente alla ricerca sulla natura e la diffusione del
culto della Grande Dea anatolica,[39] non ha più bisogno di giustifi-
cazioni la definizione di "santuario", già da noi adottata per descri-
vere il monumento acrense.

Le dodici nicchie di diversa grandezza e variamente decorate con
una o più figure ad alto rilievo, si dispongono su due piani, rispettivamente il superiore scandito da undici nicchie e l'inferiore dalla
dodicesima, lungo un costone roccioso di livello diseguale, visibil-
mente adattato con opportuni tagli nella roccia (Figs. 1–2). Esse, anche
per la contestuale presenza di due piccole aree semicircolari alle
estremità del monumento che presentano due basi circolari di altari,
configurano una struttura organica all'interno della quale doveva
dispiegarsi l'attività cultuale.

Di questa purtroppo permangono solo labili tracce nella notizia di
un erudito locale ottocentesco, il barone Gabriele Iudica, cui si de-
vono dei saggi di scavo nell'area antistante le sculture. Nell'opera in
cui egli descrive *Le antichità di Acre*, dichiara di aver posto in luce "fra
le quantità di ceneri, di carboni, lucerne, olle e piccole patere".[40] Se
queste ultime rientrano nel novero delle offerte votive più comuni
nei più diversi contesti cultuali, le lucerne evocano uno scenario di
riti notturni, perfettamente consono a quanto la documentazione attesta per certi aspetti peculiari del culto metroaco.

Le più recenti indagini condotte a cura di L Bernabò Brea non
hanno rivelato altro che frammenti ceramici capaci di fornire qualche elemento per datare la frequentazione dell'area sacra precisa-
mente intorno al III sec.a.C., muti tuttavia sulla vita rituale di essa.[41]

---

[38] *Arte e civiltà della Sicilia antica*, vol. II, Genova-Roma-Napoli-Città di Castello
1938, p. 125; vol. III, p. 514. Lo studioso inoltre interpreta il monumento come
riferentesi al culto di Demetra (*op. cit.*, vol. II, pp. 124–130 e figs. 113–114; vol. III,
p. 514 s. e fig. 143; Id., "Arti e Artisti della Sicilia antica", *Mem.Acc.Linc.*15 (1915),
S. 5a, pp. 557–560 e fig. 61). Per la storia delle varie esegesi dei Rilievi si veda
G. Sfameni Gasparro, *I culti*, pp. 126–128.
[39] Ci meraviglia che uno studioso come R. Turcan, nel recensire il nostro volume
sui *Culti orientali in Sicilia*, abbia potuto dichiarare che la "Mètèr d'Acrae est probablement une *Potnia thèròn* qui a quelque parenté avec d'autres Mères de la Grande
Grèce (cf. G. Zuntz, *Persephone*, Oxford 1971), mais non pas précisément avec celles
de Pessinonte" (*RHE* 1975, p. 203).
[40] G. Iudica, *Le antichità di Acre scoperte, descritte e illustrate*, Messina 1819, p. 14.
[41] *op. cit.*, pp. 111–113.

Figure 1. Veduta generale del santuario metroaco di Akrai: da G. Sfameni Gasparro, *I culti orientali in Sicilia*, EPRO 31, Leiden 1973, Tav.LXVIII,109

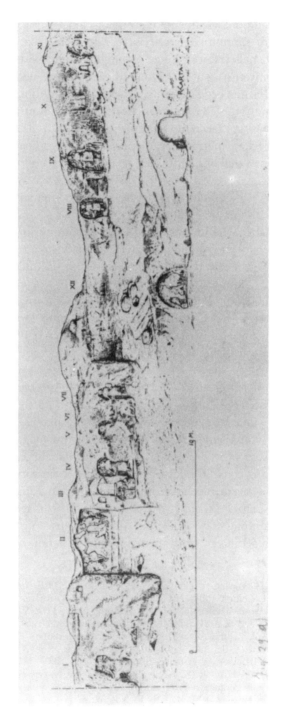

Figure 2. *Idem*: disegno di R. Carta, *ibid.*, Tav.LXIX,110

I paralleli tipologicamente e cronologicamente più prossimi a siffatta struttura di santuario rupestre a carattere metroaco possono essere individuati nelle regioni micro-asiatiche. Meno pertinente appare infatti il confronto con la grotta attica di Vari, dedicata al culto di Pan, di Hermes e delle Ninfe, essendo assai dubbia l'identificazione con la dea frigia della figura in trono scolpita su una parete di essa.[42] I monumenti cui facciamo riferimento sono tutti di indubbia ed esclusiva consistenza metroaca e di piena età ellenistica, essendo in tutti i casi gli inizi dell'impianto sacro e del relativo culto situabili nel IV– III sec.a.C.

Il primo dei santuari rupestri la cui fisionomia strutturale risulta la più vicina al complesso acrense è quello della *Meter Steunene* di Aezani (Frigia), data la natura del luogo, un promontorio roccioso lungo il quale si collocano un'ampia caverna fronteggiata da una terrazza con due larghi *bothroi* circolari, tre nicchie destinate ad accogliere rilievi votivi, numerose altre nicchie di minori proporzioni con analoga destinazione e piccole grotte (Fig. 3). Il materiale rinvenuto nell'area sacra, nel definirla come sede di culto metroaco identificabile con il santuario della Meter Steunene noto a Pausania (VIII,4,3; X,32,3), mostra che la sua vita si prolunga fino ad età imperiale romana.[43]

Parimenti significativo è il confronto con il piccolo santuario di Kapikaya presso Pergamo, costituito da una grotta nella roccia, presso cui scorre una sorgente, essendo scavate sulla parete delle nicchie per rilievi votivi[44] mentre un' analogia ancora maggiore sotto il profilo tipologico offre il complesso sacro del Panajir Dagh presso Efeso (Fig. 4). Esso consiste infatti in una vasta parete rocciosa percorsa da una ricca serie di nicchie[45] da cui provengono i numerosi rilievi votivi dalla singolare iconografia che presenta delle specifiche, anche se parziali, affinità con quella dei rilievi acrensi. Vi appare infatti la dea, talora seduta in trono fiancheggiato da leoni, con patera e largo

---

[42] Cfr. C.H. Weller et alii, "The Cave at Vari", *AJA* 7 (1903), pp. 261–349.

[43] *CCCA* I, Leiden 1987, 124 (santuario) e 125–135 (materiale). Si veda già per una prima identificazione del sito Th. Wiegand, "ΜΗΤΗΡ ΣΤΕΥΝΗΝΗ", *AM* 36 (1911), pp. 302–307 e M. Schede, "Ausgrabungen des Deutschen Archäologischen Instituts in Ankyra und Aezani", *Gnomon* 5 (1929), pp. 60–61. Un'ampia descrizione del monumento e del suo significato religioso in L. Robert, "Documents d'Asie Mineure. XVIII. Fleuves et cultes d'Aizanoi", *BCH* 105 (1981), pp. 331–360.

[44] *CCCA* I,424–425. Cfr. K. Nohlen—W. Radt, *Kapikaya ein Felsheiligtum bei Pergamon* (Altertümer von Pergamon XII), Berlin 1978.

[45] *CCCA* I,612 pl. CXXXII. Cfr. F. Naumann, *op. cit.*, pp. 214–216.

Figure 3. Santuario della *Meter Steunene* di Aezani, Frigia: da M.J. Vermaseren, *CCCA* I, EPRO 50, Leiden 1987, pl. XVII,124

Figure 4. Santuario del Panajir Dagh (Efeso): *ibid.*, pl. CXXXII,612

timpano,[46] più spesso in piedi con i medesimi attributi,[47] accompagnata da due assessori maschili, l'uno giovanile solitamente identificato dal petaso come Hermes, l'altro maturo, barbuto, secondo il tipo di Zeus.[48]

A differenza dei rilievi acrensi, scolpiti nella roccia, quelli efesini erano mobili e quindi estraibili dalle nicchie che li ospitavano. Numerose iscrizioni dedicatorie accompagnano le immagini votive, di cui ulteriori esemplari provengono anche da altre aree della città.[49]

La peculiare autoctonia micro-asiatica della tipologia della scultura rupestre e le sue connessioni con il culto della Grande Dea locale, nelle sue diverse "epifanie" e relative denominazioni, non ha bisogno di dimostrazioni. Le note rock-façades frigie, da Arslan Kaya (Küçük Kapikaya)[50] a Maltas-Malkaya[51] e Bahsis[52] fino al notissimo Monumento di Mida di Yazilikaya,[53] oggetto dell'indagine esemplare di E. Haspels,[54] sono tutte databili nel VI sec.a.C. e a loro volta si collegano con più antichi monumenti rupestri dell'area anatolica di VIII–VII sec.a.C. raffiguranti una dea in piedi o seduta.[55] Particolarmente rilevante, anche se appartenente ad una diversa tipologia artistica, è la nota statua da Büyükkale, di figura femminile con alto *polos*, accompagnata da due assessori maschili rappresentati in proporzioni ridotte ai suoi lati, i quali suonano rispettivamente il flauto e l'arpa.[56]

Tutta questa documentazione attesta l'avvenuta costituzione nel VI sec.a.C. di due moduli iconografici, che più tardi convergeranno

---

[46] Cfr., ad esempio, *CCCA* I,613 pl. CXXXIII e 617 pl. CXXXIV.

[47] *CCCA* I,614–615 pl. CXXXIII.

[48] Tra gli innumerevoli esemplari basti ricordare il rilievo *CCCA* I,616: Hermes col petaso e 614–615,644: coppia di assessori.

[49] *CCCA* I,613–685 pl. CXXXIII–CLIII.

[50] *CCCA* I,111–112, pl. XVI.

[51] *CCCA* I,118.

[52] *CCCA* I,119.

[53] *CCCA* I,168 pl. XXVIII.

[54] E.H. Haspels, *The Highlands of Phrygia. Sites and Monuments*, vols. I–II, Princeton 1971. Cfr. anche L. Robert, *REG* 85 (1972), Bulletin Epigraphique, pp. 475–482, nn. 459–474.

[55] Sulla storia dell'arte rupestre frigia basti qui ricordare i fondamentali contributi di E. Akurgal (*Phrygische Kunst*, Ankara 1955; *Die Kunst Anatoliens von Homer bis Alexander*, Berlin 1961) e la recente messa a punto di F. Isik ("Die Entstehung der frühen Kybelebilder Phrygiens und ihre Einwirkung auf die ionische Plastik", *JÖAI* 57, Beibl. 1986/87, cols. 41–108: Id., "Zur Entstehung der Phrygischen Felsdenkmäler", *AS* 37 (1987), pp. 163–178.

[56] *CCCA* I,32 pl. IV; F. Naumann, *op. cit.*, pp. 71–84; p. 295 n. 23 Taf.7,1. Si veda anche G. Neumann, "Die Begleiter der phygischen Müttergöttin von Bogazköy", *Nach.d.Akad.d.Wiss. in Gottingen*, Phil.-hist.Kl. 1959, nr. 6, pp. 101–105.

spesso in un medesimo contesto, ossia quello nord-ionico ed eolico meridionale con il tipo della dea seduta in trono, spesso all'interno di un *naiskos*, con leoncello sui ginocchi, e quello sud-ionico, con la figura in piedi. Entrambi gli schemi sono verisimilmente di origine frigia ma presto risultano sottoposti ad una più o meno profonda ellenizzazione.[57]

Il rapporto vitale con l'ambiente montano della personalità divina denominata *Kybele* o *Meter Kybele*, già in questo periodo corrispondente alla lidia *Kybaba* o *Kybebe* dalle lontane ascendenze siriache,[58] sarà più tardi riflesso nell'attributo tipico di *oreia* così frequente nella documentazione letteraria e negli innumerevoli nomi toponimici che la designano nei varii centri di culto.[59] Esso, che pure è tradotto verisimilmente in termini iconografici nella struttura del *naiskos* come figura della grotta, è espresso plasticamente nel radicamento della sua immagine ovvero del trono e della porta, che pure la rappresentano, nella viva roccia.[60]

Se la continuità di questa ideologia nell'Asia Minore ellenistica è del tutto naturale, l'interpretazione storico-religiosa del monumento acrense, situato nell'estremo Occidente greco, non può evitare il riferimento all'ambiente anatolico come il più probabile parametro cui collegare la tipologia in questione. Prima di verificare se sussistano le coordinate storiche atte a giustificare l'ipotesi di un rapporto ovvero di una vera e propria derivazione da modelli micro-asiatici per l'ideazione di tale monumento, è necessario analizzare gli schemi iconografici e i relativi contenuti ideologici dei rilievi acrensi.

Il primo ed essenziale motivo, ricorrente in tutte le sculture, con due sole eccezioni, è costituito dall'immagine di Cibele seduta in trono di prospetto, con chitone e *himation*, e recante gli attributi tipici del modio, della patera nella destra e del timpano nella sinistra, indivi-

---

[57] Sull'iconografia di Cibele, oltre l'ampia indagine di F. Naumann, osservazioni utili anche nella perspicua sintesi di F. Graf, "The Arrival of Cybele in the Greek East" in *Actes du VIIe Congrès FIEC*, vol. I, pp. 117–120.

[58] Cfr. W.F. Albright, "The Anatolian Goddess Kubaba", *Archiv für Orientforschung* 5 (1928–1929), pp. 229–231; E. Laroche, "Koubaba, déesse anatolienne, et le problème des origines de Cybèle" in *Eléments orientaux*, cit., pp. 113–128.

[59] Per la documentazione relativa ci sia permesso rimandre ai nostri precedenti lavori sul tema (*Connotazioni metroache di Demetra*, cit., p. 1165; *Soteriology*, pp. 1–4).

[60] Cfr. Ch. Picard, "Rhéa-Cybèle et le culte des portes sacrées" in L. Freeman Sandler (ed.), *Essays in Memory of Karl Lehmann*, New York 1964, pp. 259–266; D.M. Cosi, "La simbologia della porta nel Vicino Oriente per una interpretazione dei monumenti rupestri frigi", *Annali della Facoltà di Lettere e Filosofia* I (1976), pp. 113–152.

duabili nelle sculture meglio conservate e ipotizzabili con buon fonda-
mento nelle altre. A fianco del seggio della dea appaiono spesso due
leoni in posizione araldica[61] ovvero un solo animale.[62] In un caso si
può sospettare che un animale fosse raffigurato accovacciato sulle
ginocchia della dea.[63] Siffatta tipologia, a partire almeno dal VI
sec.a.C., come già notato, è pressocché canonica nell'iconografia metroaca e non ha bisogno di esemplificazioni, sebbene si possa fare
riferimento alla classificazione formulata da S.N. Svoronos a proposito
dei *naiskoi* ateniesi per l'identificazione di classi e tipi particolari.[64]

Tuttavia, ai fini della definizione delle valenze religiose del santuario acrense, piuttosto che questo comune schema iconografico, pur
fondamentale per stabilire l'identità della divina titolare del culto,
risultano essenziali le numerose presenze accessorie che intervengono
in una serie di Rilievi insieme con la Grande Dea, anche se in posizione subalterna. Di fatto, soltanto le nicchie con i Rilievi IV, VI–
VII e X–XI,[65] mostrano la sola immagine della dea seduta. I Rilievi
I, III, V, VIII e IX ispirati alla medesima tipologia e i due impor-
tanti Rilievi II e XII che invece presentano la dea in piedi, mostrano
una pluralità di personaggi la cui identificazione, pur in taluni casi
problematica, tuttavia lascia emergere una complessa e articolata
teologia ruotante attorno al personaggio centrale del culto.

Non insisteremo ora su alcuni motivi di minore importanza per la
definizione di quella teologia, o di interpretazione troppo incerta a
causa della pessima conservazione delle sculture, come è il caso delle
tracce evanescenti di quattro figure nel Rilievo I[66] ovvero dei tre
piccoli personaggi presso il trono divino nel Rilievo VIII (fedeli?).[67]
Menzioniamo soltanto, per la singolarità dello schema iconografico,
la scena del Rilievo IV che nella parte superiore, presso l'omero della
dea, mostra una seconda piccola nicchia che ospita una figura in cui
si può forse riconoscere l'immagine della stessa *Meter* accompagnata

---

[61] *I culti*, p. 130: Rilievi IV–V Cat.320–321, Tavv.LXXXIV–LXXXIX, figs. 124–
130; Rilievi VII–IX Cat.323–325, Tavv.LXXXVI–XCIII, figs. 127–134.
[62] *Ibid.*, Rilievo I Cat.317.
[63] *Ibid.*, p. 131: Rilievo I Cat.317.
[64] J.N. Svoronos, *Das Athener Nationalmuseum*, vol. III, Athen 1937, pp. 622–626.
[65] *I culti*, p. 271 Cat.320; p. 272 Cat. 22–323; p. 274 s. Cat.326–327.
[66] *Ibid.*, p. 268 s. Cat.317.
[67] *Ibid.*, p. 273 Cat.324, Tavv.XC–XCI, figs. 131–132. M.J. Vermaseren interpreta la piccola figura ignuda presso la figura femminile in trono della nicchia superiore come un "Attis fanciullo"(s.v. *Attis* in *LIMC* III,1, Zürich—München 1986,
p. 41 n. 411 fig. *ibid.*,).

da due piccoli "assessori" ignudi.[68] Se per un verso viene qui evocata la nota tipologia della duplicazione dell'immagine divina, ben attestata per la stessa Cibele nella serie dei doppi *naiskoi* provenienti soprattutto da Atene e da Delo,[69] ma costituente un motivo iconografico abbastanza diffuso nell'area greca in relazione a diverse figure divine,[70] per l'altro il rilievo acrense mantiene la sua singolarità per la diversa proporzione delle figure.

Molto congetturale rimane l'interpretazione della scena complessa del Rilievo VIII, che presenta tra l'altro un personaggio seduto su un ripiano della roccia presso la consueta figura in trono della dea. All'identificazione con il sileno Marsia proposta da L. Bernabò Brea,[71] la quale evocherebbe un personaggio parzialmente analogo a quel *propolos* agreste che è il già ricordato Pan, a suo tempo abbiamo preferito quella con Attis,[72] di cui si avrebbe una ulteriore immagine oltre quelle, più sicure, dei rilievi II e XII.

Senza poter essere peraltro troppo affermativi in proposito, aggiungiamo soltanto che appunto il Rilievo XII presenta particolari problemi esegetici.[73] Al centro della scena, ai lati delimitata da due leoncelli, è infatti un personaggio con modio che, identificabile alla dea per questo attributo e l'evidente posizione di preminenza all'interno dell'intera composizione, tuttavia è abbigliato con una corta tunica che lascia scoperte le gambe a partire dai ginocchi. Le difficoltà interpretative relative a questa figura si propongono anche, oltre che per l'immagine con gambe sovrapposte secondo un atteggiamento abbastanza frequente nelle rappresentazioni di Attis appoggiato al *pedum* pastorale, anche per il terzo personaggio della scena, identificabile come maschile per la foggia dell'abbigliamento (tunica corta e mantello) che tiene due fiaccole, l'una rivolta verso l'alto e l'altra verso il basso, fino a toccare una sorta di blocco quadrato, forse un altare. Il significato di tutto il quadro rimane oscuro per l'assenza di parametri iconografici. E' comunque confermata la singolare ricchezza figurativa e ideologica del santuario acrense, specchio di concezioni mitiche e forse anche di prassi rituali di cui in larga misura ci

---

[68] *Ibid.*, p. 271 Cat.320.

[69] Cfr. M.C. Giammarco Razzano, "Il culto di Cibele e il problema dei doppi naiskoi", *Miscellanea greca e romana* 9 (1984), pp. 63–88.

[70] T. Hadzisteliou Price, "Double and Multiple Representations in Greek Art and Religious Thought", *JHS* 91 (1971), pp. 48–69.

[71] *Op. cit.*, p. 103.

[72] *I culti*, pp. 145–147.

[73] *Ibid.*, p. 147 s., p. 175 s. Cat.328 Tav.C–CI, figs. 141–142.

sfuggono, per la mancanza di fonti parallele, le articolazioni e le valenze religiose.

Chiaramente individuabile è invece lo specifico contenuto e significato storico-religioso di un tema iconografico abbastanza costante nei rilievi acrensi, ossia quello dei due "assessori" raffigurati ai due lati della testa della dea, in proporzioni assai ridotte ma chiaramente identificabili dagli attributi (asta e scudo o timpano) come i mitici *propoloi* della dea, ossia i Coribanti frequentemente identificati con i Cureti, connessi a loro volta in maniera specifica con lo Zeus cretese e la madre Rhea, quest'ultima a sua volta presto assimilata in Grecia alla Gran Madre anatolica.

Non ripeteremo qui quanto già argomentato in proposito né riteniamo utile addurre ancora una volta la documentazione archeologica ben nota che mostra le figure in questione nella formula specifica di una "coppia" di assessori presso Cibele.[74] Parimenti superfluo sarebbe addurre le numerose fonti letterarie che conoscono un gruppo indefinito di "servitori" mitici, talora rappresentati nell'attualità da associazioni di fedeli addetti alla celebrazione del culto orgiastico della dea. Basti ricordare per tutti il notissimo *excursus* di Strabone (*Geogr.*X,3,7–23) che, interrogandosi sul problema che potremmo definire di esegesi storico-religiosa avant-lettre posto dai Cureti e dai numerosi gruppi di analoghi personaggi (Satiri, Sileni, Baccanti, Titiri, Coribanti), cioè se essi siano esseri di rango sovrumano (*daimones*) ovvero "servitori degli dei" (*propoloi theon*), adduce le varie tradizioni che, collegando i miti e i riti cretesi e frigi, considerano Coribanti, Cabiri, Dattili dell'Ida e Telchini come identici ai Cureti (*ibid.*, 3,7). Aggiunge poi che i Greci danno il nome di Cureti ai *propoloi* della "Grande Dea frigia o ancora, secondo il luogo in cui la si venera Idea, Dindimene, Sipilene, Pessinuntide, Cibele e *Kybele*" e "li chiamano anche Coribanti o, per contrazione *Kyrbantes*" (*ibid.*, 3,12).[75]

Ai monumenti citati nella nostra precedente indagine, si può aggiungere una terracotta probabilmente proveniente dall'isola di Egina, che mostra ai lati del trono di Cibele le figure di due Coribanti-Cureti riconoscibili dallo scudo.[76] Essi stanno nella medesima posizione araldica dei personaggi dei Rilievi acrensi, a differenza di tutti gli altri esempi noti, in cui essi appaiono piuttosto in movimento, nel

---

[74] *Ibid.*, pp. 132–135.

[75] Un'interpretazione del passo straboniano in H. Jeanmaire, *Couroi et Courètes*, Lille 1939, pp. 593–616.

[76] *CCCA* II,527 fig. 18a p. 168.

tipico atteggiamento di concitazione orgiastica evocato nel mito e realizzato nella prassi cultuale. Questo piccolo monumento, di cui non è nota l'esatta cronologia ma che può ritenersi tardo-ellenistico ovvero imperiale romano, costituisce il parallelo più pertinente per lo schema rigidamente frontale e statico dei Coribanti acrensi.

La complessa scena del Rilievo II (Fig. 5) si rivela decisiva per la definizione dell'orizzonte teologico sotteso all'iconografia del santuario acrense.[77] L'identificazione dei personaggi che compongono l'"assemblea" metroaca, sufficientemente sicura, delinea un quadro complesso, i cui singoli elementi trovano riscontro nell'uno o nell'altro settore dell'universo mitico e cultuale della Grande Dea anatolica. Nella sua totalità, peraltro, esso manca di adeguati paralleli, costituendosi come un *unicum*, una sorta di coagulo non altrimenti attestato di temi iconografici e ideologici variamente alternantisi nella documentazione a noi nota.

Al centro della scena appare un personaggio in piedi in posizione frontale che l'abbigliamento (chitone e *himation*), l'attributo del modio sul capo e soprattutto i due piccoli leoni in posizione araldica ai lati definiscono come Cibele. Tuttavia, mentre piuttosto anomala è la presenza di un terzo animale su cui la dea poggia il piede sinistro, singolare è soprattutto il gesto delle braccia, distese in entrambe le direzioni fino a poggiare le mani sulla testa di due personaggi che l'affiancano. Di essi, quello di sinistra è identificabile senza equivoco, per la presenza del grande *kerykeion*, come Hermes mentre nella figura di destra, con le gambe incrociate e asta o più probabilmente *pedum*, abbiamo ritenuto di poter individuare Attis, il *paredros* di Cibele che emerge chiaramente nell'ambito del culto metroaco nel mondo greco a partire dal IV sec.a.C.[78]

---

[77] *I culti*, pp. 135–144; p. 269 s. Cat.318 Tavv.LXXVI–LXXVII, figs. 117–118.

[78] Basti ricordare la notissima stele del Pireo con dedica ad Agdistis e Attis (*CCCA* II,308 pl. LXXVIII) e la celebrazione degli *Attideia* da parte della locale comunità degli Orgeoni (*CCCA* II,262). Per la ricca documentazione proveniente da questa area si veda *CCCA* II,257–322 pl. LIX–LXXXVI. Non è possibile in questa sede discutere in dettaglio la recente formula interpretativa di L.E. Roller che fa di Attis una "creazione" greca, frutto della proiezione a livello mitico della figura del Gallo, il devoto eunuco della dea, privo dunque di qualsiasi autentica ed autonoma consistenza religiosa ("Attis on Greek Votive Monuments Greek God or Phrygian?", *Hesperia* 63, 1994, pp. 245–262, pl. 55–56). La tesi, di sapore evemeristico, non è del tutto nuova. Per una diversa esegesi, fondata sulle valenze ctonio-vegetali del personaggio, nella sua specifica consistenza mitica e cultuale, ci sia permesso rinviare al nostro saggio già citato (*Soteriology, passim*).

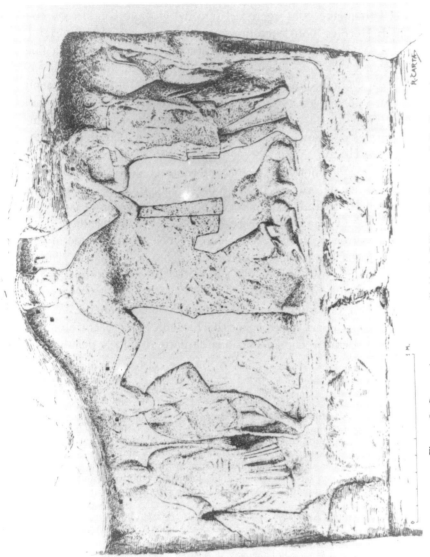

Figure 5. Santuario metroaco di Akrai, Rilievo II, disegno di R. Carta: da G. Sfameni Gasparro, *I culti*, Tav.LXXVII,118

A fianco di Attis interviene la figura della fanciulla dadofora, ben nota nella documentazione figurata come accompagnatrice della Madre divina, solitamente insieme con il giovinetto recante l'*oinochoe*, certo ad evocare il contesto rituale, peculiare del culto della dea che già Pindaro conosce oggetto dei cori notturni di fanciulle. Parimenti noto è il frequente convergere del tipo del giovane con *oinochoe* con quello di Hermes, con la costituzione di una triade che, ricorrente con particolare frequenza nei *naiskoi* attici,[79] è attestata già alla fine del V sec.a.C. da una scena singolare incisa su un medaglione argenteo da Olinto. Qui tuttavia, a differenza di tutti i monumenti metroaci, i personaggi sono raffigurati in movimento: su un cocchio trainato da leoni sta ritta la dea mentre a fianco del cocchio avanzano Hermes e la fanciulla con due grandi fiaccole, variamente identificata con Hecate[80] o con Persefone.[81] E' probabile peraltro che la scena del piccolo monumento macedone, nella sua tipica atmosfera di corsa concitata, rifletta un episodio mitico quale è quello della ricerca della figlia rapita da parte di una Demetra che da parte sua nel V–IV sec.a.C. ha assunto—in certi contesti—delle peculiari "connotazioni metroache" nell'accostamento a Cibele, contribuendo in pari tempo a quella ellenizzazione della dea frigia che risulta, tra l'altro, proprio dalla sua associazione alla coppia di "assessori" costituita dalla fanciulla dadofora e da Hermes.

Se l'esegesi del monumento da Olinto come pertinente ad una Demetra con valenze metroache (cocchio con leoni) è corretta,[82] se ne potrebbe dedurre che l'assunzione da parte di Cibele della coppia

---

[79] Il monumento più antico della serie sarebbe un *naiskos* del Pireo, datato dallo Svoronos nel IV sec.a.C. (*op. cit.*, vol. III, p. 624; vol. II, n° 284 Taf.CXIX,1554). Su tale documento in particolare si fonda la nota tesi di A. Conze ("Hermes-Kadmilos", *Arch.Zeit.*38, 1880, pp. 1–10 Taf.I–IV: *ibid.*, p. 1 s. B, Taf.2,3; cfr. Id., "Hermes—Kadmilos", *Ath.Mitt.*13, 1888, pp. 202–206). Lo studioso ritiene che il giovinetto con *oinochoe*, anche quando non rechi un attributo distintivo (petaso, *kerykeion*) sia da identificare con Hermes, definito *Kadmilos* per sottolineare sia il suo ruolo di "servitore" della dea sia le probabili connessioni con l' ambiente samotrace (ved. oltre). Per i principali monumenti relativi alla triade in questione cfr. *I culti*, p. 137 s. e in genere ora il *CCCA*.

[80] D.M. Robinson, *Excavations at Olynthus. X. Metal and Minor Miscellaneous Finds*, Oxford 1941, p. 260 ss., fig. 17a–b; *CCCA* VI, Leiden 1989, 204 e fig. 10, pl. XLV,204. Cfr. *I culti*, p. 138. H. Möobius, che pubblica un secondo analogo monumento, identifica con Hecate la fanciulla con fiaccole ("Die Göttin mit dem Löwen" in *Festschrift für Wilhelm Eilers. Ein Dokument der internationalen Forschung zum 27 September 1966*, Wiesbaden 1967, pp. 449–468.

[81] M.J. Vermaseren, *CCCA* VI p. 67 s.

[82] Cfr. G. Sfameni Gasparro, *Connotazioni metroache, cit.*, p. 1168 s.

di assessori costituita dalla vergine dadofora e dal giovinetto, spesso identificato ad Hermes, sia viceversa il segno di una sua caratterizzazione in senso "demetriaco" o comunque il frutto della decisa ellenizzazione della sua *facies* mitico-rituale.

Il rapporto della Gran Madre con Hermes, d'altra parte, è molto frequente nell'intero arco cronologico e geografico di svolgimento del culto metroaco.[83] Con particolare insistenza, indizio certo di una specifica "teologia" di cui purtroppo ci sfuggono le coordinate e le valenze specifiche, esso emerge dai rilievi efesini già ricordati in cui si configura un'ulteriore formula iconografica di tipo triadico. La dea vi è accompagnata da due assessori maschili, l'uno dei quali è appunto Hermes e il secondo il personaggio barbuto del tipo di Zeus, non meglio identificato, i quali peraltro sembrano porsi su un piano di parità rispetto alla *Meter* piuttosto che in posizione subordinata come nel caso della fanciulla dadofora e dell'Hermes definibile, con il Conze, come *Kadmilos*.

Il rilievo acrense in esame, da parte sua, fonde questo schema di peculiare valenza ellenica, con quello di ascendenza anatolica in cui interviene il paredro frigio della dea. Tuttavia, piuttosto che nella formula di coppia quale appare nel notissimo rilievo del Pireo con dedica ad Agdistis e nell'intera documentazione mitica e cultuale pertinente a Cibele, Attis è qui situato in uno schema triadico, componendosi appunto con l'Hermes che specularmente gli corrisponde a fianco della *Meter*. Ne risulta che questa ulteriore formula di triade, ben attestata del resto nella documentazione di età imperiale[84] e già ritenuta dal Picard riflesso di un "sincretismo greco-frigio" tardivo,[85] deve farsi risalire alla prima età ellenistica che si conferma momento cruciale—dopo gli essenziali prodromi di età arcaica e classica—del fenomeno di ellenizzazione del contesto metroaco ma anche di recupero delle valenze autenticamente orientali di questo contesto medesimo.

In tale dialettica di costruzione di una *facies* ellenica e di consapevole valorizzazione delle connotazioni originarie della Gran Madre

---

[83] Una documentazione nel nostro volume *I culti*, p. 139 s. Sul tema si veda più ampiamente M.J. Vermaseren, "Kybele und Merkur" in S. Sahin—E. Schwertheim—J. Wagner (edd.), *Studien zur Religion und Kultur Kleinasiens, Festschrift für Friedrich Karl Dörner zum 65. Geburtstag am 28 Februar 1976* (EPRO 66), Leiden 1978, vol. II, pp. 956–966 Taf.CCXXIII.

[84] *I culti*, pp. 136–137.

[85] Ch. Picard, "Trapézophore sculpté d'un sanctuaire thasien", *Mon.Piot* 40 (1944), pp. 107–134. Cfr. anche E. Will, *art. cit.*, pp. 105–111.

anatolica si pone anche l'ultima, significativa componente del quadro delineato dagli ignoti ideatori del santuario acrense. Ai lati estremi del Rilievo II, infatti, si pongono due figure maschili incedenti a cavallo, nelle quali si riconoscono senza equivoco quei Dioscuri che fonti letterarie, epigrafiche e monumentali collegano alla frigia Cibele[86] oltre che alla sorella Elena e ad altre figure femminili, nella formula triadica analizzata dallo Chapouthier.[87]

Anche a proposito di questo tema è superfluo ripercorrere in dettaglio l'analisi dei monumenti già ampiamente noti.[88] Piuttosto riteniamo ancora valida la suggestione avanzata da M.P. Nilsson[89] e accolta da F. Chapouthier,[90] secondo cui l'associazione dei Dioscuri con la Gran Madre frigia va interpretata alla luce dell'accostamento, talora configurato come vera e propria identificazione, dei due divini gemelli greci ai Cabiri o ai Grandi Dei di Samotracia. Anche P. Lambrechts ha ritenuto di poter affermare che la connessione Cibele-Dioscuri rispecchi una teologia di origine micro-asiatica.[91] Di fatto, abbastanza solide e antiche sono le connessioni di Cibele con la sfera mitico-cultuale dei celebri misteri samotraci e più ampiamente con l'ambito del culto cabirico[92] che, oltre Samotracia stessa e altre isole dell'Egeo quali soprattutto Lemnos e Imbros, coinvolge diverse aree del mondo greco continentale, la Beozia e Tebe in particolare.[93]

---

[86] Cfr. *I culti*, pp. 141–143.

[87] F. Chapouthier, *Les Dioscures au service d'une déesse. Étude d'iconographie religieuse*, Paris 1935. Una completa rassegna dei monumenti figurati pertinenti ai divini gemelli ora in A. Hermary, s.v. *Dioskouroi* in *LIMC* III,1, Zürich-München 1986, pp. 567–593; III,2, pp. 456–477. In particolare, per i tipi della triade Dioscuri-personaggio femminile *ibid.*, III,1, pp. 577–580 nn. 123–160; III,2, p. 466 s.

[88] Ai monumenti già esaminati nel nostro volume si può aggiungere, con J. de la Genière, che riteniamo probabile che la figura femminile tra i Dioscuri di alcuni monumenti dell'Asia Minore catalogati dallo Chapouthier come pertinenti ad Elena (*op. cit.*, p. 23 n. 1; p. 25 s. n. 3; pp. 38–40 nn. 16–18) sia piuttosto la grande dea locale. Meno sicuro è che questa sia da riconoscere in alcuni monumenti spartani analizzati dalla studiosa (*Le culte de la Mère des dieux*, cit., pp. 37–45 figs. 7–8; cfr. F. Chapouthier, *op. cit.*), p. 41 n. 20 e pp. 44–46 n. 22.

[89] *Griechische Feste*, Leipzig 1906, p. 421 s.; Id., *The Mycenean Origin of Greek Mythology*, Cambridge 1932, pp. 73 ss.

[90] *Op. cit.*, p. 17; pp. 180–184.

[91] *Le culte métroaque*, cit., p. 165 s.

[92] Cfr. *I culti*, p. 143.

[93] Per la documentazione basti rimandare alla nota monografia di B. Hemberg, *Die Kabiren*, Uppsala 1950. Un'utile raccolta delle fonti letterarie è offerta da N. Lewis, *The Ancient Literary Sources*, (Samothrace I), New York 1958, il primo di una serie di volumi che mettono a disposizione degli studiosi i risultati delle numerose e proficue campagne di scavo condotte nell'area del santuario dei misteri. La

Appunto nell'ambito dei misteri samotraci era presente quell' Hermes *Kadmilos* o *Kasmilos* che interviene spesso nella cerchia metroaca; egli talora è distinto dal gruppo dei *Megaloi Theoi* titolari del culto misterico talora invece rientra a pieno titolo in esso, quale membro di una coppia di compagni della dea dai molti nomi e dalla multiforme identità che pure fa parte di tale raggruppamento.[94]

Nella prospettiva del culto di Samotracia, il quale rimane tuttora in larga misura impenetrabile quanto ai contenuti mitici e rituali, si intreccia dunque una trama fitta e variegata di rapporti tra teologie e personaggi appartenenti anche ad ambiti storici diversi, quali sono appunto la dea dei misteri, l'anatolica Cibele, il gruppo dei Grandi Dei, talora in numero di quattro sì da inglobare la dea medesima ed Hermes *Kasmilos,* talora intesi come coppia maschile, spesso denominati Cabiri e accostati o francamente assimilati in alcuni casi ai Dioscuri.

Nel concludere l'analisi del rilievo acrense avevamo ritenuto di poter affermare che il contesto religioso samotrace "sembra porsi, nella sua tipica apertura alle associazioni fra più divinità in un unico contesto variamente composto, come il più utile parametro per comprendere l'ideologia religiosa che soggiace al Rilievo II. In esso, come in una sintesi di iconografie e dottrine teologiche diverse, abbiamo visto Cibele emergere al centro di un'assemblea di divinità di rango subalterno: Hermes, Attis, Hecate, i Dioscuri. Tutti questi personaggi sono connessi, in formule diverse, con la dea, secondo le molteplici fonti (letterarie, epigrafiche, monumentali) alle quali si è fatto riferimento. L'originalità della composizione acrense sta nella contemporaneità di queste presenze, per la quale non sappiamo addurre alcun parallelo a noi noto. E' difficile ammettere che tale complessa ed originale visione religiosa sia stata creata *in loco*; ma pur avendo indicato nel mondo di una grecità periferica e ricca di valenze "barbare" e orientalizzanti, quale è quello samotrace, un opportuno termine di confronto per una siffatta molteplicità di associazioni, non ci è possibile essere troppo affermativi in proposito e parlare di una precisa derivazione.

---

conoscenza dei contenuti religiosi di questi ultimi, peraltro, rimane tuttora sostanzialmente preclusa all'indagine critica per la scarsa espressività delle fonti in proposito. Un recente approccio al problema in S. Guettel Cole, *Theoi Megaloi. The Cult of the Great Gods at Samothrace* (EPRO 96), Leiden 1984.

[94] Cfr. H.S. Versnel, "Mercurius amongst the Magni Dei", *Mnemosyne* 27 (1974), pp. 144–151.

La più sicura conclusione che scaturisce da questa indagine è che un centro siceliota del III sec.a.C. conosceva e venerava il paredro frigio di Cibele e in pari tempo era disponibile alla comprensione di una teologia complessa nella quale rientrano delle figure che altri documenti fanno piuttosto ritenere appartenenti a serie figurative diverse".[95]

E' lecito ora chiedersi se sia possibile compiere un ulteriore passo per l'individuazione dei parametri storici cui ricondurre in maniera diretta o mediata l'articolata trama teologica che l'iconografia rivela soggiacente al santuario rupestre di Akrai. Il confronto con l'ideologia cabirico-samotrace, per la parte di essa che una documentazione discontinua, di valore diseguale e spesso d'interpretazione assai problematica, lascia trasparire, conferma quella direzione orientale che già la struttura generale del santuario, nella sua qualità di monumento rupestre, ci aveva autorizzato a percorrere.

La legittimità di tale percorso sotto il profilo strettamente storico oltre che tipologico deve essere verificata in rapporto alla situazione della Sicilia ellenistica e in particolare dello stato siracusano nella cui orbita rientra Akrai. Se, come gli elementi stilistici tuttora percepibili nel più o meno profondo deterioramento cui le sculture sono state sottoposte nel corso dei secoli fanno ritenere, il complesso figurativo acrense si situa nel III sec.a.C., il contesto storico cui collegare l'ideazione e la realizzazione del monumento non potrà essere che quello del lungo e prospero regno di Ierone II di Siracusa, cui del resto appartiene l'unica moneta rinvenuta nell'area dei Santoni in occasione degli ultimi sondaggi archeologici cui essa è stata sottoposta.

Se infatti l'epoca di quel Dionigi II che pure fonti tarde ricordano votato al culto metroaco allorché dovette rifugiarsi esule a Corinto (a. 343 a.C.),[96] appare troppo alta per situarvi la fondazione acrense, il periodo della vicenda siciliana del corinzio Timoleonte non sembra neppur esso propizio per un evento di questo tipo. Di fatto, come è stato opportunamente notato, la monumentalità dell'opera presuppone l'intervento dei pubblici poteri e in specie, nel caso di un piccolo centro come Akrai, delle autorità della vicina metropoli piut-

---

[95] *I culti*, p. 144. Si può aggiungere che la presenza dei Dioscuri nelle tradizioni religiose siceliote è antica e abbastanza diffusa. Cfr. E. Ciaceri, *Culti e miti nella storia dell'antica Sicilia*, Catania 1911, pp. 296–301

[96] Eliano, *Var.hist.*IX; Clearco in Ateneo XII,541.

tosto che di quelle locali. Il periodo della signoria di Agatocle, che pure per la trama complessa dei suoi rapporti internazionali potrebbe aver offerto spazio ad un grandioso progetto teologico e alla relativa impresa costruttiva quali sono rappresentati dal santuario acrense, tuttavia, oltre ad essere ancora cronologicamente troppo alto per situarvi questo evento, non pare idoneo a motivarlo storicamente, in considerazione degli agitati eventi politici e militari in cui il personaggio fu coinvolto.

E' a tutti noto che il lungo e sostanzialmente pacifico regno ieroniano, soprattutto dopo la stipula del trattato di alleanza con Roma del 263 a.C., sia stato segnato da grande floridezza economica, dalla conquista di una posizione di notevole prestigio internazionale di Siracusa nell'ambito delle grandi potenze politiche ed economiche del Mediterraneo e, all'interno dei propri territori, di un'intensa attività costruttiva. Di essa sono testimoni i grandiosi resti della capitale del regno oltre che la notizia di Diodoro Siculo (XVI,83). Anche Akrai sembra aver goduto i frutti del generale benessere caratterizzante il regno ieroniano e avuto parte ai progetti di rinnovamento edilizio del sovrano se, come sembra molto probabile, il teatro e il *Bouleterion* cittadini sono da attribuire a questo periodo.[97]

In questo contesto si collocherebbe anche la costruzione del santuario metroaco, quale ulteriore segno della dimensione squisitamente ellenica per un verso e di potenza internazionale dall'altro assunta dallo stato siracusano, capace di dialogare da pari a pari con i varii regni ellenistici, come risulta in particolare dai rapporti di Ierone II con l'Egitto tolemaico e dalla politica del sovrano siracusano nei confronti della grecità insulare. E' noto infatti il suo munifico intervento nei confronti di Rodi dopo il terremoto che sconvolse l'isola e la concessione dell'*ateleia* alle navi rodie che commerciavano con Siracusa,[98] con un'intensità di frequentazione notevole, come mostrano i

---

[97] L. Bernabò Brea, *op. cit.*, pp. 31–43 (il teatro); pp. 44–51 (il *Bouleuterion*). Nonostante l'impossibilità di una datazione del tutto certa dei monumenti, in particolare del teatro, essendo il *Bouleuterion* attribuibile con buone probabilità appunto al regno ieroniano, lo studioso indica in quest'ultimo il momento storico più consono alla costruzione del teatro stesso.

[98] Polibio V,88,5–6; Diodoro XXVI,8. Sul regno ieroniano ricordiamo qui soltanto i contributi di G. De Sensi Sestito, "Relazioni commerciali e politica finanziaria di Gerone II", *Helikon* 15–16 (1975–1976), pp. 187–252; Ead., *Gerone II, un monarca ellenistico in Sicilia*, Palermo 1977. In particolare per gli aiuti concessi ai Rodiesi nel più ampio quadro della politica mediterranea del tiranno siracusano *Gerone II*, pp. 165–180.

numerosissimi bolli di anfore rodie rinvenuti nella città[99] e nella stessa Akrai.[100]

Particolarmente intensi e consistenti risultano di fatto i legami della
Sicilia con Rodi, i quali trovano riflesso in varii istituti politici e am-
ministrativi sicelioti[101] mentre alcuni documenti attestano la presenza
nell'isola egea di singoli personaggi e di intere famiglie siracusane.[102]

Il raggio dei rapporti di Siracusa in particolare ma anche di altri
centri sicelioti con il Mediterraneo orientale in età ieroniana e nei
successivi secoli dell'ellenismo, peraltro, è assai ampio. Nella documentazione analizzata a più riprese da G. Manganaro essi emergono
assai fitti e articolati in particolare con Cos,[103] che poteva mandare
i suoi *theoroi* a compiere la propaganda per il locale culto di Asclepio
nell'Isola nel 242 a.C. e riceverne decreti di accettazione da parte di
comunità cittadine, quale quella di Camarina e di *Phintias Geloorum*.[104]

---

[99] G. Manganaro, "Movimenti di uomini tra Egitto e Sicilia (III–I sec.a.C.)" in
L. Criscuolo-G. Geraci (edd.), *Egitto e storia antica dall'ellenismo all'età araba. Bilancio di
un confronto*, Atti del Colloquio internazionale Bologna, 31 agosto–2 settembre 1987,
Bologna 1989, pp. 517–519: il periodo di maggiore intensità di traffici fra Rodi e la
Sicilia risulta compreso fra il 240–210 a.C. e il 146–108 a.C. Un inventario dei
bolli anforari rodii, peraltro da integrare con i ritrovamenti degli ultimi decenni, in
G.V. Gentili, "I timbri anforari rodii nel Museo Nazionale di Siracusa", *ASS* 4
(1958), pp. 18–95.

[100] Cfr. G. Pugliese Carratelli, "Silloge delle epigrafi acrensi" in L. Bernabò Brea,
op. cit., pp. 173–175.

[101] G. Manganaro, "Città di Sicilia e santuari panellenici nel III e II sec.a.Cr.",
Historia 13 (1964), p. 147 dove lo studioso conclude l'esame della pertinente documentazione affermando che "l'elemento rodiota nella compagine demografica, politica e linguistica della Sicilia ellenistica fu assai resistente. . . . Nell'opera di riordina-
mento esercitata da Timoleonte in Sicilia fu grande il rispetto per le istituzioni locali
elleniche: nella valutazione di esse va guardato a queste realtà precise e, al dil à di
Corinto, a centri migratori come Cos e alla forza dell'elemento rodiota".

[102] Cfr. D. Morelli, "Stranieri in Rodi", *SCO* 5 (1955), p. 172: quattro donne
siracusane; p. 174: un *Tyndareus*; G. Manganaro, *Movimenti, cit*, p. 515 n. 15.
E' interessante notare che un *koinon* di Sabaziasti di Rodi pose un decreto onorifico
per il siracusano Aristone (*REG* 1984, BE, 292; *SEG* 33, 1983, 639: *c.* 100 a.C.). Un
elenco dei doni di sicelioti nel santuario di Atena Lindia in B. Pace, *Arte e civiltà*, vol.
III, p. 730 s.

[103] Nell'isola sono state rinvenute le stele funerarie di una siracusana (A. Maiuri,
Nuova silloge epigrafica di Rodi e Cos, Firenze 1925, p. 94 n. 197; F.P. Rizzo, *La Sicilia
e le potenze ellenistiche al tempo delle guerre puniche*, Suppl. a Kokalos 3, Palermo 1973,
p. 25 s. n. 4) e di una cittadina di Lilibeo (G. Susini, "Tre iscrizioni inedite da
Coo", *ASAA* 30–31, NS 14–16, 1952–1954, p. 359 s. n. 2 e fig. 2; *REG* 71, 1958,
BE 368). Nell'elenco dei vincitori dei *Dionysia* a Cos, nel III sec.a.C. è menzionato
un abitante di Taormina (*SGDI* 3643; cfr. F.P. Rizzo, *op. cit.*, p. 26 s. n. 6). E'
superfluo ricordare il lungo soggiorno nell'isola del poeta siceliota Teocrito (F.P.
Rizzo, *op. cit.*, p. 28 s.) che conferma comunque la vivacità della vita culturale della
Sicilia e di Siracusa in particolare nell'alta età ellenistica.

[104] Cfr. G. Manganaro, *Città di Sicilia*, pp. 415–419. Nel decreto dei Camarinesi

L'attribuzione da parte di R. Herzog a Gelone, figlio di Ierone II, di un lungo frammento di lettera inciso sulla medesima stele recante il decreto di *asylia* di Gela è stata contestata con buoni argomenti da L. Robert.[105] Rimane pertanto incerto se anche Siracusa sia stata raggiunta dai *theoroi* dell'Asclepieio di Cos.

Analoghi rapporti sono intrattenuti con Magnesia sul Meandro che inviò anch'essa in Occidente nel 207 a.C. i suoi *theoroi* per propagandare il culto di Artemide Leucofriene; costoro giunsero anche a Siracusa.[106] Banchieri siciliani risultano attivi nelle Cicladi nel corso del II sec.a.C., in particolare a Delo,[107] e numerosi personaggi o intere famiglie siracusane o di altre *poleis* siceliote sono presenti in centri come Mileto e Smirne.[108]

In particolare si ricorderà che nella stessa Akrai un'iscrizione di II–I sec.a.C. contenente responsi oracolari riflette una trama di rapporti con una regione anatolica come la Panfilia[109] mentre l'isola di Chio fin dal IV sec.a.C., risulta meta di cittadini siracusani[110] e a sua

---

rinvenuto Cos, relativo a tale evento (R. Herzog-G. Klaffenbach, "Asylieurkunden aus Kos", *Abhand.Berlin*, Kl. f. Sprachen 1950, I, n. 12; cfr. L. Robert, *REG* 66, 1953, BE n. 152), e nel parallelo decreto di *Phintias Geloorum* (Herzog-Klaffenbach n. 13; BE 1953, n. 152) si sottolineano i rapporti di "parentela" fra le due *poleis*. Ciò verisimilmente in conseguenza della presenza di gruppi di Cos nel movimento di greci verso la Sicilia promosso da Timoleonte per ripopolare le città siceliote. Cfr. Plutarco, *Timol.*, 35 a proposito di Gela, dove l'espressione *ek Keo* è da correggere in *ek Kôi* (cfr. Manganaro, *loc. cit.*, p. 416). Agrigento era stata ripopolata con l'apporto di coloni da Elea. Sui documenti in questione si veda anche F.P. Rizzo, *op. cit.*, pp. 7–29.

[105] Herzog-Klaffenbach n. 3; cfr. L. Robert, *REG* 66, 1953, p. 156 s.

[106] O. Kern, *Die Inschriften von Magnesia am Meander*, Berlin 1900, n. 72: decreto siracusano che riconosce alla città di Magnesia il diritto di *asylia* e accoglie l'invito alla partecipazione alla festa della dea. Cfr. G. Manganaro, *Città di Sicilia*, cit., p. 419; p. 426 s.

[107] A Delo opera quale banchiere, fin dalla fine del III sec.—inizi del II sec.a.C. Timone, figlio di Ninfodoro, siracusano. Il figlio di Timone, anch'egli di nome Ninfodoro, intorno al 179 a.C. è amministratore del tesoro sacro dl tempio di Apollo nell'isola. Cfr. J. Hatzfeld, "Les Italiens résidant a Délos", *BCH* 36 (1912), p. 108; Id., *Les trafiquants italiens dans l'Orient hellénique*, Paris 1919, p. 28 s. Gli inventari dell'isola conservano notizia dei donativi di sicelioti residenti ovvero inviati da comunità cittadine di Sicilia ai santuari locali (B. Pace, *Arte e civiltà*, vol. III, p. 730).

[108] G. Manganaro, *Città di Sicilia*, cit., p. 430 s. con relativa documentazione. Per l'ampio reticolo di rapporti commerciali e culturali dei sicelioti nell'III–II sec.a.C. nell'Oriente mediterraneo si veda Id., "La monetazione a Siracusa fra Canne e la vittoria di Marcello", *ASSO* 65 (1969), pp. 283–296; "Per una storia della Sicilia romana", *ANRW* I,1, Berlin-New York 1972, p. 452 s.

[109] G. Manganaro, "L'oracolo di Maie per una carestia in territorio siracusano", *ASNP*, Cl. Lettere e Filosofia, S. III,11 (1981), pp. 1069–1082.

[110] Iscrizione sepolcrale di un siracusano residente a Chio (IV sec.a.C.): *REG* 72 (1959), BE, 313; PW, *RE* X A (1972), col. 322. Cfr. G. Manganaro, *Movimento di uomini*, cit., p. 515 n. 15.

volta interessata a rapporti commerciali con la Sicilia.[111]

Questi dati, tratti da una documentazione relativamente ampia e che comunque, per la natura fortuita dei ritrovamenti epigrafici e archeologici, costituisce solo la punta emergente di un reticolo certo assai più denso di legami della Sicilia ellenistica e in particolare dello stato siracusano con le regioni del Mediterraneo orientale, permettono di situare storicamente un monumento come il santuario rupestre di Akrai, con la sua complessa fisionomia religiosa irriducibile ai parametri noti dello stesso culto metroaco nelle regioni della Grecia continentale. E' lecito pertanto guardare ai varî centri evocati come possibili tramiti attraverso i quali una teologia micro-asiatica con i relativi schemi iconografici di espressione poté giungere fino all'estremo Occidente ellenico rappresentato dal centro siceliota.

L'isola di Chio, già nel VI sec.a.C. conquistata al culto metroaco quale è attestato dal notissimo monumento rupestre denominato Dascalopetra e "Scuola d'Omero",[112] in età ellenistica continua a prestare culto alla dea anatolica,[113] titolare di un *Metroon* insieme con il quale in un'iscrizione del 200 a.C. è ricordato un *Kabireion*,[114] essendo la contiguità delle due sedi di culto verisimilmente riflesso della tipica connessione che di frequente li interessa.[115]

Rodi, fin dal III sec.a.C. sede di numerose associazioni religiose di *Samotraikiastai*,[116] conosce anche un fiorente culto dei Dioscuri,[117] cui

---

[111] *SEG* III,92: un cittadino di Chio, Senocrito, fu onorato da Atene per avere facilitato l'acquisto di grano in Sicilia.

[112] *CCCA* II,561 pl. CLXIX. Tra l'ampia bibliografia sul monumento basti ricordare H. Kaletsch, "Daskalopetra—ein Kybeleheiligtum auf Chios" in *Forschungen und Funde. Festschrift Bernhard Neutsch*, Innsbruck 1980, pp. 223–235, Taf.44–47.

[113] Una dedica del IV sec.a.C. è posta alla *Meter Kybeleia*: *CCCA* II,560. Cfr. W.G. Forrest, "The Inscriptions of South-East Chios, I", *ABSA* 58 (1963), p. 59 n. 11.

[114] *CCCA* II,558; W.G. Forrest, *art. cit.*, p. 62. Al I sec.a.C. si può attribuire un'altra iscrizione con dedica di una *stroté* e di *kathedrai* alla *Meter*: *CCCA* II,559; W.G. Forrest, *art. cit.*, p. 59 n. 9. Varie sculture con immagini della dea in *CCCA* II,562–565.

[115] Sul culto metroaco nell'isola e le sue connessioni con la sfera cabirica si veda F. Graf, *Nordionische Kulte. Religionsgeschichtliche und epigraphische Untersuchungen zu den Kulten von Chios, Erythrai, Klazomenai und Phokaia*, Roma 1985, pp. 107–120.

[116] D. Morelli, "I culti in Rodi", *SCO* 8 (1959), p. 57; pp. 152–154. Il culto degli dei di Samotracia è attestato a Camiro, Lindo e Rodi. I documenti dell'isola menzionano anche i sacerdoti di queste divinità. Cfr. G. Pugliese Carratelli, "Per la storia delle associazioni in Rodi antica", *ASAA*, NS 1–2 (1939–1940), p. 184 s. Un'altra dedica agli dei di Samotracia da parte di uno *hiereus* in *SEG* 33 (1983), 644: I sec.a.C.

[117] D. Morelli, *I culti*, p. 42; p. 126 s. Numerose dediche provengono da Rodi fin dal III sec.a.C. Sono attestati sacerdoti, associazioni di fedeli detti *Dioskouriastai* e

pure sono votati dei *koina* molto spesso menzionati insieme con le prime. Si tratta di un culto pubblico che si sviluppa nel medesimo periodo (215 a.C.) in cui si afferma anche quello, parimenti ufficiale, degli dei di Samotracia e dei Coribanti. Questi ultimi, nella denominazione di *Kyrbantes*, ricevono dediche a Camiro fin dal II sec.a.C. e a Rodi sono titolari di un sacerdozio.[118] Anche la *Meter theon* è titolare nel II sec.a.C. di un *koinon* per la cui caratterizzazione forse non è irrilevante che sia menzionato insieme con quello degli *Ermaistai* e in una serie che contempla anche le associazioni dei *Soteriastai*, veneratori di quei "dei Salvatori" in cui si potranno identificare gli dei di Samotracia e/o i Dioscuri.[119] L'isola peraltro si rivela già toccata anche da quel primo movimento di espansione verso Occidente che interessa la dea anatolica sul finire dell'età arcaica e agli inizi del periodo classico, come attestano due terrecotte con il tipo di Cibele seduta in trono con leoncello sui ginocchi, databili tra la fine del VI e gli inizi del V sec.a.C., rinvenute rispettivamente a Rodi[120] e a Camiro,[121] mentre alcuni esemplari più recenti (IV sec.a.C.) vengono da Lindos.[122]

Anche Cos partecipa di un'esperienza religiosa assai ricca e variegata[123] che, oltre a gravitare attorno al famoso *Asklepieion*, si alimenta delle numerose tradizioni mitiche e cultuali aggregate alle molteplici personalità divine di un *pantheon* di schietta ascendenza ellenica ma pure arricchito degli apporti del vicino mondo anatolico. In questo quadro è presente anche la Madre degli dei, destinataria di pubblici sacrifici nel III sec.a.C.[124] ma presente anche nella religiosità privata se la sua immagine, nel consueto schema della dea in trono con

---

delle feste, con agoni, chiamate *Dioskouria* e associate ad *Epitaphia*. Cfr. G. Pugliese Carratelli, "Supplemento epigrafico rodio", *ASAA* 30–32 (NS 14–16) (1952–1954), p. 268 s. n. 268. Un *koinon di Dioskouriastai* anche Lindos nel I sec.a.C. e nella Perea rodia (II sec.a.C.). G. Pugliese Carratelli, *Per la storia, cit.*, p. 180.

[118] D. Morelli, *I culti*, p. 59; p. 158 s. Cfr. M. Segre, "L'oracolo di Apollo Pythaeus a Rodi", *PP* 4 (1949), p. 73: I sec.a.C.

[119] D. Morelli, *I culti*, p. 57; p. 60 e p. 160. *SIG*⁴ 1114; *CCCA* II,674.

[120] *CCCA* II,673 pl. CC.

[121] *CCCA* II,678 pl. CC.

[122] *CCCA* II,675–677. Cfr. C. Blinkenberg, *Lindos*, vol. I, *Fouilles de l'Acropole*, Berlin 1931, 681 n. 2884; 682 n. 2885; 695 n. 2956 pl. 137.

[123] Un quadro sintetico ma ben documentato in S.M. Sherwin White, *Ancient Cos. An Historical Study from the Dorian Settlement to the Imperial Period*, Göttingen 1978, pp. 290–373.

[124] *Ibid.*, p. 325. Cfr. G. Pugliese Carratelli, "Il damos coo di Isthmos" in *ASAA* 41–42 (NS 25–26) (1962–1964), p. 158 II; *CCCA* II,671.

leoncello sui ginocchi, affianca il defunto nel banchetto in un singolare rilievo funerario del II sec.a.C., verisimilmente a garanzia del
suo beato destino ultraterreno.[125]

Un culto privato dei Dioscuri è attestato nell'isola in età ellenistica,[126]
cui verisimilmente risale un rilievo che mostra i personaggi in piedi,
nel solito atteggiamento di assessori di una figura femminile[127] la cui
identificazione più ovvia (Elena), peraltro, non può ritenersi che congetturale data la varietà di presenze femminili che i monumenti mostrano insieme con i divini gemelli. Essi sono destinatari di un culto
pubblico anche a Calymnos nel II–I sec.a.C., epoca in cui l'isola era
soggetta all'influenza di Cos.[128]

L'invio di *theoroi* e di *proxenoi* a Samotracia rivela la familiarità con
i locali misteri e l'ideologia relativa[129] mentre un culto dei *Kyrbantes* a
Cos è attestato da una *lex sacra* purtroppo mutila.[130]

Né si trascurerà di chiamare in causa anche Delo, meta di tanti
negotiatores italici, greci e orientali soprattutto nel II sec.a.C. ma già
nel precedente importante centro economico e crogiulo d'incontro e
di fusione di culture e tradizioni religiose greche e orientali.[131]
E' nota l'esistenza nell'isola di un *Metroon*, come quello ateniese sede
dei pubblici archivi,[132] mentre numerose immagini della dea proven-

---

[125] L. Laurenzi, "Sculture inedite del Museo di Coo", *ASAA* 33–34 (NS 17–18)
(1955–1956), p. 80 n. 13: rilievo ellenistico. Una statua frammentaria della dea *ibid.*,
p. 90 n. 43 e fig. 91 = *CCCA* II,669, pl. CXCVIII: II sec.a.C. Un altro rilievo
frammentario è custodito nel Kunsthistorisches Museum di Vienna: *CCCA* II,670
pl. CXCVIII.

[126] G. Pugliese Carratelli in *Miscellanea Rostagni*, pp. 162–163.

[127] L. Laurenzi, *art. cit.*, pp. 144–145 n. 207 fig. 207: II sec.a.C. A parere di
A. Hermary, peraltro, il rilievo sarebbe di età imperiale (*art. cit.*, p. 579 n. 146).

[128] *SGDI* 3595. Cfr. M. Segre, "Tituli Calymnii", *ASAA* 22–23 (NS 6–7) (1944–
1945), p. 153 n. 117 pl. LXX: dedica di un *naos* e di statue ai Dioscuri e al *Demos*
da parte di un sacerdote dei Dioscuri.

[129] *IG* XII,8,171b,27 ss.; 171d,59 ss.; F. Salviat, "Addenda samothraciens", *BCH*
86 (1962), pp. 275–278.

[130] M. Segre, "Nuove iscrizioni di Coo", *Aevum* 9 (1935), p. 255.

[131] Dopo il primo inventario dei "Romani a Delo" di Th. Homolle (*BCH* 8, 1884,
pp. 75–158) e i due fondamentali contributi di J. Hatzfeld (cfr. sopra n. 107), la
documentazione dovrebbe essere aggiornata. Per un panorama complessivo dei culti
dell'isola, oggetto come è noto di scavi sistematici e di ottimi studi monografici sui
singoli monumenti nella Serie della *Exploration archéologique de Délos* a cura dell'Ecole
française d'Athènes, si veda la documentata monografia di Ph. Bruneau, *Recherches
sur les cultes de Délos à l'époque hellénistique et à l'époque impériale*, Paris 1970. Cfr. anche
M.-F. Baslez, *Recherches sur les conditions de pénétration et de diffusion des religions orientales
à Délos (IIe–Ier s. avant notre ère)*, Paris 1977.

[132] Ph. Bruneau, *op. cit.*, pp. 431–435. La più antica menzione del tempio risale
al 208 a.C.: *CCCA* II,587–599 pl. CLXXVII.

gono da varie aree, soprattutto dal santuario degli dei egiziani.[133] In essa é attestata l'esistenza di un *Kabeireion* la cui localizzazione non sembra del tutto certa,[134] mentre indubbia è l'identificazione del *Samothrakeion* il cui primo impianto risale agli inizi del IV sec.a.C. mentre nel II sec.a.C. si pone una seconda fase costruttiva.[135]

Anche una sede cultuale dei Dioscuri è spesso menzionata nei rendiconti degli *hieropoioi*.[136] Il culto pubblico dei due personaggi è attestato fin dalla fine del IV sec. o dagli inizi del III sec.a.C. e comportava varie cerimonie, fra cui l'*epikrasis*, equivalente alla comune teossenia.[137] Ad esso si accompagnava anche una vivace devozione di privati.[138] Soprattutto importante sotto il profilo storico-religioso è la circostanza che tutti e tre i gruppi divini, Cabiri, Dioscuri e dei di Samotracia, talora definiti Grandi Dei, sono titolari di un unico sacerdozio e spesso risultano identificati nella titolatura ufficiale dello *hiereus* cui è affidato il loro culto.[139] Delo pertanto mostra non solo la frequente associazione delle coppie divine in questione bensì una loro franca identificazione, certo sulla base della comune caratteristica di divinità protettrici dai rischi del mare e della guerra.

Tra le varie metropoli micro-asiatiche, tutte in vario grado sedi di fiorente culto metroaco, quali—per ricordarne solo le principali Gordion,[140]

---

[133] Incerta rimane l'identificazione con una sede di culto metroaco degli edifici scoperti sul monte Cinto e designati come santuario B e C (*CCCA* 600–602; Ph. Bruneau, *op. cit.*, pp. 242–245, pp. 475–477). Cfr. *CCCA* II,603–639, pl. CLXXVII–CXC per i monumenti (*naiskoi*, statue in marmo e pietra, terrecotte) rinvenuti in varie aree cittadine, spesso di abitazioni, e *ibid.*, 640–646 pl. CXC–CXCI per altri di provenienza ignota.

[134] Esso è definito *Kabeireion to eis Kynthon* nell'unico documento che lo ricorda (*IG* XII,144 A 90). Sui problemi della sua collocazione topografica si veda Ph. Bruneau, *op. cit.*, pp. 388–390.

[135] F. Chapouthier, *Le sanctuaire des dieux de Samothrace* (Exploration archéologique de Délos XVI), Paris 1935; Ph. Bruneau, *op. cit.*, p. 381 s., 390.

[136] Ph. Bruneau, *op. cit.*, p. 379. Lo studioso rifiuta l'identificazione del santuario dei Dioscuri con l'impianto archeologico designato con la sigla GD 123 (*ibid.*, pp. 383–386) quale era stata proposta dall'editore del monumento L. Robert, *Trois sanctuaires sur le rivage occidental: Dioscourion, Asclépiéion, Sanctuaire anonyme (Leucothion?)* (Exploration archéologique de Délos XX), Paris 1952.

[137] Ph. Bruneau, *op. cit.*, pp. 391–394.

[138] *Ibid.*, pp. 397–398.

[139] *Ibid.*, pp. 395–398. L'identificazione dei tre gruppi sembra affermata a partire dal II sec.a.C., essendo frequente, nelle dediche e nella titolatura sacerdotale, la formula *theon Megalon Samothrakon Dioskouron Kabeiron*.

[140] *CCCA* I,50–54 pl. VII–X. Si veda M.J. Mellink, "Comments on a Cult Relief of Kybele from Gordion" in R.M. Boehmer-H. Hauptmann (edd.), *Festschrift für Kurt Bittel, cit.*, vol. I, pp. 349–360; vol. II, Taf.70–73. La città è centro di culto metroaco fino ad epoca tarda. Cfr. L.E. Roller, "Hellenistic Epigraphic Texts from Gordion",

Sardi,[141] Cizico,[142] Colofone,[143] Efeso,[144] Smirne,[145] è specialmente rivelatore il caso di Pergamo,[146] per la peculiare trama di rapporti che in questa città quel culto intreccia con la sfera cabirica. La tradizione mitica attestata dal noto oracolo apollineo richiesto in occasione di una peste (II sec.a.c.),[147] secondo la quale la nascita di Zeus sarebbe avvenuta sulla rocca di Pergamo alla presenza dei Cabiri "figli di Urano", nell'implicita identificazione Cureti-Coribanti-Cabiri mostra attiva siffatta trama, confermata da una dedica agli "Dei Grandi Cabiri" rinvenuta nell'area del santuario di Zeus e della Madre.[148]

Un altare, recante l'immagine di due anfore all'interno di un *naiskos* e dedicato ai Coribanti,[149] conferma l'identificazione di questi ai Dioscuri, cui quella iconografia è tipicamente pertinente. La città, sacra ai Cabiri fin dai suoi primordi, come vogliono le testimonianze congiunte di Pausania e di Elio Aristide,[150] è sede di "misteri" in loro onore con iniziazione (*myesis*) degli efebi, e di varie cerimonie pubbliche, fra cui *kriobolia*.[151] Essa ha pure uno *hieron* dei Dioscuri[152] e una comunità di fedeli votati al loro culto.[153]

AS 37 (1987), pp. 103–133; Ead., "The Great Mother at Gordion: the Hellenization of an Anatolian Cult", *JHS* 111 (1991), pp. 128–43.

[141] *CCCA* I,455–465 pl. XCIX–CII. Cfr. G.M.A. Hanfmann-J.C. Waldbaum, "Kybebe and Artemis. Two Anatolian Goddesses at Sardis", *Archaeology* 22 (1969), pp. 264–269; G.M.A. Hanfmann, "On the Gods of Lydian Sardis" in R.M. Boehmer-H. Hauptmann (edd.), *Festschrift für Kurt Bittel, cit.*, vol. I, pp. 219–231; vol. II, Taf.43–44.

[142] *CCCA* I,278–290 e 292 (monte Dindimo). Cfr. E. Schwertheim, "Denkmäler zur Meterverehrung in Bithynien und Mysien" in S. Sahin-E. Schwertheim-J. Wagner (edd.), *op. cit.*, vol. II, pp. 810–24.

[143] *CCCA* I,598–606 pl. CXXX–CXXXI. Cfr. B.D. Merritt, "Inscriptions of Colophon", *AJPh* 56 (1935), pp. 358–397.

[144] *CCCA* I,612–685 pl. CCXXXII–CLIII. Cfr. J. Keil, "Denkmäler des Meter-Kultes", *JÖAI* 18 (1915), pp. 66–78; Id., "Vorläufiger Bericht über die Ausgrabungen in Ephesos", *JÖAI* 23 (1926), pp. 248–299.

[145] *CCCA* I,541–584 pl. CXX–CXXVIII. Cfr. C J. Cadoux, *Ancient Smyrna. A History of the City from the Earliest Times to 324 A.D.*, Oxford 1938, pp. 25–27.

[146] *CCCA* I,348–426 pl. LXXV–XCIII. Cfr. E. Ohlemütz, *Die Kulte und Heiligtümer der Götter in Pergamon*, Würzburg—Auhmühle 1940, pp. 174–191.

[147] *CIG* 3538 = Kaibel, *Epigr.*1035; *IvP* II,324; *IGR* IV, 360. Cfr. E. Ohlemutz, *op. cit.*, pp. 192–202; L. Robert, *Fleuves et cultes d'Aizanoi, cit.*, p. 359 s.

[148] *IvP* II,332. Cfr. E. Ohlemütz. *op. cit.*, p. 196.

[149] *IvP* I,68 ; E. Ohlemütz, *op. cit.*, p. 194.

[150] Pausania I,4,6; Elio Aristide II, p. 709 Dindorf.

[151] *IvP* I,252 del 125 a.C.

[152] *IvP* I,245 = *OGIS* 335; *SEG* 680. Cfr. L. Robert, "Notes d'épigraphie hellénistique", *BCH* 49 (1925), pp. 219–221.

[153] *CIG* 3540 dove si menziona una *symbiosis Dioskouriton andron*, ossia un tiaso di Dioscuriti.

La città, con il suo santuario rupestre e il complesso intreccio mitico-rituale che accomuna la Gran Madre con il gruppo dei suoi *propoloi* Coribanti-Cabiri-Dioscuri, conferma come nell'ambito della grecità micro-asiatica, con la sua simbiosi vitale di elementi tradizionali ellenici e anatolici, siano da reperire i più adeguati parametri di riferimento tipologico e verisimilmente anche storico dell'orizzonte metroaco riflesso nel singolare monumento metroaco della colonia siracusana.

La tipologia del santuario acrense risulta omologa a quella dei centri di culto metroaco che in Asia Minore in età ellenistica perpetuano le peculiari strutture rupestri delle aree sacre alla dea anatolica. La teologia soggiacente alla ricca iconografia dei rilievi, se certo riflette l'ormai netta ellenizzazione della Gran Madre e del suo ciclo mitico-rituale, comune all'intera sfera di diffusione del suo culto nell'Occidente greco e nelle stesse regioni micro-asiatiche di lunga tradizione ellenica, lascia trasparire nell'intreccio complesso degli schemi iconografici una fisionomia peculiare, irriducibile a modelli noti. Di essa sono altrove ben attestati i singoli elementi, quali il rapporto con il paredro frigio Attis, già presente nell'Atene del IV sec.a.C., ovvero con la coppia di assessori costituiti dalla vergine dadofora e dal giovinetto/Hermes e la connessione, variamente configurata, con lo stesso Hermes talora accompagnato da un secondo paredro anziano. Parimenti nota è l'associazione mitica e rituale con il gruppo dei Coribanti, a loro volta rappresentati in alcuni casi da una coppia, costituendosi in tal modo un ulteriore schema di triade che alterna con quella costituita dalla dea con i Dioscuri. Infine, in una particolare sfera mitico-cultuale, sono peculiari i legami della Madre frigia con la cerchia divina, dalla varia e sfuggente identità, che presiede ai misteri di Samotracia. A quest'ultima, di fatto, sembra da ricondurre la stessa formula di triade in cui intervengono i Dioscuri, nella loro specifica assimilazione con la coppia cabirico-samotrace.

La singolarità del monumento acrense è costituita peraltro dalla convergenza—in un unico orizzonte teologico e cultuale—di tutte le linee di questo quadro estremamente complesso e stratificato, frutto di un vario intersecarsi dei molti contesti storico-culturali percorsi dalla religiosità metroaca in una vicenda secolare. Per tale convergenza non è possibile individuare nello stato attuale della nostra documentazione alcun parallelo preciso. Essa tuttavia trova dei parametri di riferimento più pertinenti, almeno per alcune delle sue strutture, ancora nelle regioni della grecità insulare (Samotracia, Rodi, Cos, Chio) e micro-asiatica (Efeso, Pergamo).

Si potrà concludere che il piccolo centro siceliota, perfettamente inserito nell'orbita culturale siracusana e certo specchio di una componente metroaca della *facies* religiosa della metropoli piuttosto che autore originale di una così "anomala" invenzione teologica, testimonia nel cuore della grecità occidentale una tradizione metroaca ricca di valenze e di fermenti orientali. Esso comunque rappresenta, per la grandiosità del monumento e la ricchezza dei significati teologici e cultuali che in esso si dispiegano, un parametro ineludibile per quel processo, per molti versi nuovo e singolare, di diffusione in Occidente della figura e del culto della dea anatolica che viene innescato allorché la classe senatoria di Roma nel 205 a.C. si rivolge ad Attalo di Pergamo per ottenere la sacra pietra nera venerata a Pessinunte e farne oggetto di pubblica *religio* nell'Urbe, dedicandole dopo qualche anno un tempio sul Palatino, centro delle più sacre memorie religiose della Roma romulea, a sanzione del suo carattere di dea eneade, garante dei gloriosi destini della città.

THE PRESENCE OF THE GODDESS IN HARRAN

Tamara Green

The past is, as M.I. Finley wrote, "an intractable incomprehensive mass of uncounted and uncountable data,"[1] made intelligible only through the construction of meaning that is itself the product of human choice; the writing of the history of an idea arises out of the human propensity for creating unified thought. In attempting to write an account of the worship of the mother goddess in the Northern Mesopotamian city of Harran during its 3,000 year history, it is essential to keep Finley's words before us, for we must remember that not only is the history of religious experience notoriously difficult to delineate, given its ineffable quality, but that the erratic and disparate nature of the sources leave unfillable gaps in our knowledege. In our search for understanding of the role of the mother goddess in Harran, we too often are forced to try to construct a model from the scantiest kinds of evidence, especially since the divine figure of the male Moon god dominates all accounts of the city's religious life. We must search for clues around the edges of history.

The city of Harran, located at the intersection of several ancient caravan routes, was founded as a mercantile outpost by Ur in the early 2nd millennium B.C.E. Inhabited by succeeding waves of Akkadians, Babylonians and Assyrians, it was absorbed into the Persian empire after the fall of the last ruler of Babylon, Nabonidus, in the sixth century B.C.E. Several centuries later, the conquests of Alexander brought the city into the orbit of an intellectual Hellenism already partially transmuted by its contact with the Near East. And although Harran was notorious among the early Christians in the region for the persistence of its traditional cults and rites long after the official recognition of the Church, it was located near those two great centers of Syriac Christianity, Edessa and Nisibis. It was these variegated cultural traditions that the Muslims encountered when they conquered the city in 639 C.E.

---

[1] M.I. Finley, "Myth, Memory and History," *The Use and Abuse of History* (New York, 1987), 13.

Whatever the complex political history of Harran, the difficulties in tracing its religious traditions are made even more complex by the dominant presence of the Moon god Nanna/Sin in all the accounts of the city. Every ancient Mesopotamian city had one deity that it elevated above all others; and throughout its 3,000 year history, Harran was the possession of the Moon god, around whose worship the city organized its world. The empires of the Akkadians and Babylonians, of the Greeks, Romans and Arabs may have controlled successively the political life of the city, but all paid tribute, in one form or another, to its divine Lord. The god's power manifested itself in a variety of ways: as "the lamp of heaven" in the evening sky, as guarantor of political dominion, as illuminator of the divine will through prophecy, and as the embodiment of male generative power. His role as revealer of what is hidden ultimately led to his absorption into the hermetic traditions of late antiquity, and was this aspect of his divinity that ultimately provided him an entree into the mystical traditions of Islam. Nevertheless, although his masculine preeminence in the divine hierarchy tends to cast into historical shadow the other divinities worshipped at Harran for their life-giving powers, textual and archaeological evidence points to a variety of persistent cultic traditions that had their roots in the power of the feminine. Unlike the Moon god, however, whose attributes tend to be well-defined and whose importance is well-documented, the female deities mentioned in our texts are often difficult to identify with any certainty. Complicating the search is the variety of texts and archaeological evidence produced over a 3,000 year period.

The Goddess in ancient Mesopotamia

Our earliest references to Harranian religion reveal the cultic presence of several of the traditional Mesopotamian deities, most notably the protecting deity of the city. In Sumerian texts, the Moon god is called Nanna, but he has a variety of cultic titles. Su-En, contracted to Sin, seems to represent the moon in its crescent form;[2] it is an image that is distinctly masculine, for the moon's "horns" become the embodiment both of the royal crown with its political power and of the fertility of the raging bull. Despite the clearly masculine char-

---

[2] It was by this name that he was called by the Semitic successors of the Sumerians.

acter of the moon deity in Mesopotamian myth, it nevertheless can be argued that there is also evidence for a feminine aspect of the moon which manifests itself only in the full moon. If the crescent of the moon is the symbol of male virility and sexual power, the full moon perhaps may be seen to portray the gravidity of woman about to give birth; thus, within the moon's periodic nature there is a constant cycle of alternation between male and female. Those cultures which traditionally have seen the moon as feminine have connected its cycles with those of female fertility; the moon's appearance of growing fullness is a manifestation of woman's fecundity. The moon is born and dies in its masculine form, but it as female that it reaches its fullness. It has been suggested that the iconography of horned goddesses, such as the Egyptian Hathor and Isis and perhaps even the Greek Io, may in fact represent this duality of sexual natures.

A Sumerian hymn addressed to the Moon in its fullness would seem to support such an interpretation:

> Father Nanna, lord, conspicuously crowned,
>   prince of the gods,
> Father Nanna, grandly perfect in majesty,
>   prince of the gods;
> Father Nanna, (measuredly) proceeding in noble raiment,
>   prince of the gods;
> fierce young bull, thick of horns, perfect of limbs,
>   with lapis lazuli beard, full of beauty;
> fruit, created of itself, grown to full size,
>   good to look at, with whose beauty one is never sated;
> womb, giving birth to all, who has settled down
>   in a holy abode . . .[3]

In the Mesopotamian pantheon, however, the consort of the Moon god Sin, Ningal (Akkadian = great lady) is the most clearly formulated female aspect of the moon, although the textual evidence defines her role primarily in political terms, i.e., as the wife of the Moon god. On the stele of Ur-Nammu (2112–2095 B.C.E.), she is portrayed sitting next to her spouse as he confers the regalia of power to the king. It is at at Ur, and later, Harran, where Sin's political strength was centered, that she is most clearly linked to the Moon god as his spouse and as the mother of Inanna. The Harran stele of Adad-guppi, mother of Nabonidus, records an invocation to Sin and Ningal;[4]

---

[3] T. Jacobsen, *Treasures of Darkness* (New Haven, 1976), 7–8.
[4] ANET 560–562.

letters from the Sargonid period invoke the blessing of Sin and Ningal;[5]
and in a treaty between Ashurnirari V of Assyria (753–746 B.C.E.)
and Mati'ilu of Arpad, Sin of Harran and Ningal are together called
upon as witnesses.[6] In religious and mythological texts, however, Ningal
is portrayed as a deity of the reed marshes; and although in Akkadian
texts she is sometimes called "the mother of the great gods," in surviving myths, her powers seem to have been superseded by the increasing status of her daughter, Inanna, whose sexual power far
exceeds that of her mother. Whatever creative power Ningal might
have had in her origins has been sublimated to the greater political
domination of her spouse.

Although it is true that 1,500 years later Greek and Roman authors,
as well as medieval Arabic sources, in references to the cult of the
moon at Harran, often give the deity a feminine gender, such citations may represent a cultural blind spot, rather than the reality of
the female aspect of the Harranian god. Herodian reports that the
emperor Caracalla was on his way back from the temple of Selene
when he was assassinated,[7] and Ammianus Marcellinus maintains
that it was to Luna that Julian offered his prayers, adding that the
moon was especially venerated in that region;[8] whether the female
gender is one imposed by the authors' own perception of the moon's
gender, or whether the presence of a lunar goddess at Harran is a
borrowing from the Greco-Syrian pantheon cannot be determined.
It has been suggested, however, that there were at least three moon
temples at Harran, including two outside the city itself, one of which
may in fact been devoted to a female deity. At Asagi Yarimca, a
village four miles north of Harran, a stele with the disc and crescent
emblem of the Moon god and a cuneiform inscription was discovered
in 1949, and Seton Lloyd argue that this was the location of "Selene's"
temple.[9]

The fourth-century historian Spartian, in his account of the assas-
sination of Caracalla, was perhaps more precise, however, in calling
the Harranian deity Lunus. His comment that

> All the learned, but particularly the inhabitants of Carrhae (Harran),
> hold that those who think that the deity ought to be called Luna, with

---

[5] Etienne Combe, *Histoire du Culte de Sin en Babylonie et en Assyrie* (Paris, 1908), 58.
[6] ANET 3,532–53.
[7] *Historiae*, iv,13.
[8] "quae religiose per eos colitur tractus." xxiii.3.2.
[9] S. Lloyd and W. Brice, "Harran," *Anatolian Studies* I (1951), 80.

the name and the sex of a woman, are subject to women and always their slaves; but those who believe that the deity is male never suffer the ambushes of women. Hence the Greeks, and also the Egyptians, although they speak of Luna as a god, in the same way that women are included in "Man," nevertheless in their mysteries, use the name Lunus.[10]

seems to be both a recognition of the bisexual nature of all lunar deities and of the power of cultural difference.

We must remember that several millennia and many cultural layers separate the anonymous Sumerian author of the hymn to Nanna and our late antique Greco-Roman historians and philosophers. When Plutarch, for example, says of the Egyptians[11] that they take the moon as the mother of the world and ascribe to it an hermaphroditic nature, since it is impregnated by the sun and becomes pregnant and then by itself sends generated matter in the air and scatters it here and there, we must consider the Greek author's own religious or philosophical biases. Similarly, when Ephraem, a Syrian Christian contemporary of Ammianus Marcellinus, reports that the second century C.E. philosopher and Hellenophile Bardaisan of the neighboring city of Edessa "looked at the Sun and the Moon; with the Sun he compared the Father, with the Moon the Mother," this may reflect the influence of astrological doctrine upon Bardaisan's rather eclectic teachings rather than ancient Mesopotamian beliefs.[12]

The Goddess in late antiquity

After the collapse in 538 B.C.E. of the neo-Babylonian empire of Nabonidus, whose devotion to the gods of Harran is well-attested to by a variety of inscriptions, our historical sources from the Persian, Hellenistic and Roman periods reveal little about the religious life of Harran except to confirm the continuing attraction of the oracular power of its Moon god. It is only with the nominal victory of the Church in the fourth century that Harran reappears in our sources, chiefly as a useful *exemplum* for Syriac Christian writers of the wicked persistence of paganism; in fact, the obvious polemical intent of their

---

[10] *Caracalla*, vii,3–5.
[11] *de Iside*, 43.
[12] *Hymni Contra Haereses* ed. Beck, LV,10.

accounts of Harranian religion in late antiquity often makes it difficult to evaluate their usefulness. It is only at this point in the history
of Harran that the goddess emerges clearly.

Several Christian documents, including the late fourth century anonymous *Doctrine of Addai*, the hymns of Ephraem Syrus, the fifth century homilies attributed to Isaac of Antioch, and the polemical *Homily
on the Fall of the Idols* by Jacob, Bishop of Sarug (451–521), not only
make specific reference to the religion of Harran but also allow us to
consider more generally but with a great deal of caution to what
degree older particularized beliefs persisted in the face of cultural
syncretism. The divine names found in these texts present a mixture
of the familiar and the obscure, and are the best indication of the
diverse religious traditions that are characteristic of the region. Thus,
Addai rhetorically asks the Edessans:

> Who is this Nebo, an idol which ye worship, and Bel which you honor?
> Behold there are those among you who adore Bath Nikkal, as the
> inhabitants of Harran, your neighbors, and Tarʿatha, as the people of
> Mabbug, and the Eagle as the Arabians, also the Sun and the Moon,
> as the rest of the inhabitants of Harran, who are as yourselves. Be ye
> not led away captive by the rays of the luminaries and the bright star;
> for every one who worships creatures is cursed before God.[13]

Although Jacob's homily provides a slightly different list, it, too, is
nevertheless quite specific in its assignment of indvidual deities to
particular cities:

> He (i.e. Satan) put Apollo as idol in Antioch and others with him,
> In Edessa he set Nebo and Bel together with many others.
> He led astray Harran by Sin, Baʿalshamen and Bar Nemre
> By my Lord with his Dogs and the goddesses Tarʿatha and Gadlat. . . .
> Mabbug made he a city of the priests of the goddess(es)
> And called it with his name in order that it would err forever
>   (going after its idols),
> a sister of Harran, which is also devoted to the offerings;
> And in their error both of them love the springs.[14]

Finally, we have the homilies of Isaac of Antioch, which actually
deal with Beth Hur, a town founded by Harran, but which make reference to the religious beliefs of the mother city:

---

[13] *The Doctrine of Addai, the Apostle*, ed. G. Phillips, (London, 1876), 23 ff.
[14] P.S. Landerdorfer, *Die Gotterliste des mar Jacob von Sarug in seiner Homilie über der
Fall der Gotzenbilder* (Münich, 1914), 51–54; 59–62.

The founders (i.e. Harran) of the place encouraged it by its very name to exchange God for the Sun ... Look at the Sun, your savior, O city that came forth from Harran ... The Persians spared her not, for with them she served the sun; the Beduins left her not, for with them she sacrificed to ʿUzzai ... For the eyes of the Sun they were exposed, who worshipped the Sun and the Moon.[15]

And elsewhere, in describing the conquest of Beth Hur, he writes: "The demon that is called Gadlat wove his (i.e., Satan's) wrath on his servant."[16]

If these documents accurately reflect the admixture of religious beliefs in the region, it would demonstrate not only the persistent power of the Moon god and other Mesopotamian deities associated with the planets, but that other cults, both Western Semitic and Arab, had their place; that the Mother Goddess, represented in several forms and under several names, had her shrines, festivals and devotees, as did numerous local Baʿals, even if much of this tradition was now to be given further explication, at least by some Harranians, by the addition of various esoteric traditions, including astrology and "the magical arts." With the exception of Apollo, noticeably lacking are the Greek names of the deities, indicating that despite the late antique sobriquet of "Hellenopolis," traditional Harranian religion was, at least on the surface, little influenced by Greek rule.

The names of the female deities found in our texts represent the same admixture of divine attributes and functions that have become so intertwined by this period that it is difficult to sort them out except by linguistic origin: Bath Nikkal, or Inanna/Ishtar, who represents the oldest strain in Mesopotamian paganism; Tarʿatha, or Atargatis, the *Dea Syria*, whose Western Semitic origins became buried, like those of Baʾalshamen, under a host of local traditions in late antiquity; al-ʿUzza, one of a triad of Arab goddesses whose original functions cannot be clearly determined, but who was later identified with both Venus and Astarte; and Gadlat, whose name is composed of semitic elements. Nevertheless, a caveat must be noted in the following discussion of these goddesses: although the name of a deity such as Atargatis appears over a wide geographical area, it cannot be concluded necessarily that cultic practices are the same everywhere, since most often in the traditional popular religions of antiquity, the power

---

[15] *S. Isaaci Antiocheni doctoris syrorum opera omnia*, ed. G. Bickell (Gissae, 1873) I, 51–62, 99–102, 159.

[16] Isaac of Antioch, XI,167–68.

and expression of a deity are bound to the group and the place.

The *Doctrina Addai* declares that the Harranians honored the goddess Bath Nikkal, or the daughter of Nikkal (Ningal). The name has been identified as a localized form of Ishtar-Venus,[17] whose worship, of course, was widespread throughout the Near East under an increasing variety of epithets in late antiquity. We have already noted that the triadic asssociation of the Moon god, his consort and divine female child; Inanna as the daughter of the Moon god can be found in the Sumerian period, and it has been demonstrated that Sin, Ningal and Bath Nikkal were the most important deities at Harran according to "local cuneiform texts and other Akkadian traditions."[18] In her function as the planet Venus, Bath Nikkal is linked to the Moon god on the stelae of the Babylonian Nabonidus, where her sign as the morning star is found along with lunar and solar symbols.

Bath Nikkal may be a title whose use has specific meaning at Harran, and whose history there can be documented, but the ubiquitous Western Semitic Atargatis (Aramaic Tar'atha) presents greater difficulty, for the *Dea Syria* was worshipped in such a wide variety of forms and such a great number of places that it is impossible to discern any particularities of her cult at Harran during this period, except through inference. The archaeological evidence for her worship elsewhere in the region is diverse.[19] Our primary literary text, the second century C.E. *Dea Syria* attributed to Lucian, is far more specific; it describes in great detail the worship of the goddess at Hierapolis (Mabbug), a city that the *Doctrina Addai* confirms worshipped Tar'atha and which was linked to Edessa by the *Doctrine of Addai*, and called a sister to Harran by Jacob of Sarug in his homily.

Jacob's remark that "in their error both of them (Harran and Mabbug) love the springs" is the clearest statement of her function at Harran and is supported by the goddess' association everywhere with the life-giving power of water. At both Hierapolis and Edessa were ponds filled with her sacred fish; although there is no such reference for Harran, it is possible that the various wells of Harran may have been under the protection of the goddess.[20]

---

[17] H.J.W. Drijvers, *Cults and Beliefs at Edessa* (Leiden, 1980), 143.

[18] Drijvers, *Cults and Beliefs*, 41. cf. E. Dhorme, *Les Religions de Babylonie et d'Assyrie* (Paris, 1949), 54–60.

[19] See Drijvers, *Cults and Beliefs*, 76–121.

[20] Perhaps the most famous of these wells was the one at which Jacob was reported to have met Rachel when he arrived in Harran to find a bride.

The water-protecting powers of Atargatis/Tarʿatha may have led to a later association with the pre-Islamic Arab goddess, Manat, whose idol, according to the 9th century Ibn al-Kalbi, "was erected on the seashore in the vicinity of Qudayd between Mecca and Medina."[21] Finally, in the iconography of Atargatis from a number of Syrian cities, she is accompanied by a variety of male consorts. A relief found at Edessa depicting the goddess and a deity has been identified by Drijvers as Hadad, the Syrian weather god with whom she was joined at Hierapolis, but it is not known which male god, if any, served a similar function at Harran.[22]

Nevertheless, although it is tempting to extrapolate from Lucian's account of the Syrian Goddess at Hierapolis a deeper understanding of her worship in Harran and to look for broader parallels in iconography, we must take note once again of the fact that not only is ritual so often tied to place, but that at the same time her various representations in Graeco-Roman period show clear signs of an amalgamation of symbols that vary with their provenance. Thus she may be represented as the Tyche of a city (Edessa), as the consort of the Syrian storm god Hadad (Hierapolis, Edessa, and Dura-Europus), as the consort of Nergal, the ancient Mesopotamian god of the underworld (Hatra), or as Cybele seated between two lions (Hierapolis). Several coins from Harran suggest that the goddess was venerated at Harran, as at Edessa, as the Tyche of the city, although Jacob of Sarug's inclusion of both Tarʿatha and Gadlat in his list of female deities argues against this interpretation, since Gadlat is probably the Aramaic equivalent of Tyche.[23]

As Drijvers concludes in his analysis of the role of Atargatis at Edessa, "The wide range of variants in the cult of the Dea Syria most appropriately demonstrates (such) a process of religious assimilation and articulation . . . Although her cult at Edessa may have been influenced by her centre at Hierapolis, it certainly belonged to the most authentic traditions of the city."[24] The same must be held true for whatever form the Harranian worship of the goddess might have taken.

---

[21] Ibn al-Kalbi, *Kitab al-Asnam*; trans. N.A. Faris (Princeton, 1952), 12.

[22] Drijvers, *Cults and Beliefs*, 80.

[23] As Drijvers notes, "Gadlat is in all likelihood a combination of Gad and Allat." the Aramaic word *Gad* means Tyche, so that Gadlat is the name of Allat in her function of Tyche of Harran. *Cults and Beliefs*, 44. Thus, the name would seem to have a generic, rather than specific, function.

[24] Drijvers, *Cults and Beliefs*, 121.

To what extent Atargatis differs in function from the Arab goddess al-ʿUzza in this period is difficult to say. Al-ʿUzza, who according to Isidore of Antioch, was worshipped at Beth Hur, which had a large Arab population, has been identified with a number of female divinities, including Aphrodite and Astarte; she bore the Syriac epithets of *Balti* (my Lady) and *Kawkabta* (the [female] star). At Palmyra, Beltis is the consort of Bel; Astarte is the consort of Baʿalshamen at Tyre.

Given the fact that Beth Hur was founded by Harran, it is likely that the goddess had her devotees at Harran as well, although what form her worship took at Harran, as well as with which male deity she might have been associated, is impossible to determine. Her original significance in pre-Islamic Arabia remains unclear, although she was certainly worshipped at Mecca. The Koran mentions her as one of the three false goddesses whom the Quraysh had worshipped before Islam (53:19); according to the Ibn al-Kalbi, the Quraysh regarded her, along with Manah and Allat, as the daughters of Allah.

> By Allat and al-ʿUzza,
>   and Manah, the third idol besides.
> Verily they are the most exalted females
> Whose intercession is to be sought.[25]

Both al-ʿUzza and Bath Nikkal may be the "Bright Star" of the *Doctrina Addai*: "Do not be led away captive by the rays of the luminaries and the Bright Star." The name ʿUzza has as its Arabic root ʿ*zz* to be strong, which would link her to Azizos, the male version of the morning star, who was worshipped in a triad along with his twin, Monimos, the evening star, and the sun god in a number of places in northern Syria and Mesopotamia, including perhaps Edessa.[26] We have already seen the extent of Arab political domination in the region around Harran and Edessa in this period, and it is probable that they installed their gods alongside the others members of the local pantheon.

In his oration on Helios, the emperor Julian had identified Monimos and Azizos as Hermes and Ares respectively, who acted as assessors (*paredroi*) of the Sun God.[27] In Arabia, Azizos was Abd al-Aziz, which name was to become in Islam one of the epithets of Allah. What relationship these male deities had with the female al-ʿUzza is not clear, although it has been suggested that among the Semites, the Venus

---

[25] Ibn al-Kalbi, 17.
[26] Cf. discussion in Drijvers, *Cults and Beliefs*, 147 ff.
[27] Julianus, *Julian* I, ed. W.C. Wright (Cambridge, Mass., 1913), 413.

star was regarded originally as male, and later became bisexual in nature.[28] Like Azizos, al-'Uzza seems to have embodied a martial nature. The Beduin were said to have offered human sacrifice to al-'Uzza; 400 virgins were reported to have been slain at Emesa in honor of the goddess, and to her the sixth century Lakhmid prince Mundhir sacrificed the son of his enemy.

The multiplicity of goddesses and the overlap of functions as demonstrated by our textual and iconographical evidence are indicative of the various ethnic traditions that were to be found in the region: indigenous Mesopotamian, Aramaic, and Arab. To what extent these various strands were interwoven in late antiquity cannot be known. In general, however, the boundaries between the various functions of the divine feminine seem to be less clearly drawn than among the male deities; since the political function of the female was, on the whole, not as well-defined, these goddesses tended to cross social and ethnic boundaries more easily. One may also note as a corollary that none of the goddesses became as clearly identified with their Greek and Roman counterparts as did the male deities. The question of differentiation of function becomes even more complicated when we consider the references to traditional Harranian religion found in Muslim sources; and it must at once be conceded that once again the chain of continuity has been broken, for we are without evidence for Harranian religion from the time of the early Christian authors discussed above until our first Muslim sources in the 10th century. What is clear, however, is that while the transformative and prophetic powers of the Moon god provided a place for him in the esoteric traditions of late antiquity even into the Muslim period, medieval Muslim accounts of Harranian religion demonstrate that whatever the forms worship of the feminine took at Harran in the last period of the city's history, there seems to be evidence of the persistence and continuity of her much earlier traditions in Mesopotamian and Syrian religion.

The Goddess in the Islamic period

Perhaps the most difficult material to interpret is that which is found in medieval Muslim texts. Muslim interest in Harran was grounded

---

[28] J. Henninger, "Uber Sternkunde und Sternkult in Nord- und Zentral Arabien," ZE 79 (1954), 82–117.

both in the identification of Harran as the birthplace of the biblical
patriarch Abraham and as the purported source of ancient esoteric
traditions that found a home in the more radical branches of Islam.
Nevertheless, there are several Muslim authors whose antiquarian
interest in Harran provide us with further data concerning the survival of the mother goddess at Harran. The two most detailed Muslim
accounts of traditional Harranian religion are found in the *Catalog* of
the 10th century encyclopedist Ibn al-Nadim[29] and in Biruni's *The
Chronology of Ancient Nations*, written in the 11th century.[30] Although
both contain calendars which purport to be accounts of the Harranian festival cycle, the sources and dates for these lists of festival
days are unclear, and are filled with textual difficulties. Nevertheless, although there are many male divinities listed in these calendars
whose identities cannot be determined with any certainty, we can see
the persistence of those female deities found in texts of the earlier
period. It is ironic to note that these accounts contain the only descriptions we have of cultic practices in honor of the goddess at Harran.

The calendar of the *Catalog* records the following festivals of the
goddess. Also listed are the corresponding dates from al-Biruni:

1. *Catalog*: On the first three days of Nisan, the Harranians honor
   Baltha, who is Zuharah (Venus).
   Chronology: On the 2nd, is the feast of *Damis*, on the 3rd is the
   Feast of antimony. On the 5th is the feast of Balin (Balti?), the
   idol of Venus. In the *Catalog* of Ibn al-Nadim it is recorded that
   on the 30th of Adhar begins the month of Tamr, and during this
   month is the marriage of the gods and the goddesses; they divide
   in it the dates, putting kohl (antimony powder) on their eyes. Then
   during the night they place beneath the pillows under their heads
   seven dried dates, in the name of the seven deities, and also a
   morsel of bread and some salt for the deity who touches the ab-
   domen. Such a festival might then correspond to the feast of antimony mentioned in Biruni.
2. *Catalog*: On the 4th day of Kanun I (December), they begin a
   seven-day festival in honor of Baltha, who is Zuharah, whom they
   call *al-Shahmiyah* (the glowing one). They build a dome within her

---

[29] Ibn al-Nadim, *Kitab al-Fihrist*, ed. Gustave Flugel (Leipzig, 1871), 318–327.
[30] Biruni, *Kitab al-Athar al-Baqiyah ʿan al-Qurun al Khaliyah*, ed. C.E. Sachau (Leipzig,
1878); translated as *The Chronology of Ancient Nations*, C.E. Sachau (London, 1879).

shrine and adorn it with fragrant fruits; in front of it, they sacrifice as many different kinds of animals as possible. "They also [offer] plants of the water," a ritual which in all likelihood has some connection with the springtime offering, widespread in the Near East, of "gardens of Adonis" in celebration of the renewed fertility of the god.

Chronology: On the 7th is the feast of addressing the idol of Venus. In addition, Biruni lists for the same date, one month later (the 4th of Kanun II) the feast of Dayr al-Jabal (the place of the mountain) and the feast of Balti (Venus). This may be the same festival recorded in the *Catalog*, the month's difference being the product of scribal error.

3. *Catalog*: On the 30th of Kanun I, the priest prays for the revival of the religion of *Uzuz* (sic).

In addition, the feast of the "Weeping Women" in honor of "Ta-uz" celebrated in the middle of the month of Tammuz, according to the *Catalog*, must be added to the list of festivals in which the goddess is honored, for clearly this is the ancient Mesopotamian rite which reenacted the death of the fertility god Tammuz and the mourning of Ishtar. Among the goddesses mentioned in "what is in another person's handwriting" in the *Catalog* is Rabbat al-Thill, "who received Tumur (dates)." In ancient Mesopotamian religion, it was Dumuzi/Tammuz who was the power of growth in the date palm; thus, Rabbat al-Thill, the Mistress of the Herd, must be Inanna/Ishtar. The anonymous author adds that it was Rabbat al-Thill who guarded the sacred goats, perhaps dedicated to Tammuz as the shepherd god, which were offered as sacrificial victims.

Also found in Biruni, but not mentioned in the *Catalog* are:

1. On the 9th day of Tishri II (November), *Tarsa* (Tar'atha?) the idol of Venus.
2. On the 17th day of Tishri II, there is the feast of *Tarsa*. On the same day they go to Batnae (Sarug). On the 18th day of Tishri II, there is the Feast of Sarug; it is the day of the renewal of the dresses.
3. On the 25th of Kanun II, there is Feast of the idol of Tirratha (sic).
4. On the 3rd and the 7th of Ab (August), there is the feast of *Dailafatan* (Dilbat), the idol of Venus.

Although, as we mentioned earlier, it is often difficult to perceive real differences among the various female deities, since their functions and attributes tend to be all-embracing, every layer of Mesopotamian history seems to be represented by the great variety of divine female names, ranging from Akkadian to Aramaic, that are used to describe the goddess in these texts. Although the significance of many of the rituals and festivals included in the *Chronology* is difficult to interpret, it is clear that according to the author of the calendar found in the *Catalog*, the goddess retained her original identification as both earth mother and Evening Star, thus demonstrating the continuity and survival of the ancient traditions of the goddess in the city of the Moon god. The survival of these deities in these medieval Muslim texts attests not only to the power of the goddess, but the existence of religious beliefs and practices almost completely hidden from our view.

CYBELE AND HER COMPANIONS ON THE
NORTHERN LITTORAL OF THE BLACK SEA

Patricia A. Johnston

In the cities along the northern coast of the Black Sea, the presence of the cult of Cybele is attested as early as the sixth century. The worship of Cybele was introduced here by Greek colonists between the eighth and sixth centuries B.C.,[1] often through a process of syncretism with the local cult of the great mother-goddess. Maarten J. Vermaseren, in his widely read *Cybele and Attis: the Myth and the Cult* (1977), devoted little attention to this area, other than a few pages to Cybele in the Danubian Provinces. Since then a growing body of materials has been gathered, catalogued, and published concerning Cybele throughout the Roman Empire, including this region, most recently by Vermaseren himself in his posthumously published volume VI of the *Corpus Cultus Cybelae Attidisque*, which includes Thracia, Moesia, Dacia, and Regnum Bospori, all of which, at some point, touch the northern coast of the Black Sea.[2]

In his sixth volume of this collection, Vermaseren distinguishes between the Greek Cybele, worshipped in the coastal cities, and Roman Cybele, worshipped in the interior, both of them descended from the Asiatic Cybele, who had become a national Roman Goddess during the Republic. The focus in this paper will be to identify some of the characteristic aspects of Cybele and her companions in

---

[1] Strabo associated various orgiastic rites with one another and drew analogies between their gods. He observed that the rites of Phrygian Cybele resembled those of Thracian Kotys and Bendis; he also equated Rhea and Cybele, and maintained that Thracian music is Asiatic in origin. (10.3.15–16, trans. H.L. Jones, Cambridge 1954, p. 105). It is now accepted that Cybele originated in Asia Minor, where the earliest representation of Cybele, found at Çatal Hüyük, has been confirmed by carbon-dating to belong to the fifth millenium B.C. cf. M.J. Vermaseren, *CCCA*, I, Leiden 1987, #773 and p. 233.

[2] M.J. Vermaseren, *CCCA VI: Germania, Raetia, Noricum, Pannonia, Dalmatia, Macedonia, Thracia, Moesia, Dacia, Regnum Bospori, Colchis, Scythia et Sarmatia*, Leiden 1989, pp. 141–142; *Cybele and Attis: the Myth and the Cult*, London 1977. Items from *CCCA* VI will be preceded by a number sign (#). Frequent reference will also be made to M. Tacheva-Hitova, *Eastern Cults in Moesia Inferior and Thracia*, Leiden 1983, 71–15; M.M. Kobylina, *Divinités Orientales sur le Littoral Nord de la Mer Noire*, Leiden 1976.

the cities and towns along the northern shore of the Black Sea, where the Greek Cybele predominates, from the sixth century B.C. to the secc d or third centuries A.D. (The increased syncretism of the later periods make it difficult to distinguish some of these characteristics, so later periods are referred to only for the sake of comparison.) The relatively spotty nature of some of the characteristics, which may help to establish some thread of consistency, will of course necessitate occasional reference to interior sites in this region and elsewhere.

Representations of Cybele in the sixth volume of Vermaseren's catalog tend to represent her as a young goddess seated on a throne, wearing her "usual" dress, which consists of a *chiton* or tunic, a *himation* or outer garment which sometimes covers her head as well. Her headdress varies: sometimes she wears a *polos*, a flat, rounded hat which Kobylina[3] associates with Cybele's role as a chthonic deity; sometimes she wears a mural crown, resembling crenelated towers, indicating her role as protectress of cities, and sometimes she wears no headdress or it is not identifiable (because of damage to the figure). In her left hand she holds a *tympanon* (a tambourine or drum), and in her right hand she holds a *patera* from which, in several depictions, she is pouring a libation. During the Roman period the *tympanon* is sometimes replaced by a sceptre in the interior sites (but not along the coast), a phenomenon which is also seen during the same period in the cities of Asia Minor.[4]

Here, as elsewhere, Cybele is frequently accompanied by a lion: in the earliest period it tends to be a small lion which rests on her lap; as early as the late fifth century she is in a chariot drawn by a team of lions, and thereafter is also frequently depicted with one or two large lions sitting or standing beside her throne. The presence of a lion is a detail that is sometimes cited as evidence that Cybele came originally from Asia Minor. Since Greeks were not familiar with this animal and the importance attached to it in Asia Minor, other creatures, such as a hare or a kid, or the infant Attis sometimes replace the lion in her lap,[5] but in the cities lining the northern coast of the the Black Sea, this is not common. Another com-

---

[3] Kobylina, pp. 1–3.

[4] Cf. Tacheva-Hitova, p. 139 and nos. II, 110, 115, and 102 = Vermaseren #340.

[5] Tacheva-Hitova, pp. 136–7 and nos. II, 121, 122; the kid: CCCA II, #681, 4th century B.C.; the infant Attis: *CCCA* II, #683, 684, 695, all from the sixth century B.C.; the examples come from the cities of Cyprus.

mon detail here, as elsewhere, is the placement of Cybele in a *naiskos* or small shrine.[6]

Sixth-century depictions of Cybele

Five (or perhaps four) of the earliest representations in this area come from the northern litoral of the Black Sea. Near the entrance to the Black Sea they are found at Salmydessus[7] and Apollonia (#361, 362a & b, 365); the last of the items (#511) comes from Olbia.

In Vermaseren's item #361, from Apollonia, Cybele sits in a *naiskos*. There appears to be no indication of a lion. She holds a *patera* in her right hand and a *tympanum* in her left hand. The second two items, also from Apollonia (#'s 362a & 362b), consist of two separate marble reliefs depicting a goddess enthroned in a *naiskos*. Two lions in #362a are seated on her lap; the goddess in #362b is not accompanied by a lion, and may or may not be Cybele. In #365, from Salmydessos, she holds a single lion "crouching right to left across her lap."[8]

The sixth-century representation of the goddess from Olbia (#511) has Cybele sitting on a throne in her usual attire with a lion on her lap. She wears earrings, and on each of her shoulders hang three hair-tresses (instead of the more usual two), outlining a triangular forehead.[9]

The remaining two items which Vermaseren assigns to the sixth century are an inscription found at Olbia (#515), and a graffito on a vase (#589), indicating that the vase is an offering "τῇ μᾱτρί". The graffito was found at Myrmekion (near Panticapaeum, on the Crimean Peninsula). The inscription from Olbia (#515), on a vase fragment, has been summarized by Vinogradov as a message from a priest to another highly placed person at Olbia, possibly to the high priest of

---

[6] cf. Tacheva-Hitova, 136–137.

[7] Aeschylus, *Prometheus Bound* 726–727, describes Salmydessos as "the rocky jaw of the sea, hostile to sailors (ἐχθρόξενος ναύτῃσι), stepmother of ships (μητρυιὰ νεῶν)." Although for Greeks and Romans the Black Sea was known as Εὔξεινος, the 'welcoming' sea, myths associated with this region (e.g., Tereus and his treatment of the Attic sisters Philomela & Procne; Orpheus & Eurydice; Jason & Medea, etc.) suggest this is something of a euphemism. Cf. R.F. Hoddinott, *Bulgaria in Antiquity*, New York 1975, p. 33.

[8] Vermaseren, *ad* #365.

[9] Tacheva-Hitova, p. 136.

the town, reporting on an inspection tour of holy places. This person reports having found, among other things, newly damaged altars, including those of the Mother of the Gods, of the Borysthenes and of Herakles. Vermaseren suggests that this report may lend additional support to Herodotus' story (IV,76; 78) of Anacharsis, who was killed and disowned by his fellow-Scythians because he had joined the foreign cult of Cybele.[10]

Two items found in the Scythian barrows below the river Kuban should perhaps be added to Vermaseren's list of sixth-century representations of Cybele. Two of these items were found in the Kelermes mound, dated between 580 and 570 B.C., in the Kuban river valley. Artamonov has called the mounds in this region "the oldest Scythian-type barrows with rich grave goods."[11] Among the items found there is a round silver mirror with a gold-plated back. The back of the mirror consists of eight sections divided radially; in one of these sections is a "Near Eastern winged female deity" whom Artamonov identifies as Cybele. She stand "in a long dress, reaching to her heels, holding the forepaws of two lions, their tails submissively tucked between their legs."[12] Although these two lions are full-grown, it may be observed that in their behavior they are much more like the lion cubs that sit in Cybele's lap than the full grown creatures which guard her throne. This cub-like behavior, of course, serves to underscore the power of this goddess.

A second item from the same barrow is "a silver rhyton, originally covered in gold leaf and bearing an engraved design in the same East Ionian style as the mirror. . . . Its decoration was in three bands." In the second band "a figure of . . . Cybele, holding winged griffins in her lowered arms is partly visible. In the third row, the large figure of a centaur is almost intact."[13]

---

[10] The passage itself is still unpublished; cf. Vermaseren, pp. 151–152; J. Vinogradov, *Olbia. Geschichte einer altgriechischen Stadt am Schwarzen Meer*, Konstanz 1981; Jeanne and L. Robert, *Bulletin épigraphique* in *Revue des études grecques*, 1962, p. 249. Regarding the Herodotus passage, cf. Vermaseren, *Cybele and Attis: the Myth and the Legend*, London 1977, pp. 28–29.

[11] M.I. Artamonov, *The Splendor of Scythian Art: Treasures from Scythian Tombs*, Praeger: New York 1969, p. 22. He notes that the people in this area were called Maeotae, not Scythiae, but "it is precisely in these barrows that early Scythian culture is to be found in its most vivid and characteristic form." Elsewhere, commenting on the early Greek influence on Scythian art, he observes "Greek objects and motifs of Greek origin appear there simultaneously with Scythian culture." (p. 29).

[12] p. 25; cf. plates 29, 31.

[13] p. 26.

Cybele during the fifth century

Four items survive from the fifth century, two of them showing Cybele with one or two lions, and two items which show her standing rather than sitting. In #376 she holds the lion in her lap, and in #204, a silver medallion found at Olynthus and dated 460–450 B.C, Cybele stands in her chariot, which is being drawn by a team of lions. Cybele is again standing in #202, a terracotta mould from Olynthus. The last of the fifth-century items is a marble head (#538), possibly of Cybele, wearing a polos.

Fourth century and later

From the fourth century B.C. through the second century A.D. many representations of Cybele in this area have been found (approximately 136 monuments, reliefs, or statues).[14] Depictions of Cybele on the Black Sea northern littoral tend to be relatively consistent with the "usual" sixth- and fifth-century representations of her dress and her seated or standing positions. There are notable modifications to her iconography during this period, some of which reflect historical developments; these tend, however, to be found in the interior rather than in the coastal sites. The replacement of the *tympanon* by a sceptre occurs increasingly during the Roman period, beginning about the second century A.D., in the interior sites, but apparently not in the coastal sites. A marble relief (#341) from Serdica in the interior of Thrace, for example, represents various scenes in the circus: we see gladiators fighting animals, actors with masks, and fights between animals. In two of the four panels at the left-hand of the relief are Venus and Cybele, and here Cybele holds a sceptre in her left hand and a *patera* in the right; the two lions beside her throne are turned toward her.[15]

---

[14] I count the following numbers, totalling 147, for Cybele in Vermaseren's text: 6th century: 7; 5th century: 4; 4th century: 23; 3rd century: 39; 2nd century: 9; 1st century: 20. A.D. 1st century: 6; 2nd century: approx. 41. The numbers (totalling 88) for Attis: 5th century: 3 (possibly); early 4th: 1 ("possibly"); 4th/3rd century: 1; "Hellenistic" & 3rd century: 8 + 52; 2nd century: 5 or 6; 1st century: 4; 1st B.C./A.D.: 2; A.D.: 1st century: 7; 2nd century: 5 [2 + 3 (Attis with Cybele)]. These numbers are nothing more than estimates, however, since some of their identifications are not certain, and some are located in the interior rather than on the coast.

[15] Vermaseren #341; Tacheva-Hitova 103 includes an enlarged photo of the section

Another variation is the representation of Cybele seated *on* a lion: again, such variations which can be dated tend to be found in the interior, such as those from the second century A.D. (3, 7, 18, 26), which were found in Germany, and one from the fourth century A.D. (80), which comes from Noricum. Two others survive, one with no designated date from Olbia (#527), and one from Scythia (#603) which is dated sixth-seventh century A.D. It is possible that variations such as these, when found in the coastal sites, reflect a later date than when they are found in the interior.

Cybele's companions

Cybele has a broad range of companions, however, who tend to be more in attendance during one era or another. As the great mother of gods as well as mortals and all creatures, she of course appears in the company of a number of the Olympian dieties. Male deities appearing with Cybele along the Black Sea coast include not only Attis, but also Hermes, Eros, and (probably) Zeus.[16] Female deities appearing with her include Hekate/Kore/Persephone, Demeter, Artemis, and Aphrodite.

Another depiction of a goddess who has been identified as the Great Mother is found on a golden, triangular diadem found in a fourth-century tomb at Karagodeuashkh, below the River Kuban. It is decorated with three bands of figures; in the top register is "a female figure with a veil over the lower part of her face." The middle register contains what Artamanov describes as "chariot drawn by two horses, seen from the front with an upright human figure in it." The bottom register shows the seated figure of "presumably a goddess" wearing a conical headdress like the triangular diadem on which it appears. Blawatsky and Kochelenko identify this goddess as "*la Grande Déese*," and the figure in the chariot above her as a "*Dieu Solaire*".[17] Vermaseren, however, omits this diadem, perhaps intentionally, since it does not include the usual icons associated with Cybele. There is

---

of this relief where Cybele is placed, as well as the entire relief; cf. her discussion on pp. 119–121.

[16] Other frequent attendants include the Thracian Rider, the Danubian Riders, and the Dioscuroi, which have been extensively treated in Tudor's volumes, Tacheva-Hitova, etc.

[17] W. Blawatsky & G. Kochelenko, *Le Culte de Mithra sur la Côte septentrionale de la Mer Noire*, Leiden 1966; frontispiece. Cf. Artamonov, p. 80, plates 318 and 320.

no lion, for example, and the goddess at the base of the headdress wears a similar triangular headdress instead of a *polos* or mural crown.

Lions, however, are absent from many other depictions of Cybele, and there is at least one well-known rock-carved depiction of her in Lydia which has been described as having a cone-shaped hat.[18] Depictions of Cybele and the solar god or Helios or Sol on the same piece appear to be uncommon, both here and elsewhere.[19] There are, however, three depictions in *CCCA* I, which is devoted to Asia Minor, of the two deities together. From the Roman period in Phrygia, #139 contains busts of Luna and Sol on the pediment, with Cybele, lions, and the Dioscuri on the upper part of the monument. The lower part of this monument shows Cybele with the Thracian Rider. A second- or third-century A.D. white marble stele, also from Phyrgia (#197), depicts, in the pediment, a seated Cybele with lions seated on either side. Sol is depicted below her in a *quadriga*, and a female bust is above the horses. From Lydia, a white marble relief (#485) depicts "Artemis-Cybele" in a vault, in the company of Demeter and Victory. Among the many details on this complex work is a crescent moon and, just outside the vault, a solar disc.

Attis, Cybele's youthful lover, is first attested alone during the fourth or early third century in this region at Olbia (#525),[20] where a red terracotta figurine representing Attis seated on a rock and playing the syrinx has been found. A great many represenions of Attis have been found in the coastal cities (at least 88 in Vermaseren's catalog). The depictions of Attis vary from a conservatively attired youth to a wanton little child similar to the Eros-Cupid figure that frequently appears in hellenistic and Roman poetry. A key detail in identifying Attis is his pointed Phrygian cap. Thus #210, which depicts a seated woman in *chiton* and *himation* holding a sleeping baby is identified as "possibly Cybele and Attis," in part because of the infant's cap, although a Phrygian cap could represent other cults as well.[21]

---

[18] Vermaseren, *CCCA* I, 440.

[19] *CCCA* II (Greece) and *CCCA* VI contain no examples; *CCCA* I (Asia Minor) contains three: #139 contains busts of Luna and Sol on the pediment, with Cybele, lions, and the Dioscuri on the upper part of the monument; the lower part shows Cybele and the Thracian Rider.

[20] The earliest representations of Attis in Vermaseren's catalog are three isolated heads of Attis (#'s 207, 208, 214), from the fifth century. As Tacheva-Hitova points out (p. 141), however, the linkage of heads with Attis is not always reliable, since the Phrygian cap, the sole sign of identification, could be related to other cult-figures.

[21] Vermaseren, p. 68, #210. Cf. Tacheva-Hitova in previous note.

Attis is believed to have been accepted into the cult of Cybele relatively late,[22] not only in the coastal cities of the Black Sea, but also in other parts of the world where Cybele was worshipped. In mainland Greece, inscriptions found in the Piraeus indicate that an institution was established by foreigners to worship Cybele and her cult during the fourth century B.C. Attis was adopted into the cult, but "the appointment of a priestess underlines the absence of a priest. It was not until A.D. 163/4 that a State priest was appointed side by side with the priestess, which may indicate that at that time, under Marcus Aurelius, the cult was taken over by the Roman State." In Asia Minor, the earliest attestations of his presence also appear to belong to about the fourth century B.C.[23]

Attis is represented in two very different typologies. In one, he is depicted as a youth or young man, fully clothed in *tunica manicata*, *anaxyrides*, and a long cape, which frequently covers his head, and this cape in turn is covered by his Phrygian cap. This Attis frequently plays or holds a syrinx. Often he is in a funerary setting, where he stands with his legs crossed, in an attitude of mourning, resting his head on one hand while the other props up the elbow of the hand supporting the head. Often he leans upon a shepherd's crook or has one nearby.

At other times, as at Callatis (#405) he is depicted wearing a short cape on his shoulders and a Phrygian cap but has the round face of a very young child; his belly is bare and his genitals are exposed. This Attis suggests a mischievous child, very much like the romanticized, Eros-Cupid figure of hellenistic and Roman literature and art. Sometimes this Cupid-like Attis merges with other deities, such as Eros himself, wearing wings, or even as Mithras. In the Mithraic cult, depictions of Mithras in the tauroctony usually show an intent young man, more like the somber, syrinx-playing or mourning Attis.

---

[22] Lambrecht's argument that Attis was not originally a god, has been attacked by a number of scholars, including Vermaseren; cf P. Lambrechts, *Attis: von Herdersknaap tot God*, Brussel 1962. G. Thomas, "Magna Mater and Attis," *ANRW* II.17.3 (1984) 1500–1535, traces the development of the idea of resurrection with regard to Attis, when seems to be firmly established approximately by the time of Firmicius Maternus and the Neo-Platonists, i.e., the fourth century A.D. By this time, "Attis is now conceived of as a higher cosmic god, even the Sun-god. . . . At the solstice . . . symbolically Cybele is seen to have paled before the ascendant Attis and to have become the subsidiary element of the divine couple," according to Thomas (p. 1521). cf. G. Sfameni-Gasparro, *Soteriology and the Mystic Aspects in the Cult of Cybele and Attis*, Leiden 1985, 26–60.
[23] Vermaseren, *CCCA* II, 68–70, ad #257; cf. Sfameni-Gasparro, 49.

But when Mithras is merged with Attis, the childlike face and round belly seem to be the inherited characteristics that these two deities share. Sometimes the figure is identified as "Attis *or* Mithras," as in #474, where a male body rising from a stone (a common depiction of Mithras, who, like Cybele was born from stone) is "possibly" Attis but "possibly Mithras."[24]

Vermaseren notes hermaphroditic tendencies in the child-like figure (#405, hellenistic, from Callatis) which he calls "Attis-Dionysus;" not only are the child's belly and genitals bare, but he has rounded breasts which are also bare. Attis-Dionysus holds in his right hand a bunch of grapes, whence the association with Dionysus. In his left hand he holds a cock, which is another common piece of Attis iconography. Elsewhere (e.g., #555 [n.d.], #558 [1st century B.C., #'s 575, 584, 587 [1st century A.D.]) Attis rides on the cock. Vermaseren suggests that the cock may allude to the *gallus* or *archigallus*,[25] which is plausible, since the Latin word *gallus* means "barnyard cock." It is therefore not surprising if the cock alludes to the Pessinuntine priests of Attis and Cybele, and who look to Attis to justify their practice of self-castration.

Two hellenistic busts of Attis survive from Olbia (#528 and 529); their faces are somewhat child-like. These busts wear *fibulae*, and the hands appear to be crossed over the chest and holding a torch. From the same period, possibly also from Olbia, is a statue which is identified as an actor representing a *gallus*. This figure wears a long himation over the back of his body; his stomach and genitals are exposed. He holds a *silex* with his right hand and "with his left hand his *pudenda* (emasculation)."[26] During the hellenistic period and later, Attis is most often depicted in this Attis-Eros mode, with belly and genitals exposed, and wearing the Phrygian cap which identifies him as

---

[24] Blawatsky & Kochelenko show two statuettes of child-like figures in the gesture of killing a bull which they identify as "Mithra-Attis" (figs. 8 & 9), from Panticapeum. They argue that the cult of Mithras only penetrated the Bosporus under the guise of Mithras-Attis, and that Mithras-Attis was unable to occupy a place of importance because of the competition from Sabazios (pp. 12–13). For the idea of men being born from stone, cf. Vergil, *Georgics* I.61–63: . . . *quo tempore primum/Deucalion vacuum lapides iactavit in orbem,/unde homines nati, durum genus.* cf. P.A. Johnston, *Vergil's Agricultural Golden Age: A Study of the Georgics*, Leiden 1980, pp. 9–12; I. Borzák, *"Von Hippokrates bis Vergil,"* in *Vergiliana: Recherches sur Virgile*, ed. H. Bardon and R. Verdière, Leiden 1971.

[25] Vermaseren ad #97, p. 32.

[26] Vermaseren ad #530.

Attis. Sometimes this infantile Attis is winged, as in #581 and #597, the latter from the first century B.C. or A.D., the former slightly later, and in that case he is identified as Attis-Eros.

Cybele and Attis

There are surprisingly few representations of Attis *in the presence of* Cybele. The earliest joint appearance of the two deities in Vermaseren's catalog appears to be a gilt silver plaque, found in Mesembria in southern Thrace, on the coast of the Aegean Sea from the fourth century B.C. This plaque (#335) was found inside a storage jar in an area which apparently was a cult site for the worship of Demeter and Cybele together with several other silver plaques depicting Cybele.[27]

In #335, Cybele is seated on a low throne in a *naiskos* with two columns and a pediment. On Cybele's right stands a large female figure holding two flaming torches, identified as Hecate; on Cybele's left a small, standing youth, wearing only a shoulder-cape, is identified as Hermes. A lion sits next to the throne, behind the youthful Hermes, and a male and a female worshipper stand in the foreground, before the goddess. Above the peak of the pediment, separated by the roof-top from the gathering below, a small, childlike figure plays the syrinx. His legs are crossed, and he wears a peaked cap. He is identified as Attis.

In the second century B.C. the two deities are next seen together in a relief (#491) found not in the coastal cities but in Potaissa, in Dacia. Again, as in #335, the two figures are separated, this time by a straight horizontal line which separates the lower half of a female figure (which *may* be Cybele) in the upper section from the figure of Attis, in what is identified as an attitude of mourning in the lower section: here Attis stands fully-clothed, cross-legged, and supporting his chin on his right hand, as he leans his elbow on a *pedum* (a shepherd's crook). He wears a Phrygian cap, and a syrinx and a dolphin are depicted on the wall behind him.

Their next joint appearance in this area is the only one which

---

[27] Vermaseren, p. 98 ad. #334. The other Cybele items found there are #336 (Cybele with two lions), #337 (Cybele in the presence of Hermes, Hecate and worshippers), and #338 (Cybele with a lioness and male worshippers).

actually takes place in a coastal site, and this does not occur until the second century A.D., on the disc of a terracotta lamp from Olbia (#526).[28] Here Cybele sits on her throne, wearing a mural crown, with a *tympanum* in her left hand. According to Vermaseren, her right hand rests on her knee. On either side of her is a seated lion. Attis (fully clothed) stands on her right holding a syrinx, and on her left is a shape that looks like a torch but is identified as a pine tree. The figures are framed by a stele, and the letters TAM[29] are inscribed on the base.

Cybele with deities other than Attis

Thus, between the sixth century B.C. and the second century A.D. we have a total of three[30] items on which both Attis and Cybele appear, and only one of these comes from the northern coastline of the Black Sea. The earliest of these items, which comes from the coast of the Aegean Sea, is dated to the fourth century B.C. (in this case, they may be even earlier than the artifacts found at Athens or in Asia Minor), and the representation of Attis there is the sort one would more usually associate with the hellenistic period. The other two figures of Attis are the more somber, fully-clothed figures.

What then of Cybele's other companions? Cybele appears in this region in the company of a number of other gods, as well as mortals, animals, and sea creatures, but the lions are undoubtedly her most constant companions. In the fourth century, Hermes is a frequent companion, both individually and, with Hekate, forming a triad with the Goddess. This pair is seen in three, and possibly four, items

---

[28] For a photograph of the lamp, see Kobylina, *Div.Or.* p. 21 no. 12; Derewitzky - Pavlovsky - von Stern, *Museum Odessaer Ges.*, p. 44 and pl. XVII, 1. It should be noted that Kobylina (p. 20) believes Cybele holds a phialos (*phiale*) in her right hand, and wears a *kalathos* on her head.

[29] There is no explanation what these letters symbolize. The inverse abbreviation (in #376a), Μαθ, is read as Μά(τηρ) Θ(εῶν). #376 is a fragment of a *krater* which shows a lion, a wild boar, and a tree, dated to about 400 B.C.

[30] A possible fourth item is #210, mentioned above, a figurine depicting a woman in a *chiton* and an *himation*. She sits on a low throne with a footstool and holds a sleeping child on her lap. Her head is missing, but the head of the child has a pointed cap, suggesting this "Possibly Cybele and Attis" (Vermaseren, p. 68). No date is assigned to it. From fourth century A.D. Byzantium, a white marble relief shows Cybele between Attis and Hermes, wearing a mural crown; to the right of Hermes is a goddess identified as Demeter, wearing a *polos*.

belonging to the fifth and fourth centuries B.C.[31] On the fifth-century medallion mentioned earlier (#204), Hermes and a female figure who carries two torches accompany Cybele, who, in a charioteer's long *chiton*, drives a team of lions. A winged Victory flies toward her with a wreath. Hermes, who leads the procession, is identified by the *caduceus* he carries. He wears a short cape (a *chlamys)* and the broad-brimmed hat (*petasus*) of an ephebe. It should also be observed that, in this region of the world, whenever Hermes appears with Cybele, her headdress is a *polos*, which appears to be associated with their interactive chthonic relationship (Hermes and Hekate, of course, being two deities who regularly descend into the underworld).[32]

When the third deity in the triad with Hermes and Cybele is a female deity, Vermaseren has tended, in this volume, to identify her as Hekate, except in #204, where it is disputed whether she is Persephone or Demeter. Vermaseren concludes that it is Persephone, and that the medallion depicts Cybele's "descent into the Underworld."[33] Möbius[34] argues, however, that the female figure who regularly accompanies Hermes in #204 is Hekate. Hekate, like Persephone (= Kore), regularly carries a torch or torches. These two goddesses are closely related in Greek mythology, sometimes as cousins, or sisters, and, although they also appear together as separate entities (e.g., #198), they are also sometimes the same person, so that there may not be sufficient material here to make a finer distinction concerning this particular piece. Hermes' most frequent partner when he attends Cybele in the Black Sea region, however, based on the materials found, can certainly be said to be Hekate.

In Vermaseren's catalog, two, and possibly three items survive from the fourth century. Two of them (#335, 337) were among the mate-

---

[31] 5th century: #204; 4th century: #'s 335, 337, 450, 520, 588.

[32] The only possible exception which I could find is #335: Vermaseren identifies her headdress here as a *polos*, but the photograph, which is quite good, suggests the brick-work of a mural tower, which, if it is a mural crown, could perhaps have something to do with Attis' appearance here.

[33] This phrase makes me uncomfortable; I have not been able to trace any extant mythological or religious tradition whereby she actually *descends* into the Underworld; the traditional number of figures able to descend and return again is strictly limited (Hercules, Theseus, Orpheus, Aeneas; Dionysus only in Aristophanes' comedy—unless there is some other source of which I am not aware). Her chthonic role seems fairly well established, particularly when she is accompanied by Hermes and Hekate, but I have yet to find a myth wherein she actually goes down there.

[34] H. Möbius, "Die Göttin mit dem Löwen," in *Festschrift W. Eilers*, Wiesbaden 1967, 459 ff. and fig. 5.

rials found at the Demeter-Cybele cult site in Mesembria, in south-ern Thrace, as mentioned earlier. #335 is the gilt silver plaque on which Cybele is seated on a low throne, between a large female figure, identified as (possibly) Hekate, on Cybele's right, and, on her left, a smaller male figure identified as (possibly) Hermes. This male figure is clothed only in a shoulder-cape. A male and a female wor-shipper stand in the foreground, facing the goddess in profile, and above the pediment sits a naked, childlike Attis, playing the syrinx. While the small male figure before her may indeed be Hermes, it is curious that he should be so much smaller than Hekate, since he is usually equal in size to the deity with whom he jointly attends Cybele. Another curious detail is that he holds in his hands something that looks very much like a plough. Demeter, of course, taught the art of ploughing to Triptolemus, who taught this skill to the rest of human-kind. It may be reasonable to consider whether this goddess may be a blend of Demeter and Cybele, particularly since this was found in a cult site for the two goddesses, and to raise the possibility that this figure may represent Triptolemos.

A shape similar to what appears to be a plough can be detected at Hermes' feet in #337, a silver plaque from the same cult-site at Mesembria. Here, however, the photograph is less clear, and may merely represent the folds of his long cape. In this plaque, Hermes and Hekate stand outside the *naiskos* which houses the goddess, Hermes to her right and Hekate to her left, and mortal worshippers stand behind them, on either side of the shrine. Within the shrine, on either side of the goddess, are two other naked, bearded, male fig-ures which are not mentioned by Vermaseren. They appear to be holding items which correspond in angle and shape to the items held by the deities outside the *naiskos*, *e.g.*, the figure on Cybele's left appears to hold something similar to Hekate's torches, and the figure on Cy-bele's right has what may be a scythe, which would correspond to a similarly shaped line emerging from under Hermes' right arm. Here, too, except for his long cape and hat, Hermes appears to be naked.

The third item (#450), from the end of the fourth century, is iden-tified as "a fragment of a marble *naiskos*... possibly from Tomis." Here Cybele is depicted seated on her throne, a large *tympanon* to her left, with the bust of a bearded male figure standing behind her. The fragment breaks off just below her breasts, and the top of the *naiskos* is not readily visible in Vermaseren's photograph. Bordenache reconstructed this fragment on the basis of a number of votive offerings at the sanctuary of Cybele in Ephesus, and demonstrated that the bearded male figure standing behind her is probably Zeus and that Hermes very likely was once represented standing to her right. In Greece and Asia Minor are numerous such figures, so that there is ample evidence to support the thesis that there was a third male member of the triad, namely Hermes, with Cybele and Zeus. Only one such item survives in the coastal cities (#450), and this one relies on its similarity to the figures found at Ephesus. The surviving evidence would appear to indicate that this triad was not as widespread among the coastal cities as elsewhere.[35]

Hermes, then, when compared to Attis, appears in the presence of Cybele rather frequently in *CCCA*, VI. At least five of the Hermes appearances belong to the fourth century B.C. His appearance with her in these early centuries is also found in other volumes of *CCCA*, particularly volumes I (Asia Minor) and II (Greece and the Islands). At Ephesus, moreover, Hermes is Cybele's *only* companion in at least seven different items (#'s 616, 617, 634, 651, 678, 681, 684), most of them belonging to the fourth century B.C. (#634 and 678 have no date; #681 is hellenistic).

Conclusion

Cybele has of course a number of other companions who have not been addressed in this paper—the Thracian Rider, the Danubian Riders, and the Dioscuri have all, at one time or another, been identified as companions of the great Goddess. A certain amount of syncretism between the successive companions may have taken place, and Attis, with his bipolar typologies, seems to embody many of the characteristics shared in those transitions. Although a fuller study will have to be made of this proposition with regard to the Rider gods, the evidence advanced here suggests that the frequency of Hermes' presence is diminished as Attis becomes prominent, during the hellenistic period. In some regions, however, such as this coastal area, Attis is not as frequent a companion as his myth would imply, and

---

[35] B. Bordenache, *Sculture greche e romane del Museo nazionale di antichità di Bucarest. I. Statue e rilievi di culto, elementi architettonici e decorativi*, Bucarest 1969, p. 38 no. 59 and pl. XXVI. cf. *CCCA*, I (e.g., 613, 614, 615, 637, 643, etc.); Tacheva-Hitova, p. 90, no. 41; Vermaseren, p. 132 *ad* #450.

therefore Hermes is not completely displaced. Thereafter a branching and multiplication of regional companions seems to develop; the Rider gods, who tend to be much more closely tied to a specific region than a Greco-Roman deity such as Hermes would be, retain some of the characteristics of Hermes and Attis: the Thracian Rider holds sway in Thrace, the Danubian Riders in Dacia, while the Dioscuri, like Hermes not associated with a specific location, provide a direct Greco-Roman link for the other Rider gods. Mithras, although associated with Cybele indirectly, through his syncretism with the childlike Attis, also has ties with Cybele insofar as she is equated with Terra, who is found on frescoes such as the one at Capua, where she gazes with apparent approval at the sight of Mithras killing the bull.

When the lion(s) is replaced with different animals or even with the infant Attis, a very clear diminishment of her power, I believe, is taking place. The lions signal her command over wild creatures, and implicitly over tame ones, too. The hare is also wild, but much less fierce. The kid is a domesticated animal, and of course a human infant is a completely defenseless and dependent creature.

Her *tympanon* characterizes the exuberant dancing and singing that characterizes her ritual. When this is replaced by a sceptre, the symbol of civil authority, she becomes a very different kind of deity, for with the sceptre her spiritual authority is becoming highly formalized, more legal than spiritual.

These changes, however, appear to have arrived later in the cities and towns along the coast of the Black Sea, than in the interior ones, a rather surprising conclusion, which tends to belie the sort of truism once ascribed to Cato the Elder, the conservative Roman statesman. Cato reportedly observed that long-lasting cities should never be founded on the coastline since ships can sail up the the city with no advance warning of the sea-borne host. An advancing, marching army makes a great deal of noise and even causes a the land to shake, so that it can be detected well in advance of its arrival. Even more insidious to a coastal city, however, is the readiness with which morals are corrupted and undermined not only by foreign merchandise and morals, but even more by the enticement of other lands, with the result that, even if the inhabitants of the town stay at home, *animo tamen exultant et vagantur* (Cicero, *de re publica* 2.1–4). Inhabitants of the coastline of the Black Sea, by contrast, appear to have settled with their Goddess and to have retained her cult's traditional iconography (and, presumably, its ritual), and to have been influenced far less by foreign ideas than were those who settled in the interior, where most of the changes in the cult tend to happen first.

BIBLIOGRAPHY

M.I. Artamonov, *The Splendor of Scythian Art: Treasures from Scythian Tombs*, Praeger: New York 1969.

I. Berciu et C.C. Petolescu, *Les Cultes Orientaux dans la Dacie Méridionale*, Leiden 1976, (EPRO 54).

W. Blawatsky & G. Kochelenko, *Le Culte de Mithra sur la Côte septentrionale de la Mer Noire*, Leiden 1966, (EPRO 8).

B. Bordenache, *Sculture greche e romane del Museo nazionale di antichità di Bucarest. I. Statue e rilievi di culto, elementi architettonici e decorativi*, Bucarest 1969.

I. Borzák, *"Von Hippokrates bis Vergil,"* in *Vergiliana: Recherches sur Virgile*, ed. H. Bardon and R. Verdière, Leiden 1971.

Z. Gočeva and M. Oppermann, *Corpus Cultus Equitis Thracii (CCET) I: Monumenta Orae Ponti Euxini Bulgariae*, Leiden 1979; *Corpus Cultus Equitis Thracii (CCET) II,I: Monumenta inter Danubium et Haemum Reperta*, Leiden 1981 (EPRO 64).

H. Graillot, *Le culte de Cybèle, Mère des Dieux, à Rome et dans l'Empire romain* (Bibliothèque des Ecoles françaises d'Athènes et de Rome, vol. 107), Paris 1912.

R.F. Hoddinott, *Bulgaria in Antiquity*, New York 1975.

P.A. Johnston, *Vergil's Agricultural Golden Age: A Study of the Georgics*, Leiden 1980, (Mnemosyne Suppl. 60).

M.M. Kobylina, *Divinités Orientales sur le Littoral Nord de la Mer Noire*, Leiden 1976, (EPRO 52).

P. Lambrechts, *Attis: von Herdersknaap tot God*, Brussels 1962.

H. Möbius, *"Die Göttin mit dem Löwen,"* in *Festschrift W. Eilers*, Wiesbaden 1967.

G. Sanders, *"Kybele und Attis,"* *Die Orientalischen Religionen im Römerreich (OrRR)*, Leiden 1981, pp. 264–297 (EPRO 83).

G. Sfameni-Gasparro, *Soteriology and the Mystic Aspects in the Cult of Cybele and Attis*, Leiden 1985 (EPRO 130).

M. Tacheva-Hitova, *Eastern Cults in Moesia Inferior and Thracia (5th Century BC–4th Century AD)*, Leiden 1983 (EPRO 88).

G. Thomas, *"Magna Mater and Attis,"* *ANRW* II.17.3 (1984) 1500–1535.

D. Tudor, *Corpus Monumentorum Religionis Equitum Danuvinorum (CMRED): I. The Monuments*, Leiden 1969; *II. The Analysis and Interpretation of the Monuments*, Leiden 1976 (EPRO 13).

M.J. Vermaseren, *Cybele and Attis: the Myth and the Cult*, London 1977.

M.J. Vermaseren, *Corpus Cultus Cybelae Attidisque (CCCA)* (EPRO 50):

I: *Asia Minor*, Leiden 1987.
II: *Graecia atque Insulae*, Leiden 1982.
VI: *Germania, Raetia, Noricum, Pannonia, Dalmatia, Macedonia, Thracia, Moesia, Dacia, Regnum Bospori, Colchis, Scythia et Sarmatia*, Leiden 1989.

THE NAME OF CYBELE'S PRIESTS THE "GALLOI"

Eugene N. Lane

> Singula adferunt errorem cum pluribus rebus aut hominibus eadem appellatio est (ὁμονυμία dicitur), ut 'gallus' avem an gentem an nomen \<fluminis> an fortunam corporis significet incertum.—Quintilian, 7.9.2.

> Single words bring about error when there is the same name for several things or people (it is called "homonymy"); for instance, it is uncertain whether "gallus" refers to a bird, a people, the name \<of a river>, or a condition of the body. (N.B.—the addition of "fluminis" is mine.)

The term γάλλος (gallus) is used for the emasculated priests of the goddess commonly called Cybele, and also (by Lucian) for those of the Syrian Goddess (Atargatis). That it is also used for the Gauls, and that a branch of the Gallic race was ruling in Cybele's home city of Pessinus from *c.* 266 B.C.[1] onwards, and that the priests of Pessinus bore Gaulish names has been viewed as a mere coincidence, both in antiquity and the present day.[2] But is it?

---

[1] E.V. Hansen, *The Attalids of Pergamum*[2], Ithaca, N.Y., Cornell U.P., 1972, p. 31. On the Galatians see also the relevant chapter in R.E. Allen, *The Attalid Kingdom, A Constitutional History*, Oxford, Clarendon Press, 1983, 136–144.

[2] In the famous correspondence with the Pergamene kings, 163–156 B.C., Dittenberger, *OGIS* 315; C.B. Welles, *Royal Correspondence in the Hellenistic Period*, New Haven and London, Yale U.P., nos. 55–61; discussed F. Stähelin, *Geschichte der kleinasiatischen Galater*[2], Leipzig, Teubner, 1907, 75–85; Hansen, *op. cit.*, 126 ff. In these letters a high-priest with the hieratic name of Attis has a brother with the obviously Celtic name of Aiorix. The treatment of the matter in S. Mitchell, *Anatolia*, Oxford and New York, Oxford U.P., 1993, I, 47–50, is typical, but, if one examines it, very odd. He follows the argument originally advanced by Stähelin that the priests who met Manlius Vulso (see below note 16) in 189 B.C. were anti-Gallic Phrygians. He further says that the Gauls were interested in the political importance of the priesthood, and that "their earliest appearance as holders of the office coincided with the. . . . end of the ancient practice of castrating the high priests." Actually, as we will show, their earliest appearance as high priests more or less coincides with the beginning of the tradition about castrated priests. He also states that "the appearance of Celts in the temple organization by the mid-second century B.C. is certain proof that they had adopted the indigenous cult of Cybele and her consort Attis"—this in spite of the absence of Attis as an object of worship in Pessinus or Anatolia in general, as has been shown by Lynn Roller (see note 6). Most oddly, Mitchell nowhere even seems to take notice of the coincidence of the priests' name with that of the Gauls!

The name for the priests seems to occur first in a possibly apocryphal witticism attributed to the philosopher Arcesilaus (c. 318–242 B.C.) by Diogenes Laertius (4.43.2):

πρὸς τὸν πυθόμενον διὰ τί ἐκ μὲν τῶν ἄλλων μεταβαίνουσιν εἰς τὴν Ἐπικούρειον, ἐκ δὲ τῶν Ἐπικουρείων οὐδέποτε, ἔφη, "ἐκ μὲν ἀνδρῶν γάλλοι γίνονται, ἐκ δὲ γάλλων ἄνδρες οὐ γίνονται."

To the person who asked why people went from other schools to that of Epicurus, but never from the Epicureans, he said, "Galloi are made from men, but never men from galloi."

If this anecdote is genuine, then it shows that the word as applied to the priests had gained currency by the date of Arcesilaus' death. Anyone who has read Diogenes Laertius, however, realizes that his account is an uncritical stringing-together of anecdotes, often mutually contradictory, and likely to contain anachronisms.

We are on somewhat firmer ground with some of the epigrams of the Greek Anthology. Apparently the two earliest of these are by Dioscorides—A.P.6.220[3] and A.P.11.195.[4] According to Gow and Page[5] this poet probably flourished in the late third century B.C. The first epigram has to do with a gallus called Atys[6] who scared away a lion with his drum-playing:

Σάρδις Πεσσινόεντος ἀπὸ Φρυγὸς ἤθελ᾽ ἱκέσθαι,
    ἔκφρων μαινομένην δοὺς ἀνέμοισι τρίχα,
ἁγνὸς Ἄτυς Κυβέλης θαλαμηπόλος· ἄγρια δ᾽ αὐτοῦ
    ἐψύχθη χαλεπῆς πνεύματα θευφορίης
ἑσπέριον στείχοντος ἀνὰ κνέφας, εἰς δὲ κάταντες
    ἄντρον ἔδυ νεύσας βαιὸν ἄπωθεν ὁδοῦ.
τοῦ δὲ λέων ὤρουσε κατὰ στίβον, ἀνδράσι δεῖμα
    θαρσαλέοις Γάλλῳ οὐδ᾽ ὀνομαστὸν ἄχος.

---

[3] A.S.F. Gow and D.L. Page, *The Greek Anthology: Hellenistic Epigrams*, Cambridge, Cambridge U.P., 1965, Dioscorides 16. For this group of poems, see A.S.F. Gow, "The Gallus and the Lion," *JHS* 80, 1960, 88–93. The author is particularly concerned in this article with the identification of the objects dedicated to the goddess, such as the mysterious θαλάμη ("chamber"). He concludes that the reference is probably to the τύποι καὶ προστηθίδια (images and breastplates) of Polybius (see below)—i.e., the aedicula-like pectorals known from later figured representations to have been worn by the priests of Cybele.

[4] Gow and Page, *op. cit.*, Dioscorides 36.

[5] *Op. cit.*, II, p. 5.

[6] It should be noted that the high-priest from Pessinus, in the correspondence noted above (note 2), is also called Attis. On the original use of Attis (Atys) as a personal name, rather than that of a divinity, see Lynn Roller, *Source*, 7, 1988, 43–50.

ὃς τοτ' ἄναυδος ἔμεινε δέους ὕπο καί τινος αὔρη
  δαίμονος ἐς τὸν ἐὸν τύμπανον ἧκε χεῖρας,
οὗ βαρὺ μυκήσαντος ὁ θαρσαλεώτερος ἄλλων
  τετραπόδων ἐλάφων ἔδραμεν ὀξύτερον,
τὸν βαρὺν οὐ μείνας ἀκοαῖς ψόφον. ἐκ δ' ἐβόησεν
  "Μῆτερ, Σαγγαρίου χείλεσι πὰρ ποταμοῦ
ἰρὴν σοὶ θαλάμην ζωάγρια καὶ λαλάγημα
  τοῦτο τὸ θηρὶ φυγῆς αἴτιον ἀντίθεμαι."

Chaste Attis, the chamber-guard of Cybele, furious, giving over his
mad hair to the winds, wished to come to Sardis from Phrygian Pessinus.
The wild blasts of his harsh ecstasy grew cold in him as he made his
way through the evening darkness, and he took refuge in a sloping
cave, leaving the road a bit. A lion rushed after his tracks, a fear to
courageous men and an unnamable grief to a gallus. He then remained
speechless out of fear, and by the inspiration of a spirit put his hands
upon his drum. When this beat heavily, the most courageous of quad-
rupeds ran swifter than the deer, not standing to hear the heavy sound.
He cried out, "Mother, by the banks of the Sangarius river I dedicate
a holy chamber as an offering for saving my life, and this noisy instrument, the reason for the beast's flight."

The second has to do with a dancer who took the part of a Gallus
and won a contest—unworthily—over the author, who took a traditional tragic part:

Γάλλον Ἀρισταγόρης ὠρχήσατο, τοὺς δὲ φιλόπλους
  Τημενίδας ὁ καμὼν πολλὰ διῆλθον ἐγώ·
χὡ μὲν τιμηθεὶς ἀπεπέμπετο, τὴν δὲ τάλαιναν
  Ὑρνηθὼ κροτάλων εἰς ψόφος ἐξέβαλεν.
εἰς πῦρ ἡρώων ἴτε πρήξιες, ἐν γὰρ ἀμούσοις
  καὶ κόρυδος κύκνου φθέγξετ' ἀοιδότερον.

Aristagoras danced the part of a gallus, whereas hard-working I went
through the business about the Temenids, fond of sailing. And he went
away with the prize, and one sound of the castanets did away with
poor Hyrnetho. Then to the fire deeds of heroes, for among the un-
appreciative even a lark sings better than the swan. (Larks do sing
better than swans, by the way, so the whole poem may be ironic.)

A third early Hellenistic epigram is among those falsely attributed to
Simonides—*A.P.*6,217.[7] It treats the same subject as Dioscorides'

---

[7] Gow and Page, *op. cit.*, "Simonides" 2; cf. II, 517. *A propos* of this poem Gow
and Page note (II, 518) that the name γάλλος was unknown for votaries of Cybele
before the third century B.C., and use this as an argument against Simonides'
authorship.

epigram on the gallus who put the lion to flight, and is either an imitation of or the inspiration for Dioscorides' poem, but in either case not far off in date.

Χειμερίην νιφετοῖο κατήλυσιν ἡνίκ' ἀλύξας
  Γάλλος ἐρημαίην ἤλυθ' ὑπὸ σπιλάδα
ὑετὸν ἄρτι κόμης ἀπεμόρξατο, τοῦ δὲ κατ' ἴχνος
  βουφάγος εἰς κοίλην ἀτραπὸν ἷκτο λέων.
αὐτὰρ ὁ πεπταμένη μέγα τύμπανον ὅ σχέθε χειρὶ
  ἤραξεν, καναχῇ δ' ἴαχεν ἄντρον ἅπαν,
οὐδ' ἔτλη Κυβέλης ἱερὸν βρόμον ὑλονόμος θὴρ
  μεῖναι, ἀν' ὑλῆεν δ' ὠκὺς ἔθυνεν ὄρος
δείσας ἡμιγύναικα θεῆς λάτριν ὅς τάδε Ῥείᾳ
  ἐνδυτὰ καὶ ξανθοὺς ἐκρέμασεν πλοκάμους.

When, avoiding the wintry snowfall, a gallus came to an abandoned cave, he wiped the rain from his hair, and on his tracks came a cattle-eating lion down the hollow trail. But he beat the great drum which he held in his outstretched hand, and the whole cave sounded with the noise, nor did the forest-dwelling beast dare withstand the holy sound of Cybele, but quickly it darted up the wooded mountain, fearing the half-woman worshipper of the goddess, who hung up to Rhea his garments and his yellow locks.

The theme then becomes a commonplace in epigrams of later times, which I forbear quoting.[8] Before, however, we pass from the subject of galli mentioned in Hellenistic epigrams, we must turn our attention to a famous fragment sometimes attributed to Callimachus († c. 240 B.C.):[9]

Γάλλαι μητρὸς ὀρείης φιλόθυρσοι δρομάδες
  αἷς ἔντεα παταγεῖται καὶ χάλκεα κρόταλα.

Gallai, thyrsus-fond runners of the mountain mother, for whom instruments and bronze castanets clash.

---

[8] See *A.P.*6,218 (= Gow and Page, Alcaeus of Messene 21) and *A.P.*6,219 (= Gow and Page, Antipater of Sidon 64). Gow and Page date these poets respectively to the early and the mid-second century B.C. (II, pp. 7, 32). Other even later poems of the Anthology also refer to galli. They are by Erycius (*A.P.*6,234) and Antistius (*A.P.*6,237). The latter continues the commonplace of the gallus who terrifies the lion. It is also worth noting that one of these epigrams (*A.P.*6,218) calls the priest a Μητρὸς ἀγύρτης, an older name, attested in the fourth century B.C. (There is a play by the comedian Antiphanes called Μητραγύρτης.) Perhaps the term "gallus" is a later substitution in an already existing topos. The poem, does, however, assume that the priest was castrated, something which would point to the custom's being practiced before the coming of the Gauls (see footnote 27, below).

[9] Frag. 761 Pfeiffer, under Fragmenta Incerti Auctoris.

This is the only place where the feminine form is used. It is nowhere specifically stated that this passage is by Callimachus. The source of it is Hephaestion XII,3, p. 39, 1, who cites it as an example of Galliambic verse. He does not attribute the passage to Callimachus, but states that the meter is called γαλλιαμβικόν or μητρῳακόν, διὰ τὰ πολλὰ τοὺς νεωτέρους εἰς τὴν μητέρα τῶν θεῶν γράψαι τούτῳ τῷ μέτρῳ (because the more recent poets wrote a lot of things in honor of the mother of the gods in this meter). George Choiroboscus (a sixth-century grammarian who *inter alia* wrote a commentary on the second-century metrist Hephaestion) indicates that Callimachus wrote in this verse-form. (He may have written in it before it acquired its name.) It is at all events exceeding the evidence by quite a lot to attribute these verses to Callimachus.[10]

It is on this passage and on the quip ostensibly by Arcesilaus, cited above from Diogenes Laertius, that Franz Cumont bases his categorical denial that the galli can have taken their name from the Gauls.[11] Now the Gauls invaded Asia Minor in 278–7 B.C. and before 266 the Tectosages were settled around Ancyra, perhaps the Tolistobogii around Pessinus.[12] Admittedly it is not until the famous correspondence of 163–156 B.C. between the Attalid kings and the priests of Pessinus that we see that the cult of Pessinus is completely gallified,[13] but we must recognize that we have little idea of what the Gauls found on occupying Pessinus, or how soon they started assimilating it or making it their own. Even if one assumes that the passages attributed to Arcesilaus and Callimachus are genuine, it does not seem out of the question that if the Gauls started making the cult their own almost as soon as they arrived in Galatia, particularly if they expanded or even introduced the striking custom of the eunuch priests, the fact would have been unknown to these authors before they both died *c.* 240 B.C.[14] (As we will see later, we will have to admit that Callimachus knew at least about the renaming of the river of Pessinus as Gallus.) And since they are quite possibly apocryphal,

---

[10] For the whole matter see R. Pfeiffer, *Callimachus*, Oxford, Clarendon Press, 1941, I, p. 478.

[11] In his article, s.v., Galloi, in RE.

[12] Hansen, *op. cit.*, 29 and 31.

[13] Hansen, *op. cit.*, p. 126.

[14] Remember that there is no evidence for the custom early on, e.g. in Herodotus, and that even Attis joins Cybele iconographically only in the later fourth century B.C. (Friederike Naumann, *Die Ikonographie der Kybele in der phrygischen und der griechischen Kunst*, Tübingen, Verlag Ernst Wasmuth, 1983, 239 ff. See also Lynn Roller, Hesperia

we can allow another twenty or so years, until the time of Dioscorides, for the news to have gotten about.

Galli first appear on the pages of history in the events of the early second century B.C. First (Polybius, 21.6.6; cf. Livy 37.18.9) in reference to a threatened siege of Sestus by C. Livius Salinator in 190 B.C.:

Ἐξελθόντες μὲν Γάλλοι δύο μετὰ τύπων καὶ προστηθιδίων ἐδέοντο μηδὲν ἀνήκεστον βουλεύεσθαι περὶ τῆς πόλεως.

Two galli, coming out with images and breastplates, begged that he plan nothing irremediable about the city.

This passage has remained remarkably uncommented-on. If nothing else, it shows that the custom of eunuch priests and their name, galli, had spread to the coastal regions of Asia Minor even before it is specifically attested at Pessinus! Phocaea is closely involved with these events in Livy's account, and it might be suggested that the galli in question were from that city, rather than from Sestus itself. As in Dioscorides' epigram, galli may have traveled far in their holy missions. A rock-cut sanctuary of the goddess, of uncertain date, is known at Phocaea.[15]

Next in reference to the expedition of Manlius Vulso into Galatia in 189 B.C. (Polybius, 21.37.5):

καὶ παρ' αὐτὸν τὸν ποταμὸν (Sangarius) στρατοπεδευσαμένου (i.e. Manlius) παραγίνονται Γάλλοι παρ' Ἄττιδος καὶ Βαττάκου τῶν ἐκ Πεσσινοῦντος ἱερέων τῆς Μητρὸς τῶν θεῶν, ἔχοντες προστηθίδια καὶ τύπους, φάσκοντες προσαγγέλλειν τὴν θεὸν νίκην καὶ κράτος.

And when he encamped right by the river, there came galli from Attis and Battakes the priests of the mother of the gods, having breastplates and images, saying that the goddess proclaimed victory and power.

Livy, 38.18.9, tells the same story, also using the term Galli.[16]

63, 1994, 245 ff., especially footnote 81.) There is of course the difficulty that there is likewise no evidence for the custom of eunuch priests among the Celts before their establishment in Asia Minor. See also footnote 25, below. The question is beyond the scope of this article to solve.

[15] Naumann, op. cit., 153–4.

[16] The theory (which originated with Stähelin) that these galli welcomed the Romans since they were non-Celts opposed to the Celtic rulers is gratuitous (Hansen, op. cit., 89–90). At least one Galatian prince, Eposognatus, was on the Pergamene-Roman side, and the priests could have sided with him. See also the criticism of S. Mitchell's treatment of these events in note 2. Note that in this passage also Attis appears as the hieratic name of a priest, rather than as that of a divine being.

Now, as we have observed, the ancients, just like the moderns, were unwilling to connect the name of the priests with that of the ethnic group. There seems to be only one ancient authority who makes the obvious connection: namely Jerome, commenting on a Hebrew word which he translates "effeminatos."[17] He says:

> Hi sunt quos hodie Romae, matri, non deorum, sed daemoniorum servientes, Gallos vocant, eo quod de hac gente Romani truncatos libidine in honorem Atys (quem eunuchum dea meretrix fecerat) sacerdotes illius manciparint. Propterea autem Gallorum gentis homines effeminantur, ut qui urbem Romanam ceperant, hac feriantur ignominia.

> These are those whom nowadays at Rome they call galli—they serve the mother not of the gods but of demons—because the Romans freed some priests of this race who were deprived of their sex-drive in honor of Atys, whom the harlot goddess made a eunuch. On this account therefore men of the Gallic race are made effeminate, that those who seized the city of Rome might be struck by this disgrace.

Rather the ancients generally connected the priests' name with a river Gallus, generally said to flow by Pessinus. Actually, although there are numerous references to the river, with or without connection to the priests, there is only one author (and the lexicographical tradition dependent on him), to my knowledge, who specifically gives a reason for making the connection. That is also the earliest, Ovid, *Fasti* 4,361 ff.:

> "Cur igitur Gallos qui se excidere vocamus,
>   cum tanto a Phrygia Gallica distet humus?"
> "Inter," ait, "viridem Cybelen altasque Celaenas
>   amnis it insana, nomine Gallus, aqua.
> qui bibit inde, furit."[18]

> "Why then do we call Gauls (galli) those who have castrated themselves, when the Gallic land is so far from Phrygia?"
>   "Between," she (Erato) said, "green (Mount) Cybele and high Celaenae, there flows a river with insane water, called 'Gallus.' Who drinks of it goes mad."

Strabo knows of the river, but does not connect it with the priests (12.3.7):

---

[17] *In Osee* I,4 = Migne, PL 25,851C. Although the Migne footnote of 1884 takes Jerome to task for this opinion, it was still honored by Mommsen in *Röm. Geschichte* I[8] 869 (*non vidi*), according to Cumont s.v. Galloi in RE.

[18] Ovid can hardly be pressed on geographical matters. Celaenae is of course in an entirely different part of Anatolia from Pessinus. On Cybele as a name for

διέξεισι (ὁ Σαγγάριος) δὲ τῆς Ἐπικτήτου Φρυγίας τὴν πλείω, μέρος δέ τι καὶ τῆς Βιθυνίας ὥστε καὶ τῆς Νικομηδείας ἀπέχειν μικρὸν πλείους ἢ τριακοσίους σταδίους, καθ᾽ ὁ συμβάλλει ποταμὸς αὐτῷ Γάλλος, ἐκ Μόδρων ἔχων τῆς ἐφ᾽ Ἑλλησπόντῳ Φρυγίας.

(The Sangarius) goes through most of Phrygia Epictetus and part of Bithynia, so that it is a little over three hundred stades from Nicomedia and the point where the Gallus River flows into it, coming from Modra of Hellespontine Phrygia.

Pliny, *Natural History* 5,147, enumerating the geographical features of Galatia, connects the name of the river with the priests but fails to give a reason:

Flumina sunt in ea praeter iam dicta Sangarium (neuter, sic!) et Gallus, a quo nomen traxere matris deum sacerdotes.

There are rivers in it (Galatia) in addition to those already mentioned— the Sangarius and the Gallus, from which the priests of the mother of the gods drew their name.

Elsewhere (6,4) Pliny, describing river which flow into the Black Sea and other landmarks of its coast, makes the Gallus into a tributary of the Sangarius:

Sangarius fluvius ex inclutis; oritur in Phrygia, accipit vastos amnes, inter quos Tembrogium et Gallum, idem Sagiarius plerisque dictus.

The Sangarius River is one of the famous ones. It arises in Phrygia and receives vast tributaries, among them the Tembrogius and the Gallus. It is called the Sagiarius by most people.

In this passage there is no mention of the connection with the priests.

---

mountains, see particularly Mary Jane Rein's contribution to this volume. On the Ovid passage in particular, see C. Brixhe, *Die Sprache* 25, 1979, 43–44. The later lexicographers Sextus Pompeius Festus (dependent on Verrius Flaccus, of the Augustan period) and Vibius Sequester closely represent the same tradition as Ovid.

Festus, *De verborum significatione* 7,71:

Galli qui vocantur Matris Magnae comites, dicti sunt a flumine, cui nomen est Gallo: qua qui ex eo biberunt, in hoc furere incipiant, ut se privent virilitatis parte.

The companions of the great mother, who are called galli, take their name from a river called Gallus, because those who have drunk from it begin to go mad this way, that they deprive themselves of their virile organ.

Vibius Sequester, *De fluminibus*, no. 170 (Parroni):

Gallus in Phrygia, unde qui bibit insanit more fanatico.

The Gallus is in Phrygia; who drinks from it goes mad in a fanatic fashion.

Note verbal echoes of Ovid, even though there in no mention of priests.

There is a third passage from Pliny, 31,9, citing Callimachus:

In Aenaria insula calculosis mederi.... idem contigit in Velino lacu potantibus, item in Syriae fonte iuxta Taurum montem auctor est M. Varro et in Phrygiae Gallo flumine Callimachus, sed ibi in potando necessarius modus, ne lymphatos agat, quod in Aethiopia accidere his qui e fonte Rubro bibere Ctesias scribit.

On the island of Aenaria those with bladder-stones can be cured.... and the same thing happens to those who drink at the Veline Lake, and in Syria at a spring near Mount Taurus—as M. Varro says—and in the Gallus River of Phrygia—as Callimachus says—, but there one must limit one's drinking, lest it drive people crazy, as Ctesias says happens in Ethiopia to those who have drunk from the Red Spring.

Note that this reference to Callimachus, whom we have already studied, does not connect the name of the river with that of the priests. On the other hand, the reputation that this river had for causing insanity if its waters were overimbibed may lie behind Ovid's tradition. The reference to the curing of bladder-stones, which is the only thing specifically attributed to Callimachus, is unparalleled in other sources.

Herodian the historian (1,1,11,2) also mentions the river in connection with the priests, but does not give a specific reason for the connection. Note that like Firmicus Maternus (see below) he places it right at Pessinus.

Πεσσινοῦντι πάλαι μὲν Φρύγες ὠργίαζον ἐπὶ τῷ ποταμῷ Γάλλῳ παραρρέοντι, ἀφ' οὗ τὴν ἐπωνυμίαν φέρουσιν οἱ τῇ θεῷ τομίαι ἱερωμένοι.

At Pessinus the Phrygians once held their orgies on the Gallus River which flows by it, whence the holy eunuchs of the goddess take their name.

Firmicus Maternus, *De errore profanarum religionum* 3, also speaks of the river as being near Pessinus, but does not connect the priests:

Phryges, qui Pessinunta incolunt circa Galli fluminis ripas, terrae ceterorum elementorum tribuunt principatum et hanc volunt omnium esse matrem.

The Phrygians, who inhabit Pessinus around the banks of the Gallus River, attribute to Earth primacy over the other elements and assert that she is the mother of all.

Martianus Capella, VI,687, seems, like Strabo (and Pliny?), to be talking of a Bithynian river. Unlike Strabo, he connects it with the priests:

Nam Bithynia initium Ponti est et ab ortu Thraciae adversa a Sangari flumine primos habet habitatores, qui fluvius alio fluvio Gallo miscetur, a quo Galli dicuntur, ministri matris deum.

For Bithynia is the beginning of Pontus and has its first inhabitants of Thracian origin, opposite the Sangarius River, which joins with another river, the Gallus, whence the ministers of the mother of the gods have the name "galli."

So far the references to the river from a pretty much purely geographical point of view. Hereafter, however, (note that our account is not strictly chronological) things become more complicated. We encounter 1) Neo-Platonic allegorical interpretations, and 2) a mythographical tradition professing to go back to a certain Timotheus and/or Alexander Polyhistor. We find ourselves making the acquaintance also of a certain Gallus, a mythological character, presumably the prototype of the castrated galli. Notably, Gallus is absent from the earliest of the accounts of the Attis myth, that of Pausanias—which does not claim "Timotheus" as a source—, but appears in Arnobius' and Stephanus Byzantinus' accounts, which explicitly claim "Timotheus" as their source,[19] as well as in that of Herodian Grammaticus.

First, the Neo-Platonic accounts. Sallustius Philosophus (1,4), for instance, continues mentioning the river, but has it as the place where the Mother of the Gods fell in love with Attis, and proceeds to read arcane meanings into it, which do not concern us here:

εἰ δὲ δεῖ καὶ ἕτερον μῦθον εἰπεῖν, τὴν μητέρα τῶν θεῶν φασι τὸν Ἄττιν παρὰ τῷ Γάλλῳ κείμενον ἰδοῦσαν ποταμῷ, ἐρασθῆναί τε καὶ λαβοῦσαν τὸν ἀστερωτὸν αὐτῷ περιθεῖναι πῖλον, καὶ τοῦ λοιποῦ μεθ' ἑαυτῆς ἔχειν. . . . . ὁ δὲ Ἄττις τῶν γινομένων καὶ φθειρομένων δημιουργός, καὶ διὰ τοῦτο παρὰ τῷ Γάλλῳ λέγεται εὑρεθῆναι ποταμῷ· ὁ γὰρ Γάλλος τὸν γαλαξίαν αἰνίττεται κύκλον, ἀφ' οὗ τὸ παθητὸν ἔρχεσθαι σῶμα.

If one must tell another myth, they say that the mother of the gods, seeing Attis lying by the Gallus River, fell in love with him, and taking the starry cap put it on him, and for the rest of time kept him with herself. . . . . . Attis is the creator of things that come into being and are destroyed, and that is why he is said to have been found by the Gallus River. For the Gallus hints at the galaxy, from whence the changeable body comes.

---

[19] The passage in Pausanias is VII,17,9–12. Note that Pausanias also says that because of Attis' death, the Galatians in Pessinus refuse to eat pork. Clearly Pausanias is of the opinion that the Galatians have been Cybele-and-Attis worshippers for a long time if they have let the related story that Attis was killed by a boar influence their dietary habits, as Lynn Roller has kindly pointed out to me.

In a similar vein, the Emperor Julian mentions the Gallus River, only to invest it with esoteric meanings. He also mentions Gallus, a god or hero, who is the prototype of the galli. As to the river, he follows the same tradition as Sallustius:

> ὃν (the antecedent seems to be a conflation of Attis and Gallus) δή φησιν ὁ μῦθος ἀνθῆσαι μὲν ἐκτεθέντα παρὰ Γάλλου ποταμοῦ ταῖς δίναις, εἶτα καλὸν φανέντα καὶ μέγαν ἀγαπηθῆναι παρὰ τῆς μητρὸς τῶν θεῶν. . . . . . ἀλλ᾽ εἰ τὴν κορυφὴν σκέπει τοῦ Ἄττιδος ὁ φαινόμενος οὐρανὸς οὑτοσί, τὸν Γάλλον ποταμὸν ἄρα μή ποτε χρὴ τὸν γαλαξίαν αἰνίττεσθαι κύκλον; (*On the Mother of the Gods*, 165 B.C.).

> The myth says he flourished, being exposed by the swirls of the Gallus River, and then seeming handsome and tall he was loved by the mother of the gods. . . . but if this apparent heaven covers the top of Attis' head, is it not necessary for the Gallus River to hint at the galaxy?

Clearly for these last authors, the existence or non-existence of a geographically fixable Gallus River is immaterial, so long as there is such a mythological river which can be identified with the Milky Way.[20]

Julian, as we said, also mentions a mythical eponym, Gallus, and there also exists a textually confused passage or Arnobius, V,5–7 and 13, already alluded to, naming "Timotheus" as his source, in which Agdistis, incensed at the marriage of Attis to a king's daughter, sends madness upon the whole assemblage at the wedding, and both Attis and the father-in-law castrate themselves. Gallus suddenly appears, apparently as the father-in-law's name, although he remains nameless in Pausanias' earlier parallel account of the myth (VII,17,10–12).

Stephanus of Byzantium, s.v. Γάλλος, joins the tradition of the galli being named after the river together with that in which Gallus appears as a mythical figure, and names sources:

> Γάλλος, ποταμὸς Φρυγίας. οἱ περίοικοι κατὰ μὲν Τιμόθεον Ποταμογαλλῖται, κατὰ δὲ Προμαθίδαν Ποταμογαλληνοί, οὓς παρατίθεται ὁ Πολυίστωρ ἐν τῷ περὶ Φρυγίας τρίτῳ· καὶ ὅτι τὸν Γάλλον καὶ τὸν Ἄττιν ἀποκόψαι τὰ αἰδοῖα, καὶ τὸν μὲν Γάλλον ἐλθεῖν ἐπὶ τὸν Τηρίαν ποταμὸν καὶ οἰκῆσαι καὶ τὸν ποταμὸν Γάλλον καλέσαι· ἀπ᾽ ἐκείνου γὰρ τοὺς τεμνομένους τὰ αἰδοῖα Γάλλους καλοῦσι.

---

[20] Gallus as the (divine) prototype of the galli occurs too frequently in Julian's *On the Mother of the Gods* for me to quote all the passages: 159A–B, 161C, 165D, 168D, 169A.

Gallus, a river of Phrygia. The nearby inhabitants according to Timo-
theus are Potamogallitai, according the Promathidas Potamogallenoi.
Both of them are quoted by Polyhistor in the third book about Phrygia.
And <he also says> that Gallus and Attis cut off their genitals, and
Gallus came to the Terias River and settled there and called the river
Gallus. From him (it?) they call those whose genitals are cut galli.

Note that Gallos is here said to be a new name for a river previously called Terias.

The Timotheus of Stephanus and Arnobius is generally held to be
the same as the Eleusinian Eumolpid who helped Ptolemy I found
the Sarapis-cult.[20] If this is so, it proves that the Cybele-and-Attis
story was known in late-fourth-century Alexandria, perhaps with a
mythical character Gallus involved, or well before the coming of the
Gauls to Anatolia. But the identification is by no means certain, and
the name quite reasonably common—77 entries in the RE. All that
we can say with reasonable likelihood is that "Timotheus" preceded
Alexander Polyhistor, and that only if Stephanus can be assumed to
have known what he was talking about.[21]

It should be observed here in passing that the writers of the Real-
Encyclopädie are inconsistent in their treatment of the identity of our
Timotheus. Under Timotheus 14 (col. 1338), we find him listed as a
separate entity—"Schrieb nach Arnob. V.5 über den Kult der Magna

---

[21] It is odd that Stephanus names "Timotheus" and Promathidas as sources of
Alexander Polyhistor, whereas Herodian Grammaticus, generally acknowledged to
be Stephanus' source (see note 22), does not. For Promathidas, see F. Gisinger's
article in RE, s.v. He is apparently a historian of Heracleia Pontica, of the time of
Pompey, thus not long before Alexander Polyhistor. Can one thus also assume that
the "Timotheus" in question is of the same period?—that is assuming that Stephanus
has any basis whatever for the elaboration of the source he depends on otherwise,
and that his statement does not simply represent a conflation of Herodian's tradition and that of Arnobius. In that case, one would be free to place Timotheus after
Polyhistor, even seeing in him a Neo-Platonist, something which would explain his
late appearance in the tradition. Or, assuming that Polyhistor does indeed mention
Timotheus as a source, he may have used him only for the ethnic noun, not for the
myth of Attis, for that is all a strict reading of Stephanus implies. In that case
Arnobius (or his source) may have been the one who credits the myth to Timotheus.
At all events, a close reading of the sources discourages jumping to conclusions. For
an uncritical exaggeration of the role of Timotheus, assumed to be the Eumolpid,
see, e.g., T. Zielinski, The Religion of Ancient Greece, Oxford University Press, 1926,
120–121.
  The texts of Arnobius and Pausanias, although important for the myth, do not
mention the galli as priests, nor do they speak of the river. For that reason they
are not given here. The reader may find an interesting parallel presentation of the
two accounts in H. Hepding, Attis, seine Mythen und sein Kult, RGVV 1, Geißen 1903,
37 ff.

Mater" (Laqueur). Yet under Timotheus 19 (col. 1342), we find Weinreich hesitantly making the identification with Timotheus the Eumolpid ("muß wohl. . . . sein"). Later in the same article Weinreich dissociates a hymnographer of uncertain date, known from Macrobius, from the Eumolpid, and at the same time comments on the disparity of tone between the Sarapis-story, a genuine product of the Eumolpid, and that of Cybele and Attis.

Herodian Grammaticus[22] has exactly the same story to tell as does Stephanus, except that he does not trace his sources any farther back than Polyhistor (*Grammatici Graeci* 3,1,156–7):

Γάλλος ὁ ποταμὸς Φρυγίας·—λέγει δὲ ὁ Πολυίστωρ ἐν τῷ περί Φρυγίας τρίτῳ, τὸν Γάλλον καὶ τὸν Ἄττιν ἀποκόψαι τὰ αἰδοῖα καὶ τὸν μὲν Γάλλον ἐλθεῖν ἐπὶ τὸν Τηρίαν ποταμὸν καὶ οἰκῆσαι καὶ τὸν ποταμὸν Γάλλον καλέσαι. ἀπ᾽ ἐκείνου γὰρ τοὺς τεμνομένους τὰ αἰδοῖα Γάλλους καλοῦσιν—καὶ ἔθνος.

Gallus is a river or Phrygia. Polyhistor says in the third book about Phrygia that Gallus and Attis cut off their genitals and that Gallus came to the Terias River and settled there and called the river Gallus. From him (it?) those whose genitals are cut they call galli. Likewise a race.

But there is another passage of the same author often overlooked in the discussion (*G.G.*3,1,243, line 11 f.):

Πεσσινοῦς πόλις Γαλατίας ἀπό τινος Γάλλου Πεσσινοῦντος· τινὲς δὲ ἀπὸ πηγῆς ῥεούσης τοῦ λόφου τοῦ ἐν ᾧ ἐτάφη ὁ Μαρσύας.

Pessinus is a city of Galatia named after some gallus (Gaul?) called Pessinus. Some people say it is from a spring flowing from the hill in which Marsyas was buried.

It is uncertain whether the Gallos from which Pessinus takes it name is supposed to be a Gaul or a gallus, but it is interesting to see even the name of the city is capable as being viewed as something which came about in historical times. The second clause is equally interesting as with its mention of Marsyas it gets us back to Celaenae, which Ovid so far has been the only one to mention in connection with the river. It is, admittedly, a little of a geographical stretch to see how a river at Celaenae could give its name to the city of Pessinus, but it is noteworthy to see the tradition resurfacing.[23]

---

[22] Stephanus' source: see Lentz, *Grammatici Graeci* 3,1,cxxxvi ff.
[23] I list here some other, less informative references:
Ammianus Marcellinus (26,8,3), speaking of a retreat which the emperor Valens

What do we make, then, of this jumble of partially self-contradictory information concerning rivers? The best attempt has been made by M. Waelkens.[24] He ends up seeing at least three, possibly four, rivers by this name: 1) a river of Philomelion, known numismatically, 2) a large river of Bithynia, tributary to the Sangarios (presumably that referred to by Strabo, the second passage of Pliny, and Ammianus Marcellinus)—this river may have to be separated into two, however, in order to satisfy the details of all sources—, and 3) the river of Pessinus, likewise a tributary of the Sangarius. This is definitely the river referred to by Herodian and Firmicus Maternus, and was earlier called the Terias, the name mentioned by Herodian Grammaticus and Stephanus of Byzantium, the sources dependent on Alexander Polyhistor. It is also presumably that referred to by Ovid and the tradition represented by the first passage of Pliny and Martianus Capella (who may have conflated it with the Bithynian river).[25] I would submit that the confusion with Celaenae and Marsyas, evidenced in Ovid and the second passage of Herodian Grammaticus (overlooked by Waelkens), suggests the possibility of a fourth (or fifth) river by that name.

Waelkens points out that the excavations of Pessinus reveal a channelized river running through the city. Currently it is an intermittent stream, coming down from the mountains to the north and losing itself in the fields before reaching the Sangarius, 20 or so km. away.

---

made from Chalcedon to Ancyra, has him shaking off the pursuing enemy "per. . . . fluminis Galli sinuosos amfractus" (through the winding reaches of the Gallus River).

Claudian, without naming the priests, joins the tradition making the Gallus a tributary of the Sangarius (*In Eutropium*, II,262–264):

> Dindyma fundunt
> Sangarium, vitrei puro qui gurgite Galli
> auctus Amazonii defertur ad ostia Ponti.

> Mount Dindyma pours forth the Sangarius, which increased by the pure stream of the glassy Gallus, flows down to the mouth of the Amazonian Pontus.

The *Etymologicum Magnum*, s.v. γάλλος, gives as an alternative explanation of the word: Ἡ ἀπὸ Γάλλου ποταμοῦ τῆς Φρυγίας, παρ' ὃν (οἱ γάλλοι) ἐτελοῦντο.

Finally, Makarios Chrysokephalos, a 14th-century paroemiographer, tells us (*Proverbia* III,92): Γάλλοι γὰρ καλοῦνται οἱ ἀποτετμημένοι, ἤτοι ἀπὸ τοῦ ποταμοῦ Γάλλου ἢ ὅτι ἀποπεπτώκασιν εἰς ἑτέραν φύσιν.

I do not include here all the uninformative lexicographical references, e.g., Hesychius or Suidas.

[24] *Byzantion*, 41, 1971, pp. 349–373. Waelkens knew all of the sources listed above except Herodian Grammaticus.

[25] As well as Festus, Vibius Sequester, the Etymologicum Magnum, Makarios Chrysokephalos, and presumably Claudian, mentioned only in footnotes 18 and 23 above.

This is the Gallus of Herodian and Firmicus Maternus, and is also the river shown on coins of Pessinus from the reign of Antoninus Pius. It is the Gallus of the Neoplatonists Julian and Sallustius. It is also the Terias of the tradition dependent on Alexander Polyhistor. In short it is the river of all the mythological lore. Granted that its importance may be exaggerated by authors who wish to magnify the myth, it may actually have been a somewhat more significant stream in antiquity.

Now there is nothing inherently impossible in the same name being applied to rivers in various parts of Asia Minor. Cf. the two lakes Askania and the case of Coloe.[26] The map of the United States is littered with rivers bearing such names as Rocky, Red, White, Black, Salt, etc. In that case, Gallos would represent some physical characteristic of the river, in an indigenous language. But I think a stronger case can be made (except perhaps in the case of the river of Celaenae) for the rivers to have taken their names from the Gauls, as the Gauls passed through and occupied Bithynia on their invasion of Asia Minor, and were (as we have seen) high priests of Pessinus. Even Philomelion lay in the province of Asia just over the border from the Galatian kingdom before its annexation by Rome in 25 B.C. The strongest evidence that this is actually the case is the statement of Polyhistor that the name of the river was new, having supplanted the name Terias—not (we would say) when a mythical eponymous priest Gallus came to it, but when the Gauls as a people settled there. Probably the new name of the river simply meant the "Galatian River."

Admittedly, then, on Pliny's evidence—see the third Pliny passage above—the change in the river name and (possibly) its reputation for causing insanity would have already been known to Callimachus, although the name as used for the priests and the connection of the insanity with self-castration would not yet have joined the account. There is nothing inherently impossible about Callimachus' awareness of what we might call a formative version of the later story. He died late enough for the re-naming of the river(s) to have reached his ears. (But note again that the only characteristic of the river directly attributed to Callimachus by Pliny is its otherwise unattested curative power—we are dealing with a confused tradition here.)

After all, if the whole region could change from being part of

---

[26] For Askania, see E.N. Lane, *Numen*, 22, 1975, pp. 235–236; for Coloe, see E.N. Lane, *Anatolian Studies*, 25, 1975, pp. 105–108.

Phrygia to being Galatia, why not see a change in river-names after the Gallic invasion? Support for this idea comes likewise from the fact that, in the second passage of Herodian Grammaticus, the name Pessinus also appears to be new, and the passage seems to indicate that the city takes its name from a Gaul (or a gallus?) called Pessinus, clearly a contrived eponymous founder. (It might then be worthwhile to look for a Celtic explanation of the name, but that is a task which I leave to the Celtic philologists.)

In sum, then, there is no compelling reason not to make the obvious connection of Gauls with galli, and with the river(s) in question, and thus to reduce to two the homonyms listed at the outset by Quintilian. The passage of Diogenes Laertius and the epigram falsely attributed to Callimachus, previously used to show that the name of the galli antedates the advent of the Gauls, are neither of them reliable, although it does seem to be the case that Callimachus knew of the renaming of the river. Likewise, the attribution of Arnobius' mythological account to Timotheus the Eumolpid, something which would likewise prove the antecedence of the name to the arrival of the Gauls, is entirely arbitrary, and, as admitted by Weinreich, somewhat unlikely on general stylistic grounds. Furthermore, there is the evidence of Polyhistor that Gallus as a river-name was an innovation. What applies to the river could equally well, or better—since we are talking about transference of names from people to people this time—apply to the priests. The obvious thing, then, is to assume that the Gauls gave their name to the priesthood, even though they may not have created it. If most ancient authorities are of a different opinion, it is probably because our proposed solution is too obvious, and their aetiology, involving such picturesque details as a river that causes madness, makes for better stories.[27]

---

[27] One cannot treat this subject without examining the entire tradition of eunuch priests in Anatolian and Near Eastern religion. There seems to be less evidence for it than is generally thought. The "Megabyzoi" of Artemis of Ephesus have generally been held to be an example of this phenomenon. But as it shown by the article by James O. Smith in this same collection, the evidence for them, and especially for their being eunuchs, vanishes under close inspection. In particular, the archaic so-called Megabyzos ivory statuette from Ephesus has been shown to be a woman (A. Bammer, *JÖAI* 1985, 57). The silver statuette of a priest from Elmali, of the Phrygian period, now in the Antalya Museum (Engin Özgen et al., *Antalya Museum*, Ankara 1988, no. 41) has also been held to represent a eunuch, but that is a mere surmise.

Eunuch priests of the Syrian Goddess are known from Apuleius' *Metamorphoses* and Lucian's *On the Syrian Goddess*, both works of the second century A.D., although only Lucian uses the term γάλλοι for them. Indeed, Lucian's account includes an elaborate aetiological story for the origin of this practice, set in Hellenistic times. Relevant also is the account of the Syriac-writing historian Bardasanes that a King Abgar of Edessa—presumably of this time of Caracalla—abolished the practice of self-emasculation in honor of Atargatis. (See Fergus Millar, *The Roman Near East*, Cambridge, Mass., Harvard University Press, 1993, 475–76.) There can be no doubt but that self-castration was practiced in this cult also, but there is no more reason to project it into the immemorial past any more than there is in the case of the devotees of Cybele.

THE GODDESS CYBELE IN FUNERARY BANQUETS AND WITH AN EQUESTRIAN HERO

Elpis Mitropoulou

I have concerned myself several times in the past with the goddess Cybele and with Attis. (Apart from the studies which I refer to below there is another one insufficiently known to archaeological circles: E. Mitropoulou, Τερρακόττες του θεού Αττη, Αφιέωρωμα εις μνήμη Κ. Βουβέωρη, *ΑΡΕΤΗΣ ΜΝΗΜΗ*, Athens 1983, pp. 219–249 (Ελληνική Ανθρωπιστική Εταιρεία, no. 35, in which I discuss 38 figurines of Attis, 18 of which were unpublished. I divide the figurines of Attis into different types). Now I will concern myself with other facets of Cybele's iconography. Be it noted in advance, however, that the name "Cybele" is used only as a convenient and conventional, if somewhat misleading, term for a goddess probably better referred to simply as the Great Mother, or Mother of the Gods.

A. *The goddess Cybele in funerary banquets*

Friederike Naumann has already treated Cybele as she is represented in funerary banquets (p. 193–194). Her treatment however is extremely summary and mentions only two examples. Therefore we have considered it necessary to concern ourselves with the same subject, having additional examples which lead us to certain significant conclusions. We have attempted to locate the beginning of this subject, that is, the representation of Cybele in funerary banquet reliefs.

Catalogue:
K1. Marble relief in Bursa Museum, no. 8500, from Sultaniye village, Karacabey. Graeco-Persian, early fifth century B.C. Height: 2.45; width 0.55; thickness 0.12. There are three zones. The upper one is a banquet scene. In the middle zone a youth with a pointed Persian hat leads a wagon that probably is carrying some kind of grain, which has just been reaped, and is being taken to the threshing floor. In the third zone is a scene of deer-hunting, and below it an Aramaic inscription. The details were shown in color.

In the first zone we have to the right two seated musicians, playing a lyre, and (according to the catalogue) a flute, or possibly a bagpipe-like instrument. Although this scene has been interpreted as a man (husband) reclining and a woman (wife) seated, it seems to me that the man is standing with his hands open in an attitude of worship. Thus he is the dedicant. The seated female figure holds a round object in each hand (pomegranates?), as is perhaps also the case in the next relief. To the left of the seated woman are two figures, a man holding a towel (according to the catalogue), and a woman holding a disk with fruit, which must have been painted. Behind them is a tripod with cauldron. The second zone has been considered to represent a funeral carriage followed by three mourning women, but it seems to me that the three figures are in a well-known attitude of prayer, rather than mourning, and that the carriage is transporting grain. Thus the family would have offered this relief to the goddess of the fertility of the earth to ask for the prosperity of their fields and their farming, The deity is probably "Cybele," Aphrodite, or another similar divinity. *In the absence, however, of a reading of the Aramaic inscription, all this must remain tentative.* (Further publication rights are reserved, and the existing photograph does not reproduce the inscription well enough to permit reading.)

Bibliography: Exhibition catalogue, *The Anatolian Civilizations, II, Greek/ Roman/Byzantine*, Istanbul. May 22–October 30, 1983, no. B141.

K2. Marble banquet relief in Istanbul, Archaeological Museum no. 5763, from Daskyleion (Aksakal, Manyas) in Mysia, Graeco-Persian, early fifth century B.C. Height:, 2.21; width, 0.62; thickness 0.20.

It is a tall, narrow stele. Again there are three zones. The top one apparently was an anthemion with palmette and volute, but is now broken off. The second one represents a carriage followed by two female figures in an attitude of worship. The carriage here is similar to that on our no. K1. Our three examples show a wagon where only grain can be transported and there is a cover for adverse weather conditions. The bottom zone is a banquet scene. On the right is a tripod with traces of a vase. Next to it is a youth, clad, probably a cup-bearer, ready to take the drinking bowl from the male figure on the couch and fill it with wine. On the couch is a bearded male figure, reclining on two pillows, with a himation around the lower part of his body. In his left hand he holds a fruit or an egg which he has just received from his female companion who sits next to him on the couch. The seated female figure wears earrings and a mural crown over a long veil which runs down over her chiton. She rests her feet on a long footstool, and in her left hand she holds a flower. Behind her is a young girl (priestess?), wearing a long chiton with overfold, and holding in her left hand a basket with fruit and in her right a piece of fruit which she is preparing to give to the seated female figure. As the female figure wears a mural crown, it is unlikely that she is simply the deceased or a relative of the deceased. She is probably rather a goddess who is concerned with the fertility of the earth and is at the same time the goddess of the city, of order, and of punishment. In other words, she is the Great Mother, otherwise known as "Cybele." (fig. 1)

Bibliography:
N. Doluney, *Istanb.A.Müz.Yil.*13/14, 1967, 19 ff. 103 ff., pl. 3, 8, 5, 10.
E. Akurgal, *Ir.Ant.*6, 1966, 147 ff. pl. 36.37.
J. Borchardt, *Ist.Mitt.*18, 1968, 196 ff., pl. 40.1.
J.M. Deltzer, *RA* 1969, 201, fig. 2
H. Moebius, *AA* 1971, 445 ff., 451 ff., fig. 2.
B. Fehr, *Orientalische und Griechische Gelage* (1971) 967 ff., pl. 363.364.
Pfuhl-Moebius, I, no. 4, pl. 2 (with further bibliography).
Anatolian Civilizations, p. 57, no. B. 142 (only second frieze illustrated).

K3. Relief of gray marble in Istanbul Museum, no. 5762, from Daskyleion. Pfuhl-Möbius date this stele later than the preceding ones on stylistic grounds, largely on the basis of the remains of the anthemion, to the last third of the fifth century B.C. At the bottom there is a tenon for insertion into a base, at the top a badly damaged anthemion. There are three friezes: The topmost shows what Pfulh-Möbius call a "verhängter Sarkophag mit hohem Deckel" on a carriage to the right, in front of it a man, and behind it presumably two women. The frieze is continued on the sides of the stele: to the right is a laden mule, and to the left are a man and a woman riding mules. The woman holds a swaddled child on the lap. The middle frieze seems to have portrayed a funerary banquet, with a woman seated facing right, a reclining man, and behind the woman a servant in front of a hanging animal (?). The third frieze contains remains of a hunting scene, apparently never completed. The carriage of the first frieze is exactly the same as in the preceding examples. We would be inclined to the opinion that this is a votive stele referring to the Great Mother.

Bibliography:
N. Doluney, *loc. cit.*, 28 f., 106 f., pl. 3, 5; 6, 11–13.
G.M.A. Hanfmann, *BASOR* 184, 1966, 10 ff.
J. Borchhardt, *loc. cit.*, 194 ff., pl. 40,2.
H. Möbius, *loc. cit.*, 449 f., fig. 3.
Pfuhl-Möbius I, no. 74, pl. 19, with further bibliography.

K4. Marble relief in Museum of Afyon Karahissar, no. E 1858, from Altin Tas (Phrygia), Graeco-Persian, *c.* 460 B.C. Height, 0.94; width 0.66; thickness, 0.22.

The relief is divided into three zones. The upper zone shows two facing sphinxes with poloi. Between them is a tree. The middle zone shows to the right a figure lying on a couch. It appears to be female. Behind her stands a figure in a long gown, who is crowning her. At the end of the couch sits another female figure, who holds a flower. Behind this figure stands a youth holding a fan, creating a breeze for the seated figure. Behind him, two worshippers approach from the left, apparently a father and son. Behind them is a table with offerings. In the third zone, which is damaged, there is a procession of four musicians with flutes and cymbals, and behind them can be distinguished the horns of a bull, apparently for sacrifice. (fig. 2)

Bibliography:
MAMA VI, no. 369, pl. 65.
Seidl, *Das Totenmahlrelief*, no. 566.
R.N. Thönges-Stringaris, *AM* 80, 1965, 94, no. 170.
Pfuhl-Moebius, I, no. 75, pl. 19, with further bibliography.
Anatolian Civilizations, p. 59, no. B. 145.

K5. Votive relief in Cos Museum, no. 12. From Cos. The shape of the relief is unusual. It is oval, without any frame. Dimensions: 0.43 × 0.29 – 0.22 × 0.065 × 0.01. Marble; end of fourth century B.C.

This relief in the upper zone shows a banquet scene to the left with a divine couple identifiable either as Zeus Meilichios and Hera Meilichia, or as Asclepius and Hygeia. The male divinity reclines to the left and holds in his right hand a rhyton and in his left a phiale. He wears a himation which covers the lower part of his body. At the end of the couch a female divinity is seated looking at him. She wears a chiton and long himation over it. Her feet rest on a footstool. She holds in both hand a long, unusual object. In front of them is a rectangular table full of food. Next to them to the right is the goddess Cybele. She is seated and her feet rest on a footstool. She wears a Doric belted chiton and a himation over it; she also has a polos. In her right hand she holds a phiale and in her left a tympanon. There is a lion in her lap. To the right in the lower frieze is a male worshipper, wearing a long himation. His right hand is raised in a gesture of prayer. In front of him is a huge snake coiled upwards toward the god, reaching as far up as his left shoulder.

Bibliography:
Laurenzi, *ASAtene* 33/34 (1955/56) 80, no. 13.
Stringaris, *loc. cit.*, no. 154, pl. 23, fig. 1.
Mitropoulou, 1977, p. 137, no. 62, fig. 62.
Neumann, p. 193, no. 423.

(From Cos also there is another banquet relief with a huge snake— Pfuhl-Moebius fig. 1546. It is possible that both reliefs represent the divine couple Zeus-Hera or Asclepius-Hygeia. Pfuhl and Moebius consider this to be a funerary stele.)

K6. Votive relief in Corfu Archaeological Museum. From Corfu. 360– 350 B.C. Only a fragment from the upper left is preserved. It shows a banquet scene. It is hesitantly included here. It shows a male worshipper, a cup-bearer, and a goddess seated at the end of a couch, whom Vermaseren considers to be Cybele, because of the polos. I do not however find this identification plausible. There was also a reclining male figure on the couch, but all that is preserved is the upper part of the rhyton held in his right hand.

Bibliography:
Stringaris, *loc. cit.*, no. 187, p. 11, 1.
Vermaseren, *CCCA* II, no. 519, with further bibliography.

K7. Votive relief, found in Italy, Pieve di Vallechia (Pietzasante), Lucca, National Museum. Height, 0.665; width, 0.731; thickness, 0.08. It is of Greek marble and dates to the second century B.C.

To the left is a banquet scene with a god reclining on a couch towards a goddess who sits on the end of the couch. He wears a long himation which comes round the lower part of his body. The goddess wears a chiton with a himation over it. The divinities are again probably to be identified as Zeus Meilichios and Hera Meilichia or as Asclepius and Hygeia. In front of them there are traces of a rectangular table and perhaps part of a coiled snake under it. To our right is Cybele seated on a throne with a high elaborate back with three acroteria. To her left are traces of her tympanon. In the background is a curtain behind which three armed men appear from the chest upwards. They carry shields and wear helmets. They move to the left. They are probably to be identified as Corybantes. Pfuhl and Moebius consider this to be a grave relief.

Bibliography:
S. Ferri, *NSc* 1947, 46 ff., fig. 1.
Pfuhl-Möbius, pl. 268, fig. 1869.
O. Walter, *ÖJh* 31, 1938/9, 73, fig. 28.
Seidl, no. 403.
Stringaris, p. 92, no. 161.
Vermaseren, *CCCA* IV,84, pl. 77, no. 204.
Neumann, no. 424.
Turcan, pl. VII.

K8. A votive banquet relief from the Athenian Agora. Agora Museum Athens S732. Found in late fill, section T 535, 73/ΛΔ April 24, 1936. Dimensions 0.10 × 0.125 × 0.034 × 0.01. It is of Hymettian marble and shows traces on the back of a fine point chisel. Only the left middle fragment is preserved. It shows a banquet scene which includes a divine couple (Zeus and Hera?), Cybele, and cup-bearer. To the right, which is broken, one can reconstruct a god lying on a couch. At the end of the couch sits a goddess who is preserved as far as the waist. She wears a chiton and a himation and holds an object which presumably is incense for a censer which would have been on a table in front of the divine pair, but is now lost. Behind her we see the goddess Cybele. The figure is preserved as far as the waist. She wears a chiton and a himation. With her left hand she holds a tympanon from underneath. Behind her is a cup-bearer of whom only the head is preserved. Previously unpublished. Early third century B.C. (fig. 3)

(There is another votive relief of approximately the same period from the Agora, Agora Museum Athens S1101, where the figures probably are Zeus and Hera accompanied by a large coiled snake— Mitropoulou 1976, p. 113, no. 53, fig. 53.)

K9. Previously in the collection of the Evangelike Schole, Smyrna. A banquet scene showing a seated goddess with polos. At the top left are the busts of three armed figures (riders?) with shields. Although this piece is generally considered to be a grave relief, I think that it can be considered votive and that the main figures are Cybele, her priests, and the Corybantes. It is of late Hellenistic date.

Bibliography: Pfuhl-Moebius, p. 126, fig. 21.

K10. Marble banquet relief in the Alexandria Museum, no. 3460. Dimensions unavailable. To the right is a goddess seated on the end of a couch, wearing a polos, a chiton, and a large himation. She holds with both hands a large tympanon over a square table, of which only the left part and one leg are preserved. Behind her is an animal followed by two worshippers. End of fourth century B.C. or beginning of third century B.C. (fig. 4)

Bibliography: Kater-Sibbes, *Mitteilungen DAI Abt.Kairo*, 1975, pl. 101b.

Cf. the temple with Cybele which one can see on the example Vermaseren *CCCA* III, pl. XCIX, fig. 201.

K11. A terracotta mold votive banquet relief in the Louvre, Paris, no. 1083, from Collection Greau.

To the right is Dionysus reclining on a couch. He is represented in an archaic style, especially his head with its ornamentation. He wears a long chiton. With his right hand he holds a mesomphalos phiale. His left arm from the shoulder and the left part of his body are missing. Cybele is seated at the end of the couch. She wears a chiton and a himation over it, which is drawn over the back of her head. With her left hand she holds a tympanon from above. She rests her feet on a lion. Between and behind them is a horse which looks at Cybele. Only the head and the neck are visible. As the head of Dionysus is similar to archaic terracotta heads of this divinity from Taras, it is possible that our relief came from there.

Bibliography:
Gardner, *Sculptured Tombs*, p. 101.
Winter, I, 204, 5.
JdI 37 (1922) p. 204, fig. 1.

B. *Cybele with a mounted god or hero*

K12. Marble votive relief in Bucharest, Archaeological Institute, formerly in National Museum. From Tomis (Constanta). Second century A.D. Dimensions: 0.33 × 0.52 × 0.11.

To our right is Cybele seated on a throne with a high back. She wears an Ionic belted chiton and a himation, as well as a mural crown, as protectress of the city. Her feet rest on a footstool. With her right hand she holds a phiale and with her left a tympanon. On each side of her stands a lion. Next to them is a rectangular altar, and behind it is a tree with coiled snake which moves to drink from a phiale which is held by a rider. He wears a short chiton and a chlamys which flies out behind him. Below the horse is a dog.

Bibliography:
M. Tacheva, *Thracia ECMI TH* pl. XXXIV, fig. 55a.
D.M. Tudor, *CNA* 11, 1935, 109, 113.
R. Vulge, *Histoire ancienne de la Dobrogea*, Bucharest 1939, pl. XXXIII, fig. 57.
Al. Stefan, "Problèmes du syncrétisme religieux concernant le cavalier thrace en Dobroudja à l'époque romaine", *Le monde thrace, Actes du II. Congrès International de Thracologie, Bucharest 1979* (Paris-Rome-Montreal 1982) pp. 140–150, pp. 140, 142, pl. I, 1.
Vermaseren, *Cybele and Attis*, fig. 77.
Opperman in Vermaseren, ed., *Die orientalischen Religionen im Roemerreich*, Leiden 1981, p. 531, fig. 1.
Vermaseren *CCCA*, VI, 1989, no. 446, pl. CVI

K13. A marble votive relief from Tomis (Constanta), in Constanta Archaeological Museum, Height, 0.33; width, 0.52; thickness, 0.11. 2nd or 3rd century A.D.

Similar to the one mentioned above. To the left we have two columns with Corinthian capitals, and inside them a mounted hero with dog and bow. Outside to our right is Cybele seated on a throne with high back, putting her hands on two lions, which flank her.

Bibliography:
G. Florescu, "Monuments antiques du Musée régional de Dobrugea", *Dacia* V–VI (1935–36), p. 430, no. IX, and fig. 9.
Hampartunian, *Corpus Cultus Equitis Thracii (CCET)* IV,46, no. 30.
Tacheva-Hitova, 98 f., no. 56.
Scorpan, no. 38, fig. 38.
Vermaseren, *CCCA* VI, no. 433, pl. CIV.

K14. A marble votive relief perhaps from Tomis or surroundings, in London, private collection. Second or third century A.D.

There is a two-line inscription on the plinth:

Γλυκονιανὸς Λυσονίου/ θεῶ(ι) Καρίω(ι) εὐχήν

To our right Cybele is seated on a stool. She wears a belted Ionic chiton and a himation, as well as a polos. Her right hand rests on a tympanon holding a patera, and her right offers liquid from a phiale to a coiled snake. From our left a rider approaches. He wears a short chiton and a flying chlamys. In his left hand he holds a double-headed ax.

Bibliography:
Sotheby's Catalogue, 1st July 1969, p. 54, no. 113.
Vermaseren, *CCCA* VII, fig. 90.

K15. Marble votive relief in Constanta, Muzeum Regional, 15762. From the collection of H. Slobozianu. Height, 0.36; width, 0.51; thickness, 0.93 (?). Only the lower left part is preserved. From our left a rider approaches an altar, next to which a goddess is seated. Of the goddess only a small portion is preserved, not enough for a certain identification, but Vermaseren considers her to be Cybele. Third century A.D.

Bibliography:
Scorpan 67, no. 33, fig. 33.
Tacheva-Hitova 107, no. 75.
Vermaseren, *CCCA* VI, pl. CIII, fig. 432.

Discussion of salient iconographic features displayed by these pieces:

I. *The Carriage*

There is a carriage on our reliefs nos. K1, K2 and K3. From Daskyleion, where our nos. K2 and K3 originated, there is another relief (Pfuhl-Moebius no. 1) with a similar scene, now in Istanbul Archaeological Museum 5761 and 5764. It has been dated by a number of scholars to 500 B.C., by others to the third quarter of the fifth century and even by Dentzer to 400 B.C., but we do not think there should be a 100-year diference between the two pieces. Rather they both belong shortly after 500 B.C. The carriages on our reliefs K1, K2, and K3 are completely different from the one on the second relief from Daskyleion. That on the second relief from Daskyleion is square in shape and has three columns on the long side. What is significant is not a presumed difference in date between the two reliefs, but a difference in the purposes to which the carriages were put. The one was used to carry people and the other to transport grain. The carriage with columns is one in which people can travel. The closed carriage of nos. K1, K2, and K3, on the other hand, was used to transport grain and protect it from adverse weather conditions.

II. *Polos and Mural Crown*

Cybele always appears with one or the other of these types of headgear. She usually wears a polos as on our nos. K4, K5, and K11. She wears a mural crown in our examples K2, K12, and K13. This indicates that she is the protective goddess of a city. I mention only a few of the long list of possible parallels:

1. A bronze relief from Razgrad (Abritus) in Bulgaria: R.F. Hoddinott, *Bulgaria in Antiquity: an Archaeological Introduction*, London 1975, p. 165, fig. 109.
2. A bronze relief from Valène (Drône): Vermaseren, *CCCA* VII, no. 109, pl. LXXVI.
3. A marble votive relief in the Louvre, Paris, MA 2871, from the Choiseul Collection. It has the inscription: ANΔIPHNH. . . . .: *JHS* 22 (1902) 191, fig. 2; Schwertheim p. 814 ff., pl. CXCIII, fig. 25; Vermaseren, *CCCA* I, no. 339, pl. LXXII. For the inscription cf. Strabo, XIII 614: ὑπὸ δε τοῖς ’Ανδρείωροις (a place in the Troad)

ἱερόν ἐστι Μητρὸς θεῶν ᾿Ανδρειρηνῆς ἅγιον καὶ ἄντρον ὑπόνομον μέχρι παλαιᾶς.

4. A votive relief from Cyzicus with representation of Cybele and Hermes, bearing the inscription. . . . . λον θεῶι ἀνδειρεῖδι/Περγάμου: Vermaseren, *CCCA* I no. 286.
5. Terrracotta statuette from Olynthus, Thessaloniki AM 524: Vermaseren, *CCCA* V, no. 201.
6. A terracotta mold from Olynthus in New York City, collection of Prof. Simkovitch of Columbia University: Vermaseren, *CCCA* V, no. 203.

III. *Fan*

The fan is particularly characteristic of the art of the Middle East, where, because of the heat, fans were frequently used. The fan may be held by Cybele herself, as in the first of the examples cited below, or by the seated female figure in a banquet relief, as in the second example, or by a girl standing behind the female figure, as in the remaining examples.

1. Bronze votive relief in Sofia AM 3849, second century A.D.: Vermaseren, *CCCA* VI, no. 377, pl. XCIV. In this case the fan has sometimes been held to be a leaf.
2. A banquet relief from Kyzikos in the Louvre, Paris, MA 2854 where the female companion of the reclining male figure holds a fan (or leaf) in her left hand: Stringaris pl. 26,2.
3. A banquet relief in Oxford, Ashmolean Museum: Michaelis, no. 142; Pfuhl-Möbius no. 1629. A girl standing behind the seated female figure holds a fan.
4. A banquet relief in London, British Museum 733: Pfuhl-Möbius, p. 136, fig. 27.
5. A marble banquet relief in Delos: *BCH* 1906, p. 6541, fig. 1.
6. A votive banquet relief in London, British Museum 725. In this case both the girl standing behind the female companion of the reclining male figure, as well as the female companion herself, may be holding fans. The relevant part of relief is broken off, but if we compare this figure with the figure on the previous relief we will see that the position of the hand is the same. It is also possible that the seated female figure held a distaff. The way the hand is turned on relief no. 2 above lends credence to this interpretation. In this case too the object has been interpreted as a leaf.

7. Bronze votive relief, possibly from Africa, in Paris, Bibl. Nat. 616. In this case Cybele holds the fan. Roman: Vermaseren. *CCCA* II (1982) no. 308, pl. LXXV.

IV. *Curtains*

The idea of curtains behind the main figure in votive reliefs first appears in the Hellenistic period, and increases in the Roman period. It is more frequent in grave art of Asia Minor than in that of mainland Greece.

1. A votive relief in the Vatican Museum, presumably of the 3rd century B.C.: unpublished.
2. A banquet relief from Teos: Stringaris no. 140, pl. 28, fig. 2.
3. A Capitoline votive relief M617: H. Stuart, *Museo Capitolino* 113, fig. 63. (I have doubts about the genuinity of this relief, which I discuss elsewhere, specifically in a lecture given in Berlin in 1988, at the invitation of Humboldt University and the Pergamon Museum.)

V. *Throne with very high back*

There are many examples which show Cybele seated on a throne with a very high back which reaches as far as her neck, but there are no other examples with a chair-back so high as to reach the level of her head, or with elaboration at the top. We can see a high-backed throne, for instance, in the Cybele-procession from Pompeii, Vermaseren *CCCA* IV, pl. IX–XVII, fig. 42, and on a silver bracelet, probably from Asia Minor, in Boston, Museum of Fine Arts. nos. 61–1130. The idea has, of course, passed on to Christianity, where one sees it in representations of the Virgin Mary, and in the episcopal thrones. Some examples in funerary art are provided by Pfuhl-Möbius pl. 167, fig. 1107 (third century B.C.) of unknown origin, and pl. 135, figs. 901 and 904 (*c.* 150 B.C.) both from Samos.

VI. *The flower*

A flower is held by the female figure at the end of the couch on our K2. There are very few other examples, to our knowledge, of votive reliefs on which the figures hold flowers.

1. Cybele holds a flower on a gem which shows her seated wearing a mural crown, while a lion gazes at her: Miller, LXIII, fig. 807.
2. A bronze relief with Cybele and Attis in Berlin, Pergamon Museum 8169-90, on which Attis holds a flower: *AA* 7, 1892, III, no. 15; Vermaseren, *CCCA* III, pl. CLXVIII, fig. 304.
3. Relevant also is the well-known votive relief from the Piraeus in Berlin, Pergamon Museum 1612. This relief of the late 4th century B.C. shows Cybele and Attis, and is the earliest example of Attis being illustrated in art: Vermaseren, *CCCA* II (1982), no. 308, pl. CLXXXVI. Naumann, no. 552, pl. 40, fig. 1. It was previously thought that Cybele in this relief held a pomegranate flower, but Vermaseren realized that it was a jug. Naumann (1983, pp. 240-241) and Roller (1994, p. 256) have emphasized the similarity between this vessel and that carried by the Phrygian Matar.
4. Other divinities may also hold flowers, such as the Eumenides, in a relief from the Argos Museum: Harrison, p. 281, fig. 72. The flower is an obvious symbol of the fertility of nature and as such is still in use especially at Easter time. A similar thought lies behind divinities holding ears of grain, such as the mother goddess, Potnia, from the Citadel House in Mycenae: J. Chadwick, *The Mycenaean Religion* p. 93, fig. 40.

VII. *The tree*

There is a tree shown on our K4. A similar tree may be seen with a Mother Goddess (Cybele) on the votive relief from Vezirhan, Bilecik, in Ankara, AM 6219/71.27, a Greco-Persian work of the end of the fifth century B.C.: *Anatolian Civilizations* p. 60, no. B 146. The tree in this case seems to serve as the goddess's headdress. I forbear mentioning trees in religious scenes on Hittite and other Near Eastern seals.

VIII. *The sphinx*

On our K4 there is a tree and on either side of it a sphinx with polos. A possible parallel is provided by an ivory inlay from Arslan Tash in the Louvre, Paris, showing two ram-sphinxes with double crown and between them a sacred tree: J. Chadwick. *The Mycenaean World*, 1976, p. 319, fig. 379. In Greco-Roman art we have a sphinx with Cybele on a relief from Thasos, Thasos Museum 18: Vermaseren, *CCCA* II, no. 529, p. CLIX. Likewise there is a large sphinx next to

Cybele's armchair in a statue from Baalbek, now in Istanbul AM: S. Ferri, *Arte Romana sul Danubio*, 1933, p. 291, fig. 542. To be compared also is the statue of Cybele found in Panticapaeum on Mount Kaya, s. of Döğer; on the pediment here are two sphinxes: first century B.C., Vermaseren, *CCCA* I, no. 104, pl. XIV.

IX. *The snake*

In our relief K 14 the Great Mother offers liquid from a phiale to a snake. Likewise in our K5 the snake is connected with the reclining figure who may be the chthonian Zeus Meilichios. (See Burkert, p. 159, for the chthonian aspect of Zeus and his connection with Demeter.)

1. In the archaic period we have the Great Mother and snake on the shrine-model relief block from Sardis, Manisa Museum 4029, which is generally held to represent a shrine of Cybele: G.M.A. Hanfmann—N.H. Ramage, *Sculpture from Sardis, the finds through 1975* (1978), 15 ff., no. 7, figs. 20–50; D.G. Mitten, *BASOR*, 174 (1964) 39–43, figs. 25–26; Naumann, no. 34, pl. 12, fig. 3: Rein, figs. 6 and 7; Vermaseren, *CCCA* I, no. 459, pl. CI.

2. Relief in the Louvre, Paris, MA 3592, from Kula in Lydia. This relief has three friezes. In the second one, according to the inscription, the figures are Demeter, Artemis, and Nike. "Artemis" rests her hands on the heads of two lions. Between "Demeter" and "Artemis" is an eagle inside a crescent. Over "Demeter" is a coiled snake, and another one is coiled next to "Artemis". "Artemis'" throne also has two coiled snakes: Vermaseren, *Cybele and Attis*, fig. 16; I. Diakonoff, *BABesch* 54 (1979) p. 150, no. 30, fig. 32. It is obvious in this case that we have syncretism, and that "Artemis" has taken over the iconography of the Great Mother (Cybele).

3. A votive relief in Paris, Louvre, MA 3316, of the late Roman period, where Cybele offers liquid from a phiale to a snake: Vermaseren, *CCCA* I, no. 104, pl. XIV.

4. It is perhaps unnecessary to point out that snakes accompanied fertility goddesses also in the Minoan period, such as the well-known, and frequently illustrated, faience statuette from Knossos of the New Palace period in the Herakleion Museum. Examples can also be adduced from Mesopotamia and India.

X. *Tympanon and lion*

A. The tympanon is connected with Cybele in our K5, K7 (?), K8, K10, K11, K12.

a. Cybele holding a tympanon from below occurs on nos. K5, K7 (?), K8, and K12. The prototype may be the statue of Cybele in the Athens Metroon or that in the Piraeus.

b. On our K11 Cybele holds a tympanon from above. This is also a common type, and perhaps derives from the Pergamene cult-statue of Cybele.

c. In our no. K14, Cybele leans on the tympanon with her left hand. This type is less common than the two preceding, but examples can be adduced from Rizzo, pl. Acc. B, 4; a gem, Rizzo, p. 95, fig. 20; a marble statue in Bursa, AM, Pfuhl-Moebius, no. K557, pl. 42; also from Vermaseren, *CCCA* IV, no. 45, pl. 19, and no. 268, pl. 107.

d. There is no parallel to my knowledge for Cybele holding the tympanon with both hands over a table in banquet relief, such as we see in our no. K10.

B. Lion

a. Cybele is represented with a lion on her lap in our K5.

b. Cybele has two lions, one on each side of her in our K12 and K13.

c. Cybele rests her feet on a lion in our no. K11.

C. Tympanon and lion

a. In our K5 Cybele holds the tympanon from below and has a lion on her lap. This is a very common type.

b. In our K12 Cybele holds the tympanon from below and has two lions, one on each side of her. This type is common.

c. In our K11 Cybele holds the tympanon from above and has a lion under her feet. This combination is unique.

The statue of Cybele from Moschato (*Εφ. Αρχ.* 1973, 213, p. 89), the statue from Gordion (Neumann no. 626, pl. 47,4) and the terra-cotta statuette from Pergamon (*AA* 1960, 465, fig. 42) show Cybele holding the typanum from above. Obviously the original idea derives from the Moschato example.

The idea of Cybele resting her feet on a lion (although to my knowledge there are few examples of it) goes back to Middle Eastern civilization where we see various divinities standing on animals. The idea of course is to show the power of the divinity over the animal and nature in general. (The idea is carried over into Christianity, where Christ or a saint such as St. George may put his foot on the back of a reclining human figure. This represents the triumph of good over the prostrate evil.)

Other examples of Cybele with her feet on the back of a lion are provided by

1. A marble votive relief from Samos, Pythagoreion, now in Kastro of Tigani. Late 2nd century B.C.: Vermaseren *CCCA* II, no. 572.
2. A marble naiskos from Pannonia in the National Museum of Slovenia, Ljubljana, no. 7923, Vermaseren *CCCA* VI, no. 124.
3. A terracotta figurine in the Vienna Kunsthistorisches Museum, no. 1112, of Roman date: Vermaseren *CCCA* VII, no. 178.
4. A naiskos showing Cybele with her feet on the back of a lion, from Ephesus: J. Keil, *OeJh* 18 (1915) 63, fig. 37; Reeder, p. 434, fig. 9.
5. A statuette from Soli, Cyprus, of the second century A.D., in which Cybele rests her feet on a lion: Nicolaou, p. 174, l. XXVI, 8.
6. A curved relief from the sanctuary of Akrai in Sicily. Cybele looks as if she were dancing, and has her left foot on the back of a lion: Vermaseren, *CCCA* IV, no. 154.
7. A Hellenistic bronze matrix in the Metropolitan Museum of Art, New York no. 20.2.24: Reeder p. 424, fig. 1.

Other relevant examples involving various divinities include

8. The Hittite Kubaba (whose relation to Cybele it is beside the point to discuss here), shown on the orthostat from Malatya in Ankara, where both Kubaba and her consort have animals under their feet. 950–750 B.C.: Naumann, no. 1, pl. 1, fig. 2.
9. The relief on the orthostat from Carchemish, also showing Kubaba. Ninth century B.C.: Naumann, no. 2, pl. 1, fig. 3.
10. The three gods standing on the backs of animals in the frieze of the sanctuary of Yazilikaya, near the Hittite capital of Bogazköy, illustrated H. Frankfurt, *The Pelican Book of Art*, 1963, p. 226, fig. 261.

Further examples can be multipied from Phoenician and ancient Mesopotamian civilizations.

XI. *The musicians*

There are four categories of musicians: flute players, lyre players, cymbal players, and bagpipe players. The first two can be seen in our K1. The second and third can be seen on our K4, although the bagpipe player there has been misidentified as a flute player.

First among parallels I would like to cite five examples of reliefs showing dinners, music, and dancing in the festivals of various divinities. (I have collected them previously, for another article.) All are of Hellenistic or Roman date, none classical.

1. A votive relief dedicated to the Great Mother (Cybele) and to Apollo. It was said to be from Nicaea in Bithynia, but Perdrizet showed that it must come from Triglia near Mudanya in Mysia. It is now in the National Archaeological Museum of Athens, no. 1485, and is of Hellenistic date (Mitropoulou 1988, no. 2).
2. A relief from Bursa, Archaeological Museum 2579, showing Asclepios and Hygeia (Mitropoulou 1988, no. 3).
3. A relief from Panterna, near Cyzicus, in the British Museum, London. It shows Apollo Kitharoidos, Dionysus, and Zeus Hypsistos, and is of Roman date (Mitropoulou 1988, no. 4).
4. A relief from Çanakkale, Çanakkale Museum no. 2653. Perhaps Athena figured in the broken part, in so far as we can assume from the broken inscription. (Mitropoulou 1988, no. 5).
5. A bronze relief in New York showing Cybele with musicians and dancers: Reeder, figs. 1 and 3, mentioned above already as an example of Cybele with her feet on the back of a lion.
6. A terracotta votive naiskos from Kalymnos, now in London, showing Cybele, Pan, and a cup-bearer: *AM* 13 (1888) pl. V., p. 205.
7. A relief from Cyprus, specifically from the temple of Golgoi, in the Metropolitan Museum of New York, no. 74.51.1238. It is of Roman date and shows Apollo Kitharoidos. In this case there is not just single dancer, as in the other examples, but a number of people, as there are in contemporary rural religious dances (Mitropoulou 1988, no. 6).

Other parallels may be provided by the following:

8. A limestone statue group from Büyük Kale which stood in a niche in the southeastern city gate. It is now in the Ankara Museum. We see a flute player and a lyre (or harp) player (could one call them Couretes?) accompanying a native Mother Goddess with a

very high polos and a pomegranate as symbol of fertility. It is from the post-Hittite period, and may represent the earliest version of the Phrygian Mother Goddess. (Vermaseren, *CA* pl. 10; Vermaseren, *CCCA* I pl. IV, fig. 32; Naumann no. 23, pl. 7, fig. 1; Rein, p. 31, pl. 183).

(This goddess shows many similarities to the goddess from Salmanköy in Ankara, of which only the head, with high polos and a star, is preserved, and probably represents the same divinity: Naumann no. 24, pl. 7, fig. 2; Rein, p. 31. The goddesses in naiskoi shown by Naumann as no. 18, pl. 5, fig. 2; no. 19, pl. 5, fig. 3; and no. 20, pl. 5, fig. 4 also show the same divinity, but are not relevant here as they do not involve musicians.)

Vermaseren, *CCCA* I, pl. IV, fig. 32 (a terrra-cotta figurine from the neighborhood of Eskisehir in the Istanbul Museum) provides a statuette of Cybele with musicians, and pl. XXXVII, fig. 200 (as well as no. 277, pl. LVIII) one of Cybele with a double-flute player, second century A.D.

9. A coin from Patras where we see a goddess wearing a mural crown and two smaller-scale female figures on either side of her, who are represented dancing. Although there are admittedly no musicians here, music must have been present in order for the dancing to be carried out. (Pausanias, ed. Papachatzis, *Achaika*, p. 104, fig. 56.) There is also from Patras a relief, now in the National Museum, Athens, with eight Corybantes dancing (*ibid.*, p. 105, note 1; Thomopoulos, p. 157, 5), as well as a temple of the Mother of the Gods, in which Attis was also worshipped. The statue of Cybele was of stone, whereas that of Attis was said not to be visible. From Patras there is likewise a statuette of Roman times with a seated Cybele holding a cornucopia. A lion is at her right side: Δελτίον 29 (1973–4) Χρονικά Β ΙΙ, 406, pl. 260b (P. Angelopoulou).

Cymbals

A. Simple cymbals
Cymbals can be seen on our no. K4. Attis is also connected with cymbals. Here we will mention some other examples where Cybele appears in connection with cymbals.

1. Bronze medallion from Lydia (?). Brussels, Museé du Cinquante-naire. Late Roman. Bust of Cybele, two lions. There are two cymbals in the tympanon: Vermaseren, *CCCA* I, no. 493, pl. CVIII.
2. Votive relief from Rome, in Vatican Museum, no. 3378: Vermaseren, *CCCA* III, no. 257, pl. CXLIX.
3. Terracotta lamp from S. Italy, Museo Civico di Storia ed Arte, no. 4059: Vermaseren, *CCCA* IV, no. 144, pl. XLVI.
4. Circular marble oscillum from Sousse. Sousse, Municipal Museum: Vermaseren, *CCCA* V, no. 73, pl. XXVII.
5. Reddish terracotta vase with two medallions, probably found in the Rhône valley. St. Germain-en-Laye, Musée des antiquités nationales 9864: Vermaseren, *CCCA* V, no. 383, pl. CXXIX.
6. Bronze bust of Cybele, found in the village of Tours, near Abbéville. Paris, Bibl. Nat. 611. First century A.D.: Vermaseren, *CCCA* V, no. 468 (no photo).
7. Bronze medallion, found at Csaksar. Székesfehérvár AM, no. 3516. Bust of Cybele, to the right a pair of cymbals, to the left a pair of flutes: Vermaseren, *CCCA* IV, no. 123, pl. XXX.
8. A terracotta mold from Olynthus. Cybele holds a cymbal with her right hand and a torch with her left. Fifth to fourth century B.C. Thessaloniki, AM 524: Vermaseren, *CCCA* VI, no. 211, pl. XLIV.
9. A similar mold in the collection of Prof. Simkovitch of Columbia University, New York. Fourth century B.C.: Vermaseren, *CCCA* VI, no. 203, pl. XLV.

B. Cymbals with a dedication to the Mother of the Gods

10. Marble relief from Cyzicus. Paris, Louvre 2850. Two cymbals hanging from a tree and a long inscription describing how the dedication was made to Meter Kotiane by a gallus called Soterides in thanks for the escape from captivity of his brother, who had been captured while taking part in a campaign of Julius Caesar in Libya in 46 B.C.: Vermaseren, *CCCA* I, no. 287, pl. LXII.

C. Cymbals accompanying Cybele in conjunction with other deities

11. A votive relief showing Cybele with Hermes and Hecate, now lost. In the field were a crescent and two cymbals: Vermaseren, *CCCA* I, no. 893, p. 262, fig. 46.

12. The well-known red-figure volute crater by Polygnotus in the Ferrara Archaeological Museum which shows Cybele with Dionysus, Muses, musicians, etc., also includes cymbals: Vermaseren, *CCCA* IV, no. 213, pl. LXXXXVIII.

D. A priest of Cybele with cymbals

13. A relief found between Lanuvium and Ganzano in 1736. Rome, Museo Capitolino no. 1207: Vermaseren *CCCA* III, no. 466, pl. CCXCVII.

E. A priestess of Cybele (?) with cymbals

14. A grave relief in the Ashmolean Museum, of 150 B.C. Two cymbals, a tympanum, and a snake are present: Vermaseren, *CCCA* I, no. 574 (no photo); Pfuhl-Moebius, I, p. 233, no. 898, pl. 134.

XII. *Corybantes*

Corybantes (or Couretes) appear on our no. K7 and K11. Couretes were represented as armed warriors carrying shields and protecting the goddess Rhea and the child Zeus from Kronos. From the sixth century B.C. onwards they were identified with the Asiatic Corybantes, or followers of Cybele (see I.M. Linforth, "The Corybantic Rites of Plato," *CPCP* 13 (1949) 19–57; Reeder, p. 434). According to Strabo (472.19) Corybantes was merely the Asiatic name for the figures who in mainland Greece were called Couretes. Further syncretism took place with the Cabeiri, the Great Gods of Samothrace, and the Dioscuri (who, however, were always two in number. For the whole matter see B. Hemberg, *Die Kabiren*, Uppsala, 1950.) There are several additional examples where the Corybantes are illustrated with Cybele:

1. A Hellenistic marble votive relief in Athens, Acropolis Museum 2455: Vermaseren *CCCA* II, no. 190, pl. 38.
2. A Hellenistic marble votive relief from the Piraeus, Piraeus Museum E15/1165: O. Walter. *OeJh* 31 (1938) fig. 22; Vermaseren *CCCA* II, no. 270, pl. LXIII; Reeder p. 434.
3. A fragmentary marble votive relief from Potidaea in the Polygeros Museum. It is of Attic workmanship and dates to 330 B.C. It shows one of the Corybantes, and six worshippers: Θ. Στεφανίδου,

"Αναθηματικό ανάγλυφο από την Ποτείδαια," *Μακεδονικά* 13 (1973) p. 107 ff., pl. 1.

4. A marble votive relief from the temple of Cybele in Patras, Athens National Museum. It shows eight Corybantes dancing with their instruments: Thomopoulos, p. 198; Papachatzes, Attica, p. 105.

5. A marble votive relief from Lebadeia in Athens National Museum no. 3942, dated 350–340 B.C.: Vermaseren *CCCA* II no. 432, pl. 127.; Naumann no. 422, pl. 28, fig. 1.

6. A bronze relief from Sorento in Naples Museum: Vermaseren *CCCA* IV, fig. 76.

7. A votive relief from Amphipolis in Thessaloniki, AM 738. On the pediment are three standing Couretes with a shield and a lance each: Vermaseren *CCCA* VI, no. 291, pl. LXIX.

8. A plaster votive relief in the Cairo Museum: Ch. Picard, *MonPiot* 49 (1957) p. 41, pl. V; Naumann no. 141, pl. 31,1; Vermaseren *CCCA* V no. 28, pl. 13.

9. A marble votive relief in London, British Museum no. 788: Vermaseren *CCCA* VII, fig. 69, pl. 51.

10. A terracotta votive relief, previously in the collection of the Polytechneion, Athens, now presumably in Athens National Museum: Winter, III, 2, p. 175, 4.

11. Reliefs in the rock-cut sanctuary of Akrai in Sicily: Vermaseren, *CCCA* IV, fig. 161c; fig. 153b; fig. 160, pl. 59.

12. Bronze votive relief from Mesembria, in Komotini Archaeological Museum 1589, of Hellenistic date: *Πρακτικά* 1973, πιν. 82a . . . *Μακεδονικά* 13 (1973) 112–113; *BCH* 98 (1974) 681, 684, fig. 245.

13. A lamp from south Italy now in Trieste, Museo Civico, 4059: Vermaseren *CCCA* IV, no. 144, pl. 46.

14. The well-known silver lanx from Parabiago near Milan. Cybele is on a chariot drawn by lions. Among the other figures are three dancing Corybantes. The date is probably second century A.D.: Vermaseren *CCCA* IV no. 268, pl. 107.

15. A marble floor in Paris, Bibliothèque Nationale: Schauenberg, *Helios* (1955) pl. 29; Vermaseren, *Attis*, p. 37; *CCCA* IV, no. 465, pl. 155.

16. A relief from Rome, Villa Albani, dated 43 A.D.: Vermaseren, *CCCA* III, no. 9, pl. IX.

17. The Hellenistic bronze matrix in New York, which we have already mentioned: Reeder p. 424, fig. 1.

18. A relief from Thasos, Thasos Museum no. 18: Vermaseren *CCCA* II, no. 529, pl. 159.
19. A gold triangular diadem, found in the Nablus region. Jerusalem, Israel Museum no. 76.63.50. One of the Couretes is dancing, holding a shield and a dagger: Vermaseren, *CCCA* I, no. 896, pl. CXCVIII.

Couretes protecting the child Zeus can be seen on a Roman-period terracotta relief, H.B. Walters, *Catalogue of the terracottas in the Department of Greek and Roman Antiquities in the British Museum*, p. 378, D 501, pl.

(There are also some banquet reliefs, which have nothing to do with the Great Mother, but still have three armed warriors in the upper part of the relief. A good example is a banquet relief from Teos previously in the Evangelical School of Smyrna, which shows two reclining male figures and behind a curtain the busts of three armed men with shields: Pfuhl, *JdI*, 1905, p. 123, no. 2, fig. 20; Stringaris K140; Pfuhl-Möbius, no. 1908.)

XIII. *The divine couple*

The reliefs K1, K2, K3, and K4 have been thought to be grave reliefs and the two figures on the couch to be the deceased. We rather believe that on K1 we have a reclining goddess and on K2 and K3 a reclining god with his partner. A banquet scene with a reclining female figure is quite rare, but there are some parallels. (See Mitropoulou 1974 for further discussion.) The reclining female figure can be Demeter, Isis, Tyche, or Hygeia.

a. *Demeter and Kore*

1. A votive relief in Mytilene Museum, 3823, showing Demeter and Kore: Mitropoulou 1974, no. 1, fig. 1.
2. A votive relief from the Naucratis Museum, now in London, BM 728. It shows Demeter and Kore: Mitropoulou 1974, no. 2, fig. 2.
3. A relief in Stanford University Museum 21449. It has been thought to be a grave relief, but this possibility is ruled out by the presence of worshippers. The reclining deity wears a chiton with a himation over it, and holds a drinking rhyton. There is a female partner seated at the end of the couch, as well as a male

partner. Three worshippers follow: a father with his two sons. If the reclining deity is female, as can be concluded from her breasts, then the deities in question are Demeter, Kore, and Euboulos. In the upper left corner there is the head of a horse. It is interesting that the reclining figure, even though female, holds a rhyton: *DAI Mitteilungen Kairo* 1975, pl. 98b.

b. *Isis*

4. A relief from Thasos in the Louvre, Paris, MA 3575 (MND 266). It represents Isis with a high polos, and presumably her priestess. Three symbols of Isis including a sistrum, are hanging on the wall: *BCH* 26 (1902) 477, fig. 45; Fr. Dunand, *Le culte d'Isis dans le bassin oriental de la Mediteranée, II: Culte d'Isis en Grèce*, 1973 p. XX fig. 2.

c. *Tyche*

The goddess Tyche takes on the character of the Great Mother or Cybele in the Hellenistic period, and competes with her as the goddess who rules over all life and death. She becomes the city goddess in many places, and her best-known representation is the Tyche of Antioch (illustrated, Burkert, *Greek Religion*, p. 168).

5. A relief in Palermo, National Museum 1551. Tyche is reclining holding a horn of plenty and offering liquid to a snake. There is an inscription: ΔΙΟΜΗΔΗC ΕΠΟΕΙ. From the lunate sigma of the inscription we conclude that the relief is of the Roman period: Mitropoulou 1976, p. 122, no. 69b.

6. Coins of Alexandria in Egypt showing Tyche reclining within a naiskos and holding a rudder. An example is provided from the reign of Antoninus Pius (138–161 A.D.), with obverse head of Antoninus Pius, R. Plant, *Greek Coins and their Identifications*, 1979, no. 2063.

d. *Hygeia*

7. A marble votive relief from Ephesus in the Ephesus Museum. With her right hand she offers food to a snake. There is also a cup-bearer and the head of a horse. The piece is to be dated to the late fourth century B.C.: Mitropoulou, 1976, p. 65, no. 80, fig. 80.

The interpretation of the reclining god in the banquet reliefs, such as our K3 and K4, is perhaps to be suggested by the fact that in other cases Cybele is shown with more definable gods. For instance on K5, the Great Mother may be shown with the chthonian couple, Zeus Meilichios and Hera Meilichia. We also find the Great Mother with Zeus to her left and Hermes to her right in numerous representations, of which one example is

1. A votive relief from Kayalt Dag at Bayramic. Roman: Vermaseren, *CCCA* I, no. 334, pl. LXXI.

Other reliefs showing the Great Mother with Zeus are

2. one from Tenos in the Benaki Museum, Athens, dated to the second century B.C.: Vermaseren, *CCCA* II pl. 176, fig. 583.
3. one in the Hermitage, St. Petersburg: J. Keil, *OeJh* 18, 1915, 74, no. M, fig. 46; Vermaseren, *CCCA* VII, no. 64, pl. XLV.
4. Also, a marble statue of the Great Mother from Tomis in the Bucharest Museum. Here she is seated with Zeus standing to her left in a much smaller size. The Corybantes are also present: Bordenache, no. 61, pl. 28, fig. 61, and finally
5. A marble relief from Cyzicus in London, BM 788, of early Roman date: Mitropoulou 1977, 138, note 29; Vermaseren *CCCA*, I, fig. 69.
6. A votive relief in Bursa, AM (1007) 3231, Hermes and other deities are also present: Vermaseren, *CCCA* I, no. 430, pl. XCIV.

The Great Mother is also found with Dionysus, such as in our no. K11. Other instances of this are found

1. On a red-figured volute krater of the painter Polygnotus. 440–430 B.C. in the Ferrara archaeological museum, from grave 128 in the Valle Trebba, discussed previously. It shows Cybele and a bearded Dionysus seated close together, as well as a priestess, Maenads dancing, and two flute-players: Vermaseren *CCCA* IV, no. 213, pl. LXXXVIII (with the misleading identification Dionysus-Sabazius).
2. and on a votive relief from Lebadeia in the Athens National Museum, of Hellenistic date: Vermaseren *CCCA* II, no. 432, pl. CVVVII.

As Burkert says (p. 179), "Meter Kybele is seen as one with the Dionysian throng. The abandonment of ordered existence, the procession to the mountain, and the ecstatic dancing go to establish the identity."

XIV. *A god being crowned*

On our K4 a female figure crowns the reclining deity who presumably is the Great Mother. Similar scenes are to be found

1. on a votive banquet relief from Eleusis, in Athens National Museum 1519. Here there are two banquet scenes, one of them with Zeus Meilichios and Hera Meilichia, and the other with Kore, who crowns Demeter with a wreath. All the gods are seated, none of them reclining: Svoronos, pl. 88; Mitropoulou, 1977, p. 131, no. 60, fig. 60, with further bibliography and discussion.

(In later Roman banquet reliefs, such as Pfuhl-Moebius pls. 242, 243, we can see one of the reclining figures holding a wreath towards his partner.)

2. On the relief of the apotheosis of Homer, signed by Archelaus of Priene, from Bovillae, Italy: B.S. Ridgeway, *Hellenistic Sculpture* I (1990), p. 257, pl. 133.
3. On a relief in the Louvre, Paris, MA 3592, from Kula in Lydia, with "Demeter," "Artemis" (Anaeitis), and "Nike," discussed already above. There are three friezes. In the first of them we see a coiled snake and in the two corners a round floral decoration. In the second are the three goddesses indicated by the inscription. "Artemis" (Anaeitis), who has the iconography of the Great Mother, rests her hands on the heads of the two lions which flank her. On her head is a crescent moon. Her chair has two coiled snakes. Between her and "Demeter" is an eagle inside a crescent. Over "Demeter" is a coiled snake, and another one is coiled next to "Artemis." What makes this interesting syncretistic relief relevant here is that Nike is crowning "Artemis." It is illustrated and discussed by, I. Diakonoff, "Artemidi Anaeiti anestesen," *BABesch* 54 (1979) pp. 139–188, esp. p. 150, no. 30, fig. 32; Vermaseren, *CA* pl. 16; *CCCA* I, no. 485, pl. CVII. If the bird in the crescent, generally taken as an eagle, can be taken as a hawk, then we would have a closer connection between this piece and the earlier Phrygian representations of the Great Mother.

BIBLIOGRAPHY

Anatolian Civilization	*Anatolian Civilization II, Greek/Roman/Byzantine, Catalogue of the Exhibition, Istanbul. May 22–Oct. 30, 1983.*
Bordenache	G. Bordenache, *Sculture grece e romane del Museo Nazionale di Antichità di Bulgaria. I statue e relieve di culto, elementi architettonici e decorativi,* 1969.
Burkert, Gr. Rel.	W. Burkert, *Greek Religion,* 1985.
Despinis	Γ. Δεσπίνις, *Συμβολή στη μελέτη του έργου του Αγορακρίτου,* 1971.
Jeanmaire	H. Jeanmaire, *Couroi et Courètes,* Lille, 1939.
Farnell	L.R. Farnell, *The Cults of the Greek States.*
Hanfmann-Ramage, Hanfmann	George M.A. and N.H. Ramage, *Sculpture from Sardis, The Finds through* 1975, 1978
Hanfmann-Waldbaum	Hanfmann, George M.A. and Jane C. Waldbaum, "Kybele and Artemis, Two Anatolian Goddesses at Sardis," *Archaeology* 22 (1969) 264–269.
Harrison	Jane Ellen Harrison, *Themis. A Study in the Social Origins of Greek Religion,* repr. 1963.
Huyghe	R. Huyghe, *Larousse Encyclopedia of Prehistoric and Ancient Art,* 1962.
Kater-Sibbes	J.G.F. Kater-Sibbes in *Mitteilungen des Deutschen Archälogischen Instituts, Abteilung Kairo,* 1975.
Larousse	*Larouse World Mythology,* ed. Pierre Grimal, 1981.
Loukas	Ι. Λουκάς, *Η Ρέα Κυβέλη και οι γονικές λατρείες της Φλύας,* 1988.
Linforth	I.M. Linforth, "The Corybantic Rites of Plato," *CPCP* 13 (1946) 19–57.
Mitropoulou, 1974	E. Mitropoulou, *Three Unusual Banquet Reliefs.* Athens 1974.
Mitropoulou, 1976	E. Mitropoulou, *Horses' Heads and Snakes: Banquet Reliefs and their Meaning,* Athens 1976.
Mitropoulou, 1977	E. Mitropoulou, *Deities and Heroes in the Form of Snakes,* Athens, 1977.
Mitropoulou, 1983a	Ε. Μητροπούλου, "Ανάγλυφο Κυβέλης από το Μουσείο της Σπάρτης", *Πρακτικά του α΄ τοπικου συνεδρίου λακωνικών σπουδών, Μολάοι, 5–7 Ιουν. 1982,* Athens, 1982, p. 16 ff.
Mitropoulou, 1983b	E. Mitropoulou, "Different Types of Cybele etc.", *Concilium Eïrene XVI, Proceedings of the 16th International Eirene Conference, Prague 31.8–4.9.1982,* 1983, pp. 191–208.
Mitropoulou, 1986	Ε. Μητροπούλου, "Ο Αττις και η Κυβέλη", *Πρακτικά του 2ου τοπικού συνεδρίου αχαϊκών σπουδών, Καλάβρυτα 25–27 Ιαν. 1983,* Athens 1986, pp. 191–208.
Mitropoulou, 1988	"Feasting at Festivals", *Akte des XIII internationalen Kongresses für klassische Archäologie,* Berlin 1988.
Mollard-Besques	*Catalogue raisonné des figurines et reliefs en terre-cuite grecs, étrusques, et romains, III, Epoques hellénistique et romaine, Grèce et Asie Mineure,* Paris 1972.

Moortgat	Anton Moortgat, *The Art of Ancient Mesopotamia*, 1969.
Naumann	Friederike Naumann, *Die Ikonographie der Kybele usw.*, Istanbuler Mitteilungen, Beiheft 28, Tübingen, 1983.
Nicolaou	Ino Nicolaou, "Evidence for the Cult of Cybele in Cyprus," in *Studies Presented in Memory of Porphyrios Dikaios*, Nicosia 1979, pp. 169–177.
Nilsson	M.P. Nilsson, *A History of Greek Religion*, 1949.
Papachatzis, Attica	Ν. Παπαχατζή, *Παυσανίου Περιήγησις, Αττικά*, Athens 1974
Papachatzis, Achaika	Ν. Παπαχατζή, *Παυσανίου Περιήγησις, Αχαϊκά*, Athens 1980.
Petrocheilos	Ιωάννης Πετρόχειλος, "Αναθηματικά γλυπτά της Κυβέλης από τον Πειραιά," *Arch.Eph.* 1992, pp. 21–65.
Pfuhl	E. Pfuhl, "Das Beiwerk auf den ostgriechischen Grabreliefs," *JdI* 20 (1905) pp. 123 ff.
Pfuhl-Moebius	E. Pfuhl and Hans Moebius, *Die ostgriechischen Grabreliefs*, Mainz, 1977.
Rein	Mary Jane Rein, *The Cult and Iconography of Lydian Cybele*, Dissertation, Harvard University, 1993.
Reeder	E. Reeder, "The Mother of the Gods in a Hellenistic Bronze Matrix," *AJA* 91, 1987, pp. 423–440.
Roller, 1988	L.E. Roller, "Phrygian Myth and Cult", *Source* 7 (1988), pp. 43–50.
Roller, 1991	L.E. Roller, "The Great Mother at Gordion, The Hellenization of an Anatolian Cult," *JHS* 111 (1991), pp. 128–143.
Scorpan	C. Scorpan, *Cavalerul Trac*, 1967.
Seidl	J. Seidl, *Das Totengrabrelief*, Dissertation Wien, 1942.
Stringaris	Rhea Thoenges-Stringaris, "Das griechische Totenmahl," in *AM* 80 (1965), pp. 1–99.
Svoronos	J.N. Svoronos, *Das Athener Nationalmuseum*, 1903–1937.
Thomopoulos	Στ. Γ. Θωμόπουλος, *Ιστορία της πόλωες των Πατρών*, Athens 1880.
Tacheva-Hitova	M. Tacheva-Hitova, *Eastern Cults in Moesia Inferior and Thracia*, EPRO 95, Leiden 1983.
Turcan	Robert Turcan, *Les Cultes orientaux dans le monde romain*, 1989.
Vermaseren, *CA*	M.J. Vermaseren, *Cybele and Attis*, 1977.
Vermaseren, *CCCA*	M.J. Vermaseren, *Corpus Cultus Cybelae Attisdisque*, EPRO 50, Leiden, 1977–86.
Winter	Fr. Winter, *Die Typen der figürlichen Terrakotten*, 1903.

Figure 1

Figure 2

Figure 3

Figure 4

PRIVATER DANK – SILBERVOTIVE AUS NORDAFRIKA

Friederike Naumann-Steckner

"Il n'y a pas possibilité d'imaginer ni d'établir des catégories dans l'ex-voto. Celui-ci affecte le plus souvent la figure réduite d'un membre, d'un objet usuel. Les sanctuaires sont remplis de ces figurines en cire, en bois, en marbre, ou encore de membres postiches, de béquilles, de bandages, qui témoignent d'un soulagement obtenu, ou encore d'images rappelant un péril évité. Parfois c'est une promesse qu'on veut tenir d'une manière solennelle et durable par une plaque de marbre gravée". Mit diesen Worten leitet Henri Leclercq sein Lemma "ex-voto" im Dictionnaire d'archéologie chretienne et de Liturgie (1922) ein. Seine Beobachtungen sind noch immer gültig und können ohne Einschränkung auf die griechisch-römische Antike übertragen werden.

Der Gottheit um eine Bitte zu verstärken oder als Dank ein würdiges und dauerhaftes Geschenk zu machen, scheint ein uraltes Anliegen des Menschen. Die großen Anatheme sollten neben der Frömmigkeit auch das wirtschaftliche Vermögen des Stifters bzw. der weihenden Gemeinde deutlich werden lassen.[1] Größere Städte errichteten in wichtigen Heiligtümern Schatzhäuser für die Weihgaben ihrer Bürger.[2] Bothroi in oder bei den Tempeln zeugen davon, daß unbrauchbare oder altmodische kleinere Geschenke der Gläubigen auf würdige Weise zur Seite geräumt werden mußten, um Platz für neue Gaben zu schaffen.[3]

Eine besondere Form der exvota sind kleine und dünne Metall-, oft Silberplättchen mit Bild, von denen schon E. Will bemerkte, daß sie wegen der mäßigen Erhaltung nur ein unvollkommenes Bild der

---

[1] EAA I, Roma 1958, s.v. anathema (S. Ferri).
[2] Pausanias VI,19,1 ff. X,11,1 ff.
[3] U. Zanotti-Bianco – P. Zancani Montuoro, Capaccio, Not.Scavi 1937, 299 ff. M. Launey, Le sanctuaire et le culte d'Héraklès à Thasos, Études Thasiennes I, École française d'Athènes (Paris, 1944) 174 ff. T. Linders – G. Nordquist (Hrsg.), Gifts to the Gods. Symposium Uppsala 1987 (Uppsala, 1987). S. auch die Rezension 'Votive Deposits in Italy: New Perspectives on Old Finds' von B. Ginge, JRA 6, 1993, 285 ff.

ursprünglichen Vielfalt und Verbreitung zuließen.[4] Aus Anlaß der
Veröffentlichung der Funde im Dolichenusheiligtum von Mauer an
der Url hat R. Noll Material, Form, Darstellung und Adressaten der
sehr verstreut publizierten römischen exvota in einer Liste zusammen-
gestellt.[5] Bezieht man griechisch-hellenistische Votivbleche[6] und Matrizen aus Moesien und Thrakien[7] ein, so ergibt sich ein etwas ande-
res Bild.

Eine Erwerbung der Archäologischen Gesellschaft für das Römisch-
Germanische Museum Köln erweitert unsere Kenntnis und verän-
dert dieses Bild erneut ein wenig. Die sieben Bleche stammen nach
zuverlässiger Angabe aus Nordafrika (Mitteltunesien).[8] Je ein Blech
zeigt die auf dem Löwen reitende Kybele bzw. Fortuna-Tyche in
einer Aedikula, zweimal ist eine Göttertrias zu sehen, auf drei Blechen die Büste der Minerva.

Die Votive bestehen alle aus sehr dünnem, fast folienartigem Blech.
Die beiden Trias-Votive und die drei Minerva-Votive sind jeweils
über dem gleichen Model gearbeitet, auch wenn sich dabei manche
Details stärker oder schwächer ausgeprägt haben. Die leicht unterschiedliche Größe der Minerva-Votive läßt erkennen, daß die Punz-
reihe am Rand nicht zum Model gehörte, sondern in einem zweiten
Arbeitsgang separat nach Blechgröße zugefügt wurde. Die Rücksei-

---

[4] E. Will, Le relief cultuel gréco-romain (Paris, 1955) 37 ff.

[5] R. Noll, Das Inventar des Dolichenusheiligtums von Mauer an der Url. Der
römische Limes in Österreich 30 (Wien, 1980) 72 ff. Ergänzungen bei H.J. Kellner –
G. Zahlhaas, Der römische Tempelschatz von Weißenburg in Bayern (Mainz, 1993)
69. Ältere Zusammenstellung: J. Toynbee, A Londinium Votiv Leaf or Feather and
its Fellows, Collectanea Londiniensia. Studies in London Archaeology and History
presented to Ralph Merrifield (London, 1978) 129 ff. Nachzutragen ist: J. Corrocher,
Sources et installations thermales en Bourbonnais, in: Les eaux thermales et les cultes
des eaux en Gaule et dans les provinces voisines. Actes du colloque 1990, Aix-Les-
Bains, hrsg. von R. Chevallier (Tours-Turin, 1992) 177 ff. Abb.17. I. Fauduet,
Sanctuaires associés à l'eau en Gaule Centrale, ebd. 199 ff. E. Künzl – S. Künzl,
Aquae Apollinares/Vicarello, ebd. 273 ff. Katalog Dieux guérisseurs en Gaule romaine,
hrsg. von C. Landes (Lattes, 1992) 224 ff.

[6] Treasures of Ancient Macedonia. Ausstellung Thessaloniki 1978 (Athen, 1978),
105 Nr. 434–457. K. Reber, Antike Kunst 26, 1983, 77 Taf.21.

[7] V.P. Vasilev, Bronzene Matrizen aus Mösien und Thrakien. Recherches sur la
culture en Mesie et en Thrace. Bulgarie 1e–4e siècle. Bulletin de l'institut d'archéologie
37, 1987, 177 ff.

[8] Erworben 16.8.90. Inv. Nr. RGM 90,514a–g. Hansgerd Hellenkemper, Köln,
danke ich für die Erlaubnis zur Publikation, ausführliche Diskussion, zahlreiche
Literaturhinweise und die kritische Durchsicht des Manuskripts, François Baratte,
Paris, und Kenneth Painter, London, gaben vielfältige Hinweise, wofür ich herzlich
Dank sage. Thomas Quaink, Römisch-Germanisches Museum Köln, reinigte und
restaurierte die Votive.

ten der Votive sind mit eingefärbtem Epoxyharz dick verstrichen, so
daß keine Arbeitsspuren mehr festzustellen sind.[9]

Eine energiedispersive Röntgen-Mikroanalyse (EDAKS) im Elektro-
nenrastermikroskop ergab folgende Materialzusammensetzung (in %).[10]

		Ag	Cu	Cl
Kybelevotiv	Inv. 90,514b	43,79	56,21	–
Fortuna-Tychevotiv	Inv. 90,514c	42,67	52,27	5,06
Votiv mit Trias	Inv. 90,514d	82,96	17,04	–
Votiv mit Trias	Inv. 90,514e	90,96	7,07	1,97
Votiv an Minerva	Inv. 90,514a	39,35	54,08	6,57
Votiv an Minerva	Inv. 90,514f	76,15	23,85	–
Votiv an Minerva	Inv. 90,514g	36,56	59,55	3,89

Bei der Interpretation der EDAKS kann das Chlor vernachlässigt
werden, da es sich sekundär aus dem Boden an dem Metallblech ab-
gelagert hat.[11] Der sehr unterschiedliche Gehalt der Votive an Silber
und Kupfer besagt, daß die Votive nicht aus demselben Rohblech
gefertigt sind: entweder waren die Model über lange Zeit in Ge-
brauch oder aber die Votive wurden jeweils aus kleinen Resten von
Silber/Kupferblech geschnitten, das für andere Zwecke geschlagen
worden war.

Alle Votive weisen Nagellöcher auf, die in der Regel von vorne
nach hinten ausgestanzt oder durchgebohrt sind; je nach Position
der Löcher waren die Votive wohl mit zwei, drei oder vier Nägeln
(auf einem Holzträger) befestigt worden. Ein zusätzliches Loch bei
einem der Minervavotive kann freilich nicht, wie bei einem der Trias-
votive, als Ersatz für ein ausgerissenes Loch angesehen werden; vielleicht wurde das—kleinere—Loch notwendig, weil der Nagel an der

---

[9] An den einfacheren Silbervotiven aus Water Newton stellte Jane Lang, British
Museum Research Laboratory, folgenden Arbeitsvorgang fest: ". . . they were not
pressed into moulds but were all hammered out from sheet metal. The resulting
sheets were then cut to shape with shears. For the decoration the metal was sometimes
worked from one side and sometimes from both; but there is no bruising of the
metal, and so it must have been backed with pitch or a similar material during
working. To make the Chi-Rho on plaque no. 10, a broad central vertical line was
drawn lightly on the back. Dots were punched on to the line from the back with a
finely pointed tool. The relief was then emphasised with neater lines drawn on the
front. The surrounding 'veins' were worked from front and back . . ." (Briefliche
Mitteilung von K. Painter am 9, September 1993).

[10] Kurt Hangst, Museum für Ostasiatische Kunst, führte die Analyse am Physika-
lischen Institut der Universität Köln durch. Er half mir auch bei der Interpretation.

[11] Bereits kleine Unterschiede in der Lagerung können stark differierende Auf-
nahme von Chlor bewirken.

Abb. 1a

Abb. 1b

vorgesehenen Stelle keinen Halt fand. Das Tyche-Votiv war ursprünglich wohl nicht mit Befestigungslöchern ausgestattet; die beiden Löcher sind in unregelmäßiger Position und Form von hinten nach vorne durch das Blech gestoßen.

Nagellöcher finden sich an relativ wenigen Votiven: beispielsweise an den Blechen aus Mesembria, den Augenvotiven aus Wroxeter und Alésia, an Votiven in Form von Tabulae ansatae und an den christlichen Votiven aus dem Schatzfund von Ma'aret en-Norman; ein Votiv aus diesem Fund und zwei aus Mesembria sind mit einer Hängeöse versehen.[12] Für die Votive aus Weißenburg wird vermutet, daß sie in einem Ständer aus organischem Material eingeklemmt aufgestellt waren.[13]

Kybelevotiv, RGM Inv. 90,514b (Abb. 1a). Erh. max. H. 6,2 cm, erh. max. B. 4,8 cm. Das Blech ist allseitig bestoßen, rechts unten fehlt ein größerer Teil. Aus drei Fragmenten zusammengesetzt. Ein Nagelloch rechts oben; ein zweites links oben ausgerissen.

Kybele sitzt frontal auf einem seitlich stehenden Löwen, der den Kopf dem Betrachter zugewandt hat. Sie trägt eine niedrige Mauerkrone. In der rechten, zur Seite gestreckten Hand hält sie die Spendeschale, die linke ruht im Schoß. Vor der Göttin—zu ihren Füßen— steht ein Altar(?) mit auskragender, geschwungener Deckplatte, ihr zur Seite ein Thymiaterion(?). Über ihrer rechten Schulter ist ein liegender Halbmond zu sehen. Spuren oberhalb der Darstellung scheinen anzudeuten, daß das Bild von einem Perlkreis eingefaßt war, was freilich nicht zu der horizontalen oberen und unteren Kante paßt.

Auf dem Löwen reitend wurde Kybele seit der Mitte des 4. Jahrhunderts dargestellt.[14] Ob die Übertragung des Kultbildes von Prokonessos

---

[12] Treasures (*Anm.*6) Nr. 452.453. K. Painter, A Roman Gold Ex-voto from Wroxeter, Shropshire. Antiquaries Journal 51, 1971, 329 ff. Katalog Dieux guérisseurs (*Anm.*5) 224 ff. Nr. 101.102.104.107. J. Kellner, Die Römer in Bayern (München, 1972) 109 Abb.50. Die Schweiz zur Römerzeit. Katalog Colonia Raurica 1957 (Hrsg. von R. Fellmann, Basel 1957) Abb.12.13.15.16.17. M. Mundell Mango, Silver from Early Byzantium (Baltimore, 1986) 242 ff. Ein Votiv in Form einer Tabula ansata, wohl aus Kleinasien, war mit einem Kettchen vermutlich an dem Weihgeschenk befestigt, s. Idole. Frühe Götterbilder und Opfergaben/Katalog der Ausstellung München 1985 (Mainz, 1985) Nr. 96. Die Löcher in der Mitte des P bei einigen Votiven aus Water Newton sind wohl nicht als Nagellöcher zu deuten, vgl. K.S. Painter, The Water Newton Early Christian Silver (London, 1977) z.B. Nr. 10.11.13.16, s. auch Nr. 12.15.17.

[13] Kellner-Zahlhaas 1993 (*Anm.*5) 70 mit *Anm.*222.

[14] F. Naumann, Die Ikonographie der Kybele in der phrygischen und der griechischen Kunst (Tübingen, 1983) 233 f. M.J. Vermaseren, Matrem in leone sedentem (Leiden, 1970) war mir nicht zugänglich.

nach Kyzikos Anlaß war, dort Statere mit dem Bild der reitenden Kybele zu prägen, läßt sich nicht schlüssig beweisen.[15] Verbreitet war dieses Bild erst in hellenistischer und römischer Zeit, wo es—möglicherweise seit Claudius—zur Ausstattung der Spina im Circus maximus in Rom gehörte.[16]

Silberne Kybelevotive stehen in einer langen Tradition. Der größte erhaltene Bestand stammt aus einem Demeter-Heiligtum im thrakischen Mesembria.[17] In dem kleinen, an die Stadtmauer angebauten Gebäude wurden u.a. Terrakottastatuetten, schwarzgefirniste Keramik, Münzen und eine rotfigurige Pelike gefunden, die 24 bronzene, silberne, goldene und vergoldete Votivplättchen enthielt. Bleche mit Adoranten-Darstellungen und Augen überwiegen, neben einzelnen Votiven mit dem Bild von Demeter und Kore, der Nymphen, einer Hand und eines Widders lassen sich drei mit Sicherheit Kybele zuordnen.[18]

Ein Votivblech zeigt die thronende Kybele mit Polos, Schale und Zepter in einem Naiskos, umgeben von einem Löwen, Hermes und dem "Mädchen mit den Fackeln"; Adorant und Adorantin sind vor die Göttin getreten.[19] Bei einem zweiten Votiv hält die Göttin im Tempel zwischen Hermes und Mädchen den Löwen auf dem Schoß; Adoranten, in unterschiedlichem Maßstab gebildet, flankieren das Tempelchen.[20] Diesen beiden Votivblechen aus Mesembria ähnelt ein (stark fragmentarisch geborgenes) Silbervotiv aus Eretria, das Kybele zwischen Hermes und Kore zeigt und das K. Reber ebenfalls ins 4. Jahrhundert v. Chr. datiert.[21] Die Silberbleche wurden sicherlich über bronzenen Matrizen gepreßt, wie man sie aus römischer Zeit kennt: insbesondere eine Fundstelle bei Abritus hat zahlreiche solcher Ma-

---

[15] H.v. Fritze, Nomisma VII (Berlin, 1912) Taf.VI,18.

[16] J.H. Humphrey, Roman Circuses (London, 1986) 273 ff. Beispiele für Marmor-, Ton-, Silber- und Bronzestatuetten, Marmor- und Tonreliefs, Lampenbilder: M.J. Vermaseren, Corpus Cultus Cybelae Attidisque (Leiden, 1977–1989), *EPRO* 50, I Nr. 365. II Nr. 43. III Nr. 330.439.470. IV Nr. 37.143. V Nr. 12–14.56.67–71.398. VI Nr. 3.18.26.80. VII Nr. 3.52.126.134. Naumann a.O. Kat. Nr. 610–617. Greek and Roman Sculpture in Gold and Silver, Museum of Fine Arts, Boston (Boston, 1974) Nr. 77. Dieser (unvollständigen) Zusammenstellung läßt sich keine lokale Präferenz gerade dieses Kybeletypus ablesen.

[17] A.K. Vavritsa, Praktika tes en Athenais Archaiologikes Etaireias 1973 (1975) 77 ff. mit Taf.89–96. Vermaseren, *CCCA* VI Nr. 334 mit Lit.

[18] Treasures a.O. (*Anm.6*) Nr. 446.447.448. Vielleicht auch 453.

[19] 11,9 x 9,2 cm, Vavritsa a.O. Taf.92 α. Treasures a.O. Nr. 447. Vermaseren, *CCCA* VI Nr. 335.

[20] 6,8 x 4,6 cm, Vavritsa a.O. Taf.94 α. Treasures a.O. Nr. 448. Vermaseren, *CCCA* VI Nr. 337.

[21] 6,3 x 7,4 cm, Reber, a.O. (*Anm.6*) 77 Taf.21.

trizen für Votive der unterschiedlichsten Gottheiten erbracht.[22] Matrizen für Votive an Kybele sind die Bronzeplatte "aus Thessaloniki" in Lyon und die Doppelmatrize für Kybele und Artemis-Luna (?) in Sofia;[23] von einer im Typus genau entsprechenden Einzelmatrize für Votive an die letztgenannte Gottheit vermutet Vermaseren, daß sie in Afrika erworben wurde.[24] Das sehr detaillierte Gipsrelief im Ägyptischen Museum Kairo könnte ein—hellenistisches—"Zwischenmodel" zur Verbreitung des Typus—in diesem Fall einer besonderen Variante—sein.[25] Nach solchen Modeln wurden freilich nicht nur Votivgaben aus dünnem Silberblech, sondern sicherlich auch der stabilere Priesterschmuck und Kastenbeschläge gearbeitet.[26]

Ein drittes, einfacheres Votivblech aus Mesembria ist annähernd dreieckig und wird von einer gepunzten Perlreihe eingefaßt. Dargestellt ist die stehende Göttin zwischen zwei Löwen.[27] Ähnlich schlicht gibt ein bronzenes Votivplättchen (oder ein Model?) das Götterbild auch im 2. oder 3. Jahrhundert n. Chr.: frontal thronend, die Füße auf einem liegenden Löwen, die Hände auf zwei sitzenden Tieren.[28] Ob auf einem weiteren Votiv aus Mesembria in der thronenden Gottheit mit Zweig in der Linken, auf die sechs Adoranten zugehen, ebenfalls Kybele zu sehen ist, wie M.J. Vermaseren annimmt, mag offen bleiben.[29] Auf einem runden Medaillon unbekannten Zwecks aus gepreßtem Silberblech, das aus Olynth stammt,[30] ist Kybele, begleitet von Hermes und dem "Mädchen mit den Fackeln", den

---

[22] Vasilev, Matrizen (*Anm.*7) 117 ff.

[23] Vermaseren, *CCCA* VI Nr. 198. Naumann a.O. (*Anm.*14) Nr. 444. V.P. Vasilev, Matrices en bronze dans la toreutique romaine provinciale des IIe–IIIe siècle, Annales de l'université Jean Moulin. Lettres Actes du IVe Colloque International sur les bronzes antiques (1976) 187 Abb.5. Vermaseren, *CCCA* VI Nr. 377.

[24] Vermaseren, *CCCA* VII Nr. 108. Vasilev, Matrizen (*Anm.*7) 183 f. mit *Anm.*21.

[25] Naumann a.O. (*Anm.*14) Nr. 441 mit Lit. Zu Technik und Verbreitung s. Vasilev, Matrizen (*Anm.*7), 177 mit *Anm.*1.3.

[26] sog. Priesterkrone in Berlin mit Kybele- und Sabaziosrelief; Bronzetafel, abgebildet in den "Böttigerschen Papieren"; Vermaseren, *CCCA* III Nr. 304. Zu den Kästchen s. H. Buschhausen, Die spätrömischen Metallscrinia und frühchristlichen Reliquiare. Wiener Byzantinische Studien 9 (Wien – Köln – Graz, 1971).

[27] 6,7 x 5,2 cm, Silber. Treasures (*Anm.*6) Nr. 446. Vermaseren, *CCCA* VI Nr. 336 Taf.84.

[28] Sotheby's Antiquities, London 9, 12, 1985, Nr. 120.20 x 14 cm.

[29] Vermaseren, *CCCA* VI Nr. 338 Taf.85. Treasures (*Anm.*6) Nr. 453 Taf.62. Die im Naiskos stehende, eine Schlange fütternde Göttin auf einem Votivblech aus Tekija ist wahrscheinlich nicht Kybele, s. Vermaseren, *CCCA* VI Nr. 382 zu D. Mano-Zissi, Les trouvailles de Tekiya (Belgrad, 1957) 94 Nr. 34 Taf.23.

[30] Vermaseren, *CCCA* VI Nr. 204 mit Abb.10. Naumann a.O. (*Anm.*14) 229 ff. mit Parallelen zur Darstellung.

Löwenwagen lenkend dargestellt; Nike mit Kranz fliegt auf die Göttin zu, ein Stern im Halbmond ist in den Zwischenraum gesetzt. Das Bild wird von einem feinen Perl- und von einem Buckelkranz eingefaßt. Möglicherweise war auch das Bild der löwenreitenden Kybele auf dem Kölner Votiv von einem entsprechenden Perlkranz umgeben, von dem noch wenige Reste zu sehen sind. Mit dem Medaillon aus Olynth verbindet das Kölner Votivblech schließlich noch der Halbmond. Er ist für Kybele allerdings nicht charakteristisch, sondern findet sich eher bei Darstellungen, bei denen die Göttin synkretistisch mit anderen Gottheiten vermischt oder verbunden ist— etwa den Bronzematrizen in Sofia und in Paris und bei zwei Büsten- und einer Bendismatrize aus Abritus;[31] als Giebelspitze ziert er bei exvota den Naiskos der Donauländischen Göttertrias und den von Jupiter Dolichenus und Juno Regina und ist—mit Stern—über dem Naiskos des Sabazios zu sehen.[32] Bei zahlreichen der aquitanischen, Mars geweihten Votivblechen aus dem Hortfund von Hagenbach ist eine große Lunula ein wesentlicher Bestandteil des Votivs.[33]

Auch in Afrika war in römischer Zeit der Kult der Kybele verbreitet. Vielleicht besaß Kybele in Karthago am Tempel der Tanit/ Dea Caelestis, mit der sie auch gleichgesetzt wurde, ein Heiligtum.[34] Augustinus berichtet von Feiern am Tag der Lavatio der Berecynthia mater in Karthago.[35] Die in Afrika gefundenen Bildwerke der Kybele unterscheiden sich nicht von den römischen Kybelebildern in anderen Provinzen;[36] auf dem Löwen reitend ist die Göttin nur auf Mosaiken mit Zirkus-Darstellung und auf dem Spiegel kleiner Tonlampen

---

[31] Vasilev, Matrizen (*Anm.*7) Abb.19.27.13.14.5.

[32] G. Ristow, Festschrift für Klaus Wessel (1988) 237 ff. K. Gschwantler, Römisches Österreich 11/12, 1983/84 Taf.9 Abb.15. E. Schwertheim, Die Denkmäler orientalischer Gottheiten im römischen Deutschland. *EPRO* 40, (Leiden, 1974) Taf.106. Lunula und Stern sind über Nero-Helios zu sehen auf einem Goldplättchen aus Gorgippia, das als Teil eines Priesterdiadems gedeutet wird, s. Rome face aux Barbares. Centre Culturel Abbaye de Daoulas (1993) 130 Nr. 63.01. M. Almagro, Las necrópolis de Ampurias II (Barcelona, 1955) 199 f. Taf.XI. Zur Deutung s. auch E.N. Lane, Corpus Cultus Jovis Sabazii III, *EPRO* 100 (Leiden, 1989) 22.

[33] H. Bernhard, H.J. Engels, R. Engels u.R. Petrovszky, Der römische Schatzfund von Hagenbach (Mainz, 1990). So auch bei einem Votiv aus Thun-Allmendigen und einem Sabazios-Votiv aus Heddernheim, G. Behrens, Mainzer Zeitschrift 36, 1941, 18 Nr. 1 Abb.17,11 und Nr. 11 Abb.17,13.

[34] Roscher, Mytholog.Lexikon 2,2 Sp.2927 f. s.v. Meter. Metroon am Ostabhang der Byrsa in Karthago: Vermaseren, *CCCA* V 34 Nr. 92. Ein Heiligtum der Magna Mater ist in Mactar belegt.

[35] Augustinus, De civ. dei II 4.

[36] Vermaseren, *CCCA* V Nr. 34–154; auf dem Löwen: Nr. 56.57.60.62–71. 76.83.101.106.109–111.113.116.133.137.

dargestellt, deren Model wohl von Werkstatt zu Werkstatt getauscht oder verhandelt wurden.

Votiv an Fortuna-Tyche, Inv. RGM 90,514c (Abb. 1b). Erh. H. max. 6 cm, B. 5,1 cm. Das Blech ist oben und unten abgebrochen und an der linken. Seite der Göttin stark verletzt. Zwei zur Vorderseite durchgestochene Nagellöcher sitzen an der breitesten Stelle.

Es handelt sich um ein palmblattförmiges exvoto: der Naiskos in der Mitte ist beidseitig von aufsteigend geripptem Blech umgeben. Fortuna-Tyche steht frontal in einem Tempelchen, bekleidet mit einem langen Gewand und einem über die linke Schulter gelegten, um den Unterkörper geschlungenen Mantel. In der Rechten hält sie das auf eine Kugel gestützte Steuerruder, die Linke war vermutlich erhoben. Spuren eines Füllhorns sind nicht auszumachen.

"Toto quippe mundo et omnibus locis omnibusque horis omnium vocibus Fortuna sola invocatur ac nominatur, una accusatur, rea una agitur, una cogitatur, sola laudatur, sola arguitur et cum conviciis colitur: volubilis, a plerisque vero et caeca existimata, vaga, inconstans, incerta, varia, indignorumque fautrix, huic omnia expensa, huic omnia feruntur accepta, et in tota ratione mortalium sola utramque paginam facit, adeoque obnoxi sumus sorti, ut sors ipsa pro deo sit, qua deus probatur incertus." So beschreibt Plinius, n.h. II.V.22, Charakter und Wirken der Göttin Fortuna. Ihre Erscheinung in Rom charakterisiert Plutarch, de fortuna Romanorum 4: sie werde ohne Flügel, ohne Sandalen, ohne die unzuverlässige und instabile Kugel dargestellt, das Ruder, das sie führe, sei nicht doppelt. Und sie halte das berühmte Horn der Fülle in der Hand ...

Darstellungen der Fortuna (-Tyche) in ihren verschiedenen Aspekten finden sich häufig auf kaiserzeitlichen Münzen. Typische Münzen, auf denen das Bild der Göttin dem exvoto in Köln ähnelt, wenngleich die Göttin auf den Münzen den Kopf meist zur Seite gewandt hat, sind beispielsweise ein Sesterz Kaiser Vespasians mit Fortuna redux aus dem Jahr 71 n. Chr., ein Aureus des Nerva mit Fortuna Augusti von 96 n. Chr.,[37] Denare Hadrians wohl aus dem Jahre 118 n. Chr. und ephesische Goldprägungen desselben Kaisers, ein Denar des Antoninus Pius von 152/3 n. Chr., ein Aureus

---

[37] H. Mattingly – E.A. Sydenham u.a., The Roman Imperial Coinage (London, 1923 ff.) 422 var. J.P.C. Kent – B. Overbeck – A.U. Stylow, Die römische Münze (München, 1973) Nr. 230 R.H. Mattingly, Coins of the Roman Empire in the British Museum (London, 1923 ff.) III,5 Nr. 36 Taf.1,19.

des Severus Alexander aus dem Jahr 231 n. Chr., schließlich ein Antoninian des Postumus von 267 n. Chr.;[38] in Trier geprägte Folles für Constantius' Verteidigung der Rheingrenze im Jahre 299 n. Chr. und im Jahre 309/310 n. Chr. in Siscia ausgegebene Folles scheinen als letzte das Bild der Fortuna zu tragen.[39]

Silberne exvota für Fortuna-Tyche kennt man in größerer Zahl. Dem Kölner Votiv gleicht besonders das Votiv Inv. 2771 aus dem Depotfund von Tekiya:[40] auch hier ist der schlichte Naiskos von unregelmäßig gefälteltem Silberblech umgeben und das sehr gedrungene Götterbild, obwohl im Stil anders, hat die gleichen Attribute. Der Schatz von Weißenburg enthielt drei Votive an Fortuna, alle größer und mit ihren Palmblattaufsätzen auch reicher als die Votive in Köln und aus Tekiya; zweimal steht die Göttin mit Füllhorn und Steuerruder unter einer Bogenarkade, beim dritten Votiv ist zusätzlich das Glücksrad an ihrer Seite und die Göttin ist in einem Tempelchen mit teilweise tordierten Säulen und verziertem Giebelfeld dargestellt.[41] Auf dem sehr reichen Silberrelief aus Niederbieber stehen Fortuna und Mars, jede Gottheit in ihrer Aedikula, sozusagen als Bekräftigung über der zentralen Figur des Merkur,[42] auf dem Silbervotiv für die donauländische Göttertrias im Römisch-Germanischen Museum Köln schließlich nimmt Fortuna-Tyche zwischen Fisch, Hahn und Widderkopf das Giebelfeld ein.[43] Während der Widderkopf Sol, der Hahn Luna zuzuordnen sind, die die seitlichen Giebelakrotere bilden, darf man den Fisch wohl auf die im Hauptfeld stehende große Mutter beziehen: von den Matrizen aus Abritus geben zwei die Büste einer Göttin mit Fisch.[44] Die Nähe mag gleichwohl auch auf den Synkretismus der beiden schicksallenkenden und segenspendenden Göttinnen anspielen.[45]

---

[38] Mattingly a.O. III 262 Nr. 170 f. Tafel 50,8.9; 395 Nr. * Taf.75,2. IV 115 Nr. 791 Taf.16,17.VI 188 Nr. 739 Taf.25. A.S. Robertson, Roman Imperial Coins in the Hunter Coin Cabinet, University of Glasgow (Oxford, 1977 ff.) IV 92 Nr. 56 Taf.24.

[39] C.H.V. Sutherland, R.A.G. Carson, The Roman Imperial Coinage VI (London, 1967) 149.185.480.

[40] Mano-Zissi a.O. (Anm.29) Nr. 37 Taf.26.

[41] Kellner – Zahlhaas, Weißenburg 1993 (Anm.5) 67 ff. Nr. 35.36.37. Inv. 1981, 4366; 1981, 4367; 1981, 4369.

[42] P. La Baume, BJb 177, 1977, 567 Abb.2. Römer am Rhein. Ausstellung Köln 1967 (Köln, 1967) Nr. C 210.

[43] Ristow, a.O. (Anm.32).

[44] Vasilev, Matrizen (Anm.7) Abb.9.14.

[45] Ristow a.O. (Anm.32) 244.

Abb. 2

Formal ganz ähnlich ist schließlich die Fortuna auf dem Beschlagblech eines scrinium aus Trier, das ja auch technisch ähnlich gearbeitet ist.[46]

Fortuna-Tyche in ihren verschiedenen Aspekten wurde von Einzel-
personen, den unterschiedlichsten Personenkreisen und Körperschaften
angerufen; auffällig zahlreich sind Weihungen des Militärs und—
zusammen mit Merkur—von Gewerbetreibenden; die Verehrung läßt
sich nicht auf bestimmte Regionen eingrenzen. Für Afrika sei nur an
den Fortuna-Tempel in Thugga und an die Tyche neben Jupiter-
Septimius Severus und Juno-Julia Domna am Tetrapylon von Leptis
Magna erinnert.

Votive mit Trias, Inv. RGM 90,514d,e (Abb. 2). Inv. 90,514d:
erh. H. 6,5 cm, B. 9,6 cm, beide oberen und die rechte untere Ecke
bestoßen, mehrere Risse. Zwei Nagellöcher unten erhalten.

Inv. 90,514e: erh. H. 6,3 cm, B. 9,8 cm, beide oberen und die
rechte untere Ecke bestoßen, tiefer Riß an der mittleren Aedikula.
Links oben ein Nagelloch neben einem ausgerissenen Nagelloch, links
unten ein weiteres.

---

[46] Buschhausen a.O. (*Anm.*26) 49 f. Nr. *A* 18. Siehe auch S. 77 Nr. 36, Beschlag
mit frontal stehender Fortuna.

Das Silberblech ist durch drei Aedikulen gegliedert, die Stützen bilden glatte Säulen mit nicht ausgearbeitetem Kapitell, die beiden äußeren Giebel haben glatte Simen und Geisa, beim mittleren bilden Zweige das Gebälk.

In der linken Aedikula steht Merkur, nackt bis evtl. auf ein Schultermäntelchen, den Petasos auf dem Kopf, einen Beutel in der rechten Hand, den Caduceus im linken angewinkelten Arm.

Die mittlere Aedikula nimmt eine stehende, langgewandete Frau mit Kopfbedeckung ein. In der erhobenen linken Hand hält sie einen Stab mit knospenartigem Ende, die rechte ist gesenkt, ein Attribut nicht auszumachen. Zu Füßen der Stehenden befinden sich zwei Gegenstände, links ein Zylinder mit zugespitztem Aufsatz, rechts ein spindelartiger Gegenstand.

In der rechten Aedikula schließlich steht ein bärtiger Gott mit Modius und einem kurzen, geschürzten Gewand; ein Mantel fällt ihm von der Schulter bis zu den Waden. Der Gott hält links ein Zepter mit Knauf; an seiner rechten Seite steht ein zylindrischer Gegenstand mit Querholm, wohl ein Altar.

Silbervotivplättchen an mehrere Gottheiten sind nicht selten. Erwähnt wurde bereits das Votiv aus Niederbieber mit zwei kleinen Aedikulen für Tyche und Mars über einer größeren für Merkur.[47] Zwei Aedikulen nebeneinander weisen auch eine Matrize aus Abritus und eine Matrize in Sofia auf; bei ersterer steht Juno-Hera neben Jupiter-Zeus, bei der anderen thront Kybele neben Artemis-Luna, doch konnten über dieser Matrize evtl. auch unabhängige Einzelvotive gepreßt werden.[48] Mindestens zwei Aedikulen zeigte ein fragmentarisch erhaltenes Votiv, das 1789 mit weiteren 50–60 Fragmenten in einer Urne bei Stony Stratford gefunden wurde.[49] Auf der linken Seite sieht man Mars mit Helm, Rüstung und Stiefeln, in der Rechten den Speer, die Linke auf einem Schild; in der anderen Aedikula ist an Flügeln, Palmzweig und wehendem Gewand Victoria zu erkennen. Drei Naiskoi nebeneinander sind schließlich auf einem Goldplättchen aus Ratiaria eingepreßt.[50] Die darin stehenden Personen—zwei weiblich, eine männlich—sind nicht zu benennen, da Attribute fehlen. Neben-

---

[47] s. *Anm.*42.

[48] Vasilev, Matrizen (*Anm.*7) Abb.4.19.

[49] H.B. Walters, Catalogue of the Silver Plate, Greek, Etruscan and Roman in the British Museum (London, 1921) S. 63 Nr. 239.

[50] Vasilev, Matrices (*Anm.*23) 189 mit Abb.9.

einandergereiht findet man Aedikulen auch auf scrinia-Blechen: der bereits genannte Beschlag aus Trier zeigt Apollo, Bacchus, Fortuna, Mercur und Jupiter oder Poseidon, ein jeder in seinem Tempelchen.[51] Und bei einem Beschlagblech aus Mathay in Saint-Germain-en-Laye ist der mittlere Giebel über der Mänade spitz, während Bacchus und Mars rechts und links unter Perlbandbögen stehen.[52]

Bei anderen Votiven sind mehrere Gottheiten in einem Tempel vereint, so bei zwei Votiven aus dem Schatzfund von Weißenburg Minerva, Merkur und Apollo,[53] auf einem Votiv aus London-Moorgate drei Matronen.[54] Eine Regel für die Zusammenstellung bestimmter Gottheiten läßt sich bei Votiven aus so unterschiedlichen Regionen natürlich nicht feststellen, es wird sich jeweils um lokale Kultgemeinschaften handeln. Eine Deutung der Dreiergruppe auf den neuen Kölner Votiven kann also nur von der Ikonographie der Dargestellten ausgehend, versucht werden.

Leicht identifiziert werden kann Merkur in der linken Aedikula. Bis auf die Kopfflügel statt des Petasos ist er auf dem Votiv aus Niederbieber in gleicher Weise dargestellt,[55] Petasos mit Kopfflügeln hat er auf drei Votiven aus Weißenburg[56] und einem aus Tekiya,[57] ohne Petasos zeigt ihn schließlich eine Matrize aus Kravenik bei Veliko Tarnovo.[58] Ziegenbock und Hahn fehlen allerdings auf den Votiven in Köln.[59]

Den Gott in der rechten Aedikula charakterisieren Bart, kurzes Gewand und Kopfbedeckung. Bei Mars, bei dem unter den Pteryges des Panzers stets das kurze Gewand sichtbar wird, würde man Helm und Schild erwarten—wie beispielsweise bei den Votiven aus Barkway, Stony Stratford, Niederbieber und Weißenburg.[60] Vulkan trägt auf

[51] Buschhausen a.O. (*Anm.*26) 49 f. Nr. A 18.

[52] ebd.171 Nr. A 106.

[53] Kellner – Zahlhaas a.O. (*Anm.*5) 71 Nr. 29; 30 Taf.57; 58.

[54] R. Merrifield, The Roman City of London (London, 1965) Taf.89. London in Roman Times (London, 1930) 47 Taf.20. M. Green, The Religions of Civilian Roman Britain. A Corpus of Religious Material from the Civilian Areas of Roman Britain. (Oxford, 1976) Taf.XVIb.

[55] s. *Anm.*42.

[56] Kellner – Zahlhaas a.O. (*Anm.*5) 71 f. Nr. 29.30.31.

[57] Inv.2773. Mano – Zissi a.O. (*Anm.*29) 106 Nr. 39. Taf.27.

[58] Vasilev, Matrizen (*Anm.*7) 180 Nr. 20 Abb.20.

[59] Auf den scrinia-Blechen sind sie Attribut des Gottes, vgl. Buschhausen a.O. (*Anm.*26) Nr. A 18.A 19.A 65.

[60] Walters a.O. (*Anm.*49) 59 ff. Nr. 231–234.237.239–241. BJb 177, 1977, 567 Abb.2. Kellner – Zahlhaas a.O. (*Anm.*5) 76. Nr. 39. Auf scrinia-Beschlägen: Busch-

Votiven aus Barkway zum kurzen Gewand den lang herabfallenden
Mantel, dazu aber einen spitzen Pilos, Zange und Hammer—kein
Zepter mit Knauf.[61] Jupiter Dolichenus ist entweder bis auf den Mantel
nackt, trägt auch keine Kopfbedeckung und hält außer dem Zepter
das Blitzbündel—so auf drei Votiven aus Heddernheim[62]—oder er
wird in orientalischer Art auf dem Stier stehend mit Labrys und Blitzbündel wiedergeben.[63] Den—bartlosen—Gott in Panzer und kurzem
Gewand auf einem Votiv aus Pessinus deutet Walters als Mithras;[64]
Mithras zeichnen außerdem die Hosen aus, die man auch bei Sabazios
auf einem Votiv aus Ampurias sieht.[65] Sarapis schließlich, zu dem
der Modius paßt, ist in der Regel mit langem Chiton, selten nur mit
Himation wiedergegeben—nicht aber in kurzem Gewand.[66] Die ge-
nannten Götter wurden in Afrika mehr oder weniger stark verehrt,
vielfach mit einheimischen Gottheiten identifiziert oder an sie angeglichen;[67] die nicht übermäßig stark belegte Verehrung der orientalischen
Gottheiten nahm nach der Stationierung römischer Soldaten zu.[68]
Einen Hinweis darauf, daß in dem Gott in der rechten Aedikula

---

hausen a.O. (*Anm.*26) Nr. A 21.A 65.A 106. Der sitzende Mars kann hier außer
Betracht bleiben, vgl. J. Werner, Die beiden Zierscheiben des Thorsberger Moor-
fundes (Berlin, 1941) Taf.8. Ders., Germania 27, 1943, 96 f. Taf.22. s. auch
G. Bauchhenß, LIMC II,1, 1984 s.v. Ares/Mars III.

[61] Walters a.O. (*Anm.*49) 61 f. Nr. 235.236.

[62] Schwertheim a.O. (*Anm.*32) Nr. 78.81.82.

[63] ebd. Nr. 80. Noll a.O. (*Anm.*5) Nr. 7.

[64] Walters a.O. (*Anm.*49) 58 Nr. 229. Toynbee a.O. (*Anm.*5) 135 stellt ihn neben
den Kriegsgott von Palmyra.

[65] Almagro a.O. (*Anm.*32) 199 f. Taf.XI. E.N. Lane – M.J. Vermaseren, Corpus
Cultus Jovis Sabazii, II *EPRO* 100 (Leiden 1989) 85. Zu Kultgemeinschaften s.
Lane (*Anm.*32) 13 ff.

[66] W. Hornbostel, Sarapis *EPRO* 32 (Leiden, 1973) passim. z.B. auf goldenen
Votivblechen aus Douch/Oase Khargeh, M. Reddé, Le trésor de Douch. Comptes
rendus des seances de l'Académie des Inscriptions et Belle lettres 1989, 428–445.

[67] G.-Ch. Picard, Les religions de l'Afrique Antique (1954). s. dazu M. le Glay,
Les syncrétismes dans l'Afrique ancienne in: F. Dunand – P. Lêvêque, Les syncrétismes
dans les religions de l'antiquité, *EPRO* 46 (1975) 123 ff. Cicero, de natura deorum
1,84, sagt in bezug auf Vulcan: "ut primum, quot hominum linguae, tot nomina
deorum: non enim, ut tu Vellaius quocumque veneris, sic idem in Italia Volcanus,
idem in Africa, indem in Hispania. Lane (*Anm.*32) 39.

[68] M. Leglay, Les religions orientales dans l'Afrique ancienne. in: Les Confér-
ences visites du Musée Stephane Gsell (Paris 1956). Jupiter Dolichenus in Afrika:
M. Hörig – E. Schwertheim, Corpus Cultus Iovis Dolicheni, *EPRO* 106 (Leiden,
1987) Nr. 615–631. Mithras in Afrika: M.J. Vermaseren, Corpus Inscriptionum at
Monumentorum Religionis Mithriacae (The Hague 1956) 87–98. Zu Sabazios:
R. Fellmann, Der Sabazios-Kult. in: Die orientalischen Religionen im Römerreich,
EPRO 93 (Leiden, 1981) 316 ff.

Abb. 3

evtl. Ba'al-Saturn gesehen wurde (z.B. die Harpe), gibt es m.E. bei der Darstellung nicht.[69]

Die Göttin in der mittleren Aedikula ist durch das Knospenzepter, vielleicht auch den Giebelschmuck aus Blattreihen als Vegetations- oder Fruchtbarkeitsgöttin charakterisiert. Mit dem sog. Tannzweig- muster gegliederte Giebelgeisa sind bei den Votivblechen nun nicht selten, sie kommen sowohl an der Aedikula des Mars auf einem Votiv aus Barkway und an Votiven aus Tekiya wie auch an Matrizen aus Thessaloniki, Razgrad und Abritus vor, und auch eine Tonmatrize aus Montana hat diese Geisonzier.[70] Ein richtiger Blattschmuck ziert die Giebel der Naiskai von Hygieia und Diana bei goldenen Votiven aus Germisara/Geoagion und den Grottenrand der Mithrashöhle auf einem versilberten Bronzevotiv aus Stockstadt, was F. Drexel als In- diz für pannonische Herkunft wertet;[71] bei dem scrinium aus Kai- seraugst sind die Bögen über Minerva und Mercur mit Blattreihen geschmückt.[72]

Erkennt man in der Kopfbedeckung einen Helm, so sprechen doch das Fehlen von Aegis mit Gorgoneion, die deutlich als Knospe, nicht als Spitze ausgebildete Bekrönung des Stabes und die geringe Größe des freilich schildartig gewölbten Gegenstandes zur Linken der Ste- henden gegen eine Deutung als Minerva.

Vom Bild der langgewandeten Frau mit Knospenzepter ausge- hend, ist eine auch nur einigermaßen begründbare Identifikation mit Juno, Ceres, Ops, Caelestis, Tanit oder Astarte nicht möglich. Auch die Göttinnen auf zwei goldenen exvota ehemals Sammlung L. Pol- lak—die eine mit Zepter im rankengeschmückten Naiskos, die andere evtl. mit Füllhorn und pilosartiger Kopfbedeckung—sind nicht zu benennen.[73]

---

[69] M. Leglay, Saturne Africain I.II (Paris 1961.1966) *passim*.

[70] Walters a.O. (*Anm.*49) 59 Nr. 232. Mano-Zissi a.O. (*Anm.*29) Nr. 34 Taf.23, Nr. 35 Taf.24. Vermaseren (*Anm.*16), *CCCA* VI Nr. 198. W. Gerassimowa-Tomawa, Beitrag zur thrakischen Religion und Ethnographie, Dritter internationaler thrakolog. Kongreß I (1984) 286 Abb.3. Vasilev, Matrizen (*Anm.*7) Abb.4.6.9–11.13.14. L. Ognenova-Marinova, Un atelier plastes imagenarius à Montana. Recherches sur la Culture en Mésie et en Thrace. Bulletin de l'institut d'archéologie 37, 1987, 173 ff. Abb.5.

[71] Goldhelm, Schwert und Silberschätze. Reichtümer aus 6000 Jahren Rumäni- scher Vergangenheit. Ausstellung Frankfurt 1994 (Frankfurt a.M., 1994) 217 f. Nr. 87.1 und 2. Schwertheim, Denkmäler a.O. (*Anm.*32) Nr. 117g. F. Drexel in: W. Schleiermacher, Germania 12, 1928, 54, *Anm.*8.

[72] Buschhausen a.O. (*Anm.*26) Nr. A 19.

[73] L. Pollak, Catalogo della Collezione oggetti di scavo del fu Prof. P. Sarti (Rom 1906) Nr. 260.261.

Votive an Minerva, Inv. RGM 90,514a; 9,514f; 90,514g (Abb. 3).
Inv. 90,514a, H. 8,3 cm, B. 5,4 cm. Oben links und unten beidseitig
Verletzungen, quer gerissen. Das Votiv war möglicherweise ursprünglich mit vier Nägeln in den Ecken befestigt; das unregelmäßige Loch
unten in der Mitte könnte von einer zweiten Befestigung, nachdem
die seitlichen Löcher ausgerissen waren, stammen.
Inv. 90,514f, H. 7,4 cm, B. 5,7 cm. Oben links und unten beidseitig beschädigt, links oben ein kleines und ein großes Nagelloch,
rechts oben und in Höhe des Schriftfeldes ein Befestigungsloch.
Inv. 90,514g, H. 7,6 cm, B. 5,4 cm. Oben links, rechte Kante
und rechte u. linke untere Ecke beschädigt. Das Nagelloch links oben
ausgerissen und durch ein etwas tiefer angebrachtes ersetzt, das Nagelloch unten links zur Vorderseite durchstoßen.
Die drei Votive zeigen dieselbe Darstellung: eine Büste der Minerva.
Die Göttin hat auf dem lang herabfallenden Haar einen Helm mit
Helmbusch und ist in ein faltenreiches Ärmelgewand gekleidet, über
dem sie die Aegis mit Gorgoneion trägt. Neben dem Kopf sind beidseitig ein sechsstrahliger Stern über einem Halbmond zu sehen. Unter
der Büste sitzt ein bei allen drei Votiven leeres Schriftfeld.
Durch Helm und Gorgoneion ist Minerva, deren Bild dem der
Athena angeglichen wurde, leicht zu identifizieren. Unter den bekannten Silbervotiven ist nur eines mit ihrem Bild: ein Votiv aus dem
Tempel—einem Dolichenus-Heiligtum—in Maiden Castle, Dorches-
ter.[74] Es zeigt ein Gesamtbild der Göttin: Minerva mit Helm, Speer,
Schild und Aegis mit Gorgoneion steht frontal in einem abgegrenz-
ten Feld. An der Basis meint C.D. Drew einen Inschriftenrest zu
erkennen. Danebenzustellen ist eine 11 cm hohe, 1 cm dicke Bron-
zeplatte der Sammlung H. Scheufelen, "wohl zur Herstellung von
Silberreliefs", wie G. Hafner schreibt.[75]
Silbervotive mit Büsten sind relativ häufig belegt, so ein rundes
Votiv aus Pessinus mit Sol-Büste im Perlkranz, bekrönt von einem
"Palmblatt", ein rechteckiges Votiv mit Zeus/Jupiter-Büste im Medail-
lon und ein palmblattförmiges Votiv mit Selene/Luna-Büste aus
Tekiya sowie Votive mit Luna—und mit Venusbüste aus Vichy.[76]

---

[74] Toynbee, a.O. (*Anm.*5) 138 Nr. 22 mit *Anm.*26. A.B. Cook, Zeus III,2 (Cambridge, 1940) 1098 Abb.877. Green (*Anm.*54) 276 Taf.VIII h.
[75] G. Hafner, Die Bronzen der Sammlung H. Scheufelen (Mainz, 1958) Nr. 415.
[76] Walters a.O. (*Anm.*49) 58 Nr. 228 Abb.66. Mano-Zissi a.O. (*Anm.*29) Nr. 36
Taf.25 und Nr. 38 Taf.27. Corrocher a.O. (*Anm.*5).

Dazu kommen mehrere Matrizen mit Büsten einer Göttin, meist im Epiphaniegestus, aus Abritus.[77]

Gerade Minerva wurde auch in anderen Gattungen oft zur Büste verkürzt, so an Gerätschmuck, als Zierknopf, Möbelzier oder Messergriff.[78] Dem stark schematisierten, vereinfachten Bild kommt das Brustbild der Roma auf Kontorniaten noch am nächsten, wobei Roma manchmal mit Aegis, manchmal mit nackter Brust abgebildet wurde[79]. Die Bedeutung von Mond und Stern neben Minerva bleibt unklar, Parallelen wurden bei dem Kybele-Votiv genannt. Die Gestirne könnten als allgemeines Zeichen der Göttlichkeit oder der aeternitas gewertet werden, doch steht ein Beweis dafür noch aus.[80]

Datierung und Einordnung

Kybele-, Fortuna/Tyche- und das Merkurbild der Trias-Votive gehen auf Bildformen zurück, die im Hellenismus geschaffen wurden oder sich verfestigt haben und die, mehr oder weniger abgewandelt, bis in die Spätantike für kleinere Götterbilder—insbesondere an Gerät—beibehalten wurden.[81] Anders die Minerva-Votive. Vergröberungen wie die rudimentäre Form des Helmes, das unförmige Gesicht mit den hervorquellenden Augen, der großen Nase und dem nur als Kerbe angegebenen Mund, die abrupte Abkürzung von Körper

---

[77] Vasilev, Matrizen (*Anm.*7) Abb.8.9.10.11.12.13.14.23 (aus Opaka).

[78] A. Leibundgut, Die römischen Bronzen der Schweiz II. Avenches (Mainz, 1976) Nr. 71. III Westschweiz, Bern und Wallis (Mainz, 1980) Nr. 110. G. Faider-Feytmans, Les bronzes romains de Belgique (Mainz, 1979) Nr. 251–253.283. H. Menzel, Die römischen Bronzen aus Deutschland. I. Speyer (Mainz, 1960) Nr. 55. II. Trier (1966) Nr. 183e. III. Bonn (Mainz 1986) Nr. 207.218.312.314.332.337.371. R. Fleischer, Die römischen Bronzen aus Österreich (Mainz, 1967) Nr. 27–35. H. Rolland, Bronzes antiques de haute provence (Paris, 1965) Nr. 72.73.

[79] B. Kleer, Roma auf Kontorniaten, in: Spätantike und frühes Christentum. Ausstellung Frankfurt 1984 (Frankfurt, 1984) S. 70 ff.

[80] Mond und Stern erscheinen beispeilsweise auf der Rückseite hadrianischer Münzen, s. Mattingly a.O. (*Anm.*37) Taf.55,13.14.15; 57,1.2; 70,6, dazu S. CXXXVI.CLV. Ein Stern ist auch auf der "Begrüßungsszene" zwischen Mann und Frau auf einem Kastenblech aus Trier dargestellt, s. Menzel a.O. (*Anm.*78) Trier, Nr. 298 Taf.95.

[81] Bestes Beispiel für diese Kontinuität sind die kleinen Medaillons mit Büsten paganer Gottheiten an den sog. Hochzeitsgürteln, wohl des 6. oder 7. Jhs. n. Chr., vgl. M.C. Ross, Catalogue of the byzantine and early medieval antiquities in the Dumbarton Oaks Collection II (Washington, 1956) 37 ff. Nr. 38 Taf.30–32 mit Zeit- und Stildiskussion.

und Armen sind vor dem 4. Jahrhundert nur im 'barbarischen' provinziellen Kunsthandwerk denkbar.[82] Ähnliche Stilmerkmale weisen dann die Athena auf einem Goldarmband im Metropolitan Museum of Art oder die Büsten und Gorgoneia auf Beschlagblechen des 4. Jahrhunderts auf.[83] So ist anzunehmen, daß die Kybele-, Fortuna-Tyche- und Trias-Votive nach hellenistisch-römischen Vorbildern, die Minerva-Votive als eigene Schöpfung eines provinziellen Handwerkers vielleicht im 3. Jahrhundert entstanden sind.[84]

Die silbernen Votivbilder stehen in einer langen Tradition, frühe Belege sind freilich nur schwer greifbar. Ob die ausgeschnittenen und gravierten Bronzeplättchen aus dem Hermesheiligtum Kato Symi/ Symi Viannou auf Kreta bereits dazu zu rechnen sind, muß offen bleiben.[85] Silberne Blechvotive sind aber sicherlich in einer attischen Inschrift aus der 1. Hälfte des 2. Jahrhunderts v. Chr. gemeint, die G. Hirschfeld besprochen hat:[86] es wurde der Antrag gestellt, die "Typoi" des "Heros Jatros" einzuschmelzen und daraus eine Oinochoe zu gießen. Aus den Gewichtsangaben vermutet Hirschfeld, daß es sich bei den "Typoi" um gepreßte Gliedmaßen, wohl auf Silberblech, gehandelt hat. Eine Vorstellung von deren Aussehen vermitteln, neben den Augenvotiven aus Mesembria, vielleicht die 57 Gold- und 20 Silbervotive ehemals Sammlung L. Pollak, die stilisierte Augen, Brüste und Gesichter wiedergeben.[87] In ihrer Nachfolge stehen die

---

[82] Age of spirituality. Hrsg. von K. Weitzmann (New York, 1979) 181 Nr. 160. Romans and barbarians. Museum of Fine Arts Boston (Boston, 1976) 70 Nr. 95. M. Vilimkova, Roman art in Africa (Boston, 1963) Nr. 33–36.

[83] Romans and barbarians 182 Nr. 205. Buschhausen a.O. (*Anm.*26) Nr. A 9.A 33.A 50.A 60.A 61 s. auch A 82 mit Porträts.

[84] Diskussion der Zeitstellung der wenigen Stücke mit bekanntem Fundzusammenhang: Toynbee a.O. (*Anm.*5) 144. Toynbee kommt zu dem Schluß, daß die bei ihr aufgeführten Votive nicht genauer eingeordnet werden können als 2.–3. Jahrhundert n. Chr., das grobe Minerva-Votiv aus Maiden Castle jedoch in der 2. Hälfte des 4. Jahrhunderts entstanden ist. Möglicherweise wurden die Votive in verschiedenen Werkstätten hergestellt.

[85] J.A. Sakellarakis, Museum Heraklion. Illustrierter Führer (Athen 1979) 106 f. Kellner und Zahlhaas a.O. (*Anm.*5) 69 rechnen silberne Idole des 2. Jahrtausends aus Kleinasien und urartäische Bronzebleche mit vereinfachten Menschenbildern zu den frühen Votiven.

[86] G. Hirschfeld, Hermes 8, 1874, 350 ff. Zur Praxis, Weihegaben einzuschmelzen s. Decret CIG II² 839 und B.D. Meritt, Hesperia 16, 1947, 164 ff. Nr. 64; ders., Hesperia 32, 1963, 33 ff. Nr. 32. Der Thesauros faßt "Typos" weit: "itidem = 'Typos' in numo argenteo aureove dicitur Nofa quae impressa est." Moderne Beispiele s. W.H.D. Rouse, Greek Votive Offerings (Cambridge, 1902) 237.

[87] s.o. *Anm.*17. Pollak a.O. (*Anm.*73) Nr. 252.254. Weitere Augenvotive z.B. Dieux guérisseurs (*Anm.*5); Fauduet (*Anm.*5).

modernen Gliedervotive, die insbesondere R. Kriss aus den unterschiedlichsten Ländern, besonders mit katholischer und orthodoxer Bevölkerung, gesammelt hat:[88] Augen, Arme, Lungen, Beine, andere Körperteile, für deren Heilung der Gläubige Dank aussprach.

Auf Votive mit dem Bild der Gottheit bezieht R. Noll die Inschrift auf einem Altar aus dem Tempel der Noreia im Glantal:[89] der Decurio der ala I Thracum, G. Fabius Modestus aus Rom, hat der Noreia Augusta eine Silberschale im Gewicht von 2 1/3 Pfund und "emblemata Noreiae aurea uncias duas" geweiht. Es sei in diesem Zusammenhang daran erinnert, daß auch die Votive aus Allmendingen bei Thun, Innichen, Carnuntum, Wroxeter und einige Votive aus Mesembria aus Goldblech sind.[90] Drei Inschriften aus Afrika nennen schließlich eine palma argentea:[91] zwei der silbernen Votive offensichtlich in Form eines Palmzweiges wurden in Henchir Kasbat Saturn, ein weiteres in Maxula Aesculap geweiht. Das Wort "palma" ist dabei eine treffende Beschreibung für Votive wie insbesondere Nr. 38 und Nr. 39 aus Tekiya,[92] kann aber natürlich auch auf Votive bezogen werden, die wie die Dolichenus-Bleche aus Mauer an der Url einen "lilienförmigen"[93] oder noch stärker differenzierten Abschluß haben.[94]

---

[88] Wallfahrt kennt keine Grenzen. Katalog der Ausstellung im Bayerischen Nationalmuseum München (München, 1984) 31 Nr. 23a.e.f.k.m.t.u. L. Kriss-Rettenbeck, Bilder und Zeichen religiösen Volksglaubens (München, 1963) Abb.386.388.389.

[89] R. Noll, ÖJh 38, 1950, Beibl. 142 (*CIL* III,4806). Emblema bedeutet nach dem Thesauros Linguae Latinae freilich in der Regel "de figuris et ornamentis argenteis (aureis) in vase quolibet illigatis".

[90] ebd. S. 135. R. Lunz, Urgeschichte des Oberpustertales (Bozen, 1977) Abb.55. R. Noll, Eine goldene Votivgabe für Sol aus Carnuntum. Römisches Österreich. Jahresschriften der Österreichischen Gesellschaft für Archäologie 3, 1975, 167 ff. Painter, Wroxeter (*Anm.*12) 329 ff. Treasures (*Anm.*6).

[91] Inscr.Lat.Afr.256, aus Henchir Kasbat, im Bardo-Museum. Weihgeschenk an Saturn: palma argentea im Wert von * XXV. Inscr.Lat.Tunesien 709, aus Henchir Kasbat. Weihgeschenk an Saturn: palma argentea im Wert von * X. Inscr.Lat.Tunesien 868, Maxula (Radès). Weihgeschenk an Aesculap: palma argentea. s. auch F. Baratte, Les trésors de temples dans le monde romain in: Ecclesiastical silver plate in sixth century Byzantium, hrsg. von S. Boy u.M. Mundell Mango (Washington, 1993) 114 mit *Anm.*37. François Baratte, Paris, danke ich für diese Angaben.

[92] Mano-Zissi a.O. (*Anm.*29) Nr. 38.39.

[93] Noll, Mauer an der Url a.O. (*Anm.*5) Taf.20.21. Zur Formdiskussion s. R. Noll, ÖJh. 38, 1950 Beiblatt 126 ff.

[94] Als "Siegeszeichen" war der Palmzweig auch im christlichen Kult und sogar der kaiserlichen Repräsentation ein geeignetes Geschenk, s. Toynbee a.O. (*Anm.*5) 144.146 mit Hinweis auf das Insignienbild des Comes sacrarum largitionum in den Notitia Dignitatum, B. Overbeck, Argentum Romanum (München, 1973) 57.

Abb. 4

Der uralte Brauch wurde bruchlos in den christlichen Kult hinu-
bergetragen, wie nicht nur Theodoret von Kyros und Paulinus von
Nola bezeugen,[95] sondern in frühchristlicher Zeit auch der Schatzfund
von Water Newton[96] und eine Gruppe von Votiven aus Syrien in
der Walters Art Gallery belegen.[97] Die Votivgaben des 17.–20. Jahrhunderts sind noch in vielen orthodoxen und katholischen Kirchen,
insbesondere in Griechenland, Italien und Lateinamerika zu sehen
(Abb. 4). Form und Darstellung haben sich nur wenig gewandelt.
Dominierten—soweit die geringe Materialbasis solche Aussagen über-
haupt zuläßt—in der römischen Antike palma-förmige Votive, Votive
mit dem Namen der Gottheit und des Stifters[98] und Bleche mit dem
Bild der Gottheit vor Votivblechen mit Körperteil oder Adoranten,
so sind unter den neuzeitlichen Votiven solche mit dem Abbild oder
Symbol des Gegenstandes, für den eine Gunst erbeten oder Dank
gesagt wird, besonders häufig (Körperteil, Baby, Person, Tier, Auto).
Sie alle können durch ein Herz als allgemeine Dankesgabe vertreten
werden. Votive mit Maria und Kind sind vergleichsweise selten.[99]

Die Karte (Abb. 5) gibt—ohne zeitliche Differenzierung—die Fund-
orte der mir bekannten Votivbleche. Die Fundpunkte belegen natürlich
nicht die Verbreitung der Votive, sondern vielmehr Ausgrabungs-,
Konservierungs- und Publikationsstand. Es bleibt jedoch auffällig, wie
bereits J. Toynbee betonte,[100] daß die palma-förmigen römischen
Votive überwiegend aus den Provinzen mit keltisch durchmischter
Bevölkerung stammen und sich in Gebieten, in denen Truppen sta-
tioniert waren, häufen. Die Hinzunahme der vorrömischen und der
christlichen Votive, der Model sowie der literarischen Belege modi-
fiziert dieses Bild. Hinzu kommt, daß viele Votive offensichtlich nicht
"im Tempelschatz" am Ort, an dem man sie stiftete, gefunden wurden,
sondern als Beutegut weit verschleppt.[101] Die meisten Votive fanden

---

[95] Theodoret von Kyros, Graec.affec.cur.8,64. Paulinus von Nola, Carmen XIV,
Corpus scriptorum ecclesiasticorum latinorum (1866–) 30.7.

[96] Painter, Water Newton (*Anm*.12) Nr. 10–27.

[97] G. Vikan, Byzantine pilgrimage art. Dumbarton Oaks 1982, 45 mit Abb.38.
Mundell Mango, Silver (*Anm*.12) 240 ff. Nr. 71.72.

[98] Auffällig bei den Schatzfunden von Vichy, Hagenbach und auch Mauer an
der Url, s. F. Baratte, Le trésor d'argenterie gallo-romaine de Notre-dame – D'Allen-
con (Paris, 1981) Taf.38; Bernhard – Engels – Engels a.O. (*Anm*.33); Noll a.O.
(*Anm*.5).

[99] Wallfahrt a.O. (*Anm*.88) 159 f. Nr. 233.234 (Mariazeller Muttergottes).

[100] Toynbee a.O. (*Anm*.5) 143.

[101] Bernhard – Engels – Engels a.O. (*Anm*.33).

sich in Schatz- oder Hortfunden, manche als Streufunde, wenige lassen sich einem Heiligtum zuordnen.[102] Nur das goldene Votiv von Innichen stammt vermutlich aus einem Privathaus,[103] die beiden versilberten Bronzeplatten von Ampurias aus einem Brandgrab.[104] Für die Matrizen aus Abritus ist eine Werkstatt als Fundort wahrscheinlich, ein Nachweis liegt jedoch nicht vor.[105] Der Erhaltungszustand der Votive in Köln—insbesondere die ausgerissenen Nagellöcher und die Ersatzlöcher für eine zweite Verwendung—lassen darauf schließen, daß sie aus einem Heiligtum stammen, vielleicht einer Tempelanlage, die von Kultstätten anderer Gottheiten umgeben war.[106]

---

[102] Am klarsten Mesembria und Germisara, sicher Alésia, Stockstadt, Mauer an der Url und Carnuntum, wahrscheinlich Bewcastle, Maiden Castle, Vichy, Weißenburg und Pessinus, vielleicht auch Barkway. S. auch Toynbee a.O. (*Anm.*5) 143.

[103] Lunz a.O. (*Anm.*90).

[104] Almagro a.O. (*Anm.*32) 199 f. Abb.1.2 und Taf.XI.

[105] Vasilev, Matrizen (*Anm.*7) 177. G.I. Kazarov, AA 37, 1922, 187 ff.

[106] Viele der geschlossenen Funde von Votivblechen enthalten Votive an verschiedene Gottheiten, bei denen keine ausgeprägte Kultgemeinschaft nachgewiesen ist, z.B. Barkway: Mars und Vulkan; Stony Stratford: Jupiter, Vulkan, Apollo, Mars, Victoria; Vichy: Jupiter, Sabzios; Weißenburg: Apollo, Minerva, Merkur, Fortuna, Mars, Herkules, Luna, Victoria, Genius; Mauer an der Url: Jupiter Dolichenus, Herkules.

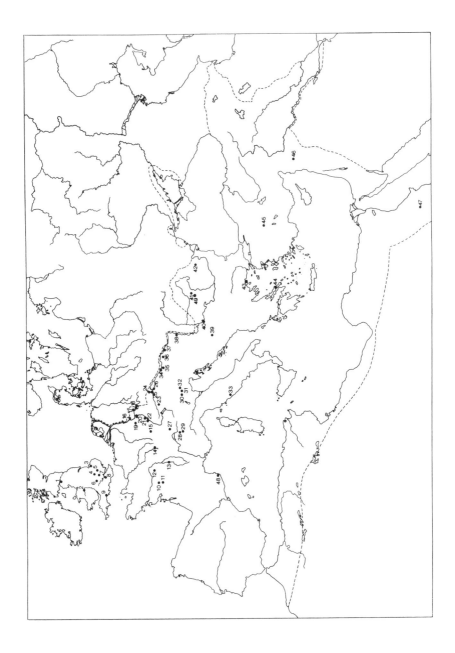

Legende zur Karte

1 Bewcastle
2 Wroxeter
3 Water Newton
4 Godmanchester
5 Cavenham Heath
6 Stony Stradford
7 Barkway
8 London
9 Maiden Castle
10 Notre Dame d'Allençon
11 Antigny
12 Pouille
13 Vichy
14 Alesia/Alise Sainte Reine
15 Deneuvre
16 Niederbiber
17 Heddernheim
18 Stockstadt
19 Dhronecken
20 Kleinwinternheim
21 Neupfotz (Rheinzabern)
22 Hagenbach
23 Isny
24 Weißenburg
25 Kastell Böhming
26 Kastell Eining
27 Thun-Allmendingen
28 Martigny
29 Großer St. Bernhard
30 Mechel/Valemporga di Meclo
31 Sanzeno
32 Innichen/San Candido
33 Vicarello
34 Linz a.d. Donau
35 St. Margarethen i. Lavanttal
36 Mauer a.d. Url
37 Carnuntum
38 Adony
39 Ilidze bei Sarajevo
40 Tekiya
41 Apulum
42 Barboşi
43 Mesembria
44 Eretria
45 Pessinus
46 Ma'arat en Norman
47 Douch/Oase Khargeh
48 Ampurias
49 Germisara/Geoagion

·

"Γαλλαῖον Κυβέλης ὀλόλυγμα" (*ANTHOL.PALAT.*VI,173).
L'ÉLÉMENT ORGIASTIQUE DANS LE CULTE DE CYBÈLE*

Panayotis Pachis

Certains épigrammes de *l'Anthologie Palatine* constituent des témoignages caractéristiques concernant la présentation du culte de Cybèle
pendant les temps hellénistiques. Ces épigrammes appartiennent au
IIIᵉ–IIᵉ siècle avant J.-C., et leurs auteurs présentent d'une manière
unique la physionomie mystique-orgiastique des cérémonies de la
déesse phrygienne, qui lui est, d'ailleurs attribuée dans les témoignages d'écrivains dès l'apparition de son culte en Grèce.[1] Cette forme
du rite-culte continue de constituer encore pendant cette époque,
comme nous constaterons à la suite de notre étude, la manière principale de son expression.

L'élément qui constitue l'indice le plus significatif de ce groupe
d'épigrammes est la référence concrète aux Galles, la présentation
des prêtres eunuques de la déesse.[2] Cette particularité pourrait être
considérée comme une innovation qui se présente pour la première

---

* Les abréviations des noms de revues sont celles de *l'Année Philologique.*
Je voudrais remercier en particulier le professeur Eugene N. Lane pour ses con-
seils précieux pendant la rédaction de cet article.
[1] Cf. H. Hepding, *Attis seine Mythen und sein Kult* (RGVV 1, Giessen 1903) 710, où
sont réunies les références de *l'Anthologie Palatine.* Voir aussi A.S.F. Gow, *The Greek
Anthology. Hellenistic Epigrams*, vol. II (Cambridge 1965); I.U. Powell, *Collectanea Alexandrina*
(Oxford 1970 [1925]); Lloyd Jones and Parsons (edd.), *Supplementum Hellenisticum* (Texte
und Kommentare. Eine altertumwissenschaftliche Reihe, 11, Berlin-New York 1983).
Cf. aussi M.J. Vermaseren, *Cybele and Attis* (London 1977) 126, A.S.F. Gow, "The
Gallus and the Lion", *JHS* LXXX (1960) 88–93; G. Sfameni Gasparro, "Significato
e ruolo del sangue nel culto di Cibele e Attis", in *Atti della Settimana di Studi "Sangue
de antropologia biblica nella letteratura cristiana"*, Roma 29 novembre–4 dicembre 1982,
cur. F. Vattioni (Roma 1983), vol. I, 219 n. 71; ead., *Soteriology and Mystic Aspects in
the Cult of Cybele and Attis* (Études Préliminaires aux Religions Orientales dans l'Empire
Romain, 103, [dans la suite *EPRO*], Leiden 1985) 20; H. Hepding, *Attis* 139–140.
[2] H. Hepding, *Attis* 160–165, 217–220; H. Graillot, *Le culte de Cybèle, Mère des
Dieux à Rome et dans l'Empire romain* (Paris 1912) 287–319; F. Cumont, "Gallos", *RE*
XIII (1910) col. 675, 681sq.; A.D. Nock, "Eunuchs in Ancient Religion", *ARW* XXIII
(1925) 25–33, repr. in Z. Stewart (ed), *Essays on Religion and the Ancient World*, vol. I
(Oxford 1972) 7–15; J. Carcopino, "La réforme romaine du culte de Cybèle et
d'Attis II. Galles et Archigalles", *Aspects mystiques de la Rome païenne*, (Paris 1942) 76–
109; G. Sanders, "Gallos", *RAC* VIII (1972) 993–1025; G. Sfameni Gasparro,

fois selon les témoignages qui concernent les écrivains à l'époque hellénistique. Même une référence pareille était inconcevable pour les Grecs de l'époque classique, parce que ces prêtres provoquaient une répugnance particulière. Cette réaction s'observe à partir du moment où le culte est apparu sur le territoire grec. Le culte de la déesse est connu en Grèce à la fin de l'époque archaïque et était présenté principalement par les prêtres missionnaires mendiants (μητραγύρτης)[3] qu'il faut considérer comme les responsables principaux de l'extension du culte dans toute la Méditerranée. Ils rôdaient sans organisation concrète et n'appartenaient pas à un temple. Le poète comique Kratinus (Ve siècle avant J.-C.), confirme leur caractère par le terme "ἀγηρσικύβελις" (prêtre ambulant et mendiant de Cybèle).[4] Le même auteur

---

Soteriology, 26–43; W. Burkert, *Ancient Mystery Cults* (Cambridge 1987) 35–36; G. Sanders, "Les Galles et le Gallat devant l'opinion chrétienne", M.B. de Boer-T.A. Edridge (edd.), *Hommages à M.J. Vermaseren* (*EPRO* 68) vol. III, 1062–1091. Cf. aussi Plinius, *HN* 35,165: "... *Matris Deum sacerdotes,... qui galli uocantur...*".

[3] Pour répandre le culte en Grèce, cf. E. Will, "Aspects du culte et de la légende de la Grande Mère dans le monde grec", *Eléments orientaux dans la religion grecque ancienne. Colloque de Strasbourg 22–24 mai 1958* (Paris 1960) 95–111; G.M. Sanders, "Gallos", 987,990; W. Burkert, *Structure and History in Greek Mythology and ritual* (Berkeley-Los Angeles 1982 [1979]) 103; I.K. Loucas, Η Ρέα-Κυβέλη και οι γονιμικές λατρείες της Φλύας (Chalandri [Athènes] 1988) 18; R.E. Wycherley, *The Athenian Agora, III: Literary and Epigraphical Testimonia*, (Princeton 1957) 156 n. 492, G. Sfameni Gasparro, "Connotazioni metroache di Demetra nel coro dell Elena (vv. 1301–1365)", M.B. de Boer-T.A. Edridge (edd.), *Hommages à M.J. Vermaseren*, 1154–1158, ead., *Soteriology*, 12; M.J. Vermaseren, *Cybele and Attis* 99.

Cf. aussi Photius, *Lexicon* "Μητρῷον" (ed. S.A. Nader, vol. I, 1864–65, 422): "..... μητραγύρτης ἐμύει τὰς γυναῖκας τῇ μητρὶ τῶν θεῶν"; Suidas, *Lexicon*, (ed. A. Adler, vol. III, 1953); Pollux, 3,11; Diod.Sic.3,13, Plutarque, *Marius*, 17; Clearch. fr. 47 (Wehrli) = Athenaios, *Deipnos*.541cd; cf. aussi Apuleius (*Metam*.VIII,24) qui décrit exactement ces prêtres de la déesse.

[4] Kratinus, Δραπέτιδες, fr. 66 (62) (ed. R. Kassel-C. Austin, *Poetae comici Graeci*, vol. IV, Berlin-New-York 1983, 154–155): Hesych. A 461 ἀγερσικύβελις Κρατίνος ἐν Δραπέτισιν (ἀνδραπέτησιν) cod.Corr.Bergk.Rel. 46) ἐπὶ Λάμπωνος. Τὸν αὐτὸν ἀγύρτην καὶ κυβηλιστὴν εἶπεν, οἱονεὶ θύτην καὶ μάντιν. κύβαλιν γὰρ ἔλεγον τὸν πέλεκυν (lac.Ind.Bergk). ὅθεν καὶ Λύσιππος ἐν Βάκχαις (fr. 6K) τὸν αὐτὸν (ὡς add.Bergk.) ἀγύρτην κωμωιδεῖ... Suid. κ 2595 κυβαλίσαι πελεκῆσαι. Κυβηλὶς γὰρ ὁ πέλεκυς (hucusque = Phot. p. 183, 4 = Hesych. K 4377) codd.). καὶ ἀγερσικύβλις ὁ θύτης. Κρατίνος ἐν Δραπέτισιν (-τησιν codd.) ἐπὶ Λάμπωνος εἶπε τὸν ἀγύρτην καὶ κυβηλιστήν. Phot. (b,z) α 146 = Lex.Bachm. p. 21, 17 ἀγερσικύβηλιν Κρατίνος Λάμπωνα τὸν μάντιν ὡς καὶ θύτην. Κυβαλὶς γὰρ ὁ πέλεκυς. οἱ δὲ ἐγερσικύβηλιν (ἀγ- Phot. Z, om. B) ἐν τῷ δράματι γράφουσιν, τὸν ἐφ᾽ ἑαυτὸν ἐγείροντα τὸν πέλεκυν. Et.Magn. p. 8, 9 Et.Sul. α 49S) Lass—Liv. ἀγερσικύβηλιν Κάβηλις λέγεται ὁ πέλεκυς ὁ μαντικὸς (cf. Lex.Bachm. p. 9, 15). οἱ δὲ τὸν ἐφ᾽ ἑαυτὸν ἐγείροντα τὸν πέλεκυν. ἢ θύτην. ἄγερσις γὰρ ἀνερμον ἢ ἀθροισμόν. Κρατίνος ἐν Δραπέτισιν.

Cf. aussi "*mihi quidem Cratinus videtur scripsisse, ut notaret Lemponem tamquam sacrificulum stipem colligentem, tamquam avarum hominem et alieni appetentem*" Bergk.Vid. Ad fr. 352 et de Lampone ad fr. 62. Etiam Cratini *verba esse ante* Bergkium et Meinekium putabatur, recte siquidem Hesychius his verbis explicationenm adiungit. 'Hunc ipsum' Lamponem,

les caractérise aussi comme théoporteurs (κήβυβος). Selon le témoignage de Photios, les Ioniens les appelaient *metragyrtai* dans un passé
indéterminé; "maintenant" (νῦν) le terme *Galles* est en usage.[5] C'est
justement ce témoignage qui nous oblige à nous demander pendant
quelle période ce changement du nom des prêtres de Cybèle est survenu. Nous croyons même que cela devrait être extrêmement important, étant donné que, d'après le passage susmentionné de Photios,
cette innovation a eu lieu dans le milieu où le culte de la déesse
apparut originellement. Or, il ne faut pas oublier que c'est justement
par ce nom que les prêtres du culte seront principalement connus
dans le monde gréco-romain au sens large du terme. Par conséquent,
selon les données de la recherche contemporaine, nous croyons que
l'hypothèse la plus possible serait que le changement de leur nom est
survenu juste après l'invasion de *Galates* en Asie Mineure au IIe siècle
avant J.-C.[6] Ce n'est donc pas du tout par hasard que ces prêtres
sont désignés précisément par leur nouveau nom, comme l'on a déjà
mentionné plus haut, dans les épigrammes de l'*Anthologie Palatine*, qui
appartiennent à un époque postérieure.

Cette caractéristique est d'ailleurs aussi connue par les sources qui
témoignent de l'entrée du culte de Cybèle à Athènes. D'après les
témoignages postérieurs de Photios, de Suda, de Julien et de certains
commentateurs, qui sont considérés comme les plus importants témoignages de cet événement, les Athéniens ont exécuté l'un de ces prêtres, car il enseignait à leur femmes le culte de la déesse. La mort de
ce prêtre a provoqué le courroux de la déesse et la peste dans la
ville. Cette situation a pris fin seulement quand les Athéniens ont

---

cf. Quae mox de Lysippo dicit. Sic etiam Sudae verba intellegenda. Incertum tamen
utrum in eadem fabula an in alia his verbis usus sit poeta cf. Hesych. (ἀγύρτης),
κ 4374 (κυβηβικὸν τρόπον), fr. Adesp.869K), 4375 (κυβηλιστάς), 4376 (κύβηλις), cf.
Phot. p. 183, 5 "δόλιον ἀγύρτην Oedipus Sophocleus Tiresiam compellat *Or.388*".
Cf. Plat. *Rep.*364b, Hippocr. *Morb.sacr.*1,10; cf. Arist. *Rhetor.*1405a20; cf. W. Burkert,
Mystery Cults, 35.

[5] Kratinus, Θράτται fr. 9 (82 ed. Th. Cock, I,38), cf. aussi Photius, *Lex.*183,1:
"κύβηβον" : "Κρατῖνος Θράτταις. Τὸν θεοφόρητον. Ἴωνες δὲ τὸν μητραγύρτην καὶ γάλλον
νῦν καλούμενον. Οὕτως Σιμωνίδης (ed. A. Meineke, *Fragmenta poetarum comoediae antiquae*,
Berlin 1840, II,65), cf. Gesneri, *Thes.L.Lat.*V. Cybebe et Cybèle. Voir aussi E. Laroche,
"Koubaba, déesse anatolienne et le problème des origines de Cybèle", *Eléments orientaux dans la religion grecque ancienne*, 115 n. 2; G. Sfameni *Gasparro, Soteriology*, 15 n. 35.

[6] Voir C. Schneider, *Kulturgeschichte des Hellenismus* (München 1967) vol. I, 810–
814. Mes remerciements au professeur E.N. Lane pour cette information qu'il m'a
fournie par lettre (28.3.1995).

expié en construisant, au centre de la ville, un temple, hommage à la déesse.[7]

Cet incident, présenté d'une façon concrete dans les témoignages susmentionnés, doit être considéré plutôt avec défiance, en tant que non correspondant à la réalité historique, étant donné que les écrivains qui le citent sont d'une époque postérieure.[8] Cependant, on ne peut pas contester l'importance des ces témoignages pour la compréhension des circonstances de l'entrée du culte de Cybèle dans le territoire grec. Leur particularité devient plus accentuée si on les considère comme le résultat d'une élaboration survenue à des périodes postérieures. Par cette approche, nous croyons qu'on peut comprendre la réalité historique concernant l'acceptation des cultes étrangers par les Grecs pendant, en principe, les temps classiques.[9] D'ailleurs, nous essayons ainsi, comme dans des cas pareils, d'expliquer l'entrée d'un culte étranger dans le milieu des cités grecques. Les Grecs, et plus particulièrement les habitants d'Athènes, étaient généralement méfiants à l'égard des cultes étrangers et, surtout, de ceux dont le rite venait en opposition avec la religion traditionnelle. Ils croyaient que l'entrée d'un nouveau dieu pourrait perturber le *status quo* religieux mais aussi social de leur cité, ce qui entraînerait la rage des dieux du panthéon traditionnel. La manière dont le culte en question a été accepté dans le milieu de la cité d'Athènes, ainsi que les circonstances sous lesquelles il a été répandu, peuvent être mieux

---

[7] Cf. Photius, *Lex.*; Suidas, "βάραθρον"; *Schol. in Arist. Plutus*, v. 431; Julien, *Discours sur la Mère des dieux*, 1,159ab; Plutarque, *Nicias*, 13,34, R.E. Wycherley, *The Athenian Agora*, 155 n. 488, 156; M.J. Vermaseren, *Corpus Cultus Cybelae Attisque, Graecia atque Insulae* (dans la suite *CCCA*) (*EPRO* 50, Leiden 1982) vol. II, 3–109. Cf. aussi M.J. Vermaseren, *Cybele and Attis* 72; M.P. Nilsson, *Geschichte der griechischen Religion*[3] (dans la suite *GGR*) (München 1976) vol. I, 688; P. Boyancé, *Études sur la religion romaine* (Rome 1972) 223 et surtout n. 2; R. Turcan, *Les cultes orientaux dans le monde romain* (Paris 1989) 37; F. Graf, "The Arrival of Cybele in the Greek East", *Actes du VIIe Congres de la FIEC* (Budapest 1983), vol. I, 117–120, I.K. Loukas, Η Ρέα-Κυβέλη, 15–23; G. Sfameni Gasparro, "Significato e ruolo del sangue", 219.

[8] Voir M.P. Nilsson, *GGR* I,630; D.M. Cosi, "L'ingresso di Cibele ad Atene e a Roma", *Atti* XI (N.S.I.) 1980–1981 (Centro di ricerca e documentazione sull'antichità classica, Rome 1984), 81–91; G. Cerri, "La Madre degli Dei nell' Elena di Euripide : tragedia e rituale", *Quaderni di Storia* 18 (1983) 155–195 et surtout 160–180, 183. Par contre, M.J. Vermaseren (*Cybele and Attis* 32–33) croit à la base historique précisément de ces témoignages postérieurs de Photios et de Suda.

[9] Voir W. Burkert, *Griechische Religion der archaischen und klassischen Epoche* (Religionen der Menschheit, 15, Stuttgart 1977) 273–278; H.S. Versnel, *Ter Unus. Isis, Dionysos, Hermes: Three Studies in Henotheism* (Inconsistencies in Greek Religion, I, Leiden 1990) 102–123; R. Garland, *Introducing New Gods* (London 1992).

comprises si nous considérons un témoignage postérieur, mais très caractéristique, provenant de Julien, qui écrit: "on dit en effet que les Athéniens outragèrent Gallos et le chassèrent pour innovation en matière de religion, ne comprenant pas à quelle Déesse ils avaient affaire, et qu'elle était adorée chez eux sous les noms de la Déô, Rhéa et Déméter" (λέγονται γὰρ οὗτοι περιυβρίσαι καὶ ἀπελάσαι τόν Γάλλον ὡς τὰ θεῖα καινοτομοῦντα, οὐ ξυνέντες ὁποῖόν τι τῆς θεοῦ χρῆμα καὶ ὡς ἡ παρ'αὐτοῖς τιμωμένη Δηὼ καὶ Ῥέα καὶ Δημήτηρ).[10]

La disposition méfiante, voire hostile, à l'égard des cultes étrangers, et surtout orientaux, a atteint son point culminant principalement après les guerres perses. C'est précisément à partir de cette époque que prédomine l'idée que tout élément étranger pourrait être une menace continue, comme de l'invasion perse. Ce fait pourrait expliquer la disposition des Athéniens envers le culte de la déesse, ce qui avait pour résultat une expansion plutôt limitée de celui-ci dans le milieu de leur cité.[11] Par contre, il est remarquablement répandu dans d'autres cités grecques, comme par exemple dans le Pirée, ainsi que sur le reste du territoire grec.[12]

Il en résulte qu'il est donc normal que, pendant l'époque classique, absolument aucune relation n'ait existé entre le mythe et les cérémonies, éléments dont la synthèse sera la base du rituel de ce culte à des époques postérieures. Cela est d'ailleurs véritable par les témoignages qui sont liés à l'ambiance cultuelle de la déesse et qui datent de cette période. Ces informations nous permettent de comprendre d'ailleurs la répugnance particulière que provoquait chez les Grecs de l'époque classique le rite du culte tel qui se pratiquait, très probablement, de la même façon que dans son berceau originel, en Asie Mineure.

Parmi les particularités qui font leur apparition après l'entrée et la propagation du culte de la déesse dans l'espace grec, et surtout dans le milieu de ses bandes sacrées, prédomine une image de la déesse en tant que Mère-déesse miséricordieuse qui assiste et secourt ses

---

[10] Julien, *Or.*VIII,(V),159a–b (ed. G. Rochefort, I, 102–103).

[11] Voir Lynn E. Roller, "Attis on Greek Votive Monuments. Greek God or Phrygian?", *Hesperia* 63,2 (1994) 245–262 et surtout 252.

[12] En ce qui concerne les témoignages épigraphiques sur le culte de Cybèle dans le Pirée, voir W.S. Ferguson, "The Attic Orgeones", *HThR* 37 (1944) 64–144 et surtout 107–115; R. Garland, *The Piraeus from the fifth to the first Century B.C.* (London 1987) 235–237; M.J. Vermaseren, *CCCA* vol. II, nos. 258–266, pp. 68–70; L.E. Roller, "Attis on Greek Votive Monuments", 257 n. 77.

fidèles dans les moments difficiles de leur vie.[13] Cependant, l'autre aspect de son image, celui lié à son élément orgiastique, n'est pas abandonné. D'ailleurs, c'est cet élément-là qui révèle son origine orientale. Nous croyons que la coexistance de ces deux images sur le visage de la déesse exprime, de façon tout à fait réussie, son caractère omnipotent et absolu dans le milieu cultuel de la réalité grecque. Cela peut être mieux compris même à l'aide de ses représentations cultuelles. D'ailleurs, depuis des temps très anciens, l'art constitue l'un des moyens principaux pour la compréhension de la réalité cultuelle de la Grèce ancienne. Nous pouvons donc, également dans le cas présent, éclaircir, à l'aide des représentations de la déesse, les conditions d'acceptation et d'adaptation d'une divinité étrangère dans le milieu cultuel de la réalité grecque des temps classiques. Ainsi, en ce qui concerne la façon dont la déesse en question est représentée, nous pourrions signaler l'évolution suivante depuis son milieu cultuel originel en Asie Mineure, jusqu'à l'époque de la propagation de son culte sur le territoire grec: pour la première fois au cours du VIe siècle avant J.-C. et dans le milieu des cités grecques de l'Anatolie, se développe un type de représentation plus simple, semblable à celui rencontré plus tard dans le milieu de la Grèce continentale.[14] Cependant, son hellénisation s'achève à la fin du VIe siècle avant J.-C., ce qui a donné la figure connue de la déesse, rencontrée dans le monde grec et plus tard dans l'ensemble du monde greco-romain; à la base de celle-ci était la statue célèbre créée par Agorakritos au Ve siècle avant J.-C. qui se trouvait dans l'Agora d'Athènes.[15] Cette pratique d'héllenisation continue et atteint son point culminant dans l'esprit du syncrétisme et de l'œcuménisme de l'époque hellénistique et, sur-

---

[13] Voir M.J. Vermaseren, *CCCA* vol. II, nos. 273, 275, 276; cf. aussi L.E. Roller, "Attis on Greek Votive monuments", 38.

[14] Pour la propagation du culte de Cybèle de l'Asie Mineure dans l'espace grec, voir S. Reinach, "Statues archaïques de Cybèle", *BCH* 13 (1989) 543–560; E. Will, "Aspects du culte et de légende de la grande mère dans le monde grec", 95–111; F. Naumann, *Die Ikonographie der Kybele in der phrygischen und der griechischen Kult* (Ist Mitt, Beiheft 28, Tübingen 1983) 136; L.E. Roller, "Phrygian Myth and Cult", *Source* 7 (1988) 43–50 et surtout 45–47; ibid., "Attis on Greek Votive Monuments", 249.

[15] En ce qui concerne cette statue de la déesse, voir les témoignages de Pausanias I,3,5; Arrian, *Periplous* 9; Plinius, *HN* 36,17. Cf. aussi A. Von Salis, "Die Göttermutter des Agorakritos", *JdI* 28 (1913) 1–26; G. Despinis, Συμβολή του έργου του Άγορακρίτου (Athènes 1971) 111–123; F. Naumann, *Die Ikonographie der Kybele*, 159–169; L.E. Roller, "Attis on Greek Votive Monuments", 249. Cf. aussi la représentation sur un cratère en figure rouge provenant d'Athènes, Spina, *ARV²* 1052, no. 25.

tout, romaine. Un exemple illustrant très bien ce phénomène est celui d'Isis, dont la figure a subi une hellénisation complète depuis son entrée et propagation en Grèce.[16]

Il faut signaler que les auteurs grecs du Ve siècle avant J.-C. évitaient de manière systématique les diverses appellations de la déesse qui rendaient évidente son origine orientale. De cette facon, Cybèle acquiert une figure nouvelle qui caractérisait les déesses grecques. Elle s'identifie alors à la déesse crétoise Rhéa, à la grecque Mère des dieux et des hommes, allors que, plus tard, son association avec Déméter est un exemple caractéristique de l'association de divinités analogues.[17] Cette association justement correspond à l'image d'une divinité omnipotente qui, avec son caractère absolu, domine sur la vie et la mort des règnes animal et végétal, ainsi que sur les hommes. Ces trois noms de la déesse, Mère des dieux, Rhéa et Cybèle, proviennent d'un fond religieux commun et ils s'identifient à certains degrés. Ces noms designent la meme déesse qui dans ce syncrétisme particulier des cultes homologues retrouve pendant cette époque son unité.[18] Il faut souligner ici que cette association est possible principalement grâce à la nature commune et analogue de ces divinités. Cela peut être mieux compris, si on tient compte du témoignage de Julien concernant l'entrée de la déesse dans la cité d'Athènes, temoignage déjà mentionné.

A ce propos il faut aussi faire remarquer qu'à part les essais permanents de la part des Grecs, pour helléniser le caractère de la déesse ayant comme base les données du panthéon grec, on remarque encore une forte résistance dans le nouveau milieu où se répandait le culte de la déesse. Cette résistance concerne la conservation de certains éléments qui discernent particulièrement la figure initiale de la déesse. Dans ces éléments, c'est l'élément orgiastique qui prédomine. C'est exactement cette forme qui la place dans l'ensemble des déesses qui viennent à cause de leur caractère en opposition avec le respect du religieux tel qui s'exprimait pendant les années classiques. Ce fait

---

[16] Voir Johannes Eingartner, *Isis und ihre Dienerinnen in der Kunst der römischen Kaiserzeit* (Supplements to Mnemosyne, 115, Leiden 1991).

[17] Voir M.P. Nilsson, *GGR* I,298; I. Loucas, Η Ρέα-Κυβέλη, 139–147.

[18] Cf. M.J. Vermaseren, *Cybele and Attis* 22; R. Duthoy, *The Taurobolium. Its Evolution and Terminology* (*EPRO* 10, Leiden 1969) 63–64; I.K. Loukas, Η Ρέα-Κυβέλη, 21–23; N. Papachatzis, Παυσανίου Ελλάδος περιήγησις (Athènes 1974) vol. I, 184–185; E. Wycherley, *The Athenian Agora*, 150–160 n. 456–519; D. Sabbatucci, *Il misticismo greco*[2] (*nuovi* saggi, n. 71, 2, Roma 1979) 215–226. Voir aussi Hesiodus, *Theog.*453, Pindare, *Nemean* 6,13; Strab. *Geogr.*X,3,1; Soph. *Phil.*391–393.

a eu comme résultat dans quelques régions la mise en relation de
son rite avec les indices qui distinguent les cultes qui ont un vif caractère mystique-orgiastique. Il se poursuit ainsi l'acquisition de l'expérience qui exprime la relation profonde et réciproque qui se crée
entre l'élément divin et l'élément humain. Cette influence de l'un sur
l'autre s'exprime principalement dans le culte de la déesse par la
participation d'un groupe particulier de fidèles qui atteignent une
situation qui se caractérise comme "*enthousiasmos*".[19] Aussi le seul élément qui caractérise particulièrement pendant cette époque la vie
cultuelle du rite métroaque est la manie sacrée qui constitue l'aspect
principal de l'ensemble mystique du culte.

Comme nous l'avons déjà dit, les relations écrites sur les Galles
commencent au IIIe siècle avant J.-C. Mais l'élément qui continue à
jouer un rôle dans le rite, comme on peut le comprendre dans ce
cas particulier, c'est la situation d'enthousiasme des fidèles et non
pas la pratique des cérémonies qui aboutit à la tres naïve offrande
du caractère viril des prêtres à la déesse. Au contraire, par les témoignages concrets des épigrammes qui existent dans l'*Anthologie Palatine*,
les prêtres ou les prêtresses avaient coutume de donner des offrandes, mais celles-ci étaient complètement différentes de celles que nous
avons citées plus haut. Leurs actes doivent être considérés comme
une preuve qui manifeste leur soumission et leur respect envers la
toute-puissante déesse phrygienne.

Dans le même esprit, on a le témoignage de Rhianos de Crète, qui
est compris dans les épigrammes de *l'Anthologie Palatine*.[20] Cet écrivain
qui, selon Suda, a vécu au milieu du IIIe siècle avant J.-C., nous donne
les informations les plus caractéristiques sur le rituel du culte:

---

[19] Pour le caractère mystique-orgiastique du culte, cf. U. Bianchi," Prolegomena
I: Mysticism and mystery Religions", U. Bianchi (ed.), *Mysteria Mithrae* (dans la suite
MM) (*EPRO* 80, Leiden 1979) 7; G. Sfameni Gasparro, "Il mitraismo nella feno-
menologia misterica", *ibid.*, 314.

Pour la définition des concepts "mystique" et mystérique" par rapport à la Grèce
et au Proche-Orient ancien, cf. U. Bianchi, "Initiation, mystères, gnose (Pour l'histoire de la mystique dans la paganisme gréco-oriental)", C.J. Bleeker (ed.), *Initiation*,
(Leiden 1965) 154–171; id., *The Greek Mysteries* (Leiden 1976) 18, id., *Prometeo, Orfeo,
Adamo* (Roma 1976) 59sq., 71–94, 129–143, 188sq., id., "Prolegomena", 360;
G. Sfameni Gasparro, "Riflessioni ulteriori su, Mithra 'dio mistico'", *in MM* 397–
408, ead., "Soteriologie dans le culte de Cybèle et d'Attis", U. Bianchi-M.J. Vermaseren (edd.), *La soteriologia dei culti orientali nell Impero Romano*. *Atti del Colloquio In-
ternationale su La soteriologia dei culti orientali nell Impero Romano, Roma 24–28 settembre
1979* (dans la suite *CSCO*) (*EPRO* 92, Leiden 1982) 478 n. 5.

[20] Rhianus Cret. *Anthol.Palat.*VI,173 = H. Hepding, *Attis* 7. Cf. aussi I.U. Powell,
Collectanea Alexandrina, 18–19, A.S.F. Gow-D.L. Page, *The Greek Anthology*, 506–507,
Suidas, *Lexicon*, "Ριανὸς, ὁ καὶ Κρής, ὦν Βηναῖος (Βήνη δὲ πόλις Κρήτης)· οὗτος δὲ ἦν τῆς

Achrylis, la prêtresse phrygienne qui si souvent a laissé flotter ses boucles sacrées au milieu des torches de résine et poussé de sa bouche ces clameurs profondes que les Galles font entendre en l'honneur de Cybèle, a consacré ces cheveux à la déesse des montagnes en les suspendant aux portes de son temple, maintenant qu'elle a arrêté ses pieds ardents de fureur.

Ἀχρυλὶς, ἡ Φρυγίη θαλαμηπόλος, ἡ περὶ πεύκας
πολλάκι τοὺς ἱεροὺς πλοκάμους,
γαλλαίῳ Κυβέλης ὀλολύγματι πολλάκι δοῦσα
τὸν βαρὺν εἰς ἀκοὰς ἦχον ἀπὸ στομάτων,
τάσδε θεῇ χαίτας περὶ δικλίδι θῆκεν ὀρείᾳ,
θερμὸν ἐπεί λύσσης ὧδ' ἀνέπαυσε πόδα.[21]

On voit, donc, que la personne qui joue le premier rôle dans cette épigramme est une femme, la prêtresse de la déesse, qui s'appelle Archylis et désignée par le terme θαλαμηπόλος (prêtresse de chambre), et non pas les prêtres Galles.[22] De cette façon l'auteur veut peut-être révéler la répugnance qui a encore été provoquée par les prêtres du culte métroaque, auprès des citoyens des villes grecques. C'est pour cela qu'il présente dans son épigramme une femme comme la personne principale. Les femmes sont celles qui, comme nous le verrons par la suite, jouent le premier rôle dans les cérémonies mystiques offertes à la déesse par les Grecs. Ce comportement pourrait être considéré comme une indication du respect religieux qui caractérise les conceptions de l'époque de l'auteur. De cette façon il prend soin de rester fidèle aux principes de la mentalité grecque, à laquelle le culte s'est d'ailleurs adapté et s'est, ensuite, répandu dans l'espace grec. Sa façon de s'exprimer est aussi très significative de la disposition des Grecs à l'égard des cultes étrangers mais également de la dévotion de l'auteur à la religion de ses ancêtres.

παλαίστρας πρότερον φύλαξ καὶ δοῦλος, ὕστερον δὲ παιδευθεὶς ἐγένετο γραμματικὸς σύγχρονος Ἐρατοσθένους, ἔγραψεν ἐμμέτρως ἐξάμετρα (Meineke, *Anal.Alex.*201) ποιήματα... Ἡρακλείδα ἐν βιβλίοις δ'". D'après Suidas, Rhianos était contemporain d'Eratosthène qui est mort pendant le règne de Ptolémée V Epiphanès (an de succession 204/5 avant J.C.); Lloyd Jones and Parsons (edd.), *Supplementum Hellenisticum*, 346–347, Stephanus Byzantius, "Βήνη. πόλις Κρήτης ὑπὸ Γορτύνην τεταγμένη. Τὸ ἐθνικὸν Βηναῖος", Pausanias IV,6,1: "τοῦτον γὰρ τῶν μεσσηνίων τὸν πόλεμον Ῥιανός τε ἐν τοῖς ἔπεσιν ἐποίησεν ὁ βηναῖος καὶ ὁ πρινηεὺς Μύρων"; cf. aussi N. Papachatzis, *Παυσανίας* (Athènes 1979) vol. III, 9–11, 52.

[21] *Anthologie Grecque.* Première Partie, *Anthologie Palatine*, tome III (livre VI, texte établit et traduit P. Waltz, Paris 1931, 31).

[22] Cf. Suidas, "θαλαμηπόλος" (II,681): "ἡ περὶ τὸν θάλαμον ἀναστρεφομένη, καὶ φυλάττουσα... ἡ νεωκόρος Ἀχρυλὶς ἡ Φρυγίη θαλαμηπόλος, ἡ περὶ πεύκας πολλάκι τοὺς ἱερούς χευάμενη πλοκάμους". Une autre épigramme de Dioscur. (*Anthol.Palat.*VI,220 = H. Hepding, *Attis* 7) parle d'un Galle qui s'appelait Attis et qui est désigné comme : "ἀγνός... Κυβέλης θαλαμηπόλος".

Bien-sûr, il ne faut pas oublier que de même, dans ces épigrammes, nous observons une évolution sur la forme du culte qui surviendra
pendant l'époque héllénistique. Cette évolution est liée à l'apparition
d'Attis aux côtés de Cybèle. Selon ces témoignages littéraires, avec
son bien-aimé confidant apparaissent aussi les prêtres eunuques de la
déesse.[23] Attis apparaît pour la première fois dans l'espace grec au
cours du IVe siècle avant J.-C. Sa représentation dans le cadre de
l'art cultuel est, le plus souvent, nettement orientale, même si elle ne
correspond pas du tout au milieu oriental originel du culte, selon les
chercheurs contemporains.[24] Ainsi comme nous avons pu constater,
l'auteur Rhianos fait une comparaison entre la disposition de la prêtresse et celle des Galles. L'auteur veut ainsi peut-être présenter aussi
d'une manière indirecte la réalité qui continue encore d'être un élément complètement étranger à la pensée grecque, et de cette façon
crée alors une image unique dans son genre et peut-être plus accor-
dée à une époque postérieure.

De plus, il est intéressant pour cet auteur, suivant probablement
l'exemple des autres auteurs de l'*Anthologie Palatine*, de montrer dans
ces épigrammes l'offrande par la prêtresse de ses cheveux à la déesse.[25]
Cette action se réalise peu avant qu'elle abandonne les services du
culte métroaque. On pourrait supposer que cela est lié exactement à
l'habitude grecque du service annuel des prêtres dans le rite de religion
traditionnel.[26] Certaines similitudes se voient—au delà du cadre de
la religion officielle—aussi dans le rite des autres cultes orientaux,
qui ont commencé à se propager dans l'espace grec pendant l'époque hellénistique. Ainsi, nous trouvons le culte d'Isis et de Sérapis,

---

[23] G. Sfameni Gasparro, *Soteriology*, 26–28; 49; P. Foucart, *Des associations religieuses
chez les Grecs. Thiases, Eranes, Orgeons* (Paris, 1873 [réimpr . . . New York 1975]), 84–
101 et inscr. n. 418, cf. le catalogue des inscriptions en ordre chronologique in
W. Scott Ferguson, "Attic Orgeones", 108: *IG* II²,1316 (246/45 B.C.?); 1301 (220/
19, B.C.); 1314 (213/12 B.C.); 1315 (211/10 B.C.) = H. Hepding, *Attis* no. 9, 79–
80; *IG* II², 1328 I (183/82 B.C.) = H. Hepding, *op. cit.*, no. 10, 80–81; *IG* II²,1327
(178/77 B.C.); 1328 II et 1329 = H. Hepding, *op. cit.*, no. 11, 81 et les deux inscriptions de 175/74 B.C. et *IG* II²,1334 (70 avant J.C.).

[24] Voir L.E. Roller, "Attis on Greek Votive Monuments", 252–253.

[25] Cf. H. Hepding, *Attis* 710, voir aussi notamment Thuillos, *Anthol.Palat.*VII,223,13
(ed. P. Waltz, Paris 1960, 152sq.): "ἡ κροτάλοις ὀρχιστρὶς Ἀριστίον, ἡ πεύκαις / καὶ τῇ
Κυβέλῃ πλοκάμους ῥῖψαι ἐπισταμένη, λωτῷ κερόεντι φορουμένη". Pour l'habitude de
l'offrande des cheveux aux dieux cf. W. Burkert, *Griechische Religion*, 120–121;
S. Eitrem, *Opferritus und Voropfer der Griechen und* Römer (Kristiania 1915, Nachdr.
Hildesheim-New York 1977) 34 4–415; W.H.D. Rouse, *Greek Votive Offerings. An Essay
in the History of Greek Religion* (Cambridge 1902).

[26] W. Burkert, *Griechische Religion*, 157–163; N. Papachatzis, Η θρησκεία στην αρχαία
Ελλάδα (Athènes 1987) 177–178.

c'est-à-dire des prêtres et des prêtresses dont le service est soit annuel soit à vie. Il faut rappeler que le cas du service à vie suit naturellement la tradition orientale des cultes que nous étudions.[27]

Une autre explication qu'on pourrait donner à l'épigramme de Rhianos sur la prêtresse est la suivante: la prêtresse est arrivée à la fin de sa vie, et prend des forces, peu avant de mourir en pratiquant avec l'aide de la déesse ses cérémonies. Ce qui a une importance particulière, dans toutes les explications qu'on peut donner, c'est le respect particulier que la prêtresse montre envers la déesse en prodiguant ses services zélés. Sa soumission se déclare par la pratique des cérémonies et encore plus en consacrant ses cheveux longs au temple de la déesse. La prêtresse accroche ses cheveux, selon les informations des auteurs, aux flambeaux qu'elle tenait souvent pendant les cérémonies nocturnes. Il vaut encore noter que ce flambeau provenait de pins du petit élysée qui existait autour du temple de la déesse.[28] Après, elle les pose à l'entrée du thalame c'est-à-dire dans le souterrain du sanctuaire de la déesse, afin qu'ils constituent la preuve éternelle du respect religieux et de la dévotion envers la déesse toute-puissante.

Cette offrande, comme on a déjà mentionné plus haut, et, d'après les informations de Nicandre, peut être considérée comme analogue à celles des Galles qui déposent leurs membres coupés dans le thalame du culte métroaque.[29] Cet acte est considéré comme une preuve

---

[27] F. Cumont, *Die orientalischen Religionen im römischen Heidentum*[7], (Stuttgart 1975) 38–39; W. Burkert, *Mystery Cults*, 31–53.

Pour les prêtresses au culte de Cybèle voir aussi H.R. Goehler, *De Matris Magnae apud Romanos cultu*, (Diss. Leipzig, Meissen 1886) 39–51; Fr. Bömer, *Untersuchungen über die Religion der Sklaven in Griechenland und Rom* (Abhandlungen der Akademie der Wissenschaften und die Literatur in Mainz, Geistes und Sozialwissenschaftliche Klasse, Jg. 1963, Nr. 8), vol. 4 (Wiesbaden 1963) 29–37; H. Graillot, *Le culte de Cybèle, Mère des Dieux, à Rome et dans l'Empire romain* (BEFAR, 107, Paris 1912) 238–253; M.J. Vermaseren, *Cybele and Attis* 104–111; id., *CCCA* vol. II, 14 n. 23, 64–65 n. 245, 75 n. 262, 76–78 n. 263, 146 n. 469; G. Thomas, "Magna Mater and Attis", *ANRW* II 17.3 (1984) 1525–1533. Cf. aussi *IG* III³,2361 = *SIG*³ 1111 lin. 70: "... ἱέρεια Ὡραίας διὰ βίου".

Pour le culte de Isis/Sarapis, voir L. Vidman, *Sylloge Inscriptionum Religionis Isiacae et Sarapiacae* (RGVV XXVIII, Berlin 1969), index s.v. Isiastai, Sarapiastai, Anubiastai, hiera-phoroi, melanophoroi, pastophoroi; id., *Isis und Sarapis bei den Griechen und Römern* (RGVV XXIX, Berlin 1970), 69–94; H.B. Schönborn, *Die Pastophoren in Kult der ägyptischen* Götter (Meisenheim am Glan 1976).

[28] Des bois de pins semblables, se trouvaient également autour des temples de la déesse dans le milieu originel du culte en Asie Mineure. Sur le bois de pins consacré sur l'Ida à Cybèle, voir surtout Vergil, *Aen.*IX,85sq.; Sen. *Troad.*1734sq. e.

[29] Voir Nicandri *Alexipharmacon*, 68 et *schol. ad loc.* = H. Hepding, *Attis* 89. Cf. aussi P. Pachis, "Kernophoros", *SMSR* 50 (n.s. VIII,1) (1984) 125–129; I.K. Loucas, Η Ρέα Κυβέλη, 155–168.

suprême de leur offrande et de leur soumission à la volonté absolue qui constitue un trait particulier de l'image orientale de la déesse. De toute façon il ne faut pas oublier que dans le premier cas nous avons une offrande complètement indolore, tandis que la consécration des Galles était particulièrement pénible et que son résultat marquait leur vie entière. Mais il faut remarquer que leur acte se réalisait pendant une période transitoire de leur vie. Dans le premier cas, nous avons des indications concernant la mort biologique de la prêtresse et dans le deuxième, nous avons la mise à mort de la vie précédente de l'homme social qui était impie et son entrée dans une nouvelle situation qui s'oppose à la sphère d'influence par le sacré. Naturellement il faut que nous parlions aussi des offrandes traditionnelles des cheveux et des habits des Galles à la déesse.[30] C'est encore une acte par lequel ils voulaient montrer exactement leur relation intime avec la déesse. Nous croyons, donc, qu'il est bien naturel que la prêtresse demande ainsi le secours de sa déesse-protectrice, qui règne, avec sa présence omnipotente, sur la vie et la mort, afin de franchir le seuil de la mort sous sa protection continue. D'ailleurs, il ne faut pas oublier le secours et l'assistance remarquables que celle-ci offrait en tant que mère-déesse, aux hommes et, surtout, à ses fidèles. C'est précisément ce trait de miséricorde qui la distingue, comme on a déjà mentionné, de l'élément orgiastique, caractéristique de son origine orientale, particulièrement après la diffusion de son culte dans l'espace grec.

Des offrandes telles que celle de la prêtresse, citée dans l'épigramme que nous examinons peuvent être examinées dans le cadre des "rites de passage".[31] Nous croyons que, par cette approche la particularité

---

[30] Cf. Simonid. (*Anth.Pat*.VI,217) qui témoigne que les prêtres consacrent : "ἔνδυτα καὶ ξανθοὺς πλοκάμους"; Erycius, *Anth.Pal*.VI,234 = H. Hepding, *Attis* 10: "Γάλλος ὁ χαιτάεις, ὁ νεήτομος, ὑπὸ Τυμώλου Λάδιος ὀρχηστὰς μάκρ᾽ ὀλολυζόμενος, τᾷ παρὰ Σαγγαρίῳ τάδε Ματέρι τύμπαν᾽ ἀγαυᾷ τ᾽ ὀρειχάλκου λάλα κύμβαλα καὶ μυρόεντα βόστρυχον, ἐκ λύσσας ἄρτια παυσάμενος"; Suidas, (III,555): "Ὄρεια οὐδετέρως, τὰ τοῦ ὄρους. ὅς ταδ᾽ ὄρεια ἔνδυτα καὶ ξανθοὺς ἐκρέμασε πλοκάμους καὶ Φώτιος ὁ Πατριάρχης ὄρεια σοι τὰ δῶρα, κάστανα καὶ ἀμανῖται" et "Γάλλος ἀπόκοπος ἐν ἐπιγράμμασι· γάλλος ὁ χαιτήεις, ὁ νεώτομος, Ὅς ποτε Τμῷ Λάδιος ὀρχηστὸς μακρὰς ὀλολυζόμενος". Voir aussi A.S.F. Gow, "The Gallus and the Lion, *Anth.Pal*.VI,217–220,223", *JHS* LXXX (1960) 88–93 et surtout 89–90; S. Eitrem, *Opferritus und Voropfer*, 347. Pour l'apparition des Galles en gènéral, cf. M.J. Vermaseren, *Cybele and Attis* fig. 65; id., *CCCA* vol. III, fig. CCXCVI, CCXCVII. Pour de pareilles offrandes dans l'ancienne religion grecque, cf. aussi Aesch. *Ag*.1268; Eur. *IA* 1073, *Ion* 223, *Tr*.257.

[31] Cf. Arnold van Gennep, The *Rites of Passage* (London 1977 [1909]), E. Leach, *Kultur und Kommunikation. Zur Logik symbolische Zusammenhänge* (Suhrkamp Taschenbuch

de cette prêtresse peut être comprise. Ainsi, pendant les céremonies dont on parle, l'homme essaie de maintenir sa relation personelle avec le lieu sacré, par le moyen de telles offrandes, mais en même temps, cherche à exprimer les relations de supériorité et de subordination, existant entre le domaine du sacré et celui du profane. L'homme sent le besoin de demander l'assistance des dieux, particulièrement pendant des périodes de transition qui laissent leur marque sur sa vie personnelle (naissance, adolescence, marriage, mort). Il pense qu'une telle transition à une nouvelle situation s'effectuera en toute sécurité seulement avec l'aide et l'assistance sans limites des dieux. Il croit que l'incertitude et, très souvent, même la crainte provoquées par le changement peuvent être surmontées seulement avec la protection des dieux, dont il demande le secours. D'après W. Burkert qui a commenté le témoignage que nous examinons, "par la consécration de ses cheveux, la personne cède une partie de soi—il s'agit bien-sûr d'une perte indolore qui est très vite réparée—exactement comme le sacrifice comprend un élément de la conscience lourde et de la réparation, de la même façon ici, l'angoisse créée par les changements de la vie devient un symbolisme de délivrance des forces qui, jusqu'alors, régissaient la vie humaine".[32] Cette offrande de l'homme à un tournant de sa vie reste dans l'espace du sanctuaire et a un caractère permanent, puisqu'elle est le plus souvent accrochée en haut. De cette façon, l'offre au-delà du désir de parade, montre ainsi, de façon marquée, la reconnaissance d'un acte supérieur.

L'offre des cheveux aux dieux de la part des hommes est un phénomène très répandu dans le monde grec.[33] Dès l'époque homérique on trouve ce genre d'offrandes dans le cadre de cérémonies funèbres.[34] Dans de nombreuses régions les garçons et les filles coupent leurs cheveux et les consacrent à une divinité, un fleuve, un héros-dieu local,[35] quand ils atteignent leur majorité,[36] ou, même, avant

---

Wissenschaft, 212, Frankfurt/M 1987) 98–100; U. Bianchi (ed.), *Transition Rites. Cosmic, Social and Individual Order* (Storia delle Religioni, 2, Roma 1985).

[32] W. Burkert, *Griechische Religion*, 121.

[33] Pour la signification de l'offre des cheveux en Grèce, voir W.H. Rouse, *Greek Votive Offerings* (Cambridge 1902), 241–245; L. Sommer, *Das Haar in Aberglauben und Religion der Griechen* (Diss. München 1912), Evans, *The Palace of Minos*, IV (London 1936) 480; S. Eitrem, *Opferritus und Voropfer der Griechen und Römer*, 344sq.

[34] Voir Homer, *Il.*23,135, et 151; *Od.*4,196–197, et 24,46; Herodot.IV,34; Soph. *El.*52,448sq.; Eur. *Hél.*90sq., *Or.*96; Pausanias I,43,4; Kallim. *Hymn* IV,296sq. Cf. aussi M.P. Nilsson, *GGR* I,136,149,180–181.

[35] Voir M.P. Nilsson, *GGR* I,136,238.

[36] A. Brelich, *Paides e Parthenoi*, (Incunabula Graeca XXXV, Roma 1981 [1969])

leur mariage.[37] Les offrandes de ce genre sont aussi un phénomène ordinaire, chaque fois que l'homme se trouve face à un danger (naufrage, maladie, etc.).[38] Leur importance devient même plus primordiale quand il s'agit des divinités qui protègent la vie des hommes d'une manière absolue. On peut comprendre cela si on prend en considération que la déesse Artémis qui était la protectrice des enfants et de l'accouchement, rassemblait des offrandes de cheveux. De plus, les gens avaient coutume à consacrer leur cheveux à la déesse en faisant un vœu, et tout particulièrement quand ils affrontaient un danger.[39] C'est ainsi qu'Artémidore nous dit: "cela indique des chagrins d'un caractère personnel ou quelque affliction soudaine qui a provoqué une grande douleur; car les gens qui se trouvent dans des situations pareilles nécessairement se coupent les cheveux" (τῶν ἰδίων πένθη ἢ αἰφνίδιόν τινα συμφορὰν μεγάλων κακῶν ἀναπλέων σημαίνει· οἱ γὰρ ἐν τοιούτοις γενόμενοι ἑαυτοὺς ἀνάγκη περικείρουσι).[40] Cette action doit être considérée, comme on a déjà mentionné plus haut, comme une sorte de sacrifice (*aparché*) que les hommes étaient accoutumés à pratiquer envers les dieux.

Nous trouvons aussi ces offrandes dans le rite d'autres cultes de caractère mystique-orgiastique, comme le culte dionysiaque. Euripide dit dans les *Bacchantes* que "sacrées sont mes mèches, soignées pour le dieu" (ἱερὸς ὁ πλόκαμος τῷ θεῷ δ'αὐτὸν τρέφω).[41] Ce témoignage nous permet de comprendre la valeur qu'avait la consécration faite par les hommes envers les dieux. Et pour cela ils soignent leurs cheveux pour pouvoir à un moment donné les consacrer aux dieux. Cet acte

---

31, 34, 37, 71–72 n. 59, 80–81 n. 88, 115, 129, 358–360, 446–447, 464; M.P. Nilsson, *GGR* I,136–138; F.T. van Straten, "Gifts for the Gods", 89. Cf. aussi Theophr. *Char.*21.3.

[37] Voir Aphrodite Avagianou, *Sacred Marriage in the Rituals of Greek Religion* (European University Studies, XV,54, Bern-Berlin-Frankfurt/M-New York 1991), 3, 11–12. Cf. Aussi Hesych. s.v. "γάμων ἔθη. τὰ προτέλεια καὶ ἀπαρχαὶ καὶ τριχῶν ἀφαιρέσεις τῇ θεῷ ἀπὸ μιᾶς τῶν γάμων τῆς παρθένου".

[38] Voir F.T. van Straten, "Gifts for the Gods", in H.S. Versnel (ed.), *Faith, Hope and Worship. Aspects of Religious Mentality in the Ancient World* (Studies in Greek and Roman Religion, 2, Leiden 1981) 90, 97–98. Cf. aussi Pausanias II,11,16; Robuck, *Corinth* XIV, no 116.

[39] Cf. *Anth.Pal.*VI,59,200,201,271,274,276sq., 280; Herodot.IV,34. Voir aussi S. Eitrem, *Opferritus und Voropfer*, 365; M.P. Nilsson, *GGR* I,137–138, 493; A. Brelich, *Paides e Parthenoi*, 447.

[40] Artemid. *Oneir.*I,22 cf. aussi Plut. *Qu.Rom.*267A–C: "καὶ γὰρ παρ' Ἕλλησιν ὅταν δυστυχία τις γένηται, κείρονται μὲν οἱ γυναῖκες κομῶσι δ' οἱ ἄνδρες".

[41] *Bacchae*, 494, cf. E.R. Dodds (ed.), *Euripides Bacchae* (Oxford 1989 [repr.]), 139, voir aussi Eur. *Bacch.*112 et E.R. Dodds, *op. cit.*, 81, Eur. *Hipp.*202, Aesch. fr. 313.

était pratiqué primitivement par les femmes et par les hommes pour montrer leur foi envers les dieux. Mais plus tard, à partir du Ve siècle, il caractérisait seulement le tempérament religieux des femmes.[42] Elles se distinguaient par leur sensibilité particulière et s'adressaient aux dieux, en leur consacrant comme vœu leur cheveux longs ou seulement des boucles de cheveux. C'est de cette façon qu'elles voulaient montrer leur reconnaisçance infinie envers la divinité, en donnant ce qui était pour elles le plus précieux. Cet acte constitue l'offrande suprême d'une partie de la personnalité entière des fidèles (*pars pro toto*), et l'habitude d'accrocher leurs cheveux aux portes des temples des dieux était assez répandue chez les Grecs et chez les Romains.[43] Un tel geste est témoigné dans l'épigramme de l'*Anthologie Palatine* que nous étudions, mais aussi dans une série d'épigrammes contenues dans le VIe livre de la même collection.[44] Nous pouvons ainsi comprendre qu'il s'agit d'une action de piété qui caractérise le rite de la religion traditionnelle et les cultes mystiques.

De plus, dans notre épigramme nous observons qu'il existe une description réaliste de l'ambiance dans laquelle se pratiquaient les cérémonies. On y voit la nature sauvage et la disposition orgiastique des fidèles qui étaient représentées par la prêtresse de la déesse. L'ambiance entière dans laquelle se réalisaient d'ailleurs tous ces témoignages, comme nous verrons par la suite, pourrait être considérée comme une expression des efforts que donnent les fidèles pour entrer dans un milieu dominé seulement par la déesse. Il y a aussi un ordre constant dans lequel les hommes chantent des hymnes et expriment d'une manière paradoxale leur reconnaissance et leur soumission envers la Grande Mère de la nature et des êtres humains.

Il nous faut encore parler, en prenant comme cause le témoignage concret de Rhianos, du rôle que jouent les femmes dans le rite, où

---

[42] S. Eitrem, *Opferritus und Voropfer*, 348–349, cf. *PLG* 208, nr. 5 (Bergk.): "ἃς καὶ ἀποφθίμενας πᾶσαι νεοθᾶγι σιδάρῳ ἄλικες ἱμερτὰν κράτος ἔθετο τὴν κόμαν", Theodor. Prodr.VI,439sq.: "ἔκκοψον ἄκραν τῇ θανούσῃ τὴν κόμην, σπεῖσον πικρὸν δάκρυον ἐκ βλεφαρίδων".

[43] S. Eitrem, *Opferritus und Voropfer*, 379–380; Christian Jacob, "Paysage et bois sacrés : ἄλσος dans la *Périégèse de la Grèce de Pausanias*", in *Les bois sacrés*. Actes du Colloque international du Naples (Collection du Centre Jean Bérard, Naples 1993) 31–44, et surtout 39; Claudia Montepaone, "*L'alsos/lucus*, forma idealtipica artemidea: il caso di Ippolito", *Les bois sacrés*, 69–79, et surtout 72–74; Olivier de Cazanove, "Suspension d'ex-voto dans les bois sacrés", *Les bois sacrés*, 111–126, et surtout 115, 120, 122. Cf. aussi Plinius, *HN* XXVIII,86.

[44] *Anthol.Palat.*VI,35,57,96,106,168,221,255,262,331.

leur vive sensibilité avait une importance particulière. Il faut encore
ajouter que les manifestations religieuses des femmes à l'époque classique et dans les années postérieures renferment plus de passion que
la religion traditionnelle qui se caractérise justement comme andro-
cratique.[45] Les femmes, bien qu'elles aient eu une petite influence
dans la formation de la religion officielle, jouaient souvent un rôle
assez important dans les formes mystique-orgiastiques. Cela nous
permet de conclure qu'à ces cultes participaient principalement des
individus, ou des groupes sociaux qui ne participaient pas normalement à la vie publique ni au culte de la ville. Cet événement nous
montre encore une fois que la religion avait aussi un aspect senti-
mental qui éclatait à la fin. Et pour cela justement que M.P. Nilsson
dit que les femmes jouent un rôle de dissolvant dans la religion grecque traditionnelle.[46]

Les cérémonies de la déesse sont habituellement pratiquées dans
une ambiance orgiastique, qui est accentuée, comme nous verrons
plus tard, par l'usage d'instruments musicaux divers, de la danse et
de cris de délire. La description de l'épigramme de Rhianos nous
introduit, d'une manière très caractéristique, dans un milieu pareil.
Cette situation effrénée est indiquée précisément par la mention du
cri fort jeté par la prêtresse pendant la pratique de ces cérémonies.
Il se rendait par le terme "ὀλολυγμός", c'est-à-dire "cri fort de joie".[47]

---

[45] W. Burkert, *Griechische Religion*, 350, 365–370; G. Sfameni Gasparro, *Misteri e culti mistici di Demetra* (Storia delle Religioni, 3, Roma 1986) 223–307, B. Gladigow, "Die Teilung des Opfers", *Frühmittelalterliche Studien*, 18 (1984) 26–27; P. Ardesmann, "Thesmophorien", *RE* VIA1 (1936) col. 1518; P. Foucart, *Associations religieuses*, 58–66; M.P. Nilsson, Ελληνική λαϊκή θρησκεία (ελλην. μεταφρ. Ι. Θ. Κακριδής) (Βιβλιοθήκη του φιλολόγου, 8, Athènes 1979) 92–94, Ulrike Huber, *Die staatlichen Frauenfesten Athens*, (Magisterarbeit Tübingen 1984); G. Duby-M. Perror (ed.), *Geschichte der Frauen*, vol. I: Antike, Pauline Schmitt Pantel (Hrsg.) (Frankfurt/M.-New York 1993).
Pour la participation particulière des femmes en-tant que prêtresses dans le culte de Cybèle voir M.J. Vermaseren, *CCCA*, vol. II. Pour l'interdiction des femmes à participer au culte public de la ville, cf. aussi W. Burkert, *Griechische Religion*, 382–388, Sokolowski, *LSCG* 82,96; *LSS* 56,63,66,88,89; *LSAM* 42; R. Wächter, *Reinheitsvorschriften im griechischen Kult* (Giessen 1910) 125–129.
[46] Cf. M.P. Nilsson, Ελληνική λαϊκή θρησκεία, 94.
[47] Cf. Eur. *Bacch.*24–25,689–690; E.R. Dodds (ed.), *Bacchae* 66,162; *Etym.Magn.* "ὀλολυγή· φωνὴ γυναικῶν ἥν ποιοῦνται ἐν τοῖς ἱεροῖς εὐχόμεναι"; Pollux.I,28; Eur. *Or.*1137, *Heracl.*782, *Aesch.Th.Ag.*28 cf. 595, *Ch.*387. Cf. aussi *Orphei Hymni* (ed. G. Quandt, Berlin 1962 [1955] 15); Eust. *ad Od.*4,767. Le terme "ὀλολυγή" apparaît pour la première fois au culte de la déesse Athena, cf. Hom. *Il.*6,301. Voir aussi M.J. Vermaseren, *The Legend of Attis in Greek and Roman Art* (*EPRO* 9, Leiden 1966) 42, A.S.F. Gow ("The Gallus and the Lion", 91) qui se réfère au terme "λαλάγημα".

A ce cas concret, ce terme a comme but principal d'exprimer la reconnaissance de la prêtresse envers la déesse et en même temps la situation particulière où elle se trouve. Il faut encore accentuer que cet "ὀλολυγμός" est aussi lié au cri des femmes qui est souvent aussi particulièrement caractéristique pendant les cérémonies qui concernent les morts. Des réactions semblables sont, d'ailleurs, ordinaires pendant les sacrifices, où les femmes y assistant jettent de hauts cris aigus. Ce cri indique clairement un impératif émotif. Ce cas a fourni à un chercheur contemporain l'occasion de lier le témoignage que nous examinons aux cérémonies qui ont un caractère mortuaire d'Attis. Il est possible, comme le prétend le chercheur, que les clameurs profondes que les Galles font entendre—le "γαλλαῖον ὀλόλυγμα" de Rhianos (A.P.VI,173) et le "ἰδαῖος ὑλαγμός" de Nicandre (Alex.220)— puissent s'interpréter comme des chants funèbres.[48]

Dans ce cas concret, ce que l'auteur veut révéler, c'est seulement la situation de la manie sacrée dans laquelle se trouve la prêtresse de la déesse. Cela se voit d'ailleurs aussi par le fait que ce cri cérémonial qui est rapporté dans les divers témoignages comme "ἀλαλαί" s'unit principalement aux cultes qui ont un caractère mystique-orgiastique.[49] D'ailleurs, l'emploi susmentionné du terme "ὑλαγμός", qui signifie "aboiement", par Nicandre vise à décrire le plus clairement possible l'état particulier atteint par les fidèles au cours de ces cérémonies.[50] Ainsi, Pindare dit: "et que s'élèvent les sourds gémissements des Naïdes, et les cris de délire et les hourras qu'accompagne la brusque secousse du cou rejeté en arrière" (Ναΐδων ἐρίγδουποι στοναχαὶ μανίαι τ'ἀλαλαί . . .).[51] Contrairement à la citation de Rhianos les cérémonies orgiastiques se réalisaient avec l'accompagnement des instruments que tenaient les fidèles. Ceci apparaît dans les témoignages des auteurs du Vᵉ siècle avant J.-C.[52] L'importance que ces instruments avaient pour le rite du culte était tellement grande que leur

---

[48] D. Cosi, "Salvatore e salvezza nei misteri di Attis", *Aevum* L (1976) 69 et surtout n. 169. D'après *LSJ*, "ὀλολυγμός" le terme est utilisé "rarely of lamentation". Voir aussi *Ant.Pal.*VII,182.

[49] Menandr., fr. 326 (ed. Kock); Lucian., *Tragop.*30sq., *Dion.*4; Livius, 39,10; Aristoph. *Lys.*1291–1294; Eur. *Bacch.*592–593; Pind. *Ol.*7,68. Cf. aussi R. Kanicht, *Euripides Helena*, vol. II (Kommentar) (Heidelberg 1969), 350–351.

[50] Voir *LSJ*, s.v. ὑλαγμός.

[51] Pind. *Dithyr.*II, fr. 70b (ed. B. Snell, *Pindari carmina cum fragmentis*, Leipzig 1964, pp. 74–75); L.A. Farnell, *Pindar. Critical Commentary to the works of Pindar*, Amsterdam 1961, repr. [1932]), 423.

[52] Diod.Sic.5,49,1; Apol.Rhod.I,1138–1140 et *schol.ad.loc.* Luc. *Dial.deor.*20 (12),

utilisation est sous-entendue dans tous les témoignages. En écoutant le son des instruments, une situation orgiastique naît chez ceux qui participent aux cérémonies et généralement dans toute l'assemblée; ceci, selon les témoignages des auteurs, était d'ailleurs connu dans tout le monde hellénique.[53]

Parmi ces témoignages la relation faite par Pindare possède une place particulière. Il y décrit l'atmosphère des cérémonies pour la déesse.[54] La description de l'ambiance cultuelle trouve son sommet dans un autre témoignage du même auteur, qui se rapporte au culte de Dionysos à Thèbes. Comme nous le savons, la divinité de Dionysos est analogue quant au caractère orgiastique, à la Grande Mère et c'est précisément pour cette raison qu'elles sont comparées, en tant que cultes analogues.[55] Cela devient plus clair, si on prend en considération le témoignage de Strabon qui dit que dans ce cas on "réunit donc en commune description les rites des Grecs dans le culte de Dionysos et ceux des Phrygiens dans celui de la Mère des dieux" (τὴν κοινωνίαν τῶν περὶ τὸν Διόνυσον ἀποδειχθέντων νομίμων παρὰ τοῖς Ἕλλησι καὶ τῶν παρὰ τοῖς Φρυξὶ περὶ τὴν Μητέρα τῶν θεῶν συνοικειῶν ἀλλήλοις) (X,3,12). Et la cérémonie d'ailleurs de la Grande déesse asiatique était elle aussi restée proche de la cérémonie dionysiaque. La musique frénétique des tambourins, des cymbales, des cliquettes et des flûtes, des instruments qu'utilisaient les Ménades du culte de Dionysos, était la seule qui pouvait créer l'ambiance nécessaire à la pratique des cérémonies métroaques. Il est alors assez normal que dans une telle sorte de culte domine la description que Pindare nous donne de manière caractéristique, "voici que, près de l'auguste

---

233–234; Strab. *Geogr.*X,3,17; Athenaios, *Deipnos.*636a; Eur. *Palamid.* fr². 586 (ed. Nauck, 545), *Hél.*1313sq., 1346,1352, *Bacch.*5559; Eumel. fr. 10 (ed. Kinkel); Apollod. 3,5,1; Eupol. fr. 1, 15. Cf. aussi M.P. Nilsson, *GGR* vol. I, pp. 160–161, G. Sfameni Gasparro, *Soteriology*, 9–11, ead., "Helena", 1151, 1158–1159, 1162, 1164; E.R. Dodds, *Bacchae* 76–77, R. Canicht, *Euripides Helena*, II,350–351; I.K. Loucas, Η Ρέα- Κυβέλη, 19–20 et surtout n. 38.

[53] Arist. *Pol.*VIII,1340a10: "[τὰ δ᾽Ολύμπου μέλη] ποιεῖ τὰς ψυχὰς ἐνθουσιαστικάς"; G. Sfameni Gasparro, "Helena", 1151–1152 et n. 18; E. Moutsopoulos, "Euripide et la philosophie de la musique", *REG* LXXV (1962) 420–425, 436–438; G. Quasten, *Musik und Gesang in den Kulten der heidnischen Antike und christlichen Frühzeit* (Liturgiegesch. Quellen und Forschung, 25, Münster i.W. 1930) 45–58.

[54] Pindare, *3 Pyth.*137–140.

[55] Cf. Strab. *Geogr.*X,3,13: "ἡ κοινωνία τῶν περὶ τὸν Διόνυσον ἀποδειχθέντων νομίμων παρὰ τοῖς Ἕλλησι καὶ τῶν παρὰ τοῖς φρυξὶ περὶ τὴν Μητέρα τῶν θεῶν", Aesch. *Edonoi*, fr. 71 (ed. Mette); Eur. *Palam.* fr². 586 (ed. Nauck, 545); E.R. Dodds, *Bacchae* 76–77, 83–85 et passim; R. Kanicht, *Euripides Helena*, II,331sq., 357; G. Sfameni Gasparro, "Helena", 1152–1153, 116–1165; ead., *Soteriology*, 11–19 et surtout 15.

Mère, les timbales rondes ouvrent le ban, et que bruissent les cymbales, et la torche ardente, dont la blonde résine entretient la flamme" (σεμνᾷ μὲν κατάρχει/Ματέρι πὰρ μ[εγ]άλα ῥόμβοι τυπάνων,/ἐν δὲ κέχλαδ[εν] κρόταλ᾽ αἰδομένα τε δᾷς ὑπὸ ξαν[θα]ῖσι πεύκαις).[56] C'est le même esprit d'ailleurs qui s'exprime dans l'hymne homérique consacré à la Mère des dieux. Dans cet hymne, la majestueuse déesse se présente baignée dans la joie. "Elle aime le son des cymbales et des tambourins, ainsi que le trémissement des flûtes" (ᾗ κροτάλων τυπάνων τ᾽ἰαχὴ σύν τε βρόμος αὐλῶν).[57] Le lien qui existe entre les instruments et la personne de la déesse est tellement grand que Cybèle dans toutes les sources est caractérisée par ces instruments. C'est d'ailleurs pour cette raison que l'on utilise des instruments concrets pour son culte. Cela est visible aussi dans l'hymne orphique consacré à la déesse Rhéa qui y est caractérisée comme déesse "χαλκόκροτος".[58] Pour ce point particulier il faut que nous rapportions aussi l'importance de l'utilisation des tambourins dans le rite du culte métroaque. Les tambourins qui se caractérisent comme des instruments orientaux, étaient souvent qualifiés de "βυρσοτενῆ".[59] Ils étaient tellement appréciés par la déesse qu'elle y fut plusieurs fois appelée "τυμπανοτερπής".[60] On retrouve cela dans un certain nombre de témoignages qui sont liés d'une manière directe ou indirecte au rite du culte. Euripide dans les *Bacchantes*, en décrivant les habitudes qui prédominaient dans le culte de Dionysos, dit que ces tambourins sont considérés comme une invention des Kourètes qui étaient les compagnons constants de la déesse. Ils les laissaient, d'après l'auteur, entre les mains de la déesse afin qu'ils constituent son symbole permanent.[61] On trouve aussi la même idée dans les témoignages des trouvailles archéologiques.

---

[56] *Dithyr.II*, fr. 70b (ed. B. Snell, *Pindari carmina cum fragmentis³*, Leipzig 1964, vol. II, 74–75). Voir aussi Diogène Athenaeus, *TrGF* I 45 F1, *TrGF* II 629, II, 188 f.; Emilio Suárez de la Torres, "Expérience orgiastique et composition poétique: le *dithyrambe* II de Pindare (Fr. 70B Snell-Maehler)", *Kernos* 5 (1992) 183–207.

[57] *H.Hom. ad Matr.*3. Cf. T.W. Allen-R. Halliday-E.E. Sikes, *The Homeric Hymns²* (Oxford 1936) 394–395; J. Humbert, *Homère Hymnes*, (Paris 1967).

[58] *Orph.H.*14,3 (p. 14), 38,1 (p. 30): "χαλκοκρότους Κουρῆτες"; Hesychius, *Lexicon*, "χαλκόκροτος".

[59] Eur. *Bacch.*124,205. En ce qui concerne la signification des tambourines dans le cadre du culte de la déesse, voir aussi Aisch. *TrGF* III 57,10; Eur. *HF* 889, *Hélèn.*1347; *Cyc.*65,205; *TrGF* II,629,9. Cf. E.R. Dodds, *Bacchae* 83–84; R. Kanicht, *Euripides Helena* II,351–353; F. Naumann, *Die Ikonographie der Kybele* 136, L.E. Roller, "Attis on Greek Votive Monuments", 246.

[60] *Orph.H.*27,11 (p. 23).

[61] Eur. *Bacch.*123–124, cf. E.R. Dodds, *Bacchae* 84–85.

Selon ces témoignages les tambourins constituaient le moyen principal de l'équipement sacerdotal de la déesse.[62]

Mais l'instrument qui saisit d'un transport divin, tant dans la poésie que dans l'iconographie plastique, est la flûte. Aristote la caractérise comme l'instrument orgiastique par excellence.[63] Il se caractérise d'ailleurs par son lien avec la pratique des cérémonies orgiastiques et à cause de son bruit profond, comme "βαρύδρομος" (la flûte au bruit profond).[64] Cet instrument d'après une tradition est considéré comme une invention de l'époque de Kronos.[65] Pausanias dit aussi, de manière caractéristique, que le chant de la Mère qui s'accompagnait de sa flûte, était une invention de Marsyas.[66]

Ce serait une exagération si on rapportait au cas présent les témoignages postérieurs des Grecs et des Latins où on trouve la description de toute l'atmosphère qui se créait grâce à l'utilisation de ces instruments dans le rite du culte. Nous pensons qu'il vaut mieux ne faire mention que des autels que consacraient les fidèles pendant la pratique de la cérémonie de taurobole.[67] Les instruments y sont souvent représentés accrochés aux branches d'un pin sacré qui avait une très grande importance pour le rite du culte métroaque. Ce fait nous permet de comprendre encore une fois la place particulière que ces instruments prenaient dans les cérémonies du culte et constitue encore une preuve de la capacité de la musique à provoquer chez

---

[62] Cf. M.J. Vermaseren, *CCCA* vol. I–VII (Leiden 1987–1989), où se trouvent réunies les représentations relatives à la déesse.

[63] Arist. *Pol.*VIII,1341a,21–22: "οὐκ ἔστιν ὁ αὐλὸς ἠθικὸν ἀλλὰ μᾶλλον ὀργιαστικόν, ὥστε πρὸς τοὺς τοιούτους αὐτῷ καιροὺς χρηστέον ἐν οἷς ἡ θεωρία κάθαρσιν μᾶλλον δύναται ἢ μάθησιν", cf. *ibid.*, 1342b16.

[64] Eur. *Hélèn.*1350–1352, cf. R. Kanicht., *Euripides Helena* II,353, voir aussi, Athenaios, *Deipnos.*, 185a.

[65] M. Rocchi, *Kadmos e Harmonia un matrimonio problematico* (Storia delle Religioni, 6, Roma 1989), 31; M. Wegner, *Das Musikleben der Griechen* (Berlin 1949) 32sq. Voir aussi Nonn. *Dion.*XLV,43; Catull.63,22; Lucr.2,620.

[66] X,30,9: "οἱ δὲ ἐν Κελαιναῖς ἐθέλουσι μὲν τὸν ποταμὸν ὃς διέξεισιν αὐτοῖς διὰ τῆς πόλεως ἐκεῖνόν ποτε εἶναι τὸν αὐλήτην, ἐθέλουσι δὲ καὶ εὕρημα εἶναι τοῦ Μαρσύου τὸ μητρῷον αὔλημα· φασὶ δὲ ὡς καὶ τῶν Γαλατῶν ἀπώσαιντο στρατείαν τοῦ Μαρσύου σφίσιν ἐπὶ τοὺς βαρβάρους ὕδατί τε ἐκ τοῦ ποταμοῦ καὶ μέλει τῶν αὐλῶν ἀμύναντος", cf. Steph.Byz. "Πεσσινοῦς"; Diod.Sic.3,58,23; Apollod.1,4,2. Voir aussi M.J., Vermaseren, *Cybele and Attis* 19.

[67] R. Duthoy, *The Taurobolium*, 9–11 no. 5, 11–13 no. 6, 14, no. 11, 15–16, no. 17, 17–18, no. 22, 22–24, no. 33, 24, no. 34; M.J. Vermaseren, *CCCA* vol. II, no. 389 (pl. CXVII, CXXI) no. 390 (pl. CXXI, CXXII) vol. III, no. 226 (pl. CXIX) n. 236 (pl. CXXII, CXXIII) no. 239 (pl. CXXIV), no. 241b (pl. CXXVII, CXXIX, CXXX, CXXXI) no. 357 (pl. CCVII, CCIX); id., *The Legend of Attis* 26 et pl. XV; I.K. Loucas, Η Ρέα-Κυβέλη, figs. 6–7, 10–11.

les hommes des sentiments orgiastiques. Ceci était d'ailleurs connu dans tout le monde ancien, particulièrement chez les fidèles qui participaient aux cérémonies qui avaient un caractère orgiastique. Ménandre d'ailleurs nous informe que les hommes à cause de l'influence que la déesse elle-même exerçait sur eux à travers le son orgiastique de la musique, ressentaient une sorte de *"manie"*.[68]

Mais l'élément qui complète d'une manière particulière l'image du caractère inspiré du culte est la réalisation par les fidèles de danses frénétiques.[69] Les fidèles étaient particulièrement tentés par les danses métroaques qui constituaient un des éléments principaux du culte de la déesse. D'ailleurs ces danses, qui se réalisaient dans le cadre particulier du culte orgiastique constituent un des principaux moyens pour provoquer des sentiments religieux chez les participants à la cérémonie. A son époque Lucien disait: "il est impossible de trouver même un culte mystèrique ancien qui ne possède pas l'élément de la danse" (τελετῶν οὐδὲ μίαν ἀρχαίαν ἔστιν εὑρεῖν ἄνευ ὀρχήσεως)[70] et nous pensons qu'il a raison en ce qui concerne les cérémonies mystique-orgiastiques. Une des manières de theomixie ou union du fidèle avec le divin, qui était le but principal de cérémonie, était l'enthousiasme. Le fort rejet de la tête en arrière est plus fréquent que vers l'avant. L'exaltation de la danse se manifeste aussi par les nombreux mouvements et les cheveux déliés.[71] Cette image est confirmée par une série de petites statues qui représentent, comme on le croit, les partisans du culte métroaque. Ces trouvailles proviennent de sites archéologiques de Grèce et d'Asie Mineure. Ces figurines portent

---

[68] *Theophoroumene*, 25sq. (ed. A. Koerte, *Menandri Reliquiae*, vol. I, Leipzig 1957, 101).

[69] Cf. Eur. *Phoen.*655, *Bacch.*482; Platon. *Symp.*215e, *Ion* 555e; Apollod.2,2,2; E. Rohde, *Psyche. Seelenkult und Unsterblichkeitsglaube der Griechen*[2] (Darmstadt 1980) (repr. Nachdr. Freiburg-Tübingen 1898) vol. I, 287; P. Boyance, *Le culte des Muses chez les philosophes grecs. Études d'histoire et de psychologie religieuses*, (Paris 1936) 64sq., M.J. Vermaseren, *CCCA* vol. II, 17, no. 49, 117, no. 379, vol. V, 5, no. 9, 38, no. 104, 41–42, no. 115; E.R. Dodds, *Bacchae* XV,87,159. Voir aussi Dionysos qui danse au monte Parnasse (Macr. *Sat.*1,18 4); cf. Eur. fr[2]. 752 (ed. Nauck), Aristoph. *Ran.*1211sq.

[70] Lucian, *de salt.*15.

[71] M.J. Vermaseren, *The Legend of Attis* 43 et n. 1, 49; S. Eitrem, *Opferritus und Voropfer*, 398–399; H. Graillot, *Le culte de Cybèle*, 304. Cf. Aisch. *TrGF* III 57; Soph. *Ant.*152,1154; *OT* 1093; Eur. *HF* 680–686, 889 f.; *Ion* 1079, 1084; *Hélèn.*1312f., 1345; *Phoin.*655,788–791,1756; *Bacch.*114,189,190,195,205,220,323,379,862; Eur. *N*[2] 752; Pratinas, *TrGF* I 4F3,1.5.17; *TrGF* II 629,6; Philodamos, *Paian* 8sq., 19sq., 40, 133sq., 146sq.; Serv. *ad Aen.*X,22: *"Semper Galli per furorem motu capitis comam, rotantes ululatu futura pronuntiabant"*.

des habits orientaux, elles ont les mains levées et la tête tournée en arrière (*"oklasma"*).[72] Ce fait nous permet de comprendre qu'il s'agit d'un témoignage montrant clairement la place caractéristique de la danse et l'ambiance qui s'instaure durant la cérémonie. Cette danse de la manie pratiquée par les fidèles de Cybèle est comparable aux danses analogues des Corybantes, les accompagnants constants de la déesse. Dans l'ambiance cultuelle de Samothrace ils se caractérisent aussi précisément, à cause de leur nature, comme "βητάρμονες" (danseurs).[73] Le terme "βητάρμων" (danseur) se trouve pour la première fois chez Homère[74] et plus tard chez Apollonius de Rhodes.[75] Chez le dernier, ce terme qualifie les Argonautes en armes qui ressemblent à la troupe mythique des Corybantes, quand ils dansaient en l'honneur de Cybèle. D'ailleurs le caractère intense de ses manifestations montre d'une manière toute particulière leur origine orientale.[76]

La danse pratiquée par les partisans de la déesse et surtout par les femmes pourrait être liée à une autre cause. Il nous est possible de supposer qu'elle pourrait constituer une partie des cérémonies magiques qui visaient principalement à faciliter la germination.[77] C'est d'ailleurs un phénomène assez fréquent et nous le trouvons dans l'atmosphère cultuelle des divinités de la fécondité. Un tel acte peut trouver place dans le cadre de la magie homéopathique dont les données jouent un rôle particulier dans la vie des hommes qui vivent dans les régions agricoles. Il est alors normal que les fidèles agissent de la sorte. De ce fait ils essayaient peut-être de rendre favorable la

---

[72] M.J. Vermaseren, *The Legend of Attis* 48–53 et pl. XXVIII,2,3,4, XXIX,1,2, XXX,1,2, XXXI,1,2, XXXII,1,2,3, XXXIII,1,2,3, XXXV,2,3; M.J. Vermaseren-M. De Boer, "Attis", *LIMC* III (1986) 22–44, et surtout nos. 56–76, 240–278. Voir aussi la représentation du cratère en figure rouge d'Athènes, Spina, A*RV*[2] 1052, no. 25.

[73] Strab. *Geogr.*X,3,21; Verg. *Aen.*IX,617,X,552; Horat. *Od.*I,16; Etym.Magn. "βητάρμονες". Cf. Aussi M. Rocchi, *Kadmos e Harmonia*, 33,71, G. Sfameni Gasparro, *Soteriology*, 15, n. 37.

[74] Hom. *Od.*8,250, cf. 383; Eust.ad *Hom.Od.*VIII,250,264, *Schol.Hom.*VIII,250: "παρὰ τὸ ἐν ἁρμονίᾳ βαίνειν ἤτοι ὀρχησταί ... ἀπὸ τοῦ βαίνειν ἁρμοδίως".

[75] Apoll.Rhod.3257sq., 4,1142; cf. aussi P. Boyance. *Études sur la religion romaine*, 222, n. 4.

[76] Pour des habitudes pareilles qui ont survécu à l'entourage de l'Asie Mineure, cf. R. Turcan, *Les cultes orientaux dans le monde-Romain* (Paris 1989) 37. Nous rencontrons pareilles habitudes d'une part chez les Montanistes (W. Schepelern, *Der Montanismus und die phrygishen Kulte*, Tübingen 1929, 146sq.) et d'autre part dans le mysticisme musulman (Sufism), voir Gr. D. Ziakas, Ο μυστικός ποιητής, *Maulana Jalaladin Rumi* και η διδασκαλία του, (Thessalonique 1987 [1973]).

[77] E.R. Dodds, *Bacchae* XIII–XVI; M.P. Nilsson, *GGR* vol. I, 161–162; U. Bianchi, "Prolegomena", *MM*; N. Papachatzis, Η θρησκεία στην αρχαία Ελλάδα 171–172.

déesse qui règne d'une manière absolue sur la nature et les hommes. Le fait que tous les ans à une certaine époque, une telle danse se réalisait peut nous conforter dans cette idée. C'est par cette manifestation que les hommes de certaines régions voulaient symboliser et rendre favorable la production annuelle de leurs biens. C'est pour cette raison que les fidèles réalisaient souvent ces danses pendant le printemps, au temps où la nature entière manifeste la grandeur de la déesse. Euripide met en scène une telle situation, quand il décrit dans les *Bacchantes*, avec les couleurs les plus vives, la disposition d'esprit qui dominait les fidèles pendant les danses orgiastiques. C'est autant l'intensité qui prédomine que, comme dit l'auteur, "toute la terre deviendra une bande de danseurs" (γᾶ πᾶσα χορεύσει) (v. 114). Naturellement il faut signaler que l'auteur de ce dernier témoignage se réfère au rite du culte de Dionysos. Mais ceci ne pourrait certainement pas constituer un facteur suspensif qui nous empêcherait de comprendre la nature particulière du culte métroaque. D'ailleurs il ne faut pas oublier, comme nous l'avons déjà dit et comme nous le verrons par la suite, que ces deux cultes sont considérés comme similaires à cause de leur nature orgiastique. L'image du témoignage d'Euripide peut sans doute être comparée à un témoignage archéologique postérieur: la tablette en argent de Parabiago qui remonte au IVe siècle après J.-C.[78] Dans cette trouvaille on retrouve l'intensité et le mouvement que présente l'entourage naturel et cosmique qui se trouve sous la surveillance de la Grande Mère. Le témoignage archéologique susmentionné constitue une preuve de plus en ce qui concerne la modification du caractère originel de la déesse, selon "l'esprit du temps" de la basse antiquité. Il existe encore une autre découverte qui confirme la place particulière de la déesse. Elle se trouve dans la collection des monuments du culte métroaque qu'a présentée M.J. Vermaseren. Ce témoignage provient de Colonos Agoraios à Athènes (IIe siècle avant J.-C.) et le chercheur le caractérise comme "terracotta polos".[79] Sur cette trouvaille on trouve quatre femmes qui dansent devant une divinité féminine qui, sans aucun

---

[78] Voir Luisa Musso, *Manifattura suntuaria e commitenza pagana nella Roma del IV secolo: indagine sulla lanx di Parabiago* (Roma 1983) 13, 15, 22–49, 87–88, 106–148; M.J. Vermaseren, *The Legend of Attis* 27–28, id., *Cybele and Attis* 72 et pl. 53; A. Levi, *La patera d'argento di Parabiago* (R. Istituto d'Archeologia e Storia dell'Arte. Opere d'Arte, fasc.5, Roma 1935), id., "La lanx di Parabiago e i testi orfici", *Atheneum* (N.S.) XV (1937) 187–198 et pl. 1–3.

[79] Cf. M.J. Vermaseren, *CCCA* vol. II, 719, no. 36 (pl. IV,36).

doute, est Cybèle. Ce témoignage pourrait encore constituer une confirmation indubitable de la place des femmes dans le rite des cultes de la fécondité. Des actions de ce type doivent être considérées comme des efforts pour rendre favorable la déesse, et pour fortifier les forces séminales de la nature. Il faut dire également que l'on essaie ainsi de ramener la nature à l'harmonie perdue et d'assurer le bonheur de l'ensemble de la communauté sociale en général.

Le lieu où se réalisaient les cérémonies orgiastiques de la déesse était—comme nous l'avons déjà dit à propos de l'épigramme de Rhianos—les élysées sacrés et les montagnes, qui constituent l'expression principale de la nature libre, où régnait la déesse. Ceci est justifié d'ailleurs aussi par l'expression "μήτηρ ὀρεία" (Mère qui règne sur les monts) que nous trouvons dans les témoignages du Ve siècle avant J.-C., ce qui veut dire que la déesse domine des milieux entourés de montagnes escarpées de forêts denses et de lieux isolés.[80] Dans ce site naturel, tous les élements de la nature, les règnes végétal et animal, ainsi que les hommes s'inclinent avec crainte devant la majesté absolue de leur mère. La relation particulière de Cybèle avec le monde des montagnes, des forêts et de la nature sauvage en général, peut être mieux comprise, si on prend en considération son rapport étroit avec Pan, ce dieu des forêts singulier, protecteur de la vie pastorale. Le culte simultané de ces deux dieux fait son apparition dès le Ve siècle avant J.-C. Cela est évident principalement grâce à un nombre de témoignages archéologiques concernant le domaine cultuel, qui représentent le dieu comme la personne qui est toujours le *paredros* de Cybèle.[81] De même, on trouve le culte commun de deux divinités dans un grand nombre de textes de cette période. Ce caractère se retrouvait par ailleurs dans l'hymne orphique qui est lui consacré.

---

[80] Eur. *Or.*1453, *Hipp.*141–144 et *Schol. in Hipp.*144 (ed. E. Schwartz, vol. II, 24); Soph. *Phil.*391–394 et *Schol. in Phil.*391, (ed. P.N. Papageorgius, *Scholia in Sophoclis Tragoedias vetera*, Leipzig, 1888, 362); *Schol.Pind. III Pyth.*139b (ed. A.B. Drachmann, *Scholia vetera in Pindari Carmina. Scholia in Pythonicas*, Amsterdam 1967 [repr.], vol. II, 81); Timoth. fr. 15 in D.L. Page, *Poetae Melici Graeci* (Oxford 1962) 401, n. 791; Diod.Sic.3,58,3; Nonn. *Dion.*XIII,137,XVII,63,XLIII,22; Apol.Rhod. *Argon.*1,1118–1119; Aristoph. *Av.*746; Suidas, (III,555): "Ὀρεία· ἡ ἐν ὄρεσιν ἀναστρεφομένη. τάσδε θεῇ χαίτας περικλεῖδι θῆκεν ὀρεία τῇ ἐν ὄρεσι"; *IG* IV²,I,131,16. Cf. aussi G. Casadio, "I Cretesi di Euripide e l'ascesi Orfica", *Didattica del Classico*, Nr. 2 (Foggia 1990), 287–310, voir surtout 292, 293; G. Sfameni Gasparro, "Helena", *passim*; R. Kanicht, *Euripides Helena* II,358–359.

[81] En ce qui concerne la relation entre Cybèle et Pan, voir F. Brommer, "Pan in 5. und 4. Jahrhundert v. Chr.", *Marburger Jahrbuch für Kunstwissenschaft* 15 (1949/1950) 5–42, et surtout 5, 12, 30–35; P. Borgeaud, *The Cult of Pan in Ancient Greece*

D'après cet hymne elle se caractérise comme: "Mère des Dieux, nourrice de tous, honorée comme les dieux. . . ." (ἀθανάτων θεότιμε, θεῶν μῆτερ, τροφὲ πάντων . . .).[82] Il est alors naturel que ce milieu soit le lieu suprême où se réalisent les cérémonies qui ont comme but principal de glorifier sa grandeur.

Euripide dans *"Hélène"*, commence un hymne à la Grande Mère avec la description: "Mère des Dieux, qui règne sur les monts" (ὀρεία . . . μήτηρ θεῶν).[83] Selon nous on trouve ici de la meilleure manière la fonction de la physionomie orientale dans la forme grecque. L'auteur présente dans son œuvre, d'une manière très caractéristique, une sorte de syncrétisme religieux, par lequel coexistent, dans l'espace grec, les cultes de deux divinités semblables, liées aux notions de fertilité et de fécondité. Il ne faut pas bien-sûr oublier les différences entre les caractères des deux divinités. L'une est associée à la nature sauvage et sans ordre, alors que l'autre, particulièrement dans le milieu cultuel d'Éleusis, est liée à la propagation de la culture des céréales et au développement de la civilisation. Cette œuvre d'Euripide présente, donc, les deux type de culte, c'est-à-dire le caractère mystique-orgiastique du culte de Cybèle, ainsi que la nature mystique-initiatique du culte d'Éleusis. Ces deux types de religiosité sont les plus significatifs de la manière par laquelle le Grec des temps classiques essayait de concevoir sa relation réciproque avec le milieu divin. C'est précisément cette figure de la déesse qui règne sur les montagnes et l'environnement naturel au sens large du mot qui est présentée par l'auteur que nous examinons.[84] C'est cette déesse encore qui court avec manie sur son char tiré par des lions, dans les forêts ombragées,

---

(Chicago/London 1988) 52–53, 82–83; J.A. Haldane, "Pindar and Pan: Frs. 95–100 (Snell)", *Phoenix* 22 (1968) 18–31, L.E. Roller, "Attis on Greek Votive monuments", 252; M.J. Vermaseren, *CCCA* II, nos. 66, 180, 182, 339 (Athènes), no. 279 (Piraeus), no. 432 (Leibadia); E. Suárez de la Torre, "Le Dithyrambe II de Pindare", 196–198. Cf. Aussi Pindar, *3. Pyth.*137–140, Fragm.95 (Snell); Schol.*3. Pyth.*137–139 (attribue à Aristodemos); Pausanias IX,25,3; Eurip. *Hippol.*141–144.
Contre cette union Cybèle-Pan dans le culte local de Béotie s'est élevée récemment F. Bader, "Autobiographie et héritage dans la langue des dieux : d'Homère à Hésiode et Pindare", *REG* 103 (1990–1992) 383–408.

[82] *Orph.H.*27,1 (pp. 22–23).

[83] Vv. 1301–1307: "ὀρεία ποτὲ δρομάδι κώλῳ μάτηρ θεῶν ἐσύθη ἀν' ὑλέαντα νάπῃ/ ποτάμιόν τε χεῦμ' ὑδάτων/βαρύδρομόν τε κῦμ' ἅλιον πόθῳ/τᾶς ἀποιχομένας ἀρρήτου/ κούρας" cf. R. Kanicht, *Euripides Helena.*, II, 338–339, H. Grégoire, Euripide, vol. V, *Hélène-Les Phéniciennes* (Paris 1950) 946.

[84] Voir G. Cerri, "La Madre degli Dei nell' Elena di Euripide", 155–195; Anton F. Harald Bierl, *Dionysos und die griechische Tragödie* (Classica Monacensia, 1, Tübingen 1991), 163–172.

dans les vallées creuses, dans les rivières. Sur son passage frénétique les arbres s'inclinent devant elle. Ces images nous permettent de comprendre que la sauvage et inquiète déesse ne laisse en paix ni le règne végétal, ni le règne animal ni les hommes. La nature se trouve comme la déesse elle-même en extase et ce fait se passe particulièrement au printemps et en hiver. Pendant ces périodes tous les milieux se soumettent à l'implacable volonté de la Grande déesse.[85] Cette situation est présentée d'une manière des plus expressives par la trouvaille archéologique de Parabiago dont nous avons déjà parlé. Dans ce témoignage sont présentés d'une manière caractéristique l'espace cosmique et la nature qui se trouvent sous le pouvoir de la déesse majestueuse. Ainsi ne faudrait-il pas oublier que dans le cas présent, l'artiste, en obéissant à l'esprit de son époque, ait adapté sa représentation de la déesse à l'interprétation symbolique que donnaient les Stoiciens (Cornutus), les Epicuriens (Lucrèce) et la pensée postérieure des néoplatoniciens.[86]

Ces fêtes, comme nous l'indiquent les témoignages des auteurs, se réalisent à la lumière de tisons pendant la nuit. La marche cultuelle dans la montagne visait à faire se rencontrer des fidèles et la Grande Mère et à étudier la nature sauvage et dominée par la déesse.[87] Ce fait est confirmé par un commentaire de la troisième ode pythique de Pindare qui date de l'époque hellénistique. Dans ce commentaire, il existe une description qui montre le style particulier des cérémonies "nocturnes, puisque les mystères en son honneur ont lieu pendant la nuit" (ἐννύχιαι δέ, ἐπεὶ νυκτὸς αὐτῇ τὰ μυστήρια τελεῖται).[88] L'heure nocturne d'ailleurs, comme nous verrons par la suite, et la marche dans la montagne assurent la situation mystique des cérémonies de la troupe. De cette facon, les pannychides de la Grande Mère qui se distinguent par leur caractère mystique-orgiastique et qui se pratiquent dans un lieu naturel isolé doivent être considérés comme

---

[85] F. Cumont, *Orientalische Religionen*, 46–47; M.J. Vermaseren, *The Legend of Attis* 26–27 et pl. XIV,3,4; G. Sfameni Gasparro, "Helena", 1166–1168; R. Kanicht, *Euripides Helena*, II, 338; C. Christou, *Potnia Theron* (Thessalonique 1968). Cf. aussi Soph. *Phil.*400–401: "μάκαιρα ταυροκτόνων λεόντων ἔφεδρε" et *Schol. in* 401.

[86] Cf. supra n. 78.

[87] Pind. *3 Pyth.*137–140; Herod.IV,76 = H. Hepding, *Attis* 6; Eupol. fr. 1, 15. Cf. G. Sfameni Gasparro, "Helena", 1163, ead., *Soteriology*, 20; P. Lekatsas, Διόνυσος (Athènes 1971) 39–41.

[88] Pind. *3 Pyth.*137–140, cf. *Schol. in* 140 (ed. A.B. Drachman, *Scholia vetera in Pindari Carmina*, 81).

un effort d'expression libre des adeptes du culte, au-delà des lieux de la religion traditionnelle.

Les marches nocturnes dans les montagnes, les flambeaux et le sens de la présence permanente de la déesse préparent les éclats de délire amenés par les cris de la cérémonie, la danse et la musique. L'agitation commence avec la musique qui éclate dans la tranquillité de la montagne et de la nuit. Les tambourins, les cymbales en cuivre, les flûtes, provoquent de plus en plus la musique démoniaque, d'une manière orgiastique jusqu'à ce que s'unissent les sons des cliquettes, des battements des mains et des longs cris des adeptes. La danse frénetique les saisit par des sauts, les mains se secouent, le corps se convulse, la tête se rejette en arrière avec des cris effrayants. Dans cette course frénétique et cette danse, la manie captive toute la nature. Dans l'extase se délie l'ordre du Monde.[89] Toute cette situation est rapportée par les témoignages des auteurs qui donnent à la déesse le surnom de Cybèle Dindymène.[90] C'est de cette manière qu'ils font allusion à son berceau micrasiatique originel où ces caractéristiques sont particulièrement vives. Ce climat d'ailleurs de l'entourage phrygien qui présente des altérations climatologiques brutes pendant l'alternance des saisons constitue le lieu idéal où le drame de la nature devient perceptible aux fidèles. C'est dans ce lieu que se déroulent les cérémonies, comme nous le transmettent d'ailleurs aussi les témoignages des épigrammes de l'*Anthologie Palatine* qui proviennent de l'époque alexandrine. Ainsi les fidèles pénètrent dans un lieu où la présence de la déesse est extrêmement forte, et ceci constitue un moyen qui contribue essentiellement à la charge émotionelle des fidèles et à leur libération—comme nous l'avons déjà dit—par rapport aux liens de l'entourage quotidien. C'est exactement dans ce lieu qu'ils

---

[89] P. Boyancé, *Études sur la religion romaine*, 224; E.R. Dodds, *The Greek and the Irrational*[6] (Berkeley-Los Angeles 1968 [1951]) 75–82; H. Jeanmaire, Διόνυσος. Ιστορία της λατρείας του Βάκχου (ελλην. μεταφρ. Α. Μέρτανη -Λίζα, Patras 1985) 148–286; P. Lekatsas, Διόνυσος, 37–39, 41–49; R. Turcan, *Cultes orientaux*, 37–38, 45; M.J. Vermaseren, *Cybele and Attis* 19 (Il cite l'entrée d'un temple de Smyrne qui se trouve aujourdhui au Musée de l'Hermitage (St. Petersburg). Sur les piliers ("*antae*") de l'entrée du temple que nous avons cité, il y a des représentations de Mainades); G. Sfameni Gasparro, "Helena", 1152, 1162, 1169, 1179; ead., *Soteriology*, 9–18; E.R. Dodds, *Bacchae*, 115–116, 201–205; E. Rohde, *Psyche*, II, 40–43. Cf. aussi Eur., *Bacch.*359, 981–1015; *Hipp.*141–144, et *Schol.ad loc.* (Ed. E. Schwartz, vol. II, 1891, 23–24); Hipp. *Morb.sacr.*I,VI,360,13sq; Apol.3,5,1; Martial, *Ep.*V,41,3,XI,84,4.

[90] M.J. Vermaseren, *CCCA*, vol. III, 62–64, no. 24, 100, no. 355; R. Duthoy, *The Taurobolium*, 21, no. 28. Cf. Diod.Sic.3, 58–59, 8; *Anthol.Palat.*VI,51 = H. Hepding, Attis 8; Catull, 63, 13; Martial, *Ep.*II,81.

peuvent la rencontrer et c'est pour cette raison qu'ils essaient de l'obtenir en imitant la manie de la nature. Et ils croient que plus vite ils arriveront à cette situation plus réussie sera leur identification avec elle. Leur désir s'exprime dans le culte par le surnom donné aux fidèles de "Κύβηβος" (kybèbos), c'est-à-dire de théophore.[91] De cette manière ils se déclarent possédés par la Grande-Mère. Cette déesse a d'ailleurs la possibilité d'animer le fidèle, comme dit Euripide, d'un transport divin.[92] Avec cette possibilité elle entraîne l'homme comme l'orage, avec comme résultat de le faire échapper au milieu étroit où il se meut ordinairement. Ainsi le fidèle peut s'identifier à la déesse qui se distingue par son caractère maniaque suprême. D'ailleurs son surnom de "Κυβήβη" (Kybèbe) montre la particuliarité de sa physionomie.[93] Le temps et l'espace n'ont dans cette situation aucune importance pour l'être humain. Le fidèle se meut déjà dans une autre dimension qui lui donne la capacité de se sentir comme un dieu.

L'identification du fidèle avec l'entourage sauvage et isolé où se pratiquent ces cérémonies, peut être considérée comme une sorte d'échappée hors de la civilisation, et comme une marche où le fidèle a pour but principal d'arriver, à travers une situation chaotique, à l'eudaimonia recherchée. C'est alors de cette façon que se manifeste la majesté de la déesse, à ceux qui ont montré le respect qu'il fallait et la soumission à la mère absolue et souveraine de la nature et des hommes. Selon nous cette action des fidèles pourrait s'étendre au cadre général des "rites des passages" dont nous avons déjà parlé.

C'est qui fait se mouvoir le fidèle, c'est l'idée qu'en vivant dans des situations spécifiques et hors de la communauté, il lui est possible de se trouver aussi hors du monde humain. La situation d'ailleurs de la manie a pour résultat principal la transformation de la personnalité du fidèle. Un texte de Philon, qui appartient à un époque postérieure, décrit cette état où arrive le fidèle de Cybèle comme une "νηφάλιος μέθη" qui est provoquée sans l'influence du vin.[94] Cet état justement contribue sans aucun doute à la création des liens

---

[91] *Etym.Magn.*: "κυβηβεῖν . . . αἰτία ἐνθουσιασμοῦ τοῖς μύσταις", voir aussi G.M. Sanders, "Gallos", col. 987; 990.

[92] Eur. *Hipp.*141–144.

[93] Κυβήβη: Herod.V,102; Hipponax, fr. 125; cf. aussi *cybebe*: Verg. *Aen.*X,22; κυβέλη: Eur. *Bacch.*79; κύβηλις: Hippon. fr. 167 (ed. H. Began). Cf. W. Burkert, *Structure and History*, 102–104, 120; R. Turcan, *Cultes orientaux*, 35–36; E. Laroche, "Koubaba, déesse Anatolienne", *Elements orientaux*, 113–128.

[94] Philon, *De opificio. mundi*, 71: "μέθη νηφαλίῳ κατασχεθεὶς ὥσπερ οἱ κορυβαντιῶντες",

d'une relation réciproque avec la déesse. Par cette relation, le fidèle acquiert le salut auquel il aspire tellement.

Après cet état d'agitation qui mène le fidèle à un état d'exaltation vient la sérénité. Il faut dire que ce passage de la situation chaotique où le fidèle était par la manie à la situation physiologique est caractérisé par le terme "ἀπομαίνεσθαι".[95] De cette manière est montré le passage par le fidèle de l'intensité à la mesure qui caractérise sa vie quotidienne. Le temps sacré où est entré le fidèle est terminé pour lui et il retourne au cadre du temps commun (profan) et quotidien. L'élément qui continue à le fortifier est le sens de la protection permanente de la déesse. C'est pour cette raison que nous croyons que le fidèle continue à s'identifier avec la déesse. D'ailleurs cette sérénité qui succède à la manie caractérise particulièrement la figure de la Grande Mère, car l'autre aspect qui la distingue est celui de la sérénité et de la souffrance.[96]

Ceci est normal puisque la déesse aussi présente dans sa physionomie l'aspect analogue. Ainsi la manie a-t-elle des résultats bienfaisants pour le fidèle, quand il se trouve dans les cadres du rite cultuel. Le même phénomène constitue parallèlement une punition implacable pour l'homme impie. La Grande-Mère est caractérisée par sa double nature; compatissante et solidaire de ceux qui lui sont entièrement fidèles, mais, au contraire, cruelle avec ceux qui manquent à leurs obligations. Cette situation se déclare d'une manière caractéristique dans la variante phrygienne du mythe du culte.[97] Selon le récit mythique, Attis et les autres protagonistes arrivent à une situation de manie effrénée qui a pour eux des résultats tragiques. Cette situation maniaque d'Attis est appellée par Ovide *"perbacchatus"*.[98]

---

cf. P. Boyancé, *Eléments sur la religion romaine*, 203; G. Filoramo, *A History of Gnosticism* (Cambridge, MA-Oxford 1994 [1990]) 32.

[95] Aretaeus, 3, 6, 11; Caelius Aurel.152. Voir aussi R. Renehan, *Greek Lexicigraphical Notes* (Göttingen 1975) 37.

[96] R. Turcan (*Cultes orientaux*, 40–41) qui se rapporte à Agdistis : "assuma dans son récit les aspects négatifs et violents de la Mère amoureuse d'Attis. Chez Arnobe, Cybèle joue un rôle normalisateur"; G. Sfameni Gasparro, *Soteriology*, 31–43 et surtout 41; P. Pachis, Το νερό και το αίμα στις μυστηριακές λατρείες της ελληνορωμαϊκής εποχής (Diss. Thessalonique 1988) 93.

[97] Cf. Agatharch., *de fluv.*X,5 (ed. F. Dübner, 88), XII,1,89,XIII,1,90; Eur. *Bacch.*882; E.R. Dodds, *Bacchae* 188; G. Sfameni Gasparro, *Soteriology*, 69, 87 et nos. 11, 123 (où elle se réfère au résultats actifs de la manie).

[98] R. Turcan, *Cultes orientaux*, 39; M. Meslin, "Agdistis ou l'Androgyne malséante", M.B. Boer—T.A. Edridge (edd.), *Hommages à M.J., Vermaseren*, vol. II, 772, n. 27; Arnob. *adv.Nat.*V,7 = H. Hepding, *Attis* 40,109. Voir aussi la qualification *"raptus"*

Pour terminer il faut aussi mettre l'accent sur le fait que ces cérémonies, au moins pendant les époques classique et hellénistique,
n'étaient pas encore liées à l'initiation des fidèles. Ce fait est certain,
bien que, selon certain témoignages qui appartiennent au Ve siècle
avant J.-C., et à l'époque où les épigrammes de l'*Anthologie Palatine*
sont écrites, les cérémonies nocturnes soient appelées "μυστήρια".[99]
Ainsi, selon ces relations précises il faut insister sur le fait que le
terme "μυστήριον" (mystère) est lié dans ces cas spécifiquement à la
signification de l'entourage isolé et le caractère nocturne du culte.
De cette manière se manifeste l'effort pour l'isolement qui protège
l'ensemble des fidèles de la déesse des yeux impies, des personnes
qui n'appartiennent pas à leur troupe sacrée. Ces deux éléments dont
nous avons parlé constituent d'ailleurs des indices qui président de
manière supreme aux cérémonies de la Grande-Mère.[100] Les cérémonies du culte métroaque se caractérisent également, particulièrement à l'époque que nous examinons, comme "ὄργια" (orgia).[101] Ce
terme a pour but principal de manifester, outre la forme mystique
de son rite, ce que Strabon décrit comme: "toutes les manifestations
de caractère orgiastique ou relevant du délire des Bacchants, ainsi
que toutes les danses et les rites propres à la célébration des mystères
initiatiques" (τὸ ὀργιαστικὸν πᾶν καὶ τὸ βακχικὸν καὶ τὸ χορικὸν καὶ τὸ
περὶ τὰς τελετὰς μυστικόν).[102]

---

d'Attis; Catul.63. Cf. E. Parratote, "Motivi soteriologici nella letteratura latina della
tarda d'éta republicana", *CSCO*, 334.

[99] G. Sfameni Gasparro, "Dai misteri alla mistica : Semantica di una parola", *La
Mistica. Fenomenologia e rifflessione teologica* (Roma 1984) 73–113; ead. *Soteriology*, 14,
nos. 20–25, 31–32; ead., "Ancora sur termine TELETH. Osservazioni storico-
religiose", *Filologia e forme letterarie. Studi offerti a Francesco della Corte*, vol. V (Urbino
1987) 137–152; cf. aussi Philod. *Anthol.Palat.*VII,222 (ed. P. Waltz, Paris 1960, 152);
Thuillos, *Anthol.Palat.*VII,223,1–3 (*op. cit.*, 152sq.); P. Foucart, *Des associations religieuses*, 158–159.

[100] Cf. Soph. *Ant.*1012sq., *Trach.*765sq.; L. Ziehen, "orgia", *RE* 35 (1939) col. 1026–
1029; G. Sfameni Gasparro, *Soteriology*, 9–19.

[101] En ce qui concerne la signification du terme "ὄργιον", voir A. Motte –
V. Pirenne-Delforge, "Le mot et les rites. Aperçu des significations de ὄργια et de
quelques dérivés", *Kernos* 5 (1992) 119–140.

[102] *Geogr.*X,3.10.

PHRYGIAN MATAR: EMERGENCE OF AN
ICONOGRAPHIC TYPE[1]

Mary Jane Rein

The earliest Greek representations of the mother goddess Kybele are
in the form of a simple architectural frame or "naiskos" containing
an image of the goddess. These so-called "Kybele naiskoi" emerge
in western Anatolia during the middle decades of the sixth century
B.C. The source for their iconography can be recognized in a series
of Phrygian stelai from the vicinity of Ankara and in the rock-cut
monuments of the Phrygian highlands.[2] A variety of literary, inscrip-
tional, and lexical references, documenting the Greek belief that Kybele
came from Phrygia, complement these iconographic origins.[3] In particular, several late Classical lexica, such as the Suda and Stephanos
of Byzantium, derive the name Kybele from a mountain in Phrygia
named *Kybeleia*.[4] The aim of this paper will be to demonstrate that
the iconography of these Phrygian monuments is shaped by this conception of the goddess as "mountain mother". A review of the Greek
Kybele naiskoi will suggest, in turn, that their standard architectural
format is dependent for meaning on the mountain imagery of the
Phrygian monuments.[5] The colonizing history of the important Ionian
city Miletus in the region of the Hellespont and Propontis will, moreover, emerge as a significant factor in this Greek adaption and dis-
semination of the Phrygian image of the mother.

---

[1] This study was originally presented as a paper at the 94th Annual Meeting of
the Archaeological Institute of America: *AJA* 97 (1993) 318 (abstract). I am grateful
to Professors Lynn Roller and Eugene Lane for their valuable assistance in providing additional bibliography and advice.

[2] R. Temizer, "Un bas-relief de Cybèle découvert à Ankara," *Anatolia* 4 (1959)
183–187; C.H.E. Haspels, *Highlands of Phrygia* (Princeton 1971) 110–111; M.J. Mellink,
"Comments on a Cult Relief of Kybele from Gordion," *Beiträge zur Altertumskunde
Kleinasiens: Festschrift für Kurt Bittel*, ed. R.M. Böhmer and H. Hauptmann (Mainz am
Rhein 1983) 349–360, esp. 359.

[3] Diodorus 3.58.1; Etym.Mag. s.v. Kybelon; Hesychius s.v. Kybeleia; Hipponax,
fr. 167 (Degani); St. Byz. s.v. Kybeleia.

[4] References to a Phrygian mountain named Cybele also occur in Virgil, *Aeneid*
III.111; XI. 768 and Ovid, *Fasti* 4.249, 363.

[5] A corpus of Kybele representations is included in F. Naumann, *Die Ikonographie
der Kybele* (Tübingen 1983).

The Phrygian iconography of the Mother serves as a clear complement to the Greek sources which derive the name Kybele from a
mountain located in Phrygia. The natural rock outcroppings of the
Phrygian highlands furnish numerous cliff faces designed in the form
of a building façade with a prominent doorway. These monuments
celebrate a goddess identified from inscriptions in old Phrygian as
Matar.[6] On the best known of these façades, the so-called "Monument of Midas," usually dated to the late eighth century, Matar is
mentioned three times and the doorway, now empty, would originally have contained her image.[7] The relevance of this Phrygian
Mother to Greek Kybele is demonstrated by two inscribed monuments from the Highlands on which the goddess is named Matar
Kubileya.[8] This titular compound resembles the common designation for the Greek Mother, "Meter Kybele". These inscribed Phrygian
monuments, therefore, supplement and confirm the sources which
represent Kybele as Phrygian in origin.[9]

That the Phrygian form Kubile is the source for the Greek theonym
Kybele has been recognized since the late nineteenth century.[10] The
decipherment of Hittite hieroglyphs in the 1920's led the semiticist
William Albright to recognize a further resemblance between the Greek
theonym Kybele and that of the North Syrian goddess Kubaba.[11]
The full extent of this phonetic similarity was explored in a seminal
article by Emmanuel Laroche, in which he proposed that the Phrygians were responsible for transforming the north Syrian theonym into
the form eventually adapted by the Greeks.[12] This suggestion correctly preserves the Phrygian intermediary advertised by the ancient
sources. Political and cultural relations between Karkemish,[13] the chief
site for the worship of Kubaba, and the Phrygian capital, Gordion,
strengthen the view that the theonym Kubaba was somehow the inspiration for the Phrygian form Kubile.

---

[6] C. Brixhe and M. Lejeune, *Corpus des Inscriptions Palaéo-Phrygiennes* (Paris, 1984)
W–01a–b; W–04; W–06; B–01; M–01c–e.

[7] Brixhe & Lejeune, M–01c–e; Haspels 73–76, figs. 8, 598.

[8] Brixhe & Lejeune, W–04; B–01.

[9] For a discussion of the evidence pertaining to the Phrygian cult of the Mother,
see L. Roller, "Phrygian Myth and Cult," *Source* 3–4 (1988) 43–50.

[10] W.M. Ramsay, "Studies in Asia Minor," *JHS* 3 (1882) 33 ff.; S. Reinach, "Cybèle
à Kyme," *BCH* 13 (1889) 556–558.

[11] W.F. Albright, "The Anatolian Goddess Kubaba," *Archiv für Orientforschung* 5
(1928–1929) 229–231.

[12] E. Laroche, "Koubaba, déesse Anatolienne, et le problème des origines de
Cybèle," in *Éléments orientaux dans la religion grecque ancienne* (1960) 113–128.

[13] H. Güterbock, "Herrin von Karkemiš," *JNES* 13 (1954) 109 ff.

Figure 1. Stele of Kubaba from Karkemish, Courtesy of the British Museum

Phrygian depictions of the mother appear, moreover, to have been adapted from late Hittite representations of Kubaba. The pivotal monument for illustrating this iconographic relationship is a stele from Karkemish in which the frontal pose of the goddess and her placement within a frame are suggestive of the Phrygian type of naiskos with standing, frontal representation of the mother (figure 1).[14] A further similarity between the north Syrian and Phrygian goddesses can be recognized in their shared association with the hawk. In Luwian hieroglyphic, the writing used in the late Hittite period at Karkemish, Kubaba is spelled with the phonetic element KU—followed by a logogram of a hawk.[15] The hawk is also a standard attribute in the iconography of Phrygian Matar, as well as the subject of numerous votive offerings from Gordion.[16] This predatory bird expresses an important quality of the mother goddess who oversees the cycle of life and death.

These iconographic and other similarities have tended to support the reasoning that Kubaba is an immediate ancestress of Matar Kubile.[17] Close examination, however, reveals that the phonetic resemblance is superficial. Claude Brixhe's study of the old Phrygian corpus emphasizes the fact that in the two inscriptions in which "Matar Kubile" is apparently mentioned, the true reading is actually "kubileya". He interprets Kubileya as a feminine adjectival epithet, corresponding in form to the Latin masculine Pompeius/feminine Pompeia.[18] Kubileya therefore serves to modify the real Phrygian theonym, which is simply Matar. Kubilon/-a can be understood here as referring to (a) specific mountains in Phrygia or as the generic Phrygian word meaning mountain(s). Matar Kubileya can thus be translated either as "Mother from Kubilon/-a" or "Mountain Mother." Brixhe further suggests that Kybele as theonym represents a blending of "kubeleya" and Kybebe. This reading requires a reassessment of Laroche's hypothesis regarding a linguistic relationship between Kubaba

---

[14] L. Woolley and R.D. Barnett, *Carchemish* III (London 1952) B62, 254; Mellink, 354–355.

[15] J.D. Hawkins, "Kubaba, A. Philologisch," *Reallexicon der Assyriologie* V (1980) 257–261.

[16] R.S. Young, *et al.*, *Three Great Tumuli* (Philadelphia, 1981) pl. 28.

[17] Most references to Kybele's origins depend upon Laroche's conclusions, cf. P. Chantraine, *Dictionnaire Étymologique de la langue Grecque* I (Paris, 1970) 598.

[18] I owe this comparison to Professor Calvert Watkins, who kindly discussed the linguistic evidence with me; see also, Brixhe, no. 32.

and Kybele. Indeed, Brixhe suggests that the epithet Areyastin, which also occurs on one of the monuments in the Highlands,[19] might be understood as another Phrygian epithet for Matar.[20] Other thus-far unattested names are also possible as epithets. The similarity of the Syrian name and the Phrygian toponym is, nonetheless, undeniable. Perhaps syncretism and Phrygian knowledge of the cult of Kubaba, in the context of the late eighth century alliance between Gordion and Karkemish, helped to promote a preference for the similar-sounding epithet Kubile.[21]

The phonetic similarity observed between Kubile and Kybele remains unaffected by this new reading. Phrygian influence on the Greek theonym seems likely, beginning with the slightly variant form Kybelis which appears in a fragment of the Ephesian poet Hipponax.[22] The accustomed form, Kybele, first occurs in Pindar,[23] although Meter remains the most common designation in the ancient sources. In fact the syntactic unit Matar Kubile (or Matar Areyastin) is comparable to the many Greek compounds in which Meter is qualified by a mountain name.[24] The form Kybebe, which occurs in Hipponax, as well as in Herodotus and Charon of Lampsakos, is probably a transliteration of the Lydian form Kuvava. This is suggested by the fact that the fragments of Hipponax include many Lydian words, while Herodotus uses this version expressly in reference to the Lydian goddess. In the case of Lydian Kuvava there is a more transparent relationship to Hittite Kubaba.[25] Kybebe survives in both Greek and Latin sources as an alternative literary form whose earlier history

---

[19] Brixhe and Lejeune, W–01a.
[20] Brixhe, 43.
[21] Mellink, 359.
[22] Hipponax, fr. 125 (Degani).
[23] Pindar, fr. 80 (Snell).
[24] Meter Oreia: Eur. *Hippolytus* 144; Eur. *Helen* 1301; Schol, in, Arist. *Birds* 876; Kall fr. 761.1 (Pfeiffer); J. Keil, *ÖJh* 23 (1926) 258–261; Meter Idaia: Eur. *Orestes* 1453; Dindymene: Hdt. 1.80; Strabo, 12.5.3; Sipylene and Idaia: Strabo 10.3.12. In addition, Lynn Roller brings to my attention that Kybelaia is attested several times as a Greek toponym, possibly in reference to two mountains, one in Erythrai, and one on Chios: Strabo 14.1.33; Hekataios (*FGrHist* 1 F230); H. Engelmann and R. Merkelbach, *Inschriften von Erythrai und Klazomenai*, vol. II, 365–366.
[25] R. Gusmani, "Der Lydische Name der Kybele," *Kadmos* 8 (1969) 158 ff. and *Neue Epichorische Schriftzeugnisse aus Sardis*, Sardis M3, (Cambridge, Mass. 1975) 28–30; Herodotus 5.102; Hipponax no. 167 (Degani); Photius s.v. kybelos, *FGH* 262 F5. I.M. Diakonoff discusses the linguistic background for long a and long e in early Lydian words transmitted from Hittite in "On Cybele and Attis in Phrygia and Lydia," *Acta Antiqua Academiae Scientiarum Hungarica* 25 (1977) 336–337.

and transmission remain quite separate from the more commonly known form of the name.[26]

This early instability of the theonym and its late appearance in Greek sources, confirm the reports that Kybele's origins were non-Greek. Yet the concept of the Great Mother is a very ancient element in Greek religion. The goddess-centered worship of Minoan Crete is well known and involves worship in caves and on mountain peaks. Although the name of this Bronze Age goddess is unknown, a tablet from Pylos preserves a reference to the "Mother of the Gods" in linear B, ma-te-re te-i-ja.[27] In Hesiod, the Mother emerges as the earth mother Gaia or as the mother of the gods Rhea. When the Greeks, long familiar with a great goddess, came into contact with Phrygian Matar they must have recognized and conflated their own mother goddess with her. The point of contact that facilitated this fusion was certainly in Anatolia, as has long been suspected.

A key piece of evidence is furnished by an inscribed sherd, reading Qubalas, excavated from a late-seventh-century stratum of the south Italian city, Lokri Epizephyri.[28] Worship of the Mother is well attested at this site in later periods, and the form Qubalas may be an early adaptation of Kubile, the epithet for the Phrygian Mother. Guarducci proposes that the cult was introduced to the west by Colophonians, who fled Anatolia after their city was taken by the Lydian King Gyges.[29] This scenario implies that the cult of Kybele was known to the Greeks of western Anatolia by the mid-seventh century. The Greek adoption of the Phrygian goddess, however, requires a situation of cultural contact.

Archaeological and literary evidence demonstrate that there was active Phrygian communication with the Greek world by the end of the eighth century. Herodotus mentions the throne of the Phrygian king Midas, still seen at Delphi in his day. A fragment of Aristotle further records that Midas married an Aeolian Princess, Hermodike, daughter of King Agamemnon of Kyme.[30] The probable burial mound of Midas, at Gordion, contained several bronze bowls inscribed in

---

[26] Vergil, *Aeneid* 10.220; cf. Servius *ad loc.*

[27] J. Chadwick and M. Ventris, *Documents in Mycenaean Greek* (Cambridge, 1973) 410.

[28] M. Guarducci, "Cibele in un' epigrafe arcaica di Locri Epizefiri," *Klio* 52 (1970) 135–138; the initial Q- reflects the use of the koppa in place of the kappa before o and u, L. Jeffery, *Local Scripts of Archaic Greece* (1989) 2nd edition, ed. A. Johnston, 33.

[29] Herodotus 1.14; Strabo 6.1.14; Guarducci, 137.

[30] Herodotus 1.14; Oscar White Muscarella, "King Midas of Phrygia and the

old Phrygian script, using an alphabet considered by many as an adaption from the Greek alphabet.[31] Metal goods of Phrygian manufacture are also found in this period in the major Greek sanctuaries. East Greek fibula types and pottery are, in turn, recognized from the Cimmerian destruction level at Gordion.[32] The means which allowed for this exchange of Phrygian and Greek goods are not certainly established, athough they are often imagined as traveling by overseas trade. Overland trade is also likely along river valleys, such as that of the Hermus river, which provide convenient and passable routes from the interior of Anatolia to the Aegean coast. The other probable overland route lies in northwest Anatolia, along the coast of the Black sea.

The region of the Pontos and Propontis becomes a focus for Greek colonization from the late eighth through the sixth centuries B.C. Miletus, the leader in this effort, founded such important cities as Kyzikos, Sinope, and Trapezus. I suggest that these colonies, located along the borders of the Phrygian Empire, facilitated the Greek adoption of Phrygian customs, including worship of the Phrygian mother. The cult of Meter is extensively documented throughout this region during the Hellenistic and Roman periods.[33] The early history of the cult of Meter in this region of northwest Anatolia is likely to be greatly clarified by the current excavations at Troy, where an archaic sanctuary of Kybele is presently a focus of excavation and research.[34] Ancient sources on the Milesian colony of Kyzikos provide further evidence for the worship of Meter in northwest Anatolia. The epithet Dindymene originates in connection with Kyzikene Mt. Dindymos, and a sanctuary on its peak devoted to the great mother was reputedly a foundation of Jason and the Argonauts.[35] Herodotus also reports on rites for Meter within the city of Kyzikos.[36] Close religious ties, which are characteristic of relations between a colony and its mother city, support the thesis that the worship of Kybele

---

Greeks," in *Anatolia and the Ancient Near East, Studies in Honor of Tahsin Özgüç*, ed. K. Emre, *et al.* (Ankara, 1989) 337.

[31] Young *et al.*, 275.

[32] Muscarella, 333–344.

[33] E. Schwertheim, "Denkmaler zur Meterverehrung," in *Studien zur Religion und Kultur Kleinasiens*, ed. S. Şahin, *et al.* (Leiden 1978) 791–837.

[34] C. Brian Rose, "Greek and Roman Excavations at Troy, 1991–1992," *AJA* 97 (1993) 341.

[35] Apoll.Rhod., *Argonautica* 1.985; Paus.8.46.4; Strabo 12.8.11.

[36] Hdt.1.476.

was introduced to the Greeks from Phrygia, through Milesian contact with her northwest Anatolian colonies.

Excavations at Miletus have thus far yielded sixteen naiskoi representing Kybele, a quantity which far exceeds the number of naiskoi found at any other east Greek site. Four of these, recovered over the last decade, postdate the corpus of Kybele representations compiled by Naumann.[37] Nor does this corpus include three Milesian examples in the Berlin Museum,[38] nor at least three more naiskoi, currently on display in the on-site museum at Miletus.[39] As a leader of the Ionian league, Miletus must have exercised considerable religious influence over the other Greek cities of coastal Anatolia. Her prolific sculptural workshops were also the source of a distinctive style. She is credited with the invention of the seated male and female statuary types and the seated Kybele may have developed from these, since the Phrygian prototype is always standing.[40] The seated version becomes the standard Kybele type in Aeolis and later emerges as the Classical type associated with the cult image of the Metroon in the Agora of Athens—this is also the preferred type on Chios, where the rock monument known as the seat of Homer is actually a seated Kybele.[41] Through her northern colonies Miletus was certainly in contact with Phrygian traditions. In this climate, it is easy to assign her the role as primary adapter and disseminator of the Phrygian image of the mother.

The simple architectural frame of the Greek naiskoi is clearly derived from the Phrygian iconography of Matar. The type of building façade depicted on these rock monuments conforms to the contemporary architecture of Phrygia, as suggested by doodles of houses with similar gabled roofs and curling akroteria discovered on one of the megara at Gordion.[42] On the best preserved of the Greek naiskoi

---

[37] V. von Graeve, "Milet," Ist.Mitt 36 (1986) 45–47, taf.11 and "Neue archaische Skulpturfunde aus Milet," in Archaische und klassische griechische Plastik, ed. H. Kyrieleis (Mainz am Rhein 1986) 21–25, pl. 6.

[38] C. Blümel, Die archaisch griechischen Skulpturen der Staatlichen Museen zu Berlin (Berlin 1963) Nr. 44–45.

[39] Miletus inv. nos. 261; 263; 800. A naiskos in the Museum courtyard and a weathered block stored with fragments of classical architecture in a shed beside the Museum, appear to be reused naiskoi; neither have Museum inventory numbers.

[40] R. Özgan, Untersuchungen zur archaischen Plastik Ioniens (Bonn, 1978) 23–25; 29–41.

[41] H. Kaletsch, "Daskalopetra—ein Kybeleheiligtum auf Chios," in Forschungen und Funde: Festschrift für Bernhard Neutsch, ed. F. Krinzinger et al. (Innsbruck 1980) 223–235.

[42] Mellink, 356–359.

Figure 2. Miletian Kybele Naiskos, Courtesy of Professor Volkmar von Graeve

Figure 3. Kybele Naiskos from Etlik, Ankara,
Courtesy of the Ankara Archaeological Museum

recently discovered from Miletus (figure 2),[43] traces of a painted meander on the projecting frame may even mimic the geometric decoration commonly seen on the façades of the Phrygian highlands and on the stelai from Ankara (figure 3). The design of the façade seems to derive from its conception as an entrance into the mountain dwelling of the goddess. The emergence of this iconographic type definitely occurs among the monuments of the highlands, where Phrygian architectural elements are applied to the iconography of the mother goddess standing within her shrine.[44]

The iconography of Matar in the Phrygian Highlands begins with the so-called stepped altars or throne monuments. These are flat, aniconic representations with squared bodies and rounded heads that are free-standing or incised on the rock face. That they represent the Phrygian Mother Goddess seems likely from their prominence throughout the Highlands. Some which are designed with two identical figures may represent the Mother Goddess with consort, or the doubling may simply increase her potency. An example from a shrine in the east Phrygian city of Boğazköy is decorated with scenes of hunters and wildlife which reflect the goddess' concern over the cycles of nature.[45] The schematic form of these representations enhances the expression of natural power, as does their placement in a landscape where the presence of the goddess must have been sensed throughout. Their aniconic form is reminiscent of the stone described by Roman sources, which was worshipped at the Phrygian sanctuary of the Mother at Pessinus until it was brought to Rome.[46] This unworked rock, possibly a meteorite, was not only considered an appropriate representation of the goddess but was also her most famous image.

In a different, probably later, type of monument the Phrygian goddess is represented in human form. This development of her anthropomorphic representation was probably inspired by late Hittite iconography.[47] Nevertheless these façade monuments clearly remain within the old stepped-altar tradition. The relationship to the rock landscape

---

[43] von Graeve, "Neue archaische Skulpturfunde aus Milet," 23, fig. 1.

[44] M.J. Mellink, 357, observes that the Phrygian façade was designed to give an architectural framework to the goddess' natural mountain dwelling, although she also stresses the likelihood of a temple prototype, perhaps located at Gordion and possibly to be recognized in the excavated building, Megaron 2.

[45] K. Bittel, "Phrygisches Kultbild aus Boğazköy," *Antike Plastik* II (1963) 8.

[46] *contra* Naumann, who, in her discussion of the ancient evidence concerning the Pessinuntine stone, concludes that its aniconic form had no precedent, 283–285.

[47] Mellink, 354–356.

remains a primary feature. Linking the two types is also their common use of a stepped approach, as well as their orientation toward
the rising sun. Preserved in several niches is a worn female figure
carved from the cliff face, in one piece with the façade. In other
façades, in which the niche is now empty, a similar draped female
figure can be reconstructed on the basis of tenon holes and background weathering.[48]

An affinity for entrances and boundaries also emerges in the highlands as a meaningful element in the iconography of the Phrygian
Mother. This is not only expressed by the goddess' consistent presence in the doorway. At Midas City, the façade monuments favor
the edges of the settlement—as though encircling it for protective
purposes. A sculptural group of the goddess and her two companions, originally set into a naiskos within the east Phrygian gateway at
Boğazköy was incorporated into the fabric of the city wall.[49] In this
position, at the interface of interior and exterior space, the goddess
served as both protectress of the city and guardian of those depart-
ing. A similar dichotomy is expressed in her cult, in which she is
both the protectress of wild, mountainous places and patroness of
the city. It is therefore understandable that her worship involved
portable naiskoi and outdoor monuments.

The doorway depicted on these rock façades represents an entrance
into the mountain and evokes the goddess' natural cave dwelling.
The association of the mother with her mountain home becomes so
total that her image need not even be included—as is evident from
a small-scale representation of a Phrygian building façade inscribed
on a cliff face at the site of Fındık in the Highlands—labelled in old
Phrygian as Matar. One of two Phrygian monuments inscribed with
the name Matar Kubile is the cliff monument at the site of Germanos
which bears the longest extant inscription in old Phrygian and is
located in a remote area of Bithynia (figures 4 and 5). The goddess'
power must have been very potent to bring worshippers to this distant spot, which today is approached by jeep but must finally be
reached on foot. The representation of the niche is diminished to a
summary entrance into the rock. The unadorned cliff face at Germanos stands for the mountain which represents the goddess' home
and by metonomy the goddess herself. This imagery is similarly ex-

---

[48] Haspels, 75.
[49] Bittel, 8–21.

Figure 4. Inscribed rock monument at Germanos,
Courtesy of Professor Claude Brixhe

MARY JANE REIN

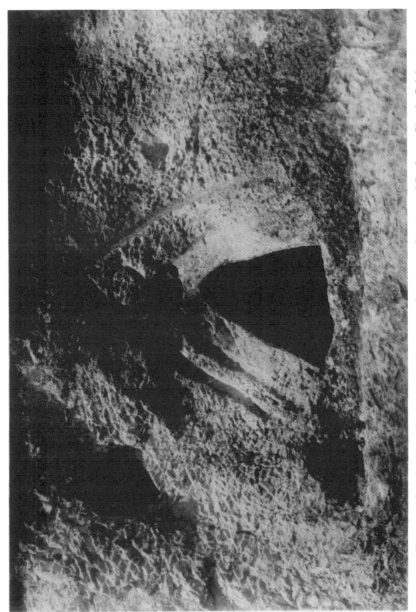

Figure 5. Detail of inscribed rock monument at Germanos, Courtesy of Professor Claude Brixhe

pressed by the mountain epithet Kubile which in Greek becomes interchangeable with the name Meter.

On a cliff in the Köhnüş valley of the highlands, another niche labelled Matar Kubile, is carved with a wide opening in the form of the mouth of a cave. This is reminiscent of the gloss on Kybele in Hesychius which reads ἄντρα καὶ θάλαμοι—"caves and inner chambers". This definition is an extension of Kybele's association with the mountain. In the more sophisticated iconography of the façade monuments, the entrance to the cave is reinterpreted as a real Phrygian building façade. Yet the meaning remains the same as that conveyed in Pausanias' description of the Phrygian site of Steunos at Aizanoi, where there was a cave consecrated to Meter Steunene, in which a statue of the goddess stood.[50] This cave has been discovered and excavated and is a vivid illustration of the goddess dwelling within her mountain home.[51]

These meaningful features of the iconography of the Mother clearly take shape in a Phrygian setting and correspond to the more abbreviated imagery of the east Greek naiskoi. The design of the Greek naiskos makes little sense without reference to the mountain meaning conveyed by the Phrygian rock monuments. The opportunities for cultural contact between Greeks and Phrygians are suggested by the foundation of Milesian and other Greek colonies in northwest Anatolia. The Greeks adopted both the iconography and meaning of the mother within her natural mountain dwelling—this is expressed by the many archaic Greek Kybele naiskoi, and this is also the sense behind her name, which the Greeks long remembered as a Phrygian borrowing.

---

[50] Paus.10.32.3.
[51] R. Naumann, "Das Heiligtum der Meter Steunene bei Aezani," *Ist.Mitt* 17 (1967) 218–247.

THE ANCIENT MOTHER OF THE GODS
A MISSING CHAPTER IN THE HISTORY
OF GREEK RELIGION*

Noel Robertson

I. *Introduction*

The subject of the missing chapter is a goddess familiar to everyone who has explored Greek literature, art, or documents. She dwells in the mountains, and sits enthroned between two lions, and is worshipped with tumultuous rites. Her name, however, will vary according to the sources we consult.

In the actual record of cult—inscriptions, Pausanias, any sort of antiquarian comment—her constant title is Μήτηρ (τῶν) θεῶν "Mother of the Gods" or simply Μήτηρ "Mother". Literary sources—poets, historians, and the rest—often agree, and further describe her as Μήτηρ ὀρεία "mountain Mother". But in place of these transparent titles they also use the names Ῥέα "Rhea" and Κυβέλη "Cybele". "Rhea" was always current, from Homer onwards. Yet it never occurs in cult, with a single unexplained exception, a civic cult on Cos, where "Rhea" makes a contrast with the usual title elsewhere on the island. "Cybele" appears towards 600 B.C., first as a *graffito* on a sherd, then in the poet Hipponax; from the late fifth century it has an ever increasing vogue. Whereas the origin of "Rhea" is unknown, that of "Cybele" is not in doubt. It is Phrygian, and means something like "rock" or "mountain"; in a Phrygian inscription an adjective form serves as epithet of the native Phrygian Mother. But like "Rhea" it is almost never used in cult in the Greek world (including Hellenistic and Roman Anatolia).

The goddess so named is not a new-comer to Greece, nor do her

* The argument has already been briefly indicated in M. Silver (ed.), *Ancient Economy in Mythology. East and West* (Savage, Md. 1991) 8–10, and at *Festivals and Legends. The Formation of Greek Cities in the Light of Public Ritual* (Toronto 1992) 27–30. I thank Professor Lane for allowing me to honour the memory of a scholar whose seven volumes, *Corpus Cultus Cybelae Attidisque*, are a resource unmatched in the study of any other major deity in the Greek and Roman world.

characteristic rites undergo any significant change at any time, in so
far as they belong to the general custom of Greek cities (from the
fourth century onward, certain elements of Anatolian worship were
brought to Greece by private persons). Any Greek deity, be it Zeus
or Apollo or Demeter, is revealed to us by a gradual process during
the Archaic and Classical periods, as literature and art develop, and
as documents appear. Literature speaks of "Rhea" and the "Mother"
from the outset. The enthroned figure with lion or lions is rendered
in sculpture and terracottas from the mid sixth century onward. The
Mother's shrines, if we gather up all the indications, are found throughout the Greek homeland and the colonies. At a few places, notably
Athens and Thebes, the evidence is early; and the cult is carried
from a mother city to its colonies, notably from Miletus to Cyzicus.
It is not surprising that one of the few major deities named in Linear B is Μήτηρ θεῖα "Mother of the Gods" ("Divine Mother", as it
is sometimes translated, is not plausible as a cult title).

The Mother then is age-old in Greece. Yet this is not the picture
presented in the handbooks and elaborated by current research. It is
always assumed that the Anatolian cult of "Cybele" was introduced
to Greece in the late Archaic period or at the beginning of the fifth
century, when the Mother happens to be suddenly illuminated at
Athens and at Thebes, by the remains in the Agora and by several
passages of Pindar. Some have even maintained that begging eunuch priests arrived at the same time. Quite recently, since Locri in
Italy yielded a sherd inscribed with the name "Cybele", conjecture
has traced various routes by which the cult may have passed from
Phrygia to Ionia, then to the Greek peninsula, and finally to Magna
Graecia. And we are often told as well that the Anatolian Mother
coalesced in Greece with some vestige of a putative "great mother"
formerly worshipped by Minoans and perhaps Mycenaeans. The
insubstantiality of these notions is well evinced by the name "Cybele",
which is by far the favourite name in modern accounts, and yet was
scarcely ever used by ancient worshippers.

The misunderstanding of the Mother has led to other misunder-
standings. They concern the god Cronus and the infant Zeus. Cronus
is a vivid figure of myth, the Mother's consort and the chief representative of an older world (for the other Titans are plainly fictitious
and secondary). Yet he is virtually unknown in cult, except as a
consequence of his literary renown. And yet again we find a festival
"Cronia", a month "Croniôn", places called "Cronian", the personal
name "Cronius". The fullest studies have arrived at opposite results.

On the one view, he is a high god, a very ancient one, dispossessed by Zeus; on the other, he is a mere personification of the old days, though no one has been able to say why the old days should be called "Cronus". The infant Zeus belongs to the same story, as the Mother's child who in the best-known version is hid and reared in a mountain cave on Crete. A huge edifice of speculation now exists about a mystic fertility spirit worshipped in a cave, where he dies and is reborn each year. For anyone who seeks to understand Greek religion, Cronus and the infant Zeus are what Wilamowitz called "agonizing" problems.

The purpose of the present essay is to demonstrate, with the strictness that the term implies, that the Mother was always a principal deity in Greek cities, and had a function as practical and important as the other principal deities. The demonstration relies on two forms of evidence for the same thing: the antiquarian and documentary notices referring to the Mother's festivals, and the aetiological myths arising from these festivals. Festivals are the essential mode of worship in the ancient Mediterranean and Near East, and in many other societies. Apart from festivals, the term "cult" is an abstraction. A god's festival or festivals are celebrated at the time his help is wanted. The direct evidence for ancient festivals, as for all ritual and custom, is painfully limited. But aetiological myth is abundant and also, when properly handled, quite as revealing as any literal report. We shall see how to handle it as we proceed.

The Mother has two seasonal festivals, in spring and summer. The direct evidence, including the calendar of months at some Ionian cities, shows that they are very old. So do the related myths and legends, among them some very familiar stories. The stages of the argument are as follows: the direct evidence for the spring festival (§ II), and its aetiology (§ III); the direct evidence for the summer festival (§ IV), and its aetiology (§ V); our conclusion (§ VI).

II. *The spring festival Galaxia*

The festival Galaxia is attested at Athens and, in virtue of the month-name Galaxion, on Delos and Thasos.[1] Only at Athens are we informed of the deity honoured by the festival: the Mother of the Gods.

---

[1] The Delian calendar: A.E. Samuel, *Greek and Roman Chronology* (Munich 1972) 99. The Thasian: Samuel 130; F. Salviat, *BCH* 82 (1958) 215–18. Earlier studies of

Thus the lexica, and thus the record of offerings by the Councillors, and by the ephebes in the late second century.[2] It is noteworthy that in both literary and epigraphic sources the Mother alone is named, mostly with her full title, ἡ Μήτηρ τῶν θεῶν; there is no mention of Cronus, her partner in myth.

On Delos and Thasos the festival will again be hers. Paros should be added to the tally, for it is very likely, if not quite demonstrable as yet, that the Thasian calendar was adopted without change from the mother city.[3] There is plenty of evidence for the Mother at all these places. On Delos it is, as usual, Hellenistic;[4] on Paros it goes back to the fourth century,[5] and on Thasos to the Archaic period.[6]

At Athens the calendar date does not appear. On both Delos and Thasos, however, the month Galaxion takes the place of Elaphebolion, March/April. Other indications agree. A sacrificial calendar of the Imperial period, issued by some private group in Athens, honours Cronus on 15 Elaphebolion.[7] Here it is indeed Cronus and not the Mother; but the name was doubtless substituted by the author of the calendar, who inclines to picturesque deities of the countryside.

Further afield, at Olympia, Cronus receives sacrifice at the spring equinox, in the month Elaphius.[8] It is likely again that Cronus has superseded the Mother. Her cult is well attested at Olympia, but Cronus is more prominent in local myth, inasmuch as Mount Cronius, though named for the summer festival, was inevitably understood as his abode.

---

the Galaxia are confined to Athens: A. Mommsen, *Feste der Stadt Athen* (Leipzig 1898) 449; L. Deubner, *Attische Feste* (Berlin 1932) 216.

[2] Bekker, *Anecd.*1.229, Hsch., s.v. Γαλάξια. Councillors: Theophr. *Char.*21.11, ἐθύομεν οἱ πρυτάνεις τῆι Μητρὶ τῶν θεῶν τὰ Γαλάξια (Wilamowitz: τὰ γὰρ ἄξια mss.). Ephebes: *IG* 2² 1011 line 13 (107/6 B.C.), ἔθυσαν δὲ καὶ τοῖς Γαλαξίοις τῆι Μητρὶ τῶν θεῶν.

[3] M. Wörrle, *Chiron* 13 (1983) 352–7.

[4] P. Bruneau, *Recherches sur les cultes de Délos* (Paris 1970) 431–5; Vermaseren, *CCCA* 2.188–204 nos. 587–646, pls. 177–91. Bruneau assumes that "the Metroum" is always the same in Delian documents; but the chapel associated with the Egyptian gods is likely to be distinct from "the Metroum on Delos" where public records were kept, just as at Athens.

[5] O. Rubensohn, *RE* 18.2 (1949) 1855–6 s.v. Paros; Vermaseren, *CCCA* 2.205 nos. 647–9; F. Naumann, *Die Ikonographie der Kybele* (Tübingen 1983) 196–202,343, pls. 28–9. According to the Parian Chronicle (*FGrHist* 239 A 10), the Mother and her Phrygian tunes are as old as the reign of Erichthonius.

[6] F. Salviat, *BCH* 88 (1964) 239–51; Vermaseren, *CCCA* 2.169–76 nos. 529–48, pls. 159–67; Naumann, *Ikonographie* 147–9,308–9, pl. 21.

[7] *IG* 2² 1367 (= *LSCG* 52) lines 23–6.

[8] Paus.6.20.1; cf. Dion.Hal. *Ant.Rom.*1.34.3–4.

On Thera a cult foundation of the fourth century prescribes sacrifice to the Mother on the fifth of Artemisius and the fifth of Hyacinthius.[9] Although the calendar of Thera is not in order, these dates very likely match the spring and summer festivals; the common month-name Artemisius *vel sim.* seems always to come in spring, in the place of Elaphebolion or Munichion. Cos likewise honours "Rhea" at two junctures in the year, in the month Pedageitnyus and in some later month, on a day before the tenth.[10] The month Pedageitnyus may correspond to Anthesterion.

The festival business is little known. As we might expect, there was a banquet. Athens' Councillors and ephebes are said to offer sacrifice, and an ox is specified on Thera.[11] But the distinctive ritual was something else. The festival name Γαλάξια, a differentiated form of *γαλάκτ-ια, means "Milk-rites". According to the lexica already cited, a porridge was made of boiled milk and barley meal, also called γαλαξία. It was obviously an offering to the goddess and per-haps also a refreshment for the worshippers. Long after, milk was consumed at the spring festival of Magna Mater: whether the cel-ebrants drank it or ate a milky mixture does not appear.[12]

In either case, as an offering or as a meal, the porridge requires a suitable vessel, and this can only be the bowl, *phialê*, which is one of the Mother's attributes. Athens' famous statue of the Mother, attributed to either Pheidias or Agoracritus, holds a *phialê* in the right hand and a tympanum in the left, a pose that was widely adopted thereafter.[13] As the tympanum evokes the summer festival, the *phialê*

---

[9] *IG* 12.3.436 (= *SIG*[3] 1032, *LSCG* 134) lines 15–18.

[10] *Heil.Gesetz. Cos* 2 (*SIG*[3] 1026, *LSCG* 151 B) lines 2–5. The offerings in this month are to be the same "as are prescribed in Pedageitnyus". The present month is not Carneius, as some have thought. The biennial Carneia which are referred need not be concurrent; cf. n. 1 to *SIG*[3] 1026. Admittedly, the order of the Coan months cannot be firmly settled without reference to inscriptions still unpublished; yet it is clear that Carneius preceded Pedageitnyus in the same semester. For a provisional arrangement, see M. Segre, *ASAtene* n.s. 6/7 (1944/45) 170; Samuel, *Chronology* 112; S.M. Sherwin-White, *Ancient Cos* (Göttingen 1978) 193 n. 110. As to the day of the month, see n. 175 below.

[11] In the private calendar from Athens (n. 7 above), where the offerings are al-most entirely vegetarian, there is the usual cake, and then, in Sokolowski's restora-tion, ἐπι[πλά]σεις βοῦν "you shall fashion an ox" (out of a measure of flour).

[12] Sallust.4, γάλακτος τροφή. Cf. H. Hepding, *Attis* (Giessen 1903) 197–8; Nilsson, *GGR*[2] 2.645. Since Sallustius interprets the "feeding on milk" as a symbol of rebirth, it would not be to his purpose to mention any mixture. Hepding thinks of a mix-ture of milk and honey, which as Usener showed was a baptismal sacrament in the early church.

[13] For this type, see Naumann, *Ikonographie* 159–69. It is true that many a deity

will evoke the one in spring. In ephebic inscriptions a *phialê* is dedicated to the Mother year by year; the occasion is specified only once
as the Galaxia, but will always be the same.[14] It was also a customary dedication at the Mysteries of Eleusis, where iconography suggests that the *phialê* was a familiar implement of ritual.[15]

At this point the direct evidence for the spring festival has been
exhausted. Most of it, consisting of documents and of a single entry
in the lexica, refers to the Athenian instance, and even there it is
so slight that with only a little less luck we would never have heard
of the festival at all. Nonetheless, there can be no doubt that it
was very widely celebrated. For the Mother herself was very widely
worshipped, as both literature and inscriptions go to show, and the
worship, as with other gods, consisted of calendar festivals at the
appropriate seasons. The Mother's summer festival has left fuller traces,
for reasons that will emerge hereafter. But the spring festival was
just as integral to the worship, and can be postulated wherever the
Mother occurs.

Every festival has a purpose; we should note the purpose here before going any further. The purposes are always practical. Various
gods promote the various resources and livelihoods of the community, and are summoned to help at the appropriate time. As the
Mother is a pastoral goddess, ruling the hills and mountains where
animals are grazed, she will be asked to produce a favourable environment for this immensely important undertaking. The need is for
water sources and green herbage, and is especially felt at two seasons, in spring and summer. Spring shows what the conditions are,
and whether the animals will flourish in the months ahead. Summer
threatens ruinous heat and drought. Hence the Mother's two festivals.

---

is depicted as holding a *phialê* and pouring libation, a gesture that evidently signifies
a blessing. But despite Naumann 70–1, the Mother's *phialê* requires a more specific
explanation.

[14] *Hesperia* 24 (1955) 228–32 lines 27–8, 125–6 (128/7 B.C.); *IG* 2² 1006 lines
23–4, 79–80 (123/2); *Hesperia* 16 (1947) 170–2 no. 67 line 31 + *IG* 2² 1009 line 37
(117/16); *IG* 2² 1011 line 13 (107/6), naming the Galaxia; 1028 lines 40–1 (102/1);
1029 lines 24–5 (97/6); 1030 lines 35–6 (after 97/6).

[15] For a list of *phialê* dedications, see Chr. Pélékidis, *Histoire de l'éphébie attique* (Paris
1962) 212, 223 (Demeter and Core), 225 (the Mother), 246 (Dionysus), 277. The
dedication to Dionysus was not typical, occurring in only one year, but both at
Athens and at Peiraeus. In Eleusinian ritual, a *phialê* came into use at more than
one juncture, for in scenes of Heracles' initiation a priest holds a *phialê* containing
fruits or poppy-heads, and in other scenes a *phialê* with liquid contents is held by
one of the Eleusinian goddesses or by Triptolemus. In this case the significance of
the ephebic dedication can only be conjectured, but it was once known to everyone.

The "Milk-rites" of spring are a magic means of inducing nature, both earth and sky, to yield abundant moisture. The related myth, as we shall see in a moment, says that Zeus himself, the sky god, is nursed on the milk of a mother goat. Myth is a projection of magical practice and belief. Consider for a moment the more prolific myths attending the winter festival of Dionysus; for they express the same magic notion.[16] The purpose there is to revive the ravaged vine, rather than grass and foliage; a mimic suckling is again the means. The myths say either that the infant Dionysus was nursed by nymphs on the mountain Nysa, an ideal version of all upland vineyards, or that when Dionysus arrived at a given city the royal women were nursing new-born sons. The myths also tell how Maenads or legendary celebrants cause milk and other nourishing liquids to gush from the earth. There is a general similarity in the respective rites of Dionysus and of the Mother, which comes to be embroidered in myth. It is due to a common background of very ancient magic.

III. *The birth of Zeus as* aition *of the spring festival*

Besides direct, literal evidence for Greek ritual, there is another kind that waits to be recognized and exploited: aetiological myth. It is said or implied of almost every festival we know of that it began at some moment long ago when the god first arose and displayed his power, or when he first came among men, or when men first sought help from the god. A given story and a given festival have the same wide currency. Just as (say) Athena or Demeter or Apollo is worshipped everywhere at the same season, so the stories about the advent of each, or about man's need of each, are recorded at many far-flung places. A story will show local variations, but the common features are always striking; they correspond to the leading features of the ritual which the story explains.

Stories do in fact exist for both the Mother's festivals, the Galaxia of spring and the Cronia of summer (to use the Ionian names). But it is only with the latter that the aetiology is either explicit or obvious (§ V). To anticipate conclusions, the ritual of summer was all frenzied movement and noise—leaping, whirling, howling, clashing, thumping. And such, says the story, was the conduct of the divine or

---

[16] See Robertson, *AncW* 26 (1995).

human principals who established the rite. Such was the conduct of
the Mother in her grief; of the Curetes who concealed her child; of
the Corybantes when they healed Dionysus; even of the Argonauts
at Cyzicus. The motives and the circumstances vary, but the principals are always seen enacting the same ritual. The best-known versions are associated with the places where the Mother is best known—
with Athens, Crete, Arcadia, Phrygia, Cyzicus.

For the spring festival we have no acknowledged aetiology. But
aetiology there must have been. Now at all the centres of worship
where the madcap stories were told to explain the summer festival,
another class of story is also told. It is a story of the Mother's giving
birth, and of the bathing and swaddling and nursing of the child,
who is Zeus. Birth and nursing are implicit in the festival name Galaxia "Milk-rites". Furthermore, the birth story and the commonest
version of the madcap story, the dance of the Curetes, make a connected sequence, the rearing of Zeus, which can only derive from
related festivals. On these grounds, we may infer that the birth story
constitutes the missing aetiology of the spring festival.

Let us then examine some versions of the story, so as to establish
that they do indeed arise from the worship of the Mother. The story
is attested at many places in the homeland and in Ionia, and further
off in Lydia and Phrygia;[17] Pausanias knew of places beyond count-
ing (4.33.1). In Lydia and Phrygia it is clear almost at a glance that
the story goes with cults of the Mother rather than of Zeus.[18] This
is weighty but not conclusive, since the story, insofar as it is Greek,
will be adventitious. We must find places in Greece where details
survive about the Mother's sanctuaries and their ritual. As everyone
knows who has considered such matters, that is a stern requirement.
The search will take us to 1) Crete, 2) Arcadia, 3) Athens, 4) Thebes,
5) Cyzicus.

1) Crete should be considered first, for it is here, in a mountain
cave, that Zeus is hid and nursed in Hesiod, who was so authorita-
tive that other versions barely survived as local curiosities.[19] Yet Hesiod

---

[17] For general surveys, see H. Schwabl, *RE* Suppl. 15 (1978) 1207–16 s.v. Zeus;
H. Verbruggen, *Le Zeus crétois* (Paris 1981) 27–49.

[18] Rapp, *ML* 4 (1915) 91 s.v. Rhea, citing others before him, points to the correspondence between Anatolian instances of the birth story and "the main cult-sites
of the Phrygian Kybele".

[19] *Theog.*477–84. Lines 481–3 or 481–4 have often been condemned as clumsy or
redundant, but without them the passage will lack a mountain cave (line 483) and
even a mountain (line 484), which both seem essential in view of the later tradition.

does not make it clear whether Zeus was born as well as nursed in the cave on Crete, or was carried there as a babe in arms by Rhea or even Gaea.[20] Because of this ambiguity, later sources sometimes say either that Zeus was brought to the mountain cave from a birthplace outside Crete, or that he was born on one Cretan mountain and nursed on another.[21] Hesiod's ambiguity is deliberate; it follows from his using a local *aition* in the general narrative of the succession in heaven.

Crete is first mentioned as the babe's destination, whether to be born or only to be nursed, because this distant place will serve as a refuge from Cronus. Hesiod next describes a particular site, a cave "on the Aegaean mount", said to be at Lyctus. This was a shrine where the birth story was told, and the local story was undoubtedly complete in itself and included both birth and nursing. When later sources set the story at a given site, it is usually complete; to say that the infant was transferred from one place to another is only a means of accommodating Hesiod. As we shall soon see, the story is told as an *aition* at various shrines on the mainland, including one at Thebes. There can be little doubt that it was told at many places in Hesiod's day. But for the sake of the narrative he situates the nursing, a protracted business, at a site on Crete which was probably the furthest one he knew of.[22]

No one after Hesiod points to Lyctus, later called Lyttus, or speaks of "the Aegaean mount". Instead, we are told how Zeus was nursed in a cave on Mount Ida, either by nymphs or by a goat. We cannot name the poet who first spoke of Ida, but he was early. It has not been noticed that the Idaean version is presupposed by a fragmentary passage of [Hesiod's] *Catalogue of Women*, in which Pasiphae is consigned by Zeus to the nymphs of Ida, obviously to be nursed and reared (fr. 145 M-W lines 1–2). This derivative episode shows that when the *Catalogue* was composed, in the later sixth century, Ida was generally accepted as the mountain where Zeus was reared. Thereafter

---

[20] "Hesiod is curiously non-committal about where the birth actually occurred", says West on line 481.

[21] Transferred from elsewhere: Callim. *H.Jov*.33–4; etc. Transferred within Crete: Diod.5.70.2; etc.

[22] Famous far-away cult sites are used to a similar purpose in the episode of Aphrodite's birth from the sea. "First she appeared on holy Cythera, and then she came to sea-girt Cyprus", etc. (*Theog*.192–200). Though her advent was celebrated every spring at every coastal shrine (cf. Ath.9.51, 394F–395A, apropos of Eryx), only Cythera and Cyprus fit the scale of the narrative.

the story is evoked by the mere epithet "Idaean" used of Zeus and the nymphs and also the Curetes.[23] The birth as distinct from the nursing is never expressly assigned to Ida—this no doubt in deference to Hesiod.[24]

From the early Hellenistic period, either the birth or the nursing or both are sometimes assigned to Mount Dicte, and Zeus, less commonly the other figures, have the epithet "Dictaean".[25] Here much less is said about a cave; indeed it seems very likely that any purported cave on Dicte is mere confusion, whether wishful or inadvertent, with the one on Ida.[26] Our literary sources are vague about the topography of Crete, for the island was seldom visited by other Greeks. Yet they all share the notion that the infant Zeus was at home at just one great site.

When we turn to the realities, it is Mount Ida that can show by far the most frequented cave sanctuary of Greek and Roman times, and according to two late dedications (cited below) it belongs to "Idaean Zeus".[27] As others have observed, some of the votive objects are inspired either by the story of Zeus' rearing in the cave or by the ritual behind it. A bronze tympanum, several cymbals, and sixty-odd shields, many finely decorated, evoke the dance of the Curetes, which is also depicted on the tympanum, even if the bearded god and his attendants are rendered in Oriental style.[28] The cave is on the north flank of Ida, about twenty miles west of Cnossus. It owes much to the long-enduring power of this Dorian city.

No other likely candidate has ever been found. The mountain south of Lyttus, modern Lasithi, has the Minoan cave sanctuary of Psychro, now famous, but it was rarely visited in the historic period.[29] The

---

[23] The name "Idaean Zeus" first occurs in Euripides, who associates him with "the Mountain Mother" and the Curetes: Porph. *De Abst.*4.19 (Eur. *Cretes* fr. 472 Nauck[2]/79 Austin/635 Mette); cf. *Hypsipyle* p. 28 Bond/fr. 1032 Mette; *Bacch.*120–9. *Cretes* was about Pasiphae, but whether Euripides adverted to her upbringing does not appear.

[24] "Zeus is never said to have been born on Mt Ide": so A.B. Cook, *Zeus* (Cambridge 1914–40) 2.932 n. 1, typically exact and acute. But he gives a wrong reason, that Dicte had priority.

[25] Callim. *H.Jov.*4–6,47–51; Apoll. *Argon.*1.509,1130; Arat. *Phaen.*33–4; etc.

[26] Cf. West on *Theog.*477 and again *The Orphic Poems* (Oxford 1983) 128.

[27] For general accounts of the cave and its furnishings, see Cook, *Zeus* 2.935–9; Verbruggen, *Zeus crétois* 71–5,77–81,84,91–9. For a bibliography, B. Rutkowski, *The Cult Places of the Aegean* (New Haven 1986) 69 no. 10.

[28] For these items, see E. Kunze, *Kretische Bronzereliefs* (Stuttgart 1931); J.N. Coldstream, *Geometric Greece* (London 1977) 286–8. As to the tympanum, cf. n. 226 below.

[29] Psychro has forfeited the name "Dictaean Cave", or should do, now that Dicte

suggestion has been made that "the Aegaean mount" is the ancient name of Lasithi, otherwise unknown.[30] Yet Hesiod's term cannot have been a name in common use, else we should find some trace in antiquarian comment. If it was descriptive, with whatever meaning, it could as well refer to Ida.[31]

Finally, Mount Dicte was somewhere near the eastern end of the island, and the cult of Dictaean Zeus at Palaikastro was shared by the easternmost cities.[32] There is however no Dictaean cave; although there were many Minoan cave sanctuaries in this area, none lasted into Greek times. It must be the regional cult of Zeus that is mentioned in the Linear B tablets at Cnossus (there is no evidence of continuity on the temple site, but perhaps none should be expected).[33] In those days, Palaikastro was an important metal-working centre.[34] The memory survived in the legend of the bronze giant Talos, whom Apollonius places at Palaikastro.[35] Zeus was responsible for Talos, but Zeus the high god, not the cave-child.

is fixed in eastern Crete. According to West on *Theog.*477, any of three Minoan cave sanctuaries on Lasithi, including Psychro, may have been intended—for he considers this a "Minoan cult myth" (see his note on *Theog.*453–506). Yet even if it were, we could not believe that the myth clung to some vacant cave on Lasithi as late as Hesiod, but thereafter moved to Ida. For it was in Hesiod's day, and for some time before and after, that the Idaean cave received its richest offerings. Note in passing that a shrine of the Curetes referred to in the treaty between Lato and Olus could be relevant (*ICret* 1 XVI 5)—if in fact it stood near the boundary with Lyttus "on the north-east flank of Dikte" [i.e. Lasithi], as we are encouraged to think by R.F. Willetts, *Cretan Cults and Festivals* (London 1962) 209. But this location is only a wild guess.

[30] So, e.g., M. Guarducci, *ICret* 3 p. 6; West on *Theog.*484; G.L. Huxley, *GRBS* 8 (1967) 85.

[31] Wilamowitz, *Isyllos von Epidauros* (Berlin 1886) 109 n. 2, and again *Der Glaube der Hellenen* (Berlin 1931–32) 1.127, would read Αἰγείωι to give the sense *Ziegenberg* (though he did not think that a definite mountain was meant). It seems quite possible that Αἰγείωι was altered to the familiar name Αἰγαίωι. Yet this too must once have been descriptive. The αἰγ- words in early poetry are studied by R.L. Fowler, *Phoenix* 42 (1988) 95–113.

[32] On the location of Dicte, see Cook, *Zeus* 2.929–30; Verbruggen, *Zeus crétois* 137–8. On the cult at Palaikastro, Guarducci, *ICret* 3 II. Huxley, *GRBS* 8 (1967) 85–7, without disputing that Dicte is a mountain, holds that this was also "the Minoan name" for the palace of Kato Zakro and survived later as a name for the region of Zakro. The hypothesis seems not to remove any of the difficulties in Greek sources, but rather to create new ones.

[33] In KN Fp 1 + 31, offerings dated to a certain month, "Dictaean Zeus" comes first in a list of deities. In other tablets offerings are dispatched "to Dicte". For discussion, see S. Hiller, *RE* Suppl.1006–7 s.v. Zeus, and also Schwabl, *ibid.*, 1450–1.

[34] This has only just been recognized: S. Hemingway, *BSA* 87 (1992) 141–51.

[35] Apoll. *Argon.*4.1638–88. Other sources do not say where Talos was at home, but we may assume that Apollonius follows a usual tradition.

On this evidence it is fair to say that all our sources who have any
awareness of the matter associate the birth story with the same cult
site, the cave on Ida. In Hesiod's day Lyttus was perhaps the leading
city on the whole island.[36] If it overshadowed Cnossus, it might well
be mentioned instead, together with the cave. As for Dictaean Zeus,
he is suddenly enswathed in the birth story in the early third century, at the hands of Callimachus, Apollonius, and Aratus. The hymn
which summons the *kouros* and his band to their annual appearance
on Dicte was composed about the same time.[37] In all these sources
the mountain setting is vague or even contradictory, as between Ida
and Dicte.[38] Surely the story was arrogated for Dictaean Zeus in a
spirit of rivalry. It had brought enormous renown to Idaean Zeus, a
deity with important shrines in several cities of central Crete and
even further off.[39] In the third century the Ptolemies opened new
horizons for the cities of eastern Crete.[40] Regional interests were
expressed then, as at the time of the Cnossus tablets, in the worship
of Dictaean Zeus. But now he was proudly cast as the principal of
that famous story.

In sum, it was solely the cave on Ida that gave rise to the Cretan
version of the birth story. We may readily imagine that on Crete, as
elsewhere in Greece, there were other sanctuaries where the birth

---

[36] "The oldest of the cities on Crete, and by general consent the mother of the
finest men", says Polybius at the moment of its destruction by Cnossus (4.54.6). In
the legends of the Second Messenian War, the Cretan archers who capture Aris-
tomenes come "from Lyctus and other cities" (Paus.4.19.4). Archaeological evidence
is slim: J. Boardman in *CAH*[2] 3.3.229.

[37] *ICret* 3 II 2; M.L. West, *JHS* 85 (1965) 149–59; Guarducci in *Studi in onore di
D. Levi* (Catania 1974) 2.32–8 = *Scritti scelti* (Leiden 1983) 38–44. The date assigned
by editors on grounds of dialect, metre, and orthography is the fourth or third
century B.C.

[38] As to Callimachus and his fellows, see ns. 25–6 above. The hymn says, Δίκταν . . .
ἕρπε "come to Dicte": it is here that we sing while standing round your altar, and
it is here that the Curetes once took the child from Rhea. Yet the sanctuary where
the hymn was inscribed in two very late copies is by the harbour of Palaikastro; it
was shared by Itanus, Praesus, and Hierapytna, referred to in the hymn as πόληας
ἁμῶν "our cities", which the arriving *kouros* is asked to prosper. Since the sanctuary
is not really "Dicte", and is not a likely setting for the birth story, it is hard to
believe that the poet was acquainted with any authentic ritual to match the story.
The scattered finds from the sanctuary, fully listed by Cook, *Zeus* 2.930, are not
revealing for our purpose.

[39] See Verbruggen, *Zeus crétois* 140.

[40] Itanus as the easternmost received a Ptolemaic garrison; cf. R. Bagnall, *The
Administration of the Ptolemic Possessions outside Egypt* (Leiden 1976) 117–23. The harbour
of Palaikastro ocuppies a strategic position, illustrated by the route of the Argonauts:
Cyrene, Carpathus, Palaikastro, Anaphe (Apoll. *Argon*.4.1625–1718).

story was handed down by local worshippers; nor need they have been caves, any more than such sanctuaries elsewhere. Yet so far as we can see, no other instance was ever noticed in Greek literature. Accordingly, to inquire about the ritual background is to inspect the Idaean cave.

Only two lettered dedications have been found in the cave, a terracotta plaque of the second or third century after Christ, and a vase inscribed even later: both are addressed to "Idaean Zeus".[41] Legend describes the cave as his, even apart from the birth story. Minos went up to the cave every nine years to converse with Zeus, his father, or on a sceptical view to give the appearance of obtaining his laws from Zeus.[42] Epimenides and Pythagoras went there too, and Porphyry, in the fullest account, speaks of strange magic rites.[43] Pythagoras "came with black fleeces, and stayed there for the customary twenty-seven days, and sacrificed to Zeus, and gazed upon the throne that was spread for him each year, and inscribed a dedication on his tomb", which is quoted (the tomb need not detain us, for this celebrated monument is not located in the cave by any other source).

It seems natural to conclude that this was a sanctuary of Zeus. Every modern scholar has done so. But then consequences follow which cannot possibly be considered natural. The god thus revealed is thought to be very different from Zeus as we see him elsewhere.[44] He is a god of vegetation, reviving each year along with his domain in nature, perhaps first dying, then coming back to life in a miraculous rebirth. And many think that this pattern was also expressed in the form of initiation rites conducted in the cave, either for maturing adolescents or for members of a secret society.[45] In earlier days the cult was usually traced back to Anatolia, especially Phrygia, or to other eastern lands. Now it is claimed as a Minoan heritage.

---

[41] *ICret* 1 XII 1 (plaque); G. Daux, *BCH* 81 (1957) 632 (vase).

[42] Pl. *Leg.*1 *init.*, 624A–625A, [pl.] *Minos* 319; Diod.5.78.3; Dion.Hal. *Ant.Rom.*2.61.2 ("Dicte" instead of "Ida" is inadvertent); Str.10.4.8, p. 476 (Ephorus *FGrHist* 70 F 147); Max.Tyr.38.2; Iambl. *VPyth* 5.25–7; schol. *Od.*19.179.

[43] Diog.Laert.8.1.3; Porph. *VPyth* 17. It is Porphyry again who quotes Euripides' *Cretes* to show that "the prophets of Zeus on Crete" were vegetarians (n. 23 above).

[44] The notion of a mysterious Cretan cult of Zeus appears in every handbook of Greek religion and in every discussion of such topics as initiation rites and purification, Epimenides and Pythagoras and the Orphics, so that references are superfluous. Instead, see Verbruggen, *Zeus crétois*, where the notion is combatted as well as can be done by focussing on Zeus, without reference to the Mother.

[45] Unhappily, Verbruggen, *Zeus crétois*, remains committed to initiation rites. It is worth remarking that M.P. Nilsson, who was most effective in promoting the Minoan

The Idaean cave does not warrant these hypotheses. The fundamental question is, what deity was worshipped here with characteristic rites? It is in fact the Mother, not Zeus, who would be fitly honoured with the votive objects that evoke a frenzied dance, tympanum and cymbals and shields. We shall see further on that the Curetes, clashing spear on shield, are projected from her summer festival (§ V). As to tympanum and cymbals, both instruments are notoriously brandished by her worshippers; the tympanum is her constant attribute in art. Several bronze bowls, *phialai*, were also dedicated in the cave,[46] and are equally appropriate to the Mother (cf. § II). Still other votive objects point to female worshippers and a female deity, but do not show who she was.[47]

A find seemingly unpublished is an Archaic limestone statue of a seated goddess.[48] It came from the small, dark upper chamber where lamps were used in Roman times. Here too is a rock formation resembling a throne. Now Pythagoras, says Porphyry, τόν τε στορνύμενον αὐτῶι κατ᾽ ἔτος θρόνον ἐθεάσατο "gazed upon the throne that was spread for him each year", scil. for Zeus. If it was a privileged sight, it must have been out of the way, as in the upper chamber. At Athens "to spread a throne" is a ceremony honouring the Mother, probably at her spring festival; we shall come to it below.

These are signs that the Idaean cave was once a sanctuary of the Mother.[49] In the course of time Zeus seems to have supplanted her as the presiding deity. Hesiod will be largely responsible, for in the connected story of the succession in heaven it is the episode of the Cretan cave that assures the triumph of Zeus. Cnossus and Ida fell

---

fertility spirit, expressly set himself against the related notion of initation rites: *The Minoan-Mycenaean Religion*² (Lund 1950) 548–9. Yet when W. Burkert, *Lore and Science in Ancient Pythagoreanism* (Cambridge, Mass. 1972) 151, informs us that "There were 'caves of Zeus' in Crete, sites of the initiatory ceremonies of secret societies", he adduces Nilsson, *GGR*² 1.261–4 as if in direct support of this point (*ibid.*, n. 173). That is almost libellous.

[46] Kunze, *Kret.Bronzereliefs* 1.31–2 nos. 69–73, 212–16, pls. 44, 47–8.

[47] Verbruggen, *Zeus crétois* 83, cf. 78,80,99, thinks that Zeus was preceded by "an anonymous goddess".

[48] See Verbruggen, *Zeus crétois* 74, citing S. Marinatos, who uncovered it in 1956. I ought to say that I have not been able to consult E. Platakis, Τὸ Ἰδαῖον ἄντρον (Herakleion 1965). Verbruggen was chided by a reviewer for failing to make use of this work.

[49] We may also reflect that the association of Idaean Zeus with Bacchic and no doubt Orphic mysteries, which first appears in Euripides (as cited in n. 23), is much more understandable if the rites of the cave sanctuary are simply those of the Mother, for she and Dionysus are flagrant kindred spirits.

heir to a Panhellenic reputation that was bound to influence the local cult. Zeus was in any case, in his normal range as weather god and as guardian of the social order, as prominent on Crete as in the rest of Greece;[50] he must have been worshipped at other sites on Ida. But despite modern theories, his nature did not greatly change with his role in the cave.

2) In Callimachus and Pausanias, Arcadia is bound up just as closely as Crete with the birth story. Here we are given several definite locations. On Mount Thaumasius near Methydrium—either Madara or Ayios Ilias, the two mountains flanking the city—Rhea presented Cronus with the swaddled stone; she also sought the protection of armed Giants, congeners of the Curetes, who go with the summer festival; on the mountain summit was a cave sacred to Rhea.[51] The river that runs by Gortys was for a certain stretch near its source called Lusius "Washing-place" because it served to wash the infant Zeus.[52] It was on Mount Lycaeus, in a certain wooded area, that Rhea gave birth; she then washed the child in the source of the river Neda, and handed him over to local Nymphs, including Neda.[53] The river Lymax "Scouring", a tributary of the Neda, got its name when Rhea on being delivered was cleansed by the Nymphs.[54] The bathing and rearing were also situated on Mount Ithome nearby, again at the hands of the Nymphs, again including Neda; here too the babe was hidden by the Curetes.[55]

Methydrium, Gortys, Lycaeus, Ithome, Neda: these are all towards the southwest of the Arcadian plain, the area which Callimachus calls by the old name Parrhasia. For literary purposes this area was singled out as the Arcadian birthplace, and the details were suitably adjusted. In Callimachus Zeus is born in Arcadia and reared in Crete. In Pausanias the different sites have somewhat different roles in the story. The harmonizing effort is obvious when Methydrium concedes that Zeus was born on Lycaeus, but insists that the stone was tendered on Thaumasius. Another moment has been isolated in the lexical

---

[50] Verbruggen, *Sources pertaining to the Cult of Zeus in Crete* (Louvain 1979), and *Zeus crétois* 127–54.

[51] Paus.8.36.2–3; Steph.Byz. s.v. Θαυμάσιον. On the Giants vis-à-vis the Curetes, see F. Vian, *La Guerre des géants* (Paris 1952) 239–40; M. Jost, *Sanctuaires et cultes d'Arcadie* (Paris 1985) 245.

[52] Paus.8.28.2.

[53] Callim. *H.Jov.*10–17,32–41; Paus.8.36.3,38.2–3.

[54] Paus.8.41.2.

[55] Paus.4.33.1.

entry *Geraistion*, said to be "a place in Arcadia" where "Zeus was swaddled".[56] Now local legends do not grow up in this way, as discrete episodes of a longer narrative. We must infer that the complete story of the birth and rearing (with whatever detail) was once told at each site: apropos of Ithome Pausanias remarks that the story was common to innumerable places and peoples.

We can also see that the cult to which the story was attached is the Mother's. On Thaumasius, we have a cave of Rhea; in the woods of Lycaeus, "a sacred place" called "the Couch of Rhea"; at the foot of Ithome, in the later city of Messene, a statue of the Mother made by Damophon, and a *megaron* of the Curetes.[57] Zeus the weather god is worshipped on Lycaeus and Ithome, as on so many mountains; but these shrines have nothing to do with the birth story.

The Mother is fairly prominent in other parts of Arcadia, not only in the southwest.[58] At Lycosura, on a spur of Lycaeus at the southeast, the Mother has a place in the sanctuary of the Arcadian goddess *Despoina* "Mistress": an altar in front of the temple; an emblematic pair of lions in the temple's mosaic floor; among the reliefs of Damophon's great statue, another pair of lions flanking a tympanum, and groups of both Curetes and Corybantes.[59] In the agora of Megalopolis Pausanias saw a ruined temple and a small statue.[60] Near Asea, at the reputed source of the Alpheius, he notes a roofless temple and two stone lions; a battered statue of the Mother that was found here in the nineteenth century may be as early as the beginning of the sixth century.[61] Wee see her again in western Arcadia. In the Alpheius valley, on the road to Olympia, a rustic priestess with prophetic powers lends colour to a speech of Dio Chrysostom.[62] Azania at the northwest was renowned for "Idaean howling", i.e. for its celeb-

---

[56] *Et.Magn.* s.v. Γεραίστιον. The place is often associated with Arcadian Gortys on the ground that Zeus is nursed by Nymphs called *Geraistiades* at Cretan Gortyn.

[57] Cave on Thaumasius: Paus.8.36.3. Sacred place on Lycaeus: Callim. *H.Jov.*11–14. Monuments in Messene: Paus.4.31.6,9.

[58] On her cults in Arcadia, cf. H. Graillot, *Le Culte de Cybèle* (Paris 1912) 509–11, 515–16; Jost, *Sanctuaires* 523.

[59] Paus.8.37.2,6; Jost, *Sanctuaires* 523 (mosaic and sculptural fragments).

[60] Paus.8.30.4.

[61] Paus.8.44.3. For the statue, see J. de La Genière, *MélRome* 97 (1985) 711–14, and *CRAI* 1986, 33–35, and *StItal* n.s. 10 (1992) 98. From Achuria near Tegea there is a small altar of Roman date dedicated "to the Great Mother": *IG* 5.2.87; Jost, *Sanctuaires* 523.

[62] *Or.*1.53–4.

ration of the summer festival.[63] The Phrygians of Aezani, who also worshipped the Mother, were proud to say that they had migrated from this corner of Arcadia.[64]

The Mother's ritual and its aetiology were probably much the same throughout Arcadia, but for some reason literary folk concentrated on the southwest. Elsewhere, in the plain of Mantineia, Pausanias tells a local tale about a spring Arne "Lamb", presumably a cult-site.[65] When Rhea bore Poseidon, she set him down among a flock of lambs browsing round the spring; "and she pretended to Cronus that she had borne a horse, and gave a foal to swallow instead of the child, just as she later gave him instead of Zeus a stone wrapped in swaddling clothes". The reason for contriving this odd variation of the familiar story is doubtless that the latter had been preempted by the spokesmen of southwest Arcadia. The details of the story— the spring, the flock, the expiatory foal—are unmistakably inspired by ritual.

3) After Arcadia, we hear of two other places in the homeland where the cult of the Mother was deeply rooted and the story was told of Zeus' birth and rearing: Athens and Thebes. At both places the evidence for the Mother is much earlier than elsewhere, going back to the Archaic period. And although the birth story is not explicitly connected with the cult, the connexion is very probable.

The Mother has three notable shrines at Athens: one in Agra, the rural district beyond the Ilissus adjoining the southeast sector of the city, the earliest Dark-Age community; another in the excavated Agora at the northwest, an area developed in the later sixth century; and yet another on the Museum hill at the southwest corner of the city. There were other shrines in the countryside.[66] One element of the aetiology is perfectly clear. The chorus of Euripides' *Helena* describe

---

[63] Stat. *Theb.*4.292, *Idaeis ululatibus aemulus Azan.* Lact.Plac. *ad loc.*, *"aemulus"*, *quia in illo monte Azanio ut Iupiter ita etiam Mater deorum colitur ritu Idaeo. "Azan": apud Arcades Curetes hoc nomen habent de monte Azanio. unde vulgo in sacris deae magnae . . . dicitur Azan.*

[64] Paus.8.4.3,10.32.3. A coin of Aezani, with Cybele holding a miniature Zeus and the Curetes dancing round her, shows that the birth was situated here, doubtless in the cave mentioned by Pausanias, which has been explored and published; see R. Naumann, *Ist.Mitt* 17 (1967) 218–47; L. Robert, *BCH* 105 (1981) 352–60; Vermaseren, *CCCA* 1.44–7 nos. 124–36, pl. 17.

[65] Paus.8.8.1–2 (*FGrHist* 322 F 4); cf. Fest. s.v. Hippius, p. 101 Müller; *Et.Magn.* s.v. Ἄρνη, Tzetz.Lycophr. *Alex.*644 (Theseus *FGrHist* 453 F 1).

[66] Shrine in Agra: § IV. In the Agora: H.A. Thompson and R.E. Wycherley, *The Agora of Athens* (Princeton 1972) 30–1, 35–8; Vermaseren, *CCCA* 2.3–48, nos. 1–179, pls. 1–34. For the Museum hill, see below. In the countryside: Graillot, *Cybèle*

the Mother's frenzied roaming, after the pattern of the summer festival (lines 1301–52); but in this Athenian version she searches for her daughter, as if she were Demeter—a tribute to the overarching renown of Eleusis (§ V).

Athens' version of the birth of Zeus, which has not been recognized as such, is ascribed to the legendary poet Musaeus. Musaeus' best-known work in later times was a *Theogony*, in which "Zeus at his birth was entrusted by Rhea to Themis, and Themis gave the babe to Amaltheia, and she put him to suck at a goat which she had, and the goat nurtured Zeus".[67] In the sequel, Zeus, Amaltheia, and the goat are all transferred with the help of Gaea to "one of the caves on Crete", so that Hesiod is duly accommodated, in much the same fashion as in Callimachus' *Hymn to Zeus*. The goat, moreover, becomes the centre of attention as the source of Zeus' *aigis*, the dreadful "goatskin" of epic poetry that is now used to defeat the Titans. We can ignore these embellishments, the Cretan cave and the *aigis*. The words quoted are a full and sufficient account of Zeus' birth and rearing.

Musaeus "He of the Muses" was a pseudonym, a rather naked one, used to authenticate religious poetry, especially healing charms and oracles, so that he became the inventor of these things.[68] In early days he probably did service in various quarters, but by the late fifth century he had been appropriated beyond appeal by Athens, as father and preceptor of the Eleusinian hero Eumolpus.[69] It was on the Museium hill that he sang and was buried after a long

---

503–8; S. Solders, *Die ausserstädtischen Kulte und die Einigung Attikas* (Lund 1931) 52. In Attic art the Mother goes back to the later sixth century. There is a small seated statue and terracotta figurines, both from the Acropolis: Naumann, *Iconographie* 145–6,308; de La Genière, *MélRome* 97 (1985) 696, and *CRAI* 1986, 32. It would be unreasonable to ask for anything earlier.

[67] Eratosth. *Catast*.13 (Musaeus *Vorsokr* 2B 8); Hyg. *Astr*.2.13.4; schol.Germ. *Arat*. p. 73 Breysig; schol.Arat. *Phaen*.156; Lact. *Inst.Div*.1.21.39. Cf. Diod.5.70.5 (*FGrHist* 468 [Crete app.] F 1).

[68] Ar. *Ran*.1033; pl. *Protag*.316D, *Rep*.2,364E; cf. Hdt.7.6.3; schol.Ar. *loc. cit.* (Philochorus *FGrHist* 328F 208; Soph. *TGrF* fr. 1116).

[69] The earliest witness, but an emphatic one, is [Eur.] *Rhes*.945–7. Musaeus is a favourite on red-figure vases, hob-nobbing with the Muses and Apollo (*LIMC* s.v.). The words which Beazley reads and restores on a scroll read to Musaeus by Linus, θεῶν αἱ[ειγενετάων, would make a suitable opening for a theogony, if only they were sure: *AJA* 52 (1948) 340 (*LIMC* no. 11). It is sometimes maintained, as by Jacoby, *FGrHist* IIIb Suppl.1.575, that Musaeus originates in Athens or Attica. This would make it more likely still that the Museium hill is named after him, as suggested below.

life.⁷⁰ Now the name Μουσεῖον for the hill is rather puzzling, for there is no trace hereabouts of any cult of the Muses, which one would expect to be the origin of the name.⁷¹ The name appears to be due to the association with Musaeus. It must then have replaced some earlier name; but given Musaeus' celebrity, that does not seem impossible. In any case, it appears that the inspired prophet was associated with just this part of Athens because his activity suited the pre-existing worship of the Mother. We should examine the remains on the hill. They have never been fully understood.

On the northwest slope is a rock-cut inscription, of the fourth or third century B.C., that evokes Musaeus' oracles: ἔπος δὲ φωνή.⁷² This must be the abbreviation of a hexameter tag like ἔπος δὲ [φθέγξατο] φωνή "the voice uttered a word". One of the few verbatim fragments of Musaeus, two hexameter lines describing the operation of the Delphic oracle when it belonged to Gaea and Poseidon, contains a similar phrase, φωνὴ πινυτὸν φάτο μῦθον "the voice spoke a wise word".⁷³ Here the voice is Gaea's (or "Chthonia's"), and exemplifies the primary mode of Delphic prophecy, an inspired utterance by the Pythia; it is juxtaposed in the next line with the taking of omens from the sacrificial fire. The lines are quoted by Pausanias from the

---

⁷⁰ Paus.1.25.8. He also had a grave and epitaph at Phalerum (Diog.Laert.1.3; *A.P.*7.615; schol.Ar. *Ran.*1033); here as in Philochorus he is son, not father, of Eumolpus. The significance of the Phalerum monument is moot: cf. E. Kearns, *The Heroes of Attica* (London 1989) 17 n. 48, 187.

⁷¹ The Museum hill first enters history in 294 B.C., when it was fortified by Demetrius. Yet it figures as a landmark in Cleidemus' account of the Amazon invasion, i.e. in the mid fourth century: Plut. *Thes.*27.1,3 (*FGrHist* 323F 18: the "fragment" should begin with 27.1, not 27.2). W. Judeich, *Topographie von Athen*² (Munich 1931) 424, connects the hill with the Ilissian Muses, quite unfeasibly; cf. Wycherley, *GRBS* 4 (1963) 173–4, and *The Stones of Athens* (Princeton 1978) 171.

⁷² S.N. Dragoumis, *AthMitt* 23 (1898) 202–4; A.A. Papayiannopoulos-Palaios, Ἀρχαῖαι Ἑλληνικαὶ Ἐπιγραφαὶ (Athens 1939) 76 no. 14; W. Peek, *AthMitt* 67 (1942) 150–1 no. 324; not in *IG* 2²; cf. *SEG* 41 (1991) no. 232. The date is Peek's, who says "the inscription is certainly no later". Dragoumis proposed either a connexion with Musaeus or "the notion of an echo". The latter is preferred by Judeich, *Topographie*² 398, and by Peek 151, even though both Dragoumis and Peek admit, to their honour, to making repeated attempts to raise an echo with no success. According to N.I. Pantazopoulou, *Polemon* 3 (1947–48) 121, the inscription recalls the *mētragyrtês* who preached and perhaps prophesied about the Mother (of which more below); cf. Papayiannopoulos-Palaios, Ἐπιγραφαὶ 77 and *Polemon* 3 (1947–48) 96.

⁷³ Paus.10.5.6 (*Vorsokr* 2B 11). "Straightway Chthonia's voice spoke a wise word; with her was Pyrcon, servant of the glorious Earth-shaker". Chthonia stands for the Pythia, Πύρκων for the Delphic officiant called πυρκόος, who watched the sacrificial fire (Hsch. s.v.). The second element is the root (σ)κο- of κοέω (cf. *schauen, show*), so that the word is a synonym of θυηκόος (Attic θυηχόος), θυοσκόος.

Eumolpia, which may or may not be the same as the *Theogony*.[74]

As for the sanctuary of the Mother, one limit is marked by another rock-cut inscription at a different point on the northwest slope, this one by a professional hand of the fourth century: ἱερὸν Μητρός "shrine of the Mother".[75] The Museium hill is also given as the provenance of two roof tiles stamped with a dedication to the Mother by scions of a family prominent in the later second century B.C.[76] Other such tiles have been found in the Agora and undoubtedly belong to the large new Metroum that was constructed there shortly after the middle of the century, with the help as it seems of Attalus II, who is responsible for the great stoa opposite.[77] So tiles may have drifted by chance from the Agora to the Museium hill. But it is just as simple to suppose that the sanctuary here was refurbished at the same time, since every cult of the Mother was deserving of attention in the days when Athens courted Pergamum.[78]

Our shrine has also been suggested as the setting of a strange story, first mentioned by Julian in his oration on the Mother, about a *mêtragyrtês* who was rebuffed or murdered by the Athenians and then vindicated by the founding of "the Metroum".[79] But all our sources plainly mean the shrine in the Agora; for the rest, the details are so uncertain and obscure that the starting point is impossible to discern.

---

[74] Both the *Theogony* and the *Eumolpia*, as represented by express citations, contain Athenian material, as distinguished by M.L. West, *The Orphic Poems* (Oxford 1983) 42–3 (he identifies the two works without ado).

[75] A.N. Skias, *EphArch* 1899, 239–40 no. 2; Papayiannopoulos-Palaios, Ἐπιγραφαὶ 76–7 no. 15; Peek, *AthMitt* 67 (1942) 149–50 no. 323; not in *IG* 2²; cf. *SEG* 41 (1991) no. 121. In the spelling of ἱερόν I follow Peek.

[76] *IG* 2² 4870; cf. Wycherley, *The Athenian Agora. Literary and Epigraphical Testimonia* (Princeton 1957) 159 no. 514; A.N. Oikonomides, *The Two Agoras of Ancient Athens* (Chicago 1964) 75; Vermaseren, *CCCA* 2.63 no. 242.

[77] See Thompson and Wycherley, *Agora of Athens* 36–8; C. Habicht, *Hesperia* 59 (1990) 574–5.

[78] It is a curiosity that another of these tiles was found in a Cerameicus grave of the second century after Christ: Peek, *Kerameikos* 3. *Inschriften, Ostraka, Fluchtafeln* (Berlin 1941) 17 no. 12; Vermaseren, *CCCA* 2.67 no. 252.

[79] Jul. *Or.*5.159 A; cf. Phot., Suda s.v. Μητραγύρτης; Suda s.v. βάραθρον; Apost.11.34; schol.Ar. *Plut.*431. That the story refers to the Museium hill is confidently stated by Papayiannopoulos-Palaios, Ἐπιγραφαὶ 77, 81, and *Polemon* 3 (1947–48) 94–6; Pantazopoulos, *Polemon* 3 (1947–48) 119–22; Oikonomides, *Two Agoras* 75–6. Yet they do not consider, or even acknowledge, the pointers to the Agora: the place became the record office, says Julian; it became both the council-hall and the record office, say the lexica. The Agora receives its due from other scholars, but this is not the end of the matter. The lexica, though not Julian, further describe the scene as a pit, or even as "the Pit" for casting out cadavers (Suda s.v. βάραθρον: the

The inscription naming the shrine will mark its eastern limit. The other, evoking Musaeus' oracles, is about 150 m. to the west. Just below it on the hillside is a remarkable but little noticed installation.[80] A floor about 13 m. wide and 10 m. wide has been levelled in the native rock. Seven thrones, with a footstep beneath, have been carved in a row in the rising ground on the long side, each separated from the next by a common arm. On the short side, at the corner, is a bench. This has been explained as a meeting room for a council, or as a law court, or simply as a place to rest, a "primitive exedra".[81] But councils, law courts, exedras are all of common occurrence, and never take a form such as this. No secular explanation can be satisfactory.

The Mother is worshipped everywhere in rock-cut shrines, and is commonly depicted as sitting on a throne; some of the shrines include her seated figure in relief. There are also rock-cut thrones, single ones, on mountains in Greece and in western and central Anatolia, some on remote and barely accessible heights, which are probably hers, though definite proof is lacking.[82]

The seven thrones invite comparison with other multiple forms. It is just at Athens and a few places nearby that we find a peculiar kind of votive relief, the double *naiskos*—twin images of the goddess sitting on adjacent thrones, mostly beneath a single pediment.[83] The twin images are as nearly identical as befits the sculptor's art. Both

---

story appears to be a last-minute insertion by the lexicographer), where the *mêtragyrtês* was first flung on his head and then, after the pit was filled in, commemorated with a statue. Until these details are accounted for, it is rather wishful to hold up the story, and many do, as illustrating some dramatic turn in religious feeling.

[80] Cook, *Zeus* 1.145–7 (drawings); Judeich, *Topographie*² 397; Papayiannopoulos-Palaios, Ἐπιγραφαὶ 77, and *Polemon* 3 (1947–48) 95–6 (photograph); Pantazopoulos, *Polemon* 3 (1947–48) 121; Oikononomides, *Two Agoras* 76. No one but Oikonomides claims to see "traces of the filled pit", as in the story of the *mêtragyrtês*.

[81] Cf. n. 80. Council-room: Papayiannopoulos-Palaios, Pantazopoulos. Law-court: Cook, Oikonomides. Neither council-room nor law-court, but "a kind of primitive exedra, a place for recreation and rest": Judeich.

[82] They are surveyed by Cook, *Zeus* 1.135–48, who treats them all as thrones of Zeus, like the mountains themselves, though he does not quite exclude the Mother. "The throne of Pelops" on Mount Sipylus is in the same area, on the north face beside a main road, as the excavated sanctuary of Mother *Plastênê* and the prehistoric, seemingly Hittite, rock-cut image which Pausanias knows as the Mother; cf. § V.

[83] Vermaseren, *CCCA* 2 nos. 62, 172, 183, 193, 238–9, 241, 341, 454, 461, 478, 611, cf. also 590, and *CCCA* 7 nos. 14, 21, 63, 142; Naumann, *Ikonographie* 188–90, 334–6, pl. 30. Of the examples with known provenance, a dozen come from Athens, and one each from Delos, Delphi, Isthmia, Corinth, Troezen. T. Hadzisteliou

wear the same *polos* and robe and hold the *phialê* in the right hand;
both even have the right leg advanced. The difference between them
is therefore an artistic variation: the one holds a sceptre and has a
lion at her side, the other holds a tympanum and has a lion in her
lap.[84] For the purpose of the dedication, a double image is better
than a single one.

In some of the Mother's rock-cut shrines there is a determined
repetition on a larger scale, rows of niches that were somehow essential to the worship. It is true that many rupestral shrines have niches
for votive plaques; but these of the Mother go far beyond the norm.
There are three Ionian examples, at Phocaea, Ephesus, and Samos,
and a Dorian one at Acrae in Sicily.

At Phocaea the shrine extends over a rocky slope traversed by
rock-cut stairs, and the niches, a hundred or so, are in several groups;
each group is neatly arranged, and sometimes the ground in front
has been levelled.[85] Most niches are empty, but a few have traces of
the Mother in relief. At Ephesus the niches are all together on the
northeast side of Panayir Dagh, in several ascending rows near the
bottom of the slope.[86] In one the Mother appears in faint relief, but
many niches were fitted with marble reliefs dowelled into the rock.
Samos town has two larger sanctuaries and two smaller ones with
groups of niches, likewise fitted with reliefs.[87]

The shrine at Acrae near Syracuse is the most informative, for
here the niches have rock-cut images in fairly high relief. There are
indeed many empty niches as well, mostly small ones; but most of
these are clearly secondary, adjoining the others. Eleven large niches
with images of the Mother are carved in a row on a hillside over a
stretch of about 50 m., and yet another at a lower level.[88] All the

---

Price, *JHS* 91 (1971) 53–6, in her study of "double and multiple representations",
makes a special category for "Cybele", but it includes a quite disparate item, Hittite
seals, and overlooks the restricted range of the double *naiskos*.

[84] It seems misguided to say, as does Naumann, *Ikonographie* 190, that the twin
images express "two fundamentally different characteristics" of the Mother, solemn
majesty and wild abandon.

[85] E. Langlotz, *ArchAnz* 84 (1969) 377–85; Naumann, *Ikonographie* 153–5, pl. 20.

[86] Vermaseren, *CCCA* 1.184–9 nos. 612–31, pls. 131–4; Naumann, *Ikonographie*
214–16,346–9, pls. 32–4.

[87] Naumann, *Ikonographie* 217.

[88] L. Bernabò Brea, *Akrai* (Catania 1956) 89–113, pls. 17–22; G. Sfameni Gasparro,
I Culti orientali in Sicilia (Rome 1973) 126–49, 267–76, pls. 76–104; Vermaseren,
CCCA 4.61–6, pls. 52–63; Naumann, *Ikonographie* 202–8, 344–5, pl. 30. The niches
(1–11 from left to right, and 12 below) with a single seated image of the Mother are

images save two (the one in the lower niche, and another in the upper row) show her in the usual seated pose, mostly holding *phialê* and tympanum and flanked by lions. Admittedly, the niches are not of uniform size and proportions, and half of them also contain smaller images of the Mother's attendants.

These other shrines resemble the seven thrones on the Museum hill in being carved on rocky slopes.[89] But it is not sufficient to simply mention them, for they are enigmatic in themselves. The seven thrones, the multiple niches, somehow served the Mother's ritual, and so did the double *naiskos*. It is in ritual that a common explanation must be sought.

It was the custom to "spread a throne", στρωννύειν θρόνον, i.e. to make it comfortable with covers and perhaps pillows, obviously for the goddess: the worshippers saw her, with the eye of faith, sitting on the throne, just as she does in art. The custom is best known from the records of a private group at Peiraeus, and in a different form was adopted in Corybantic healing;[90] yet these instances are secondary to the Mother's public festival. Porphyry, as we saw above, describes it as an annual rite at the Idaean cave. More than one throne might be prepared. The Peiraeus group resolve "to spread two thrones in the finest possible way", and the activity is spoken of in the plural, as στρώσεις "spreadings".[91] The goddess was even better pleased and honoured when the gesture was repeated. It is repeated with solemn show in the sculptural type of the double *naiskos* and in the official resolve at Peiraeus.

To judge from the seven thrones and the multiple niches, the gesture was repeated often by a festival crowd. On the Museum hill the

---

4,6–7,10–11. Those with the Mother seated and attendants standing are 1,3,5,8–9. Those with both the Mother and attendants standing are 2,12 (the principal figure in 12, badly damaged like many others, has a short tunic, and only the *polos* and nearby lions suggest the Mother). Attachment holes in the rock show that several of the images had metal ornaments—crowns, collars, bracelets.

[89] Another possible instance should be mentioned in passing. According to F. Graf, *Nordionische Kulte* (Vevey 1985) 318,420, a shrine similar to those of Phocaea and Ephesus can be recognized at Erythrae. He points to "votive niches cut in the rock" beside a terrace on the south slope of the acropolis, but their number and disposition are not stated.

[90] See Hepding, *Attis* 136–8,183–4; Nilsson, *GGR* 2² 641–2. For the Corybantic rite, see also O. Immisch, *ML* 2.1 (1894) 1615–18 s.v. Kureten; I.M. Linforth, *Cal.Publ.Cl.Ph.*13 (1946) 123–4,156–7. An early tragedy, perhaps Sophocles' *Tympanistae*, told how Dionysus was cured of madness by this means, so as to explain his affinity with the Mother. See Robertson in *CIV* ² 14 (1995).

[91] *IG* 2² 1328 lines 9–10,1329 lines 15–16.

empty thrones may have been spread by seven bands of worshippers; a sevenfold organization appears elsewhere in Athenian ceremony.[92] In the other shrines the figures in the niches, whether carved in the rock or rendered on tablets, probably looked on while the ritual was performed nearby. At Acrae the ritual setting can still be made out. The niches face a narrow strip of level ground, and at three symmetrical points—at either end and in the middle—there is a broader area, comparable to the rock-cut floor on the Museum hill.[93] At either end, beyond the niches, a semicircular floor has been cut into the rock, and at the centre of the floor an outcrop of rock has been left to make a rough circular base. In the middle of the row, or more precisely between the seventh and eighth niches, there is another artificially levelled area with another rough-hewn circular base. The bases have been taken as altars or altar foundations, but would do as well to support wooden thrones.[94] The three areas imply three groups of worshippers, conformable with the usual division of Dorian cities into three *phylai*.[95]

No date is mentioned for the celebration at Peiraeus, but the group was busiest in spring; this must have been the festival time.[96] The task of spreading a throne is one for women. At Peiraeus it was doubtless in the hands of one or other of the female officiants named in the record: φιαληφόροι , ζάκορος, πρόπολος.[97] We expect the custom to be reflected in the festival aetiology. Now in the story of the birth of Zeus Rhea is always helped by other women—by Gaea, Themis, Amaltheia, or by local Nymphs;[98] the action differs in this respect from the other great birth story, of Leto and the twins, in which the mother gives birth in a solitary place. These women are

---

[92] See Robertson, *Festivals* 124–5 (on the Oschophoria), and *HSCP* 95 (1993) 235–8 (on the Anthesteria).

[93] These areas are described and illustrated in Bernabò Brea, *Akrai* 91 (drawings by O. Puzzo), 111–13 (site report by C. Laviosa), pl. 22; Sfameni Gasparro, *Culti orientali* 128–9,267,273, pls. 70–73,89,102–4.

[94] A hole is noted and shown in the top of the middle base (Bernabò Brea, *Akrai* 111, pl. 22.4). If sculpted stone altars had been set up on the rock, as suggested by Laviosa (*ibid.*, 111, cf. 140), one would expect to find cuttings at the circumference. But perhaps the rock surface is too damaged for any to survive.

[95] The threefold division is evident at both Acrae and Syracuse: N.F. Jones, *Public Organization in Ancient Greece* (Philadelphia 1987) 172–6.

[96] See W.S. Ferguson, *HThR* 38 (1944) 107 n. 49.

[97] *IG* 2² 1328 lines 10–11 (naming also αἱ περὶ τὴν θεὸν οὖσαι ἐν τῶι ἀγερμῶι), 16–17; *IG* 2² 6288 line 1.

[98] For a list of such figures, see H. Schwabl, *RE* Suppl.15 (1978) 1214–16 s.v. Zeus; Verbruggen, *Zeus crétois* 39–46.

not said to deliver the child, only to care for Rhea after the delivery. They correspond to the real-life officiants who spread the throne.

The rock-cut thrones on the Museum hill are likely to be early. Although the inscription naming the shrine was carved in the fourth century, we cannot suppose that this conspicuous area, close to a main road and a city gate, was then available for any unwanted use. It was the shrine of the Mother that drew Musaeus to the spot, with his oracles and his *Theogony*.

4) The birth of Zeus was also located at Thebes, at a place so called, Διὸς Γοναί "Birth of Zeus".[99] The place happens to be mentioned in our sources as the destination of Hector's bones after they were brought from Ophrynium in the Troad at the bidding of an oracle, as a remedy for plague. And it was the appropriate place, since Zeus in the *Iliad* acknowledges Hector as a special favourite, because of his copious sacrifices.[100] Lycophron expressly says that it was Hector's merit in sacrificing that caused Zeus to translate the hero to his own γενεθλία πλάξ "natal ground", a periphrasis for the place-name.[101] Even a verse oracle quoted by Pausanias, which is probably a later embroidery, speaks of the translation as due to Διὸς ἐννεσίῃσι "Zeus' commands". The story of the translation is then both consistent and credible. It would be normal for Thebes when afflicted to make inquiry of an oracle, and normal for the oracle to suggest a striking new observance and a suitable point of attachment.[102] The cobweb theories that have been spun round this cult of Hector can be brushed away.

---

[99] Lycophr. *Alex.*1189–1213, with schol.vet.; schol.Hom. *Il.*13.1 (Aristodemus *FGrHist* 383F 7); cf. [Arist.] *Pepl.* fr. 640 Rose³ no. 46; Paus.9.18.5.

[100] Hom. *Il.*22.170–3,24.66–70, cf. 4.48–9,24.33–4.

[101] *Alex.*1191–5. Further on, Lycophron says that in consequence of the oracle Hector will be worshipped as a healing deity, and as such "you will dwell in the Islands of the Blessed, a mighty hero", νήσοις δὲ μακάρων ἐγκατοικήσεις μέγας ἥρως (1204–5). We are told elsewhere, and on good authority, that "Island of the Blessed" was a term for Thebes' acropolis (Armenidas *FGrHist* 378F 5). Lycophron now uses it as a general designation for Thebes so as to produce a fanciful analogy between the Theban cult hero and the epic denizens of the Islands of the Blessed. The schol *ad loc.* quotes two unprepossessing hexameters, allegedly an inscription at Thebes: "These are the Islands of the Blessed, where once the very finest, Zeus king of the gods, was born by Rhea at this place here". The term is again a general designation; whether Lycophron was indebted to the lines, or they to him, does not appear. We should not infer, though many do, that there was any difference of opinion about the site of Zeus' birth and Hector's grave or about its name.

[102] The very plausible circumstances are ignored or disputed by scholars who start from some inflexible presupposition. For F. Pfister, *Der Reliquienkult im Altertum*

Hector was summoned to Thebes to deal with plague.[103] The site where he was installed must have been appropriate also to his healing mission. Now the birth story, we have found, goes with the cult of the Mother. She is often a healing deity, and was conspicuously so at Thebes; for Pindar in the *Third Pythian* thinks of her as a last hope for the ailing Hiero (lines 77–9).[104] An argument can be made for equating the Mother's shrine with the site of the birth story and of Hector's grave. It is conjectural, but nonetheless straightforward.

Pausanias came to Hector's grave outside the Proetidian gate, on the road to Chalcis, "beside the fountain called after Oedipus" (*loc. cit.*). The area of the gate and the line of the road are approximately known, and the fountain is usually identified as one that was much admired in the nineteenth century.[105] It flowed from the foot of a hill on the south side of the road. Admittedly, Pausanias does not mention the birth story or the place-name "Birth of Zeus". In his time, when Thebes was near the end of its agonizing history and habitation was restricted to the Cadmeia, the grave must have been the only monument worth pointing to and explaining. "Birth of Zeus", however, was the older name for this site at the northeast, beside a main road leading into the city.[106]

(Giessen 1909–12) 1.193–4,2.440–1, Thebes' cult of Hector is indigenous and primary, like every other local cult, so that any translation story must be a hoax. It is a further step, a giant one, to cast the Homeric Hector as a victim of *Sagenverschiebung*, a doctrine which still receives a friendly nod from L. Ziehen, *RE* 5A 2 (1934) 1514–15 s.v. Thebai 1. For J.E. Fontenrose, *The Delphic Oracle* (Berkeley 1978) 391, the story is necessarily false because the oracle is versified and is not attested by a contemporary source. On these preposterous criteria see Robertson, *Phoenix* 36 (1982) 358–63. In the present case Fontenrose is well refuted by his own tabulations (p. 27), which show cult foundations, including translations, to be far commoner in "historical responses" than in "legendary" ones, 73% against 29%. For some other opinions, see A. Schachter, *Cults of Boiotia* (London 1981–) 1.233–4 (Hector's grave), 3.145–6 (the place-name "Birth of Zeus").

[103] So Lycophr. *Alex.*1205, ἀρωγὸς λοιμικῶν τοξευμάτων; at 1207 Apollo as author of the oracle is called ἰατρός. Not surprisingly, he also gives aid in war, again according to Lycophron (1210–11). Aristodemus and the oracle in Pausanias are vague but not contradictory, citing misfortunes and the assurance of future prosperity. Most scholars insist that on this point the story fluctuates wildly (cf. n. 102).

[104] For the cult of the Mother at Thebes, see Graillot, *Cybèle* 509–11; Wilamowitz, *Pindaros* (Berlin 1922) 270–2; Ziehen, *RE* 1532–4 s.v. Thebai 1; L. Lehnus, *L'Inno a Pan di Pindaro* (Milan 1979) 7–18, 49–55; Schachter, *Cults of Boiotia* 2.137–41.

[105] On the gate and the road, see S. Symeonoglou, *The Topography of Thebes* (Princeton 1985) 190,239; on the fountain, *id.*193–4,302–3.

[106] There should be no temptation to equate the place-name "Birth of Zeus" with the hills southwest of the fountain, as does Symeonoglou, *Thebes* 12, following Keramopoullos. If Lycophron's πλάξ has any particular meaning, the place was low and flat.

As Pindar prays to the Mother to cure Hiero, he imagines her shrine and festival. She it is "whom girls beside my own porch hymn through the night, together with Pan, as a powerful goddess", τὰν κοῦραι πὰρ ἐμὸν πρόθυρον σὺν Πανὶ μέλπονται θαμὰ σεμνὰν θεὸν ἐννύχιαι. The scene of worship is located in three emphatic words, πὰρ ἐμὸν πρόθυρον. Most commentators have always taken this as the "porch" of Pindar's own house.[107] And a story was told of how Pindar had been moved by a vision to set up an image of the Mother "beside his house", and of how the Thebans had been directed by an oracle to make it a civic shrine. And Pausanias was shown, somewhere on the west side of Thebes, both the ruins of Pindar's house and an adjoining shrine of the Mother with a notable statue.[108] No one with sense can doubt that the story is a fiction, and the ruins a sham, addressing chiefly those three emphatic words, perhaps also a lost hymn to the Mother.[109] The conclusion will hold even if we believe that Pindar was a deeply religious person and presented his convictions in his poetry. Literature and life never made such a perfect match as between the *Third Pythian* and the vision, the oracle, the ruins.

Still, those words confront us: what do they mean? I would have sailed to Syracuse, Pindar tells Hiero, had it been of use (lines 63–76); but as it is, I will offer prayer at home.[110] "Beside my own porch" describes the Theban setting of the Mother's worship. Now even if Pindar did happen to live beside the shrine, it would be odd to say so in this context, by way of locating the shrine for Hiero and the audience at Syracuse. It has been suggested lately that the words only mean "right at hand" (or "right at foot", as the Greeks said);[111] but πρόθυρον "porch" is much too definite to be so used. It suggests a monumental entrance, as to a palace or a sacred precinct, and Pindar uses the word elsewhere to add a note of grandeur.[112]

---

[107] See the doxography and discussion in Lehnus, *Inno a Pan* 7–18.

[108] The story: schol.Pind. *Pyth.*3.137a,137b (Aristodemus *FGrHist* 383F *13), 138,139b; *V.Pind.Thom.*1; cf. Philostr. *Im.*2.12.2–3. The ruins: Paus.9.25.3.

[109] Unless it is even wiser to suspend judgement, as Lehnus, *Inno a Pan* 18–55, appears to do.

[110] The *persona* behind these two first-person statements has actually been taken as the Syracusan chorus by some skirmishers on the hard-fought field of Pindaric criticism. Yet it seems very clear that Pindar is speaking for himself; cf. G.B. D'Alessio, *BICS* 39 (1994) 138–9.

[111] So D.C. Young, *Three Odes of Pindar* (Leiden 1968) 48–50, followed by W.J. Slater, *GRBS* 12 (1971) 145, for whom it expresses a Syracusan point of view (cf. n. 110).

[112] E.g., *Isthm.*8.2, of a great house on Aegina, where the victory celebration takes

He is fond of architectural metaphors, and in two of its eight occurrences πρόθυρον does not denote a literal "porch", but a figurative one. Corinth is the "porch of Isthmian Poseidon"; Heracles drives Geryoneus' cattle "up to the Cyclopean porch of Eurystheus", i.e. to the ground beneath the walls, or in front of the gate, of the Mycenaean citadel of Tiryns.[113] For Pindar then a "porch" may be any grand approach. When contrasted with distant Syracuse, "my own porch" will refer to Thebes and to some familiar, impressive approach to the city, scil. a stretch of road leading to a gate.

The Greeks gave much attention to an approach of this kind, usually called προάστιον.[114] That word in turn is applied by Pindar to the abode of the blessed in the underworld: φοινικορόδοις δ' ἐνὶ λειμώνεσσι προάστιον αὐτῶν, "in fields of crimson roses is their *proastion*" (*Threnus* 7.3). "Suburb", the standard English rendering, is not really apt for a district especially frequented and adorned. But as the only English word for a city district distinct from the rest of the city, it must do duty here, and again for *prothyron* in the *Third Pythian*: "their suburb", "my own suburb". The porch or suburb is Pindar's own as a part of Thebes; he does not mean that he lives right there.

Thus the Mother's shrine was beside a main approach to Thebes. But on which side? One immediately thinks of the shrine mentioned by Pausanias, next to the purported ruins of Pindar's house. Yet this cannot be the shrine of the *Third Pythian*, for two reasons. First, although it stood outside the city as Pausanias knew it, scil. the shrunken settlement on the Cadmeia, it was well within the perimeter of the earlier city. Pausanias puts it just beyond the stream Dirce; in the fifth century Thebes extended much further west.[115] Indeed it must have been inside the city when first associated with Pindar; for it was there that one would look for the poet's house. Second, Pausanias

---

place; *Paean* 6.135, of the royal dwelling of Aegina daughter of Asopus; *Nem*.5.53, of the precinct of Aeacus on Aegina's Colonna hill, where an actual *propylon* has been excavated—see G. Welter, *Aigina* (Berlin 1938) 52.

[113] *Ol*.13.5; fr. 169.7. At *Ol*.6.1–3 the operation of building a porch is compared to praising the victor.

[114] Cf. Thuc.2.34.5, the Academy road near the Dipylon gate; Hdt.3.142.2, a certain showplace at Samos.

[115] For the western limits, see Wilamowitz, *Pindaros* 27–8,35–6; F. Schober, *RE* 1439–41 s.v. Thebai 1; F.E. Winter, *Greek Fortifications* (Toronto 1971) 108 n. 18; Symeonoglou, *Thebes* 120–2, and his "sites" nos. 257, 259, also nos. 156, 239, 250. Note too that the shrine was evidently *not* on the main road leading west, which Pausanias picks up a moment later (9.25.4). Symeonoglou, *Thebes* 134–5,140–1, 198–9,251–2, offers hypothetical locations for both the shrine and Pindar's house.

gives the cult epithet as *Dindymênê,* which is proper to the Anatolian Mother (§ VI); Pindar clearly means the native Mother, the companion of Pan.[116] So we are free to equate the "porch" with the road to Chalcis, and the Mother's shrine with the place called "Birth of Zeus".

5) The birth story is again associated with the Mother at Cyzicus in the Propontis, a colony of Miletus. When Apollonius brings the Argonauts to Cyzicus, he speaks first of the mountainous peninsula north of the city, usually called Ἄρκτων νῆσος "Isle of bears", but by Apollonius Ἄρκτων ὄρος "Mount of bears".[117] The scholiast explains that Zeus' nurses were here turned into bears, a detail which, though unattributed, will come from one or more of the local historians—of Cyzicus, Miletus, Heracleia—who dealt with the birth story.[118]

Now a similar bear transformation is recounted as a catasterism: the Great and Little Bears, also called Helice and Cynosura, are two Idaean nymphs who nursed Zeus. So Aratus, whose scholiast adds another item from "a Cretan tale about (the constellation) Draco", viz. that Zeus himself became the snake between the Bears, after taking this form to evade Cronus.[119] The bear catasterism was also known to the Naxian chronicler Aglaosthenes, since he gave the name Cynosura to one of the Idaean nymphs—and this was part of his own version of the birth story, in which Zeus was stolen away from Crete to Naxos for safe-keeping.[120]

It was conjectured long ago that the source of both Aratus and his scholiast is [Epimenides], who has much to do with Ida and the birth of Zeus. Even sceptics still regard the bear catasterism as distinctly Cretan; sometimes it is flatly said that the story was transferred from

---

[116] Despite Lehnus, *Inno a Pan* 40–1, we can hardly suppose that the epithet had been wrongly used in the old shrine (*un falso commemorativo,* he says).

[117] Apoll. *Argon.*1.941, with schol.936–41a. "Mount of bears" recurs at Str.12.8.11, p. 575.

[118] Agathocles *FGrHist* 472 F 1a–c (*On Cyzicus*); Maeandrius 491 F 3 (*History of Miletus*); Promathidas 430 F 1 (*On Heracleia*); Callistratus 433 F 2 (*On Heracleia*).

[119] Arat. *Phaen.*30–7, with schol.46 (Epimenides *Vorsokr* 3 B 22–3/*FGrHist* 468 [Crete app.] F 3a), whence Diod.4.80.1–2; cf. Eratosth. *Catast.*2, schol.Germ. *Arat.* pp. 59, 114 Breysig, Hyg. *Astron.*2.2.1 (Aglaosthenes *FGrHist* 499 F 1). Coins of the Roman province of Crete show either Zeus or Augustus beside seven stars, which Svoronos identified as the Great Bear, in token of the catasterism; but the interpretation is dubious at best. See Verbruggen, *Sources* 34–5,46 fig. 20.

[120] Eratosth. *Catast.*30, schol.Germ. *Arat.* pp. 90–1 Breysig, Hyg. *Astr.*2.16.2 (Aglaosthenes *FGrHist* 499 F 2). Since Aglaosthenes F 1–2 is cited both times with the title of his work, *Naxiaca,* there is no room for the old conjecture, revived by Le Boeuffle in his edition of Hyginus (Paris 1983) 155 n. 2, 166 n. 10, that this is really Laosthenidas, an authority on Crete (Diod.5.84.4, cf. *FGrHist* 462).

Crete to Cyzicus.[121] But the opposite development is far more likely.
Aglaosthenes shows that the catasterism was familiar enough to be
adopted in an eclectic account. The scholiast's source, who took in
Draco as well as the Bears, was eclectic too. A snake transformation
is not otherwise imputed to Idaean Zeus, and the term "Cretan tale"
used by the scholiast was doubtless prompted by Aratus' mention of
Idaean nymphs. Versions of the birth story that are clearly native to
Crete speak of goats, bees, even dogs. But it is hard to see why they
should also speak of bears; actual bears are not, I believe, recorded
on the island.[122]

At Cyzicus, on the other hand, the peninsula and its bearish name
were famous. Surely it was here that the notion first arose of nurses
turned into bears, as Cyzicus' own contribution to the various animal characters of the birth story. The birth story, let us note, must
have been quite firmly located on the "Mount of bears" before it
could inspire such an unlikely notion.[123] Thereafter the Cyzicus version became a favourite and was turned to other uses.[124]

The "Isle of bears" or "Mount of bears" was also known as Mount
Dindymus, the modern Kapu Dagh, with an elevation of 800 m.[125]
It was sacred to the Mother. In Apollonius the Argo is shut up in
Cyzicus by the Etesian winds until the Mother sends a sign and the

---

[121] For a sampling of opinion, see W. Gundel, *RE* 12.2 (1912) 2859–61, s.v. Helike
3, and *RE* 12.1 (1924) 39–40 s.v. Kynosura 6, and, with F. Boll, *ML* 6 (1937)
871,874,883, s.v. Sternbilder; J. Poerner, *De Curetibus et Corybantibus* (Halle 1913) 248–
50; M. Pohlenz, *RE* 11.2 (1922) 2012 s.v. Kronos; Jacoby on *FGrHist* 468 F 3–5
and 499 F 1–2; Schwabl, *RE* Suppl.15 (1978) 1212–13 s.v. Zeus; Verbruggen, *Zeus
crétois* 42–3.

[122] Verbruggen, *Zeus crétois* 43 n. 92, makes the same observation, but suggests
that the story came to Crete from the Peloponnesus. Note however the cave Arkoudia
on the promontory of Akrotiri, named for a stalagmite that resembles a bear: Rutkowski, *Cult Places of the Aegean* 68–9 no. 7.

[123] The case is different when Agathocles of Cyzicus says that Rhea got the stone
for tricking Cronus from Proconnesus (*FGrHist* 472 F 1c)—i.e. from the famous
marble quarries which give the Sea of Marmara its name. Such a story hardly required any prompting from a local cult, though one did exist (Paus.8.46.4). So too
at Chaeroneia it may have been something about the shape of the rock called Pet-
rachus that attracted the story (Paus.9.41.6). But the name "Mount of bears" could
never have been explained by the birth story unless the story was already there.

[124] The other catasterism deriving from the birth story is the nursing goat as the
star Capella in Auriga, for which Musaeus is cited, unjustifiably no doubt (cf. n. 67
above). Which catasterism came first, Capella or the Bears (who then brought with
them Draco)?

[125] For the topography and nomenclature, see F.W. Hasluck, *Cyzicus* (Cambridge
1910) 6,22–4,158; E. Delage, *La Géographie dans les Argonautiques d'Apollonios de Rhodes*
(Paris 1930) 92–113.

Argonauts respond (*Argon*.1.1078–1158). They establish her shrine on the very summit of Dindymus, and also enact her summer festival for the first time, as young men leaping and whirling in armour and clashing swords on shields, which was their means of drowning out some ill-omened sounds. Both Cyzicus and its territory to east and west were renowned for the worship of the Mother; she has several epithets, not only *Dindymênê*, denoting local sites and functions.[126] The premier cult however was that of Dindymus. More will be said later, apropos of the summer festival (§§ IV–V); but one or two points must be anticipated.

Although here as elsewhere in the Greek world the Mother acquired some Anatolian traits, she is undoubtedly Greek in origin. The local historians already cited mention an element of the cult common to Cyzicus, Heracleia, and Miletus—subordinate figures named Titias and Cyllenus—so that the Mother must have been brought from home by Greek colonists of the seventh and sixth centuries.[127] In Herodotus' account of the Scythians, the Mother's rites at Cyzicus and those of Dionysus at Olbia are represented as characteristic Greek customs that are odious to the steppe folk, even more than the ways of other foreigners (4.76–80). Their attitude is illustrated *per contrariam* when Anacharsis, a rare Scythian Philhellene, conducts his own celebration of the Mother's festival, but is shot while doing so. The story would lose all point if the Greeks themselves were known to have adopted the Mother's rites from somewhere else.

When Apollonius describes how the Argonauts honour the Mother on Mount Dindymus, we learn, first, that her ritual includes a wild noisy dance or whirligig, behaviour otherwise attributed to the Curetes or Corybantes, and second, that this is indeed the Mother's ritual, and has nothing to do with Zeus. The ritual belongs to her summer festival, since its effect in the narrative is to allay the Etesian winds. Now if Mount Dindymus is also the setting for Zeus' birth and nursing, this story like the episode in Apollonius originates in the cult of the Mother. The ritual behind the birth story is clearly not the summer festival, as in Apollonius. It can only be the spring festival.

---

[126] For the Mother's cult at Cyzicus and environs, see Drexler, *ML* 2.2 (1897) 2856–8 s.v. Meter 11; Hasluck, *Cyzicus* 214–22; Graillot, *Cybèle* 374–7; Vermaseren, *CCCA* 1.90–8.

[127] The Mother is well attested at Miletus and several colonies, not only Cyzicus and Heracleia, but does not appear in the section on "cults" in N. Ehrhardt, *Milet und seine Kolonien*² 1.127–91. She has been dismissed as an alien.

IV. *The summer festival Cronia*

The festival Cronia is somewhat better known than the Galaxia, and has attracted far more comment from scholars.[128] The festival name is attested for Athens, Thebes, and Rhodes, and the month-name Cronion for several places on the Ionian coast and islands—for Colophon and Magnesia-on-the-Maeander, for Naxos and Samos and the Samian colonies Perinthus and Minoa on Amorgos.[129] On the word of Macrobius, Cyrene has a summer festival of "Saturnus";[130] this is very likely another instance. Macrobius also quotes a passage of Accius' *Annales* tracing the Saturnalia to the Greek festival and citing the name "Cronia".[131] Accius consulted a Greek source, who supplied the information that the festival was celebrated by "most of Greece and especially Athens".

As usual, the evidence is best for Athens. The festival is named in documents as well as literature, and Philochorus and Plutarch provide reliable comment; it may be that Accius drew on Philochorus. The Cronia of Thebes and Rhodes, let it be said at once, have both been doubted. The former receives a bare mention in the Plutarchan *Life of Homer*; the latter is reported with scandalous detail by Porphyry. Both can be fully vindicated.

The festival falls in summer, but at any time from early to late in the season. At Athens the date is 12th Hecatombaeon (July/August), approaching midsummer.[132] On Samos and at Perinthus, however, the month Cronion corresponds to Scirophorion, the previous month at Athens. At Magnesia-on-the-Maeander, again, an unrelated ceremony is scheduled for the time "when sowing begins, on the first day of the month Cronion".[133] Here Cronion must correspond to

---

[128] M. Mayer, *ML* 2.1 (1894) 1512–19 s.v. Kronos; Mommsen, *Feste* 32–5,402, 404; Nilsson, *Gr. Feste* 37–9, and *RE* 11.2 (1922) 1975–6 s.v. Kronien, and *GGR²* 1.512–13; Pohlenz, *RE* 1983–4 s.v. Kronos; Wilamowitz, *Sitz.Berlin* 1929, 36–9 = *Kl.Schr.*5.2.158–62; Deubner, *Att. Feste* 152–5; Jacoby on Philochorus *FGrHist* 328 F 97; F. Bömer, *Abh.Mainz* 1961, 4.174–5,181–3; P.P. Bourboulis, *Ancient Festivals of "Saturnalia" Type* (Thessalonica 1964) 11–12,26,35.

[129] Colophon: *ÖJh* 8 (1905) 163 line 11; *AJP* 56 (1935) 375 line 80; cf. L. Robert, *REG* 86 (1973) 71. Magnesia-on-the-Maeander: n. 133 below. Naxos: Samuel, *Chronology* 105. Samos: Samuel 121. Perinthus: Samuel 88–9. Minoa on Amorgos: n. 143 below.

[130] *Sat.*1.7.25. Cf. Vermaseren, *CCCA* 5.17–19 nos. 35–42, pls. 15–17.

[131] *Ibid.*, 1.7.37 (Acc. fr. 3 Morel), *Maxima pars Graium Saturno et maxime Athenae/ conficiunt sacra, quae Cronia iterantur ab illis* etc.

[132] Dem.24 *Timocr.*26, with schol.

[133] *IvMagnesia* 98 (*SIG³* 598, *LSAM* 32) lines 14–15.

Boedromion (September/October), the Athenian month most associated with the sowing; for the sowing could not well begin, even by anticipation, as early as the first of the preceding month, Metageitnion.

On Rhodes, Porphyry gives an exact date for a disputed instance: μηνὶ Μεταγειτνιῶνι ἕκτηι ἱσταμένου "in the month Metageitnion, on the sixth day" (De Abst.2.54). For the moment, let us simply ask what date this is. Strange to say, it has always been supposed that by "Metageitnion" Porphyry means not the Attic month (August/September) but the like-named month at Rhodes, Pedageitnyus, which fell in middle or late winter.[134] Yet just a few lines further on, in dating a festival at Salamis on Cyprus, Porphyry signals his use of the local calendar: μηνὶ κατὰ Κυπρίους Ἀφροδισίωι "in the Cypriot month Aphrodisius". If Porphyry is careful to identify as Cypriot a month named after the island's presiding goddess, which moreover hardly occurs anywhere else, he will not refer off-handedly to a Rhodian month homonymous with an Attic one, but occupying a place in the calendar which no one could know but a Rhodian. In general, it is safe to assume that literary sources use the Attic calendar.[135] Porphyry then dates the Cronia of Rhodes to 6th Metageitnion.

For the sake of completeness, an observance may be mentioned which is not guaranteed by the festival name. Thera honours the Mother on the fifth of Hyacinthius as on the fifth of Artemisius.[136] As already said, the dates appear to match her two festivals, in summer and spring respectively.

Other indications point to middle or late summer. Fresh figs and honey are in use at Cyrene. Philochorus and Accius both speak of masters and servants feasting together, in the country as in the city; it is the summer lull in the farmer's routine, which follows the ingathering of the grain. In Macrobius' rendering of Philochorus, the

---

[134] That Porphyry means the Rhodian month is assumed by all who are cited in n. 167 below. In Nilsson's arrangement of the Rhodian calendar, which is generally followed, Pedageitnyus corresponds to Gamelion: Samuel, *Chronology* 108. In Bischoff's arrangement, it corresponds to Anthesterion: *RE* 10.2 (1919) 1582 s.v. Kalender.

[135] Hegesander of Delphi tells of curious customs and conditions, as he is wont to do, at Apollonia in Chalcidice, and assigns them to the successive months Anthesterion and Elaphebolion: Ath.8.11,334E–F (*FHG* 4.420). If Elaphebolion is a local month, Apollonia diverges from the rest of Chalcidice and indeed from everywhere but Athens, and conjecture must ensue about some unrecorded Athenian penetration. Yet scholars have always been happy to take this route: most recently, D. Knoepffler, *J.Sav.* 1989, 34–5.

[136] See n. 9 above. Calendars on Cos have entries for both "Rhea" and "the Mother of the Gods", but the time of year does not appear (ns: 10, 175).

season is indicated by the phrase *et frugibus et fructibus iam coactis*.[137] The pair *fruges* and *fructus* is generally taken as rhetorical amplitude; for summer fruits ripen at various times, and the olive harvest, the only one in Attica worth mentioning, comes much too late to be joined with the grain. This may be right. But it is just as likely that Philochorus spoke of the festival as celebrating a variety of crops. As we shall see, a variety were in fact displayed in the ritual vessel called *kernos*.

At Cyzicus the Mother is honoured at the time of the Etesian winds, a notorious obstacle for those sailing from the Aegean to the Black Sea. The Argonauts institute her festival (admittedly, the festival name is not recorded) after the winds have held them back for twelve days.[138] The date will be sometime in late July or August.

The calendar evidence definitely shows that the Cronia came at somewhat different times in different places: in Athenian terms, in Scirophorion, Hecatombaeon, Metageitnion, and as late as the first day of Boedromion. It must be that the purpose of the festival allowed or encouraged these differences. We shall find that the festival was meant to moderate the summer weather. But the kind of weather that was wanted might vary according to local conditions and practices.

A fundamental point about the festival can be established at once with the aid of inscriptions. It was addressed to the Mother of the Gods, and to her alone. It is true that Athens' Cronia are defined, in a scholium to Demosthenes, as ἑορτὴ ἀγομένη Κρόνωι καὶ Μητρὶ τῶν θεῶν "a festival conducted for Cronus and the Mother of the Gods".[139] But "Cronus" was inevitable; he is the Mother's consort, and the festival appears to bear his name. Now the Galaxia, unlike the Cronia, do not evoke "Cronus", and are defined simply as ἑορτὴ Ἀθήνησιν Μητρὶ θεῶν ἀγομένη "a festival at Athens conducted for the Mother of the Gods".[140] The suspicion then is very strong that Cronus is intrusive. Inscriptions remove all doubt.

A Council decree of 184/3 B.C., enacted on 21 Hecatombaeon, shortly after the Cronia, commends the *prytaneis* for sacrificing to "the

---

[137] *Sat.*1.10.22 (Philochorus *FGrHist* 328 F 97).
[138] Apoll. *Argon.*1.1078–1102, 1132–3, 1151–2. When the winds fall, the Argo makes way by oar. But they rise again during the beat up the Bosporus, entailing another *aition*: *Argon.*2.498–59. The duration of the winds was commonly put at forty days, but as high as sixty.
[139] Schol.Dem.24 *Timocr.*26, cf. Phot. s.v. Κρόνια.
[140] Bekker, *Anecd.*1.229, cf. Hsch. s.v. Γαλάξια.

Mother of the Gods".[141] Their first sacrifice was the invariable one to the Council deities, and their next at the festival, so that the passage runs: καὶ τ[οῖς ἄλλοις θεοῖς οἷς πάτριον ἦν· ἔθυσαν] | [δὲ καὶ τ]ἐι Μητρὶ τῶν θε[ῶν ... The next words were probably τὰ Κρόνια, for the occasion needs to be plainly stated: "And they also sacrificed to the Mother of the Gods at the Cronia". There is no likelihood at all that "Cronus" was named in second place after the Mother as a further recipient of sacrifice. Some other observance was mentioned in the rest of the lacuna.

Another Council decree, conjecturally assigned to 267/6 B.C., commends the *prytaneis* for sacrificing "at the Cronia".[142] It was enacted a bit later in the year, probably after the Panathenaea at the end of Hecatombaeon. Once more, the Cronia directly follow the offering to the Council deities: τοῖς [θεοῖς] οἷς π|[άτριον ἦν· . . . . 25 . . . .]ν τὰ Κρ[όνια· ἔπεμψαν] δὲ κτλ. The 25 missing letters were supplied as follows by Meritt: τῶι δὲ Διὶ εὐσεβῶς συνετέλεσα]ν. Yet "Zeus" has nothing to do with the Cronia, nor is the expression warranted by any parallel. The analogy of 184/3 B.C. dictates the restoration: ἔθυσαν δὲ καὶ τἐι Μητρὶ τῶν θεῶ]ν. We have just the same clause as before: "And they also sacrificed to the Mother of the Gods at the Cronia".

A document of Minoa on Amorgos shows us that the festival Cronia for which the Samian month is named belongs to the Mother. The month is twice referred to in a set of regulations for the Mother's cult.[143] The officials here appointed are to offer sacrifice in the month Cronion; repayments of loans (the Mother lends out money) are to be received by the assembly in the month Cronion.[144] Cronion is festival time. The Mother's cult was an important one at Minoa, for

---

[141] B.D. Meritt and J.S. Traill, *The Athenian Councillors* (Princeton 1974) 154 no. 180 lines 9–10. Dem. *Prooem*.54 also speaks of the *prytaneis* sacrificing to the Mother, but without any indication of the calendar date. It was customary to dismiss the whole Council for the day (Dem.24 *Timocr*.26).

[142] Meritt and Traill, *Councillors* 91–2 no. 81 lines 5–6.

[143] *LSCG* 103 A 16, B 36 (Vermaseren, *CCCA* 2.205–8 no. 650). Earlier publications do not include the smaller fragments.

[144] R. Bogaert, *Banques et banquiers dans les cités grecques* (Leiden 1968) 200, thinks that Cronion is the fourth month of the year, and Panemus, when interest is paid, the last month. This arrangement was produced by conflating the attested months of Aegiale, Arcesine, and Minoa, and is untenable. The calendar of Minoa is the Samian, distinct from the others: Robert, *REG* 42 (1929) 28 = *Op.Min.Sel*.1.538, and *REG* 46 (1933) 438 = *Op.Min.Sel*.1.564. It is in any case natural to suppose that Cronion and Panemus are successive months.

these regulations are issued by the city. It is on the temple antae that records of the loans will be displayed, evidently a very public spot.[145] At Sardis too, in the same period, the antae of the Metroum were used for inscribing public documents of outstanding interest.[146] To be sure, the inscription speaks of the festival or the rites as "Metroa", so that the actual name Cronia may have fallen out of use.[147] The cult of the Mother, like the month-name Cronion, is to the fore both on Samos and at its colonies.[148] Amorgos has produced a fine example of an early votive *naiskos*.[149]

According to inscriptions, then, our festival honours the Mother, not Cronus or the pair Cronus and the Mother. This evidence is decisive against literary sources who speak of Cronus or Saturnus in a cursory fashion. It must be admitted, however, that Philochorus in describing the Athenian festival insists on the pair Cronus and Rhea and matches them with another pair, Zeus and Ge. This is in fact a theological interpretation of certain shrines and festivals at the south-east corner of the city—of the Mother and the Cronia, of Zeus and the Olympieia. To understand Philochorus we must examine the actual shrines. Our conviction that the Mother alone is honoured by the festival will be reinforced.

"The Mother in Agra", as she is called in Athenian documents, is an old cult in the oldest part of Athens, the settlement on the Ilissus bank singled out by Thucydides (2.15.3-5), together with the "Field", Agra, on the opposite bank. She is named in a calendar of sacrifice found on the Acropolis, datable to the period 480-460 B.C., and several times in the later fifth century, in virtue of the treasures which belonged to the shrine.[150] In the mid fourth century the Attic chronicler Cleidemus referred to "the Metroum in Agrae" and gave some account of the Mother.[151] A "priest of the Mother of the Gods" ap-

---

[145] *LSCG* 103 B 39–44,52.

[146] A Sardian decree of 213 B.C. contains a provision for inscribing the text "on the antae of the temple in the Metroum" and shows that several blocks and fragments bearing important documents belong to these antae: P. Gauthier, *Nouvelles Inscriptions de Sardes* 2 (Geneva 1989) 47–9 no. 2 lines 4–5.

[147] *LSCG* 103 B 54.

[148] Samos: Vermaseren, *CCCA* 2.182–6 nos. 566–80, pls. 170–75. Perinthus: Vermaseren, *CCCA* 6.109–10 nos. 369–72, pl. 93.

[149] Vermaseren, *CCCA* 2.208 no. 652, pl. 192; Naumann, *Ikonographie* 137,303 no. 65.

[150] Calendar: *IG* 1³ 234 line 5. Decree, accounts, inventory: *IG* 1³ 138 lines 11–12; 369 line 91; 383 line 50.

[151] Bekker, *Anecd.*1.327 (Cleidemus *FGrHist* 323 F 9); Philodem. *De Piet.* p. 23 Gomperz (Cleidemus F 25).

pears in Athenian documents over long ages;[152] he most likely served the shrine in Agra. In all this the Mother stands alone, without her mythical consort.

A separate element is added by a lexicon, doubtless from an Attic chronicler; it could very well be Cleidemus. Κρόνιον τέμενος· τὸ παρὰ τὸ νῦν Ὀλύμπιον μέχρι τοῦ Μητρῴιου τοῦ ἐν Ἄγραι "Cronian precinct: the one beside the present Olympieium as far as the Metroum in Agra".[153] The precinct, it appears, lay between the sanctuary of Olympian Zeus and the Ilissus; the Metroum must have been close beside the river on the south bank. The name "Cronian precinct" does not imply the god Cronus. It comes from the festival Cronia: shrines called Pythium, Delium, Olympieium, Diasium, Thesmophorium are all named for festivals.[154] It is easy to believe that the festival celebration required an area more extensive or more accessible than could be found on the hilly south bank. Finally, another old shrine was somewhere nearby, on the south side of the sanctuary of Zeus: that of Olympian Ge, which serves as a landmark.[155] It must have been conspicuous.

Here then is the setting which inspired Philochorus' theological interpretation. *Philochorus Saturno et Opi primum in Attica statuisse aram Cecropem dicit, eosque deos pro Jove Terraque coluisse*, etc. "Philochorus says that Cecrops first set up in Attica an altar to Cronus and Rhea and honoured those gods in place of Zeus and Ge". Sweet gentle Cecrops, author of many amiable customs, was just the man to give Cronus his due. And he gave Athens a unique pattern of worship: beside the shrines of Olympian Zeus and Olympian Ge, the Cronian precinct and the Metroum in Agra.

Pausanias, coming later, brings a complication. He does not mention the Mother in Agra, much less the Cronian precinct. Instead, he notes "a temple of Cronus and Rhea" right in the sanctuary of Olympian Zeus (1.18.7). He places it, as also the "precinct" of Olympian Ge, "in the enclosure", i.e. inside the strong Hadrianic wall which closes off the sanctuary but for a single gate. An immediate

---

[152] *IG* 2² 4595, a dedication of 328/7 B.C.; *IG* 2² 1817 = Meritt and Traill, *Councillors* 323–4 no. 466 lines 9–10, a catalogue of *prytaneis, paullo ante a.* 220/1 A.D.; *IG* 2² 5134, a theatre seat.

[153] Bekker, *Anecd.*1.273. Cf. Jacoby, n. 12 to Philochorus *FGrHist* 328 F 97; Wycherley, *Testimonia* 153 no. 472.

[154] By analogy, we may infer that shrines (or towns) called, e.g., Dium, Artemisium, Heracleium were named for the festivals Dia, Artemisia, Heracleia.

[155] Thuc.2.15.4; Plut. *Thes.*27.6; Paus.1.18.7.

problem is that no trace of either has been found in the enclosure, and that other sources seem to separate the santuaries of Ge and Zeus.[156] In matters of topography, when they are finally decided, Pausanias is more often proven right than wrong. But even if he erred somewhat in locating the temple, it is clear that htis is not the site in Agra. And yet that site is very close. A change has taken place.

In the time of Pausanias the Olympieium and its environs had been completely transformed by Hadrian's vast building program. Pausanias turns from the Olympieium to several other works; it is still uncertain whether they all stood in this area.[157] In any case, some new building was undertaken south of the Olympieium and along the south bank of the Ilissus, where Hadrian's gymnasium may have stood. If older monuments were to be saved, they could only be dismantled, transported, and reassembled elsewhere. The excavators of the Agora discovered that under the early Empire, from Augustus to Hadrian, whole buildings and large parts of buildings had been removed from their original sites and re-erected on open ground in the square.[158] Another item to be added to the tally is the fountainhouse Enneacrunus. It was in the southeast sector of the Agora that Pausanias saw the original Enneacrunus, which he assigns to Peisistratus (1.14.1).[159] Earlier writers without exception speak of it as a landmark in southeast Athens, beside the Ilissus.[160]

---

[156] See Wycherley, *GRBS* 4 (1963) 163–5, and *Stones of Athens* 165, 168.

[157] Paus.1.18.9, cf. 1.5.5: a temple of Hera and Zeus *Panhellênios*, a Pantheon, a building with one hundred columns of Phrygian marble, a gymnasium. For a survey and critique of opinion, see D. Willers, *Hadrians panhellenisches Programm: archäologische Beiträge zur Neugestaltung Athens durch Hadrian* (Basel 1990). According to Willers, the "Panhellenic program" was centred on the Olympieium; he discounts the importance of both the Pantheon and the temple of Zeus *Panhellênios*, which may or may not be the precinct excavated by J. Travlos south of the Olympieium (p. 65). The building with one hundred columns is probably the "Library" north of the Roman Market, as commonly thought (p. 18); the gymnasium was at or near Cynosarges (p. 14). It is evident that any firm conclusion must wait for new discoveries.

[158] Translated whole: the temple of Ares, the altar of Eirene (not Zeus *agoraios*) next to the Eponymi. Translated in part: the Southwest Temple west of the Odeium; the Southeast Temple west of the Panathenaic Way. For summary accounts, see Thompson and Wycherley, *Agora of Athens* 160–8; J.M. Camp, *The Athenian Agora* (London 1986) 184–7.

[159] It has not been convincingly located on the ground. The excavators fastened first on the Southwest Fountain House, then on the Southeast Fountain House, but are still uneasy. For different shades of opinion, see Thompson and Wycherley, *Agora of Athens* 197–9; Camp, *Athenian Agora* 42–3; *Agora Guide*⁴ (Princeton 1990) 164–6.

[160] Wycherley, *Testimonia* 137–42. For the probable site, see Travlos, Πολεοδομικὴ ἐξέλιξις τῶν Ἀθηνῶν (Athens 1960) 54, and *Pictorial Dictionary of Ancient Athens* (New York 1971) 114–15, 204, 340.

The temple of Cronus and Rhea, in order to be noticed by Pausanias, must have been old and stately; more recent construction, especially Roman, he generally ignores.[161] Though a temple is not attested for the Mother in Agra, one was needed for the cult treasures which we hear of in fifth-century inscriptions.[162] Philochorus speaks of an "altar" only because no other element could be carried back to Cecrops. If then the Mother's temple was moved in the time of Hadrian from the Ilissus bank to the enclosure of the Olympieium, it may be thought surprising that Pausanias does not say so. It was not his way. He does not say it of Enneacrunus, that famous landmark. He does not say it of the temple of Ares with all the statues proper to it. (1.8.4), though this was a Doric temple about as large as the Hephaesteium, which it much resembles. As he extols the monuments of the past, it is not fitting to tell what hands have been laid upon them lately.

Thus Philochorus, far from showing that Cronus was included in the festival, confirms that the Mother alone was honoured, in this case the Mother in Agra. With that fact established, we may turn to the two disputed instances of the Cronia, at Thebes and on Rhodes.

The Plutarchan *Life* says of Homer, "Sailing to Thebes for the Cronia—this is a musical contest conducted there—he came to Ios".[163] The contest at Thebes is only an excuse for bringing Homer to Ios, where fishermen pose a riddle and he dies of bafflement. In the Herodotean *Life* he meets a similar fate while sailing from Samos to Athens, and in the *Contest between Homer and Hesiod* while visiting Creophylus.[164] The Cronia of Thebes are sometimes dismissed out of hand.[165] "Such an invention", says Wilamowitz, "cannot be taken seriously just because one cannot say how the inventor came by it". No doubt the principle is generally sound, but we should hesitate to apply it here. The *Lives* of Homer are full of genuine antiquarian material which is put to surprising use.

---

[161] Travlos, *Pictorial Dict.*335–9, identifies the temple with a Roman one of the second century after Christ, Pausanias' own day, which stood between the Olympieium and the Ilissus—well outside the Hadrianic enclosure. It does not seem a likely candidate, and I withdraw the endorsement I gave before, at *Festivals* 28.

[162] Note in passing that the Stuart and Revett temple, sometimes claimed as the Metroum, has now been shown to be the Palladium shrine: Robertson in M. Dillon (ed.), *Religion in the Ancient World. New Themes and Approaches* (Amsterdam 1995).

[163] [Plut.] *V.Hom.*4, p. 242 Allen.

[164] [Hdt.] *V.Hom.*34, p. 215 Allen; *Cert.Hom. et Hes.* pp. 237–8 Allen.

[165] Wilamowitz, *Sitz.Berlin* 1929, 39 = *Kl.Schr.*5.2.163; Schachter, *Cults of Boiotia* 1.189 n. 1 (read "Agrionia"?), 2.118.

Now that the Cronia are revealed as a festival of the Mother, it would be doubly unwise to reject this testimony. For the Mother was prominent at Thebes (cf. § III), and Pindar describes the revelry of her summer festival, i.e. the Cronia: pounding tympana, clashing cymbals, flaming pine-torches.[166] At most we shall question the "musical contest", which the *Life* asserts in parenthesis. It could be authentic. At the Cronia, any such event would be as zany as the rest of the festival; it would be like the fishermen's riddle. But since Homer went everywhere to perform in musical contests, it is also possible that another one was freely attributed to the Cronia of Thebes. The fact remains that the festival was a famous occasion.

The Cronia of Rhodes appear in Porphyry as the first of many examples of human sacrifice (*De Abst.*2.54). "On Rhodes, in the month Metageitnion, on the sixth day, a human being was sacrificed to Cronus. After long prevailing, this custom was changed. For one of those who had been condemned to death by public process was kept in confinement until the Cronia, and when the festival came round they led the fellow outside the gates up to the statue of Aristobule, and gave him wine to drink and slaughtered him", προαγαγόντες τὸν ἄνθρωπον ἔξω πυλῶν ἄντικρυς τοῦ Ἀριστοβούλης ἕδους, οἴνου ποτίσαντες ἔσφαττον.

"Cronus" was bound to be mentioned, both as eponym of the Cronia and because a little further on Porphyry speaks of the Phoenician Cronus, i.e. Baal, as receiving human sacrifice. It is, however, obvious and agreed that Cronus is superseded by Aristobule. The main ingredients are therefore the festival Cronia, the goddess Aristobule, and the practice of executing a condemned man after plying him with drink. We can of course dismiss the allegation of earlier human sacrifice in a form that was wholly unredeemed; Porphyry goes on to the usual cases of human victims commuted to animals or figurines. It is the festival as known to Porphyry's source, after the supposed commutation, that needs to be explained.

Nilsson gave an explanation that others have found acceptable.[167] "Aristobule" is Artemis, for in the only other occurrence of this name,

---

[166] Pind. *Dith.*2.8–11 (the festival is transposed to Olympus). Besides the legend that the Mother's statue stood at Pindar's door, Philostratus knows another, that Pindar's birth was attended by an uproar of the Mother's cymbals and tympana (*Im.*2.12.2).

[167] *Gr.Feste* 38 and *GGR*² 1.400,512. Cf. Pohlenz, *RE* 1985 s.v. Kronos; D. Morelli, *I culti in Rodi* (Pisa 1959) 113,157; Bömer, *Abh.Mainz* 1961, 4.194.

in Plutarch's account of Themistocles, it is said to be an epithet conferred on her by Themistocles when he established a new shrine to commemorate his own "best counsel" in defending Greece.[168] The sixth is Artemis' holy day. The human victim, Nilsson then infers, is a *pharmakos* "scapegoat", a ritual otherwise ascribed to the Ionian festival Thargelia honouring Artemis and Apollo, and at Athens to the sixth of the month. The festival name "Cronia" will be secondary, arising from the dreadful reputation of the Phoenician Cronus.

There are fundamental objections. The execution of a criminal does not much resemble the expulsion of a *pharmakos*, who was driven beyond the furthest limits of the community, not simply led outside a gate.[169] If a *pharmakos* was sometimes killed, and this is disputed, it was not at a shrine. Nor does the season agree. The Attic and Ionian *pharmakos* purifies the city in the month Thargelion, May/June, before the ingathering of the grain. If Metageitnion is a Rhodian month, as Nilsson thought, it will fall in winter; if Athenian, in mid summer. It is also misguided to equate Aristobule with Artemis. Porphyry speaks of Aristobule *tout court*, as a goddess known by this name alone; further on he uses the plain names of other Greek gods and heroes, and also gives a full title, "the *ômadios* Dionysus on Chios". Aristobule is in fact well known on Rhodes, as we are about to see. On the other hand Athens' "Artemis Aristobule", as described by Plutarch, is much too obscure and enigmatic to be of help.[170]

Rhodes has a great many private associations that are named for the gods they worship, among them Ἀριστοβουλιασταί.[171] It is true

---

[168] Plut. *Them*.22.2, and *De Hdt.Mal*.37,869C–D.

[169] The terms "scapegoat" and *pharmakos* are used too freely by some scholars, as if this were a broad category of victims; cf. Robertson, *CIV*² 9 (1990) 434–8. Only the original, restricted sense is relevant here.

[170] Her shrine, says Plutarch, was near Themistocles' house in Melite, at the place where public executioners dispose of bodies and contaminated things. This must be just outside a city gate, as at Rhodes. H. Usener, *Götternamen* (Bonn 1895) 51, suggested that "Best-counsel" was a euphemism for the death sentence, and I went along at *RDAC* 1978, 205 n. 1. But now this meaning seems to me unlikely; nor can I believe that the Greeks associated executions with Artemis or any other goddess. The story of Themistocles' founding the shrine in self-advertisement could not have been concocted unless "Best-counsel" were taken, as is natural, in the most general sense. In recent years, an excavated temple within the city, on the road from the Agora to the Peiraeic Gate, has been quite fancifully claimed as Plutarch's shrine (it is indeed a temple of Artemis, to judge from the finds and the westward orientation). Travlos, *Pictorial Dict*.121, notes that the temple stood near a fork leading to yet another gate; but even if this gate had something to do with executions, the location is still not right.

[171] *IG* 12.1.163; G. Pugliese Carratelli, *ASAtene* n.s. 1/2 (1942) 151 no. 6;

that some names include epithets, e.g. *Athanaïstai Lindiastai, Diosataby-riastai, Diossôtêriastai*, and true again that on occasion the epithets stand alone, e.g. *Atabyriastai, Paphiastai*. These epithets, however, are familiar ones, deriving from public cults of great renown; it is most improbable that "Aristobule" had equal standing as an epithet of Artemis. In any case, Artemis is not commonly worshipped by private associations.[172] Now a deity who is a favourite of such associations elsewhere, as at Athens and Peiraeus and on Delos, is the Mother. Yet on Rhodes she appears in this role only once, and her worshippers are oddly denoted by a genitive, Ματρὸς θεῶν, even though they appear in a series of names of the usual sort, ending in *-astai* and *-istai*.[173] If the Mother's association had another name of the usual sort, the only one available is *Aristobuliastai*.

Porphyry names the festival as "the Cronia". He also names the god "Cronus", and this name, as all agree, is unwarranted: it comes either from the festival name "Cronia" or from the festival custom of putting someone to death. But even if "Cronus" comes from the festival custom, "the Cronia" certainly does not. The actual festival of this name was once widely celebrated and was always known to the learned; we cannot suppose that Porphyry's source used it simply as an expressive term for the unspeakable. Nor can we suppose that Porphyry himself ventured to use it so; for then his source must have provided the true name, and Porphyry would not suppress it. If the festival name is reliable, then we expect to meet the Mother. The superlative title Aristobule "Best-counsel" will suit her as well as any other deity. It may be that the name "Mother of the Gods" was avoided on Rhodes. For on neighbouring Cos the goddess is always styled "Rhea" in civic documents, a striking departure from cult practice everywhere else.[174]

All the other details are conformable. The Athenian month Metageitnion (August/September) is well within the seasonal range of the Cronia. The sixth day is close to other Dorian instances. On Cos,

---

V. Kontorini, Ἀνέκδοτες Ἐπιγραφὲς Ῥόδου 2 (Athens 1989) 73–5 no. 10 (*SEG* 39.737). For a list of these associations, see F. Hiller von Gaertringen, *RE* Suppl.5 (1931) 832–4 s.v. Rhodos.

[172] As Nilsson remarks, *GGR*² 2.118.

[173] *IG* 12.1.162.

[174] "Rhea" is named in the civic calendar of the late fourth century, and in other documents of Hellenistic and Roman date: A. Maiuri, *Nuova Silloge Epigrafica di Rodi e Cos* (Florence 1925) nos. 450 line 4, 460 line 5, 475 line 8. It is only in a deme calendar that we hear of "the Mother of the Gods" (n. 175).

again, it was some day before the tenth,[175] and on Thera it was the fifth in both Artemisius and Hyacinthius, probably the spring and summer festivals. As for the execution, the salient point is that the doomed man was first regaled and stupified with wine. It was a gesture of indulgence and remission, such as festivals encourage. And it was suited to the Cronia, a time of merry-making.

So far, we have learned from direct evidence that the festival honours the Mother at some fitting time in summer. But if we inquire of the same sources about the purpose and the manner of honouring the Mother, they tell us next to nothing. The festival is simply depicted as a time for jolly companiable feasting. At Athens, masters and servants dine together (Philochorus and Accius *apud* Macrobius); at Cyrene, celebrants wear crowns of figs and exchange honey cakes (Macrobius). At Athens, again, servants are riotous as they dine at the Cronia, or as they go about in procession at the country Dionysia; οὐκ ἂν αὐτῶν τὸν ὀλολυγμὸν ὑπομείναις καὶ τὸν θόρυβον, "you could not abide their howling and uproar".[176] As "howling" does not fit our fuller picture of the country Dionysia, it must go with the Cronia. This is a significant detail.

Howling (ὀλολυγή, ὀλόλυγμα, ὑλαγμός, ululatus), no less than tympana and cymbals, typifies the Mother's worship, though it is not elsewhere assigned to the Cronia. When Statius in the *Thebaid* surveys the several regions of Arcadia, that ancient land, he reminds us of some presiding deities, Hermes of Cyllene and Athena *alea* of Tegea; at Azania in the northwest it is the Mother, with her "Idaean howling".[177] Hellenistic poets speak of female votaries whose howling deafens and terrifies;[178] they are as disagreeable as the servants in Plutarch. Later still it is Phrygian worshippers who are said to howl, or the Galli, the Mother's disreputable priesthood. In Lucian Phrygians howl, Lydians shriek to the flute.[179]

---

[175] See n. 10 above. In Nicander an officiant goes shouting through the streets "on the ninth" (*Alex.*217–20); but we cannot assume, with Paton and Prott, that this was the day on Cos. A different day, the twentieth of an unknown month, is given in the local calendar of the deme Isthmus: *ASAtene* n.s. 25/26 (1962/63) 158 no. 2 (*LSCG* 169 B I; Vermaseren, *CCCA* 2.215 no. 671, pl. 199) lines 6–10.

[176] Plut. *Non posse suav.vivi* 16,1098B.

[177] *Theb.*4.292–3.

[178] Nic. *Alex.*219–20; *A.P.*6.173 (Rhianus *Hell.Ep.*7) 3–4.

[179] Phrygians: Arrian *FGrHist* 156 F 82; Lucian 69 *Podagra* 30–5 Macleod. Galli: *A.P.*6.903 (Antipater of Sidon *Hell.Ep.*64) 17–18; Luc. *Bell.Civ.*1.566–7; Mart.5.41.3. In Antipater a Gallus on meeting a lion howls and strikes his tympanum. Three

We see from these examples that in the course of time howling came to be thought of as vulgar or foreign or effeminate. But in early days Greeks like others howled for a ritual purpose. Howling happens to go unmentioned in Herodotus' account of the frenzied behaviour which the Scythian Anacharsis observed at Cyzicus and imitated later (4.76.2–5); yet it would suit the occasion. Cyzicus was celebrating the Mother's festival, including a pannychis, when Anacharsis stopped there on his return voyage; he vowed to do exactly the same if the Mother brought him safely home. We are reminded of the Argonauts, who first established the festival for that very purpose, to obtain safe passage. Afterwards, Anacharsis went to the Woodland, the peninsula opposite Olbia, where an altar of the Mother is actually attested by a document of the mid sixth century.[180] "He began to conduct the festival in its entirety for the goddess, holding a tympanum and attaching images to himself". The performance took some time; before it was over Anacharsis had been observed and reported and shot.

Such is the summer festival as presented by sources who speak of it by name or who seem to refer directly to the ritual. We are left with a question, the meaning of the name Κρόνια. It cannot be answered with complete assurance; but even to pose the question is a distinct advance. It arises from the fact established above, that the festival deity is the Mother of the Gods, and she alone. The god Κρόνος is simply deduced from the festival name, as if it meant "rites of Cronus", just as (say) "Apollonia" means "rites of Apollo". The notional god had a great vogue in stories of the Golden Age and the succession in heaven. But he was seldom admitted to cult.

Although some festival names are formed from the names of gods ("Apollonia", "Artemisia", "Athenaea", and so on), a huge majority are formed from descriptive terms for ritual actions. I say a huge majority, because not only are there many such names, but they include all the commonest ones, which are found throughout a whole dialect group, or more widely still, among Greeks everywhere. Consider the chief festivals of Apollo, Dionysus, Artemis, Demeter. The names are not "Apollonia", etc., but rather "Thargelia" and "Pya-

---

other poems on this theme mention only the tympanum, which is then dedicated; so the howling is a fine touch.

[180] J.G. Vinogradov, Olbia (Constanz 1981) 14–18; J. and L. Robert, REG 95 (1982) 356 no. 234; Vermaseren, CCCA 6.151–2 no. 515. The document, still unpublished, is a twelve-line graffito on a Fikellura sherd recounting a tour of the

nopsia" among Ionians, "Carneia" among Dorians; "Lenaea" and "Anthesteria" among Ionians, "Agriania" *vel sim.* among Dorians and Aeolians; "Laphria", cf. "Elaphia", "Elaphebolia"; "Thesmophoria".

The name "Cronia", as we have seen, was widespread in Ionia, and very likely occurred as well at Thebes, Rhodes, and Cyrene. By this token it must belong to the class of festival names that are drawn from ritual actions. It denotes some ritual distinctive of the Mother, as (say) "Thargelia" denotes a ritual distinctive of Apollo. But to say what it was is very difficult. All the festival names mentioned above are in fact obscure and disputed, even though some are ostensibly explained by ancient sources. It goes without saying that all these names are Greek, since they describe what Greeks did, and on public occasions.

But we must bear in mind that when a word is once adopted as a holy name, it is likely either to be reserved for that use, or to be differentiated in form from its ordinary counterpart. To take an example which can hardly be contested, the festival name Τρεφώνια/ Τροφώνια < *Τρέφων/Τρόφων means "(rites) of the Nourisher", and therefore matches the ordinary word τροφεῖα < τροφεύς. Both sets of forms are entirely natural and regular; yet they were differentiated from of old. Κρόνια like some other common festival names has no obvious meaning, but may still be only a differentiated form.

Hesychius glosses a term κέρνεα as τὰ τῆι Μητρὶ τῶν θεῶν ἐπιθυόμενα (the meaning of ἐπιθυόμενα is discussed below). The noun κέρνος, from which the adjective κέρνεος is formed, denotes a vessel characteristic of the Mother's rites. Nicander's female votary who goes howling through the streets is lavishly entitled κερνοφόρος ζάκορος βωμίστρια Ῥείης: "*kernos*-bearer" is the most definite indication in the series.[181] In a poem of Alexander Aetolus, Alcman looks back without regret to his Lydian homeland, where he would not have been a famous poet but rather a servitor of the Mother, either a κέρνας "*kernos*-man" or a priest banging the tympanum.[182] Long after, Magna Mater is served by female *cernophor(i)*.[183] Later still, in the third and

---

Woodland in which the altars of the Mother, Borysthenes, and Heracles were found to be damaged. Vinogradov is inclined to blame the Scythians.

[181] *Alex.*217. At [Plut.] *De Fluv.*13.3, in a story of the Mother's rites on Ida in the Troad, Hercher conjectures [κερνο]φόρου as a title of the woman Ida, who goes mad. But the text can be mended in various ways.

[182] *A.P.*7.709, Plut. *De Exil.*2,599 E (Alexander Aetolus *Coll.Alex.* fr. 9, *Hell.Ep.*1).

[183] *CIL* 10.1803 (Vermaseren, *CCCA* 4.9 no. 15), Puteoli; *CIL* 2.179 (*CCCA* 5.68–9 no. 184), Olisipo.

fourth centuries, the *cernus* is associated with the ritual of *criobolium* and *taurobolium*.[184] In Clement's formula of the Phrygian mysteries the initiate avows that he has borne the *kernos*.[185]

Clearly the *kernos* was important to the Mother, just as the *kistê* and the *liknon* were important to Demeter and Dionysus. How it was used does not appear from these sources. Indeed it can hardly have been used in the same way for six centuries, down to the days of *criobolium* and *taurobolium*. The mystic formulas in Clement show that all such implements had come to be emblematic of age-old ritual, and could be simply mentioned or displayed with powerful effect (in the Phrygian formula, the initiate eats out of the tympanum and drinks out of the cymbal).

The *kernos* is treated by Athenaeus as a generic type of vessel.[186] Yet the illustration which survives in our epitome of Book 11 is again drawn from ritual. Polemo in his work Περὶ δίου κωιδίου *On the skyey fleece* described the *kernos* as a composite vessel with many small cups containing a variety of vegetables and liquids, and untreated wool (eighteen items in all). Celebrants "carry round" the *kernos* and afterwards take a taste of the contents, "like one who has carried the *liknon*". Polemo's description is now applied by archaeologists to an actual vessel, a bowl with a fringe of cups around the belly, which has been found in large numbers in a votive deposit at Eleusis and scattered round the Athenian Agora, especially near the Eleusinium, and is depicted on the Niinnion plaque.[187] It does seem reasonable to say that this is a *kernos*, and, on the evidence of the plaque, that women carried it in Eleusinian ritual. Perhaps then Polemo had his

---

[184] *CIL* 6.508 (Vermaseren, *CCCA* 3.53 no. 235), Rome; J. Le Gall, *Karthago* 9 (1958 [1960] 121–3 (*CCCA* 5.40–1 no. 114), Utica; *CIL* 8.23400, 23401 (*CCCA* 5.28–30 nos. 79–80), *BAC* 1968, 220–1 (*CCCA* 5.30–1 no. 80d), *BAC* 1951/52.196 (*CCCA* 5.31 no. 81), all from Mactar. Cf. Leonard, *RE* 11.1 (1921) 325–6 s.v. Kernos; A.D. Nock, *CAH* 12.423–4; J. Rutter, *Phoenix* 22 (1968) 238; R. Duthoy, *The Taurobolium* (Leiden 1969) 74–83, 99–102.

[185] *Protr.*2.15.3. For the background, see Hepding, *Attis* 184–94; A. Pastorino on Firm.Mat. *De Err.Prof.Rel.*18.1 (Florence 1969).

[186] Ath.11.476,476E–F (Ammonius fr. 6 Tresp/*FGrHist* 361 F 2), 11.56,478C–D (Polemo fr. 88 Preller/fr. 2 Tresp).

[187] J.J. Pollitt, *Hesperia* 48 (1979) 205–33, pls. 65–72, publishes the Agora examples and reviews the discussion. But it is time to close the file on the "gold *kerchnoi*" of Eleusinian inventories. Like the *kerchnia* of other inventories, they are some kind of jewelry: see H.G. Pringsheim, *Archäologische Beiträge zur Geschichte des eleusinischen Kults* (Munich 1905) 69–72; Leonard, *RE* 316–17 s.v. Kernos; T. Linders, *Op.Ath.*17 (1988) 229–30.

eye on Eleusis.[188] But as we have just seen, the *kernos* was always regarded as distinctive of the Mother; so it is just as likely as that Polemo agrees in this, as everyone assumed before the Eleusinian vessels came to light.

Polemo helps us with more abbreviated notices in the lexica. "The *kernophoros* dance" in Pollux is one in which the dancers carry a vessel called *kernos*, said to resemble a *liknon* or *escharis*.[189] Here and in Polemo the better-known *liknon* is adduced because it too was filled with fruits and carried round; *escharis* perhaps means "tray". A scholiast on Nicander (*loc. cit.*) offers a surprising definition of a *kernos*: μυστικοὺς κρατῆρας ἐφ᾽ ὦν λύχνους τιθέασι "mystic mixing-bowls on which they set lamps".[190] As this does not suit his author, and is otherwise unparalleled, it seems very likely that the scholiast has misunderstood a notice like that of Pollux. Finally, Hesychius' expression τὰ... ἐπιθυόμενα is best understood as "things that are offered thereon", scil. on a *kernos*.[191]

If the kernos of Polemo and the lexica is the Mother's, a definite picture emerges. The individual cups were filled with a large variety of nourishing vegetables and liquids. We should not call them "first fruits", since they include several cereals and several legumes and olive oil and wine, which are gathered or produced at different times. Everything that was available was brought forth from the household stores: *frugibus et fructibus iam coactis*, as Macrobius says. Then the vessels were carried round amid howling and clashing and banging (so Nicander and Alexander Aetolus), or held up in a whirling dance (so the lexica). The purpose can hardly be in doubt.[192] It is a means of increasing nature's potency and abundance. Other rites at other seasons

---

[188] Though the "skyey fleece" was used at Eleusis, it had a wide range elsewhere. It would not be surprising to find it in the Mother's ritual (but at *IvErythrai* 206 line 12, the "fleece", *pokos*, is only a perquisite of the priest or priestess of the Cyrbantes).

[189] Poll.4.103 (om. B). Cf. Ath.14.27,629D, a madcap dance called κερνοφόρος.

[190] O. Rubensohn, *Ath.Mitt.*23 (1898) 288–90, suggests that a cake and candle were set in the middle of the Eleusinian *kernos*; yet the scholiast cannot be thus interpreted. K. Latte, *De Saltationibus Graecorum* (Giessen 1913) 81, envisages a nocturnal rite, but only as a late and secondary development. According to Leonard, *RE* 317–18, 325, s.v. Kernos, the scholiast describes a second type of vessel so called, which has no relation to the other; this is too trusting by far.

[191] In late Greek θύω, θυσία denote offerings in general, not burnt offerings. In earlier use the prefix ἐπι- of ἐπιθύω signifies either that the offerings are placed "upon" something, or that they are made "besides" other offerings: cf. J. Casabona, *Recherches sur le vocabulaire des sacrifices en grec* (Aix-en-Provence 1966) 98.

[192] Cf. Latte, *De Salt.Gr.*81–2.

aim at a like effect, and call for particular fruits, flowers, sprays, and branches to be carried round. None is so exuberant as the Mother's summer festival.

To sum up, *kernea* "things of the *kernos*" are "things that are offered thereon to the Mother of the Gods". The *kernos* is important to the Mother; its importance consists in the rite named after it. The rite was probably a leading element of the frenzied dance and din conducted by both male and female celebrants (cf. § V). We may therefore entertain without discomfort the possibility that the festival name Κρόνια is a differentiated form of κέρνεα. The *Ablaut* is within the normal range (cf. e.g. θνητός/θάνατος, κέλομαι/κλόνος).

The origin of the name Κρόνια was forgotten in the course of time: so was the origin of many other ritual names, even transparent ones like Τροφώνια. As a result, the festival was thought to honour an eponym Κρόνος, whose features were suggested by the ritual and the season. This was the summer lull, when the farmer rested from his labours, especially those of cereal farming. The gods who prosper such labours, notably Zeus, Demeter, and Poseidon, are honoured when they are needed, but not during the summer lull. Our festival then was at once a time of merry-making (though the revel had a magic purpose) and a respite from the round of toil which is the dispensation of Zeus. While the other gods were away, "Cronus" was at hand. He seemed to personify an older, simpler, kinder way of life.

As the festival is actually addressed to "the Mother of the Gods", the notional Cronus will be her consort. In the original belief, "the gods" whom the Mother bears are lesser powers of nature, projected in myth as the Curetes. But it was natural to say that Cronus and the Mother were the parents of the next generation, the gods we know, with Zeus at their head. Zeus alone has the epithet Κρονίων or Κρονίδης; nor is there any collective plural, Κρονίωνες or Κρονίδαι. The epithet therefore goes back to a time when the succession in heaven was not worked out in any detail; no particular group had been designated as children and grandchildren of Cronus.[193]

On the other hand, the formula Κρόνου πάις ἀγκυλομήτεω is a fairly late variant, since it contains the contraction -εω and competes in position with the old formula πατὴρ ἀνδρῶν τε θεῶν τε.[194] The epithet

---

[193] Cf. Wilamowitz, *Sitz.Berlin* 1929, 48–9 = *Kl.Schr.*5.2.176–7.
[194] See B. Hainsworth in *The Iliad: A Commentary* (Cambridge 1985–93) 3.30.

ἀγκυλομήτης is likely to reflect Cronus' role in the developed succession story. Authorities are divided between the traditional meaning "with crooked counsel" and the modern suggestion "with curved sickle"; a decision is not easy.[195] If the latter is right, the sickle is the one Cronus wields in the story, and nothing more. It cannot be an attribute of cult or a token of the season.[196] The festival Cronia falls in summer, and even the earliest instances, in Scirophorion, are well past the reaping of the grain, and past the ingathering as well. But on balance, the derivation from a word for "sickle" is not quite convincing,[197] and the traditional meaning seems preferable. It has been objected that ἄγκυλος, unlike σκολιός, does not occur in a figurative sense in any early writer.[198] It is however a vivid word, and Cronus' character called for a choice description: this benevolent ruler of the Golden age assailed both his father and his children. A hooked or sharply curved shape might be thought to apply.

Thus far the explicit notices of the Cronia, together with Cronus.

V. *The roaming Mother and leaping warriors as* aitia *of the summer festival*

Like so much of ancient ritual, the Mother's summer festival is richly illustrated by aetiological myth. And the aetiology is explicit. With

---

[195] "With curved sickle": Cook, *Zeus* 2.549–50; E. Risch, *LfgrE* s.v.; West on Hes. *Theog*.18. Frisk, *Gr.Etym.Wörterb.* s.v. μῆτις, and Chantraine, *Dict.Étym.* s.v. ἀγκ-, uphold the traditional etymology.

[196] The sickle of the succession story (but not the epithet) is so explained by Nilsson, *BSA* 46 (1951) 122–4 = *Op.Sel*.3.215–19, and *GGR*² 1.514. Nilsson thinks of the Cronia as a "private festival", an occasion for merry-making with no prescribed ritual, so that it could be celebrated at any suitable time. But even on this view (which must now be given up) the recorded dates are not a suitable time for a harvest fête. Despite Nilsson, "the sickle of Cronus" is not a standing attribute at all. It does not appear in art until the Roman period: E.D. Serbeti, *LIMC* 6 (1992) s.v. Kronos nos. 3–3a, 20, 26 (coins), 14–19, 27, 29 (gems), 13 (Pompeian wall painting). Serbeti also registers, as no. 4, a Hellenistic bronze cup from Macedonia, said to be "lost". But M. Mayer, *ML* 2.1 (1894) 1557 fig. 6 s.v. Kronos, in the only publication of this object (a drawing after a photograph), described it as highly suspect, so much so that it is not worth mentioning again.

[197] It seems necessary to postulate an original *ἀγκυλ-αμήτης (so Risch). But then the word could not be reinterpreted as ἀγκυλομήτης "with crooked counsel" unless it were first mispronounced.

[198] So West: Lycophr. *Alex*.344 is almost the only instance, and is based on the epic epithet. M. van der Valk, *GRBS* 26 (1985) 10 n. 25, would counter this by saying that the meaning "intricate" as a rhetorical term "is far earlier". But he gives no early examples, nor does *LSJ* or *TLG*, and a rhetorical term cannot be early enough to signify.

the spring festival, we resorted to inference; the story of Zeus' birth
and nursing was seen to be the *aition* mainly because it is attached to
the Mother's best-known cult-sites. So are the stories we are about
to consider; but there is no need to establish the connexion on the
ground. The stories declare their purpose. Long ago, the Mother
roamed in a frenzy, and the festival has been celebrated ever since.
Long ago, a band of youthful warriors cut a caper and made a din,
and the festival has been celebrated ever since.

There are then two kinds of story, about the Mother and about a
band of warriors, which are inspired by two classes of officiants, women
and young men. The stories about a warrior band are much commoner, and are also somewhat varied. Besides the mythical Curetes,
we meet legendary warriors: the Argonauts at Cyzicus, Pelops and
his band at Olympia, the native foes of the first settlers at Erythrae.
It is evident that the young men were always the outstanding performers at the festival. Accordingly, like other impressive elements of
public ritual, they could be removed from their proper context and
put to different use. They became the Corybantic healers at Athens,
and the guild of Curetes at Ephesus; neither have anything to do
with the Mother.

The following stories will be considered in detail for their bearing
on the Mother's ritual: 1) the roaming Mother at Athens, 2) the
Curetes on Ida, 3) Pelops' band and the Idaean Dactyls at Olympia,
4) the Argonauts at Cyzicus and the native troop at Erythrae.

1) The story of how the Mother roamed and her festival began is
told in two versions, in a chorus of Euripides' *Helena* and in a hymn
inscribed at Epidaurus.[199] It is common to both that the Mother roams
through the mountains in a frantic state of mind until Zeus intervenes and a revel begins, so that the Mother is appeased. These
details signal a sudden change in the natural world, as we shall see
in a moment. But first we must grasp the details.

In the hymn it is the Mother herself who revels as Zeus thunders.
ὁ Ζεὺς δ' ἐσιδὼν ἄναξ τὰν Ματέρα τῶν θεῶν κεραυνὸν ἔβαλλε—καὶ ἁ τὰ
τύμπαν' ἐλάμβανε—πέτρας διέρησσε—καὶ ἁ τὰ τύμπαν' ἐλάμβανε. "Lord
Zeus, when he saw the Mother of the Gods, would hurl lightning—
and she would take up the tympana—and he would split rocks—and
she would take up the tympana".[200] Then Zeus with kindly banter

[199] Eur. *Hel.*1301–52. Hiller von Gaertringen, *IG* 4.1² 131; P. Maas, *Epidaurische Hymnen* (Halle 1933) 8–21 no. 3; Page, *PMG* 935.
[200] *PMG* 935 lines 9–14, 11, 13 καὶ τὰ τ. *lapis*: καὶ ἁ (χά) Wilamowitz. Zeus and the

invites the Mother to rejoin the other gods; after protesting for a moment, she agrees.[201] There is a similar transition in the chorus of *Helena*, as Zeus again takes charge. "Zeus, to soothe the Mother's grim temper, gives a command" (lines 1339–40). He tells an array of goddesses to celebrate a revel. The Charites howl, the Muses more conventionally sing; Aphrodite takes up cymbals, tympana, and flute so as to accompany the howling.[202] Nothing more is said about the Mother; she has been appeased.

As stories go, this one lacks originality. In outline it is the story told of Demeter in her *Homeric Hymn*. She too roams and grieves; Zeus intervenes and causes her to relent.[203] The parallel with Demeter is reinforced, though by different means, in both the Epidaurian hymn and the chorus of Euripides. In the hymn, the Mother refuses at the last to rejoin the other gods unless she is awarded half of each of the three elements—sky, earth, and sea. Demeter and Core, we recall from the *Homeric Hymn*, rejoin the other gods at the last after a similar condition is met, that Core shall go beneath the earth for a third part of the year, and come up for the other two parts.[204] In both cases it is a question of three parts or shares. Euripides' contribution is more peculiar. The reason why the Mother is distraught, and makes

---

Mother alternate as subjects. Maas deletes the καὶ clause both times as intrusive ("About the origin of the interpolation I venture no surmise"). This produces three pairs of four-line strophes; but even so the last pair is not convincing. And it spoils the meaning.

[201] Zeus' speech is grammatically incomplete, and Page marks a lacuna after line 18; R. Herzog *apud* Hiller offers a supplement. Again, the text is better as it stands; the ellipse is deliberate and effective.

[202] Howling: ἀλαλᾶι (1344), ἀλαλαγμῶι (1352). Cymbals: χαλκοῦ δ᾿ αὐδὰν χθονίαν (1346). Tympana: τύπανα... βυρσοτενῆ (1347). Flute: βαρύβρομον αὐλόν (1351). R. Kannicht, *Euripides. Helena* (Heidelberg 1969) 2.352, doubts whether cymbals are meant by "the earthen sound of bronze", partly because, he says, "Aphrodite can strike only one of the two instruments", scil. cymbals and tympanum. But she may wield both successively; a moment later she has the flute "in her hands" (1350). It is certainly no improvement to suggest that the phrase denotes the tympana of the next line by a kind of "proleptic apposition", *vorweggenommene Apposition*. G. Sfameni Gasparro in M.B. de Boer and T.A. Edridge (eds.), *Hommages à M.J. Vermaseren* (Leiden 1978) 3.1151,1160, cites Kannicht but speaks without misgiving first of *crotali*, then of *cembali*.

[203] In the *Homeric Hymn* Demeter is twice placated, first by the people of Eleusis and then by Zeus, and accordingly the institution of her festival is reported twice, before and after Zeus intervenes (lines 292–300, 473–82); it is the necessary conclusion to both episodes. The Mother's story as we have it contains no local episode like the visit to Eleusis.

[204] *PMG* 935 lines 19–24. *Hom.H.Cer.*398–403,463–5. The Epidaurian hymn says μέρη, τὸ τρίτον μέρος (lines 20, 23); the Homeric says τρίτατον μέρος, τὴν τριτάτην... μοῖραν (lines 399, 464). See also n. 207 below.

her way through a wild mountain landscape, and even rides in a chariot drawn by lions, is that her daughter, *koura*, is gone, having been abducted under Zeus' permission.[205] No one but Euripides would have ventured on such mystifying syncretism.

Two conclusions follow from our comparison of Euripides, the Epidaurian hymn, and the *Homeric Hymn to Demeter*. First, the story of the Mother's roaming originates at Athens, for it plainly evokes the *Homeric Hymn*, which glorifies Eleusis. Second, the story is earlier than both Euripides and the Epidaurian hymn, for they embroider it in quite different ways. We may also conjecture that there was more to the story than appears in either of these derivative versions. A cult *aition* is normally tied to a given cult-site; the story ends when the local cult and festival are established. We shall soon see that other *aitia* are tied to Cnossus and Ida, to Cyzicus, to Olympia, to Erythrae. In our story the Mother must have come to some cult-site in Athens or Attica. Perhaps it was at Agra or on the Museum hill; or perhaps it was somewhere outside Athens, as at Phlya or Anagyrus.[206]

Both versions of the story depict the howling frenzy of the Mother's female votaries, though they are not labelled as such. They are represented in the hymn by the Mother herself, and in Euripides by the array of goddesses. For the first time we also learn the purpose of the revel, to effect a change in nature.

In the Epidaurian hymn Zeus hurls lightning and splits rocks; i.e., rain falls from the sky, and springs flow from the earth. On a strict view, splitting rocks and producing springs is a task for Poseidon; but for the sake of brevity the hymn ascribes it to the weather god on high. If then the Mother's revel coincides with rain and rushing waters, these are the desired end. The point is also made at the last when the Mother demands a share in all the elements, beginning with the sky, and when she is addressed in the poet's farewell as ἄνασσα ... Ὀλύμπου "queen of Olympus".[207]

---

[205] *Hel.*1306–7,1312–18,1322,1336,1341–2. Euripides follows a different version of the rape, in which Core is abducted from a ring of dancers, and Athena and Artemis try to help her, and Zeus warns them away with a lightning flash. None of these details, not even the lightning flash, has any further significance for the Mother. Maas, *Epid.Hymnen* 19–21, and Kannicht, *Eur.Helena* 2.342–3, go half way towards equating Zeus' intervention in the rape with his intervention in the story of the Mother.

[206] Cf. n. 66 above.

[207] *PMG* 935 lines 25–6. Maas, *Epid.Hymnen* 13–14, takes a different view. "The hymn depicts the time when the new gods are still ranged beside the old", as in

Apollonius, apropos of the Mother's festival at Cyzicus, describes her power in like terms. "It is she who rules the winds, the sea, the whole earth to its very depths, even the snowy seat of Olympus. And when she ascends from the mountains into the wide sky, Zeus himself, son of Cronus, gives way to her, and so do the other immortals as they honour the dread goddess".[208] These are striking words—ὅτ' ἐξ ὀρέων μέγαν οὐρανὸν εἰσαναβαίνηι "when she ascends from the mountains into the wide sky"—which express the worshippers' belief. From a Mediterranean point of view, nature is at its worst at this time of year. The other gods are ineffectual, and the Mother is summoned to provide all the forces that can help—fair winds, cool skies, fertilizing rain and springs.

In Euripides too the Mother controls nature. Commentators duly note that a motif which he shares with the *Homeric Hymn* is the failure of crops and the omission of sacrifice as a consequence of the goddess' anger, the Mother's instead of Demeter's. But they have not observed that the motif is greatly elaborated, so that it suits the Mother's pastoral domain. Cereal crops are mentioned first, and a starving population, just as in the *Homeric Hymn*.[209] Thereafter we are told that the Mother "allows no green pasture of leafy curls to shoot up for grazing animals . . . and keeps the fresh springs of clear water from gushing forth" (lines 1330–1, 1335–6). If nature now languishes, it will flourish as soon as the revel begins. It is for the sake of cereal crops that Demeter is honoured at the time of autumn sowing. But it is to counter the parching heat of summer, to revive the vegetation and the water sources, that the Mother is honoured at her own season.

Whereas Euripides leaves the sequel unmentioned, Apollonius describes it fully.[210] The Mother is greatly pleased by the revel of the Argonauts, "and the fitting signs appeared. Trees shed abundant fruit,

---

Hesiod's succession story, so that Zeus must settle with them; the Mother asks for the same power she enjoyed as Cronus' spouse. Maas also compares "the hymn to Hecate" in Hesiod's *Theogony*, in which Zeus grants Hecate a role in all three elements (lines 413–14). Finally, he postulates a common source for the Epidaurian hymn and Hesiod: an epic hymn to the Mother. Yet the Epidaurian hymn has not a hint of the succession story and the rivalry of old and new. Apollonius, as we are about to see, clinches the seasonal background. The Mother's "shares" are therefore a separate dispensation, like those of Demeter and Core.

[208] *Argon.*1097–1102. The lines are echoed at *H.Orph.*14.10–11 (of Rhea).

[209] *Hom.H.Cer.*305–12; Eur. *Hel.*1327–9,1332–4.

[210] *Argon.*1.1141–3,1145–8. The miracle of lines 1144–5 is that wild beasts leave their lairs and come up with tails wagging. They too belong to the pastoral domain; herdsmen watch for predators and hunt game (cf. *Hom.H.Ven.*158–60, skins of bear

and around their feet the earth unbidden sent up shoots of tender grass . . . She caused another miracle, since Dindymus had never yet flowed with water, but then it gushed up for them from the thirsty summit, unceasing". The purpose of the summer festival could not be more plainly stated.[211]

It follows that the revel is a magic action. The worshippers leap and whirl and howl, they bang the drum and clash the gong, to stimulate the natural world. Women can operate such magic, and so can young men, whom we come to next.[212]

2) The infant Zeus is guarded in the cave on Ida by the Curetes, warriors who leap and whirl and clash their arms. Our sources regard the cave as sacred to Zeus; but it can be argued that the Mother was there first (§ III). Now when the mythical Curetes are associated with real-life ritual, Zeus does not come into it at all. Instead, the Curetes are said to be the prototypes of armed dancers in the cult of the Mother.[213] So the argument about the cave is strikingly confirmed.

The epic *Danais* spoke of the Curetes as "attendants of the Mother of the Gods".[214] Euripides in the *Bacchae* tells how the Curetes and Corybantes, having invented tympana and flutes, handed them over to Rhea, alias the Mother.[215] Demetrius of Scepsis in his downright fashion held that both Curetes and Corybantes were young men "recruited for the war dance in the rites of the Mother of the Gods".[216] Lucretius drew from some Greek source a picture of actual armed dancers who attend the Mother in procession; he describes them as *terrificas capitum quatientes numine cristas* "shaking dreadful plumes with a movement of their heads", and says that they recall the Curetes who

---

and lion on Anchises' couch). Both the Epidaurian hymn (*PMG* 935 lines 17–18) and Euripides (*Hel.*1310) allude to the Mother's way with animals.

[211] Cornutus in like vein says that Rhea brings rain (*Theol.Gr.*6).

[212] On dancing and noise-making as a means of stimulating nature, see Latte, *De Salt.Gr.*50–6; W. Fiedler, *Antiker Wetterzauber* (Stuttgart 1931) 28–31,40–1,44,56.

[213] The ritual behind the dance of the Curetes has been generally taken as a festival of spring: Hepding, *Attis* 132 n. 1; Latte, *De Salt.Gr.*51; West, *JHS* 85 (1965) 155–6,158. But Preller-Robert, *Gr.Myth.* 1⁴ 135, left it open between a festival of spring and one "in the hot summer"; the latter is now proved correct.

[214] Philodem. *De Piet.* p. 42 Gomperz (*Danais* fr. 3 Bernabé/Davies).

[215] *Bacch.*120–31. First the Curetes are named, then the Corybantes; they are either identified, or associated on equal terms.

[216] Str.10.3.21, p. 473. Admittedly, Demetrius also said, by way of castigating Euripides, that the Mother's ritual was not native to Crete, but rather to Phrygia and the Troad (Str.10.3.20, p. 472). This will be a combination of ignorance and chauvinism.

guarded Zeus.[217] Ovid too says that the Curetes and Corybantes who clashed their arms are imitated by the worshippers of the Mother with their tympana and cymbals.[218] Finally, according to a pragmatic history of Crete, it was the Curetes who founded the city of Cnossus and its shrine of the Mother.[219]

It is stated by Lucretius and implied by the others that even in later days armed dancers performed for the Mother. We also learn something of how they looked and acted. They shake their plumes, says Lucretius. He does not say as well that they clash spear on shield; of the mythical Curetes he says only, *armati in numerum pulsarent aeribus aera*, "[dancing] in arms, they struck bronze on bronze in rhythm".[220] Ovid more distinctly says that in the later worship tympana and cymbals stand for the original shields and helmets; for whereas the Curetes pounded shields, the Corybantes pounded empty helmets. Apollonius imagines a like development at Cyzicus, where the prototypes are not the Curetes but the Argonauts. In founding the festival, the Argonauts struck sword on shield; nowadays the Phrygians make use of drum and tympanum.[221] In Euripides even the mythical Curetes and Corybantes wield tympana and flute rather than spear and shield.

Their undoubted attribute is a plumed helmet. Lucretius draws attention to bobbing heads and waving plumes. There is something similar in Demetrius' account. He derives the name "Curetes", correctly, from *koroi* "lads"; the "Corybantes", however, are oddly said to be named ἀπὸ τοῦ κορύπτοντας βαίνειν ὀρχηστικῶς "from their moving in the dance with a butting of the head". The gesture must have been conspicuous to inspire the etymology. In Euripides, again, the Corybantes are styled τρικόρυθες "with triple helmet", a rare word which can only refer to three plumes, such as we sometimes see in contemporary art.[222] Euripides points to the same feature as Lucretius.

---

[217] *De Rer.Nat.*2.629–43. It appears from line 640, *magnam armati matrem comitantur*, that Lucretius thinks of the dancers as going in procession, not as performing separately. But he may be speaking loosely, or at a venture.

[218] *Fast.* 4.207–14.

[219] Diod.5.66.1 (*FGrHist* 468 [Crete app.] F 1); Euseb., Hier., Syncell. *a.Abr.*54/6. Cf. Poerner, *De Curetibus* 258–9; Jacoby, *FGrHist* IIIb Kommentar 1.353–4.

[220] Line 637. Line 631, *ludunt in numerumque exsultant sanguine laeti* "they sport and leap in rhythm, delighted by blood", is a vague tribute to the warlike aspect of the actual dancers.

[221] *Argon.*1.1134–9.

[222] Cf. Eur. *Or.*1480, τρικόρυθος Αἴας. Dodds on *Bacch.*123 objects that a triple-crested helmet was too familiar to be thus singled out; "the epithet should suggest

It is also noteworthy that Ovid's rather strained aetiology puts an emphasis on helmets.

This evidence strongly suggests that the actual armed dancers of the Mother's cult were conspicuous for their plumed helmets and their way of tossing the plumes, but not for any other arms or armour, and that they made a din with tympana and cymbals, and sometimes with drum and flute, but not with spear and shield. In early days the mythical Curetes were seen in a similar light, being described as musical performers, not as warriors.[223] In the epic *Phoronis* the Curetes were said to be αὐληταί "flute-players", and native Phrygians, for the flute was often traced to Phrygia;[224] in Euripides, as we saw, they combine tympana and flute. The *Catalogue of Women* calls them φιλοπαίγμονες ὀρχηστῆρες "sportive dancers", siblings of Nymphs and Satyrs.[225] Earlier still, perhaps two centuries before these late epics, the tympanum from the Idaean cave shows the Curetes in Eastern style as winged and bearded daemons, but clashing cymbals like Greek worshippers.[226]

It was therefore a departure from the realities of cult, and from the original picture of the Curetes, when their performance was represented as a dance with arms and armour, a virtual war dance, ἐνόπλιος ὄρχησις, in which a clamour was strangely produced by clashing spear on shield, the usual arms of Pyrrhic dancers. This step was very likely taken after the time of Euripides, who shows himself

---

something alien and remote". Familiar or not, a triple crest was imposing, all the more so, if it was tossed about by frenzied dancers.

[223] Latte, *De Salt.Gr.*51 n. 3, errs on this point.

[224] Str.10.3.19, p. 472 (*Phoronis* fr. 3 Bernabé/Davies). The Curetes also appeared in the *Danais* (n. 214 above), and [Apollodorus] gives them an unexpected role in the story of Io. At Hera's bidding they spirit away the infant Epaphus, and Zeus kills them for it (*Bibl.*2.1.3.7 [2.9]). The episode implies that the Curetes were already at home at Argos, and disposed to serve Hera. Other traditional attendants of the Mother, the Idaean Dactyls, were likewise mentioned in the *Phoronis*, and again as Phrygians (fr. 2 Bernabé/Davies). Yet they must have come to Argos; for whereas they invented metal-working, Phoroneus invented its primary application, the manufacture of arms and armour (Hyg. *Fab.*274; Cassiod. *Var.*7.18). And he dedicated arms to Hera, an *aition* of her "Shield" festival (Serv. *Aen.*3.284 gives a parallel *aition*). In [Hes.] *Cat.* fr. 10a the Curetes, like Nymphs and Satyrs, appear to be offspring of Dorus and a daughter of Phoroneus; see P.J. Parsons, P.J. Sijpesteijn, and K.A. Worp in *Papyri Greek and Egyptian. Edited . . . in honour of E.G. Turner* (London 1981) 14. Finally, the temple metopes at the Argive Heraeum showed, with other subjects, "the birth of Zeus", i.e. the dancing Curetes (Paus.2.17.3). Thus we see that in Argive worship the Mother was joined with Hera.

[225] [Hes.] *Cat.* fr. 10a lines 17–19 (*olim* fr. 123 M–W).

[226] Kunze, *Kret.Bronzereliefs* 1.32 no. 74, 48–51, 196–8, 202–3, pl. 49.

unaware of it in his several references to the Curetes.[227] Nor has it left any mark on the Dictaean hymn to the *kouros*, datable to the fourth or third century;[228] the *kouros* leaps, and the worshippers sing to the accompaniment of flutes and pipes. We first hear of it in mid fourth century, in Plato's *Laws* and in Ephorus' account of Crete: it was evidently due to some historian who gave a novel and flattering account of Cretan institutions.[229] Plato and Ephorus like many later writers regard the Curetes as inventors of the Cretan form of war dance;[230] according to Callimachus they performed the πρύλις, a Cretan term for such a dance.[231] Apollonius transfers the image to the Argonauts. So this view of the Curetes quickly became standard; but it is not true to the ritual.

3) From the Curetes we turn to some less familiar instances of the Mother's male attendants. Olympia, where the Mother once was prominent, has two competing local legends, about Pelops and his band, and about the Idaean Dactyls.

Telestes of Selinus (*fl.* 400 B.C.), in lines quoted by Athenaeus, says that "the companions of Pelops", συνοπαδοὶ Πέλοπος, were the first to hymn, "the mountain Mother" in Greece, playing a Phrygian tune on the flute, and a Lydian one on the lyre; they did so "beside mixing-bowls" of wine, a detail we shall take up further on.[232] Just before this, Athenaeus explains that the Phrygian and Lydian modes were introduced to Greece "by the Phrygians and Lydians who came over with Pelops to the Peloponnesus"; the Lydians had joined him because Mount Sipylus is in Lydia, the Phrygians because they too were ruled by Tantalus. This account of the companions must derive from Telestes and should be included, beside the verbatim quotation, in his "fragment".

---

[227] See n. 23 above.

[228] See nos. 37–8 above.

[229] On this figure, see Jacoby, *FGrHist* IIIb Kommentar 1.307–8.

[230] Pl. *Leg.*7,796B; Str.10.4.16, p. 480 (Ephorus *FGrHist* 70 F 149). For other sources, see Poerner, *De Curetibus* 332–5.

[231] *H. Jov.* 52. In the dialect of Gortyn, πρύλεες meant "foot-soldiers" (schol.A, Eustath. *Il.*12.77). But Callimachus uses πρύλις again of the Amazons at Ephesus (*H.Dian.*240), and certain scholia ascribe the term to Cyprus, not Crete (schol.Pind. *Pyth.*2.127; schol.T *Il.*23.130—despite appearances in [Arist.] fr. 519 Rose³). The threads are tangled, but one leads to Crete. Cf. Latte, *De Salt.Gr.*31–2,38–9,42.

[232] Ath.14.21,625E–626A (Telestes *PMG* fr. 810). Line 4 requires emendation, either τοὶ δέ for τοῖς δέ (Musurus) or ὀξύφωνοι... ψαλμοί for ὀξυφώνοις... ψαλμοῖς (Wilamowitz); whichever is adopted, the Lydian tune is performed by the Lydian companions, not by "the Greeks", as in D.A. Campbell's rendering, *Greek Lyric* (Loeb

According to Telestes, then, Pelops came to Greece from Mount Sipylus with a band of Lydian and Phrygian followers. This was the usual view. It is mostly expressed in a rationalized form, which goes back to Hecataeus. Pelops leads a "host" of Lydians or Phrygians and brings great wealth; the wealth is in metal, from the mines of Sipylus, so that his followers are thought of as bearing arms.[233] Pausanias, however, has a version oddly similar to Telestes', though it is attached to a different cult. In the countryside east of Olympia he remarks on a shrine of Artemis *kordaka*, so called "because the followers of Pelops, οἱ τοῦ Πέλοπος ἀκόλουθοι, conducted a victory celebration at this shrine and danced a *kordax* dance native to the people round Sipylus" (6.22.1). The merry *kordax* dance no doubt bore some resemblance to the revels for the Mother.[234] In Pausanias' time Olympia had largely given up the Mother's ritual; her temple was occupied by the Emperors (5.20.9). Perhaps that is why the story of Pelops' musical companions came to be attached to a rural shrine nearby.

Pelops' home, the ancient realm of Tantalus, was Mount Sipylus. Sipylus, if any mountain, was sacred to the Mother. The oldest of all her images, says Pausanias, is "on the rock of Coddinus" on the north side; he means the prehistoric seated figure at Akpinar, of Hittite origin.[235] It is carved in the mountain face above a main road which leads south, round the east side, towards the other Hittite rock-carving at Karabel (a warrior god), likewise placed above the road. Herodotus speaks of the road at Karabel as leading north from Ephesian

---

ed.) 5.131. Nor is the hymn performed "at Greek drinking-parties" (*ibid.*, n. 1). The passage may or may not come from a poem entitled Διὸς γοναί "Birth of Zeus" (*PMG* fr. 809).

[233] Str.7.7.1, p. 321 (Hecataeus *FGrHist* 1 F 119), λαός; Thuc.1.9.2; *Exc.de Insid.*7.24 (Nicolaus *FGrHist* 90 F 10), στρατός; Tac. *Ann.*4.55.3, *populi*; Str.14.5.28, p. 680, "The wealth of Tantalus and the Pelopidae arose from the mines round Phrygia and Sipylus". According to Athenaeus, *loc. cit.*, "You can see large mounds everywhere in the Peloponnesus, but especially in Lacedaemon, which are identified as graves of Pelops' Phrygians".

[234] Bronze cymbals are dedicated to Artemis *limnatis* in Laconia or Messenia or both: *IG* 5.1.225–6,1497; *A.P.*6.280 (Anon. *Hell.Ep.*41). Cf. Nilsson, *Gr.Feste* 211–12, and *GGR*² 1.161,490. The cymbals found with other votive bronzes at Olympia are undoubtedly the Mother's; cf. n. 249 below.

[235] Paus.3.22.4. Naumann, *Ikonographie* 20–2, pl. 1; P.Z. Spanos in R.M. Boehmer and H. Hauptmann (eds.), *Beiträge zur Altertumskunde Kleinasiens. Festschrift für K. Bittel* (Mainz 1983) 1.477–83,2 pl. 98; Vermaseren, *CCCA* 1.128–9 nos. 439–40, pl. 96. Spanos sees not a seated goddess but a standing, bearded "mountain god"; this is unconvincing. He is also wrong in supposing that Pausanias' "Niobe" is the same as his "Mother of the Gods".

territory, and east from Smyrna,[236] Greeks must have followed it even in Mycenaean times. Close to the image at Akpinar, but in the plain, is the excavated sanctuary of the Mother Πλαστήνη, also mentioned by Pausanias, a native of the area.[237] Her local epithet is formed with the usual adjective ending from a word *plast-*. This can only be the Greek adjective πλαστή "moulded", used as a label for the pre-historic rock-carving. The label was presumably conferred in very early days, when carving in stone was a wonder to the Greeks.

The Mother's cult on Sipylus produces all the usual stories, of the birth and nursing of Zeus, of the dance of the Curetes. They are a constant theme with Aristeides, who lived at Smyrna; in the same breath he speaks of Pelops and Tantalus.[238] As denizens of Sipylus they are creatures of the Mother. The image at Akpinar is ascribed by Pausanias to Tantalus' other son Broteas. He also knows of a "throne of Pelops", said to be on a peak above the sanctuary of Mother *Plastênê*; it is in fact a rock-cut throne of the type discussed above (§ III).[239] Bacchylides, according to a scholiast, gave a credit to Rhea for restoring Pelops after his ordeal in the cauldron.[240]

A tale in Antoninus Liberalis, unascribed, has the effect of linking the Mother's cult on Sipylus with that on Ida, as if these were deemed the leading instances.[241] When Rhea hides Zeus in the cave on Crete, he is nursed, as often, by a goat. But Rhea also sets a golden dog to watch the goat; dogs after all are the indispensable guardians of herds and flocks, and especially of nursing mothers and their young. The dog itself is paradoxically stolen by the master thief Pandareus, who goes off to Sipylus and entrusts his prize to Tantalus, who with even worse dishonesty keeps it for himself—so that both are punished by Zeus in a strange but fitting conclusion.[242] The starting point is the

---

[236] Hdt.2.106.2. Cf. J.M. Cook, *BSA* 53/4 (1958/59) 18–19; G.E. Bean, *Aegean Turkey* (London 1966) 56–8.

[237] Paus.5.13.7; [Arist.] *De Mirab.Ausc.*162,846b 3–6, the Mother's "sacred precincts" at Sipylus; Vermaseren, *CCCA* 1.130–32 nos. 443–54, pl. 98.

[238] Arist. *Or.*17.3,18.2,21.3 Behr; schol.bT *Il.*24.615. Cf. Poerner, *De Curetibus* 282; Cook, *Zeus* 2.956 n. 2; Schwabl, *RE* Suppl.1154 s.v. Zeus.

[239] Paus.5.13.7. Frazer, *Pausanias* 3.353; Cook, *Zeus* 1.138–9; Bean, *Aegean Turkey* 63.

[240] Schol.Pind. *Ol.*1.40a (Bacch. fr. 42).

[241] *Met.*36. Other versions are reported in summary style by schol.Hom. *Od.*19.518, 20.66, schol.Pind. *Ol.*1.91a: cf. Robert, *Gr.Heldensage* 377–8; T. Gantz, *Early Greek Myth* (Baltimore 1993) 535. Though details vary, the gist of the story is the same. Rhea is not mentioned, and the guardian dog is said to belong to a shrine of Zeus on Crete: this is the Idaean cave.

[242] Pandareus was turned into a rock right where he stood, and we might expect

birth story or the Mother's ritual as common ground between Ida and Sipylus.

The other group of attendants are the Idaean Dactyls: Heracles and four younger brothers with names peculiar to Olympia.[243] Pausanias reports it as Eleian tradition that Rhea handed over the infant Zeus to these Dactyls. All five had their own altars. Three of the names, "Epimedes", "Paeonaeus", and "Iasus", and also "Acesidas" as an alternative to "Idas", appear to denote healing deities, appropriate companions for the Mother. Here then is an authentic local group;[244] at other places the Mother is attended by two or three Dactyls with other names. It is true that the Dactyls are said to have been summoned to Olympia from Ida on Crete, and to be known also as "Curetes", for whom there was a separate altar.[245] But the Cretan connexion is likely to be secondary, as at other places in the Peloponnesus (cf. § III). Despite their name, the "Idaean Dactyls" of Greek literature are clearly not native to Ida in Crete, nor yet to Ida in the Troad. The epithet doubtless comes from the common noun ἴδη "wood".[246] At Olympia one of the Dactyls is called "Idas", and Pindar knows of an "Idaean cave" as the local birth-site.[247]

Such is the aetiology, in two versions, of the summer festival at Olympia. Evidence on the ground shows how important the Mother was. She has a temple in the Altis, the only other besides those of Hera and Zeus.[248] It may seem even more significant that the votive offerings buried in the Altis, over a wide area at the west, include many bronze cymbals;[249] for they can hardly have been used in any other ritual but the Mother's.

---

it to be the one that perpetually threatens Tantalus; but the text is defective. Perhaps we should read Τάνταλον δέ . . . κατέβαλε καί {περὶ} ⟨ἐπέθηκεν⟩ αὐτὸν [scil. τὸν πέτρον] ὑπὲρ κεφαλῆς ⟨περὶ⟩ τὸν Σίπυλον.

[243] Paus.5.7.6–7,9,14.7.
[244] So B. Hemberg, *Eranos* 50 (1952) 56–8. For other opinions, see Poerner, *De Curetibus* 273–4; Ziehen, *RE* 18.1 (1939) 52–3 s.v. Olympia.
[245] Paus.5.7.6,8.1,8.2.2.
[246] So Wilamowitz, *Glaube* 1.279; Hemberg, *Eranos* 50 (1952) 45.
[247] *Ol.*5.18. In successive stanzas Pindar invokes Athena at Camarina and Zeus at Olympia, with the usual mention of local features. For Zeus they are the Cronian hill, the Alpheius river, and the Idaean cave; this last is assuredly not in Crete. See Wilamowitz, *Pindaros* 421 n. 1, and *Glaube* 1.132; Ziehen, *RE* 69–70 s.v. Olympia; *contra*, R. Hampe in G.E. Mylonas (ed.), *Studies presented to D.M. Robinson* (St. Louis 1951–52) 1.336–50. There is, however, no reason at all to equate the cave with the small Archaic temple of the Mother, which we are about to examine.
[248] A. Mallwitz, *Olympia und seine Bauten* (Darmstadt 1972) 160–3.
[249] A. Furtwängler, *Olympia. Die Bronzen und die übrigen Kleinfunde* (Berlin 1890) 70.

Her Temple does not represent the original arrangement. It dates from the early fourth century,[250] and the altar in front (at the west) is somewhat later; there was no previous construction on the site. It is, moreover, set as close as could be against the terrace supporting the treasuries, and faces slightly north of west towards the rising ground beyond them, which forms an approach to the hill Κρόνιον. The name of the hill, as of the precinct at Athens, comes from the summer festival (§ IV); the spring festival includes a sacrifice on the hilltop (§ III); the "Idaean cave" in Pindar must be sought on the hill or at its foot. Our attention is drawn away from the Altis towards the north.

The earlier history of the Mother's shrine has been reconstructed with great probability by Mallwitz.[251] At the west end of the row of treasuries is a smaller building which is older than any of them, and almost as old as the temple of Hera. It was a temple, with a round altar in front. This altar was replaced by another of the same kind before the end of the Archaic period. Then a great change took place. A large rectangular altar was built on the same spot, but with the long axis going north-south, so that it no longer served the small temple, which must have been abandoned (it came to be half-buried in the shifting earth). In fact the rectangular altar seems to be coeval with the Mother's temple in the Altis, sharing the same material and technique. The new temple and altar are not in a direct line, since this could not be managed—until the original altar site was given up entirely, and a replacement was built in front of the temple. On this showing the Mother had always been honoured at a strategic point in the sanctuary.

4) Two other stories about armed dancers are noteworthy for depicting another stage of the ritual, a great feast. The Argonauts at Cyzicus dine on cattle, warriors at Erythrae on a bull. At Erythrae it is clear that this is no ordinary sacrifice and banquet.

At Cyzicus both the dance and the feast take place in a rustic shrine on the very summit of the mountain, with a sweeping view of distant shores.[252] There is an image roughly made from the stock of a wild vine, an altar of piled stones, and a stand of oak-trees whose

---

[250] Telestes' lines on the Mother may have been composed at the time the temple was built.

[251] *Olympia* 92, 97, 155–60, and in W.J. Raschke (ed.), *The Archaeology of the Olympics* (Madison 1988) 91.

[252] Apoll. *Argon.*1.1107–51, whence [Orph.] *Argon.*601–17.

leaves are used for wreaths. Here the Argonauts perform their frenzied dance, well apart from the people of Cyzicus, who are otherwise occupied in the town.[253] The ensuing feast is briefly described
in conventional terms.[254]

At Erythrae the feast comes first and inspires the dance. This sequence is essential to the story, about a "strategem" of the Ionian
leader Cnopus by which he incapacitates the native defenders.[255] The
strategem has been excerpted as usual from an historical narrative,
in this case a local history of Erythrae. And like many other strategems
it is a ritual *aition*. The Greek passion for aetiology burns as brightly
in the pages of history as in myth and poetry. In each city each
distinctive piece of public ceremony was understood to be a re-en-
actment of some exciting moment in the past. So local history is full
of *aitia*. It happens that the sole surviving passage quoted from an
Erythraean history, by one Hippias, refers to three local festivals in
succession, all somehow contributing to the further story of Cnopus
and other rulers.[256] Hippias' account is not nearly as brisk and clear
as the strategem, which must be drawn from some other writer.

The strategem is the following. When Erythrae resists, Cnopus

---

[253] They are said to be "still", ἔτι, lamenting their eponymous king Cyzicus (lines
1137–8), whose death has just been recounted as the *aition* of a separate festival of
games, conducted somewhere in the coastal plain (lines 1015–77). Other sources too
dwell upon this episode, with various details; see Hasluck, *Cyzicus* 158–62; Robert,
Gr.Heldensage 831–6; Jacoby on Deilochus *FGrHist* 471 F 4–10. The Mother is brought
into it in a perfunctory way by Val.Fl. *Argon*.3.21–31,47, and [Orph.] *Argon*.535,546–
54,601–17,624; on this point both are elaborating Apollonius. The Mother's festival
must have come right after the festival of games; they do not appear to be integrally
related.

[254] Lines 1150–1. It is said at the start that the younger men bring the cattle
from the stalls (1107–8), thereafter, that the celebrants put on wreaths and get busy
with the sacrifice (lines 1123–4), and that they pour libation on the fire (1133–4).
These details are equally conventional.

[255] Polyaen.8.43. The strategem has lately been interpreted as a scapegoat ritual
of the kind described in Hittite texts. Such fantastic combinations are a portent of
this age; cf. Robertson, *CIV*² 9 (1990) 437.

[256] Ath.6.74,258F–259F (Hippias *FGrHist* 421 F 1): Hermes *dolios*, Artemis *strophaia*,
and a third festival left unnamed. After Cnopus is bidden by an oracle to honour
Hermes *dolios*, he is killed by usurpers whose subsequent regime is thoroughly per-
verse; above all else, they dress in extravagant and unsuitable clothes that are
described at length. The background is a festival of Hermes with unruly conduct
by inferiors; on neighbouring Samos the festival of Hermes *charidotês* gives license
to steal, especially clothes, κλέπτειν ἐφεῖται τῶι βουλομένωι καὶ λωποδυτεῖν (Plut.
Quaest.Gr.55,303D). Though Hippias is beguiling, he is far surpassed by Graf, *Nordion.
Kulte* 243–8, who ignores Hermes *dolios* and makes Artemis *strophaia* an excuse for
overheated speculation about ecstatic transvestite mysteries.

applies to the Delphic oracle and is told to bring over a priestess of Enodia from Thessaly who will know what to do. Being skilled in magic potions, she feeds a hallucinative substance to a bull; the enemy are induced to eat the bull, and succumb to the effects of the drug; hence the wild dance (πάντες ἀνεπήδων, διέθεον, ἀνεσκίρτων, "all of them began to leap, run, skip"). And because of it, Cnopus overcomes the enemy and captures the city. Such is the story in outline.

Further details belong to the ritual that suggested the story; to separate these details is to reconstruct the ritual. The bull, a sacrificial victim, is chosen from the herd as the largest and finest, and caparisoned with fillets and gold-flecked crimson cloths. (A show is made of preparing sacrifice; the enemy watch, and when the maddened bull bolts towards them, they are delighted by the opportunity.) The warriors seize the victim and sacrifice it and dine heartily. Then they perform the wild dance. Such is the ritual.

The story feigns that the original dancers were the enemy, the native defenders of Erythrae; when Cnopus finally attacked, "he killed them all".[257] Their camp, like the rustic shrine at Cyzicus, is set apart; possibly they are pictured as occupying the acropolis. It may seem odd that a civic festival is traced back to aliens. Yet other stories likewise distinguish the dancers from the community at large, as alien new-comers: the companions of Pelops at Olympia, the Argonauts at Cyzicus. Cronus himself, eponym of the summer festival, belongs to a different era from all the other gods worshipped throughout the year (cf. § IV sub fin.). The ritual was always regarded as extraordinary.

The dancers enjoy a feast. At Olympia, we may recall, it is said of Pelops' companions as they hymn the Mother, πρῶτοι παρὰ κρατῆρας Ἑλλάνων ... ἄεισαν νόμον, "they were the first to sing the tune beside the mixing-bowls of the Greeks" (Telestes PMG 810): another indication of the feast. At Erythrae the feast undoubtedly precedes the dance, for otherwise the story would have no point. Was the custom different at Cyzicus? Or did Apollonius simply disregard the custom in favour of the usual epic scenario, with heroes feasting and singing at the close of day? That seems quite possible.

Nothing in Cnopus' strategem points to the cult of the Mother.

---

[257] According to Pausanias (7.3.7), Erythrae had several waves of settlers—Cretans, Lycians, Carians, and Pamphylians—before "Cleopus" added a further assortment drawn from all the cities of Ionia. Despite Jacoby, n. 11 to Hippias FGrHist 421 F 1, the strategem cannot be reconciled with this account.

Inscriptions of Erythrae show that the Corybantes had a cult of their
own (so did the Curetes at Messene and Ephesus).[258] Both men and
women joined in the worship, under the respective guidance of a
priest and a priestess. References to the ritual, though cryptic, suggest high festivity; one procedure is κρατηρισμός, mixing bowls of
wine. It appears that the revelry could be abstracted, as it were,
from its larger purpose in the worship of the Mother. But in later
times even the festival Cronia was little more than merry-making.

VI. *Conclusion*

We have seen that the Mother was worshipped from of old at two
great festivals, in spring and summer, when her pastoral milieu was
in need of magic efforts. The festival names, or the derivative months,
are the plainest indication. The characteristic ritual can be recognized at a few far-flung places, even though literature is always chary
of such glimpses. But above all, the worship is imprinted in several
familiar myths. The summer festival produces the eponym "Cronus"
and his curious nature, both kindly and cruel. The spring and summer festivals together inspire the story of Zeus' birth and rearing, of
the mother goat and the guardian Curetes. There is also a wide
range of local legends to show how the Mother's cult first arose at a
given city.

As a pastoral goddess the Mother is on a footing with other principal deities who preside over staple livelihoods. She falls behind
Demeter as goddess of cereal farming and Dionysus as god of viti-
culture only because these livelihoods were of more general concern
in the historical period. But in Mycenaean times animals were pas-
tured on a very large scale; we may guess that the Mother was more
important then. Pasturing was also the dominant way of life in
Anatolia, and this accounts for a remarkable feature of Aegean and
Anatolian religion, which has not been properly grasped. The Mother
is deeply rooted in both Greece and Anatolia, just as deeply as the
pastoral regime. For other Greek gods counterparts of some sort can

---

[258] *IvErythrai* 201a 62–6/*LSAM* 25 lines 108–12 ("Corybantes"); *IvErythrai* 206/
LSAM 23 ("Cyrbantes"). Cf. Poerner, *De Curetibus* 306–9; Graf, *Nordion. Kulte* 319–
34. Curetes at Messene: Poerner 272; W. Otto, *De Sacris Messeniorum* (Halle 1933)
61–2. At Ephesus: Poerner 284–95; D. Knibbe, *RE* Suppl.12 (1970) 286–7 s.v.
Ephesos, and *Forschungen in Ephesos. Der Stadmarkt* (Vienna 1981) 70–100.

be found (and were) in Anatolia as elsewhere; but they are not in any sense the same. The Mother *is* the same. It is partly that she goes back to the time when the whole area was inhabited by people of related stock, and partly because pasturing itself changed little over long ages. The goddess and her magic rites did not need to be adapted to new conditions.

No discovery of prehistoric archaeology has ever caused such a shiver of recognition as a terracotta statuette from Çatal Hüyük, datable to the first half of the fifth millennium.[259] The Mother, with her motherly features exaggerated to the utmost, is enthroned between two mountain cats; an emerging head between her feet seems to depict the act of birth. All the peoples of Anatolia whom we can name arrived long after this. Hittites, Phrygians, Lydians, each in turn found the Mother already present. We may be sure that the first Greek speakers in the peninsula did so too. Çatal Hüyük ought to have given pause to those who declare that the cult of the Mother spread across Anatolia from east to west in the early Iron Age, and was introduced to Greece in the Archaic period.

As soon as the Greeks came to the coast of Anatolia, and this was in the Late Bronze Age, they could not fail to be struck by the likeness of the Mother there and in the homeland. This would not induce them to adopt any Anatolian cult (which means in effect to adopt the local ritual, chiefly the festivals); for they were already fully served in this respect. There is no evidence or likelihood that any Greek city, as distinct from private groups, ever adopted any element of the Anatolian worship of the Mother, in the way that Athens adopted the ritual of Adonis and Bendis. Instead, the Greeks chose to bandy names, Phrygian "Cybele" and Lydian "Cybebe", and also tales of how their own Mother came from the east.

The names and the tales are as early as the seventh and sixth centuries. Semonides and Hipponax speak of κύβηβος, Κυβήβη, Κύβηλις, and]ς ϼυβάλας is inscribed on a sherd at Locri.[260] In the epic *Phoronis* both the Idaean Dactyls and the Curetes are transmogrified into Phrygians; yet in the *Catalogue of Women* the Curetes (like the Satyrs and the Nymphs) have about the purest blood in Greece, as offspring of

---

[259] J. Mellaart, *Çatal Hüyük* (London 1967) 183–8; Vermaseren, *CCCA* 1.233 no. 773, pl. 168.
[260] Sem. fr. 36 Bergk/West; Hipp. frs. 127, 156. Guarducci, *Klio* 74 (1970) 133–8 = *Scritti scelti* (Leiden 1983) 20–5; Vermaseren, *CCCA* 4.51–2 no. 128 (but the date should be "end of the *seventh* century").

Dorus and a daughter of Phoroneus.[261] By the fifth century the Mother's Phrygian origin is commonplace, and she has taken Dionysus with her.

The names and tales are tendentious, and were not accepted by everyone. Herodotus rejects them outright. It is true that he has views of his own about the origin of the Greek gods, which leave no room for any Anatolian contribution. But in the case of the Mother he seems to follow ordinary opinion. As we saw, the story of Anacharsis presupposes that the wild revels of the Mother's summer festival at Cyzicus are wholly Greek: they are indeed the last Greek custom to be fancied by this Scythian Philhellene, and they cost him his life. Thus Book 4; in Book 5 he refers to the native Anatolian Mother, in the person of Κυβήβη of Sardis.[262] There is no doubt that "Cybebe", the *Kuvav* of Lydian inscriptions, is another form of the Mother; she is unmistakably rendered in a late Archaic relief, close to the time Herodotus speaks of.[263] He calls her ἐπιχωρίη θεός "a local goddess". In such a question Herodotus should have the last word.

---

[261] *Phoronis* frs. 2–3 Bernabé/Davies; [Hes.] *Cat.* fr. 10a line 19 (*olim* fr. 123). Cf. § V.

[262] Hdt.5.102.1.

[263] *Kuvav*: R. Gusmani, *Kadmos* 8 (1969) 158–61, and *Neue epichorische Schriftzeugnisse aus Sardis* (Cambridge, Mass. 1975) 28–30. Relief: G.M.A. Hanfmann, *Sculpture from Sardis* (Cambridge, Mass. 1978) 43–50 no. 7; Vermaseren, *CCCA* 1.134–5 no. 459, pl. 101. Cf. Hanfmann, *Sardis from Prehistoric to Roman Times* (Cambridge, Mass. 1983) 91–2, and in *Festchrift Bittel* 223–5.

REFLECTIONS OF THE MOTHER OF THE GODS IN ATTIC TRAGEDY*

Lynn Roller

Meter, the Mother of the gods, occupied an ambivalent position among the deities honored with public cult in Athens. On the one hand, Meter was recognized with a prominent shrine which formed part of the Bouleterion complex in the Athenian Agora. She was one of the deities invoked with sacrifices at the start of each meeting of the Boule, and numerous votive objects from the Agora dedicated to her testify to the intense interest in her cult among the people of Athens. At the same time, Meter projected some very unattractive qualities which appear to undercut the official status of her cult. Her rites were characterized by loud raucous music and open expression of emotionalism, activities which, in the eyes of many Greeks, carried some very dubious connotations. Her Asiatic origins were never forgotten, and thus her foreign background made her position in the heart of the city center of Athens an anomaly.

An interesting reflection of these inconsistencies may be found in the treatment of Meter in Athenian drama. The goddess is prominently featured in several plays produced during the last third of the fifth century B.C., where she is alternately a powerful deity who heals and a deity who contributes to the excesses of Dionysian ecstasism. By examining the situations in which Meter appears in Athenian drama, we can gain some sense of the Athenians' engagement with the dual identity of this figure in Athenian cult. The portrayal of Meter's character on the stage also touches on the difficult problem of the Athenians' own ambivalencies towards the status of foreign deities and towards the role of ecstatic religious cults in their religious and social life.

---

* This paper is taken from ,a larger project I am working on concerning the identity of the Anatolian Mother goddess and her place in Greek and Roman cult practice. A preliminary version of this paper was presented at a colloquium at the Department of Classics, University of California, Berkeley, in February 1995. It has benefitted from the helpful comments of those present and from the comments of Eugene N. Lane.

First, some factual background on the nature of the Meter cult in Athens is in order. As is well known, Meter, the Mother, was originally an Anatolian deity, the Greek counterpart of the Phrygian goddess *Matar*. Her presence in the Greek world can be noted from the sixth century B.C., as shrines and cult objects dedicated to her become increasingly frequent in Greek cities on the west coast of Anatolia, their colonies in the Greek west, and on the Greek mainland.[1] In Greek literature Meter's presence becomes visible and vivid in Homeric Hymn 14, where she is addressed as the Mother of the Gods. The hymn describes her as a deity who delights in the shrill cry of flutes and tympana, the clanging roar of lions and wolves, and the echoing mountains and wooded hollows. Pindar, who held Meter in high regard, presents a similarly lively picture; he describes the nocturnal festival of the goddess with its choruses, and vividly portrays the spirited music and dance which accompany the goddess's rites.[2]

Athenian interest in Meter is first evident with the appearance of a series of terracotta figurines from the Athenian Acropolis depicting a seated female figure with a lion on her lap, the standard Greek iconography of Meter; these date from the second half of the sixth century.[3] Her presence in the city's religious life became formalized

---

[1] The earliest clear evidence for Meter in the Greek world is an inscribed sherd of the late seventh or early sixth century B.C. bearing her name from the South Italian city of Lokri, Guarducci 1970. On the spread of the Meter cult in Ionia, see Naumann 1983 and Rein 1993; on Meter in the Peloponnesos, see La Genière 1985, 1986.

The goddess's Greek name, Meter, stems directly from her Phrygian predecessor, although within the Greek world, this deity also acquired a new name, Kybele, a word which, although derived from the Phrygian adjective *kubeliya*, one of the goddess's epithets in Phrygia, was never used as her name in Anatolia. The name Kybele was used to address the goddess in several passages in Greek literature (Pindar, frag. 80; *Bacchae* 78–79), but in cult texts and dedications she was always Μήτηρ, the Mother, or the Μήτηρ θεῶν, the Mother of the gods. The earliest Greek representations of Meter also show close affinities with the visual iconography of her Anatolian predecessor, but such representations become increasingly Hellenized during the course of the sixth century B.C., as the standard Phrygian image of *Matar*, a standing female figure dressed in Phrygian costume and holding a bird of prey, gives way to a seated figure wearing a chiton and himation, usually shown holding a tympanum on one arm and a small lion which rests on her lap. On the Phrygian nomenclature of the Mother goddess, see Brixhe 1979; her Greek nomenclature is well discussed by Henrichs 1976. On the development of the Greek iconography of Meter from its Phrygian prototype, see Naumann 1983.

[2] Pindar *Pythian* 3.77–79; *Dithyramb* 2.9–12.

[3] For the terracotta figurines, see Winter 1903: I, 43, n. 4; 50, n. 2a, b, c, 3. Naumann 1983: no. 111, pl. 19,3, identified a statuette depicting a seated female figure from the Athenian Acropolis as a sixth century B.C. Kybele votive, but dam-

through the construction of a shrine dedicated to her in the Athenian Agora, erected at the end of the sixth century B.C. This shrine apparently formed part of the building on the west side of the Agora traditionally identified as the Old Bouleterion, which should perhaps be restored facing east towards an altar.[4] Part of the foundations of this structure would later be reused for a Hellenistic Metroon, constructed c. 150 B.C., and since the identity of the Hellenistic building is secure through the discovery of several roof tiles stamped "Sanctuary of the Mother of the gods", it seems highly probable that its late sixth century B.C. predecessor was also a Metroon.[5] The original Metroon was evidently planned as part of a building program in the Agora begun shortly after the reforms of Kleisthenes in 508 B.C.,[6] a circumstance which implies that Meter had already found a place in civic cult practice. The original Metroon was destroyed during the Persian invasion in 480 B.C., but the ruined building was soon repaired and placed in service by c. 460 B.C.[7] In the latter part of the fifth century B.C. a new Bouleterion was constructed, slightly to the west of the older structure, but the older building was left standing and continued in use as a depository for state archives. From at least the late fifth century B.C. this archive depository was regularly

---

age to the figure's lap has erased any trace of an object such as a lion, making this identification tentative, cf. the comments of La Genière 1985: 696, n. 15.

[4] Stephen G. Miller has drawn my attention to several problems with the standard reconstruction offered for the west side of the Agora in the late sixth century B.C. by Thompson and Wycherley 1972: 29–38, pl. 4. The free-standing building which Thompson and Wycherley propose to identify as a Metroon, built in the late sixth century, may not be a single structure at all, since the foundation walls are of different materials and different heights. Miller suggests a more probable reconstruction, that the so-called Old Bouleterion was in fact a Metroon from the building's inception; the building would have faced, not north, but east onto an altar in the Agora, as did its successor, the Hellenistic Metroon. This reconstruction will be argued at greater length in Miller, *Historia* forthcoming. On the early altar, the predecessor of the altar in front of the Hellenistic Metroon, see Thompson 1966: 177. I am grateful to Professor Miller for sharing his work in progress with me.

[5] Thompson and Wycherley 1972: 29–38, one such tile is illustrated on pl. 30c.; for a full bibliography, see Travlos 1971: 352. The suggestion of Boersma 1970: 31–33, that the earliest temple was dedicated to Zeus Eleutherios is not convincing. The state archives of Athens comprised a shrine to Meter from at least the late fifth century B.C. (a problem discussed more fully below, cf. Athenaios 9.407b–c), and it seems unlikely that Zeus was displaced from his home by Meter less than a hundred years later.

[6] Thompson 1937: 135–140, 205–207. A date of c. 500 B.C. for the earliest building program in the Agora has recently been re-emphasized in a thorough study by Leslie Shear, Shear 1993: 418–422.

[7] Shear 1993: 429.

called the Metroon.[8] During the same period the Agora Metroon acquired a major cult statue, made by Agorakritos, a pupil of Pheidias. The work does not survive, but numerous small copies of it demonstrate that the piece followed the standard visual iconography of Meter, depicting her as a seated figure holding a tympanon on her arm and a lion in her lap.[9]

Thus the cult of Meter was intimately linked to the social and political institutions at the heart of the Athenian democratic government: Meter's sanctuary was a key part of the Bouleterion complex, and she was one of the deities honored with sacrifices at the start of the meetings of the Boule.[10] Yet when we meet Meter in Athenian drama, the picture we receive is significantly at odds with the established Meter of political cult. Meter's name occurs, usually in a prayer or hymn sung by the chorus, in eight (or possibly nine) works of Athenian drama ranging from c. 430 B.C. to the end of the century. They are: Euripides' *Cretans* (performed c. 430 B.C.), and *Hippolytos* (428 B.C.), and *Palamedes* (415 B.C.); Aristophanes' *Birds* (414 B.C.); Sophokles' *Philoktetes* (409 B.C.); Euripides' *Helen* (412 B.C.) and *Bacchae* (405 B.C.); a fragment of a play by Diogenes, produced near the end of the fifth century (Nauck p. 776) and a fragment of unknown authorship and date.[11] The goddess herself never appears as a character on the stage. Instead, it is her *rites* which are the focus of attention. These are quite distinctive, and differ from the standard type of rites held for the major Olympian deities: they are *orgia*, or mystery rites to be revealed only to the initiates (*Bacchae* 78–79), they are held at night (*Cretans* frag. 79 [Austin] 13–14, *Helen* 1365, *Bacchae* 146–147), and they involve the use of loud percussion instruments such as tympana and krotala (*Helen* 1308), flutes (*Helen* 1351), and free expression through dance (*Bacchae* 130–134).[12] The Mother could also appear with her lions (*Philoktetes* 391–394 and regularly in the goddess's visual iconography), whose roaring, so pleasing to her (as

---

[8] Athenaios 9.407b–c = Wycherley 1957: no. 470, a reference to Alkibiades altering a document in the Metroon. On the excavation and identification of the building, see Thompson and Wycherley 1972: 35–38.

[9] Cf. Pliny, *NH* 36.17; Pausanias 1.3.5; Arrian, *Periplous* 9. For modern attempts to reconstruct the statue, see von Salis 1913, Despines 1971: 111–123, Naumann 1983: 159–169.

[10] Aischines 3.187; Demosthenes, *Prooimia* 54; Pausanias 1.3.5; for the full ancient testimonia, see Wycherley 1957: 150–160, nos. 465–519.

[11] Kannicht and Snell 1981: frag. 629.

[12] On dance, note the observations of Hall 1989: 132–133.

stated in Homeric Hymn 14), her worshippers tried to imitate through the aural effect of these instruments. While the rites of Meter could be coupled with indigenous Greek divinities such as Demeter and Dionysos (about which I will say more later), their origin was usually placed on the edge of the Greek world, in Crete (*Cretans*), or, more often, in the goddess's Anatolian homeland, in Lydia (*Philoktetes, Bacchae*), in Phrygia (*Birds* through the link with Sabazios, *Bacchae*, Diogenes fragment), or on Mt. Ida, in Hellespontine Phrygia (*Palamedes, Helen*).[13]

To an extent these conflicting impressions of the status of the Meter cult in Athens reflect a broader dualism in Greek cult practice. The formal cults of the Greek community occupied a pivotal role as one of the powerful binding forces of Greek society,[14] serving to reinforce an individual's identification with a group, whether genos, deme, or polis. In contrast, the free-wheeling character of the music and dance movements in the Meter cult and the open expression of emotion which these enabled are typical of an ecstatic cult. The rites of an ecstatic cult were powerful precisely because they were the antithesis of normal Greek civic cult practice and its socially binding tendencies. While the formal public cults of the Greeks created boundaries between those within and those outside the group, one of the chief characteristics of an ecstatic cult was that it cut across boundaries of family group, gender and political affiliation.[15] As a result, such ecstatic rites were often an object of suspicion, even of mockery and derision. A vivid example of this is Demosthenes' use of such rites as a form of political attack on his opponent Aischines; in his speech *On the Crown*, the orator derides Aischines for dancing in the streets, handling snakes, and shouting out ritual cries, in other words, engaging in activities typical of an ecstatic cult.[16] The Phrygian background of Meter contributed substantially to this suspicious reaction, for the goddess's foreign origins meant that her cult cut across the

---

[13] Both *Palamedes*, frag. 586 Nauck, and *Helen* 1323–24, refer to Ida, without stating specifically whether Mt. Ida on Crete or Mt. Ida near Troy is meant; in both plays, however, the plot is closely connected with Troy and the Trojan war, while having no reference to Crete at all, and so it seems almost certain that this is Trojan Ida.

[14] Note Hdt.8.144, where a shared religious tradition is listed as one of the three major cohesive institutions of the Greeks.

[15] The ecstatic cult of Dionysos is the clearest example of this, cf. Segal 1978: 186–187, Vernant 1985: 48.

[16] Demosthenes, *On the Crown* 260.

ultimate boundary that even the Eleusinian Mysteries did not cross, the line between Greek and non-Greek. The ecstatic rituals of the Meter cult became, not only the bizarre actions of a few individuals, but also an example of the degenerate behavior associated with an inferior foreign people.[17]

The polarities between public civic cult and private ecstatic cult appear to have become more pronounced during the second half of the fifth century B.C. as the lines separating Athenian citizens and non-citizens, Greeks and barbarians, men and women, were more sharply drawn.[18] Because of these dichotomies, the two conflicting images of Meter, the respected political deity and the wild barbarian outsider, seem to have created further uncertainty concerning this deity's role in Athenian cult practice. We see the two sides of Meter most clearly, not in the historical or archaeological record, but in Attic tragedy, where, as has been indicated above, the rites of Meter suddenly become a noticeable factor during the late fifth century. In these plays we see a very mixed picture of Meter. In *Hippolytos* (141–144), Meter is one of the deities thought responsible for Phaedra's disturbed mental state. In *Philoktetes* (391–402) the chorus invokes the goddess in a lying oath, part of the plot to trap Philoktetes. In contrast, in Aristophanes' *Birds* (873–876) Meter appears in a more positive light as she, along with Sabazios, is hailed as a patron deity of the new ornithological polis.

In addition to these brief references, two plays in particular, the *Helen* of Euripides, produced in 412 B.C., and the same author's *Bacchae*, produced in 405 B.C., give especially prominent treatment to the Meter cult. While the specific mechanism for integrating Meter into the subject of the play is quite different in the two works, both share a focus on the goddess's Asiatic side combined with the coupling of her rites with a well-established Greek deity.

Let us start with the earlier of these two works, *Helen*. In lines 1301–1368, at a suspenseful point in the drama, the chorus breaks away from the machinations of Helen and Menelaus and their impending escape from Egypt to recount a familiar story, that of the rape of Persephone and Demeter's fruitless search for her daughter.

---

[17] Hall 1989: 103.
[18] On the increasing polarity in fifth century Athenian society between Greeks and foreigners, citizens and non-citizens, men and women, see Hall 1989 and Cartledge 1993.

The choral narrative, however, departs from the best-known telling of this story, that found in the Homeric Hymn to Demeter, at several key points. The goddess who searches is called Mother (Meter) or the Great Mother, and only in one case Deo (= Demeter, *Helen* 1343). She desists from her search, not in Eleusis but on the snow-clad peaks of Mt. Ida. It is Aphrodite, not Iambe or Baubo, who causes the Mother to forget her mourning and laugh, and she accomplishes this not through jokes but through the raucous musical instruments of ecstatic rites. After the Mother's wrath is assuaged, the question of Persephone's rape disappears entirely, as the chorus suggests that Helen has landed in her current predicament, imprisonment in Egypt, because she failed to honor the Great Mother and recommends attention to the cleansing rituals of the Mother and Dionysos.

This singular chorus, which at first seems totally inconsistent with both the light-hearted tone and the escapist subject matter of the rest of the play, has attracted considerable attention, although little agreement on its meaning. Several critics have dismissed it entirely as frivolous and irrelevant to the *Helen*, some even suggesting that Euripides interpolated this chorus from another work.[19] More thoughtful analyses of the chorus have, however, shown its general thematic suitability to the subject of this work.[20] The chorus's theme of rape and resistance is directly applicable to Helen's sojourn in Egypt, for Helen was, as she tells us, metaphorically raped by Paris and actually raped by Zeus, via Hermes, and taken forcibly to Egypt. The allusion to Trojan Ida inevitably reminds us of the Homeric Helen, the adulterous wife so familiar from the *Iliad*. The role of Aphrodite, goddess of beauty, who first makes the Mother laugh, also alludes to Helen, for Aphrodite was the divinity most closely associated with the beautiful Helen, alternately supporting her in the *Iliad* (*Iliad* 3.413–417) while opposing her in this play (*Helen* 884–886). The chorus implies that by following the example of her patron deity and placating the Asiatic Mother of the gods, Helen will reinstall herself in the favor of Aphrodite, an outcome desired by Helen herself (*Helen* 1097–1106). The link between Helen and Aphrodite reinforces the message of the second antistrophe, where the chorus asks how Helen

---

[19] Dale 1967: 147, "the complete irrelevance of this motif to the rest of the play"; Austin 1994: 177–183.
[20] Scott 1909; Zuntz 1958: 226–227; Kannicht 1969: 327–359, esp. 328; Sfameni Gasparro 1978; Cerri 1987–88.

got into such a fix, namely being wrongly detained in Egypt. "Did
you trust too much in your beauty?" (*Helen* 1368), they ask, as they
advise her to turn to the rites of the Mountain Mother for relief.[21]

The most striking feature of this choral ode is, however, its conflation
of Demeter with Meter. The identification of the Olympian deity
with the Phrygian Mother of the gods starts with the first strophe.
The goddess who searches for her daughter is named the ὀρεία Μάτερ
Θεῶν, the Mountain Mother of the gods (*Helen* 1301–1302), the clas-
sic definition of the Anatolian goddess Mother Kybele, the mountain
goddess both in her Phrygian homeland and in Greece.[22] The symbols which the Greeks associated with the rites of the Phrygian goddess are ubiquitous throughout the chorus. Shrill krotala, Meter's
instruments, (*Helen* 1308) resound as the Mother yokes wild beasts to
her chariot (1310–1311), a reference to her most common visual attribute, the lion.[23] The snow-clad slopes of Ida set the stage both for
the Mother's wrath and for the appeasement of this wrath, an allusion to one of Meter's most common epithets, Meter Idaia, a geographical inference which spoke directly to her Phrygian origins.[24]
The goddess's wrath is appeased by the ox-hide tympana, and the
deep-toned flute, the instruments which Homeric Hymn 14 assures
us are most pleasing to Meter.

To an extent the blurring of boundaries between Demeter, the revered deity of the Eleusinian Mysteries, and Meter, the uncivilized
foreigner, continues a process of assimilation of the two divinities
found throughout the Greek world from the late sixth century B.C.,
noticeable in the use of common cult artifacts and symbols.[25] By the
late fifth century the bonds between the two extended beyond the
use of shared symbols and iconography to the point where they were

---

[21] This seems a direct allusion to the better known Helen of Homeric epic and
undercuts this Helen's protest that she knows nothing of Asian Troy. Note the remarks of Zuntz 1958: 224–226; Cerri 1987–88: 60.

[22] The Mountain Mother in Anatolia, Haspels 1971: 110–111, and in Greece,
Homeric Hymn 14.5; Euripides, *Hippolytos* 141–144.

[23] To denote the chariot, the poet chose the word σατίνας, probably a Phrygian
word.

[24] Euripides, *Orestes* 1453, an invocation spoken by the Phrygian slave; cf. Strabo
10.3.12,10.3.20.

[25] The evidence from Athens includes the presence of vessels similar to those
used in the rites of Demeter found near the old Metroon, Thompson 1937: 205–
208, Nilsson 1967: 726, and an Attic black-figured olpe of the late sixth century
B.C. which depicts Demeter and Kore holding a stalk of wheat while accompanied
by a lion, Meter's symbol, Metzger 1965: 22, no. 43.

explicitly equated in literature, by Pindar and Melanippides.[26] The two goddesses were also closely affiliated in Attic cult practice, as can be seen through the key role played by one of Meter's sanctuaries, the Metroon in Agrai, in the preliminary rites of the Eleusinian Mysteries.[27] Moreover, Meter's function as the keeper of Athenian laws and statutes parallels a similar status for Demeter, in her capacity as Demeter Thesmophoros, the bringer of law. What stands out in the third chorus of *Helen*, however, is not only the syncretism between the two Mother deities, but the frequent references to Asiatic venue in the traditional tale of Greek Demeter. The site of Demeter's appeasement, in Asia on the slopes of Mt. Ida, is a clear allusion to both Phrygia and Troy. This places the activity of one of Attica's most hallowed shrines, Eleusis, in a barbarian land. Such syncretism of sacred place as well as of deity is, to my knowledge, unparalleled in Greek literature; it equates the sacred, unspoken rites of Demeter (*Helen* 1308), not just with Asiatic barbarians, but with Phrygians, a people whose name was widely used in the fifth century as a synonym both for Trojans and, indirectly, for Persians, still the most formidable barbarian enemies of the Greeks.[28] Moreover, the healing of the Mother's wrath, according to the second antistrophe, can be accomplished by the ivy, fawnskins, and all-night Bacchic revelry, the rites of Dionysos, which the *Bacchae* assures us are of Asiatic origin. To find a healing for her woes, Helen must turn not to her Greek homeland, as she claims she wishes to, but to Asia.

This integration of Asiatic deities and rituals into Greek cult is even more pronounced in the *Bacchae*. In this play Meter appears only tangentially, as one of the deities whose worship reinforces that of Dionysos. Her Phrygian tympana, inventions both of Meter and of Dionysos (*Bacchae* 58–59), are the appropriate accompaniment to the god's dance. The celebration of the mystic rites, the *orgia*, of the Great Mother Kybele, is the mark of one who has been blessed with

---

[26] Pindar, *Isthmian* 7.3–4; Melanippides, Page, *PMG*: frag. 764; Derveni Papyrus, col. XVIII, line 8, published in *ZPE* 47 (1982) supplement. For commentary on the passage, see Kannicht 1969: 330. For discussions of the relationship of Demeter and Meter, see Graf 1974: 155, n. 24, van Straten 1976, and Versnel 1990: 108, although, unlike Versnel, I see the process as one of bilateral assimilation rather than the deliberate acculturation of a foreigner.

[27] Travlos 1971: 112.

[28] The Phrygians as synonymous with Trojans, Hall 1988, 1989: 38–39; on the merging of Trojans and Persians in fifth century B.C. imagery, Bacon 1961: 71–72, 101, and Hall 1989: 68–69.

initiation into the mysteries of Dionysos (*Bacchae* 77–79). While Dionysos insists throughout the play that he is Greek-born, a god of and for the Greeks, and that the tragic end of the Greek king Pentheus results from Pentheus' failure to recognize that fact, the play also makes clear that Dionysos's rites are Asiatic rites, particularly closely associated with the Anatolian cultures of Phrygia and Lydia (*Bacchae* 13–17, 64–65). Indeed, it is their foreign character, their stark and unflattering contrast with Greek rituals, which causes Pentheus to reject them.

Apart from specific references to Meter, the goddess is present in the broader story line of the *Bacchae* in a very different way. The plot of the *Bacchae*, a narrative of resistance to a foreign deity and the ensuing consequences of such resistance, shows remarkable similarity to a peculiar story purporting to record the circumstances of the founding of the Athenian Metroon. We first learn of this tale from a scholiast on Aischines' oration against Ktesiphon; the scholiast cites a work entitled Philippics whose authorship is uncertain, but surely was part of the anti-Macedonian literature from the second half of the fourth century B.C. The scholiast records that the Athenians made a part of the Bouleterion a sanctuary of Rhea (the Mother of the gods) on account of that Phrygian man: μέρος τοῦ βουλευτηρίου ἐποίησαν οἱ Ἀθηναῖοι τὸ Μητρῷον, ὅ ἐστιν ἱερὸν τῆς Ρέας, διὰ τὴν αἰτίαν ἐκείνου τοῦ Φρυγός.[29] The earliest narratives recounting this story in any detail are, however, all much later than the event they propose to explain: the story appears in the Orations of the fourth-century A.C. Roman emperor Julian, and in the works of Byzantine lexicographers, with the fullest account found in the works of Photios, writing in the ninth century A.C.[30] Photios' narrative agrees with the account of Julian, but offers more extensive detail:

μητραγύρτης. ἐλθών τις εἰς τὴν Ἀττικὴν ἐμύει τὰς γυναῖκας τῇ μητρὶ τῶν θεῶν, ὡς ἐκεῖνοί φασιν. οἱ Ἀθηναῖοι ἀπέκτειναν αὐτὸν ἐμβάλλοντες ἐπὶ βάραθρον ἐπὶ κεφαλήν. λοιμοῦ δὲ γενομένου ἔλαβον χρησμὸν ἱλάσασθαι τὸν πεφονευμένον. καὶ διὰ τοῦτο ᾠκοδόμησαν βουλευτήριον, ἐν ᾧ ἀνεῖλον τὸν μητραγύρτην. καὶ περιφράττοντες αὐτὸν καθιέρωσαν τῇ μητρὶ τῶν θεῶν ἀναστήσαντες καὶ ἀνδριάντα τοῦ μητραγύρτου. ἐχρῶντο δὲ τῷ μητρῴῳ ἀρχείῳ καὶ νομοφυλακείῳ, καταχώσαντες καὶ τὸ βάραθρον.

---

[29] Σ Aischines 3.187 = Wycherley 1957: 151 no. 467.
[30] Julian 5.159a; Suda, s.v. μητραγύρτης; Photios, s.v. μητραγύρτης. The ancient testimonia on the Metroon have been collected by Wycherley 1957: 151–160.

Metragyrtes: a certain man came to Attica and initiated the women into the mysteries of the Mother of the gods, as some say. The Athenians killed him by throwing him into a pit on his head. When a plague occurred they received an oracle ordering them to propitiate the murdered man. And because of this they built the Bouleterion, [on the spot] on which they killed the metragyrtes. Having made a fence around him (the Suda says "around it," i.e., the building), they consecrated it to the Mother of the gods, and set up a statue of the metragyrtes. They used the Metroon for an archive and repository of law, and they filled up the pit.

In its present form this narrative exemplifies a resistance myth, a well-known myth-type describing the initial rejection and ultimate triumph of a new deity or its representative. Such a resistance myth is precisely the plot of the *Bacchae*.[31] The narrative recounting the establishment of the Meter cult in Athens assigns the role filled by Dionysos in the play to the metragyrt, the begging priest of Meter. Both narratives take as their main theme the actions of a stranger who comes to town (Thebes or Athens) to introduce a new deity and new religious rites. The activities of the stranger incur the wrath of the dominant political force in the community, the king (*Bacchae*) or the male citizens of Athens (metragyrt story), and these capture the stranger and kill him, or attempt to do so. The deity then reacts violently, punishing a larger group, the family of Pentheus (*Bacchae*) or the city of Athens (metragyrt story), including the morally innocent as well as the guilty. Thus the new deity is revealed to be both powerful and genuine, brushing aside all challenges to its authority.

The purpose of such a tale is not to condemn the deity's priest, but to praise the deity, and the concept of resistance to the deity forms an opportunity for the deity to demonstrate its power and overcome all challenges to its authority.[32] In such a tale, the resisting agent is shown in the commission of a religious crime.[33] His chief fault is largely one of omission, namely that he does not recognize the deity, or does not recognize the deity's messenger, the stranger

---

[31] Hall 1989: 152.

[32] Ancient parallels for this myth-type are numerous, ranging from the rejection of Apollo's priest in the opening scene of Homer's *Iliad* to an anecdote connected with the cult of the Magna Mater in Rome, Plutarch, *Marius* 17.9, Diodoros 36.13, discussed by Versnel 1990: 105, nt. 35. Another example is the *logos* of Anacharsis, Herodotos 4.76, which exhibits the same pattern of introduction, resistance, and death of the deity's celebrant.

[33] Burnett 1970: 19.

(in the first 800 lines of the *Bacchae*) or the priest of Meter (metragyrt story). The agent of resistance at first seems justified in his actions, because he is (he believes) upholding the moral norms of the community; in both cases these are unstated, but include the assumption that men should be dominant over women and that Greeks should be dominant over foreigners. "Should I enslave myself to women?" Pentheus asks (*Bacchae* 803), reminding us that the metragyrt came to attempt to convert the women of Athens, an action which supposedly provoked his execution. Likewise, when told by the stranger (Dionysos) that all the barbarians celebrate his *orgia*, his mystic rites, Pentheus retorts that this merely shows how foreigners are much more foolish than Greeks (*Bacchae* 402–403). This too is a point featured in the metragyrt tale, where the Phrygian background of the priest and deity makes the metragyrt doubly offensive.

The swift and disproportionately severe punishment meted out to the resisting agent seems all the more unusual, given that these attitudes, the dominance of men over women and of Greeks over foreigners, typify values that were, one assumes, widely shared by Euripides' audience. To an extent this is a motif of the traditional myth-type: the deity or his/her agent who comes down to earth and walks around in human form is never recognized or suitably entertained by the dominant individual or social group in the community, but only by someone of low status.[34] Yet in both the *Bacchae* and the metragyrt legend this circumstance goes beyond the conventions of the resistance myth, for it defines the very essence of an ecstatic cult. The power of such a cult lies precisely in its capacity to undermine the standard social order built upon maintaining the barriers of gender and ethnicity. In both the *Bacchae* and the metragyrt tale, a cult which breaks down gender and racial barriers tests the city in a very special way. The city can only restore the basis of its social order if it accepts the new deity which appears to threaten the city.

Thus in these two plays, the *Helen* and the *Bacchae*, the poet has deliberately broken down the barriers between the 'Asiatic' and the Greek form of religious experience by integrating the story of a respected Greek civic deity, Demeter or Dionysos, with the rites and symbols of the foreign deity Meter. The message here may be less a direct comment on the Phrygian origin of Meter; the poet's descriptions of 'Asiatic cult' and 'Asiatic ecstasism' in this context are not

---

[34] Burnett 1970: 25–27.

literal descriptions of Phrygian rites (it is unlikely that most Athenians knew much about Phrygia), but rather a definition of a type of religious experience, one which lay outside the closed boundaries of Greek civic cult and one which many Greeks saw as the antithesis of Greek cult practice.[35] The poet affirms that such an ecstatic cult and the open, all-inclusive nature of its rites, is (or should be) firmly grounded in the Greek experience. Both plays suggest that the loud raucous music and pulsing rhythm of the goddess's instruments, foreign to Greek ears, are the proper way to address an important native Greek divinity. In both works the rites of foreigners, specifically of Phrygians, have become the most effective way to confront the crisis experienced by the protagonist. And in both plays, one seeks a resolution of a crisis, not in the dominant moral or social values of a community's elite, but in a healing ritual brought by a foreign deity.

In giving this reading of Meter in Greek tragedy, I would like to suggest that in their references to the Phrygian goddess, the tragic poets, particularly Euripides, were part of a contemporary debate on the question of whether the open expression of religious rapture was truly Greek, or a product of inferior foreigners.[36] In the case of Meter the debate may have taken on added vigor because the goddess's principal shrine in Athens was located in the heart of the Athenian Agora, where her temple was used as a repository for the laws and documents of the Athenian democratic council. The statement of the Aischines scholiast, that the Athenians made a part of the Bouleterion into a Metroon *because of that Phrygian!* (emphasis mine),[37] implies a close relationship between the Metroon and the workings of the Athenian Boule, a point affirmed by the archaeological evidence. At the same time this passage strongly implies that the presence of a Phrygian deity, worshipped with (supposedly) foreign ritual and emotional excess, in the heart of Athens, had, by the late fifth century B.C., come to

---

[35] Hall 1989: 152–154.

[36] This debate has been vigorously pursued by a number of modern scholars as well, who have found the music, dance, and open expression of emotion in the Meter cult unbecoming to their notions of Greek religious ritual. In particular, several scholars have rejected the possibility of a Metroon in the Athenian Agora *c.* 500 B.C. on the grounds that an ecstatic cult of Oriental origins would have been too offensive to Athenian sensibilities, see Picard 1938: 97; Cerri 1983; Frappicini 1987: 25; Francis 1990: 112–120. The issue of Meter's Oriental qualities and their impact on Athens is well summarized by Versnel 1990: 105–111; see also Dodds 1960: xxii–xxiii.

[37] Note also the comments of Versnel 1990: 106, n. 37.

be seen as an embarrassment. The increasing association of Meter's rites with so-called "oriental" practices had given the goddess's cult a strong taint of inferiority it did not have a century earlier, and this was explained through attributing the deity's presence as a circumstance forced upon the city for their failure to recognize the deity's power.

Apart from this general debate, was there a particular historical circumstance behind the frequent notice given to Meter's rites in so many late fifth century plays? Some have wondered whether the references to Meter presuppose a commentary on a contemporary event, the actual murder of a priest of Meter. This interpretation is supported by several details in Photios' story. The negative image of the metragyrt is well documented in sources of the fourth century B.C. and later.[38] In addition, the method of execution used on the priest implies historical veracity, for the act of throwing a convicted criminal into an open pit was a form of capital punishment carried out in Athens in the fifth century and earlier, but had been abandoned by the end of the fourth century B.C.[39] The tale's historicity is further supported by a scholiast on Aristophanes' *Ploutos*, which offers an alternative explanation for the priest's murder: τὸν Φρύγα τὸν τῆς Μητρὸς ἐνέβαλον ὡς μεμηνότα ἐπειδὴ προέλεγεν ὅτι ἔρχεται ἡ Μήτηρ εἰς τὴν ἐπιζήτησιν τῆς Κόρης. (They [= the Athenians] threw Meter's Phrygian [into the pit] because they considered him mad, since he proclaimed that the Mother was coming on her quest for Kore.)[40] This implies that the priest was executed, not only because he supported a foreign deity, but because he was charged with profaning the Eleusinian Mysteries by ritually assimilating the cults of Meter and Demeter.[41] Yet this close correlation between the rites of Meter and of Demeter is precisely what is recounted in the third chorus of the *Helen*, where the Mountain Mother searches for τᾶς ἀρρήτου κούρας, the maid whose name cannot be spoken (*Helen* 1306–1307), a formula specifically referent to the Eleusinian Mysteries.[42] Here Euripides has equated

---

[38] Aristotle, *Rhetoric* 1405a, defines the office of metragyrt as ἄτιμος, dishonorable. Athenaios 12.541e, describing Dionysios of Syracuse, comments that he spent his last days as a metragyrtes, a mark of how low the former Sicilian tyrant had sunk. Similarly disparaging remarks were made about a metragyrtes of Ptolemy IV, cf. Plutarch, *Cleomenes* 36.
[39] For the evidence, see Cerri 1983: 161–162.
[40] Σ Aristophanes, *Ploutos* 431 = Suda, s.v. βάραθρον.
[41] Cerri 1983: 165; Versnel 1990: 109.
[42] Cerri 1983: 157.

the mysteries of the Phrygian goddess with those of Demeter in a manner highly reminiscent of this scholiast's passage. One wonders if the poet may have used this play to comment on an actual contemporary event, much as he used *The Trojan Women* to comment on the excesses of the Peloponnesian War.[43] And even if the metragyrt legend is not literally true, it forms a plausible record of the general climate of hostility to the foreign origins and perceived emotional excesses of the Phrygian Mother's rites.

Yet Euripides chose to stress, not hostility, but the inclusive and intrinsically Greek nature of the Meter cult. In this way as in so many other ways, the tragic poet was at odds with the prevailing attitudes of his times. To him, the Phrygian goddess is not the representative of a marginal group, but the deity of the whole city, as she is physically placed in the city center, the Agora. The practices of her cult, far from being eccentric, form the center of public life. The cult of Meter is able to take part in both aspects of Greek cult practice, as the goddess is worshipped both as a civic cult of the polis and a deity of private ecstasism. The poet stresses that the foreign deity is necessary to the city precisely because of that deity's ability to break down barriers between public and private cult.

The irony is that Euripides' voice was lost on his immediate successors. By the fourth century B.C. the negative picture of Meter's

---

[43] Such a literal historical reading of the metragyrt tale, while denied outright by Wilamowitz 1879: 195 n. 4, Will 1960: 101, n. 2, and Bömer 1963: 10, n. 4, has recently been strongly defended by Cerri 1983 and Versnel 1990. The chief drawback to this interpretation has been the difficulty of fitting the legend into the framework of Athenian history. There are two schools of thought concerning the chronological context into which the legend should be placed, either the late sixth century B.C. (Versnel 1990: 105–111; Nilsson 1967: 725–727), the date of the Athenian Metroon's foundation as attested by the archaeological record, or 430 B.C., a date which assumes that the plague mentioned in Photios' account is the plague at the outset of the Peloponnesian War (Foucart 1873: 64–66; Picard 1938: 97; Cerri 1983; Frappicini 1987: 25; Francis 1990: 115–118). Both of these suggestions have significant and obvious drawbacks. Neither the original construction of the Metroon nor its subsequent history shows any sign of any resistance to the cult of Meter in Athens, in fact quite the opposite, as the sanctuary of the goddess was revived in the fifth century and given an important cult statue and a special political status as archive center. And a date of *c.* 430 B.C. relies on a contrived coincidence (there may well have been more than one plague in Athens!) and is undercut by the fact that no contemporary source mentions the event. As I have noted above, the legend does not record a literal record of the introduction of Meter's cult into Athens, but the negative public reaction of at least some Greeks to this ecstatic cult during the late fifth and fourth centuries. The late sources and contrived nature of the metragyrt story preclude a firm judgement on the question of its historical accuracy.

rites, and, by implication, the negative picture of foreigners associated with the goddess's ecstatic rites, was axiomatic, enshrined in a number of fourth century literary works.[44] In the Hellenistic period such a point of view was to be expressed even more forcefully.[45] The plea from the Greek playwright Euripides to allow the healing properties of Asiatic emotionalism to penetrate the barriers of self-centered Hellenic political interests was ultimately unsuccessful.

BIBLIOGRAPHY

Austin, N. 1994. *Helen of Troy and her Shameless Phantom* (Ithaca and London).

Bacon, H. 1961. *Barbarians in Greek Tragedy* (New Haven).

Bömer, F. 1963. *Untersuchungen über die Religion der Sklaven in Griechenland und Rom* IV (Mainz).

Boersma, J.S. 1970. *Athenian Building Policy from 561/0 to 405/4 B.C.* (Groningen).

Brixhe, Claude. 1979. "Le nom de Cybèle," *Die Sprache* 25: 40–45.

Burnett, A.P. 1970. "Pentheus and Dionysus: Host and Guest," *Classical Philology* 65: 15–29.

Cartledge, P. 1993. *The Greeks. A Portrait of Self and Others* (Oxford).

Cerri, G. 1983. "La Madre degli Dei nell'*Elena* in Euripide," *Quaderni di Storia* 18: 155–195.

————. 1987–1988. "Il Messaggio dionisiaco nell'*Elena* di Euripide," *Annali dell'Istituto Universitario Orientale di Napoli. Sezione Filologico-Letteraria* 9–10: 43–67.

Dale, A.M. 1967. *Euripides' Helen. Text and Commentary* (Oxford).

Despines, G.I. 1971. Συμβολὴ στὴ μελέτη τοῦ ἔργου τοῦ Ἀγορακρίτου (Athens).

Dodds, E.R. 1960. *Euripides' Bacchae. Edition, Introduction and Commentary* (Oxford).

Foucart, P. 1873. *Des associations religieuses chez les grecs* (Paris).

Francis, E.D. 1990. *Image and Idea in Fifth-Century Greece* (London and New York).

Frappicini, N. 1987. "L'arrivo di Cibele in Attica," *Parola del Passato* 42: 12–26.

Graf, F. 1974. *Eleusis und die orphische Dichtung Athens in vorhellenistischer Zeit* ((Berlin).

Guarducci, M. 1970. "Cibele in un' epigrafe arcaica di Locri Epizefirî," *Klio* 52: 133–138.

Hall, E. 1989. *Inventing the Barbarian* (Oxford).

Haspels, C.H.E. 1971. *The Highlands of Phrygia* (Princeton).

Henrichs, A. 1976. "Despoina Kybele: ein Beitrag zur religiösen Namenkunde," *Harvard Studies in Classical Philology* 80: 253–286.

Kannicht, R. 1969. *Euripides' Helena. Text und Kommentar* (Heidelberg).

Kannicht, R. and B. Snell. 1981. *Tragicorum Graecorum Fragmenta*, vol. 2 (Göttingen).

---

[44] This is particularly true of fourth century comedy, cf. Antiphanes, *Metragyrtes*, frag. 154 (Kock II 74), cf. also frag. 159, the metragyrtes as a magician. Other examples cited by Versnel 1990: 109. Note also the sources cited above, note 38.

[45] Examples include an anecdote popular with Hellenistic epigrammatists, the encounter of the Gallos with a lion, of which five examples survive, *Anth.Pal.*6.217–220 and 237. Kallimachos also commented on the exotic behavior of Meter's followers; note *Iambos* 3.35 (Pfeiffer frag. 193), where the poet refers to one who "tosses Phrygian hair to Kybebe (*sic*) and cries out to Adonis", and *Iambos* 4.105 (Pfeiffer frag. 194), where the laurel tree swears "by the Mistress (Δέσποινα) to whom cymbals resound."

La Genière, J. de. 1985. "De la Phrygie à Locres Épizéphyrienne: les chemins de Cybèle," *Mélanges de l'École francaise de Rome. Antiquité* 97: 693–717.

———. 1986. "Le culte de la mère des dieux dans le Péloponnèse," *Comptes rendus de l'Académie des Inscriptions et Belles-Lettres*: 29–46.

Metzger, H. 1965. *Recherches sur l'imagerie athénienne* (Paris).

Miller, S.G. forthcoming. "Old Bouleterion and Old Metroon in the Classical Agora of Athens," *Historia. Einzelschriften* (forthcoming).

Naumann, F. 1983. *Die Ikonographie der Kybele in der phrygischen und der griechischen Kunst. Istanbuler Mitteilungen*, Beiheft 28 (Tübingen).

Nilsson, M.P. 1967. *Geschichte der griechischen Religion* I (3rd ed., Munich).

Picard, C. 1938. "Le complexe Métrôon-Bouleterion-Prytanikon, à l'Agora d'Athènes," *Revue Archéologique* 12: 97–101.

Rein, M.J. 1993. "Phrygian *Matar*: Emergence of an Iconographic Type," *American Journal of Archaeology* 97: 318.

Salis, A. von. 1913. "Die Göttermutter des Agorakritos," *Jahrbuch des deutschen archäologischen Instituts* 28: 1–26.

Scott, W. 1909. "The 'Mountain-Mother' Ode in the *Helena* of Euripides," *Classical Quarterly* 3, pp. 161–179.

Segal, C. 1978. "The Menace of Dionysus: Sex Roles and Reversals in Euripides' *Bacchae*," *Arethusa* 11: 185–202.

Sfameni Gasparro, G. 1978. "Connotazioni metroache di Demetra nel Coro dell' « Elena » (vv. 1301–1365)," *Hommages à Maarten J. Vermaseren*, M.B. de Boer and T.A. Eldridge, editors (Leiden) III: 1148–1187.

Shear, T.L. 1993. "The Persian Destruction of Athens," *Hesperia* 62: 383–482.

Straten, F.T. van. 1976. "Assimilatie van vreemde goden: archeologisch bronnen-materiaal," *Lampas* 9: 42–50.

Thompson, H. 1937. "Buildings on the West Side of the Agora," *Hesperia* 6: 1–226.

———. 1966. "The Annex to the Stoa of Zeus in the Athenian Agora," *Hesperia* 35: 171–187.

Thompson, H. and R.E. Wycherley. 1972. *The Athenian Agora* XIV. *The Agora of Athens: the History, Shape and Uses of an Ancient City Center* (Princeton).

Travlos, J. 1971. *Pictorial Dictionary of Ancient Athens* (Tübingen).

Vernant, J.-P. 1985. "Le Dionysos masqué des *Bacchantes* d'Euripide," *L'Homme* 25,1: 31–58.

Versnel, H.S. 1990. *Ter Unus. Isis, Dionysos, Hermes: Three Studies in Henotheism. Inconsistencies in Greek Religion* I (Leiden).

Wilamowitz-Moellendorff, U. von. 1879. "Die Galliamben des Kallimachos und Catullus," *Hermes* 14: 194–201.

Will, E. 1960. "Aspects du culte et de la légende de la grande mère dans le monde Grec," *Éléments orientaux dans la religion grecque ancienne*: 95–111 (Paris).

Winter, Franz. 1903. *Die Typen der figürlichen Terrakotten* (Berlin).

Wycherley, R.E. 1957. *The Athenian Agora* III. *Literary and Epigraphical Testimonia* (Princeton).

G. Zuntz. 1958. "On Euripides' Helena: Theology and Irony," *Entretiens sur l'Antiquité Classique* 6. *Fondation Hardt*: 201–227.

THE HIGH PRIESTS OF THE TEMPLE OF
ARTEMIS AT EPHESUS

James O. Smith

The cult of Artemis at Ephesus was a unique syncretism of Greek and Oriental elements. Several types of cult officials are unique to this sanctuary. The relevant ancient evidence reveals much about some of these officials. But the high priests of this cult, the so-called "Megabyzoi," are mostly an enigma. What modern scholars "know" about them consists entirely of assumptions supported by ambiguous ancient information. Indeed, an analysis of the ancient references shows that the very existence of a class of priests who were called "Megabyzoi" by the Ephesians and the "fact" that they were eunuchs are based on ambiguous and often contradictory ancient information.

Sources

The ancient evidence for the "Megabyzoi" is, at first glance, abundant. Several writers, some as early as the fourth century B.C., mentioned them. Though most of these authors wrote during the Roman period, and some of the earlier sources are playwrights, there are still several clear references to the "Megabyzoi" at Ephesus. Archaeological evidence also seems to support the existence of this "class" of priests, but this evidence has recently been questioned.

Description of the references to Ephesian "Megabyzoi" in ancient literary and other sources

Several ancient authors clearly refer to men named Megabyzos who were priests of Artemis at Ephesus.[1] A brief description of these authors' references to the "Megabyzoi" follows.

---

[1] The citations of authors and works in this paper will be in accordance with the Oxford Classical Dictionary.

In the early fourth century, Xenophon recorded (*An.*5.3.4.2–5.3.8.3) that during his trip back to Greece from Persia, he stopped at Ephesus and left some of his booty with Megabyzos, a "*neokoros* of Artemis," for safekeeping. Megabyzos later travelled to Greece and returned the money. Diogenes Laertius gave essentially the same account, clearly drawing on Xenophon (2.51.8–12, 2.52.7–10).

Strabo (14.1.23) gave the most complete account, saying that the Ephesians had eunuch priests, whom they called "Megabyzoi." These priests were brought in from other places.

Pliny referred to the "Megabyzoi" twice. Once (*HN* 35.36.93) he referred to a painting at Ephesus of the procession of (a) "Megabyzus," the priest of Diana at Ephesus, by Apelles, and once (*HN* 35.40.131–2) to a painting (also at Ephesus) by Nicias on the tomb of a "Megabyzus," the priest of Diana at Ephesus.

Pseudo-Heraclitus (*Ep.*9) berated the Ephesians for castrating the "Megabyzos" since they could not tolerate a real man as the priest of their virgin goddess.

Appian (*BC* 5.9) mentioned a "priest of Artemis at Ephesus, whom they called Megabyzos," whom Marc Antony met during his campaigns in the East in 39 B.C.

Plautus mentioned (*Bacch.* ll.307–8) Megabulus, the father of Theotimus, a priest of Artemis at Ephesus. Several elements of this account seem inconsistent with the above-mentioned descriptions of the "Megabyzoi" at Ephesus. The name is slightly different. Megabulus *himself* is not called a priest of Artemis at Ephesus. He also had a son, which would take some explaining for a eunuch priest. But the connection of a name so similar to Megabyzus with the priesthood of Artemis at Ephesus makes it likely that Plautus here is indeed speaking of a "Megabyzus" from Ephesus. If so, this would be the earliest such reference independent of Xenophon.

Other ancient authors mention a "Megabyzus" who may have been a priest of Artemis of Ephesus but who is not specifically said to be, and who cannot be identified as another historically attested "Megabyzos." These authors include Plutarch, Lucian, and Quintilian.

Plutarch (*Alex.*42.1.5–42.2.1) mentioned a "Megabyzos" in connection with an unnamed sanctuary in Asia Minor. This man is never specifically associated with Ephesus, much less the priests of Artemis there. Also, this reference is in the context of letters from Alexander to officials such as Seleucus and Craterus, so it is likely that this "Megabyzos" is an official associated with Alexander instead of a priest. Plutarch also referred (*Quomodo adulator ab amico internoscatur* 58D, *De tranq.anim.*471 f., where he was called "Megabyzos the Persian") to a Megabyzos dressed in purple robes and gold who was painted by Apelles.[2] In this case, one can possibly identify him as a priest of Artemis at Ephesus, since Pliny, as mentioned above, said that Apelles painted a procession of "Megabyzus." It is possible, however, that this was again an official serving under Alexander.

Lucian mentioned (*Timon* 22.8) a "Megabyzos" in connection with great wealth, but did not further identify him. It is therefore unknown whether this was a "Megabyzos" from Ephesus or a priest.

Quintilian spoke (*Inst.*5.12.21) of a "Megabyzus" beside Bagoas, a well-known eunuch, as unfit models for Greek master sculptors and painters, presumably due to a bodily imperfection. But he did not identify Megabyzus as a priest, and considering Pliny's statement, mentioned above, that the "Megabyzoi" were painted by Apelles and Nicias, it is unlikely that Quintilian was here referring to a priest at Ephesus, unless he is indulging in some roundabout criticism of Apelles and Nicias.

The epigraphic evidence, however, is not fruitful at all in providing references to the "Megabyzoi." Well over four thousand ancient inscriptions have so far been found at Ephesus. A vast majority are from the Roman period, and while many of the older ones are short and/or fragmentary, many are from the fourth century B.C. or earlier. Major and minor attendants of the Temple of Artemis at Ephesus are attested by inscriptions from the Greek period, such as the Essenes,[3] the *neopoioi*,[4] the *hierokerux* (sacred herald),[5] the *kouretes*,[6] the *epheboi*,[7] and the *kosmeterai* (Mistresses of Robes).[8] But the name Megabyzus does not appear in any form in any of the hundreds of extant inscriptions found at Ephesus from the Greek period, or indeed in any of the inscriptions so far found at the city.

---

[2] Aelian (*VH* 2.2) gave the same account, except that he places it in the studio of Zeuxis, who flourished in the late fifth and early fourth centuries B.C. Plutarch's account, however, supported by Pliny, is probably correct.

[3] See Hermann Wankel, ed., *Inschriften Griechischer Städte aus Kleinasien*, Vol. 11.1–17.4, *Die Inschriften von Ephesos*, Bonn, 1979, (hereafter cited as *Inschr Eph*) Vol. 17.4, Index, s.v. "*Essen*" for a full list of the inscriptions which refer to the Essenes.

[4] *Inschr Eph* #4,l.21, 1450, 1452, 1454, 1458, 1461, 1466, 1471.

[5] *Inschr Eph* #2,l.53.

[6] *Inschr Eph* #1449.

[7] *Inschr Eph* #6.

[8] *Inschr Eph* #1449.

A sixth-century B.C. ivory statuette of a "eunuch-priest" discovered in the archaic Artemision at Ephesus certainly appears to bolster the case for eunuch high-priests there. Cecil Smith showed that this piece (his no. 10) bears a marked similarity to several other roughly contemporary Oriental-type statuettes of eunuch-priests from other parts of Asia Minor.[9] This statuette, however, has now been identified as a woman by Anton Bammer and others,[10] thus removing the only independent verification of the ancient literary evidence.

Possible sources for the references to Ephesian
"Megabyzoi" by ancient authors

An analysis of the sources used by the ancient authors who mentioned the "Megabyzoi" would be very helpful in an assessment of the probable reliability of their accounts. Such an analysis of the passages which undeniably refer to a "Megabyzus" who was a priest at Ephesus and those who *may* refer to such an individual follows. In many cases, this analysis will be no more than conjecture.

Of those who definitely refer to the "Megabyzoi" at Ephesus, Xenophon, of course, recorded a personal experience with an individual priest of Artemis at Ephesus for his account. His account served as the source for that of Diogenes Laertius.

The source of Strabo's account is uncertain, but enough is known about him that some conjectures can be made. He alone of those who wrote about the "Megabyzoi" is known to have visited Ephesus. In his description of Ephesus in which he mentioned the "Megabyzoi", he cited the Ephesian geographer Artemidorus as a source and interviewed native Ephesians. He unfortunately did not identify the source of his account of the "Megabyzoi." But considering that he mentioned them immediately after a description of the temple and its artworks, for which he used information from native Ephesians, they rather than Artemidorus are more probable to have been his source. Possibly he saw one of Pliny's paintings of "Megabyzus" there (although he never mentioned it in his account) and asked the Ephe-

---

[9] "Chap. IX. The Ivory Statuettes," in *The Excavations at Ephesus*, David George Hogarth, ed., London, 1908, Vol. 1, pp. 160, 172–3.
[10] "Neue weibliche Statuetten aus dem Artemision von Ephesos," *JOAI* 5 (1985), p. 57; Cf. U. Muss, *Studien zur Bauplastik des archaischen Artemisions von Ephesos*, 1983, p. 102.

sians about this man. His account may well have been drawn from information provided by the locals about the tomb mentioned by Pliny. If Artemidorus had been Strabo's source for his description of the cult, the latter would have given more detailed information. In his account about Ephesus, however, Strabo appeared to have drawn only geographic information from Artemidorus.

Pliny's source is far more uncertain. He probably assembled his account, as was his custom, by having books read to him, making notes, then wrote using excerpts from others' writings mixed with personal observations.[11] Since both his references to the "Megabyzoi" occurred in descriptions of paintings as part of a discussion of the development of art, his excerpted source may have been no more than a description of paintings by different artists. It would therefore not be of much use in a detailed evaluation of the "Megabyzoi" at Ephesus. Pliny could easily have misunderstood a reference to a class of "Megabyzoi" where his source did not mean to imply such a theory. Again this reference may well derive ultimately from an explanation of an artwork at Ephesus given by a native to a visitor well after the "Megabyzoi" had passed out of existence.

Pseudo-Heraclitus' sources for his mention of the "Megabyzus" at Ephesus (*Ep*.9) are unknown. Though the author pretends to be the classical philosopher, his epistles have long been accepted as later forgeries. A recent study indicated that these writings are "products of the first century and a half of the Roman Empire."[12] The author therefore probably would have had access to a wide variety of sources about Ephesus including Plutarch and possibly Pliny.

The source(s) for Appian's reference to "Megabyzos" is also unknown. It occurs in the context of Marc Antony's visit to Ephesus in 39 B.C. Appian may therefore have used the histories of Augustus, Livy, or even Nicolaus of Damascus, but not Asinius Pollio, who recorded the events only up to 42 B.C. But he may also have been familiar with Strabo and/or Pliny and their sources and may have drawn his information from them. Indeed, his historical source may only have mentioned that Antony visited the high-priest of Artemis at Ephesus and that Appian incorporated the term "Megabyzos" for this particular priest from another source.

---

[11] Pliny the Younger, *Ep*.III.5.10.
[12] Harold W. Attridge, *First-Century Cynicism in the Epistles of Heraclitus* (Harvard Theological Studies XXIX), Missoula, Montana, 1976, pp. 3-12.

Little is known about the sources of the ancient accounts which may refer to Ephesian "Megabyzoi." Lucian, Plutarch and Quintilian certainly had access to a number of sources dealing with one "Megabyzos" or another, whether or not they were Ephesians or priests. But which of these sources they utilized is totally unknown. Plautus seems to have had some garbled knowledge of the name in an Ephesian context.

A class of priests?

Modern scholars universally assume that the title "Megabyzos" came to be applied to all high-priests of Artemis at Ephesus.[13] Most of them believe that the title was already in use by the fifth century B.C. or shortly thereafter and that it continued for centuries.[14]

The ancient literary and epigraphic evidence, however, do not support the use of the title so early. None of the other "hereditary priesthoods" mentioned by Horsley[15] predate the late fourth century B.C. Dateable individuals at Ephesus named Megabyzus reflect a similar dating. The Megabyzus mentioned by Xenophon and Diogenes Laertius clearly lived during the early fourth century. The tomb of a "Megabyzus" mentioned by Pliny was decorated by Nicias, a pupil

---

[13] E. Falkener, *Ephesus and the Temple of Diana*, London, 1862, p. 330; E.L. Hicks, *The Collection of Ancient Greek Inscriptions in the British Museum, Part III: Priene, Iasos and Ephesos*, C.T. Newton, ed., Oxford, 1890, p. 84; L.R. Farnell, *The Cults of the Greek States*, Oxford, 1896, 2:481; W. Kroll, *PW*, s.v. "Megabyzos," col. 122; O. Jessen, *PW*, s.v. "Ephesia," col. 2758; E. Akurgal, "The Early Period and the Golden Age of Ionia," *AJA* 66 (1962), p. 376; D.G. Hogarth, ed., *Excavations at Ephesus: The Archaic Artemisia*, London, 1966, p. 173; G.E. Bean, *Aegean Turkey: An Archaeological Guide*, second edition, London, 1967, p. 135; A. Bammer, *Das Heiligtum der Artemis von Ephesus*, Graz, 1984, p. 254; R. Fleischer, s.v. "Artemis Ephesia," *Lexicon Iconographicum Mythologiae Classicae (LIMC)*, Vol. 2, Part 1, Zurich, 1984, p. 756; W. Burkert, *Greek Religion*, J. Raffan, transl., Cambridge, Mass., 1985, p. 97; Winfried Elliger, *Ephesos—Geschichte einer antiken Weltstadt*, Stuttgart, 1985, p. 126. Most recently, see G.H.R. Horsley, "The Mysteries of Artemis Ephesia in Pisidia: A New Inscribed Relief," *AnatSt* 42 (1992), p. 124, although Horsley interpreted the "Megabyzoi" in a different way than his predecessors.

[14] Falkener, *Ephesus and the Temple of Diana*, p. 330 (early fifth century); Magie, *Roman Rule in Asia Minor*, n. 86 2:88 (sometime during the fifth century); Hicks, *Collection of Ancient Greek Inscriptions*, p. 84 and Horsley, "The Mysteries of Artemis Ephesia," p. 124 (during the fourth century); Jessen, *PW*, s.v. "Ephesia," col. 2758 and Elliger, *Ephesos—Geschichte einer antiken Weltstadt*, p. 126 (during the Persian period).

[15] Horsley, p. 124. All of these priesthoods differ in several significant respects from the "Megabyzoi" at Ephesus.

of Antidotus who was in turn a pupil of Euphranor. Euphranor, according to Pliny, was active during the 104th Olympiad (364–361), so Nicias would probably have been active during the late fourth century.[16] Apelles, who painted the procession of a "Megabyzus" mentioned by Pliny (and probably also by Plutarch) was a contemporary of Alexander.[17] All of these references could *conceivably* be to a single individual. Only the "Megabyzus" mentioned by Appian, who must be dated to the mid-first century B.C., falls outside the fourth century.

The date at which the title may first have come into use is not clear from ancient writers. Neither Xenophon nor Diogenes Laertius stated or implied that the name was a title by the early fourth century. Plutarch stated that it was in use by the latter part of that same century. But if so, then why was Plautus, writing in the mid-third century, unaware of this? As stated above, he named the priest of Artemis at Ephesus Theotimus, not Megabyzus.[18] Appian's reference would seem to indicate that the title was still in use during the late first century B.C. Neither Pseudo-Heraclitus nor Strabo dated the beginning or ending of the application of the title, but Strabo closed his reference to the "Megabyzoi" and their female counterparts by saying, "at the present some of their usages are being preserved . . . others are not." He does not say whether the "usage" of the title "Megabyzos" (the only such "usage" he mentions) was still current, but he says that they *had* (using the imperfect tense) priests called Megabyzos, which would seem to imply that this "usage" had passed away.[19] If there were still "Megabyzoi" at Ephesus in his time, why did he not specifically say so? Indeed, in that case he probably would have spoken to them and given more information about them in his work. The literary references therefore indicate that the title was in use at most from the mid-third century B.C. to the late first century B.C.

---

[16] Pliny said that Nicias sold a later painting to Attalus I of Pergamon (241–197), which would seem to place Nicias in the late third century. But Plutarch (*Non posse suaviter vivi secundum Epicurum* 11.1093) said that he sold the same painting to Ptolemy 1, which would fit with a late fourth-century date. Plutarch's date for Nicias seems more likely to be correct.

[17] Or, according to Aelian, by Zeuxis, who painted in the late fifth or early fourth century.

[18] This would be consistent with the practice in the "hereditary priesthoods" mentioned by Horsley (p. 124), in which succession was indeed by family but in which the individual priests (and priestesses) continued to be addressed by their own names. But this would rule out any "class" of priests called Megabyzoi by the Ephesians.

[19] As Hicks (p. 84) long ago pointed out.

The "eunuch-priest" statuette from the archaic Artemision has been used to bolster the case for the antiquity of the "Megabyzoi" at Ephesus.[20] But as stated above, the identification of this statuette as a man, much less a "Megabyzos," is now doubted.

Assuming the existence of this "class" of "Megabyzoi," modern scholars have proposed various theories to explain how the name came to be applied as a title. The name is a Greek corruption of the Persian proper name *Bagabriksha*, meaning "set free by god."[21] This name would be particularly appropriate for the "Megabyzoi" at Ephesus if they were eunuchs, as will be discussed below. The name is a clear indication of Persian influence at Ephesus, which was mentioned by Plutarch, and its Persian derivation points to its antiquity.[22] These facts, along with Strabo's statement that the "Megabyzoi" were selected from the surrounding countries, have led some modern scholars to postulate that all "Megabyzoi" were Persian.[23] Several men named Megabyzus other than the priests of Artemis are known from ancient authors. Some of them lived as early as the sixth century B.C.[24] The conjecture by Falkener that the title was conferred as an honor to one of Darius I's generals has merit, as does his theory that a man of this name once served as priest of Artemis at Ephesus and that the people of Ephesus, seeking to please the Persian monarchs, made it a title named after a priest at Ephesus by that name, possibly the one who aided Xenophon, who could well have been a Persian.[25] It is entirely possible, however, that the title was given to honor an especially well-known *neokoros* of that name and had nothing at all to do with the Persian monarchy.

This discussion of how the title came to be applied, however, entirely ignores the definite possibility that there may never have been such a title. The ancient authors who claimed that the title existed

---

[20] Ekrem Akurgal, "The Early Period and the Golden Age of Ionia," p. 376.

[21] Liddell and Scott, s.v. "*Essen*."

[22] Plutarch *Lys*.3; Farnell, *Cults of the Greek States*, 2:481.

[23] Hicks, p. 84; Falkener, p. 330; Bean, *Aegean Turkey*, p. 135. Bean also pointed out (p. 130) that Ephesus had a large Persian population, which would have made it possible for the Megabyzoi, though Persian, to be recruited locally.

[24] Hdt.3.70.7,3.81.1–82.1,3.153.1,3.160,4.143–4,7.83.1,7.121.14; Xen. *Cyr*.8.6.7.5; Diod.Sic.10.19.2,11.74.5–75.1,11.77,12.3.2–3,12.4; Thuc.3.109.1.1–3.4; Phot. *Bibl*.72.39a.8–72.41b.24 *passim* (referring to Ctesias).

[25] Falkener, pp. 330–1. Horsley (p. 124) believed that the title came to be used "in recognition of the Persian origin of the family which held it from IV [century] B.C.," which presumably included one or more of the fourth-century Megabyzoi mentioned by the ancient writers who were priests of Artemis at Ephesus.

(Strabo, Pliny, Pseudo-Heraclitus and Appian) all wrote during the Roman period, long after the supposed title ceased to be used. They were therefore using second-hand information, some of it possibly received from local inhabitants. This fact may help to explain their contradictory information regarding the use of the "title."

The most weighty argument against the use of the title locally is the epigraphic evidence. As stated above, none of the inscriptions so far recovered at Ephesus contain the name Megabyzus in any form. If this name was the official local title of the high-priest of Artemis at Ephesus from the fifth century (or even the mid-third century) through the first century B.C., it would certainly be mentioned at least once in the inscriptions. As stated above, the *Essenes* and other, more minor, temple officials were mentioned many times in one form or another in the same inscriptions. This absence of any epigraphic support whatsoever makes it highly unlikely that there was a class of priests called "Megabyzus" by the Ephesians.

If the use of the title is denied, however, its mention by four ancient authors must be explained. As stated above, all of them wrote during the Roman period, after the supposed "title" ceased to be used. Of the four, only Strabo probably ever visited Ephesus, and his evidence is likely to have come from native Ephesians. Considering the placement of Strabo's reference to the "Megabyzoi" within his account about Ephesus (mentioned above), he may have seen one of the paintings of "Megabyzoi" there, asked his native guides about it, and recorded their response. Alternatively, both he and Pliny may have drawn on a source which contained information about the monuments, and both drew on the information about the paintings of the "Megabyzoi." Strabo and Pliny's faulty information about the cult practices at the temple of Artemis could have spread from them to other authors. However, the reference to Megabulus by Plautus in connection with the temple of Artemis at Ephesus seems to show that at least some in Rome knew the name in this context at least as early as the third century B.C. This leads to a third hypothesis: that the high-priests at Ephesus were *not* known by that title locally, but that people abroad heard about the famous "Megabyzos" (or "Megabyzoi") and *they* referred to them by that name. This hypothesis would detract from the reliability of Strabo, Pliny, and Appian, but it would explain the lack of the name in local inscriptions. It would also explain why the earliest Roman mention of the name in connection with Ephesus (Plautus) did not seem to indicate that the name was a title.

If this argument is accepted, however, the actual title of the priest at Ephesus is unknown. He may have been known as the *archhiereus*, which, however, is attested at Ephesus only during the Roman period. He may have merely been called the chief *Essen*, something which is also entirely unattested in the inscriptions. Or he may have gone by another, entirely unknown title.

Were they eunuchs?

Modern writers almost universally assume that all "Megabyzoi" were eunuchs,[26] following Strabo and Quintilian, often using the above-mentioned statuette of a so-called "eunuch-priest" to support their case.[27] Eunuchs are known to have served in some capacity in the temple of Hecate at Lagina in Caria,[28] though it is clear that they were not priests. Some have conjectured that the "Megabyzoi's" "condition" was manmade,[29] possibly based on the statement by Pseudo-Heraclitus that the Ephesians castrated their "Megabyzoi."

G.H.R. Horsley, however, in his recent article mentioned above, seems to doubt the assumption that the "Megabyzoi" were eunuchs. He says that "the title of the priesthood of Artemis came to be called Megabyzus in recognition of the Persian origin of *the family* which held it from IV [century] B.C."[30] He is clearly envisioning a hereditary priesthood such as that of Artemis Ephesia at Burdur,[31] or of Apollo Tarsios at some site in northeast Lydia,[32] or of Artemis at Termessos,[33] or others mentioned in his article. Most of these priesthoods date to Roman times, but he traces the beginning of one (the priesthood of Asklepios at Pergamon) to the fourth century B.C.[34] In each of these cases, father passes the priesthood to son or daughter.

---

[26] Falkener, p. 330; Hicks, p. 84; Farnell 2:481; Jessen, *PW*, col. 1258; Kroll, *PW*, col. 122; Akurgal, "The Early Period and the Golden Age of Ionia," p. 376; Bean, p. 34; Bammer, *Das Heiligtum der Artemis von Ephesus*, p. 256 n. 33; Fleischer, "Artemis Ephesia," p. 756; Burkert, p. 97; Jones, p. 94; Bennett, p. 34.

[27] Ekrem Akurgal, p. 376; Cecil Smith, "The Ivory Statuettes," in Hogarth, *Excavations at Ephesus*, p. 173.

[28] J. Hatzfeld, "Inscriptions de Lagina en Carie," *BCH* 44 (1920): 79, 84.

[29] Jones, p. 94.

[30] Horsley, p. 124. Emphasis added.

[31] Horsley, pp. 121–3.

[32] *Ibid.*, p. 122.

[33] *Ibid.*, p. 124.

[34] *Ibid.*, p. 124.

If the "Megabyzoi" are really meant to parallel these other cases, then they cannot have been eunuchs.

The case for the "Megabyzoi" being eunuchs in ancient literature is not as strong as it first appears. Strabo indisputably said that they were. But, as stated above, he was relying on second-hand data probably supplied by locals who had never met a "Megabyzus."

Quintilian's statement is even more questionable. He said that Bagoas and Megabyzus were unfit models for sculptors or painters, but did not say why. The Bagoas mentioned most often in ancient literature was a mid-fourth-century eunuch who was a high Persian official. He assassinated Darius III's two predecessors and attempted to poison Darius as well, but was caught and made to drink his own poison.[35] This is probably the Bagoas whom Quintilian paired with Megabyzos. Both men would have been Persian officials, with Megabyzos being about fifty years earlier than Bagoas. At least three other eunuchs named Bagoas are known from ancient literature,[36] and at least four who are *not* specifically called eunuchs.[37] Pliny the Elder in his *Natural History* mentioned a Bagoas (possibly the fourth-century one) who had a house in Babylon and says that his name was "the Persian word for eunuch."[38] Thus being a eunuch is assumed to be what made Bagoas an unfit model. Since Megabyzus is paired with him in this passage, it is assumed that his "defect" was that he was also a eunuch. But the evidence is far from conclusive. And even if this Megabyzus was unfit because he was a eunuch, it is doubtful that he is a priest of Artemis at Ephesus in light of Pliny's above-mentioned statements that such priests were the subject of paintings by Apelles and Nicias, two Greek master painters. So unless Pliny's account is to be wholly discredited, Quintilian must be referring to another Megabyzus, unless, as suggested above, he is indirectly criticizing these artists.

---

[35] Along with the reference from Quintilian, see Strabo 15.3.24; Diod.Sic.16.47–51,17.5.3–6, Josephus *AJ* 11.297–301; Arrian *Anab*.2.14.5–6.

[36] These include: A Persian lover of Alexander (Athenaeus *Deipnosoph*.13.60.36; Plut. *Alex*.39,67), a later official under Herod the Great (Josephus *AJ* 17.44.3–45.1), and an otherwise unknown man mentioned by Ovid (*Am*.2.1.38–2.2.1).

[37] These include: A Babylonian general under Nebuchadnezzar (Judith 12–14), a general of Artaxerxes 2 (404–359) (Josephus *AJ* 11.297–301), a Persian naval officer who served against Alexander (Arrian *Ind* 88), and a Cappadocian official who fought against the Romans during the first century B.C. (Appian *Mith* 10). Ovid's "Bagoas" mentioned above is never *specifically* called a eunuch, but the context of the poem identifies him as one.

[38] *NH* 13.9.41.

The early statue from the temple lends no support to the assumption that "Megabyzoi" were eunuchs. It is not identified by any inscription as being a "Megabyzus," and, as stated above, it is now thought by at least some to be a woman.

A great weakness in the assumption that the "Megabyzoi" were eunuchs is the reference (and lack of reference) to them in Lucian and Plautus. Lucian's use of Megabyzus as an example of tremendous wealth in his *Timon* shows that he was at least somewhat familiar with the East, though as stated above, there is nothing to indicate that this was a priest at Ephesus. Far more interesting, however, is his failure to mention "Megabyzus" in his work *The Eunuch*, in which he had several characters who were eunuchs, including one named Bagoas (*The Eunuch* 4). This indicates that he was also familiar with one of the most famous eunuchs of the Persian period. If he was aware of any famous group of eunuchs at Ephesus called "Megabyzoi," then why did he not mention them? And if the Megabulus mentioned by Plautus was indeed a "Megabyzus" from Ephesus, as argued, then how did he come to have a son? The son could have been adopted or born before his father was made a eunuch, but this would still require an explanation. Plautus seems to have been ignorant of the "Megabyzoi" being eunuchs as he was ignorant of the name being a title, or he probably would have used the peculiarity of a eunuch having a son for comic effect.

Therefore the only clear reference to the "Megabyzoi" at Ephesus being eunuchs is that of Strabo. As argued above, his statement that there was a class of priests called "Megabyzoi" locally may well rest on faulty information or at least on a faulty interpretation of the evidence at Strabo's disposal. If so, then his statement that they were eunuchs must be regarded with equal skepticism. At most one can speculate that the Megabyzos who aided Xenophon and/or one of those painted in Ephesus (if indeed all of these were not the same individual) was a eunuch and Strabo received faulty information or interpreted it incorrectly as in the case of "Megabyzus" being a title.

Conclusion

It is therefore apparent that the evidence for a class of eunuch high-priests at Ephesus called "Megabyzos" is far from conclusive. The ancient authors who mention or may mention "Megabyzoi" at Ephesus are mostly late and self-contradictory, and are entirely unsupported by epigraphic evidence. The entire account may go back ultimately to one priest, not necessarily a eunuch, in the early fourth century B.C. The evidence is insufficient and unconvincing, and it appears highly doubtful that there was a class of priests at Ephesus called "Megabyzoi" locally or that these priests were eunuchs.

LUCRETIUS' ROMAN CYBELE

Kirk Summers

In book two of his *De rerum natura* (600–60), Lucretius describes the rites for the goddess Cybele in a powerful, detailed passage that has become the standard starting point for all discussion of her cult. He describes a turreted Cybele seated on a throne that itself sits atop a chariot pulled by yoked lions. Frenzied attendants accompany her, who play their clashing, clanging music, brandish their knives stained with the blood of castration, and shake the crests of their helmets in fearsome fashion. Despite first appearances, Lucretius does not imagine a mythological scene. He refers to the worshippers who line the streets watching the goddess's lion biga go by, terrified by the display of the knives, but awed by the spectacle in general. They strew her path with bronze and silver coins as offerings, and sprinkle rose petals on her statue. He has a real, cultic event in mind.

In analyzing this passage scholars have tried to determine whether Lucretius is describing Greek, Phrygian, or Roman rites, or perhaps even all three at the same time. Typically they have followed the historian of Cybele's cult in Rome, who writes,

> Assistait-on à ce spectacle dans les rues de Rome, vers la fin de la République? Lucrèce, à vrai dire, semble plutôt n'en parler que d'après ses lectures... Il évite d'autre part toute allusion à Rome et au temps présent, comme s'il voulait conserver à son œuvre un caractère universel.[1]

From Graillot two basic assumptions emerge, one or the other of which many subsequent scholars have accepted: 1) Lucretius has taken his description *in toto* from Greek writers;[2] 2) Lucretius can be used as evidence for how the cult was practiced throughout the

---

[1] H. Graillot, *Le culte de Cybèle mère des dieux à Rome et dans l'empire Romain* (Paris 1912), 106–107.

[2] As G. Hadzsits, "Lucretius as a Student of Roman Religion," *TAPA* 29 (1918) 145–160, at 151, 157–8; D. Stewart, "The Silence of the Magna Mater," *HSPh* 74 (1970) 75–84, at 82. Jürgen Schmidt, *Lukrez, der Kepos und die Stoiker: Untersuchungen zur Schule Epikurs and zu den Quellen von De rerum natura* (Frankfurt on the Main, 1990), 113–125.

Mediterranean world at all times.[3] Both of these assumptions, I argue, are wrong. Contemporary material and literary evidence suggests that Lucretius only describes the cult as he saw it practiced firsthand on the streets of Rome every April 4th during the festival of the Megalensia.[4] He both excludes the Greek and Phrygian elements of the cult which other evidence indicates the Romans had rejected in practice, and includes some uniquely Roman elements of the cult. This shows that Lucretius was addressing his audience within the context of their own personal experiences, speaking as one Roman to another about contemporary issues.

I will be making the following arguments: 1) Lucretius is describing a procession, a *pompa* that has no counterpart in Greece for Cybele's cult; 2) he excludes all the Greek mystic elements of the cult; 3) he has a different list of musical instruments than the Greeks; 4) certain visual images that Lucretius gives are well attested in Rome for this period, but are not Greek. Pinpointing Phrygian rites precisely presents a problem, since so little evidence survives, and since they had assimilated so much Greek culture by this time, but when the evidence permits, I will compare Phrygian rites as well.[5]

Before proceeding with these four arguments, we should mention two preliminary matters. First, the cult of Cybele in the ancient world was not uniform. Throughout the centuries in Greece and Asia Minor

---

[3] For example, J. Jope, "Lucretius, Cybele, and Religion," *Phoenix* 39 (1985) 250–262, at 254, takes the expressions *per magnas terras* (608) and *magnas per urbis* (624) to prove that "Lucretius was interpreting the cult universally." On the basis of the same phrases, Jope goes so far as to say that Lucretius is not describing a specifically urban cult. Léon Lacroix, "Texte et réalités à propos du témoignage de Lucrèce sur la Magna Mater," *Journal des Savants* (Jan.–March, 1982) 11–43, ignores historical developments within the cult and assumes that Asia Minor coins from the second century A.D. can be compared with Lucretius' description.

[4] Jacques Perret, "Le mythe de Cybèle (Lucrèce 2.600–660)," *REL* 13 (1935) 332–357, has argued the Romanness of Lucretius' description, but without the benefit of accurate information about the cult as practiced in Greece and apparently no knowledge of its practice in Phrygia. He comes to the rather strange conclusion that Lucretius had a source, and that source was "œuvre d'un Romain cultivé, très au courant et de la littérature grecque et des méthodes allégorisantes, mais qui, tout en utilisant les souvenirs que pouvait lui fournir une même, avait médité sur ce qu'il avait sous les yeux, appliqué à un objet nouveau les méthodes de ses maîtres et fait œuvre originale" (p. 355). For a refutation of many of his points see P. Boyancé, "Une exégèse Stoïcienne chez Lucrèce," *REL* 19 (1941) 147–66.

[5] What little is known about Phrygian rites for Cybele has been examined by E. Ohlemutz, *Die Kulte und Heiligtümer der Götter in Pergamon* (Würzburg 1940; repr. Darmstadt 1968) 174–191; Lynn Roller, "Phrygian Myth and Cult," *Source* 7 (1988) 43–50.

the expression and practice of Cybele's cult underwent a variety of evolutionary changes, including iconographical ones. We cannot take evidence, then, from the first century B.C. and assume without corroboration that it establishes a point of practice in an earlier century. Furthermore, even within the same time period no two peoples worshipped Cybele in exactly the same way. Thus, what was commonplace in Athens at any given time may at the same time be odd in central Anatolia. The Romans inserted themselves into the historical development of the cult when in 204 B.C. they went to Pergamon to retrieve the cult symbol (a black stone) and introduce it into their own State. Once they brought her and some of her priests to Rome, however, they were horrified to discover how she was worshipped, so they tempered her rites and refused to let Roman citizens participate in them except in the role of spectators. Cybele's worship found a place on the Roman calendar, with games, dinner parties, and plays in her honor, under the control of the curule aedile, while her priests were segregated in the temple precinct.[6] Thus in many respects the worship of Cybele in Rome had no parallels in the rest of the Mediterranean world.

In the reign of Claudius the worship of Cybele took on a new form. Claudius, it appears, added several mystic elements and put more emphasis on the *lavatio* in March, the washing of the cult statue and objects in the river Almo. Still more elements were added in the mid-second century A.D. under the Antonines, so that the worship of Cybele became thoroughly mystic. Attis, the consort of Cybele, was a major addition in these later periods, at least in his new, elevated status, as were certain other, previously unattested rites, such as the taurobolium.[7] Although the evolution of the cult in the West shows definite Greek and Phrygian influence, it nevertheless continues to bear the unique marks of Roman devotees.

The second point can be formulated as a question: Does not Lucretius himself tell his readers that he is taking his information form "the old learned Greek poets who sang of Cybele" (*hanc veteres Graium*

---

[6] Many of the Roman Republican Cybele coins reflect this State control; e.g., a coin of Publius Fourius Crassipes, 84 B.C., shows a turreted Cybele on the obverse along with the inscription AED CUR, and on the reverse a curule chair.

[7] A detailed analysis of the evidence for the historical development of the cult in Rome can be found in Duncan Fishwick, "The *Cannophori* and the March Festival of Magna Mater," *TAPA* 97 (1966) 193–202. His arguments are generally accepted by M.J. Vermaseren, *Cybele and Attis: The Myth and the Cult* (London 1977) 122–123.

docti cecinere poetae, 2.600)? The participle *docentes* in 602 indicates that
he used his sources primarily for their exegesis of the myth of Cybele
rather than for their description of her rites. Cybele rides high in a
chariot, the Greek poets say, to illustrate that the earth hangs in
midair. Her devotees yoke lions to her chariot to show that offspring
should obey their parents. They put a mural crown on her head to
say that she protects cities. Likewise, in 611–617 Lucretius is interested in what *variae gentes* assert allegorically about Cybele's attributes
(*quia . . . edunt*, 612; *quia . . . significare volunt*, 614–616), not what they
relate about the visual images of her cult. From 618 onward the
reference to how others interpret aspects of the cult is dropped, while
he places his emphasis on the fear that the rites instill in the spectators (*minantur . . . conterrere metu . . . terrificas cristas*), a point he makes
often throughout the entire poem.

Still, problems remain. To what Greek poets does Lucretius refer?
The most prominent allegorizers of myth in the Hellenistic period
were the Stoics. Because they believed that the universe and everything in it was interconnected in some way, Stoic writers often drew
conclusions on matters of theology or physics by making analogies
with other, more tangible objects. Clearly, Lucretius is rejecting that
kind of approach to scientific investigation when he gives and then
rebuffs allegorical interpretations of Cybele.[8]

Nevertheless, it is difficult to picture any Stoic allegorizers that
would fit the mold of Lucretius' "old learned Greek poets" who teach
truths about physics and morality from the myth and rites of Cybele.
In general, the Stoics preferred to emphasize Zeus who pervades
everything and subsumes all other gods and goddesses into his person as aspects of himself.[9] Certainly Chrysippus used etymology to
argue that the names of the gods were meant to symbolize physical
phenomena, including the name of Mother Earth (specifically Demeter), but he did so without reference to the ethical meaning behind specific attributes or rites.[10] At any rate, he was hardly a poet.
The Stoic poet Cleanthes, in his *Hymn to Zeus* (*SVF* 1.537), treats
Zeus personally and traditionally as a providential, benevolent god,

---

[8] Guido Milanese, *Lucida carmina: Comunicazione e scrittura da Epicuro a Lucrezio* (Milan
1989) 148; Monical Gale, *Myth and Poetry in Lucretius* (Cambridge 1994) 29–31.

[9] Elizabeth Asmis, "Lucretius' Venus and Stoic Zeus," *Hermes* 110 (1982) 458–
70, at 460; cf. Diog.Laertius 7.147.

[10] Cicero *DND* 1.36–41 and 2.66. See Jope, "Lucretius, Cybele, and Religion,"
p. 251.

without the use of overt symbolism. It is more likely that Lucretius draws from a store of common attitudes toward Cybele and her rites that emerged from manifold sources—Hellenistic poems, Greek hymns, philosophy, literature and popular oral tradition—for several times in the *De rerum natura* Lucretius uses the phrase "old learned Greek poets" as a stock phrase when presenting well-known myths that have often been allegorized.[11] By it he appeals to a long tradition of mythological expression rather than the views of specific poets. In Lucretius' day the rationalizing, allegorizing treatment of Greek myths accompanied the stories as if they had always been an integral part of them, even at Rome. Dionysius of Halicarnassus, for example, immediately thinks of allegorizing after he describes Cybele's procession at Rome (οἱ μὲν ἐπιδεικνύμενοι τὰ τῆς φύσεως ἔργα δι' ἀλληγορίας, 2.20), and assumes the approach is known to all.

Likewise, the fact that Varro, Cornutus, and Ovid know variations of the same allegorizing on Cybele only shows that those symbolic interpretations were in vogue with the Romans, not that they all were looking back to a single Hellenistic source.[12] This is verified by archaeological evidence. A coin of M. Plaetorius Cestianus, curule aedile for 67 B.C., shows a globe before the head of Cybele, suggesting the symbolic connection between the goddess and the suspended earth, also noted by Lucretius (2.663). A globe depicting Cybele may have been carried in the procession itself.[13] Also, other evidence suggests that the Roman nobility, nervous about the orgiastic nature of the cult in the first place, promoted the moral lessons being drawn from it, such as *pietas* toward parents, self-discipline, and loyalty to the motherland.[14]

We must keep in mind too that the hymns which accompanied

---

[11] *DRN* 5.405,6.754. Cicero, at *DND* 1.41, possibly following Philodemus, *De pietate* 80,23 (Gomperz), has the Epicurean Velleius use *veterrimi poetae* to refer to the poets on whose texts Stoics applied their allegorical interpretations.

[12] Varro *apud* Aug. *C.D.*7.24; Cornutus, *Theologicae Graecae Compendium*, ed. C. Lang (Liepzig 1881) ch. 6–7 (composed during the reign of Nero); Ovid, *Fasti* 4.179–372.

[13] *CCCA* 4.42 shows a globe in the Pompeian procession. Vermaseren dates it to 70 A.D.

[14] Graillot, 104–105; A.K. Michels, "Lucretius, Clodius and Magna Mater," *Mélanges a Jérôme Carcopino* (Rome 1966) 675–79; R.W. Sharples, "Cybele and Loyalty to Parents," *LCM* 10.9 (Nov. 1985) 133–34. In the Republican period the Roman leaders altered the rites and significance of many divinities of foreign origins to accord better with Roman moral standards. Such is the case with the Semitic Astarte, whom the Cypriots worshipped as Aphrodite, but the Romans as Venus Verticordia. Cf. Preller, *Römischen Mythologie* (Berlin 1881³) vol. 1, 446.

the cult were sung in Greek, and they may well have promoted a
certain way of viewing Cybele.[15] In fact, before Lucretius, Roman
writers had applied the word "canere" and its cognates in a strictly
religious sense, so we can expect that in Lucretius' usage a religious
connotation would have lingered.[16] It is unnecessary, then, to assume that Lucretius could only find allegorical interpretations of Cybele among the Greeks. His Roman audience was likely familiar with
the allegorical interpretations as a significant feature of their own
cult. To be sure, Lucretius knew a longstanding tradition of poetry
and Stoic allegorizing, but he did not, as we shall see, introduce into
his depiction of the goddess's rites any elements that the Romans
did not already know.

Pompa

Of all the rituals surrounding the Cybele cult, Lucretius could not
have chosen a more Roman feature than the procession (*pompa*) itself.[17] Beginning with 2.601 he describes Cybele sitting on her throne
in a chariot driving double-yoked lions wearing a mural crown and
accompanied by frenzied priests. Until line 621, however, the reader
has no indication whether the poet has in mind the Cybele of mythic
imagination or of cult. The words *praeportant* (621) and *volgi* (622)
solve the mystery: Lucretius envisions the statue of the goddess being
guided through the streets while the priests display their knives to
terrify the hearts and minds of the spectators. He strengthens the
imagery of procession with *mortalis* in 625, adding that the spectators
throw silver and bronze coins in the chariot's path, and shower the
goddess with rose petals (627–628).

   Ovid, at *Fasti* 4.345–346, writes that Cybele entered into the city
of Rome, after her initial *lavatio*, on a wagon pulled by oxen, on
which the people sprinkled fresh flowers. Yet most scholars take an
earlier passage, *Fasti* 4.185–186, to mean that typically in the celebration of the Megalensia in April her attendants carried her through

---

   [15] Servius ad Verg.Georg.2.394; Graillot, 254–55.
   [16] J.K. Newman, "De verbis *canere* et *dicere* eorumque apud poetas Latinos ab
Ennio usque ad aetatem Augusti usu," *Latinitas* 13 (1965) 86–106.
   [17] Perhaps the inspiration for this practice, in addition to the traditional mythological picture of Cybele in a chariot, was the procession of Liber. On this see H.H.
Scullard, *Festivals and Ceremonies of the Roman Republic* (Ithaca 1981) 91.

the city on a bier: *ipsa sedens molli comitum cervice feretur | urbis per medias exululata vias.* Archeological evidence supports that interpretation. A painting from Pompeii portraying a procession in process, shows Cybele, seated on her high-backed throne, on top of a bier.[18] Although the time and place are far removed from Lucretius' Republican Rome, so that some elements have changed, the bier at least is consistent with Ovid's procession. An even later portrayal of the procession occurs on a sarcophagus of unknown provenance, dating to the later second to early third century A.D.[19] Again a bier appears on which rests the throne and footstool of Cybele, who appears on another side of the sarcophagus. Four Galli carry the bier in procession.

Scullard is probably correct, then, to assume that the entire structure—yoked lions, chariot, and statue—was placed on a bier and carried through the streets on April 4, the first day of the Megalensia.[20] A suspension of disbelief allowed many writers and artists to ignore the presence of the bier and to imagine that the lions actually pulled the chariot themselves. Whether a similar procession also followed the *lavatio* we cannot say. Our sources for the late Republic are silent on the *lavatio*, except perhaps the special case noted by Dio Cassius (48.43.5), when the Romans washed her statue in the sea.[21] Ovid mentions that the Phrygian priest of Cybele washed her and her holy implements in the river Almo the day after her arrival to Italy, and then spontaneously a parade to the city began. Arrian, writing about 136 A.D., considers the *lavatio* a strictly Phrygian practice that the Romans incorporated into their worship.[22] Unfortunately, no evidence survives to indicate what rites accompanied the Phrygian

---

[18] *CCCA* 4.42.

[19] L. Budde-R. Nicholls, *A Catalogue of the Greek and Roman Sculptures in the Fitzwilliam Museum* (Cambridge 1964) 77 f., no. 125 and pl. 41, followed by Vermaseren, *CCCA* 7.39.

[20] *Festivals and Ceremonies of the Roman Republic* (Ithaca 1981) 99–100. See also B.F. Cook, "The Goddess Cybele: A Bronze in New York," *Archaeology* (1966) 251–257, at 257.

[21] The first evidence of the traditional *lavatio* dates to 50 A.D. (*CIL* vii 2305).

[22] *Tactica* 33.4, ed. A.G. Roos: καὶ γὰρ ἡ Ῥέα αὐτοῖς ἡ Φρυγία τιμᾶται ἐκ Πεσσινοῦντος ἐλθοῦσα, καὶ τὸ πένθος τὸ ἀμφὶ τῷ Ἄττῃ Φρύγιον ⟨ὂν⟩ ἐν Ῥώμῃ πενθεῖται, καὶ τὸ λουτρὸν δ' ἡ Ῥέα, ἐφ' οὗ τοῦ πένθους λήγει, τῶν Φρυγῶν νόμῳ λοῦται. An inscription from Cyzicus survives, dating from the first century B.C., which implies that a group of priestesses, called θαλασσίαι, were responsible for washing the cult statue in the sea; see Ch. Michel, *Recueil d'inscriptions grecques* (Brussels 1900) no. 537. One thinks naturally of the proposed *lavatio* of the Artemis statue in Euripides' *Iphigenia in Tauris*.

ceremony. It is likely, however, that Lucretius is describing the procession, not of the *lavatio*, a joyous event (at least after the bathing) which later calendars placed on March 27th and which did not involve the collection of donations, but of the strictly Roman celebration and games of the Megalensia.[23]

Two coins of the late Republic prove that Romans of that time could see in their streets the very scene that Lucretius describes. In 78 B.C. M. Volteius produced five denarii, one of which depicts Cybele, who, looking very much like a statue, wears a turreted crown and sits on a throne in a chariot pulled by two lions.[24] In her left hand Cybele holds the reins (corresponding to and explaining Lucretius' *agitare* at 6.601), while in the left she holds a *patera*. Volteius did not draw his picture of the earth goddess from experiences he might have had in the East. To the contrary, the entire series of five coins he produced that year, portraying Jupiter, Hercules, Liber with Ceres, and Apollo, in addition to Cybele, represent the five major festivals for which he, as a curule aedile, would have been responsible: Ludi Romani, Plebeii, Cereales, Megalenses, and Apollinares. Therefore we have to assume that through these issues Volteius intended to remind the public of the extravagant shows he just had or would present for their benefit, as an electioneering strategy.[25]

Additionally, since on the other four coins of his series, Volteius has linked the theme of the obverse to that of the reverse, we may also assume that the obverse of the Cybele coin depicts another aspect of her cult. The helmeted figure there could only represent one of the Curetes or, more properly, Corybantes, whom Lucretius describes as "shaking the crests of the helmets by nodding their heads." The figure could not be Attis, as some have suggested, for two reasons: 1) Attis was not worshipped alongside Cybele in the Roman public cult during the late Republic (see discussion below); 2) the helmet on the coin's figure is not the typical Phrygian cap of Attis.

---

[23] For the argument see P. Boyancé, "Cybèle aux Mégalésies," *Latomus* 13 (1954) 337–42, at 339–40.

[24] Crawford 358. Préhac, F., "Mater Deum," *Revue numismatique* 35 (1932) 119–125; Turcan, Robert, *Numismatique romaine du culte métroaque* (Leiden 1983), 14.

[25] On the moneyer Volteius see T. Robert, S. Broughton, *The Magistrates of the Roman Republic* (Cleveland, 1952) vol. 2, p. 455. No extant evidence points to an aedileship for Volteius. M. Crawford, *Roman Republican Coinage* (Cambridge 1974) vol. 2, p. 729, believes that these coins would substitute for an aedileship in the cursus honorum.

The reverse of another coin, an aureus of about 43 B.C., matches Volteius' depiction of Cybele very closely.[26] Again Cybele sits on her throne in a chariot pulled by two lions. As in the case of Volteius' coin, Cybele holds a *patera* in her right hand, but now her left arms rests on a *tympanum* (cf. *DRN* 2.618: *tympana tenta tonant*). Her appearance on this coin at this time could only suggest one thing: As Cybele once ensured victory over Hannibal, the foreign invader, so now she will protect Rome against some threat on Italian soil.[27] If the figure on the front is truly Sibyl, then the meaning would have been clear, since it was the Sibylline books that first told the Romans to bring Cybele's black stone from Phrygia to Rome in 204 B.C.[28]

Although certainly belonging to a later period, a bronze group in the New York Metropolitan Museum depicts the same scene as do the coins. On a four-wheeled cart Cybele sits on her throne, holding a tympanum and patera. Two docile lions are yoked to the cart.[29] The presence of the cart raises the question whether the group suggests the *lavatio* or the procession of the Megalensia. If this is a scene from the *lavatio*, then the lions represent the oxen, mentioned by Ovid. It seems to me, however, that the scene represents the procession during the Megalensian games, without the bier. The whole cult structure that this group models, cart, throne, lions and all, would have been carried through the streets on a bier, accompanied by the foreign attendants of Cybele.

Literary sources also confirm that Lucretius was describing Roman practice. Ovid's *ipsa sedens plaustro porta est invecta Capena* (*Fasti* 4.345) gives the historical precedent for the transportation of the statue through the streets. Dionysius of Halicarnassus, writing sometime after 23 B.C.,[30] notes that Romans have not adopted many traditional Greek rituals because they viewed them as lacking in decorum, and

---

[26] Struck by the praetors L. Cestius and C. Norbanus. Crawford 491.2. The obverse shows the draped bust of a female (Sibyl?). The other two types of this issue show the curule chair on the reverse instead of Cybele, and a bust of Africa on the obverse.

[27] Livy 29.10.4–11; 8; 14,5–14; 38.18,9. Polybius 21.37.5–6; Diodorus 36.13; Plutarch, *Marius* 17; F. Bömer, "Kybele in Rom. Die Geschichte ihres Kult als politisches Phänomen," *MDAI(R)* 71 (1964), 130–151, at 136.

[28] Turcan believes that the figure on the obverse is Venus and thus suggests that the coin was meant as propaganda for the *Iulii*. He cites Dio Cassius 46.33.3 where the historian notes a certain prodigy in 43 B.C. involving the Cybele statue on the Palatine.

[29] Cook, "The Goddess Cybele: A Bronze in New York," 251–257.

[30] See Wiseman, 224, n. 1.

says that the Romans do not practice the kind of rites most often associated with the worship of Dionysus, in which the participants lose control of their senses and become possessed by the divinity. Nor do they engage in secret mysteries, or worship in the temples by night, men and women together, or use the magic associated with such rites. Instead, on the few occasions in which the Romans permitted entry to foreign orgiastic cults, they modified the rites according to their own traditions, as in the case of the Cybele cult. They established traditional Roman games and sacrifices for the mother goddess, but by law do not permit their citizens to walk in the ecstatic procession with her Phrygian priests. The foreigners alone can transport the image of the goddess through the city, while begging for money and playing their wild instruments. The important segment of the passage (2.19.3–5) reads as follows:

Οὐδ' ἂν ἴδοι τις παρ' αὐτοῖς, καίτοι διεφθαρμένων ἤδη τῶν ἐθῶν, οὐ θεοφορήσεις, οὐ κορυβαντιασμούς, οὐκ ἀγυρμούς, οὐ Βακχείας, καὶ τελετὰς
ἀπορρήτους, οὐ διαπαννυχισμοὺς ἐν ἱεροῖς ἀνδρῶν σὺν γυναιξίν, οὐκ ἄλλο
τῶν παραπλησίων τούτοις τερατευμάτων οὐδέν, ἀλλ' εὐλαβῶς ἅπαντα
πραττόμενά τε καὶ λεγόμενα τὰ περὶ τοὺς θεούς, ὡς οὔτε παρ' Ἕλλησιν οὔτε
παρὰ βαρβάροις· καὶ ὃ πάντων μάλιστα ἔγωγε τεθαύμακα, καίπερ μυρίων
ὅσων εἰς τὴν πόλιν ἐληλυθότων ἐθνῶν, οἷς πολλὴ ἀνάγκη σέβειν τοὺς πατρίους
θεοὺς τοῖς οἴκοθεν νομίμοις, οὐδενὸς εἰς ζῆλον ἐλήλυθε τῶν ξενικῶν ἐπιτη-
δευμάτων ἡ πόλις δημοσία, ὃ πολλαῖς ἤδη συνέβη παθεῖν ἀλλὰ καὶ εἴ τινα
κατὰ χρησμοὺς ἐπεισηγάγετο ἱερά, τοῖς ἑαυτῆς αὐτὰ τιμᾷ νομίμοις ἅπασαν
ἐκβαλοῦσα τερθρείαν μυθικήν, ὥσπερ τὰ τῆς Ἰδαίας θεᾶς ἱερά. Θυσίας μὲν
γὰρ αὐτῇ καὶ ἀγῶνας ἄγουσιν ἀνὰ πᾶν ἔτος οἱ στρατηγοὶ κατὰ τοὺς Ῥωμαίων
νόμους, ἱερᾶται δὲ αὐτῆς ἀνὴρ Φρὺξ καὶ γυνὴ Φρυγία καὶ περιάγουσιν ἀνὰ
τὴν πόλιν οὗτοι μητραγυρτοῦντες, ὥσπερ αὐτοῖς ἔθος, τύπους τε περικείμενοι
τοῖς στήθεσι καὶ καταυλούμενοι πρὸς τῶν ἑπομένων τὰ μητρῷα μέλη καὶ
τύμπανα κροτοῦντες· Ῥωμαίων δὲ τῶν αὐθιγενῶν οὔτε μητραγυρτῶν τις οὔτε
καταυλούμενος πορεύεται διὰ τῆς πόλεως ποικίλην ἐνδεδυκὼς στολὴν οὔτε
ὀργιάζει τὴν θεὸν τοῖς Φρυγίοις ὀργιασμοῖς κατὰ νόμον καὶ ψήφισμα βουλῆς.

And one will not see among them [sc. the Romans]—even though now their manners are corrupted—ecstatic possessions, Corybantic frenzies, begging under the guise of religion, bacchanals or secret mysteries, no all-night vigils of men and women together in the temples, nor any other such antics; rather, they act piously and with restraint in all their words and actions in respect to the gods, unlike the Greeks or barbarians. And what amazes me the most, although there has been a great influx of nations into the city, nations who feel the need to worship their ancestral gods in their traditional ways, still the city has never officially adopted any of these foreign practices, as has been the experience of many cities in the past. But even though Rome has, at the bidding of oracles, introduced certain rites from abroad, she observes them in accordance with her own traditions, after casting off all the mythical nonsense, as in the case of the rites of Cybele. Every year the aediles perform sacrifices and put on games in her honor according to Roman customs, but it is Phrygian men and women who carry out the actual rites and lead her image throughout the city in procession, begging alms according to their custom, and wearing images around their necks, striking their timbrels while their followers play tunes upon their flutes in honor of the Great Mother. But by a law and decree of the senate no native Roman walks in procession through the city decked in flamboyant robes, begging alms or escorted by flute-players, or worships the goddess with the Phrygian ceremonies.

Thus, Dionysius knows of an annual procession among the Romans very much like what Lucretius describes. The Phrygian priests lead about an image of the goddess through the city (περιάγουσιν), collecting money to the sounds of flute playing and the striking of tambourines, while the Romans look on (cf. Ovid *Pont.*1.1.39–40). The contrast between spectator and participant, of citizen and foreigner, which emerges so clearly from Lucretius' passage, also dominates Dionysius' passage.

But does Dionysius mean that the Greeks also transport the goddess in procession through their city when he attributes to them θεοφόρησις? We must keep in mind that θεοφόρησις and its cognates indicate ecstatic possession or inspiration rather than transportation of a divine image.[31] Indeed, a little noticed passage of Philodemus' *De musica* sheds light on the application of the word to the Cybele cult.[32] In a fragmentary text Philodemus makes an allusion to rites that are probably in honor of Cybele:

> τ[αράττ]ουσιν δὲ καὶ μετὰ | συ[μπλοκ]ῆς δοξῶν, αἱ δὲ τῶν | τυ[πά]νων καὶ ῥόμβων | κα[ὶ κυ]μβάλων καὶ ῥυθμῶν | ἰδιό[τ]ητες καὶ διὰ ποιῶν ὀργάνων τὸ πᾶν συμπλοκῇ | μοχ[θ]ηρῶν ὑπολήψεων ἐξοργιάζουσι καὶ πρὸς βακχείαν ἄ[γ]ουσι, καὶ ταῦτα γυναῖκας ὡς ἐπὶ τὸ πολὺ καὶ γυναι[κώδεις ἄνδρας . . .

Here Philodemus argues that certain instruments (all characteristic of the worship of Cybele), in combination with false notions of the gods (a favorite Epicurean theme), can produce the ecstatic state in impressionable minds that marks the worship of Cybele: ". . . and they cause confusion especially with a combination of opinions, and the peculiar properties of tympana, rhomboi, cymbals, and rhythms cause frenzied behavior and lead everything to Bacchic revelry, especially through such instruments combined with false notions, which <affect> women mostly and effeminate men . . ."

In related fragments both immediately before and after this one θεοφορία occurs three times. In each case the word means "ecstatic possession".[33] The fragment that follows will suffice to make the point:

. . . διὰ] λόγους συμ[βού]λο[υς? | [. . . θε]οφορίας ἢ . . . . | . . . . γίνονται, διὰ δὲ μ[έλος | [αὐτ]ὸ καὶ γλυκύτ[η]τα τοῖς | [ὅλο]ις οὐδὲν ἀπο[σ]τάζον|[τες] τῶν τοιούτων. Καὶ κα|[θίστ]ανται δέ τινες ἐκ τῶν | [θε]οφοριῶν καταυλού-με|[ν]οί πως, οὐχὶ τοῦ μέλους | [δύ]ναμιν προσφερομένου τηλικαύτην, ποῦ γὰρ | [οἷ]όν τε δόξας ἀπαλλάξαι | [φ]ρεικώδεις αὐτῇ φωνῆς | μόν[ης] προσπ[τ]ώσει; τῷ | παραδεδόσθαι καθάπερ | εἴ τι σημεῖον τὸ το[ι]οῦτο τοῦ | πεπρα[ύνθαι] ἀπὸ δα[ι]μονίο[υ | κ]αὶ χα . . .

Philodemus is discussing the power of music to affect the soul: ". . . through words they become fellow revelers (σύμ[βακ]χο[ι] rather than συμ[βού]λο[υς]?) . . . of the ecstasy or . . . but through the melody itself and its sweetness <sc. they>, not diminishing any such things as these altogether. And some people who are charmed by fluteplaying are calmed from their ecstatic states somehow, not because the melody contributes such great power (for how is it possible to set anyone free from horrible beliefs by the strike of sound alone?); as if by giving such evidence of being calmed from a demon and . . ." The conjunction of the word θεοφορία with verbs of "calming" or "soothing" indicates that it connotes a frenzied state of mind rather than physical transportation of the cult statue.[34] Certainly Dionysius has in mind this same frenzied possession when he attributes θεο-φόρησις to Greek worshippers.

No literary or achaeological evidence, in fact, points to a transportation rite in the Greek practice of the Cybele cult by Lucretius' day, despite the claim of Burkert that in Greece "the Magna Mater makes her entrance seated on an ox-drawn wagon."[35] The reference to Ovid's Fasti 3.345 provides no substantiation for Greek practice. The only appearances Cybele makes on a chariot in Greek arti-

---

[33] C.J. Vooys, Lexicon Philodemum (Purmerend 1934) vol. 1, p. 146, defines θεοφορία in Philodemus as afflatus divinus and θεόφορος as spiritum divinum in se gerens.

[34] The previous fragment has: δοκεῖ τινα | θεοφ[ορίαν ἐμ]ποιεῖν.

[35] Walter Burkert, Greek Religion (Harvard 1985) 101 and 387.

facts are purely within a mythological context. Among the examples of the archaic period, the well-known frieze of the Siphnian Treasury at Delphi (*c.* 525 B.C.) shows Cybele-Themis thrust into the forefront of the gigantomachy on a chariot pulled by lions; one of her lions attacks a giant which happens to be in the way.[36] A kantharos fragment painted by Nearchos and dating to the last half of the sixth century B.C. depicts Cybele (indicated by the letter K), clothed in fawnskin, and fighting in the Gigantomachy.[37] A gold ring of the Robinson collection, dating to the early fifth century B.C., shows a detail of the Gigantomachy including Cybele, whose chiton and mantle blow in the breeze, as she drives her chariot.[38]

The motif of the standing, driving Cybele continues into the Hellenistic period, but now attendants are added. Still on every occasion the scene is not cultic, but mythological. On the lid of a silver perfume box from Olynthos Cybele stands and drives her lion-pulled chariot, with her chiton and mantle blowing in the breeze, while Hermes and a maiden stride alongside holding torches. Above flies Nike ready to crown Cybele with a wreath.[39] Similarly, on a terracotta medallion from Etruria dating to the third or second century B.C., Cybele ascends a lion-drawn chariot with reins and whip. As on the perfume lid, Hermes and a young maiden walk alongside the chariot, and Nike prepares to crown Cybele.[40] These representations, as Naumann (p. 230) has pointed out, must have a metaphorical meaning, since the portrayal is so mythological in nature: "Die auf die

[36] Now in the Archaeological Museum at Delphi. See Vermaseren, *CCCA* II.441 and bibliography there. Also, Friederike Naumann, *Die Ikonographie der Kybele in der Phrygischen und der griechischen Kunst* (Tübingen 1983) 155–158. For the identification as Themis see V. Brinkmann, *BCH* 109 (1985) 123. A fragment from a frieze in Agrigentum shows the same scene, this time with only the tail of Cybele's lion visible, Naumann 155–156; B. Pace, Il tempio di Giove Olimpico in Agrigento," *MAAL* 28 (1922/23) col. 173–252, at 231 ff. no. 6, plate 21; F. Vian, *Répertoire des Gigantomachies figurées dans l'art grec et romain* (Paris 1951) no. 34.

[37] Naumann, 156; B. Graef, *Die antiken Vasen von der Akropolis zu Athen (1903–1933)* no. 612, plate 36. F. Vian, *Répertoire*, no. 107, plate 25.

[38] Naumann, 156; D.M. Robinson, *Excavations at Olynthos X* (Baltimore 1941) 162; idem, "The Robinson Collection of Greek Gems, Seals, Rings, and Earrings," *Hesperia* suppl.8, (Princeton 1949) 305–323, at 315, no. 17; K. Schauenburg, "Zu Darstellungen aus der Sage des Admet und des Kadmos," *Gymnasium* 64 (1957) 210–230, at 221.

[39] Dating from the second quarter of the fourth century B.C., now in the Thessaloniki Archeological Museum. Cf. Naumann, 229–230 and fig. 39.2. H. Möbius, *Festschrift W. Eilers*, ed. G. Wiessner (Wiesbaden 1967) 459, ill. 5.

[40] Vermaseren, *CCCA* IV.207 and bibliography there. Also, E. Langlotz, *Griechische Vasen: Martin von Wagner-Museum der Universität Würzburg* (Munich 1932) 899, plate 252.

Göttin zufliegende Nike mit dem Siegeskranz unterstreicht das Irreale
und gibt die Bedeutung: Kybele wird also die Siegreiche, vielleicht
als die siegreiche Stadtgöttin ausgezeichnet." Therefore, in contrast
to the typical Roman depiction of Cybele's enthroned cult statue
placed on a lion biga, the Greeks consistently showed Cybele standing, driving her chariot, and accompanied by other mythological
figures. Her blowing mantle and leaning posture add to the fanciful
nature of those depictions.

Greek literary sources do not indicate that the Greeks transported
the goddess in procession either. Indeed, several texts show that the
statue of Cybele remained in her shrine, and that her devotees pa-
raded about with her temple as their goal, in much the same way
that the devotees of Demeter proceeded up the Sacred Way to Eleusis.

Herodotus (4.76) relates how the Scythians resisted a certain Anacharsis, when he brought to their country the rites of Cybele as practiced by the Greeks: Ξεινικοῖσι δὲ νομαίοισι καὶ οὗτοι φεύγουσι αἰνῶς
χρᾶσθαι, μήτε τεῶν ἄλλων, Ἑλληνικοῖσι δὲ καὶ ἥκιστα, ὡς διέδεξαν Ἀνά-
χαρσίς τε καὶ δεύτερα αὗτις Σκύλης. Once, when in Cyzicus, where
the Argonauts were thought to have introduced the cult, he saw the
inhabitants conducting a festival to Cybele with great pomp, he vowed
that he would also celebrate the festival exactly as he saw the Cy-
zicenes do. Back in Scythia, Herodotus says, he reenacted the ritual
completely, by "carrying a tympanum and wearing images (ἐκδησά-
μενος ἀγάλματα)." We learn from Polybius (21.37) that these ἀγάλματα
were images of Cybele and Attis.[41] Significantly, Anacharsis did not
feel compelled to transport a statue of the goddess about with a biga
of lions.

Apollonius of Rhodes' (*Arg*.1.1103–1152) account adds several more
features of the practice of the cult at Cyzicus, where again the Greeks
are said to have taught the inhabitants its rites. The Greek heroes
set up a carven wood image of the goddess, and next to her built an
altar, on which they sacrificed and poured libations. The young men
danced around her altar clashing their swords on their shields, while
others whirled rhomboi and beat tympani. After the Great Mother
caused miraculous signs, such as the taming of the wild animals, to
indicate her acceptance of the rites, the heroes made a feast and

---

[41] Cf. the phrase τύπους τε περικείμενοι τοῖς στήθεσι in Dionysius of Halicarnassus, cited above. See also A.S.F. Gow, "The Gallus and the Lion," *JHS* 80 (1960)
88–93.

sang songs to the goddess. Once again we see that the parade is absent.

The remaining literary evidence for the Greek rites of Cybele indicate that the Greeks worshipped her in conjunction with the mystery cults along with Demeter, Persephone, Dionysus, and Pan. Although that evidence corroborates the previous passages, it will best be considered along with the Greek use of torches, which Lucretius does not mention, but which was the primary visual symbol of the mystery rites.

Let us return now to the archeological evidence, where we can see clearly that the devotees of the Great Mother held processions both toward Cybele and around her, but never by transporting her. A relief from Lebadea in Boeotia of the Hellenistic period depicts Cybele seated on a throne that rests on the ground. A lion sits beside the throne. A procession of figures, some divine, some human, extend rightward from the throne. Despite the attendance of Dionysus, Pan, the Curetes, the Dioscuri and Hecate, the presence of the smaller, human figures along with a table on which offerings are placed, indicates that the scene is a realistic, though idealized, portrayal of a ritual event.[42] Another relief from Philiati in Attica, and one from the Greco-Etruscan trading port of Spina in Northern Italy, repeats much of the same visual imagery. In the latter we can see flute players, women dancing, and others holding cymbals and tympani performing before a seated Cybele and another, unidentified divinity.[43] In none of these portrayals does Cybele appear on a lion biga amid a crowd of spectators. Apparently, in Greece before and during the lifetime of Lucretius the devotees of Cybele worshipped the goddess at a fixed sacred site.

Mystery rites

Lynn Roller has argued that the Phrygians of Central Anatolia, who had long worshipped the Mother Goddess in their own manner, suddenly adopted Hellenistic iconography and practice beginning in the

---

[42] Vermaseren, *CCCA* IV.432.

[43] Often thought to be Dionysus-Sabazius; Vermaseren, *CCCA* IV.214; Stella Patitucci, Osservazioni sul cratere polignoteo della tomba 128 di valle Trebba," *Arte antica e moderna* 18 (1962) 146–164.

late third century B.C. The reasons for the sudden change was political and the effect was dramatic. At once the stylized, standing
figure, with veil and high headdress and bird of prey, gave way to
the seated, enthroned goddess who holds a tympanum and patera.
This Hellenized figure is accompanied by a lion, instead of a bird of
prey, and often by a girl who holds a torch. Her clothing has changed
also into more traditional Greek clothing. Interestingly, the immediate source for the new style came from Western Anatolia, especially
Pergamon, the leading Greek city in Asia Minor, which was also the
source of the Roman cult. It was from Pergamon that the Romans
fetched the black stone (Varro *LL* 6.15).

The Romans may have been mistaken, then, to imagine they were
bringing a strictly Phrygian deity to their city; she may have possessed more Greek marks than they knew. Nevertheless, the Romans,
who knew how to make modifications of their own to the practices
of other cultures, did not bring back aspects of Cybele's worship that
were not suited to their taste, whether Greek or Phrygian.

Perhaps the most striking omission was that of the torch-bearing
maiden, which the Phrygians had assimilated from the Greeks and
applied to their existing funerary cult.[44] For the Greeks, however,
the torches had further significance beyond chthonic. Clearly, the
constant connection of Cybele with Dionysus, Demeter, and Hecate
in Greek and even Phrygian iconography, along with the appearance of torches, a traditional symbol of night rituals, shows that the
Greeks had incorporated her cult into already existing mystery religions.[45] Euripides implies this connection in his *Bacchae* when in the
parados the chorus invoke Cybele along with Dionysus and his mysteries. Likewise, in his *Cretans*, Euripides has the chorus-leader speak
of his pure life after becoming an initiate, as he puts it, of,

> Idaean Zeus, and after celebrating the thunder of night-roaming Zagreus
> (Dionysus) and the raw feast, and holding up torches for the Mountain

---

[44] L. Roller, "The Great Mother at Gordion: The Hellenization of an Anatolian
Cult," *JHS* 111 (1991) 128–143, at 140–141.

[45] On this see G. Sfameni Gasparro, *Soteriological and Mystic Aspects in the Cult of
Cybele and Attis* (Leiden 1985) 9–25. On the Phrygian side the following inscription
from Pergamon of the Roman Imperial period shows the practice of mystery rites
there: Σεκοῦνδος, μύ[σ]της Μη[τ]ρὸς Βα[[σιλ]ήας, [ἀν]έθηκε; see M. Fränkel, *Inschriften
von Pergamon* (Berlin 1895) no. 334. Strabo, *Geogr.*10.3.15–16, believes that Cybele
has had mystery rites in Phrygia from the earliest times.

Mother, and being consecrated <in the armed dances> of the Kouretes, I received the title of bacchos.[46]

The Mountain Mother is Cybele, of course, and her devotees worship her at night along with Dionysus.

Pindar also knows a connection between the mysteries of Dionysus and those of Cybele. In one fragmentary text he observes that her devotees dance and play their instruments while the torch blazes beneath the tawny pines (αἰθομένα τε δᾷς ὑπὸ ξαν[θα]ῖσι πεύκαις, frg. 79b)[47] Elsewhere, Pindar (Pyth.3.77–79) says that young maidens often sing praises to Cybele, along with Pan, during the night (μέλπονται... ἐννύχιαι).[48] Diodorus Siculus (3.55.8–9) relates how Cybele established the race of Corybantes and set up mysteries (μυστήρια) to herself on the island of Samothrace. Who fathered the Corybantes, Diodorus says, is only revealed during the secret rites: ἐν ἀπορρήτῳ κατὰ τὴν τελετὴν παραδίδοσθαι. The poet Thyillus mentions the revelling of the night festivals, the tossing of the head among the pines, and the playing of the horned flute in honor of Cybele.[49]

In some places the rites for Cybele took place in the same temple where other mystery rites were performed. Pausanias (37.1–4) writes, for example, that four stades from Acacesium one may find τὸ ἱερὸν τῆς Δεσποίνης, wherein were three altars, one to Demeter, one to Persephone, and one to Cybele. Near these three altars is one huge statue of Demeter and Persephone seated on a throne. Carved into the base of the throne are images of the Corybantes, suggesting the worship of Cybele. Apparently, the Greeks so closely identified Cybele with Demeter, in this instance, they did not feel it necessary to create a separate statue for her.[50]

From at least the time of Demosthenes, the Greeks worshipped Attis alongside Cybele with mystic rites. At De corona 259–60 the orator attacks the character and respectability of Aeschines by connecting him with certain mystery rites imported from Phrygia. At night, Aeschines would assist his mother by reading the passages from

---

[46] E. fr. 79.9–15 Austin = 472.9–15 N. The supplement of ἐνόπλοισι χοροῖς comes from M.L. West, The Orphic Poems (Oxford 1983) 153.

[47] Cf. Strabo Geogr.10.3.12–13; he cites Pindar's fragment and concludes the κοινωνία of the rites of Cybele and Dionysus.

[48] Cf. frg. 95, where Pan is called the companion (ὀπαδέ) of the Great Mother.

[49] Anth.Pal.7.223. Wiseman (1974) 132–133, 140–146.

[50] Cf. Lydus, Mens.3: ἡ Δημήτηρ... λέγεται δὲ καὶ Κυβέλη. See Farnell, Cults of the Greek States, III,312, for further references. G.E. Mylonas, Eleusis and the Eleusinian

the mystic books, clothing the initiates with fawn skin, and carrying out various odd purification rites. By day he would lead the band of revellers through the streets while handling objects with magical and chthonic properties (fennel, white poplar, snakes). With his band of revellers he shouts invocations to two Phrygian deities with whom Cybele is most often associated in Greek art:

εὐοῖ σαβοῖ
ὑῆς ἄττης ἄττης ὑῆς.

The mystic revellers appear to be invoking Attis and possibly even Sabazius, the oriental Dionysus.[51]

Several Greek reliefs show this same connection between Cybele's consort and the mystery rites. From the Piraeus a votive relief dating to the latter half of the fourth century B.C. shows Attis in traditional garb, seated, and being offered a small jug by a standing Cybele (called here by her Phrygian name Angdistis). The inscription underneath reads, 'Ανγδίστει καὶ ῎Αττιδι Τιμοθέα ὑπὲρ τῶν παίδων κατὰ πρό-σταγμα. Roller interprets the Cybele's gesture to mean that Attis is being welcomed into the cult as an honored companion, if not a divinity, who is worthy of worship.[52] Another relief of unknown provenance, dating to the second century B.C., depicts Attis and Cybele, both standing, receiving the offerings of two women who enter the temple. The veiled head of the older woman suggests she is an initiate of the goddess, since the Greeks did not wear veils normally in worship except in mystic rites. A relief from Athens likewise shows Attis as an equal partner to Cybele.[53] The many mythological stories that developed about Attis during the Hellenistic period justify and define his role within the mysteries, as a reborn divinity.[54]

Significantly, Lucretius does not mention torches in his passage,

---

Mysteries (Princeton 1961) 288–291, thinks that the two cults could not be identified. Several statues of Cybele have been found at Eleusis; see Vermaseren, *CCCA* II.371–380.

[51] Strabo, *Geogr.*10.3.18 says that these words, evoe saboe, hyes attes attes hyes, are in the ritual of Sabazius and the Great Mother. That Sabazius is equivalent to Dionysus and is connected with Cybele also, see *idem* 10.3.12–13,15. But E. Lane expresses skepticism about the relevance of this passage to the cult of Sabazius; see his *Corpus Cultus Iovis Sabazii III: Conclusions* (Leiden 1989) *passim*.

[52] Lynn Roller, "Attis on Greek Votive Monuments: Greek God or Phrygian," *Hesperia* 63 (1994) 245–262, pl. 55–56. Cf. *CCCA* 2.308.

[53] B. Holtzmann, "Collection de l'École française: sculptures," *BCH* 96 (1972) 73–99, at 94–96, no. 9, fig. 11.

[54] H. Hepding, *Attis, seine Mythen und sein Kult* (Giessen 1903) 5–97.

nor does he give any other indication of mystery rites. Likewise, Attis, who later in the imperial period becomes the focus of mystic activity within the cult, is conspicuously absent from Lucretius' account.[55] The Roman leadership would not have allowed its citizens to engage in mystery rites for Cybele. The senate had a history of resistance to mystery religions in general during the Republican period, whether they were public or private.[56] At *De legibus* 2.35–37 Cicero implies that the only nocturnal rites permitted at Rome during his day were the Eleusinian mysteries, performed in a more restrained, Roman version, and the traditional *Bona Dea* rites.[57] Since the senate permitted no Roman citizen to participate in the cult of Cybele, we can hardly believe that citizens could become initiated into it, even in a private ceremony.

Certainly, when Claudius, yielding to many foreign influences, introduced new elements into the cult and allowed Roman citizens to participate, and later when the Antonines added still more elements, we find many testimonia to mysticism.[58] Lucretius' picture, however, is consistent with all other evidence for the cult in his period, including, as we have seen, the claims of Dionysius of Halicarnassus (2.19.3): . . . οὐ θεοφορήσεις, οὐ κορυβαντιασμούς, οὐκ ἀγυρμούς, οὐ Βακχείας, καὶ τελετὰς ἀπορρήτους, οὐ διαπαννυχισμοὺς ἐν ἱεροῖς ἀνδρῶν σὺν γυναιξίν . . .

Some scholars have pointed to evidence that would suggest that individual citizens did practice private mystery rites to Cybele even in the first century B.C.,[59] and thus have argued that Dionysius of Halicarnassus was either mistaken when he said that the Romans did not carry on night revels, or only has in mind the public (δημοσία)

---

[55] For archaeological evidence that Cybele and Attis were worshipped together in procession during later periods see Donald Bailey, "Attis on a Cult Car," *Antiquaries Journal* 56 (1976) 72–3, pl. xii, and bibliography there.

[56] As in the case of the Bacchanalia affair; *CIL* 1.196 and 10.104; Livy 39.8–18. One may note also how often the Roman authorities demolished altars and statues of Isis from 59 B.C. onward, and outlawed her rites; on this see G. Wissowa, *Religion und Cultus der Römer* (Munich 1912²) 351.

[57] Only much later would Cybele be connected with Bona Dea; see H.H.J. Brouwer, "The Great Mother and the Good Goddess," *Hommages à Maarten J. Vermaseren*, vol. 1 (Leiden 1978) 142–159.

[58] The resulting rites are chronologically arranged, according to their time of introduction, by Duncan Fishwick, "The *Cannophori* and the March Festival of Magna Mater," *TAPA* 97 (1966) 193–202.

[59] Especially T.P. Wiseman, "Cybele, Virgil and Augustus," in *Poetry and Politics in the Age of Augustus*, edd. Tony Woodman and David West (Cambridge 1984) 118, 225 fn. 11.

expressions of the cult. Nevertheless, we should reexamine the evidence traditionally offered for private mystery rites in the late Republic and Augustan periods.

Those who have argued for such rites have depended foremost on the testimony of the Greek poet Thyillus. He certainly lived in Rome and knew Cicero, and he does portray the cult of Cybele in terms of a mystery religion:

Ἡ κροτάλοις ὀρχηστρὶς Ἀρίστιον, ἡ περὶ πεύκας
τὰς Κυβέλης πλοκάμους ῥῖψαι ἐπισταμένη,
ἡ λωτῶι κερόεντι φορουμένη, ἡ τρὶς ἐφεξῆς
εἰδυῖ᾽ ἀκρήτου χειλοποτεῖν κύλικα,
ἐνθάδ᾽ ὑπὸ πτελέαις ἀναπαύεται, οὐκέτ᾽ ἔρωτι,
οὐκέτι παννυχίδων τερπομένη καμάτοις.
Κῶμοι καὶ μανίαι, μέγα χαίρετε· κεῖθ᾽[...]
ἡ τὸ πρὶν στεφάνων ἄνθεσι κρυπτομένη.[60]

Aristion, dancer with castanets, who knew how to toss her braided hair while holding the pine torches of Cybele, who was carried away by the horned flute, who knew how to drink down a cup of strong wine, thrice in a row, here she takes a rest under the elms, no longer delighted by love, no longer by the tiring all-night festivals. A great farewell, revelries and frenzies: she lies buried . . . who was formerly crowned with a wreath of flowers.

We cannot assume, however, that Thyillus describes a Roman rite. Thyillus was Greek, and heavily influenced by the Alexandrian tradition.[61] Furthermore, in a letter of Cicero to Atticus (1.9), who was residing in Athens, Cicero passes along the following message from the Greek poet: *Thyillus te rogat et ego eius rogatu* Εὐμολπιδῶν πάτρια. The phrase "ancestral rites of Eumolpus' clan" indicates that Thyillus wanted some information or documentation detailing the rites of the Eleusinian Mysteries, presumably for some poem he was writing.[62] If he could seek information from Greece about the worship of Demeter, obviously he could do the same for the worship of Cybele. Aristion is, after all, a Greek name.

Similarly, Varro's *Menippean Satires* (*Eum.* frgs. 33–49) do not pro-

---

[60] I have followed the text of D.L. Page, *Further Greek Epigrams* (Cambridge 1981) 96–97.

[61] For example, see Rhianus *A.P.*6.173 (= vii in A.S.F. Gow and D.L. Page, *The Greek Anthology: Hellenistic Epigrams* [Cambridge 1965] 176).

[62] Robert Tyrrell and Louis Purser, *The Correspondence of M. Tullius Cicero* (London 1904³) vol. 1, 136; D.R. Shackleton Bailey, *Cicero's Letters to Atticus* (Cambridge 1965) vol. 1, 284.

vide any evidence for the Roman practice of the cult, rather, as Cèbe has argued, the allusions to Athens are clear.[63] The narrator has just passed the holy precinct of Serapis before he hears a noise coming from the temple of Cybele:

> Commodum praeter Matris Deum aedem exaudio cymbalorum sonitum.

This cannot take place in Rome because the cult of Serapis, while already entrenched in Athens, had not yet gained a firm footing in the city of Rome during the Republican period.[64]

The next fragment, however, has been the source of confusion. The narrator arrives at the temple, and as a yearly offering is presented to the goddess, the Galli in the temple begin to chant their hymn. The scene is described as follows:

> Cum illoc venio, video gallorum frequentiam in templo, qui dum messem hornam adlatam imponeret aedilis signo Cybelae, deam gallantes vario recinebant strepitu.

The word *aedilis* cannot refer to a curule aedile, as one might expect, since, as already noted, by law Roman citizens could not perform rites for Cybele. Cèbe suggests *aedituus* as a likely alternative, and I believe that is the best solution.[65]

Other evidence is equally weak for proving private mystery rites during the late Republic. Catullus' poem, which says more about the myth of Attis than about the rites of Cybele, was likely the result of his travels in Bithynia or the influence of an Alexandrian model.[66] Firmicus Maternus (*De errore* 18.1) and Clement of Alexandria (*Protrepticus* 2.15), both of whom connect Cybele to the mystery religions, reflect later developments of the cult under the emperors. Firmicus Maternus, in fact, wrote *c.* 350 A.D., and may well be speaking about

---

[63] Jean-Pierre Cèbe, *Varron, Satires Ménippées* (Rome 1977) vol. 4, pp. 562–565. For the text I have used A. Riese, *M. Terenti Varronis saturarum Menippearum reliquiae* (Leipzig 1865), but with reference to F. Bücheler and W. Heraeus, *Petronii saturae, adiectae sunt Varronis et Senecae saturae similesque reliquiae* (Berlin 1963[8]), and to Cèbe's own version of the text.

[64] According to Apuleius (*Met.*11.30), the soldiers of Sulla brought back with them from the East the worship of Isis and Serapis, but, though a priest of Isis Capitolina is attested for this period (*CIL* I[2] 1263), other evidence indicates that the Senate quickly suppressed public expressions of worship to them and demolished their altars and temples as fast as they were built. See K. Latte, *Römische Religionsgeschichte* (Munich 1967) 282.

[65] Cèbe, vol. 4, p. 626.

[66] Graillot, 103.

the rites of Isis and Osiris.[67] The only evidence for private worship of Cybele are the votive statues of Attis dating from the Republican period which were found within her temple. We cannot assume, however, that they point to an organized mystery religion, since the Romans were notorious for their vowing and votive offerings (cf. *DRN* 5.1202, 1229).[68] Romans could be well aware of the existence and special role of Attis in Cybele's cult without worshipping him alongside of her. We can contrast also the frequency with which the figurines of Attis and Cybele appear in private homes in Greece and Hellenized Phrygia with their complete absence from Roman homes.

The Greeks made Attis an important object of worship alongside Cybele, especially in the Hellenistic period, as is well documented. The Phrygians preferred to treat Attis as the high priest of the goddess, but still, under Greek influence, they gradually assumed the mystic elements of the cult.[69] And as mentioned, the archeological remains from the empire document the worship of Attis alongside of Cybele. Yet Lucretius' Cybele, as well as the Cybele portrayed on Republican coins, has no such consort. Significantly, Augustine reports that Varro omitted any reference to Attis in his discussion of the cult: *Et Attis ille non est commemoratus nec eius ab isto interpretatio requisita est, in cuius dilectionis memoriam Gallus absciditur.* He goes on to say that *docti Graeci atque sapientes* both discussed him and offered allegorical interpretations for his function in the cult. But Lucretius could not include him in his passage, because the Romans would have viewed his presence as odd.

Musical instruments

The musical instruments mentioned by Lucretius also indicate that he has in mind the Roman version of the cult. The procession of Cybele through the streets is accompanied by the stretched *tympana*, hollow *cymbala*, raucous horns, and hollow *tibia*. In contrast, the Greeks

---

[67] As Vermaseren, *Cybele and Attis*, 116, believes.

[68] For a discussion of the problem see P. Romanelli, "Magna Mater e Attis sul Palatino," *Hommages à Jean Bayet* (= *Latomus* 70 [1964]) 619–626.

[69] Diodorus of Siculus, 3.59.7, writes that the Phrygians, facing a plague, were told by an oracle to bury the body of the dead Attis and worship Cybele as a goddess. He adds, "Wherefore, the Phrygians made an image of the youth, since the body had disappeared in the course of time, before which they made honors

and Phrygians worshipped Cybele with a slightly different array of instruments. Diogenes Tragicus adds one to Lucretius' list and drops another:

καίτοι κλύω μὲν Ἀσιάδος μιτρηφόρους
Κυβέλας γυναῖκας, παῖδας ὀλβίων Φρυγῶν
τυπάνοισι καὶ ῥόμβοισι καὶ χαλκοκτύπων
βόμβοις βρεμούσας ἀντίχερσι κυμβάλων ...⁷⁰

Like Lucretius, Diogenes mentions the tympana and cymbala, but he excludes the raucous horns of Lucretius' account and adds rhomboi.[71] The rhombos, often translated "bull-roarer", has been described as "an oblong piece of wood to the point of which a cord is attached. The instrument is swung in a circle by the cord and emits a muttering roar which rises in pitch as the speed is increased."[72] Both the Greeks and the Romans considered it an efficacious love charm when the instrument was spun and words were chanted.[73] Furthermore, Greek writers frequently attest its use in initiation rites of various mystery religions.[74] Its use in Dionysian rites is well documented, as in those of Demeter.[75] Additionally, although Diogenes specifically refers to "the turban-wearing women of Asia," other writers show that the Greeks knew the instrument in their worship of Cybele too. Apollonius of Rhodes makes the Argonauts teach the Phrygians the

---

suitable to his suffering and propitiated the wrath of him who had been wronged. They continue doing these rites to this day." (Διόπερ τοὺς Φρύγας ἠφανισμένου τοῦ σώματος διὰ τὸν χρόνον εἴδωλον κατασκευάσαι τοῦ μειρακίου, πρὸς ᾧ θρηνοῦντας ταῖς οἰκείαις τιμαῖς τοῦ πάθους ἐξιλάσκεσθαι τὴν τοῦ παρανομηθέντος μῆνιν· ὅπερ μέχρι τοῦ καθ' ἡμᾶς βίου ποιοῦντας αὐτοὺς διατελεῖν.)

[70] *TrGF* 45 F 1.3, cited by Athenaeus 14.635-6. Cf. Strabo, *Geogr.*10.3.15: τῷ δ' αὐλῷ καὶ κτύπῳ κροτάλων τε καὶ κυμβάλων καὶ τυμπάνων καὶ ταῖς ἐπιβοήσεσι καὶ εὐασμοῖς καὶ ποδοκρουστίαις οἰκεῖα ἐξεύροντο.

[71] He also excludes the *tibia*, but other Greek authors include them. See discussion below.

[72] A.S.F. Gow, "ΙΥΓΞ, ΡΟΜΒΟΣ, Rhombus, Turbo," *JHS* 54 (1934) 1-13, at 6. Cf. Gow's note on Theoc.2.30 in *Theocritus*, (Cambridge 1950) II,44 and pl. V.1 and 2. Archytas, Diels-Kranz *Vors.*1.435 has (sc. ῥόμβοι) ἀσυχᾷ μὲν κινούμενοι βαρὺν ἀφίεντι ἄχον, ἰσχυρῶς δὲ κύκλιος ἔνοσις αἰθερία.

[73] Theoc.2.30; Luc. *Dial.Mer.*4.5; Prop.3.6.26; Ovid *Amores* 1.8.6-7.

[74] M. Eliade, *Rites and Symbols of Initiation* (1965), 8-14,21-23,142. Cf. Schol.Clem.Al. *Protr.* p. 15 P (on the authority of Diogenianus): ῥόμβος· ... ξυλάριον οὗ ἐξῆπται τὸ σπαρτίον, καὶ ἐν ταῖς τελεταῖς ἐδονεῖτο ἵνα ῥοιζῇ. *Etymologicum Magnum* 706.25: μυστικῷ σανιδίῳ ὃ στρέφουσιν εἰς τὸν ἀέρα καὶ ἦχον ἐμποιοῦσιν. For a similar description see Hesychius s.v. ῥόμβος.

[75] For Dionysian rites see A. fr. 71.8 f. M. = 57.8 f. N., E. *Hel.*1362, *Anth.Pal.*6.165.5, Orph. frg. 34 (Kern, *Orphicorum Fragmenta* [Berlin 1922] = Clem. *Protr.*2.18). For the Eleusinian Mysteries see Epiphanius (Kern, p. 110).

use of the rhombos in the cult of Cybele: ἔνθεν ἐσαιεὶ ῥόμβῳ καὶ τυπάνῳ Ῥείην Φρύγες ἱλάσκονται (Arg.1.1138–39). In the De musica passage cited above Philodemus also links the use of the tympanum and the rhombos, almost certainly in reference to the worship of Cybele. A fragment of Pindar has σεμνᾷ μὲν κατάρχει ματέρι πὰρ μεγάλᾳ ῥόμβοι τυμπάνων, which must mean something like, "the rhomboi lead the tympana in the service to the Great Mother." Whereas we find the tympanum appearing in a variety of contexts as a means to reaching a frenzied state, we must conclude that, since the rhombos was always tied to magic and initiation rites, it most properly belonged to the Cybele cult in its function as a mystery religion with no purpose outside of it.[76]

Lucretius also mentions the raucous horns (raucisonoque minantur cornua cantu, 6.619) and the hollow pipes (cava tibia) which goad the minds of the Phrygian followers. The latter instrument appears in an anonymous poem of the Greek Anthology (A.P.6.51), which, although addressed to Rhea, clearly connects her with the Great Mother Cybele from Phrygia. The poet appeals to Rhea "nurse of Phrygian lions" to show kindness to a certain Alexis, who apparently fell into a state of frenzy while worshipping the Great Mother. The instruments that aroused his mind were the shrill-toned cymbals (κύμβαλά τ' ὀξύφθογγα), the deep-toned pipes made from the crooked horn of the young steer (βαρυφθόγγων αὐλῶν),[77] and the echoing tympana (τύμπανα ἠχήεντα). Furthermore, the poet adds the bloody knives to his list of stimulants: αἵματι φοινιχθέντα φάσγανα. Respectively, those instruments are equivalent to Lucretius' cymbala concava, cava tibia, and tympana tenta. And like the anonymous Greek poet, Lucretius concludes his list of musical instruments with the bloody knives: telaque praeportant violenti signa furoris (6.620).

---

[76] Except as a child's toy (e.g., AP 6.309, Leonidas Alexandrinus).

[77] Thyillus' λωτῷ κερόεντι. Cf. Philip of Thessalonica's (Anth.Pal.6.94) λωτοὺς κεροβόας. On the instrument, which came in pairs, one of which was curved like a horn on the end. See Daremberg and Saglio's Dict. des Antiquités, s.v. tibia. Cf. Catullus' list, 63.21–22, ubi cymbalum sonat vox, ubi tympana reboant, | tibicen ubi canit Phryx curvo grave calamo, where the last instrument is again the curved pipe; Ovid's, Fasti 4.181, inflexo Berecyntia tibia cornu flabit (here cornu refers to the curvature of the tibia, as at Ovid Epist.1.1.19 and Met.3.531); and idem, 4.190, horrendo lotos adunca sono. Also Poll.4.71,74; Verg. Aen.9.116; Ovid Met.4.30; Pliny NH 16.172; Diodorus Siculus 3.58. The double Phrygian tibia appears often in connection with Cybele, as on a relief from Lanuvium (middle of the second century A.D.), for which see CCCA III.466 and Gow, "The Gallus and the Lion," 88–93 and plate viii.1.

We should note that Lucretius' raucous horn has no parallel in the Greek practice of the cult, not in the passage of the anonymous Greek poet, nor in any other Greek presentation of Cybele's rites.[78] Catullus might have known such a Greek instrument in the cult of Dionysus, but seems to be merely following Lucretius when he writes of the Bacchants,

> plangebant aliae proceris tympana palmis
> aut tereti tenues tinnitus aere ciebant.
> multis raucisonos efflabant cornua bombos,
> barbaraque horribili stridebat tibia cantu.

> 64.261–264

Catullus' statement cannot give conclusive evidence for or against our thesis, since he relates a mythological story of Dionysus, but he does show an awareness, at least, that the raucous horn is an instrument of frenzied worship.

In fact, it was the Etruscans who invented the instrument, and the Romans adopted it early on for many functions, especially military and athletic.[79] It looked like a large, rounded C held together across the middle by a rod, and was especially effective for rallying the troops or announcing gladiator troops. The Romans also used it in assemblies, at funerals, and in weddings. Yet the question still remains whether or not the Roman worshippers of Cybele blew horns in her procession.

No direct evidence supports Lucretius' claim, even for the Roman cult. We do know, however, that the Romans were using the *cornu* in private and public religious ceremonies. Perseus (*Sat.*1.99) mentions its use in the worship of Bacchus, which supports Catullus' application of the *cornu* to that cult. An inscription from the Naples area speaks of the *tubicen sacrorum populi Romani*. Since the tuba often appears side by side with the *cornu* on Roman reliefs, as on the Arch of Constantine, we may surmise that accompanied it in religious rites also.[80] It seems likely, then, that the Romans found it natural to add the raucous horn to an already existing collection of instruments attached to the worship of Cybele from earliest times.

---

[78] As Showerman has noted, p. 40.
[79] See Saglio and Daremberg, s.v. *cornu*.
[80] Mommsen, *insc.regn.Neap.*4092.

Visual Imagery

Another feature of the Cybele cult in Rome was the shower of rose petals on the Great Mother and her companions: *ninguntque rosarum | floribus umbrantes matrem comitumque catervas* (Lucr.2.627–628). Ovid places the first occurrence for this rite at the time of the goddess' original entrance into the city of Rome: *sparguntur iunctae flore recente boves* (*Fasti* 4.346). Greek and Phrygian sources do not allude to this practice, although for the Greeks the act of garlanding in sacred rites was common enough.[81] We learn from both Horace and Propertius that the Romans scattered roses at the Phrygian revelers to heighten the sense of ecstasy and divine possession. Horace writes of the preparation for a dinner party:

> insanire iuvat: cur Berecyntiae
> cessant flamina tibiae?
> cur pendet tacita fistula cum lyra?
> parcentes ego dextras
> odi: sparge rosas; . . .

> (*Odes* 3.19.18)

Horace speaks in terms of the rites of Cybele (Berecyntiae tibiae), but he is not interested in worshipping the goddess at the party, rather, he wants to conjure up the same frenzied rapture that the Phrygian companions experience. The roses, which he wants thrown, were to be directed at the revellers themselves, as Propertius indicates in the case of another drunken party:

> Miletus tibicen erat, crotalistria Byblis
> (haec facilis spargi munda sine arte rosa),
> Magnus et ipse suos breviter concretus in artus
> iactabat truncas ad cava buxa manus.

The instruments alluded to belong to Cybele's worship, although, as in the case of Horace's poem, the rites of Cybele are not directly at issue. Apparently the Romans were beginning to incorporate into their own wild parties the instruments of frenzy they saw in the Megalensia. Again the revelers throw roses, but here the poet makes clear that Byblis, the artless dancer, is herself the object of the sprinkling (*spargi*).

---

[81] And always as the antithesis of mourning: Plut. *Consol. ad Apoll.*119a, Diog. Laert.2.54.

Finally, the visual imagery of the cult at Rome best illuminates the cryptic line *munificat tacita mortalis muta salute* (2.625). Commentators interpret the passage as a reference to the statue of the goddess, which, since it is made of stone, cannot speak. Stewart argues that Cybele gives a silent greeting because

> ... she is the mythical equivalent of the mute and noncommunicative nature of the atomic universe, spelled out in realistic terms in the lines following her appearance. She may bless men with goods of which she is the source, but she does so silently and indifferently.[82]

Neither explanation, however, explains why Lucretius would twice stress the silence of her blessing (*tacita* and *muta*). Lucretius hardly needed to remind his readers that Nature lacks the power of communication, nor would he gain anything by pointing out the obvious fact that the statue was artificial. Instead, I believe Lucretius is reacting to the specific nature of the Roman portrayal of the goddess.

Livy writes that when the Romans, prompted by the Sibylline books, went to Phrygia in 204 to bring back the Idaean Mother to Rome, they were given, not a statue of the goddess, but the goddess herself in the form of a black stone: *Is* [sc. Attalus] *legatos comiter acceptos Pessinuntem in Phrygia deduxit sacrumque iis lapidem, quam Matrem dum esse incolae dicebant* ... 29.11. That black stone made its way into the temple of Victory and later into its own temple within the pomererium. Archaeological, numismatic, and literary evidence indicates that a full statue of the goddess was associated with her cult also from the outset.[83] Not until Arnobius and Prudentius, however, do we learn how the statue related to the stone in the ritual expression of the cult. Arnobius writes,

> Adlatum ex Phrygia nihil quidem aliud scribitur missum rege ab Attalo, nisi lapis quidam non magnus, ferri manu hominis sine ulla inpressione qui posset, coloris furui atque atri, angellis prominentibus inaequalis, et quem omnes hodie ipso illo videmus in signo oris positum, indolatum et asperum et simulacro faciem minus expressam simulatione praebentem. (*Adv.nat.*7.49)

---

[82] Stewart, "The Silence of Magna Mater," 78; followed by D. Clay, *Lucretius and Epicurus* (Ithaca 1983) 229.

[83] For example, the Volteius coin in 78 B.C. (Crawford 385.4) and the coin of the two praetors L. Cestius and C. Norbanus in 43 B.C. (Crawford 491.2). See also the remains of the goddess' statue (unfortunately without the head), in E. Nash, *Pictorial Dictionary of Ancient Rome* (New York, 1962²) vol. II, pp. 29 and 30.

Arnobius' passage reveals that the Romans placed the rough, black stone of the Magna Mater into the face of the goddess' statue, which had been hollowed out for the purpose. The fact that the stone "offered a face to the goddess' statue that was not at all realistic" furthers the visual imagery of a face without eyes, a nose, and, more to the point, a mouth.

A passage of Prudentius confirms Arnobius' observations:

> Nudare plantas ante carpentum scio
> proceres togatos matris Idaeae sacris.
> lapis nigellus evehendus essedo
> muliebris oris clausus argento sedet,
> quem dum ad lavacrum praeeundo ducitis
> pedes remotis atterentes calceis,
> Almonis usque pervenitis rivulum.
>
> *Perist.*10.154–60

Prudentius indicates that the stone was small and encased in silver (*nigellus . . . clausus argento*). The phrase *muliebris oris* can only mean that the stone was set in some sort of statue, while *essedo . . . sedet* recalls Lucretius' *sedibus in curru* (2.601). Since only the body of the statue survives, we must assume that Arnobius gives an accurate report. Now we understand what Lucretius saw that caused him to emphasize the muteness of the goddess and her silent greeting: a rather bizarre looking statue with a black stone for a face.

Conclusion

Early scholarship on the cult of Cybele did not proceed cautiously enough, so that many mistaken notions about her rites still persist. The Romans of the late Republic did not worship the goddess with the same rites and in the same manner as the Greeks of the same period, despite the fact that they took the cult from an Eastern Greek city. The Romans themselves believed that they were assimilating a Phrygian cult, but even so they passed laws and modified the rites according to their own temperament and designs. All that was permitted to the Roman citizenry was to watch the annual procession, enjoy the games and shows, and, at least in the case of the aristocracy, to dine together.

The Greeks had an entirely different outlook on Cybele. They had so connected her with the mystic, orgiastic worship of Demeter and Dionysus that they had merged her observances into theirs. For this reason we find in their literature and among their archaeological remains so many indications of mystic initiations and ecstatic rites. Almost a century would pass after Lucretius' day, however, before such secret, private rites took hold in Rome. Still another century would pass before all the Eastern elements made an impact on Roman practice.

Lucretius, then, must find his place within this uneven evolution of Cybele's cult if we are to understand the intent of his passage.[84] To be sure, he offered a red herring when he directed the attention of his reader to the learned old Greek poets. Still, his contemporaries would not have been fooled. They would have recognized the rowdy procession, the lion biga, and the turreted crown. They had seen her armed attendants, and had heard the raucous music, especially the Etruscan horns. They knew too the shower of roses, the collection of coins, and likely understood why Lucretius called the mother mute and her greeting silent. And they must have found the delineation of spectator and participant to be quite natural. They would not have found natural, however, talk of torches and mystery rites, bull-roarers and magic. Attis would have appeared out of place riding on the chariot next to Cybele, as would Dionysus or Pan. No, Lucretius did not transcribe the description from some ancient poet, Stoic philosopher, Callimachus, or any other Greek. If he shows the influence of Greek allegorizers, he does so according to the standards of the Roman *mos maiorum*. But the rites are wholly Roman, such that no Greek writer could have provided.

---

[84] The religious passages of Lucretius reveal a concern for contemporary issues by their attention to Roman rites. See the author's article, "Lucretius and the Epicurean Tradition of Piety," *CP* 90 (1995) 32–58. Whereas the assumption that Lucretius merely copied Hellenistic models undermines his pertinence to contemporary issues, sensitivity to the *Romanitas* of his references allows us locate his passionate appeals in a real and vital context.

MAGNA DEUM MATER IDAEA, CYBELE, AND CATULLUS' *ATTIS*

Sarolta A. Takács

Before Hannibal's victories at Lake Trasimene and Cannae, the *decemviri* consulted the *libri Sibyllini* three times in 218/7 B.C.E.[1] Unfavorable prodigies prompted two of the three consultations. The *decemviri* in charge of the books ordered purifications, sacrifices, *lectisternia*, monetary gifts to various deities,[2] and a new festival for Saturn.[3] After the Trasimene debacle, Q. Fabius Maximus began his second dictatorship with a senatorial meeting. According to Livy's account, the dictator declared that Flaminius' mistake, which led to the defeat, did not arise from "temerity and lack of experience as from neglect of traditional ceremonies, especially the taking of auspices."[4] He urged that the Sibylline Books be consulted, as Livy notes, "a rare measure unless unnatural events of the most dreadful kind were brought to the Senate's notice."[5] Thus, Livy's Fabius emerges as a second Camillus[6] and the Roman through the actions of the Senate as the *religiosissima gens* whose city was founded *auspicio augurioque*. There was a reciprocal mechanism at work that connected the divine and the human sphere. Prescribed rituals guaranteed the *pax deorum* and along reciprocal lines the *pax hominum*. Along these linear patterns of cause and effect, it hardly surprises that the *decemviri* reported

---

[1] Livy 21.62,6, 22.9.8–10, 22.36.6–9, and pl. *Fab.Max.*2.

[2] 40 pounds of gold to the temple of Juno at Lanuvium (Livy 21.62.8) and a 50-pound gold thunderbolt to Jupiter as well as gifts of silver to Juno and Minerva (Livy 22.1.17). Livy does not disclose the contents of the list of "appropriate formulae drawn from the libri Sibyllini" before the battle of Cannae (22.36.9). We only learn that "legates from Paestum brought some golden plates to Rome. They received thanks but just as with the Neapolitans, the Romans did not accept the gold." Besides sacrifices and purification rituals, which aimed to alleviate stress and, in essence, to bind the community together, the Roman state collected additional monetary sources when necessary.

[3] Livy 22.1.19–20. Cato frg. *Or.*18.7 (H. Jordan *M. Catonis Praeter Librum De Re Rustica Quae Extant* (Leipzig, 1860), 48: "Graeco ritu fiebantur Saturnalia."

[4] 22.9.7.

[5] *Ibid.*

[6] This comparison clearly reveals itself 22.14.9.

that "the offerings to Mars had been incorrectly performed, and must, therefore, be performed afresh and on a greater scale."[7] At this occasion, the introduction of the Sicilian Venus Erycina[8] and Mens occurred.[9]

The Romans appropriated and integrated into their pantheon with Venus Erycina, from an area of strategic importance to them, a deity of considerable age and, therefore, religious power. In the case of Erycina the area had been part of the *imperium* since the First Punic War, while Asia Minor was not. The latter had been, however, an important power broker in Greek (Macedonian) affairs ever since Philip V got himself involved in the Carthaginian-Roman conflict. Asia Minor also could be eyed as an eventual lucrative addition to an ever-growing empire especially in 205 B.C.E. when the Macedonian War ended and Hannibal had ceased to be a menacing antagonist. During the Second Punic War, in a time of great anxieties, we see Rome redefine its religion. This brought a Greek veneer and resulted in the increased introduction of literary competitions.

As if Hannibal's victories were not enough, two Vestal Virgins committed sexual offenses (*stupri compertae*), for which one was put to death. The other, escaping the fate of being buried alive, committed suicide. Q. Fabius Pictor was dispatched to Delphi to consult the most prestigious Greek oracle in the Mediterranean world. He returned with an answer.[10] G. Dumézil calls this "an important moment in the development of the Roman cult of Apollo."[11] Apollo, we remember, features prominently in connection with "performing arts."

---

[7] See n. 4 above.

[8] Ovid *Fast*.4.863–76. F. Bömer *P. Ovidius Naso Die Fasten* (Heidelberg, 1958), vol. 2, 284: "Der Eryx ist seit der sagenhaften Wanderung der Elymer bis zum Ende des ersten punischen Krieges einer der bedeutendsten strategischen Punkte der Insel; gleich alt und bedeutend ist das Heiligtum der Aphrodite, das entweder von Aineias (Verg. *Aen*.V,759 ff. Strab.XIII,1,53 p. 608) oder von Eryx, einem anderen Sohn der Aphrodite (Diod. IV 83. Serv. *Aen*.I,570) gestiftet sein soll. Der Aphroditenkult erscheint auf ältesten Münzen (. . .) und weist auf den Orient, speziell Phonikien-Carthago."

On the origins of the cult of Aphrodite see H. Herter, "Die Ursprünge des Aphroditenkultes," in *Éléments orientaux dans la religion grecque ancienne* (Paris, 1960).

[9] Ovid *Fast*.6.241–248 refers to Mens as well. Bömer, 353 agrees with F. Altheim *Römische Religionsgeschichte* (München, 1960), 239–40, that Mens is Roman. On the introduction of this abstract concept as a deity see also G. Wissowa *Römische Religion und Kultus* (München, 1902), 313–4.

[10] Livy 23.11.2–3.

[11] *Archaic Roman Religion*, vol. 2 (Chicago and London, 1970), 479–80. The *ludi Apollinares*, celebrated with horse races in the *circus maximus*, followed suit in 212 B.C.E. (Livy 25.12.14–5).

One would like to think that Fabius also seized the opportunity to collect data concerning the state of affairs in Greece. Unlike the Delphic oracle though, the Sibylline Books ordered unusual rites. Human sacrifice and the burial of a pair of Gauls and Greeks.[12] Nothing, however, could stop the Carthaginians. Rome's nightmare came true; Hannibal *ante portas*. When Philip V of Macedon and Hannibal forged a treaty in 215 B.C.E., Rome's prospects looked grim.

Despite the initial loss of allied Italian cities, Philip's attempt to open a second front in Greece and the Balkans, and the war in Spain, Rome rebounded all the while introducing new religious rituals and presenting generous gifts to temples following Sibylline utterings. While in the midst of crises, the Romans reshaped their religion along the lines of their new-found identity. They were in part the descendants of Trojan Aeneas; their intellectual heritage was Greek.

Pious Aeneas, son of Anchises and Venus, suited the Romans well. This wandering minor Trojan prince existed in Greek myth, a framework the Romans adopted and propagated. In essence, Aeneas and the Romans shared the same mythological "Greekness." Thus, the militarily successful Romans armed with a respectable and tangible past began more intensively to encourage the literary arts whose major proponent had been the Hellenistic world. Ultimately, Romulus' and Remus' foundation developed into a "dignus locus, quo deus omnis eat." Rome, the mistress of the Mediterranean, was the political and religious center of an empire, whose elites prized the arts as much as the successor states of Alexander's empire headed by Attalids and Ptolemies.

Dumézil's statement that "from the religious standpoint there is no crisis in the years between Saguntum and Zama"[13] focuses on the system alone, which was open and flexible. It ignores, however, the human component. There were prodigies and omens that prompted the repeated consultation of the *libri Sibyllini*. This might be interpreted as the anxieties of the uneducated masses, but, nevertheless, they forced and received the repeated attention of Rome's leadership. The human house was in disorder and needed mending. Purification rituals and sacrifices brought the community together while simultaneously reinforcing the bonds between the leaders and the led.

The last consultation of the *libri* of the second Punic War period

---

[12] Livy 22.57.6.
[13] Dumézil, n. 11 above, 458.

was prompted by a shower of stones. Simultaneously, the Delphic Pythia concurred with the Sibylline prophecy that Roman victory would come about "si mater Idaea a Pessinunte Romam aduecta foret. (If the Idaean mother from Pessinus should be brought to Rome)."[14] A delegation was despatched to Pergamum where Attalus I Soter, an *amicus* of the Roman people, resided. He honored the Romans' request and apparently handed over the meteorite from Pessinus representing the goddess.[15] Ovid presents more baffled Romans and a more hesitant Attalus in his *Fasti*

> "Mater abest, Matrem iubeo, Romane, requiras.
>   cum ueniet, casta est accipienda manu."
> obscurae sortis patres ambagibus errant,
>   quaeue parens absit, quoue petenda loco.
> consulitur Paean, "diuum" que "arcessite Matrem,"
>   inquit, "in Idaeo est inuenienda iugo."
> mittuntur proceres. Phrygiae tunc sceptra tenebat
>   Attalus; Ausoniis rem negat ille uiris:
> mira canam: longo tremuit cum murmure tellus
>   et sic est adytis diua locuta suis:
> "ipsa peti uolui. nec sit mora! mitte uolentem!
>   dignus Roma locus, quo deus omnis eat."
> ille soni terrore pauens "proficiscere!" dixit,
>   "nostra eris; in Phrygios Roma refertur auos."[16]

More explicitly than Ovid, Varro relates that the goddess was in Pergamum. The antiquarian is explaining the etymology of Megalensia and states: "Megalesia dicta a Graecis quod ex libris Sibyllinis arces-

---

[14] Livy 29.10.5.
[15] Of the ancient sources quoted in this respect, I would argue that Cic. *De Har.Resp.*27–8 does not attach the Mater brought to Rome to Pessinus. Pessinus is, in fact, still the home of the Mother of gods. ("Hac igitur vate suadente quondam, defensa Italia Punico bello atque ab Hannibale vexata, sacra ista nostri maiores ascita ex Phrygia Romae collacarunt. (. . .) qui (Clodius) accepta pecunia, Pessinunte ipsum, sedem domiciliumque matris deorum.") Starting with Diodorus Siculus (34/35.33.2) the goddess is taken from Pessinus (Strabo 12.5.3; Val.Max.8.15.3; Appian *Hann.*56; Dio frg. 57.61; *Vir.Ill.*46; Amm.Marc.22.9.5.) While on his way to battle the Persians, Julian (361–3 CE) stopped at Pessinus, where he visited the shrine of ἡ τῶν θεῶν μήτηπ and composed an oration in her honor (*Or.*5). Julian gives a brief account how τὸ ἁγιώτατον ἄγαλμα arrived in Rome (159c–161a). Although the emperor does not state it explicitly, one can but assume that in his mind the "holiest statue/image" came from Pessinus.
[16] 4.259–72: "The Mother is absent, I order you, Romans, to look for the Mother. When she comes, a chaste hand ought to receive her. The fathers went about a roundabout way because of the obscure oracle, which parent was missing, and from which place she had to be gotten. Paean was asked and he answered: "Fetch the

sita ab Attalo rege Pergamo: ibi prope murum Megalesion templum eius deae, unde aducta Romam."[17] H. Graillot already pointed out that the association of Pessinus with the epithet Idaea is odd and that Attalus' realm ended about three hundred kilometers short of Pessinus.[18] In matter of fact, Pessinus was an independent temple-state.[19] The question arises why the priest of Pessinus would have handed over the deity to the Romans becomes even more perplexing. What could they have gained? And could Pessinus have remained the cult's center without its original source of power?

In ancient religion, i.e., the concept that a holy site emanated power, which increased with time as did its prestige, it seems most likely that Attalus, should he have had the or a baetyl, would have tried to hold on to it. The mother goddess was one of the oldest deities in the area. Her sanctuary had existed since remote times and no ancient ruler and priests of the shrine would have voluntarily handed over such a powerful deity.[20] The goddess' dislocation, the severance of meteorite from its original place, meant a decrease of religious power and prestige; and, in this case, the subjugation of an ancient to a new site. One way of avoiding the former problem was to take a representative token, for example, a copy or maybe even a piece of

---

Mother of gods, she is to be found on Mount Ida." Nobles were sent. Attalus ruled Phrygia then; he denied the Ausonian men's request. I will sing of a wonder: the earth trembled with a long-lasting murmur and the goddess spoke in her shrine thus: "I myself have wanted to be taken. Don't delay! Send me willingly! Rome is a worthy place, to which each god wants to go." He said shuddering from the terror of the sound: "Depart! You will be ours; Rome traces [its origins] back to Phrygian ancestors."

[17] *De Ling.Lat.*6.15.

[18] *Le culte de Cybèle mère des dieux à Rome et dans l'empire romain* (Paris, 1912), 46: "La mention de Pesinonte, en revanche, n'a pas sa raison d'être. Elle est en contradiction avec le titre d'Idéene. A Pessinonte, la Mère des Dieux est la Pessinontide, la Phrygienne, la Dindymène, Agdistis; jamais elle n'y est l'Idéenne. (...) Il n'est pas moins étrange qu'ils soient allés chercher sur les rives du Sangarios, au pied du Dinymos, la Dame du mont Ida. D'autre part, Attale n'a jamais pu enfermer Pessinonte dans les limites de son domaine, ni seulement dans les liens d'une confédération."

[19] Graillot, n. 18 above, 45 as well as D. Magie *Roman Rule in Asia Minor* (Princeton, 1950), vol. 1, 25–6, vol. 2, 769–70 and B. Virgilio *Il "tempio stato" di Pessinunte fra Pergamo e Roma nel II–I secolo A.C.*, *Biblioteca di Studi Antichi* 25 (Pisa, 1981), 46–7, 63–9.

[20] G. Sanders, "Kybele und Attis," in *Die orientalischen Religionen im Römerreich*, ed. M.J. Vermaseren (Leiden, 1981), 276: "Es wäre erstaunlich, wenn der König-Prieser von Pessinus das Bild, auf das der heilige Charakter und die Selbständigkeit der Stadt gegründet waren, preisgegeben hätte, aber es ist denkbar, daß Pergamon, als grazialwerte Filiale des phrygischen Mutterheiligtums, Roms Wünschen entspricht."

the original, which would possess the same powers and fulfill the same functions as the original. But would the Romans have been satisfied with such a token? Would they have known or cared about the difference? The answer lies within the parameters of Roman religion. *Evocatio*, a form of which we have here, demanded the original; the Romans would have known and cared what they carried home.

Mother goddesses could be found all over Asia Minor. The region of Pergamum, for example, seems to have had three sanctuaries; one on top of the city's acropolis dedicated to μήτηρ βασίλεια, the Μεγαλή-σιον Varro mentions, and a third about thirty kilometers south-east from Pergamum, the ἱερὸν τῆς Μητρός τῶν θεῶν Ἀσπορδηνῆς, mentioned by Strabo.[21] One notices that mother goddesses, whose sanctuaries lay outside a city, usually on mountains, carry topographical epithets like Ἀσπορδηνή. With a temple inside or close to the city limits that was not necessary. The more generic μεγάλη or βασίλεια would suffice. The official name of Rome's import was Magna Deorum Mater Idaea. There is nothing relating to Pessinus in her name.

E. Gruen suggests that "[i]t was easy enough for an annalistic writer of the late 2nd or early 1st century to assume that the symbol of Magna Mater must have been sought at Pessinus. That assumption need not bind us."[22] Pessinus was and remained the major cultic center,[23] which could not have happened without the primary cultic object at hand. It was the Great Mother of Mt. Ida that came with the help of Attalus from the Troad, not Pessinus, to Rome.[24] It is

---

[21] 13.2.6. For a discussion of the sanctuaries see E. Ohlemutz *Die Kulte und Heiligtümer der Götter in Pergamon* (repr. Darmstadt, 1968), 174–91. According to Ohlemutz, the rugged area with an elevation of about 1000m can apparently be seen from Pergamum and vice-versa.

[22] *Studies in Greek Culture and Roman Policy, Cincinnati Classical Studies,* n.s. 7 (Leiden, 1990), 19. The whole chapter ("The Advent of the Magna Mater"), 5–33 provides stimulating reading.

[23] Bömer, 229: "Wenn der Stein trotzdem von Pessinus kam, gleich ob unmittelbar oder über Pergamon, dann war er also nicht der Stein, sondern ein Stein der Magna Mater."

Gruen, 19: "For Romans of the later Republic, the cult of Cybele at Pessinus was the principal functioning shrine of the goddess in Asia Minor."

[24] Sanders, 275–6: "Wird doch durch die Legende, die von Vergil zum Nationalepos ausgearbeitet wird, Roms Herkunft auf den trojanischen Helden Aneas zurückgeführt, dessen Geburt und Jugend auf dem Ida-Berg bei Troja bei Troja in engen Zusammenhang bringen mit der *Mater Deum Magna Idaea,* der "Großen Göttermutter des Berges Ida," wie ihr Titel in Rom lautet. Da das Gebiet von Troja zum Königreich Pergamon gehört und Pessinus sich bis zum Jahre 183 v. Chr. als unabhäniger theokratischer Stadtstaat behauptet, ist es durchaus möglich, daß die römische Gesandtschaft Kybeles Bild nicht in Pessinus, sondern in Pergamon erhält." Along similar lines Gruen, 32.

also conceivable that Attalus had moved the *mater Idaea* from Ilium to Pergamum prior to Rome's request.[25]

One could argue that the purpose of 205/204 B.C.E. was to ascertain Rome's acquired heritage and subsequent rightful claim to the area's major deity. The land acquisition would follow later. Pessinus was out of reach. In essence, Aeneas' descendants had claimed, following the instructions of the *libri Sibyllini* and with the endorsement of the Delphic oracle, what mythologically and intellectually belonged to them. Once Rome's sphere of interest in Asia expanded with the War against Antiochus III, Pessinus and its mother goddess, Cybele, became tangible. In essence we are dealing with two overlapping entities, the Magna Deorum Mater Idaea and Cybele from Pessinus.[26]

F. Bömer attributed the silence of sources especially to the horror Romans experienced when they saw the actual cult practices in action.[27] This makes Roman nobles look like buffoons, which they hardly were. A reason for this silence also could be that the ritual around the Magna Deorum Mater Idaea differed at first from that of Cybele, whose cult featured *galli*. In Greece, Sanders argues, the transplanted mother goddess lost her various Phrygian topo- and oronymous epithets while even her name Cybele was replaced by the title Μήτηρ Μεγάλη. This reflected the hellenization of Cybele, whose cult was thoroughly "de-orientalized."[28]

Despite it though, eunuch-attendants of Cybele did not disappear. Were these foreigners simply not bound by the new rules? Cultic rituals scarcely changed, since a change meant a tampering with what had proved to be effective and thus invited a breach in the humankind/deities alignment. No mode of hellenization could have

---

[25] Bömer, 229–30: "Es gab mehrere Baityloi. Vom Ida ist allerdings keiner bekannt." He cites Schwenn's article "Kybele," *RE* Halbband 22 (Stuttgart, 1922), where, col. 2254, the author refers to Claud. *de rapt.Pros.*1.201–5, which mentions Ida as the home of a "religiosa silex." Bömer dismisses Claudianus' reference on the grounds that this is a late source.

[26] For background reading on the origins of Cybele and her place in Greece see the articles in *Éléments orientaux dans la religion grecque ancienne* (Paris, 1960) by E. Laroche, "Koubaba, déesse anatolienne, et le probèlme es origines de Cybèle," 114–28 and E. Will, "La grande Mère en Grèce," 95–111.

[27] "Kybele in Rom," *MDAIR* 71 (1964), 132: "Der Grund für dieses völlige Schweigen in Rom ist mit Sicherheit darin zu suchen, daß die römische Öffentlichkeit, insbesondere aber eben die adligen Kreise, offenbar einen furchtbaren Schrecken bekommen hatten, als sie sahen, was sie mit der Überführung dieses Kultes angerichtet hatten."

[28] Sanders, 266–7.

prevented this. On the other hand, if the neutral and universal concept Μήτηρ Μεγάλη was sufficiently distanced from Cybele through associations, for example, with Rhea, but Cybele and her cult remained intact, there would have been no such loss of divine good will. In addition, the "hellenized" Great Mother could be represented with the attributes of Cybele, the tympanon and the lions. This did not mean that her attendants had to be and behave like *galli*. Syncretism was at work, but not on the level of ritual.

A look at Rome shows that the festival of Cybele was celebrated in March,[29] while the festivities for the Magna Deum Mater Idaea took place in early April. Her representation was initially deposited in the Temple of Victory on the Palatine on April 4. A new temple also on the Palatine, Rome's religious center, would not be ready until 191 B.C.E. The temporary home represented also a symbolic choice. Rome had emerged victorious in the East against Philip V and was successful in the West wresting control of Spain from the Carthaginians. Further, Hannibal, unable to shatter Rome's alliances in Italy and elsewhere, would lose his final battle against Rome two years later. In 205/4 B.C.E., Rome could triumphantly look into the future claiming and embracing Greek intellectual heritage mainly through a link with Aeneas. The religious expression of this was the transfer of the mother goddess of Ida to Rome. The first *ludi Megalenses* included *ludi scaenici* and were held on the dedication of the temple in 191.[30] Cicero points out that these *Megalensia* were Greek in style.[31] This would go well with the fact that the Magna Deum Mater Deorum took the iconographic attributes of Cybele, i.e., the mural crown, tympana, and lions, but did not have the orgiastic attributes of her cult. Additional support of the initial division between the celebration of the two deities is the fact that *quindecimviri sacris faciundis*, the guardians of the *libri Sibyllini*, selected the *sacerdos matris deum*. This as a reaffirmation of the ancient link as well as the state's interest in the cult of the Mater deum. An inscription like *CIL* VI 2183, which features an *archigallus Matris deum magnae Idaeae et Attis populi Romani*, comes after Pessinus' entrance into Rome's sphere of control, which

---

[29] *Arbor intrat* March 22, *sanguem* March 24, *hilaria* March 25, and *requietio* March 26. A *lavatio*, March 27, was added in the time of Augustus.

[30] Livy 36.36.4. On the problem of dating (194 or 191 B.C.E.) see J. Briscoe *A Commentary on Livy, Books 34–7* (Oxford, 1981), 276. *CIL* VI 496, 1040, 3702 = 30967

[31] *De Harusp.Resp.*12.24.

happens after the construction of the *aedes Magnae Matris*. At this point, there is an opening for a further merger between the goddess of Pessinus, Cybele, and the Magna Deum Mater Idaea.

The political circumstances of the Late Republic and those of the early Principate reshaped again Rome's religious landscape. At a time of political disintegration, literature, however, flourished. The rise of the individual and the discovery of the self ushered in a whole new era of literary output. Literature, the belles lettres, and literary performances had their roots in the period of the first two Punic Wars. Catullus, the premier example of this new group of writers, the neoterics, wrote a poem that has as its theme Cybele and Attis. Besides the beauty of this composition, which warrants a short analysis, it illustrates that Cybele and Mater Idaea had been equated.

Previous studies have already dealt in detail with poem 63's position in the Catullan corpus, its structure, meter, symbolism, and intent.[32] W.Y. Sellar called it, a quotation now often used, "the most original of all his poems. As a work of pure imagination, it is the most remarkable poetical creation in the Latin language."[33] It is the creation that fascinates not the least by the fitting of Latin words into the suspending, torque-ing rhythm of galliambics.[34] Wilamowitz' thesis that Catullus followed a Greek model has lost out, while Fedeli and Shipton have shown that Catullus reshapes imagery from Hellenistic epigrams.[35] Clearly, poets do not work in a cultural and literary vacuum; they are inspired by what was and is.

Lucretius in his *De Rerum Natura* describes Earth as the holder of the first bodies and the producer of fruits and trees for humankind. On this account Earth is called Great Mother of the gods and Mother of wild beasts, and the one Begetter of our bodies.[36] The subsequent description follows along similar lines of well established patterns.

---

[32] See Selected Bibliography.

[33] *The Roman Poets of the Late Republic* (Oxford, ³1905), 461.

[34] R.C. Ross, "Catullus 63 and the Galliambic Meter," *CJ 64* (1968/9), 145– and J.T. Kirby, "The Galliambics of Catullus 63: "That Intoxicating Meter," *Syllecta Classica* 1 (1989), 63–74.

[35] P. Fedeli, "Attis e il leone: dall'epigramma ellenistico al *c.* 63 di Catullo," (1980), 247–56 and K.M.W. Shipton, "The 'Attis' of Catullus," *CQ* 37 (1987), 444–9 (without a reference to Fedeli's earlier article).

[36] "principio tellus habet in se corpora prima (2.589) (. . .) tum porro nitidas fruges arbustaque laeta | gentibus humanis habet unde extollere possit (2.594–5) (. . .) | quare Magna Deum Mater Materque ferarum | et nostri genetrix haec dicta est corporis una (598–9)."

Lucretius tells us that ancient and learned poets of the Greeks (*ueteres Graium docti poetae*) sang of her thus. Seated in a chariot the Great Mother drives a pair of lions, while the top of her head was surrounded by a mural crown. The accompanying lions suggest the Babylonian/Assyrian Ishtar and the Phoenician Astarte. A terracotta statuette of a seated (mother) goddess giving birth with each hand on the head of a leopard or panther from Çatal Hüyük (dated around 6000 B.C.E.) pre-dates any old and learned Greek poet. The Hittites from Boğazköy revered a mother goddess, Hepatu, whom panthers flanked long before Pessinus and its goddess, Cybele, with the mural crown rose to prominence. It is this type of the mural-crowned female that a few obverses of Late Republican coinage feature.[37]

Various peoples, Lucretius continues, call this Mother, following ancient custom of worship (*antiquo more sacrorum*), Mater Idaea. They give her Phrygian troops as an escort and assign *galli*, the latter to indicate that those who violated the divine command of the Mother (*numen qui uiolarint Matris*) and have been found ungrateful toward their parents, should be thought unworthy of having children.[38] That much for Lucretius' work, which is a contemporary philosophical pendant to Catullus' poem 63.

D. Traill arranged this poem, excluding the three lines of direct address at the end, into seven corresponding segments.[39] In the first segment, lines 1–11, Attis gives himself over to Cybele's power. He succumbs to *furor*. The reader finds him/herself *in medias res*.[40] Attis, borne in a swift vessel over the deep sea, is heading for the Phrygian woodland. The protagonist's name takes the central position of the

---

[37] The goddess seated on a chariot drawn by two lions features on the reverse of M. Volteius' denarius issues (78 or 76 B.C.E.) and the aurei of L. Cestius and C. Norbanus (44 or 43 B.C.E.); see R. Turcan *Numismatique Romaine du culte métroaque*, *EPRO* 97 (Leiden, 1983), 13–16. A hiatus followed and the image does not reappear until the reign of Hadrian.

[38] 2.610–17.

[39] "Catullus 63: Rings around the Sun," *CP* 76 (1981), 211–4 and "Ring Composition in Catullus 63, 64 and 65," *CW* 81.5 (1988), 365–9. A (1–11) Attis submits to Cybele's power; onset of *furor*; B (12–26) Speech; Attis calls on comrades to worship Cybele; C (27–38) Ascent of Ida; in sleep of exhaustion *furor* abates; D (39–43) Sun dispells darkness; Sleep leaves Attis; c (44–9) With *furor* gone, Attis sees what he has done and returns to shore; b (50–73) Speech; Attis regrets leaving home and becoming a servant of Cybele; a (74–90) Cybele brings Attis back under her control; renewal of *furor*.

[40] P. Fedeli, "Il prologo dell' *Attis* di Catullo," in *Studi di poesia latina in onore di Antonio Traglia, Storia e Letteratura reccolta di Studi e Testi* 146 (Rome, 1979), 149–60 and G.N. Sandy, "The Imagery of Catullus 63," *TAPA* 99 (1968), 389–99.

opening line. The name will recur in this position with the same metrical value three more times in the nominative (lines 27, 32, and 45) and twice in the accusative (lines 42 and 88).[41] The adjective *alta* and the noun *maria* frame Attis and his vessel.

Catullus does not offer the reader Attis' point of departure, we only know his goal the Phrygian woodland (*Phrygium nemus*) and the state of his emotion (*cupide*). *Nemus* incorporates an aspect of civilization, i.e., pasture land for cattle, which the *opaca siluis redimita loca deae* of the next line do not share. This kind of playing off contrasts will occur throughout the poem, for life-giving (procreation) and the lack of it is inherent in the cult of Cybele and Attis. Catullus, from one line to another, moves from the civilized, defineable, to the obscure, unknown. Attis runs there *cupide* and *citato pede*, the speed of the vessel transferred to his feet. It is hard to ignore the allusion to Cupid, son of Venus, in the adverb positioned between the adjective *citato* and the noun *pede*. Catullus retains this construction throughout the poem. In these *opaca loca*, away from civilizing forces, Attis, incited by furious madness (*furenti rabie*), emasculates himself—the positive side of desire turned destructive. Besides the poetic rendering of the castration, there is Catullus' choice of the Greek ἴλια (*ili*) and *silex*, the flint, the type of stone best describing a meteorite.[42]

Then there is the realization of the deed. A gender change occurred, indicated by the feminine ending of the participle. Attis (she) realized (*sensit*, occupying the same central position as Attis in the opening line) that "her" limbs were left without manhood (*uiro*). The price of the initiation, the forsaking of the procreative force, is high. Attis' blood does not, as one might anticipate, nourish the ground, it stains (*maculans*) it. The negative connotation of pollution hovers in the background. It is not quite clear whether this should be interpreted as a foreshadowing that Attis will, at one point, come to his senses, which would mean that his offering to Cybele had been done without true conviction.

Blood like the *sacrum* itself (the consecrated or the accursed) had a double religious meaning. It could simultaneously purify and pollute. Emasculation did not slow Attis down. Quick (*citata*) she picks up the light tympanon with her snow-white hands—there was after all a

---

[41] T. Means, "Catullus lxiii—Position of the Title-Name "Attis," and its Possible Significance," *CP* 22 (1927), 101–2.

[42] Claudianus used it in this context.

loss of blood! *Niueus* like *tener* is a female attribute; the former also points to icy-snow covered Ida (line 70). While the delicate fingers shook the hollow bull-hides (*terga tauri caua*), trembling she began to sing to her companions. These *terga caua* could be interpreted as the bull *scrota* offered to the deity after the sacrifice.[43] Although taurobolia did not occur in Rome until the Antonine period, the presentation of the *uires* of a *sacrum* to a deity might have been a known practice.[44]

The second segment, lines 12–26, is Attis' speech to his companions. These *comites*, a word which picks up the political meaning of a magistrate's retinue, are already *galli*; Catullus uses the feminine form (*gallae*).[45] Attis, their leader (*dux*) urges them on to come to Cybele's groves (woodlands) on high (*ad alta nemora*). The first line of this new segment reverberates the *alta maria* of the poem's first line. Cybele's place has been transformed once more from a dark to a semi-cultivated place, a pasture. These *gallae*, termed a wandering flock of the lady of Dindymus (*Dindymenae dominae uaga pecora*), had followed Attis. Together they endured the swift (*rapidum salum*) and savage sea (*trucultenta pelage*). While *salum* encompasses the whole body of water, *pelagus* (πέλαγος) denotes the surface. The adjective used to describe *pelagus*, *truculenta* (*trux*), is a facial expression and usually employed with humans and animals. There on the sea, Attis' companions emasculted their bodies from utter hatred of love (*corpus euirastis Ueneris nimio odio*).

What better place than the sea, from which Aphrodite (Venus) was born, after Kronos' genitals mingled with the sea's foam? Swiftness is picked up again, when Attis exhorts the *gallae* to cheer the lady's heart with swift wanderings (*citatis erroribus*). But like *uagus*, *error* contains a notion of aimlessness. The goal, however, is clear, the Phrygian home of Cybele, Dindymus, a mountain range north of Pessinus along the Phrygian and Galatian border.

There the festivities are in full swing. The cymbal sounds, the tympana echo, a Phrygian plays the curved flute, and Maenads, Dionysus' female attendants, toss their ivy-covered heads with force (*ui*) and celebrate the holy rites with shrill shrieks (*acutis ululantibus*).

---

[43] H. Hepding *Attis seine Mythen und sein Kult* (Giessen, 1903), 191 suggests that the genitals (*uires*) of the bull were collected after the taurobolium.

[44] The many breasts of the Ephesian Artemis might represent these offerings of *scrota*.

[45] G. Sanders, "Gallos," *Reallexikon für Antike und Christentum* 8 (1972), 984–1034.

Lucretius' description of a *pompa* includes the three instruments (*tympana, cymbala concaua, caua tibia*), but *doctus* Catullus shows his mastery. His *tympana* echo at first (*reboant*, Lucretius has *tonant*) then, in a line a parallel chiastic line (29), a *tympanon* bellows back (*remugit*) and hollow cymbals resound (*recrepant*).

The Maenads are far from misplaced here, for we find the Mother of gods mentioned in Euripides' *Bacchae*.[46] These women also possess what Attis has lost through a *silex acutus* and his companions gave up on the sea, *uis*. The adjective *acutus* links the men with the female initiates, whose howls forebode disaster.[47] Although Catullus assigns the adjective *uagus* to both groupings, Attis' group is, in this segment, *pecora* while the Maenads are a structured (military) unit, a *cohors*. "It is proper for us," says Attis, "that we hurry there with rapid three measured dance (*citatis tripudis*)."[48] This allusion brings us back to the beginning of the poem.

As in the previous sections there is verbal repetition and reverberation in the third one (lines 27–38) linking it to the others. The moment Attis, the half-woman (*notha mulier*) finished singing, the celebrating throng (*thiasus*) howls, just like the Maenads, with quivering tongues. The swift chorus (*citus chorus*) climbs with hurrying foot (*properante pede*) toward green Ida (*uiridem Idam*). Attis raging (*furibunda*), panting (*anhelans*), and wandering (*uaga*) rushes (*uadit*) through the dark groves (*opaca nemora*). Here the undefinable and definable are merged.[49] The *gallae* follow suit. At this moment Attis is still like a heifer unbroken by the yoke.[50] Like the image of the *opaca nemora*, Attis' (internal) transformation is not yet complete. Deep sleep (*sopor*) covers their eyes, and finally, the *rabidus furor animi* (the mind's raging madness) leaves them.[51] *Furor* occupies the same position as *uagus* previously (line 4). It was in essence the source of it.

Sol, who cleansed (*lustrauit*) the physical world, introduces the poem's central segment (lines 39–43). While Cybele's sphere is harsh and wild, the Sun's domain is white, immaculate. He is the force who

---

[46] 78: "τά τε ματρὸς μεγάλας ὄργια Κυβέλας θεμιτεύων."

[47] The *ulula* (owl) is a bad omen. Varro *Men.*86.4: "homines eum peius formidant quam fullo ululam."

[48] The second hemistich of the galliambic has three beats to the measure. See Kirby.

[49] K.M.W. Shipton, "The Iuvenca Image in Catullus 63," *CQ* 36 (1986), 268–70.

[50] J. Glenn, "The Yoke of Attis," *CP* 68 (1973), 59–61.

[51] K.M.W. Shipton, "Attis and Sleep: Catullus 63.39–43," *LCM* 9.3 (1984), 38–41.

vigorously expelled the shadows of night. The focus is still on the feet, since Sol completes his action *uegetis sonipedibus* (vigorous sound[ing feet]), the latter usually an attribute assigned to horses. At this point *Somnus* (slumber) and not *sopor* swiftly leaves Attis, whom Pasithea had received in her pulsing bosom.

The choice of Pasithea has dual significance. First, there is the link with Sleep (Ὕπνος). Hera had promised Pasithea, one of the three Χάριτες, Hypnos (sleep) as a prize should he make Zeus fall asleep.[52] Thus, the Graces partake in Hera's sphere as protectress of marriages, and marriage is the key theme of Catullus' *carmina maiora*. Second, there is a strong connection of these Graces with fertility goddesses, which in Orchomenos, for example, were represented by baetyls. Catullus remembered this most likely from Theocritus.[53] There is yet another detail. Attis and his followers had fallen asleep without having eaten (*sine Cerere*). Ceres can be associated with Cybele. Catullus' message is once more that Attis (and his followers) do not yet completely belong to Cybele.

Freed from impetuous madness (*rapida rabie*, echoing line 38), the ever occurring swiftness now encapsulated in *rapide*, Attis realized with a clear mind (*liquida mente*) what he had done and returned ardent-hearted (*animo aestuante*) to the seashore. Both *liquida* and *aestuante* are linked to water, Attis' present goal, while the sun, which brought about the clearing of his mind, is still present in the participial form of *aestuare*. Looking at the vast sea (*maria uasta*), Attis cries out. Thus, the fifth segment concludes (lines 44–9). The choice of *uastus* might seem simple, but again it is a word that has an additional negative connotation. The Roman audience much more than we today would have understood that Catullus thus describes a sea depleted of force.

In this speech, the poem's sixth component (lines 50–73), Catullus reassigns the masculine gender to Attis. Cybele's newest attendant addresses his home country, not his parents, as his creator (*creatrix*) and mother (*genetrix*).[54] Catullus simply leaves the focus on the land; neither Attis nor the audience reading or hearing *genetrix* can disassociate it from Cybele. In a moving, intricately composed speech Attis laments leaving civilization, life, to come to the woodlands of

---

[52] *Il.*14.269.
[53] 16.104–5.
[54] S. Fasce, "Attis erifuga," *Maia* 31 (1979), 25–7.

Ida (*Idae nemora*) and live in a life-less, untamed environment among snow and frozen lairs of wild beasts (*aput niuem et ferarum gelida stabula*). But, again, *nemora* still contains the notion of (possible) cultivation and although Attis tries, he, momentarily free of untamed madness (*rabie fera carens*), cannot make out his *patria*. Despite his doubts, he is in the hands of Cybele. The physical separation from home, emphasized by the *ego* at the beginning and *domo* at the end of line 58, is complete.[55]

All of Attis' questions, in the future tense, are futile. The flower of the gymnasium (*gymnasi flos*) has left the men's world of the *forum*, *palaestra*, and *stadium*. The adolescent Attis descends back into the stage of boyhood dependancy. He is a *mulier*, which nicely corresponds to and, in terms of gender, contrasts with the *puer* at the end of the line. For a Roman there is in both a potential of sexuality, but not in an active sense. Catullus, however, does not make it that clear-cut. His description of Attis' previous, male civic life already contains cross-sexual patterns (*mihi ianuae frequentes, mihi limina tepida, mihi floridis corollis redimita domus erat*). But, unlike then, he is now devoid of any (male) sexuality (*sterilis*), he is this white-handed, tender-fingered, rosy-lipped handmaiden, and the only entity that possesses procreative power is this place of contradiction, Mt. Ida (*uiridis algida Idae niue amicta loca*), and its mistress, the castrating, yet live-giving, Cybele.

Once Attis utters his doubts, Cybele unyokes her lions and commands the one on the left, the enemy of the flock (*laeuumque pecoris hostem*), to infuriate the doubter once more. This last thematic unit (lines 74–90) completes the ring composition. Again, Catullus plays on double meaning. Naturally, a lion is the enemy of a flock (*pecus*), but Attis' followers had been labeled *pecus* earlier. In a sense, the stinging-madness-inducing lion, that so much suggests the Babylonian/Assyrian goddess of love, Ishtar, is the enemy of any social being, for it forces, like the early stages of love, a dissociation from the social grid. Again, this is simultaneously propitious and unfavorable (*laeuum*).

Catullus' Cybele exercises *imperium*, a word that must have rung of military authority in Roman ears. "Go strike your back with your tail, endure your lashes, make the whole region resound with bellowing murmuring, shake your golden mane onto your muscular neck,"

---

[55] J. Granarolo, "Catulle ou la hantise du *moi*," *Latomus* 37 (1978), 368–86.

she exhorts her helper (lines 81–3). The poet transferred the image of "celebrating" *galli* onto the lion. The image of the bull, the most primordial symbol of fertility and cultivation, is again in the background, encapsulated in the verb *mugire*. The enforcer of Cybele's command rushes (*uadit*), like Attis in the beginning, to complete his deed. He breaks up the brushwood (*uirgultum*), i.e., destroys life, until he reaches the watery region (*humida loca*), which stands in contrast to *algida loca*, at the white shore. There he sees tender Attis (central position of the line) near the white surface of the sea (*prope marmora pelagi*) and makes the ordered attack (*impetus*). Attis (*illa*) demented (*demens*) flees into the wild glens (*nemora fera*), there "she" remained a handmaiden forever. Thus, in two short sentences the story of Attis concludes.

Some critics have identified the last three lines as a hymn and envisioned the piece performed at the Megalensia.[56] Besides the fact that these lines:

> Goddess, great goddess, Cybele, goddess, lady of Dindymus, may all your fury be far away from my house, Lady, let others be incited, others driven to madness

are apotropaic and not hymnodic, it would seem an unlikely piece in praise of Cybele, for Attis' lamentation and doubts are too pronounced to belong to a celebration of the goddess. Rather, it should be seen, not so much as a Catullan therapy session,[57] as an integral part of his many-facetted cycle of love poetry. The verbal and thematic echoes are in place and have been studied in detail by others.[58]

In the study of the Magna Deum Mater Idaea and Cybele, Catullus' poem is of importance, because it shows that in the minds of Late Republican Romans, Cybele, who could also be associated with Love, resided not only on Dindymus by Pessinus but also on Ida. In short, the equation was complete.[59]

---

[56] T.P. Wiseman *Catullus and His World* (Cambridge, 1985), 198–206.
[57] R.Th. van der Paardt, "Catullus in analyse," *LAMPAS* 20 (1987), 237–51.
[58] See Selected Bibliography.
[59] I would like to thank my former colleague Ian Rutherford, who is working on a forthcoming book on ancient pilgrimage (Oxford University Press), for the many fascinating and inspiring discussions we had about ancient religion. They certainly opened, at least for me, new avenues of thought.

Catullus 63

Super alta uectus Attis celeri rate maria,
Phrygium ut nemus citato cupide pede tetigit
adiitque opaca siluis redimita loca deae,
stimulatus ibi furienti rabie, uagus animis,
5 deuolsit ili acuto sibi pondera silice,
itaque ut relicta sensit sibi membra sine uiro,
etiam recente terrae sola sanguine maculans,
niueis citata cepit manibus leue typanum,
typanum tuum, Cybebe, tua, mater, initia,
10 quatiensque terga tauri teneris caua digitis
canere haec suis adorta est tremebunda comitibus:
"agite ite ad alta, Gallae, Cybeles nemora simul,
simul ite, Dindymenae dominae uaga pecora,
aliena quae petentes uelut exules loca
15 sectam meam exsecutae duce me mihi comites
rapidum salum tulistis truculentaque pelagi
et corpus euirastis Ueneris nimio odio;
hilarate erae citatis erroribus animum.
mora tarda mente cedat; simul ite, sequimini
20 Phrygiam ad domum Cybebes, Phrygia ad nemora deae,
ubi cymbalum sonat uox, ubi tympana reboant,
tibicen ubi canit Phryx curuo graue calamo,
ubi capita Maenades ui iaciunt hederigerae
ubi sacra sancta acutis ululatibus agitant,
25 ubi sueuit illa diuae uolitare uaga cohors,
quo nos decet citatis celerare tripudiis."
simul haec comitibus Attis cecinit notha mulier,
thiasus repente linguis trepidantibus ululat,
leue tympanun remugit, caua cymbala recrepant,
30 uiridem citus adit Idam properante pede chorus.
furibunda simul anhelans uaga uadit animam agens,
comitata tympano Attis per opaca nemora dux,
ueluti iuuenca uitans onus indomita iugi;
rapidae ducem sequuntur Gallae properipedem.
35 itaque, ut domum Cybebes tetigere lassulae,
nimio e labore somnum capiunt sine Cerere.
piger his labante langore oculos sopor operit;
abit in quiete molli rabidus furor animi.
sed ubi oris aurei Sol radiantibus oculis
40 lustrauit aethera album, sola dura, mare ferum,
pepulitque noctis umbras uegetis sonipedibus,
ibi Somnus excitam Attin fugiens citus abiit;
trepidante eum recepit dea Pasithea sinu.
ita de quiete molli rapida sine rabie

45 simul ipsa pectore Attis sua facta recoluit
    liquidaque mente uidit sine quis ubique foret,
    animo aestuante rusum reditum ad uada tetulit.
    ibi maria uasta uisens lacrimantibus oculis,
    patriam allocuta maestast ita uoca miseriter:
50 "patria o mea creatrix, patria o mea genetrix,
    ego quam miser relinquens, dominos ut erifugae
    famuli solent, ad Idae tetuli nemora pedem,
    ut aput niuem et ferarum gelida stabula forem,
    et earum omnia adirem furibunda latibula:
55 ubiam aut quibus locis te positam, patria, reor?
    cupit ipse pupula ad te sibi dirigere aciem,
    rabie fera carens dum breue tempus animus est.
    egone a mea remota haec ferar in nemora domo?
    patria, bonis, amicis, genitoribus abero?
60 abero foro, palaestra, stadio et gymnasiis?
    miser a miser, querendum est etiam atque etiam, anime!
    quod enim genus figurast, ego non quod obierim?
    ego mulier, ego adolescens, ego ephebus, ego puer,
    ego gyminasi fui flos, ego eram decus olei:
65 mihi ianuae frequentes, mihi limina tepida,
    mihi floridis corollis remidita domus erat,
    linquendum ubi esset orto mihi Sole cubiculum.
    ego nunc deum ministra et Cybeles famula ferar?
    ego Maenas, ego mei pars, ego uir sterilis ero?
70 ego uiridis algida Idae niue amicta loca colam?
    ego uitam agam sub altis Phrygiae columinibus,
    ubi cerua siluicultrix, ubi ager nemoriuagus?
    iam iam dolet quod egi, iam iamque paenitet."
    roseis ut huinc labellis sonitus <citus> abiit,
75 geminas deorum ad aures noua nuntia referens,
    ibi iuncta iuga resoluens Cybele leonibus
    laeuumque pecoris hostem stimulans ita loquitur:
    "agendum," inquit, "age ferox <i> fac ut hunc furor <agitet>
    fac uti furoris ictu reditum in memora ferat,
80 mea libere nimis qui fugere imperia cupit.
    age caede terga cauda, tua uerbera patere
    fac cuncta mugienti fremitu loca retonent,
    rutilam ferox torosa ceruice quate iubam!"
    ait haec minax Cybele religatque iuga manu.
85 ferus ipse sese adhortans rapidum incitat animo
    uadit, fremit, refringit uirgulta pede uago.
    at ubi humida albicantis loca litoris adiit,
    teneramque uidit Attin prope marmora pelagi,
    facit impetum. illa demens fugit in nemora fera.

90 ibi semper omne uitae spatium famula fuit.
dea, magna dea, Cybebe, dea domina Dindymi,
procul a mea tuos sit furor omnis, era, domo:
alios age incitatos, alios age rabidos.

SELECTED BIBLIOGRAPHY

J. Basto, "Caecilius, Attis and Catullus 35," *LCM* 7.3 (1982), 30–4.

F. Bömer, "Kybele in Rom," *MDAIR* 71 (1964), 130–151.

T. Callejas Berdonés, "El carmen 63 de Catulo: la cuestión del género literario," in *Mélanges V Actes del 9e Simposi de la secció Catalana de la SEEC 1988: treballs en honor de Virgilio Bejarano* (Barcelona, 1991), 159–66.

M. de Beuter, "El simbolismo del carmen LXIII de Catulo," *Argos* 4 (1980), 105–19.

C. Deroux and R. Verdière, "L'Attis de Catulle et son excès de haine contre Vénus," *Paideia* 44 (1989), 161–88.

H. Dettmer, "Design in the Catullan Corpus: A Preliminary Study," *CW* 81.5 (1988), 371–81.

J.P. Elder, "Catullus' Attis," *AJP* 68 (1947), 394–403.

S. Fasce, "Attis erifuga," *Maia* 31 (1979), 25–7.

———, *Attis e il culto metroaco a Roma* (Geneva, 1978).

P. Fedeli, "Attis e il leone: dall'epigramma ellenistico al *c.* 63 di Catullo," in *Letterature comparate. Problemi e metodo. Studi in onore de E. Paratore*, vol. 1 (Bologna, 1981), 247–56.

———, "Il prologo dell' *Attis* di Catullo," in *Studi di poesia latina in onore di Antonio Traglia, Storia e Letteratura reccolta di Studi e Testi* 146 (Rome, 1979), 149–60.

C.J. Fordyce *Catullus* (Oxford, 1973).

J. Glenn, "The Yoke of Attis," *CP* 68 (1973), 59–61.

H. Graillot *Culte de Cybele Mère des dieux à Rome dans l'empire romain* (Paris, 1912)

J. Granarolo, "Catulle ou la hantise du *moi*," *Latomus* 37 (1978), 368–86.

E. Gruen *Culture and National Identity in Republican Rome* (Ithaca, 1992).

———, *Studies in Greek Culture and Roman Policy*, Cincinnati Classical Studies, n.s. 7 (Leiden, 1990).

H. Herter, "Die Ursprünge des Aphroditenkultes," *Éléments orientaux dans la religion grecque ancienne, Colloque de Strasbourg 1958* (Paris, 1960), 61–76.

H. Hepding *Attis seine Mythen und sein Kult* (Giessen, 1903).

J.T. Kirby, "Galliambics of Catullus 63: 'That Intoxication Meter'," *Syllecta Classica* 1 (1989), 63–74.

P. Lambrechts, "Attis à Rome," in *Mélanges à Georges Smets* (Bruxelles, 1952), 461–71.

E. Laroche, "Koubaba, déesse anatolienne et le problème des origines de Cybèle," *Éléments orientaux dans la religion grecque ancienne, Colloque de Strasbourg 1958* (Paris, 1960), 113–28.

D. Magie *Roman Rule in Asia Minor*, 2 vls. (Princeton, 1950).

M. Martina, "Odisseo, Attis e l'amore. Nota a Catullo 63.48," *Aufidus* (1987), 15–9.

T. Means, "Catullus lxiii," *CP* 22 (1927), 101–2.

G. Most, "On the Arrangement of Catullus' Carmina Maiora," *Philologus* 25 (1981), 109–120.

D. Mulroy, "Hephaestion and Catullus 63," *Phoenix* 30 (1976), 61–72.

B.-M. Näsström *The Abhorrence of Love. Studies in Rituals and Mystic Aspects in Catullus' Poem of Attis* (Uppsala, 1989).

E. Noè, "La 'rabbia furiosa' di Attis: note per una lettura semiotica della passione (Catull 63)," *GFF* 13 (1990), 35–50.

E. Ohlemutz *Die Kulte und Heiligtümer der Götter in Pergamon* (Darmstadt, ²1968).

T. Oksala, "Catullus Attis-Ballade über den Stil der Dichtung und ihr Verhältnis zur Persönlichkeit des Dichters," *Arctos* 3 (1962), 199–213.

C. Rubino, "Myth and Mediation in the Attis Poem of Catullus," *Ramus* 3 (1974), 152–75.

G. Sanders, "Kybele und Attis," *OrRR* ed. M.J. Vermaseren (Leiden, 1981).

————, "Gallos," *Reallexikon für Antike und Christentum* 8 (1972), 984–1034.

G.N. Sandy, "The Imagery of Catullus 63," *TAPA* 99 (1968), 389–99.

E. Schäfer *Das Verhältnis von Erlebnis und Kunstgestalt bei Catull* (Wiesbaden, 1966), 95–107.

K.M.W. Shipton, "The 'Attis' of Catullus," *CQ* 37 (1987), 444–9.

————, "The Iuvenca Image in Catullus 63," *CQ* 36 (1986), 268–70.

————, "Attis and Sleep: Catullus 63.39–43," *LCM* 9.3 (1984), 38–41.

David Traill, "Ring Composition in Catullus 63, 64 and 65," *CW* 81.5 (1988), 365–9.

————, "Catullus 63: Rings around the Sun," *CP* 76 (1981), 211–4.

R. Turcan *Les cultes orientaux dans le monde romain* (Paris, 1989), 36–75.

————, *Numismatique romaine du culte métroaque*, *EPRO* 97 (Leiden, 1983).

R.Th. van der Paardt, "Catullus in analyse," *LAMPAS* 20 (1987), 237–51.

M.J. Vermaseren *Cybele and Attis. The Myth and the Cult* (London, 1977).

————, *The Legend of Attis in Greek and Roman Art*, *EPRO* 9 (Leiden, 1966).

B. Virgilio *Il 'tempio stato' di Pessinunte fra Pergamo e Roma nel II–I secolo A.C.*, *Biblioteca di Studi Antichi* 25 (Pisa, 1981).

E. Will, "Aspects du culte et de la légende de la Grande Mère dans le monde grec," *Éléments orientaux dans la religion grecque ancienne, Colloque de Strasbourg 1958* (Paris, 1960), 95–111.

O. Weinrich, "Das hellenistische Attisgedicht (Catulls Attisgedicht)," in *Ausgewählte Schriften*, vol. 2, ed. G. Wille (Amsterdam, 1973), 493–527.

T.P. Wiseman *Catullus and His World* (Cambridge, 1985).

U. Wilamowitz-Moellendorff, "Die Galliamben des Kallimachos und Catullus," *Hermes* 14 (1879), 194–201.

ATTIS PLATONICUS

Robert Turcan

Comment, pourquoi un homme châtré a-t-il pu finir par personnifier et même déifier la génération? Destin paradoxal que celui d'Attis, archétype de l'eunuchisme sacerdotal, avant d'être promu par un empereur à la fonction de démiurge universel!

Il est vrai que l'argumentation allégorique avait depuis longtemps engrangé des ressources inépuisables pour sublimer les mythes les plus scandaleux et au besoin les rites répugnants qui les actualisaient.[1] Et si les chrétiens s'indignaient contre ces tours de passe-passe qui légitimaient au regard des théosophes le paganisme populaire jusqu'à rendre d'avance caduque la polémique des apologètes, eux-mêmes ne se privaient pas d'appliquer un traitement analogue aux épisodes assez peu édifiants de l'Ancien Testament.[2]

On ne voit pas indiscutablement que le drame d'Attis ait suscité très tôt une littérature, surtout pour justifier le "sacrement de l'ordre" qui assimilait au dieu ses prêtres attitrés. Pourtant Timothée[3] - cet Eumolpide d'Eleusis qui mit au service des Lagides sa compétence religieuse pour l'organisation du culte de Sérapis - avait consacré à celui de Cybèle un ouvrage exploité (directement ou indirectement?) par Arnobe au livre V de son *Aduersus Nationes*, où il transcrit du mythe phrygien une version plus détaillée que les autres connues.[4]

---

[1] J. Pépin, *Mythe et allégorie. Les origines grecques et les contestations judéo-chrétiennes*, Paris, 1958 (1976²). Sur la polémique chrétienne, voir maintenant F. Mora, *Arnobio e i culti di mistero. Analisi storico-religiosa del V libro dell'Adversus nationes*, Rome, 1994, p. 185 ss.

[2] Orig., *C.Cels*.IV,50–51. Cf. M. Fédou, *Christianisme et religions païennes dans le "Contre Celse" d'Origène* (Théologie historique, 81) Paris, 1988, p. 125 ss., 494 s.

[3] Th. Zielinski, *Les origines de la religion hellénistique*, *RHR* 88, 1923, p. 173 ss., 179 s., 186 s.; Id., *La Sibylle. Trois essais sur la religion antique et le christianisme*, Paris, 1924, p. 71 ss., 83 ss.; C. Schneider, *Kulturgeschichte des Hellenismus*, I, Munich, 1967, p. 490 ss.; II, 1969, p. 840 s.; F. Mora, *op. cit.*, p. 116 et n. 3. Je laisse de côté le problème de savoir si la version de Pausanias (VII,17,9–12) dépend aussi de Timothée par l'intermédiaire d'Alexandre Polyhistor (H. Hepding, *Attis. Seine Mythen und sein Kult* = RGVV, 1, Giessen, 1903; rééd. Berlin, 1967, p. 104, n. 2).

[4] Th. Zielinski, *op. cit.*, p. 83 ss.; G. Sfameni Gasparro, *Soteriology and Mystic Aspects in the Cult of Cybele and Attis* (*EPRO* 103), Leyde, 1985, p. 33 (n. 27), 76; F. Mora, *op. cit.*, p. 116–134.

L'expert sacerdotal, qui devait reconnaître dans la Grande Mère l'équi-valent de cette "Terre Mère" qu'était normalement pour les Anciens la Déméter des mystères, ne pouvait pas ne pas s'interroger sur le rôle et la mort d'Attis.

Arnobe[5] le tient pour un "théologien" (*non ignobilem theologorum uirum*) c'est-à-dire pour quelqu'un qui raisonne sur les dieux. Ses considéra-tions sur l'origine du rituel métroaque reposaient, paraît-il, sur le déchiffrement d'obscurs grimoires, de livres secrets sur les antiquités phrygiennes (*ex reconditis antiquitatum libris*), en même temps que des "profonds mystères" du culte pessinontien (*ex intimis eruta . . . mysteriis*).[6] Ces expressions de l'apologiste africain me paraissent impliquer une exégèse, et l'on ne peut s'empêcher de penser aux termes dont use Plotin,[7] lorsqu'à propos précisément aussi de la Grande Mère il in-voque l'autorité des "sages d'autrefois" qui élucidaient les énigmes de la mythologie dans un esprit "mystériosophique" (μυστικῶς) et en se fondant sur les rites initiatiques ou "consécrations" (ἐν ταῖς τελεταῖς). On songe également à une phrase d'Héraclite, l'exégète d'Homère, sur les "discours mystiques" et la théologie des consécrations initia-tiques: formulations excitantes et vagues, qui relèvent peut-être de ce que le Père A.-J. Festugière appelait les "mystères littéraires".[8] Je ne sais pas si "grâce à Timothée le souffle divin d'Eleusis passa dans les nouveaux mystères d'Attis", comme l'affirmait Th. Zielinski;[9] mais le symbole de l'initiation phrygienne, tel que nous le citent (avec des variantes) Clément d'Alexandrie[10] et Firmicus Maternus,[11] porte bien la marque éleusinienne. Quant au problème de savoir si l'Eumolpide déchiffrait dans le mythe une "promesse d'immortalité",[12] analogue à celle que Déméter donnait à ses mystes, il reste bien difficile à trancher.

---

[5] *Adu.nat.*V,5 (p. 253, 7 s. Marchesi).

[6] *Ibid.*, (p. 253, 10 s. Marchesi). Cf. Th. Zielinski, *op. cit.*, p. 83 = *RHR* 88, 1923, p. 186.

[7] *Enn.*III,6,19 (I, p. 366, 25 s. Henry-Schwyzer, Paris-Bruxelles, 1951). Cf. R. Harder, *Plotins Schriften*, Neubearbeitung mit griech. Lesetext und Anmerkungen fortgeführt von R. Beutler und W. Theiler, II, Hambourg, 1962, p. 163 et 457.

[8] Heracl. *Hom.alleg.*6,6 (p. 7 de l'éd.-trad. F. Buffière dans la Coll. des Univ. de France, Paris, 1962); A.-J. Festugière, *L'idéal religieux des Grecs et l'Evangile*, Paris, 1932 (rééd. 1981), p. 116 ss.

[9] *Op. cit.*, p. 84 = *RHR* 88, 1923, p. 187.

[10] *Protr.*II,15,3. Cf. M.J. Vermaseren, *Cybele and Attis, The Myth and the Cult*, Lon-dres, 1977, p. 116 s.; G. Sfameni Gasparro, *op. cit.* (n. 4), p. 78 ss.

[11] *De errore prof.rel.*18,1–2. Cf. mon éd.-trad. dans la Coll. des Univ. de France, Paris, 1982, p. 286 ss.

[12] F. Cumont, *Lux Perpetua*, Paris, 1949, p. 260 s.

Ultérieurement, on a sans doute élucubré sur l'ouvrage du savant "théologien", et Arnobe pourrait fort bien être tributaire d'un exégète latin de la version timothéenne, car il cite le "pontife Valérius" à propos du nom (*Ia*) qu'y porte la fiancée d'Attis.[13] Ce Valérius s'identifie apparemment avec l'augure M. Valérius Messala, consul en 53 avant J.-C. et auteur d'un traité où il identifiait Janus avec Aiôn, d'après Lydus[14] et Macrobe.[15] Or Messala y faisait valoir le mot grec ἴα au sens de μία "selon les Pythagoriciens",[16] et cette idée d'unité incluse dans le latin *Ianus* légitimait à ses yeux l'identification du dieu des commencements et du premier mois romain avec l'Aiôn "qui façonne tout l'univers et le gouverne...", force unifiante du ciel "qui a lié ensemble ces deux natures dissemblables" que sont les éléments lourds (eau-terre) et légers (air-feu).[17] En grec, *Ias* est aussi le nom de la violette. Dans le mythe d'Attis, c'est la fleur qui naît du sang écoulé de sa mutilation mortelle et dont on couronne le pin porté processionnellement chaque 22 mars en hommage à son sacrifice.[18] *Ia* qui se tue sur le cadavre de son bien-aimé personnifie les violettes également écloses de son propre sang. Si donc Valérius Messala renvoyait ses lecteurs à cette histoire, il faut croire qu'Attis avait pour lui un rapport avec Janus-Aiôn conçu comme *uis caeli maxima*.[19] Cette idée anticipe curieusement sur la conception développée

---

[13] *Adu.nat.*V,7 (p. 257, 6 Marchesi). Après avoir cité Timothée, Arnobe avoue sa dette envers d'autres sources (*nec non apud alios aeque doctos*). qu'il ne précise pas autrement, mais qui pourraient avoir véhiculé la substance de l'érudition timothéenne. Cf. F. Mora, *op. cit.* (n. 1), p. 116 et n. 4, 127. Mais s'agit-il d'Alexandre Polyhistor? On peut en douter.

[14] *De mens.*IV,1 (p. 64, 12 Wuensch).

[15] *Sat.*I,9,14 (p. 38, 16 ss. Willis). Sur ce M. Valerius Messala Rufus, cf. F. Münzer, dans *RE* 2. Reihe, 8 A 1 (1955), col. 166/9, *s.u.* Valerius, 268. C'était un érudit dont Pline l'Ancien et Aulu-Gelle ont utilisé les ouvrages (*De familiis, De auspiciis*): H. Bardon, *La littérature latine inconnue*, I, *L'époque républicaine*, Paris, 1952, p. 309 s. Mécène faisait de ce Valérius un interlocuteur autorisé de Virgile et d'Horace dans son *Banquet* (Deut.-Seru. *Aen.*VIII,310): cf. H. Bardon, *La littérature latine inconnue*, II, *L'époque impériale*, Paris, 1956, p. 15 s. Ce Messala est encore trop souvent confondu avec l'orateur. "On n'a pas identifié le pontife Valérius", écrit H. Le Bonniec dans son introduction à Arnobe, éd.-trad. de *l'Aduersus nationes*, Coll. des Univ. de France, Paris, 1982, p. 40. Comme il s'agit d'un connaisseur des tradition religieuses, je suis convaincu que le "pontife" se confond avec l'augure.

[16] Lyd. *De mens.*IV,1 (*supra*, n. 14).

[17] Macr. *Sat.*I,9,14 (p. 38, 19 ss. Willis). Cf. A.-J. Festugière, *La révélation d'Hermès Trismégiste*, IV, *Le Dieu inconnu et la gnose*, Paris, 1954 (réédité), p. 176 ss.

[18] Arnob. *Adu.nat.*V,7 (p. 257, 2–9 Marchesi). Cf. G. Sfameni-Gasparro. *op. cit.* (n. 4), p. 40; F. Mora, *op. cit.*, p. 125, 133.

[19] Macr. *Sat.*I,9,14 (p. 38, 22 s. Willis). Cf. A.-J. Festugière, *op. cit.*, (n. 17), p. 178: "Quand, dans ce contexte, Messala parle de la *vis caeli maxima*, on voit bien

quatre siècles plus tard par Julien dit "l'Apostat", car enfin ce "ciel"
au sens aristotélicien du terme n'est autre que le cercle du feu divin
qui enveloppe le monde, cette "quinte essence" à laquelle l'empereur
attribue la force démiurgique d'Attis (*Or.*V,166d) et qui se confond
apparemment avec l'âme du monde.[20]

Jusqu'au *Discours sur la Mère des dieux*, Attis n'a guère inspiré
théologiquement les néoplatoniciens, à commencer par le fondateur
même de l'Ecole. Pour Plotin, les eunuques qui entourent "la Mère
de toutes choses" signifient la stérilité de la matière qui a besoin de
la raison intelligible ou Logos d'Hermès pour prendre forme, car
cette prétendue "Mère" n'a aucun pouvoir créateur.[21] Julien, qui n'a
pas lu Plotin et n'en fait état qu'indirectement,[22] affirmera tout le
contraire! Quant à Attis même, Plotin l'ignore, comme Varron trois
siècles plus tôt, dans ce que nous connaissons de ses *Antiquitates rerum
diuinarum*.[23] Ce que Plotin écrit des Galles incapables d'engendrer, à
la différence de "l'être dont la virilité est intacte",[24] ne valorise pas,
même implicitement, la figure du dieu émasculé. Les "sages d'autrefois" dont il se réclame,[25] ces exégètes du sens "mystique" des mythes et des cultes initiatiques, sont les autorités invoquées par les
allégoristes stoïciens de la *physica ratio*.

Le traité de Porphyre *Sur les statues* a la même hérédité philosophique.[26] Mais le disciple et successeur de Plotin à la tête de l'Ecole
nous y parle d'Attis. Or, même si ce qu'Eusèbe et Augustin nous

---

qu'il ne s'agit plus du ciel au sens spatial, mais du principe actif qui meut le ciel,
bref, de l'Âme du ciel."

[20] J. Pépin, *Théologie cosmique et théologie chrétienne (Ambroise, "Exam." I,1,1–4)*, Paris,
1964, p. 326 s., 486 ss.; Id., *Idées grecques sur l'homme et sur Dieu*, Paris, 1971, p. 342
ss., 349 ss.; R. Brachet, *L'âme religieuse du jeune Aristote*, Paris-Fribourg, 1990, p. 138
ss. Cf. déjà Plat. *Tim.*, 34b, et A.-J. Festugière, *La révélation d'Hermès Trismégiste*, II, *Le
dieu cosmique*, Paris, 1949 (réédité), p. 256 s.

[21] Plot. *loc. cit.*

[22] J. Bouffartigue, *L'empereur Julien et la culture de son temps* (Coll. des Etudes August.,
Sér. "Antiquité"—133), Paris, 1992, p. 89.

[23] Cf. Aug. *CD* VII,25 (trad. G. Combès dans *Œuvres de saint Augustin*, 34, 5ᵉ
Série, II, Paris, 1959, p. 193) = R. Agahd, *M. Terenti Varronis Antiquitatum rerum
divinarum libri I,XIV,XV,XVI, Jahrb.f.Class.Philol.* Suppl.24, Leipzig, 1898 (réd. New
York, 1975), p. 215, 1 ss.: *Et Attis ille non est commemoratus* ... Cf. B. Cardauns, *M.
Terentius Varro, Antiquitates rerum divinarum*, Wiesbaden, 1976, I, p. 109, ad fr. 267.
Mais on trouve des allusions au culte dans les *Ménippées*: J.-P. Cèbe, *Varron, Satires
Ménippées*, 3, Rome, 1975, p. 337 s.; 4, Rome, 1977, p. 562 ss., 616, 618, 627, 635
ss., etc.

[24] *Enn.*III 6,19.

[25] Cf. P. Boyancé, *Théurgie et télestique néoplatoniciennes*, *RHR* 147, 1955, p. 197.

[26] J. Bidez, *Vie de Porphyre, le philosophe néo-platonicien*, Gand, 1913 (rééd. Hildesheim,

transcrivent de son traité peut nous paraître un peu court, l'explication porphyrienne assure un lien entre Messala et Julien. En effet, pour le néoplatonicien du IIIe siècle, Attis est le symbole "des fleurs qui s'écoulent avant de fructifier".[27] Que Porphyre ait usé d'un verbe (διαρρεόντων) qui évoque l'écoulement du sang d'où s'était épanouie la violette des guirlandes funèbres, c'est de soi un indice assez significatif.[28] Attis est la fleur d'Ionie, Ias, dont le nom évoquait pour Messala l'unité du ciel qui enserre et maintient l'univers.[29]

Officiellement favorisé à l'époque antonine, comme en témoignent et la typologie des monnaies ou médaillons et l'aménagement d'un *Phrygianum* au Vatican,[30] le culte métroaque n'a guère eu néanmoins d'impact sensible dans les milieux aristocratiques de l'*Vrbs* avant la fin du IIIe siècle. Les autels tauroboliques n'apparaissent à Rome même qu'à dater de 295 et ne s'y multiplient vraiment que dans la seconde moitié du IVe siècle.[31] C'est l'époque où, dans la tradition littéraire, Attis devient une divinité solaire.[32] Mais l'archéologie figurée prouve que, dès le IIe siècle,[33] il portait la couronne radiée en même temps que le croissant lunaire du dieu Mên (d'où son épiclèse de *Menotyrannus*.) Comme souvent, la piété populaire avait précédé les spéculations des théologiens. Ce que Plutarque écrit des Phrygiens

---

1964), p. 143 ss., 152: le traité "ne fait que continuer le jeu des 'allégories physiques' auquel se complaisait l'ingéniosité des stoïciens". Cf. F. Buffière, *Les mythes d'Homère et la pensée grecque*, Paris, 1956, p. 536 ss.

[27] *Ap.* Eus. *PE* III,11,12 (p. 214 de l'éd.-trad. E. des Places dans la collection "Sources Chrétiennes", 228, Paris, 1976); cf. III,11,15 (p. 216) et 17 (p. 218); III,13,14 (p. 240); Aug. *CD* VII,25: *Attin flores significare perhibuit (sc. Porphyrius), et ideo abscisum, quia flos decidit ante fructum.*

[28] Arnob. *Adu.nat.*V.7 (p. 256, 19 et 257, 3–9 Marchesi): *Euolat cum profluuio sanguinis uita..* Fluore *de sanguinis uiola flos nascitur . . . purpurantes in uiolas* cruor *uertitur.*

[29] Macr. *Sat.*I,9,14 (p. 38, 19 ss., Willis): *qui cuncta . . . copulauit circumdato caelo; quae uis caeli maxima duas uis dispares colligauit.* Cf. A.-J. Festugière, *La révélation d'Hermès Trismégiste*, IV, p. 179 s. (connotations stoïciennes).

[30] R. Turcan, *Numismatique romaine du culte métroaque* (*EPRO* 97), Leyde, 1983, p. 26 ss., 52 ss., 57.

[31] M.J. Vermaseren, *Corpus Cultus Cybelae Attidisque* (*CCCA* = *EPRO* 50), III, Leyde, 1977, p. 49 ss., nos. 226 ss.; p. 101, no. 357. Cf. G. Sfameni-Gasparro, *Interpretazioni gnostiche e misteriosofiche del mito di Attis*, dans *Studies in Gnosticism and Hellenistic Religions pres. to G. Quispel . . .* (*EPRO* 91), Leyde, 1981, p. 407.

[32] Arnob. *Adu.nat.*V,42 (p. 302, 3 ss. Marchesi; cf. F. Mora, *op. cit.* p. 190 s.); Firm. Mat. *De errore prof.rel.*8,2; F. Cumont, *Lux Perpetua*, p. 264; M.J. Vermaseren, *Cybele and Attis* (n. 10), p. 181.

[33] M.J. Vermaseren, *CCCA* III, p. 123, no. 394 et pl. CCXLIV. Cf. M. Floriani Squarciapino, *I culti orientali ad Ostia* (*EPRO* 3), Leyde, 1962, p. 10 et n. 2, pl. IV, 6; J. Medini, *Le culte de Cybèle dans la Liburnie antique*, dans *Hommages à M.J. Vermaseren* (*EPRO* 68), II, Leyde, 1978, p. 747 ss. et pl. CLVI.

"croyant que leur dieu dort pendant l'hiver et se réveille en été"[34] implique aussi déjà un parallèle entre l'aventure mythique d'Attis et la révolution annuelle de l'astre diurne. Si ce dieu des Phrygiens coïncide bien avec celui des Galles, il faut supposer que la légende de sa mort était réinterprétée par la dévotion locale. F. Cumont[35] appliquait l'affirmation de Plutarque à la statue d'un archigalle gisant d'Ostie qui date de la fin du IIIe siècle: "Comme Attis, le fidèle s'endort pour renaître à une vie nouvelle . . . la sépulture du prêtre couché répond à cette conception eschatologique." En tout cas, c'est la théologie solaire d'Attis assimilé à Bacchus, Osiris, Adonis ou Mithra qui s'imposera jusqu'à Macrobe,[36] Martianus Capella[37] et Proclus.[38] Firmicus Maternus[39] impute cette exégèse à la *physica ratio*, laquelle n'a rien de typiquement néoplatonicien. Chronologiquement, il est notable qu'elle s'impose parallèlement au piétisme taurobolique des clarissimes. Sur un autel datable de 315, le bonnet d'Attis a un apex en forme d'aigle, symbole du ciel.[40] Un relief d'Aquilée[41] nous montre un *pileus* richement décoré où le soleil et la lune symbolisent l'éternité en même temps que la souveraineté cosmique de *Menotyrannus*.

C'est cette dimension cosmique, inhérente aux spéculations greffées sur la version du théologien Timothée, que Julien a (si j'ose dire)

---

[34] Plut. *De Is. et Os.* 69,378e. Cf. F. Cumont, *Recherches sur le symbolisme funéraire des Romains*, Paris, 1942 (rééd. 1966), p. 362, 391. Rien d'utile dans le commentaire de J.G. Griffiths, *Plutarch's De Iside et Osiride*, Univ. of Wales Press, 1970, p. 539 s.

[35] *Op. cit.*, p. 391.

[36] *Sat.*I,21,7–10. Cf. J. Flamant, *Macrobe et le néo-platonisme latin à la fin du IVe siècle* (*EPRO* 58), Leyde, 1977, p. 665. Le problème des sources de Macrobe n'est pas élucidé, mais il ne semble pas que le traité de Porphyre sur le *Soleil* ait inspiré à l'auteur des *Saturnales* le discours de Prétextat.

[37] II,192 (p. 74, 12 Dick-Préaux): *Attis pulcher idem* . . . Cet hymne de Philologie au Soleil s'inscrit chez Martianus Capella dans un contexte chaldaïsant sur lequel j'ai insisté ailleurs. Cf. L. Lenaz, *Martiani Capellae de nuptiis Philologiae et Mercurii liber secundus*, Introduzione, traduzione e commento, Padoue, 1975, p. 46–61.

[38] Hymn.I,25: ὕλης δ' αὖ νεάτοις ἐνὶ βένθεσιν εὔιον Ἄττην. Cf. l'éd. commentée d'E. Vogt (Klass.-Philol. Studien, 18), Wiesbaden, 1957, p. 56. Ces "profondeurs extrêmes de la matière" font penser à la grotte où Attis s'unit à la Nymphe et à ce que Julien écrit du dieu comme "substance de l'intelligence féconde et créatrice qui engendre tout jusqu'au dernier degré de la matière" (161c). Mais Proclus pourrait bien, comme Julien (J. Bouffartigue, *op. cit.*, p. 355), tenir de Jamblique la notion de "matière extrême": *De myst.*VIII,3 (p. 265, 9–10 Parthey = p. 197 de l'éd.-trad. E. des Places.)

[39] *De errore prof.rel.*8,2–3. Cf. le commentaire de mon éd.-trad., p. 244.

[40] M.J. Vermaseren, *CCCA* III, p. 102, no. 358 et pl. CCXI. Cf. R. Turcan, *L'aigle du pileus*, dans *Hommages à M.J. Vermaseren* (n. 33), III, p. 1281–1292.

[41] M.J. Vermaseren, *CCCA* IV, Leyde, 1978, p. 93, no. 224 et pl. LXXXVIII.

"théorisée", mais en s'inspirant, comme il l'affirme lui-même,[42] des enseignements de Platon, d'Aristote et des *Oracles chaldaïques*. A ces sources avouées et revendiquées s'en ajoutent probablement d'autres qui se sont intégrées plus ou moins anonymement à son microcosme intellectuel, en fonction de ses lectures de jeunesse, inégalement assimilées et coordonnées.[43]

On n'a pas manqué de souligner[44] les analogies qu'offre l'exégèse de Julien avec celle qu'Hippolyte de Rome met au crédit de la gnose naassénienne.[45] D'aprés les sectaires dont l'hérésiologue rapporte en détail les spéculations théosophiques, la Mère des dieux mutile Attis pour faire monter vers elle "la puissance masculine de l'âme".[46] Attis a été "coupé" des parties matérielles de la création "d'en-bas." Il est retourné à l'essence éternelle d'en-haut. Comme Endymion, comme Adonis - deux mortels aimés par des immortelles dont l'histoire revient si fréquemment sur les sarcophages de l'époque antonine et sévérienne[47] - Attis figurerait l'âme à laquelle aspirent les êtres célestes.[48] Les Naasséniens identifient Attis avec l'homme parfait, une sorte de Christ, "l'épi vert moissonné" (comme celui de l'époptie éleusinienne), le "joueur de flûte" dont le souffle harmonieux est l'Esprit, celui qu'a enfanté la "féconde amande", le "pâtre des astres étincelants" que célébrait un hymne chanté, paraît-il, au théâtre.[49] Or, chez Julien, Attis que Cybèle a coiffé du bonnet étoilé[50] est bien celui qui rompt avec le monde d'en-bas, après avoir semblé "pencher et incliner vers la matière" (168a) et qui revient à la Mère des dieux après l'éviration: "elle le rappela à elle après lui avoir enjoint d'arrêter sa course vers l'infini" (169d). Après son aventure, la déesse le fait revenir à elle "joyeusement, ou plutôt elle le garde auprès d'elle" (171c).

---

[42] *Or*.V(8),162b–d. Cf. J. Bouffartigue, *op. cit.*, p. 365.

[43] *Ibid.*, p. 25 ss. et *passim*.

[44] *Ibid.*, p. 375 ss. Cf. G. Sfameni Gasparro, *Interpretazioni gnostiche* ... (n. 31), p. 380–394.

[45] Hippol. *Refut*.V,7,13–15 (p. 146, 64–74 Marcovich).

[46] *Ibid.*, 13 (p. 146, 66 Marcovich): καὶ αἰωνίων ἄνω μακαρία φύσις τὴν ἀρρενικὴν δύναμιν τῆς ψυχῆς ἀνακαλεῖται πρὸς αὐτήν.

[47] G. Koch, H. Sichtermann, *Römische Sarkophage*, Munich, 1982, p. 131 ss., 144 ss. Sur Endymion, cf. maintenant H. Sichtermann, *Die mythologischen Sarkophage*, Teil 2, *Apollo bis Grazien*, Berlin, 1992, p. 32–53.

[48] Hippol. *Refut*.V,7,11–12 (p. 145, 57 ss. Marcovich): ... ψυχῆς ὀρέγεται. Cf. G. Sfameni Gasparro, *loc. cit.*, (n. 31), 393 s.

[49] Hippol. *Refut*.V,9,7–9 (p. 166, 35 ss. Marcovich). Cf. G. Sfameni Gasparro, *loc. cit.*, p. 388.

[50] *Or*.V(8),165b,168c,171a (τὴν κατάστικτον τοῖς ἄστροις τιάραν). Cf. J. Bouffartigue, *op. cit.*, p. 364.

Mais cet éloignement d'Attis jusqu'aux extrémités de la matière, dans l'antre de la nymphe (165c) correspond aussi pour une part au sort des âmes qui sombrent dans le corps. Pour expliquer la fête des Hilaries, Julien ne peut que poser la question (169d): "Qu'y aurait-il de mieux disposé, de plus joyeux qu'une âme échappée de la course vers l'infini, de la génération et de l'agitation intérieure, et qui a été enlevée jusqu'aux dieux mêmes?" (ἐπὶ δὲ τοὺς θεοὺς αὐτοὺς ἀναχθείσης). Cette dernière expression est parallèle à celle de Saloustios: πρὸς τοὺς θεοὺς οἷον ἐπάνοδος.[51] On en retrouve l'équivalent dans ce même *Discours* (171c), là où l'empereur évoque la réintégration d'Attis dans le cercle des dieux (ἐπανάγει πρὸς ἑαυτὴν ἡ θεός). Mais en 172b, il s'agit d'Hélios qui fait remonter jusqu'à lui "les âmes fortunées", celles que Saloustios[52] définit comme "ayant vécu selon la vertu, heureuses de s'être séparées de l'âme irrationnelle et qui, purifiées de tout corps, communient avec les dieux et administrent avec eux la totalité du monde". Tout au long de cet hymne en prose à Cybèle, le mythe d'Attis exemplifie en quelque manière le cycle du salut des âmes qui, après leur chute temporaire dans le monde inférieur, se libèrent en faisant philosophiquement comme l'amant de la "Mère" ou comme les "eunuques volontaires" d'Athénagore,[53] qui songe évidemment à la chasteté de ceux "qui se sont faits eunuques eux-mêmes en vue du royaume des cieux" (Matt.19,12,11), et non pas aux Galles de la Grande Mère.[54] Tout comme les théologiens de la secte naassénienne[55] Julien ne manque pas de rapprocher le cas du hiérophante d'Eleusis qui "s'interdit toute génération, puisqu'il ne peut participer au progrès vers l'infini" (173d). D.M. Cosi[56] observe avec raison qu'Attis est chez Julien "la figura prototipica dell'anima umana, della sua origine e del suo destino". C'est l'acteur divin d'une anthropologie dramatisée.

La doctrine naassénienne a dû fleurir dès l'époque antonine, sous l'influence conjointe du dualisme platonicien et de l'allégorisme stoï-cien, mais en relation aussi très probablement avec le regain de vi-talité dont bénéficie alors la religion métroaque grâce aux appuis

---

[51] *De.d. et m.*IV,10.

[52] *Ibid.*, XXI,1.

[53] *Leg.*34 (p. 187, 12 Ubaldi); cf. 33 (p. 182, 9)

[54] Comme le croyait A. Audin, *Les martyrs de 177, Cahiers d'Histoire*, 11, 1966, p. 356.

[55] Hippol. *Refut.*V,8,40 (p. 163, 213 Marcovich). Cf. J. Bouffartigue, *op. cit.*, p. 376.

[56] *Casta Mater Idaea, Giuliano l'Apostata e l'etica della sessualità*, Venise, 1986, p. 110.

officiels, quand le *Phrygianum* du Vatican commence à fonctionner.[57]
Le monnayage contemporain en témoigne éloquemment.[58] Les Naasséniens prenaient en compte le phrygianisme au temps où sa popu-
larité s'imposait même au théâtre où, revêtu d'un costume presti-
gieux et la harpe en main, un acteur chantait (nous dit Hippolyte)
"les grands mystères, sans d'ailleurs comprendre le sens de ses paro-
les".[59] Ces derniers mots doivent transcrire une réflexion de l'exégète
naassénien. Il déchiffrait sans doute dans l'hymne à Attis qui suit
une tout autre signification que celle dont se contentait le public
païen ordinaire. D'après Hippolyte, les gnostiques naasséniens participaient assidûment aux "Mystères de la Grande Mère".[60] Peut-être
même se faisaient-ils taurobolier. Car l'auteur des *Philosophoumena* nous
précise qu'ils ne sont pas mutilés, à la différence des Galles; mais,
comme des eunuques, ils excluent toute relation sexuelle. Or, le
taurobole est un sacrifice de substitution, qui permet de s'assimiler
fictivement à un Attis, sans en subir la mutilation.[61] A l'époque de
Julien, les tauroboles avaient, comme on sait, les faveurs de l'aristocratie païenne.[62]

Il n'est pas impensable que, dans les années où au château de
Macellum le futur César dévorait la bibliothèque de Georges, alors
prêtre chargé de son "institution" chrétienne, Julien ait lu la *Réfuta-
tion de toutes les hérésies*, prodigieux témoignage sur l'imaginaire syncré-
tique des milieux païens touchés par les progrès de l'Evangile, et
donc propre à intéresser un adolescent lié à cette double tradition.
Après le massacre de ce même Georges (devenu évêque d'Alexandrie, il avait eu le malheur d'y détruire un *Mithraeum* afin d'y im-
planter une église), Julien s'inquiète du sort de sa bibliothèque: "On
y trouvait surtout les livres des Galiléens, en grand nombre et de
toute espèce," rappelle-t-il à Porphyre, son directeur général des fi-
nances.[63] Il écrit aussi au préfet d'Egypte:[64] "Rends-moi donc un service

---

[57] M.J. Vermaseren, *Cybele and Attis* (n. 10), p. 45 ss. La première attestation datée
est celle du taurobole de 160 dont un autel lyonnais consacre le souvenir: *CIL*
XIII,1751.

[58] R. Turcan, *Numismatique romaine du culte métroaque*, p. 31.

[59] Hippol. *Refut.*V,9,7 (p. 166, 39 Marcovich).

[60] *Ibid.*, 10 (p. 168, 63 ss. Marcovich).

[61] R. Turcan, *Les cultes orientaux dans le monde romain*², Paris, 1992, p. 57.

[62] *Supra*, n. 31.

[63] Julien, *Lettres*, 106 (36), p. 184 de l'éd.-trad. J. Bidez dans la Coll. des Univ. de
France, Paris, 1924.

[64] *Ibid.*, 107 (9), p. 185. Cf. J. Bouffartigue *op. cit.*, p. 325 s., où l'auteur insiste sur
l'intérêt de Julien pour les "commentaires".

personnel en retrouvant tous les livres de Georges. Il y en avait beaucoup sur la philosophie, beaucoup sur la rhétorique, et de plus beaucoup sur les doctrines des impies Galiléens, ouvrages que je voudrais voir anéantis: mais de peur que d'autres plus utiles ne disparaissent avec eux, qu'on les recherche, eux tous aussi, avec grand soin." Parmi ces livres "de toute espèce" pourrait bien s'être trouvé l'ouvrage d'Hippolyte, réservoir de spéculations bizarres et fantasmagoriques auxquelles Julien n'était pas de nature à rester insensible.

Mais d'autres influences ont joué qui, par une sorte de coalescence, ont formé le noyau complexe des intuitions majeures développées dans le *Discours*. Julien revendique l'originalité personnelle de son interprétation:[65] "On m'apprend que Porphyre a philosophé sur le sujet." Mais l'empereur n'a pas lu ces écrits et ne sait pas s'ils sont ou non en accord avec son propos. "Néanmoins j'imagine pour ma part que ce Gallos ainsi qu'Attis sont la substance de l'intelligence féconde et créatrice qui engendre tout jusqu'au dernier degré de la matière . . ." (161c). Effectivement, cet Attis générateur paraît bien être une "première" dans l'histoire des allégories polythéistes, encore que les Naasséniens aient ouvert la voie à des considérations très voisines.

Mais, bien avant la gnose naassénienne, Platon dans le *Timée* (34b) avait en somme identifié le ciel avec l'âme du monde, qui l'enveloppe de toutes parts comme un firmament.[66] On retrouvera dans le *Corpus Hermeticum* (X,11)[67] une comparaison significative entre le ciel intelligible qui cercle le cosmos et l'âme qui enveloppe la tête comme une membrane, ὑμήν·: "Toutes les choses qui sont attachées à la membrane de cette tête, en laquelle se trouve l'âme, sont par nature immortelles." L'âme "noétique" est donc comme le cercle immortel du feu divin. C'est la quintessence que Julien identifie explicitement ou implicitement avec Attis.[68] C'est l'âme du monde en même temps que le prototype de l'âme humaine. Comme l'éther aristotélicien aussi, l'Attis de Julien joue un rôle créateur, là où s'opère "le mélange du corps passible et du mouvement circulaire - impassible - du cinquième

---

[65] Sur la "loyauté" de Julien et son originalité relative: *ibid.*, p. 346 s. et 379.

[66] A.-J. Festugière, *La révélation d'Hermès Trismégiste*, II, p. 256 s.; J. Pépin, *Idées grecques sur l'homme et sur Dieu* (n. 20), p. 342 ss., qui renvoie (p. 344) à Plat. *Leg.*X,896a.

[67] Éd.-trad. Nock-Festugière dans la Coll. des Univ. de France, I, Paris, 1945, p. 128, n. 47.

[68] *Or.*V(8),162b,165a,166d,167d,170c.

corps" (165c) et où se fait "la catabase" dans l'antre de la Nymphe (171a).

En définitive, par conséquent, s'exprimerait dans le *Discours* une idée préfigurée par les spéculations de Valérius Messala sur Janus-Aiôn. Mais, en assimilant Attis au ciel dont il porte les astres sur la tiare, insigne de ses pouvoirs sur "l'espace sans mélange et pur jusqu'à la Galaxie" (171a; cf. 168c), Julien nous réfère à Ouranos, également châtré, et dont Cornutus[69] expliquait la mutilation dans un sens assez comparable à celui de l'exégèse explicitée trois siècles plus tard par "l'Apostat". En effet, Ouranos est le fécondateur par excellence; mais cette génération qui déborde démesurément a besoin d'être limitée, régularisée. Kronos, qui personnifie l'ordre régissant la création universelle, "voyant l'écoulement de l'élément enveloppant devenir excessif, le restreignit en rendant les exhalaisons plus subtiles. La nature du cosmos, que nous avons dit s'appeler Zeus, ayant pris de la force, fit cesser le caractère désordonné de cette transformation et y mit un terme après avoir accordé au monde lui-même une plus longue existence." G. Rocca-Serra[70] a justement marqué l'importance de l'allégorisme stoïcien qui "fournit ici, comme en d'autres circonstances, sa base à l'exégèse néoplatonicienne."

Nourri de multiples textes, Julien a le sentiment de faire œuvre originale en trouvant l'expression d'une synthèse qui met en forme et au clair la cohérence profonde d'éléments hétérogènes, graduellement sédimentés dans sa conscience d'intellectuel païen. Jamblique et les *Oracles chaldaïques* correspondent aux strates les plus récentes, les plus déterminantes aussi de sa culture théosophique. Des *Oracles*, au vrai, il ne cite expressément qu'une épiclèse du dieu solaire (ἑπτάκτις),[71] chorège des planètes qui fait remonter les âmes au ciel, comme la Grande Mère ramène Attis à ses côtés pour en faire l'aurige

---

[69] *Theol.Graec.comp.*7, p. 7, 21–28 Lang.

[70] *Les philosophes stoïciens et le syncrétisme*, dans *Les syncrétismes dans les religions grecque et romaine* (Colloque de Strasbourg, 9–11 juin 1971), Paris, 1973, p. 14 ss., en particulier pp. 21–24; trad. G. Rocca-Serra, p. 23.

[71] *Or.*V(8),172d = E. des Places, *Oracles chaldaïques*, éd.-trad. dans la Coll. des Univ. de France, Paris, 1971, p. 112, fr. 194. Cf. Procl., *In Tim.*I, p. 34, 21 Diehl. "Peut-être Mithra," écrit A.-J. Festugière (trad. de Proclus, *Commentaire sur le Timée*. I, Paris, 1966, p. 66, n. 4). Plus prudemment, J. Bouffartigue (*op. cit.*, p. 306) se contente d'affirmer: "il s'agit d'Hélios". Voir également W. Theiler, *Die chaldäischen Orakel und die Hymnen des Synesios* (Schr.d. Königsberg. gel. Gesellsch., Geisteswiss. Klass.18,1), Halle, 1942, p. 35 = *Forschungen zum Neuplatonismus*, Berlin, 1966, p. 294 s. ("der Sonnengott").

de son char (171c), et ce char évoque évidemment celui de l'âme pour un lecteur du *Phèdre*. Les néoplatoniciens ont, comme on sait,[72] abondamment glosé sur ce thème. En tout cas, c'est cette *epanodos* céleste d'Attis que nous montrent, à l'époque même de Julien ou un peu plus tard, les médaillons contorniates au type du quadrige métroaque.[73] Mais si, dans le *Discours*, Hélios ne s'identifie pas avec l'amant châtré de Cybèle, les lecteurs de Julien pouvaient songer aux idoles qui le représentaient radié.[74]

Cependant, outre la référence expresse au "Chaldéen", l'argumentation de l'"Apostat" implique, me semble-t-il, d'autres indices d'une empreinte chaldaïque indubitable sur l'imaginaire de l'empereur.

Il affirme n'avoir pas lu ce que Porphyre a écrit sur le mythe d'Attis (161c). Mais il connaît apparemment le symbolisme du dieu-fleur, car "de fait", affirme-t-il, "le mythe raconte qu'après son exposition au bord des tourbillons du fleuve Gallos, il s'épanouit comme une fleur" (ἀνθῆσαι).[75] Le nom de Florus ou d'Anthus (Anthis) se rencontre dans l'épigraphie du culte phrygien.[76] On a vu, d'autre part, que pour Julien, Attis correspond à la quintessence, c'est-à-dire à la "fleur du feu". Or c'est l'expression même que les *Oracles chaldaïques* appliquent à la membrane (ὑμήν) intellective dissociant les deux feux, sorte de diaphragme qui coïncide avec l'âme du monde.[77]

---

[72] E.R. Dodds, *Proclus, The Elements of Theology*, Oxford, 1933, §§ 205–210, Append. II et p. 304 ss.; F. Cumont, *Lux perpetua*, p. 380; J. Trouillard, *Réflexions sur l'ὄχημα dans les "Eléments de théologie" de Proclus*, REG 70, 1957, p. 102 ss. La doctrine du char ou corps lumineux de l'âme est impliquée par les fragments 120, 193, et 201 des *Oracles chaldaïques* (p. 96, 112 et 113 E. des Places). Cf. maintenant N. Aujoulat, *Le corps lumineux des païens et le corps glorieux des chrétiens chez quelques auteurs grecs*, dans *Ainsi parlaient les Anciens*, (Mélanges J.-P. Dumont), Lille, 1994, p. 263 ss.
[73] R. Turcan, *Numismatique romaine du culte métroaque*, p. 51 s. On songe naturellement aussi à la fameuse patère de Parabiago, qui date sans doute de la seconde moitié du IVe siècle après J.-C.: M.J. Vermaseren, *CCCA* IV (n. 41), p. 107 ss., no. 268 et pl. CVII; L. Musso, *Manifattura suntuaria e committenza pagana nella Roma del IV secolo. Indagine sulla lanx di Parabiago*, Rome, 1983.
[74] *Supra*, n. 33.
[75] A noter que, dans son *Discours sur le Soleil-roi* (*Or.*IV[11],134a), Julien compare les rayons de l'astre à une "fleur": ὥσπερ ἄνθος ἀκτίνες. Cf. A. Penati, *L'influenza del sistema caldaico sul pensiero teologico dell' imperatore Giuliano*, Riv. di Filos.Neoscol.75, 1983, p. 554. J. Bouffartigue (*op. cit.*, p. 375, n. 303) perçoit "peut-être" dans ἀνθῆσαι "un écho du lien établi entre Attis et la végétation". La métaphore de Julien a, je crois, une autre portée.
[76] M.J. Vermaseren, *CCCA* V, Leyde, 1986, p. 139, no. 395. Cf. R. Turcan, *Les religions de l'Asie dans la vallée du Rhône* (EPRO 30), Leyde, 1972, p. 54, 92, 96.
[77] Fr. 6 de l'éd.-trad. E. de Places (p. 68 et 124 s., n. 1). Cf. J. Bidez, *Un faux dieu des Oracles chaldaïques*, Rev. de Philol.27, 1903, p. 79–81; A.-J. Festugière, *Un vers mé-*

Comme la "fleur du feu" chaldaïque, Attis unit et sépare tout à la fois la création matérielle et l'intellect divin.

C'est aussi un dieu que l'iconographie romaine représente le plus souvent vêtu d'une tunique retroussée à la taille, quelquefois avec une ceinture, et un lecteur païen des *Oracles* ne pouvait manquer d'être frappé par l'image de cette "fleur du feu" qu'on y trouve curieusement qualifiée de "retroussée" (ὑπεζωκός).[78] On songe pareillement au Dieu de Philon d'Alexandrie qui s'est attaché en quelque sorte au-dessous de lui (ὑποζεύξας) toutes les choses du devenir, sans être lui-même contenu par aucune, tout comme l'éther d'Aristote.[79] Certes, nulle part cette "fleur du feu" n'est assimilée expressément au dieu Attis ni chez Julien, ni dans les *Oracles*. C'est Hécate qui est nommée dans un fragment cité par Damascius.[80] Mais cette même Hécate n'est autre que l'âme du monde,[81] cercle du feu divin qui l'enveloppe comme une membrane (ὑμήν), et tout le *Discours sur la Mère des dieux* implique cette identification. Si, dans une séquence que nous livre Proclus,[82] Julien a lu que la genèse de "la matière aux multiples aspects" était comme un orage atténuant peu à peu la fleur de son feu "dans les cavités des mondes", ne pouvait-il songer au dieu-fleur descendu dans la grotte où le principe humide de la Nymphe (165c) affaiblit le feu céleste? Les rayons dont parle le même oracle et qui tendent "vers le bas" (κάτω τείνειν) devaient aussi rappeler à Julien la "catabase dans l'antre" (171a; cf. 168c), image mythique de la communication divine avec la matière. Est-il impensable qu'il y ait médité en découvrant dans un autre fragment conservé par Proclus[83] cette vision des "torches épanouies" qui descendent du

---

*connu des Oracles chaldaïques dans Simplicius, Symb.Osl.*26, 1948, p. 75 ss., 77. Le Soleil des alchimistes est aussi "fleur du feu": A.-J. Festugière. *La révélation d'Hermès Trismégiste*, I, Paris, 1950, p. 261.

[78] Fr. 6, 1 (p. 68 E. des Places); 35, 3 (p. 75).

[79] Phil.Alex. *De post.Caini*, 14. Cf. P. Boyancé, *Le Dieu Très Haut chez Philon*, dans *Mélanges d'histoire des religions offerts à H.Ch. Puech*, Paris, 1974, p. 145 s.

[80] Fr. 35, 3 (p. 75 E. des Places) = Dam. *De prim.princ.*266 (II, p. 133, 5 Ruelle).

[81] Fr. 28, 32 (p. 74, n. 2), 35, 174 et les notes afférentes d'E. des Places. La *fontana uirgo* de Mart.Cap.II,205 s'identifie avec Hécate (qualifiée de πηγαία), en même temps qu'avec la "fleur du feu". Cf. L. Lenaz, *op. cit.*, (n. 37), p. 41; E. des Places, *Les Oracles chaldaïques*, ANRW, II,17,4, Berlin-New York, 1984, p. 2318. Cf. S.I. Johnston, *Hekate Soteira. A Study of Hecate's Roles in the Chaldean Oracles and Related Literature*, Atlanta, 1990, p. 91 ss., 153 ss.

[82] Fr. 34 (p. 74 s. E. des Places) = Procl. *In Tim.*I, p. 451, 19–22 Diehl. L'expression "cavités des mondes" procède du Ps.-Aristote, *De mundo*, 4, 395b 34 (E. des Places, *Oracles chaldaïques*, p. 129, n. 8), mais sans les implications doctrinales des *Oracles*.

[83] Fr. 130, 2 = Procl. *In Tim.*III, p. 266, 21 Diehl.

Père et dont l'âme cueille la "fleur des fruits embrasés" (ἐμπυρίων), issus de l'empyrée comme Attis? Nous savons par Simplicius qu'une doctrine du cinquième corps avait sa place dans la théologie chaldaïque.[84]

Assurément, l'enthousiasme de l'exégète néoplatonisant surinterprétait les mystérieux hexamètres attribués à son homonyme. Même s'il s'est efforcé d'analyser strictement la *Théologie chaldaïque* du "divin" Jamblique,[85] il a dû élucubrer et se flatte d'ailleurs ouvertement d'avoir élaboré une interprétation personnelle (αὐτὸς οἴκοθεν ἐπινοῶ).[86] C'est le fait de quelqu'un qui veut s'expliquer à lui-même et justifier rationnellement son paganisme, en fonction de sa culture, de ses préoccupations intellectuelles, des problèmes qui le tourmentent personnellement et qui n'ont rien à voir avec la piété du fidèle ordinaire. Comme tant de polythéistes plus proches qu'ils ne le croient de certains monothéistes contemporains, Julien recherche et trouve une cohérence dans la disparité déroutante des traditions païennes, grâce à la théosophie, et c'est aussi la théosophie qui permet à des chrétiens comme Synésius[87] d'intégrer à leur réflexion la lettre des *Chaldaica*.

Mais chez Julien l'élucidation du mythe phrygien procède, semble-t-il, d'une interrogation plus intime et qui dépasse la perspective générale de la "réaction païenne." Dans l'histoire d'Attis, l'empereur déchiffre peut-être quelque chose de son drame personnel: celui d'un homme qui aime le monde et qui agit dans le monde, qui admire l'ordre cosmique et la création dans sa pluralité multiforme, mais qui aspire en même temps à l'unité perdue, à la réintégration dans le feu originel de l'Intelligence absolue. Il fait son métier d'empereur. Il s'y donne avec la même ardeur généreuse que le dieu générateur descendu dans "l'antre des Nymphes", mais sans s'y abandonner ni sombrer dans la compromission indéfinie avec la matière. Julien rend grâces à Cybèle de ne l'avoir pas laissé "errer dans les ténèbres": lui aussi a fait "l'ablation" . . . (174c).

---

[84] Simpl. *Comm. in Arist.phys.*, p. 643, 27 Diels. Cf. H. Lewy, *Chaldaean Oracles and Theurgy*[2], Paris, 1978, p. 138, n. 270.

[85] J. Bouffartigue, *op. cit.*, p. 307 ss., 345 ss., 365 s.

[86] *Or.*V(8),161c. Cf. J. Bouffartigue, *op. cit.*, p. 346.

[87] W. Theiler, *op. cit.* (n. 71); E. des Places. éd-trad. des *Oracles chaldaïques*, p. 35 ss.; Id., *Les Oracles chaldaïques*, *ANRW* II,17,4, p. 2316 ss. Cf. H.-I. Marrou, *La "conversion" de Synésios*, *REG* 65, 1952, p. 474 ss.; C. Lacombrade, *Synésius de Cyrène, hellène et chrétien*, Paris, 1951, p. 60, 62 s., 156, 167 s.; J. Bregman, *Synesius of Cyrene: Philosopher-Bishop*, Berkeley, 1982.

On ne peut pas dire que l'exégèse de l'empereur ait fait école chez les néoplatoniens, sauf chez son contemporain et ami le "philosophe" Saloustios pour qui Attis est "le démiurge de ce qui se fait et se défait".[88] Le chapitre IV de son traité *Des dieux et du monde* fait très exactement écho au *Discours sur la Mère des dieux*. Pourtant, un peu moins de deux siècles plus tard, Damascius[89] attribue à Attis la démiurgie ou le soin d'organiser "ce qui est engendré". Il situe le dieu dans la sphère lunaire, comme Adonis dont le mythe dramatise semblablement le divin en devenir. Porphyre associait déjà au dieu phrygien l'amant de Vénus considéré plus précisément comme un symbole des fruits mûrs.[90] Damascius devait connaître le traité *Sur les statues*. Mais Porphyre pourrait bien s'être expliqué encore ailleurs sur ces dieux de la fructification, dans l'ouvrage dont Julien a entendu parler, sans se donner la peine de le lire (161c). Pour Damascius, Attis et Adonis comptent comme "les derniers des dieux hypercosmiques", ceux qui exercent "sur notre monde une fonction de providence". La localisation d'Attis dans le secteur "séléniaque" ne nous rappelle pas seulement l'insigne du croissant lunaire qui surmonte à Ostie l'apex de son *pileus*.[91] Le cercle de la Lune marque l'entrée dans la sphère du changement. "Observe donc l'immutabilité du cinquième corps par rapport à l'universel changement en considérant les phases de la Lune", écrit Julien (167d), lequel nous montre ailleurs (*Or*.IV,[11],150a) "la Lune contemplant à la fois les intelligibles supracélestes et parant aussi de formes le monde matériel", en détruisant "ce qu'il comporte de désordre et de confusion". C'est donc aussi le lieu d'Attis et de la génération des formes définies.

Damascius avait encore une notion relativement précise du culte métroaque, en un temps où, depuis plus d'un siècle, il avait cessé d'être célébré publiquement. Dans sa *Vie d'Isidore*, il nous conte qu'avec son ami le philosophe Dorus il s'était aventuré à Hiérapolis de Phrygie

---

[88] *De d. et m.*IV,8. Un vers précité de l'hymne au Soleil de Proclus (n. 38) pourrait postuler la lecture de commentaires apparentés à l'exégèse de Julien ou la dépendance d'une source commune: Jamblique?

[89] *De prim princ.*352 (II, p. 214, 6 s. Ruelle), traduction d'A.-Ed. Chaignet, *Damascius le Diadoque, Problèmes et solutions touchant les premiers principes* . . . III, Paris, 1898 (rééd. Bruxelles, 1964), p. 67. Cf. O. Kern, *Orphicorum fragmenta*[2], Berlin, 1963, p. 223, fr. 201. On rapproche *l'Hymne orphique* 40 (à Musée), où Attis est invoqué avant Adonis (v. 1–2).

[90] *Ap.* Eus. *PE* III,11,12,15 et 17; 13,14. Cf. Amm.XXII,9,15 (*sectarum est indicium frugum*).

[91] *Supra*, n. 33.

sous le temple d'Apollon dans un couloir souterrain qui exhalait des vapeurs mortelles. Tous deux en étaient sortis sains et saufs. C'est alors qu'endormi dans cette "ville sacrée", Damascius avait rêvé qu'il était Attis et qu'il fêtait les Hilaries à l'invitation de la Grande Mère. "Ce songe signifiait notre salut hors de l'Hadès": autrement dit, le salut de l'âme délivrée des pesanteurs terrestres.[92] Damascius avait dû lire le *Discours* de Julien, même s'il ne le cite pas.

Certes, l'empereur n'était pas vraiment une autorité philosophique. Ce qui ne l'empêchait pas d'être lu et recopié. Au demeurant, ses spéculations sur le dieu châtré n'avaient rien non plus d'une émergence *ex nihilo*, mais tout d'une convergence ou d'une syncrèse d'éléments platoniciens, péripatéticiens, stoïciens, néopythagoriciens, chaldaïques, voire gnostiques, sinon indirectement issus de gloses sur l'ouvrage perdu de Timothée...

Remarquable chez "l'Apostat" est son souci de rendre compte non seulement du mythe, des attributs ou des attributions d'Attis, mais aussi du détail de la liturgie romaine officielle (car il ne dit rien des tauroboles, à une époque où ce type de sacrifice est pourtant pratiqué sans complexe dans l'*Vrbs* par l'aristocratie païenne). Julien reconnaît dans les modalités du cérémonial, dans le calendrier du rituel, dans les particularités des abstinences autant de confirmations de son exégèse.[93] Même le pin sacré qui "se hausse pour ainsi dire vers l'éther" (169b), l'arbre au pied duquel Attis s'est mutilé et que portent les dendrophores dans la procession du 22 mars, représente la conversion de l'âme qui rompt avec le monde d'En-Bas: "Le rite nous invite donc, nous qui sommes d'une nature céleste mais qui avons été transportés sur la terre, à moissonner la vertu accompagnée de la piété dans le champ de notre conduite terrestre pour nous hâter de rejoindre l'ancestrale déesse créatrice de vie" (169b; traduction G. Rochefort). La connaissance assez précise du culte qui inspire à l'empereur cette herméneutique passionnée suppose très probablement, comme on l'a conjecturé,[94] une part d'informations puisées directement à une source métroaque, mais intégrées à une culture philosophique truffée de représentations hétérogènes.

Quoi qu'il en soit et contrairement à ce que croyait F. Cumont,[95]

---

[92] *Ap*. Phot. *Bibl*.242,131 (VI, p. 34 de l'éd.-trad. R. Henry, Paris, 1971).

[93] *Or*.V(8),168c–169c,173a–178c. Cf. J. Bouffartigue, *op. cit.*, p. 367–373.

[94] *Ibid.*, p. 373: "Manifestement, Julien tient là ses informations de première main, et s'est renseigné auprès des dépositaires du dogme".

[95] *Lux perpetua*, p. 264.

quand il écrivait que "l'eschatologie si fortement constituée du maz-
déisme transforma celle des mystères de la Grande Mère", le maz-
déisme ne joue apparemment aucun rôle dans l'argumentation de
Julien, non plus que dans l'évolution de la religion métroaque en
général. En revanche, il suffisait de reconnaître l'âme cosmique du
Timée et la quintessence d'Aristote dans la "fleur du feu" divin géné-
reusement diffusée, mais providentiellement maîtrisée, pour ne plus
s'offusquer d'une éviration mythique. Mais pour en faire la théorie
avec l'ardeur qui anime le *Discours sur la Mère des dieux*, il fallait aussi
comprendre que l'âme individuelle est solidaire de l'âme du monde,
qu'elles sont en quelque manière consubstantielles et que leurs sorts
se confondent ou sont tout au moins parallèles. C'était au fond déjà
l'idée des Naasséniens.

MAGNA MATER, CYBELE AND ATTIS IN ROMAN SPAIN

J.F. Ubiña

1. Bibliographical remarks and general view

Our knowledge of the cult of Magna Mater and Attis in Roman Spain has scarcely advanced since A. García y Bellido published, in 1967, his well-known book on oriental religions,[1] in which he emphasized some of the most noteworthy features regarding the worship in Hispania of this divine couple, namely the irregular acceptance of Cybele and Attis in the various Spanish provinces, their marked flourishing during the early Empire, and the predominance of free citizens among their worshippers (although some were of slave or indigenous descent).

However, García y Bellido's study suffers from serious limitations, pointed out by the author himself in the "Préface" (p. IX): "Quant au thème je me suis limité à . . . la réunion de matériaux qui, un jour, puissent servir de base à des théories plus étendues de caractère historique. Le présent livre n'est donc pas une histoire des religions orientales dans l'ancienne Hispanie". If we further consider that its cataloguing system is based upon purely formal archaeological criteria, it is logical that this book hardly discusses questions of great historical interest, such as the ideological function of these cults, the religious sentiments they aroused, or their relationship with traditional Roman piety.[2]

---

[1] A. Garcia Y Bellido, *Les religions orientales dans l'Espagne romaine*, Leiden 1967, pp. 23 ss. (Henceforth AGyB, ROER). We also quote in abbreviated form the following works:

CCCA = M.J. Vermaseren, *Corpus Cultus Cybelae Attidisque (CCCA). V. Aegyptus, Africa, Hispania, Gallia et Britannia* (*EPRO* 50), Leiden 1986.

DUTHOY = R. Duthoy, *The Taurobolium. Its Evolution and Terminology*, Leiden 1969.

GRAILLOT = H. Graillot, *Le culte de Cybèle Mère des Dieux à Rome et dans l'Empire Romain*, Paris 1912.

VERMASEREN = M.J. Vermaseren, *Cybele and Attis. The Myth and the Cult*, London 1977.

[2] An indication of this archaeological formalism is the classification of the representations of Attis according to the position of the legs. The poor validity of this

Although, logically, only by addressing these historical questions may we extend our knowledge of the Hispanic cults, the studies produced in the last 25 years have been confined almost exclusively to expounding epigraphic or archaeological discoveries, in which the admitted intention is merely "to up-date" the repertory of metroac evidence compiled by García y Bellido. For this reason, although the currently known information on Cybele and Attis doubles in volume that employed by the late Spanish scholar, this has not led to any theoretical reconsideration that might shed new light on their historical significance. Even worse, there has been a tendency toward a simple, uncritical accumulation of archaeological data that might lead one to overlook their unequal informative worth:[3] even though the concise catalogues may not remark upon it, the representation of a divinity as a decorative detail within a mosaic obviously does not possess the same religious significance as the celebration of a *taurobolium* for the health of the Emperor.

Consequently, our starting point will be the *corpus* produced by Vermaseren, although we shall make a historical appraisal of each of the monuments catalogued and even reject at least ten, which have also, for the most part, been questioned by the late Dutch historian.[4] In any case, since the publication of his *corpus*, there have been hardly

---

criterion obliged García y Bellido to catalogue one third of the sculptures within a special group (named "C"), vaguely characterised as ... neither fitting the characteristics of Group "A" (legs crossed) nor Group "B" (legs uncrossed). Moreover, in this latter group he includes an Attis from *Malaca* (no. 17) that should, logically, belong to Group "A".

[3] Cf. J. Alvar, "Cinco lustros de investigación sobre cultos orientales en la Península Ibérica", *Gerión* 11, 1993, pp. 313–26. As Professor Alvar is doing genuinely innovatory research into the oriental cults in Hispania, for me it is not a mere compliment, but sincere gratitude, to show my acknowledgement to him for letting me read some of his forthcoming articles as well as for his criticism of a first draft of this paper.

[4] *CCCA* nos. 155–216 (pp. 59–79). Of these 62 monuments we must reject nos. 164 and 166 ("Tomb of the Elephant" at *Carmo*), 170 (inscription consecrated in *Italica Dominae regiae*, which probably refers to Iuno), 174 (inscription in *Corduba* dedicated to various Syrian divinities), 189 (extremely deteriorated inscription from *Conimbriga*, the consecration of which to Magna Mater is very uncertain: see *infra* note 30), 199 (inscription from *Segobriga* wrongly attributed to Attis (see note 67) and 216 (a marble statue that represents, not Attis, but Ganymede or Paris). In addition, the inscriptions from Garlitos and *Egitania* (*CCCA* 180 and 188) are both very doubtful (see notes 17 and 32). On the other hand, the mosaics from *Barcino* and *Gerunda* (nos. 207 and 209), with representations of Cybele in the Circus Maximus in Rome, can only have, in my opinion, a purely decorative function (it is even possible, as Prof. J. Alvar has commented to me, that they are images of *Nemesis Dea Caelestis*).

any new metroac findings:[5] apart from the small relief of Attis from *Emerita*, which Vermaseren failed to catalogue perhaps through an oversight,[6] mention should be made, in *Tarraconensis*, of the *titulus* II/4 from the Cueva Negra (Fortuna, Murcia),[7] and the inscriptions from S. Martín de Unx (Navarra) and from Avila;[8] and, in *Lusitania*, the inscriptions from Senhora dos Martires (Estremoz, Portugal) and Robledillo de Trujillo (Cáceres).[9]

In this sense, special note should be taken of the thesis of M. Bendala on the so-called "Tomb of the Elephant" (in the Roman necropolis of *Carmo*, today Carmona, Sevilla) which, according to him,

---

[5] In my opinion, a metroac character cannot be attributed to the reliefs from Mengíbar (L. Baena del Alcazar, "Relieves romanos de Mengíbar (Jaén)", *Italica* 17, 1984, pp. 127–47), nor to the inscription from Cascais (Portugal): *Augus et/Hermes deae/masgistri/donum*. (Cf. however, the favourable opinion of J. Alvar, "Un posible testimonio de culto a Cibeles en Cascais (Portugal)", *AEArq* 59, 1983, pp. 123–130. Opposing this is J. d'Encarnaçao, "Omissão dos teónimos em inscriçoes votivas", *Veleia* 2–3, 1985–86, pp. 305–310).

[6] This is a funerary inscription to the left of which are sculpted 3 or 4 reliefs of children, of whom only two have survived: one is an image of Attis and the other of a child wearing toga and *bulla*, doubtless the deceased. The text reads: *Q. Articvleivs/Q.F. Avitvs/vixit.an.V/H.S.E./S.T.T.L.* (Cf. A. Garcia y Bellido, *Esculturas romanas de España y Portugal*, Madrid 1949, no. 321, pl. 253; *idem*, Roer, p. 59, no. 10).

[7] Agreement has still to be reached on the historical significance of the varied and invaluable inscriptions from Fortuna, which are currently the object of study. According to A.U. Stylow and M. Mayer ("Los *tituli* de la Cueva Negra. Lectura y comentarios literario y paleográfico", *Antigüedad y Cristianismo* IV, 1987, pp. 191–235, esp. 198–204 and 228–9) the cave, located in wooded countryside with abundant water, would have been a place of *incubatio* for devotees of the Phrygian gods (See, however, the more cautious and sceptical observations of A. Gonzalez Blanco, "Las inscripciones de Fortuna en la historia de la religión romana. Perspectivas histórico-religiosas", *Ibidem*, pp. 271–317).

[8] The inscription from S. Martin de Unx (Navarra) reads: *Ne(ria Helpis/<Ma(tri)> Magne v(otum) s(olvit) p(ro) s(alute)/Coemae* (See C. Castillo, J. Gomez-Pantoja and M.D. Manleon, *Inscripciones romanas del Museo de Navarra*, Pamplona 1981, no. 30, p. 56). That from Avila might allude to the dedication of a metroac sanctuary, if we accept the debatable reconstruction by E. Rodriguez Almeida (*Avila romana*, Avila 1981, no. 52, p. 139): *Oecu/Magna/e Mat/ri P(ecunia)/C(onstituta)/LXXX*. But, in my opinion, a more plausible interpretation is the one already proposed by F. Fita: *Decuma Crem(etis) f(ilia) Ari p(osuit) c(onuigi) b(ene) m(erenti) a(ram)* (BRAH 62, 1913, p. 538, no. 17) or the reading recently proposed by R. Knapp: *Decu(mus?)/magn(a)e mat/ri p(onendum)/ c(uravit)/(annorum) LXV* (*Latin Inscriptions of Central Spain*, Los Angeles 1992, no. 35, p. 38). Thus, on the basis of these two latter reconstructions, the inscription from Avila does not possess metroac connotations.

[9] The inscription from Senhora dos Martires reads: *M(atri) D(eum) s(acrum)/I(ulius) Maximi/anus a(nimo) l(ibens) p(osuit)/pro h(uius) m(onumenti) n(umini) e(rectionem)/peculium* (J. d'Encarnaçao, *Inscriçöes romanas do Conventus Pacensis*, Coimbra 1984, no. 440, pp. 521–523). The one from Robledillo de Trujillo, very fragmented, has been reconstructed as follows: *M(agnae) I(deae) M(atri)/Marce<ll>/us An(norum) XI/C(larissimus) I(uvenis) M(ater) F(ecit)/Caesius/An(norum) XXXV/H(ic) <situs est> S(it) T(ibi) T(erra) L(evis)/*

was in reality "un auténtico santuario donde recibían culto los Dioses
Todopoderosos, Cibeles y Attis, y especialmente este último por su
especial significado religioso".[10] Bendala based his thesis on the various decorative and structural elements of the tomb, as well as on its
particular orientation: the presence of a betyl (which he considers a
representation of Magna Mater), of a bas-relief (which, in his opinion,
would represent an *archigallus*) and of a sculpture of Attis; the existence of three *triclinia* for the celebration of ritual meals, and of a
pool that would be used in the ceremonies of 27 March (*Lavatio*) and
as a *fossa sanguinis* in the *criobolium* rites of mystery initiation; finally,
the peculiar orientation of a chamber, into which the first rays of the
morning sun would directly penetrate on the day of the winter solstice, led him to deduce that this would be a kind of *sanctum sanctorum*
of the sanctuary, where the devotees of Attis celebrated the *Natalis
Invicti*: Bendala considers that this evidence is decisive to prove that
this was a metroac sanctuary, in spite of the fact that the *triclinium*
inside, as he himself admits, "reproduce los rasgos característicos de
los *spelaea* mitraicos" and, furthermore, that this would be the only
known case of the followers of Attis observing this feast day.[11]

Notwithstanding the fact that his reasoning interprets archaeological data in a very forced and imaginative way, and although his
argument contains certain errors and debatable conclusions,[12] Professor Bendala's thesis has enjoyed widespread acceptance among Spanish scholars. Vermaseren (*CCCA* 164), however, made clear his doubts
about this hypothesis and commented upon the possibility that the
Tomb of the Elephant might be that of a priest of Cybele. More recently, A. Fear[13] has demonstrated that this tomb was very unlikely

---

Mavra/M(ater) F(aciendum) C(uravit) (M. Beltran, "Aportaciones a la epigrafía y ar-
queología romanas de Cáceres", *Caesaraugusta* 1975–76, p. 65, no. 45).

[10] M. Bendala, *La necrópolis romana de Carmona (Sevilla)*, Sevilla 1976, p. 53. The
thesis has been re-stated in his two valuable syntheses on oriental religions: "Las
religiones mistéricas en la España romana" in *La Religión romana en España*, Madrid
1981, pp. 285–99, and "Die orientalischen Religionen Hispaniens in vorrömischer
und römischer Zeit", *ANRW* 18,1, 1986, pp. 345–408.

[11] M. Bendala, "Las religiones mistéricas..." p. 288.

[12] For example, he "systematically" denominates Cybele and Attis as "Dioses todopoderosos" (pp. 53, 54, 57); he considers the two to have been introduced into
Rome in the year 204 B.C. (p. 54) and that they were always worshipped together
in *Carmo*; he defines the *galli* as priests (pp. 55, 61, 69 n. 52); he believes that the
Lavatio of the Goddess was performed in the same pool that was used as a *fossa
sanguinis* (p. 57), and he claims, finally, that the metroac sacrifice of the lamb ante-
dated the *taurobolium* (p. 57 and note 41).

[13] A.T. Fear, "Cybele and Carmona: a Reassessment", *AEspA* 63, 1990, pp. 95–108.

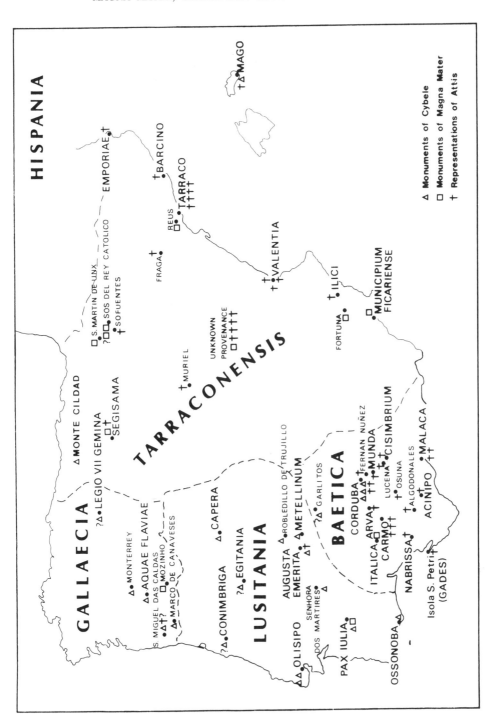

HISPANIA

Monuments of Cybele △
Monuments of Magna Mater ☐
Representations of Attis †

GALLAECIA

LUSITANIA

TARRACONENSIS

BAETICA

MAGO

EMPORIAE

BARCINO
TARRACO
REUS

FRAGA

VALENTIA

ILICI

FORTUNA
MUNICIPIUM
FICARIENSE

S. MARTIN DE UNX
SOS DEL REY CATOLICO
SOFUENTES

UNKNOWN
PROVENANCE

MURIEL

MONTE CILDAD

LEGIO VII GEMINA

SEGISAMA

CAPERA

ROBLEDILLO DE TRUJILLO

GARLITOS
METELLINUM
FERNAN NUÑEZ
CORDUBA
MUNDA
CISIMBRIUM
LUCENA
OSUNA
MALACA
ALGODONALES
ACINIPO
ITALICA
ARVA
CARMO
NABRISSA
Isola S. Petri
(GADES)

AUGUSTA
EMERITA

MONTERREY
AQUAE FLAVIAE
MOZINHO
MARCO DE CANAVESES
S MIGUEL DAS CALDAS
SENHORA
DOS MARTIRES

EGITANIA
CONIMBRIGA

OLISIPO

PAX IULIA

OSSONOBA

to be a sanctuary of Cybele due to its siting (within a necropolis), its chronology (prior to Claudius) and its architectural structures (with such limitations of space that it was not possible to hold the *taurobolium*, to burn a large pine tree, or to perform the multitudinous dances and processions). Although Professor Fear's criticism is sometimes exaggerated[14] and permeated with a caustic English sense of humour, we must agree that the Tomb of the Elephant, although it has still not revealed the religious or simply funerary significance of some of its components, should not be considered a metroac sanctuary as there is not even reason to believe it was the tomb of a priest of Cybele.

* * *

In a first consideration of the Hispanic evidence regarding Cybele and Attis, the following aspects are noteworthy:

1. All our information is of an archaeological nature and its historical and religious value disparate (inscriptions, statues, appliques and ornamental representations in mosaics). The absence of literary texts obliges us to work with evidence that is not very "eloquent" from the doctrinal point of view or from that of the religious sentiments of the faithful. It is hence inevitable that the historian must provide a personal interpretation if he wishes to go beyond the simple recording of rituals, of aesthetic and religious tastes, and of the names of a handful of dedicants whose degree of devotion is unknown.

2. Apart from 3 figurines of unknown provenance (see note 74), in the provinces[15] of *Lusitania* and *Gallaecia* we only have one repre-

---

[14] For example, Bendala never speaks of "temple" (in the contemporary sense of the word) but rather sanctuary, he never mentions the slaughter of "bulls" but of "rams", he assumes that the rituals were initially "clandestine" and, finally, he does not conceal certain "problematic" aspects emphasised by Fear. Furthermore, Fear mistakenly undervalues the solar affinities of the cult of Attis, all of which permitted M. Bendala himself to deliver a rapid riposte, reaffirming his initial hypothesis: "Comentario al artículo de A.T. Fear 'Cybele and Carmona: a Reassessment'", *AEspA* 63, 1990, pp. 109–114.

[15] Hispania was divided, from the reign of Augustus, into three provinces: *Baetica, Lusitania* and *Tarraconensis*. From this latter, which was enormous in extent and romanised to a varying degree, was separated, in times of Caracalla, the province of *Gallaecia*, in the NW of Hispania, an area of superficial romanisation where Celtic traditions maintained their strength. In the era of Diocletian, *Tarraconensis* was again divided, creating the province of *Carthaginensis*, and towards the end of the 4th century, the Balearic Islands formed a new administrative unit. In this study, we adopt

sentation of Attis, in contrast to 17 in *Baetica* and 14 in *Tarraconensis*. The cult of Magna Mater, on the other hand, seems to be more uniformly evidenced (12 monuments in *Lusitania*; 5 in *Gallaecia*; 5 in *Baetica*, and 10 in *Tarraconensis*). However, the metroac evidence of undoubted mystic character is concentrated, as we shall see, in *Lusitania*.

3. Only on two occasions do Cybele and Attis appear together: a lost inscription from *Mago* (Mahón, Menorca), of which only a 16th century copy remains, alluding to the construction of a temple for the divine couple; and a second monument, of scant "religious" value, consisting of two bronze handles of a vase found at *Segisama* (*Tarraconensis*) and decorated with the images of Cybele and Attis.[16] If, furthermore, we remember that in *Lusitania*, the province where the cult gained its most widespread acceptance, there are no significant monuments to Attis, and that the opposite is true for the East and Betic coast, it is apparent that the two deities were worshipped independently of each other. Nevertheless, the available documentation does not let us know whether this disassociation of the two cults was the result of a historical process, as almost all the monuments date from the second and early third centuries. In other words, what we know is analogous to a "photo" that, beyond doubt, reflects an important historical reality: these cults arrived in Hispania at that late date (when they had already lost their mystic character, and their rituals and religious significance had become differentiated), and disappeared—also in an almost sudden manner—in the middle of the third century, although, as we shall see, perhaps due to different causes and in different ways.

4. The monuments to each deity are of a very different nature: while Cybele was the object of public sacrifices, her cult was at times presided over by a religious hierarchy and there were sanctuaries dedicated to her, Attis is, preeminently, a god referred to in an individual, spontaneous manner on appliques, personal items and, above all, funerary sculptures and reliefs: he is never mentioned

---

as a reference the situation at the start of the third century, when Hispania was divided into the provinces of *Baetica*, *Lusitania*, *Gallaecia* and *Tarraconensis*.

[16] The most plausible transcription of the Mahón inscription (*CCCA* 215) is: *Marcus Badius Honoratus et (?) Cornelius Silvanus templum Matri Magnae et Atthini de sua pecunia fecerunt*. On the bronzes of *Segisama*, see E. Sanmarti, "Dos asas con representación metróaca del Museo Arqueológico de Barcelona", *Ampurias* 31–32, 1969–70, pp. 285–89, and *CCCA* 201.

in epitaphs and his images were never objects of worship. Accordingly, while Cybele appears as the central figure of a religious system (with its priests, rites and mythology), and her worshippers usually wanted to record their names as a mark of their devotion to her, we do not know of any who explicitly declare themselves to be followers of Attis. Moreover, the funerary monuments with representations of Attis normally belong to leading members of local aristocracies, whose public activity is reflected in the tenure of the various municipal magistracies. On the other hand, although we know of some thirty persons related to the cult of Magna Mater, none of them is recorded as ever having performed a municipal magistracy or any other prominent public function. Consequently, the differences between these cults and their distinct geographical extension through Hispania may perhaps be explained by the differing social milieux that harboured these divinities.

5. Finally, the two deities are seen to be integrated within the Roman culture of the Imperial era and thus their rites, symbols and mythological content seem to be in complete harmony with the religious feelings of traditional piety. Therefore, the main question is to clarify the historical reasons for their ephemeral expansion, that is to say, what were the spiritual satisfactions that certain sectors of the Hispano-Roman society sought from these cults.

2. *Cybele and Magna Mater*

Only on one occasion does the name *Cybele* appear in Hispanic epigraphy, and even then it is a case of a lost inscription, from *Egitania*, of which we only possess a doubtful 16th century copy.[17] Thus, strictly speaking, we should rather refer to this goddess as *Mater deum*, the usual name on Hispanic inscriptions, or otherwise as *Magna Mater*, although this denomination is rather less frequent and never

---

[17] *CCCA* 188: *P(ublius) Popil(ius) Avitus P(ublii) f(ilius) indul/gentia Pontifici(s) Ig(a)edita/nor(um) locum sepul(cri)/accepi ante/aed(em) Deae/Magnae Cybeles quam/iratam morte/sensi.* Hübner included it among the *falsae sive alienae*, but with the cautious observation *fortasse genuina* (*CIL* II,57). From then on, there have been few changes: some scholars consider it to be false, others genuine (Cf. AGyB, ROER, pp. 52–53). I wonder whether a metroac inscription really existed in *Egitania*, but in the 16th century it was copied with interpolations, such as the "explanatory" name *Cybeles* or even the strong religious sentiment in its last lines.

appears on the commemorative inscriptions of metroac rites (*taurobolia* or *criobolia*).[18] Although little importance has been accorded to this fact, I do not think it to be a trivial matter, as it is likely that behind these differing names are concealed disparate devotions, if not different deities.

In all events, the desire to eliminate the libidinous and anti-Roman connotations of the Phrygian Cybele must have favoured her frequent association and syncretism with other goddesses, especially with Venus Caelestis, Juno and Minerva.[19] In Hispania we know of some significant cases of this religious phenomenon: one inscription from Monterrey (near *Civitas Limicorum*) is consecrated *Iunoni Matris deum*,[20] another from *Legio VII Gemina* might be dedicated *Minervae et Magnae deum Matri Ideae*,[21] and the statue of Cybele found in the *Municipium Ficariense* bears on its base the inscription *Matr(i) Terrae/sacrum/Albanus disp(ensator)* (*CCCA* 195). Similarly, some Spanish historians have explained the abundance of metroac monuments in *Lusitania* in terms

---

[18] *Magna Mater* appears on the above-named inscriptions from *Mago*, S. Martin de Unx, Avila and *Emerita* (*CCCA* 185), but the latter two are of an arguable metroac nature and it is even probable that the Emeritan epigraph is of Mithraic character, according to the reading proposed by L. García Iglesias ("Notas de epigrafía emeritense", *Revista de Estudios Extremeños* 40, 1984, p. 152): *Inuic . . . /Hector Cornelior(um)/ex uisu*. The name *Mater deum*, on the other hand, appears in *Corduba* (*CCCA* 177); Garlitos (*CCCA* 180, but see note 32); *Pax Iulia* (*CCCA* 182); *Olisipo* (*CCCA* 183); *Emerita* (*CCCA* 186); *Capera* (*CCCA* 190); Marco de Canaveses (*CCCA* 191); *Aquae Flaviae* (*CCCA* 192); Monterrey (*CCCA* 193), Monte Cildad (*CCCA* 202) y Senhora dos Martires (Estremoz). Finally, *Magna deum Mater* appears in *Ossonoba* (*CCCA* 181) and *Olisipo* (*CCCA* 184).

[19] For the historical evidence in this respect, see Vermaseren, pp. 71 ff. Cf. also H. Graillot, "Les dieux tout-puissants Cybèle et Attis et leur culte dans l'Afrique du Nord", *Rev.Archeol.* (S. 4)3, 1904, pp. 322–53; H. Pavis d'Escurac, "La Magna Mater en Afrique", *BAAlger.*6, 1980, pp. 223–42 and J. Alvar, "Las mujeres y los misterios en Hispania", in *La mujer en el mundo antiguo*, Madrid 1987, pp. 245–57, p. 249, n. 7. Regarding the formula *cunctis imbuor mysteriis*, see A. Alvarez de Miranda, *Las religiones mistéricas*, Madrid 1961, p. 133.

[20] *CCCA* 193: *Iunoni/<Mat>ris/deum/(A)emilia/Flavina*. This is a singular case of devotion to the *Iuno* of *Mater deum*, a kind of female *genius* of the goddess: on "the Iuno" and the imperial cult, cf. G. Grether, "Livia and the Roman Imperial Cult", AJPh 67, 1946, 222–52, pp. 225 n. 12.

[21] *CCCA* 194: *Minervae et M(agnae) D(eum) Matri I(deae)/patriae conserv<atricibu>s et N(umini)/imp(eratoris) Caes(aris) M(arci) Aur(elii) <Cari cur>ante Casti/no v(iro) c(onsulari) de<dicatum> e(x) v(oto)*. This is, in essence, the reconstruction made at the beginning of the century by F. Fita, who even suspected that what was consecrated to the goddess was a temple (BRAH 58, 1911, pp. 229–30), but F. Diego Santos has recently proposed a very different reading which denies its metroac nature: *Minervae et I<unoni victrici ac>/patriae conseru(atrici) <pro sal(ute) Iuliae Aug(ustae)> matris/imp(eratoris) Caes M Au<r(elii) Antonini et> P. Septimi(i)/Severi <Getae>/pi(a)e fel(icis) A<ug(ustae) et*

of the syncretism of Cybele with the indigenous goddess Ataecina, whose cult enjoyed great acceptance in this province.[22]

Although this latter hypothesis is unconvincing,[23] there is no doubt that Cybele, as a Phrygian deity, is absent from Hispanic epigraphy, and it is reasonable to consider that she was also absent from Hispano-Roman religious culture, at least in any significant form. In reality, what may be deduced from our documentation, as will be made clear, is that her cult was only practised among groups of scant numerical and social relevance, and never assumed the histrionic, bloody manifestations that so upset traditional Roman piety. In fact, all the offerings, petitions and even sacrifices are addressed to *Mater Deum* or *Magna Mater*, protective deities of syncretistic character who, certainly, take on the prerogatives of the Phrygian goddess, but these are shared with those of the other classical divinities (Juno, Minerva, Venus or Earth Mother) and even—although less probably—with indigenous goddesses, such as the Lusitanian Ataecina.

In conclusion, the Hispanic sources do not permit us to individualise distinct metroac deities or cults, but they do point to a (sometimes subtle) differentiation between cults: from the monuments to the cult of a romanised Cybele (and for this reason always named in the Latin manner)[24] to those addressed to a syncretistic Mother Goddess where the Phrygian goddess has lost her personal identity, which has become compounded with that of classical or indigenous deities.

Bearing in mind this differentiation, we may affirm that Cybele only enjoyed a certain acceptance in *Lusitania*: the above quoted inscription from Robledillo de Trujillo (see note 9) and another from *Olisipo*[25] unmistakeably refer to her, and the cult is also evidenced in

---

matris senat>us et cast(ror<um et patriae . . . s>acrum (*Inscripciones romanas de la provincia de León*, León 1986, p. 45).

[22] Cf. M.-P. Garcia-Bellido, "Las religiones orientales en la Península Ibérica: documentos numismáticos I", *AEspA* 64, 1991, pp. 37–81, esp. 68–75.

[23] The main evidence vouching for the Cybele-Ataecina syncretism is the presence of indigenous names among the followers of Magna Mater. But the "indigenism" of these faithful is far from being proved and, besides, as J. Beaujeu comments, "les aires d'expansion des deux cultes ne coïncident pas et aucun document n'atteste l'assimilation ou l'association des deux divinités, en sorte que l'hypothèse reste à vérifier" ("Cultes locaux et cultes d'empire dans les provinces d'Occident aux trois premiers siècles de notre ère", *Assimilation et résistance à la culture gréco-romaine dans le monde ancien. VI Cong.int.d'Etudes Classiques*, (Madrid 1974), Bucarest-Paris, 1976, 433–43, p. 441).

[24] Cf. L. Richard, "Juvenal et les galles de Cybèle", *Rev. de l'Histoire des Religions* 169.1, 1966, pp. 51–67, esp. 55–6.

[25] Dated 108 A.D., this would be the oldest metroac inscription in Hispania:

other cities where *taurobolia* or *criobolia* were held, since we know that
from at least the time of Antoninus Pius these sacrifices were exclusively associated with the Phrygian goddess: such is the case of *Emerita*,[26]
Pax Iulia,[27] *Olisipo* (see note 25), *Ossonoba*,[28] *Egitania* (see note 17), *Metellinum*[29] and, very hypothetically, *Conimbriga*.[30] Outside *Lusitania*, the
monuments are so isolated that one can only consider devotions confined to a household setting: in *Baetica* there are three outstanding
metroac inscriptions from *Corduba*[31] and another very doubtful from
Garlitos, near the border of *Lusitania*,[32] while in *Tarraconensis* and

---

*Matri de/um mag(nae) Ide/ae Phryg(iae) Fl(avia)/Tyche cernophor(a) per M(arcum) Iul(ium)/
Cass(ianum) et Cass(iam) Sev(eram)/M(arco) At(ilio) et Ann(io) co(n)s(ulibus) Gal(lo)* (CCCA,
184; *CIL* II,179). In the same place, and possibly from the same year, there is also
the inscription *CCCA* 183: *Deum Matri/T(itus) Licinius/Amaranthus/v(otum) s(olvit) l(ibens)
m(erito)*. In fact, we do not know what type of sacrifice or offering these inscriptions
referred to, as the first epigraphic mentioning of a *taurobolium* to the Mother of the
Gods does not appear until the year 160 A.D. (*CIL* XIII,1751).

[26] *M(atri) d(eum) s(acrum)/Val(eria) Avita/aram tauroboli/sui natalici red/diti d(ono) d(edit)
sacerdo/te Doccyrico Vale/riano arcigallo/Publicio Mystico* (CCCA 186).

[27] *M(atri) d(eum) s(acrum)/duo Irinai pater et/fil(ius) criobolati/natali suo sacer(dotibus)/
Lucio Antist(io) Avito/C(aio) Antisti(o) Felicis/simo* (CCCA 182).

[28] *CCCA* 181: *M(agnae) d<e>u<m> Matri/L(ucius) Agrius/Vo<c>a<tus>/sacerd(o)s/
crinobo<lium (SIC) fecit>.*

[29] A lost inscription of which several copies exist, different but coinciding in the
mention of a *taurobolium* performed *pro salute et reditu Lupi Alboni filii* (CCCA 187).

[30] *CCCA* 189. This is a very fragmented inscription, that was reconstructed by its
editors as follows: *<Dis magnis Matris deum/*THREE NAMES OF THE DEDI-
CATOR *p>r<o/salute* PRAENOMEN *Cri>spo/<taurobolium perc>epi/<feliciter>.* (Cf.
R. Etienne, G. Fabre, P. et M. Léveque, *Fouilles de Conimbriga II. Épigraphie et Sculpture*, Paris 1976, 44 f. no. 22).

[31] *CCCA* 175:... *Clodis.../adstante Ul<pio/Heliade>* sacerdote. *Ar<am>/sacris suis
d(e)d(icaverunt) Maximo et Urbano co(n)s(ulibus)*.(234 A.D.).

CCCA 176: *Pro salute/Imp(eratoris) domini n(ostri) <M. Aureli/Severi Alexandri> Pii Felicis/
Aug(usti)./Taurobolium fecit Publicius/Fortunatus Talamas. Suscepit/chrionis Coelia Ianuaria/
adstante Ulpio Heliade sacerdo<te>./Aram sacris suis d(e)d(icaverunt)/Maximo et Urbano
co(n)s(ulibus)*.(234 A.D.).

CCCA 177: *Ex iussu Matris deum/pro salute imperii/taurobolium fecit Publicius/Valerius
Fortunatus Thalamas/suscepit crionis Porcia Bassemia/sacerdote Aurelio Stephano./Dedicata VIII
k(alendis) April(ibus)/Pio et Proculo co(n)s(ulibus)*. (25th March 238 A.D.); this appears to
be the date referred to, and not the 24th as M.J. Vermaseren himself points out in
his *Cybele and Attis*, p. 131. The exact day is important given the possibility that the
worshippers may have wished to make the sacrifice coincide with the *dies sanguinis*
(24th March) or with the *Hilaria* (25th March).

[32] F. Fita, "Epigrafia romana y visigótica de Garlitos, Capilla, Belalcázar y el
Guijo", BRAH 61, 1912, pp. 135–136 (= *CCCA* 180): *L(ucius) Tet(t)ius Setic/nas. Ma(tri)/
d(eum) m(agnae) ex v(isu)/a(nimo) l(ibens) v(otum) s(olvit)*. According to M. Pastor, however, it is not a metroac document, as its only possible reading is currently as follows: *Titius Sei.../a... M.A./s...*/. Both he and A.U. Stylow, who have studied
this inscription *in situ*, believe that it is a normal funerary stele. For professor
M. Pastor, to whom I should like gratefully acknowledge his information, it is not
conceivable that F. Fita—as I suspect—could have seen this inscription in better

Gallaecia no monument is definitive, as we only have available the doubtful references, above quoted, from *Mago* and *Legio VII*. This latter one mentions, besides, persons from the imperial court who, as occurred in *Corduba*, also suffered the *damnatio memoriae*.

The Cybeline nature of some of these monuments is confirmed by the use of the formula "ex iussu" or "ex visu", which expresses, if not an initiatory activity into the mysteries, at least a means of contact with the deity independent of the traditional rites of the classical religion: as is well known, in this time the faithful communicated with divine Saviours of greatly differing character (Cybele, Christ, Aesculapius, Serapis . . .) through visions and dreams, whether spontaneously or by means of the ritual practice of the *incubatio*.[33]

The remaining metroac monuments from Hispania (mostly mosaic and sculptural representations) should, I think, be discarded as evidence for the cult of Cybele or as having any mystic meaning. It is not by chance that this type of monument is to be found very diversely distributed within the Iberian peninsula: while in *Tarraconensis* we have eight[34] (some recent finds lead us to believe that this figure might rise in the near future), in *Lusitania*, *Gallaecia* and *Baetica* we only possess the small terracottas from Mozinho[35] and Italica (*CCCA* 169) and the head from *Myrtilis* (Portugal), at present lost, which might, hypothetically, represent Cybele.[36]

---

condition 80 years ago . . . (M. Pastor et alii, *Mirobriga. Excavaciones arqueológicas en el "Cerro del Cabezo" (Capilla, Badajoz)*, Mérida 1992, p. 35 and note 137).

[33] Cf. L. Fernandez Fuster, "La fórmula "ex visu" en la epigrafia hispánica", *AEarq* 23, 1950, 279–91 and A. Gonzalez Blanco, *op. cit.* p. 295 and notes 108 and 109 (with much modern bibliography). Inscriptions of this type have appeared in *Corduba* (*CCCA* 177), *Emerita* (*CCCA* 185) and perhaps Garlitos (see *supra* note 32).

[34] Apart from the second century marble statue of Cybele seated on a high-backed throne (*CCCA* VII, no. 96. Unknown provenance, Museo del Prado, Madrid), we know of the following monuments: inscriptions from Cueva Negra (Murcia), bronze handles from *Segisama*, mosaics from Gerona and Barcelona (all quoted above), reliefs from Sos del Rey Católico (*CCCA* 211 and 212), and the marble sculpture from Reus (*CCCA* 205).

[35] A. Tranoy, *La Galice romaine. Recherches sur le nord-ouest de la Péninsule Ibérique dans l'Antiquité*, Paris 1981, p. 334.

[36] G. Munilla, "Una estatua representando a la diosa Cibeles, hallada en la Villa Romana de 'Els Antigons', Reus", *Pyrenae* 15–16, 1979–80, pp. 277–86, esp. 284 and n. 13; cf. also M.M. Alves Dias, "Os cultos orientais em Pax Iulia, Lusitania" *Memorias de Historia Antigua* V, 1981, p. 33. For a detailed study of these monuments, see the recent works by J. Alvar: "Los cultos mistéricos en la Bética", I *Coloquio de Hª Antigua de Andalucía*, Córdoba 1993, pp. 225–36; "Los cultos mistéricos en la Tarraconense", *Col.int. de Epigrafia. Culto y Sociedad en Occidente*, Tarragona 1993, 27–46, and "Los cultos mistéricos en Lusitania", II *Cong. Pen. de Hª Antigua*, Coimbra 1990 (forthcoming).

3. *Sacrifices and offerings*

Bearing in mind that our documentation extends at least from the year 108 A.D. until 238 A.D., the evidence for metroac sacrifices is very scarce: two *taurobolia* (perhaps three) in *Corduba* and another two in *Lusitania* (*Emerita* and *Metellinum*). The *criobolium* ritual is only explicitly mentioned in the quoted inscriptions from *Ossonoba* and *Pax Iulia*. Another inscription (from *Olisipo*) does not specify whether the sacrifice was of a bull or of a lamb, and in *Corduba* it is probable that both sacrifices were performed at the same time. In *Tarraconensis*, once again, we lack reliable data, although it is possible that the anepigraphic reliefs from Sos del Rey Católico commemorate the performing of two *taurobolium* rituals.[37]

It has often been observed that the sacrifice of these animals was only accessible to worshippers of a well-off social condition, and that this might explain the scarcity of monuments. This is an inconsistent argument, as one need only remember that since the time of Moses, Jewish families sacrificed a lamb to Jahweh during Passover (Ex 12,1), without anybody feeling excluded religiously for economic reasons. The scarcity of metroac rites is thus but one more proof of the scant acceptance of Cybele among the Hispano-Romans. If we further consider that a great many of her devotees and priests bear Greek names, it is not inconceivable that this cult was restricted to some families or groups of oriental origin, settled in various municipalities within *Lusitania*. People who might be involved in the commercial life of these towns (many of them were freedmen, economically prosperous), but not connected with the military settlements, nor having any relation with the soldiers returning from oriental expeditions, as has occasionally been supposed.[38]

On the other hand, the formulae used in these sacrifices show that the devotees did not form "mystic communities", strictly speaking. On the contrary, the followers of Cybele obviously wished to

---

[37] On one of them appears "a bull's head and a star over each horn; at the left a standing person with a large vase in his right hand; he holds his left hand against his hip. At the right there is an axe. Between the axe and the standing man a dagger is represented in a rectangle" (*CCCA* 211, p. 77). The second relief only represents a bull's head and a star between its horns (*CCCA* 212, p. 78).

[38] For example, Graillot, 473; AGyB, ROER, p. 44 and A. Balil, "'Asciae' en España. Notas en torno a un rito funerario romano", *AEArq* 28, 1955, p. 128. Not even Mithras was popular in *Lusitania* (although the *Legio VII Gemina* was there), as has been shown by J. Alvar, "Los cultos mistéricos en Lusitania..." (in press).

make their ceremonies known by means of reliefs or commemorative inscriptions where it was also customary to record the names of the priests and the benefits it was hoped to obtain from the goddess. In the cases of *Corduba* (*CCCA* 176 and 177) and, possibly, *Legio VII* (see note 21) their desire for political integration is apparent, as the sacrifices are performed for the sake of the Empire and the Imperial family. It is very significant that the *damnatio memoriae* suffered by some of these inscriptions only affected the name of the Imperial family, but not the other persons who participated in the *taurobolium* nor the vocabulary of the metroac rite, which seems to indicate complete political, social and religious acceptance of the Cybeline communities and their ceremonies. In fact, we must conclude that it was precisely this "romanisation" and social acceptance that permitted Antoninus Pius and his successors to make Cybele one of the State's principal protective deities and to transform the *taurobolium* rituals into sacrifices of public interest that were rendered exclusively to this goddess.[39] It is then conceivable that the *taurobolium* in *Corduba* in the year 238 was celebrated *pro salute imperii* and thus avoided mentioning (unlike that which was celebrated four years before) the Emperor then in power, Maximinus Thrax, for the very reason that he was a usurper. In any case, Cybele's status as a protective deity of the State is explicitly recorded in the inscription quoted from *Legio*, supposing the correct reading is *Minervae et Magnae Deum Matri Ideae patriae conservatricibus* (see note 21).

Apart from this political purpose, some sacrifices were occasionally performed (irrespective of the calendar of metroac festivities) as a supplication or expression of gratitude to Cybele for some favour granted by the goddess, normally related to the saving of a life or the improvement in the health of a devotee or family member; for example, in S. Martín de Unx the rite is performed *pro salute. . . . Crispo*, in *Metellinum pro salute et reditu Lupi Alboni*, and in *Pax Iulia* and *Emerita* in commemoration of a birth (real or spiritual, as we shall see below).

---

[39] Cf. Graillot, 159 ff. and 475 (where he claims that "tauroboles provinciaux" may have been performed in *Corduba*); P. Lambrechts, "Les fêtes 'phrygiennes' de Cybèle et d'Attis", *Bull. de l'Inst. Hist. Belge de Rome* 27, 1952, 141–70, esp. 150–57; J. Beaujeu, *La religion romaine à l'apogée de l'Empire I. La politique religieuse des Antonins* (96–192), Paris 1955, 312 ff. Duthoy, pp. 63 and 116–117. But remember that the poets of the "golden Age" had already considered Cybele to be part of the ancient heritage of Rome as well as protectress of the *gens Iulia* (Cf. Graillot, 109 and Vermaseren, 86).

This apotropaic or curative power of Cybele's, together with her traditional veneration as a protectress of agrarian fertility,[40] must also have favoured her frequent identification with other classical (or indigenous) goddesses possessing similar virtues. In this way, Cybele assimilated the syncretistic goddess Magna Mater and consequently was the object of sacrifices and offerings different from the traditional Phrygian sacrifices (*taurobolia* and *criobolia*). For example, in Monte Cildad a citizen dedicated a temple to Magna Mater (*CCCA* 202), and two devotees from *Mago* dedicated another to the goddess and to her consort Attis (*CCCA* 215). On several occasions the dedicants of the inscriptions merely state that they are fulfilling a vow to the goddess.[41] In these cases the oracular character of the cult is usually made explicit, since it is the goddess herself who appears before the devotee (quite possibly in dreams, *ex visu*) and expresses her will (*ex iussu*). The *templa* consecrated to the goddess were probably the very places used by the faithful to pass the night and discover, through *incubatio*, her commands. In such a case, perhaps the priests were those who interpreted the dreams (or any other means of communication employed by the deity), who pronounced the prayers for intercession on behalf of the devotees, and who prescribed, ultimately, the divine remedies to resolve the personal, economic or social problems that troubled them.[42]

The cult of Cybele in Hispania may thus be considered one more manifestation of Roman religiosity, and not an autonomous religious system, nor even less an opponent to classical piety. Therefore, as

---

[40] According to Pliny, "immediately after Cybele became established in Rome, the crops of the next harvest were extraordinarily bountiful" (*NH* 18,4,16). Julian defines Cybele as the divine mother that protects life in all its manifestations, especially during childbirth (*Orat.*VIII,6) and Gregory of Tours relates that as late as the 4th century, the city of Autun celebrated processions, bearing the goddess, *pro salvatione agrorum ac vinearum suarum* (*In glor.conf.*76). As to Mithras and to Christ, the faithful came to Magna Mater seeking "à la fois le pain du corps et celui de l'âme" (J. Toutain, *Les cultes païens dans l'Empire romain. II. Les cultes orientaux*, Paris 1911, p. 119). For other literary sources and bibliography on this aspect of Cybele, see G. Thomas, "Magna Mater and Attis", *ANRW* II,17,3 (1984), 1500–35, p. 1521, note 105.

[41] *Ex voto* offerings are documented in Garlitos (but see note 32), *Olisipo*, Marco de Canaveses and Monte Cildad (*CCCA* 180, 183, 191, 202). As already noted, the doubtful inscriptions from *Egitania* (*CCCA* 188) and Avila refer to the consecration of an *aedes* and of an *oecus* to the goddess.

[42] J. Mangas, "Religiones romanas y orientales", in *Historia de España Antigua II*, Madrid 1978, 643; Graillot, 307 ff. Perhaps this was the reason why Tertullian (*Apol.*13) accused the priests of trafficking in the deity's favours.

Duthoy has observed, "the *taurobolium* was like similar sacrifices performed in honour of other gods",[43] and this is why they prefered to
use the verb *facere*, that is, the sacrifices were "made" for the sake of
something or someone, belonging or not to the officiant's immediate
circle, in accordance with the patterns of Roman piety. Consequently,
the greater or lesser diffusion of these cults cannot be explained by
factors of a moral or intellectual kind, as was maintined so vigorously by F. Cumont, and nor is it possible to understand the faithful
as being "converts" who have suffered a radical transformation in
their beliefs, according to the famous, modernising proposal of A.D.
Nock.[44] During the second and third centuries the metroac cults filled
no supposed spiritual vacuum within the classical religion, but on
the contrary, became faithful expressions of traditional urban paganism. It follows that their prime function was not to soothe the troubles
of the soul but to offer new channels of political and religious participation to social groups that had until then been excluded from
the municipal life, or, what amounts to the same, to extend the range
of traditional religion both socially and politically.

Precisely because it fulfilled an integrative function, the political
character of the metroac ritual did not eliminate its special content
of a mystic nature. In fact, a purely political *taurobolium* would lack
sense and religious interest, as would occur with the Christian rites
of that era in which vows were *also* made for the welfare of the
Empire and of the Emperor. Together with the epigraphic texts, the
taurobolium altars in *Corduba* (*CCCA* 176 and 177) and *Emerita* (*CCCA*
186) show representations of *paterae*, *praefericula*, *cerni* and garlands:
symbols and traditional objects of the liturgy of Cybele. In the cases
of *Corduba*, it is even possible (although it is not my own view) that

---

[43] R. Duthoy, p. 95. In other words, Cybele was a "divinité nationale", as P. Lambrechts has already shown ("Cybèle divinité étrangere ou nationale?", *Bull. de la Soc.
Royale Belge d'Anthropologie et de Préhistoire*, LXII, 1951, 44–60) or one more of the
"cultes d'empire" to use the expression of J. Beaujeu ("Cultes locaux et cultes
d'empire...", p. 433, note 1). For this reason, G. Thomas (p. 1504) suggests distinguishing between the "Roman" (or the "national") and the "Phrygian" aspects of
Cybele. But in Hispania, as we have already remarked, the Phrygian fashion has
never been verified, neither may we distinguish, in my opinion, between "mystic"
and "mysteric" cults, as proposed by E. Sfameni Gasparro ("Soteriologie et aspects
mystiques dans le culte de Cybèle et d'Attis", in *La soteriologia dei culti orientali nell'Impero
Romano*, Leiden 1982, 472–84).
[44] F. Cumont, *Les religions orientales dans le paganisme romain*, Paris 1905, cap.2; A.D.
Nock, *Conversion. The Old and the New in Religion from Alexander the Great to Augustine of
Hippo*, Oxford 1961, Chap. I.

"Thalamas" is not a *cognomen*, but that the expression "Thalamas suscepit crionis" is equivalent to "vires excepit",[45] which would ratify the important religious role played by the sexual organs and the blood of the sacrificed animal (which were undoubtedly borne or immolated in the liturgical objects engraved on the altars). In any event, it is the forms of the Roman religion that preside over the ritual, and the "mysteries" of the Great Mother are harmoniously integrated with them.

Only the *criobolium* of *Pax Iulia* seems to follow a different pattern, as here the dedicants (a father and his son, or perhaps two brothers) do not "perform" the sacrifice for the sake of anybody or in gratitude for anything but "receive" it, that is, "they are *crioboliati*", an expression equivalent to the most explicit of *sacrati* or *taurobolium percipere*. This is clearly not a case of a simple change of terminology, but also of the meaning of the ritual, which loses its character of public sacrifice and acquires a new content, of an exclusively mystic nature. Its aim is now the spiritual purification of its beneficiaries, the enigmatic *duo Irinaei*, by means of the blood of the sacrificed lamb. Until we possess data to the contrary, we must, therefore, consider that this sacrifice belongs to a later period than those previously mentioned, not earlier than the fourth century, when the "cult" of Cybele had become an authentic "religion" and the metroac sacrifices authentic "baptisms of blood", possibly through the influence of the purifying baptism of the Christians, whose presence in *Lusitania* was very important at that date.[46] The inscription from *Emerita* (*CCCA* 186, where

---

[45] The equivalence of both expressions, proposed by A. Blanco ("Documentos metróacos de Hispania", *AEspA* 41, 1968, 91–100 p. 95) implies, moreover, that each one of the two inscriptions only commemorates the celebration of a *taurobolium* in which Coelia Ianuaria and Porcia Bassemia respectively acted as *cernophorae*. Otherwise, it is to be understood that *taurobolium* and *criobolium* were performed at the same time.

[46] According to Duthoy (no. 78, p. 116), this terminology defines the third and final phase of the metroac sacrifice, and he therefore proposes dating the inscription of *Pax Iulia* between 319 and 390 A.D. Vermaseren (*CCCA* 182) concurs with this dating, but other historians, such as M.M. Alves Dias (*op. cit.*, p. 33) and J. d'Encarnaçao (*Inscriçöes romanas . . .*, no. 289, p. 359), believe that it belongs to the second or early third centuries. Cf., too, J.B. Rutter ("The Three Phases of the Taurobolium", *Phoenix* 22, 1968, pp. 226–31), who, without knowing of Duthoy's work, also arrived at the conclusion that the third and final phase of the *taurobolium*, developed in the fourth century, was characterised by its private nature. It was during this period that the devotees of Christ and of Cybele accused each other of imitating their respective initiation rites. For the literary references in this respect, see Graillot, 534 ff., but there is still nothing as lucid as the "compte rendu" of this

Valeria Avita, in the presence of an *archigallus*, dedicates an *aram tauroboli sui natalici redditi*) might possess a value similar to that of the *criobolium* of *Pax Iulia*, which was also celebrated *natali suo*. Although we cannot determine whether this dedication refers to a personal birth or, in a metaphorical sense, to a birth into a new religious life, it is likely that Valeria Avita (like the two Irinaei) is not celebrating the sacrifice in the traditional way, but that it has a mystic nature, in which case the date of this inscription (normally held to be at the end of the second century) should also be brought forward to the first decades of the fourth century, above all if we accept that what was commemorated was the day on which the *taurobolium* was received for the first time.[47]

If these later datings are correct, we would have to extend for some decades, perhaps up to a century, the documented survival of the cult of Cybele, but this does not change at all, rather it ratifies, our historical judgment concerning the shallowly rooted existence of these beliefs in Hispania, both of the traditional metroac sacrifices (performed with a political objective or for the sake of particular persons) and of the baptisms of blood (whose aim was the spiritual purification or even the faithful's rebirth to a new life). As has already been shown, in no case are there grounds for the existence of the supposed libidinous, loathsome aspects that the Christian authors, above all Prudentius and Augustine, so enjoyed to exaggerate in their descriptions of the metroac rites.[48] However, we should remember that in Hispania none of the *templa* mentioned in the inscriptions has yet been discovered, nor do we know of any *fossa sanguinis* or ritual object, such as the sacrificial knife or the *cernus*.

---

work by Ch. Guignebert in *Rev.Hist.*119, 1915, 158–65, esp. pp. 163–5. See also A. Loisy, *Les mystères païens et le mystère chrétien*, 1919, cap.IV; F. Cumont, *op. cit.*, cap.III; M. Guarducci, "L'interruzione dei culti nel *Phrygianum* del Vaticano durante il IV secolo d.Cr.", in U. Bianchi e M.J. Vermaseren (eds.), *La soterilogia dei culti orientali nell'Impero romano*, Leiden 1982, 109–22, and H. Bloch, "The pagan Revival in the West at the end of the Fourth Century", en A. Momigliano (ed.), *The conflict between Paganism and Christianity in the Fourth Century*, Oxford 1963, 202 ff.

[47] Cf. Graillot, pp. 172 and 283, and G. Sfameni Gasparro, *Soteriology and Mystic Aspects in the Cult of Cybele and Attis*, Leiden, 1985, 114.

[48] Aug. *Civ.Dei.*2,26 and 7,26; Prudentius, *Contra Symm.*1, 624–30. Cf. J. Pépin, "Reactions du Christianisme latin à la sotérilogie métroaque (Firmicus Maternus, Ambrosiaster, Saint Augustin)", in *La soterilogia* . . . 256–75; Vermaseren, 180 and, in this volume, A. Fear, "Cybele and Christ", *passim*.

4. Priests and the faithful

Epigraphy has bequeathed to us the name of one *archigallus*, Publicius Mysticus, from *Emerita*, who was probably a freedman of the city,[49] and of six (or perhaps eight) priests, half of whom appear to be freedmen of oriental origin and the other half Roman citizens.[50] As *cernophora* we are only certainly aware of Flavia Tyche of *Olisipo*, who was also probably a freedwoman of oriental origin.[51] These prosopographic references confirm that the Cybeline communities were only organised in *Lusitania*, as outside this province we only have the evidence of *Corduba*, capital of *Baetica*. In any case, it is orientals, and mainly freedmen, who held the priesthoods, with the sole exception of L. Agrius Vocatus, since the priests of *Pax Iulia* belong to the final period of the metroac religion, when it was relatively common, especially among the Roman aristocracy, to be initiated into the mystery cult of Cybele with a renewed spirituality, faced with the irresistible rise of Christianity.[52]

Some Hispanic devotees are of uncertain origin and status,[53] but

---

[49] *CCCA* 186. *Mysticus* is probably a *cognomen*, as was held by Graillot 234, note 2.

[50] It has not been established whether Marcus Iulius Cassianum and Cass(ia?) Sev(era?), from *Olisipo*, were priests (cf. GyB, Roer, pp. 45–6; *CCCA* 184) and it is even less probable that Augus and Hermes, from *Cascais*, were so, as proposed by J. Alvar (cf. note 5). Possible freedmen were Ulpius Heliadis and Aurelius Stephanus from *Corduba* (*CCCA* 176 and 177), and Doccirycus Valerianus from *Emerita* (*CCCA* 186), while among the citizens were included Lucius Agrius Vocatus from *Ossonoba* (*CCCA* 181), and Lucius Antistius Avitus and Caius Antistius Felicissimus from *Pax Iulia* (*CCCA* 182). On the other hand, given that castration or *eviratio* had been prohibited since the times of Domitian, we must suppose that none of these priests was a eunuch (*Dig.*XLVIII,8,4,2; *C.Just.*XLII,1). On this aspect see J. Carcopino, *Aspects mystiques de la Rome païenne*, Paris 1942, 76 ff. and L. Richard, "Juvenal et les galles...", p. 60, note 4. Other unclear points include the celibacy of the priesthood and whether the liturgical language was Greek.

[51] *CCCA* 184. It is probable that Coelia Ianuaria and Porcia Bassemia of *Corduba* (cf. note 45) were also *cernophorae*. Hispanic epigraphy mentions neither priestesses nor *galli* (nor does Imperial epigraphy), although Martial (III,81) quotes a *gallus* called *Baeticus* who, in the opinion of Graillot (p. 188), would be a slave born in Andalusia.

[52] Two of these illustrious aristocrats, devotees of Cybele, exercised important offices in *Lusitania*: Vettius Agorius Praetextatus was *consularis Lusitaniae* in the year 387 (*CIL* VI,1778) and Sextilius Agesilaus Aedesius was *vicarius praefectorum per Hispanias*, resident in *Emerita*, in 376 (*CIL* VI,510 = Dessau 4152). Unfortunately, we cannot confirm whether the presence of these individuals bears any relation to the worship of Cybele in this province towards the end of the fourth century.

[53] The devotee from *Conimbriga* whose name has been lost (*CCCA* 189); a dedicant whose name is difficult to reconstruct from *Legio VII Gemina* (*CCCA* 194); Marcellus from Robledillo de Trujillo and Iulius Maximianus from Senhora dos Martires (See note 9). For a general view see E.W. Haley, *Foreigners in Roman Imperial Spain:*

most of them were undoubtedly freedmen of oriental origin,[54] Romanised natives[55] and Roman citizens.[56] Some others were perhaps slaves.[57] Of the thirty or so documented devotees and priests, we do not know of any who held municipal or provincial magistracies, which appears to indicate that, contrary to the case of Attis, the local aristocracy was little inclined towards Cybele.

The social heterogeneity of these devotees shows, however, that the cult of the Mother Goddess satisfied very different spiritual needs. As has already been said, some sacrifices were performed for the sake of the Empire and of the Emperors, that is, as a statement of political loyalty. Others commemorated the birthday of a devotee, the anniversary of his religious conversion or that of his first *taurobo-*

---

investigations of geographical mobility in the Spanish provinces of the Roman Empire 30 B.C.–A.D. *284*, Columbia University 1986, 476 (facsimile of his doctoral dissertation, also available in a revised and shortened version: *Migration and Economy in Roman Imperial Spain*, Barcelona 1991).

[54] Titus Licinius Amaranthus, of *Olisipo* (*CCCA* 183); Hector Corneliorum of *Emerita* (*CCCA* 185. See *supra* note 18); . . . Clodis . . ., Publicius Fortunatus Talamas, Publicius Valerius Fortunatus Thalamas, Coelia Ianuaria and Porcia Bassemia of *Corduba* (*CCCA* 175–177). For García Y Bellido (ROER, p. 46), the bearers of the *cognomen* "Talamas" are the same person, but A. Blanco (*op. cit.*, 93) thinks it more probable that they were father and son. On the other hand, there is nothing to indicate that Porcia Bassemia was the wife of P. Valerius Fortunatus Thalamas, as is claimed by Vermaseren (*Cybele*, p. 131). Because of his position, it is also conceivable that Albanus, *dispensator* of the *Municipium Ficariense* (*CCCA* 195) was a freedman: on the figure of the *dispensator* in Hispania, see J. Muñiz Coello, *El sistema fiscal en la España Romana (República y Alto Imperio)*, Zaragoza 1982, 117 and n. 49 (with numerous literary references).

[55] Marcus Iulius Cassianus and Cassia Severa of *Olisipo* (*CCCA* 184); Lucius Tettius Seticnas from Garlitos (Badajoz) (*CCCA* 180); Lupius Albonius, of *Metellinum*, and a relative of his (*CCCA* 187); Albula Paterna from Marco de Canaveses in *Gallaecia* (*CCCA* 191); and Neria Helpis and Coema from S. Martín de Unx. Due to this "sorprendente . . . participación indígena" in the cults of Magna Mater, J. Alvar proposes distinguishing them from the "mysteric" Cybele. But none of these names is of inequivocal indigenous nature, and in any case, as Alvar himself asserts, we would always be in the presence of Romanised natives ("Los cultos mistéricos en la Tarraconense", 41–3).

[56] Publius Popilius Avitus of *Egitania* (*CCCA* 188); Aemilia Flavina from Monterrey (*CCCA* 193); Marcus Badius Honoratus and Cornelius Silvanus of *Mago* (*CCCA* 215); Caius Licinius Cissus from Monte Cildad (*CCCA* 202) and Valeria Avita of *Emerita* (*CCCA* 186). Regarding the possible connection with the *gens Valeria* of the freedmen Doccyricus Valerianus and P. Valerius Fortunatus Thalamas, and the participation of other members of this family in various mystery-cults, see J. Alvar, "Los cultos mistéricos en la Lusitania . . .".

[57] The two Irinaei, from *Pax Iulia* (*CCCA* 182); Britta from Capera (*CCCA* 190); and Gelasius and Caesaria, from *Aquae Flaviae* (*CCCA* 192). However, it has been often questioned whether all these persons were, in fact, slaves. A. Tranoy (*op. cit.*, 334) even thinks that Caesaria was a man: *Caesaria(nus)*.

lium. Finally another group was expression of gratitude to the goddess for the felicitous outcome of some venture or for recovery from an illness. Unfortunately, most of the evidence is not explicit in this respect. However this very reserve indicates that the Mother Goddess was the object of many requests of a personal or intimate nature and that all believed in her powers of assistance. During these years, therefore, the personal or spiritual function of this divinity (and probably others) was strengthened without any loss of her public or political influence. Nevertheless, this is not a case of Cybele recovering or reinforcing her original Phrygian aspects,[58] but rather of a new expression of the evolution of the classical religion in this period, when the role of spiritual and personal sentiments became more and more important, to the detriment of public and political rituals.

Although none of this allows us to speak of "mystery cults", the growing importance of this new religious dimension in fact destroyed the traditional institutional structures of worship and permitted previously marginalised groups to become fully integrated into religious life. Slaves, freedmen and women were thus able to participate actively in public rituals and even gain access to priestly positions which had been barred to them for centuries in Roman religion. The genuinely novel aspect was, then, the possibility of entering into direct contact with the deity, without magisterial intermediaries or political liturgies, although there were places especially consecrated for worship (such as the *templa* mentioned in the inscriptions) and an embryonic priestly hierarchy that officiated at the classical rituals of Cybele.

The thesis that the metroac priesthoods—and even simple participation in the rites—were a means of social and economic advancement for the oppressed and marginalised has not been proven:[59] it is difficult to understand what advancement a Roman citizen could achieve by joining an esoteric cult of limited social implantation. It seems more logical to me to interpret our information literally: even in the most solemn circumstances, as were the celebration of the rituals, these priests acted, not as "intermediaries between man and deity", but as a kind of "technician of the sacred" at the service of

---

[58] G. Thomas, *op. cit.*, 1533. Cf. also J. Gérard, "Légende et politique autour de la Mère des Dieux", *REL* 58, 1981, 153–75.

[59] J. Alvar, "Las mujeres y los misterios...", 256–7; *idem*, "Marginalidad e integración en los cultos mistéricos", in *Heterodoxos, reformadores y marginados en la Antigüedad Clásica*, Sevilla 1991, 71–90. This thesis was advanced by Graillot, 226 ff. and 558.

a small community. For this reason, they sometimes served different deities, and on some occasions one might even suspect that this religious function could have been performed by simple devotees, as seems to be the case of Marcus Iulius Cassianus and Cassia Severa from *Olisipo*, who appear as mediators of a *cernophora*, but without any explicit statement of their priestly condition.[60] A contrary case is that of the priest of *Ossonoba*, Lucius Agrius Vocatus, who not only exercised his sacred office, but also financed the *criobolium*. In any event, outside their religious communities, there is no proof that they enjoyed any special social consideration, and if we remember the restricted acceptance of these cults, it is most likely that they did not have it.

These considerations are equally valid regarding the devotees. They were mostly individuals of oriental origin who, indeed, had improved their economic and political status, as not a few were of slave descent or had been so themselves. Nonetheless, their religiosity is not a proof of their social advancement, but rather demonstrates their spiritual gratitude to the deity or simply their political faithfulness.[61] In this situation, it is not surprising that the cult should attract Roman citizens lacking *cursus honorum* (that is, to a certain point excluded from public life), who might have found some personal compensation within these communities.[62] In any case, their ritual practices

---

[60] Graillot considers Cassia Severa to be the only known priestess in Hispania, but his opinion regarding the priesthood differs from mine: "Prophète, l'Archigalle est comme le mandataire de la Mère des Dieux auprès des hommes. Le prêtre n'est que l'intermédiaire des hommes auprès de la divinité" (p. 238. On the female priesthood, see pp. 248 ff.).

[61] As Professor E.N. Lane has pointed out to me, I may appear to be contradicting myself by emphasizing the non-Phrygian nature of the Cybele-cult while, at the same time, stressing that many worshippers were orientals. This is only an apparent inconsistency, as Lane himself remarks in his criticism of a first draft of this paper: precisely because these orientals wished to become "integrated" into Roman society, they had to renounce the "less Roman" aspects of their religiosity. I am not referring, of course, to a sudden, "individual" renunciation, which might be more or less self-serving, but to the fruit of a long process of co-existence during which these orientals and their descendants (who would increasingly consider themselves to be Romans, and less and less orientals) assimilate their cult practices into the religious culture of the Empire. For this, and many other remarks and corrections, I should like to express my gratitude to Professor Lane.

[62] I do not think that these devotees would voluntarily renounce the engraving of their *cursus honorum* on their inscriptions as a gesture of piety: because of their explicit political allegiance, their religious sentiment is not comparable to—in fact, it is opposed to—that of the martyrs of Lyon who refused to state their judicial status

did not penetrate into the social fabric of Hispania (nor does it appear that this was their intention) and barely managed to survive until the Late Empire, when the cult of Cybele became an isolated stronghold of aristocratic religiosity and a brave banner of its spiritual resistance to Christianity.

It was therefore no mere coincidence that there was a relatively important representation of freedmen and women, that is, individuals of a subordinate political status, on occasions also of oriental origin and, as a result, probably lacking social integration. Indeed, approximately a quarter of the persons associated with this cult are women of a comfortable economic situation, though among them also numbered some slaves and freedwomen.[63] This feminine presence confirms the novel religious trends of the Empire referred to above, characterised by the appearance of new spiritual anxieties that affected all social classes and broke open the traditional political framework of Roman piety. What they sought was "the salvation of the soul" and, much more frequently, some corporal or material benefit, but never their social or political promotion, as this was still regulated by the traditional *cursus honorum* (in which, by the way, some Roman priesthoods occupied an outstanding rank). The subsequent disappearance of previous sexual discrimination, and the possibility that women might even attain the ranks of the priesthood, explains why authors such as Lucian (*Amores* 42) and Iamblichus (*De Myster.*III,10) spoke of Cybele as "the women's goddess". Perhaps this was no exaggeration: in *Gallaecia* all the petitions to Mater Deum were from female devotees, wherefore it is difficult not to draw comparison with the popularity later to be enjoyed by the Virgin Mary, Mother of God, among Spanish women.[64]

---

and family origin, proclaiming with enthusiasm that their only identification was that of "Christian" (*Eusebius of Caesarea, HE* V,1,20).

[63] Graillot, p. 146–47 and 285–6. Graillot observed, moreover, that of 22 *taurobolium* altars, 16 were consecrated by women and only 3 bear exclusively the names of men (*Ibid.*, 173). Regarding the situation in Hispania, cf. J. Alvar, "Las mujeres y los misterios . . .", *passim*.

[64] Vermaseren asserts (*Cybele*, 182) that in many places dedicated to Cybele, temples were later raised to the Virgin Mary, but I have not been able to confirm this circumstance in Hispania. On this point see also Ch. Guignebert, *op. cit.*, 161.

5. *Mourning Attis*

We currently know of some 40 representations of Attis, dated during the early Empire and mainly originating from *Baetica* (17) and *Tarraconensis* (22).[65] The only evidence from *Lusitania* is the funerary relief of a five-year-old boy from *Emerita* quoted above (see note 6). Epigraphic references, on the other hand, are very scarce: only the already mentioned inscription from *Mago*, at present lost, names Attis (*CCCA* 215), though it is probable that the altar in Osuna (Sevilla) with the inscription *arbori/sanctae/Q(uintus) Avidius/Augustinus//ex visu posuit*, is also the work of a devotee.[66] Likewise, a pantheistic inscription from San Miguel das Caldas (Portugal) is consecrated, among other, to *diis omnipotentibus*, the manner in which Cybele and Attis were commonly denominated during the Late Empire.[67] This could therefore be one of the last references to the cult of these deities in Hispania.

The main evidence of Attis is, then, sculptural representations and reliefs, whose two most important characteristics have already been noted: firstly, their scarcity or non-existence in *Gallaecia* and *Lusitania* (provinces where the cult of Magna Mater is well documented). This leads us to consider that, at least during the early Empire, the cult of both deities was not related in Hispania. Indeed, Attis and Cybele only appear together in the inscriptions quoted from *Mago* and San Miguel das Caldas, and in the reliefs from *Segisama* (*CCCA* 201). Nevertheless, the worshippers of Cybele, especially those who performed

---

[65] Two of these representations belong to private collections, another three cannot be located and several have appeared at recent dates, which leads us to believe that in the near future new evidence of this deity may appear. Indeed, Munilla (*op. cit.*, 279, note 3) recently reported two new representations originating from Tarragona and at present kept in the Archaeological Museum of that city.

[66] He may have been the descendent of freedmen of Syrian origin. The expression *arbori sanctae* is considered to be a synonym of *Attidi sancto* or *sancto Attidi*: see A. Blanco, *op. cit.*, 96. According to Vermaseren (*CCCA* 161), there is another tree dedicated in the Metroon at Ostia (*CCCA* III, no. 376).

[67] *CIL* II,2407 (= J. Vives, *Inscripciones Latinas de la España Romana*, Barcelona 1971, no. 365). Cf. Graillot, 475–6 and Duthoy, p. 65. On the other hand, the inscription from *Segobriga: Atthidi/M(arci) Manli(i)/Crassi V(ernae)/Anencletus/contubernali//Aemilia/Dercino cum/Attide sua/s(it) t(ibi) t(erra) l(evis)*, does not allude to Attis, as A. García y Bellido thought (Roer p. 62, no. 26), but is a simple sepulchral inscription dedicated to a female slave named Att(h)is. The dedicants are Anencletus, her spouse or *contubernalis* and Aemilia Dercino, perhaps her mistress: cf. K. Schillinger, *Untersuchungen zur Entwicklung des Magna Mater-Kultes im Westen des römischen Kaiserreiches*, Konstanz 1979, p. 55, note 1; *CCCA* 199, p. 74, and M. Almagro Basch, *Segobriga II. Inscripciones ibéricas, latinas paganas y latinas cristianas*, Excavaciones Arqueológicas en España, no. 127. Madrid 1984, pp. 164–166.

taurobolia or *criobolia*, must have known of the mythological relation of the Goddess with Attis, and even felt some kind of veneration for the young god. In fact, the above-mentioned Q. Avidius Augustinus may have been a *dendrophoros* who consecrated his ex-voto after receiving a divine command during a mystic dream (*incubatio*) and, consequently, a devotee of this divine couple.

Secondly, although most representations of Attis have a marked funerary character, there is nothing to indicate that this god was the object of worship or rituals specifically related to death. He was more a symbol, both religious and philosophical, of the uncertainties man experiences confronted by his mortality. This meditative *Attis tristis*, who is always shown in a standing position[68] and usually resting on just one leg, expresses and prompts profound meditation. But these are not the cult images of a god, but rather the expression of a stoically resigned attitude to man's inevitable end: in other words, the representations of mourning Attis have little or anything to do with the cult or the religious beliefs in this god.[69]

In fact, we do not even know of one person who explicitly declared his devotion to Attis. Very much to the contrary, his potential devotees seemed to ignore him when he was represented on their funerary monuments: in Valencia, for example, the mausoleum of an aristocratic family has yielded us two long inscriptions recording the local magistracies performed by some of their members.[70] The

---

[68] In Hispania there is no evidence of the figure of Attis in a lying attitude and/or dying, as is particularly frequent in Italy (see M.J. Vermaseren, "L'iconographie d'Attis mourant", *Festscrift G. Quispel*, Leiden 1981 (*EPRO* 91), 419–31) nor are there the sculptural proptotypes analysed by Vermaseren himself in his book *The Legend of Attis in Greek and Roman Art*, Leiden 1966, such as "Attis' birth", "Cybele's passion for Attis", and "Attis sese mutilans et moriens".

[69] As M. Bendala rightly says, "la imagen de Attis se convirtió en muchos casos en un símbolo funerario más—como la guirnalda, la corona de flores o el rostro de Medusa—, sin que su presencia signifique siempre la adhesión al culto mistérico en su sentido más profundo o comprometido (. . .). Estas son las razones por las que las figuras de Attis se concentran en las regiones más romanizadas, donde el arte romano se hace más abundante y significativo". ("Las religiones mistéricas . . . 289). Cf. J. Beaujeu, "Cultes locaux et cultes d'empire . . .", p. 441.

[70] Cf. A. Balil, *Esculturas romanas de la Península Ibérica VI*, Valladolid, 1983, pp. 27–28, and G. Pereira Menaut, *Inscripciones romanas de Valentia*, Valencia 1979, pp. 42–46, who have made the following reconstruction:

(No. 22):

L(ucio) Antonio L(uci) f(ilio)/Gal(eria tribu) Nigro/Iulia G(ai) f(ilia) Maxima/mater.//C(aio) Iulio C(ai) f(ilio) Gal(eria tribu)/Nigro aedili, de/curioni Valentino/rum Veteranorum, Iulia/ C(ai) f(ilia) Maxima patri.

text makes no allusion to Attis, although it is framed by four reliefs of this deity, whose presence only has the above-mentioned vague symbolic character. The same may be said of the inscription and the two well-known reliefs of the so-called "Torre de los Escipiones" in *Tarraco*,[71] or of the Attis represented in the mausoleum of Sofuentes (Zaragoza), that perhaps belonged to the *eques romanus* C. Atilius Aquilus,[72] or of the funerary inscription from *Emerita* (belonging to the child Q. Articuleius Avitus), adorned with a relief of a cross-legged Attis and, beside him, another relief of a boy wearing the *bulla* to remind us of his aristocratic status (cf. note 6). There is no doubt that a similar social rank must have been held by the persons incinerated in the tombs at *Carmo* where three sculptures of Attis have appeared,[73] and by the person buried in the sarcophagus of *Emporiae* (*CCCA* 210), although in this case Attis is not the main figure but merely an allegory of winter. Consequently, the most noteworthy feature of the monuments of Attis is not their religious but their social nature, as the vast majority of them belonged to members of the local elites.

On the other hand, the iconographic heterogeneity of his representations demonstrates the multi-functional nature of his symbolism, which was to a large extent similar to that of the cross among the devotees of Christianity from the third century. Besides the "funéraire Attis" (which is the most common) and the jolly representation of

---

(No. 23):

L(ucio) Antonio L(uci) f(ilio) Gal(eria tribu)/ Crescenti aed(ili), IIvir(o)/ flamini. Huic defuncto/ <ab> universo ordine Valenti/ <norum> decreta est publica lauda/ <tio et locus> sepultura<e et> funeris im/ <pe>nsa et statua ex de(creto) d(ecurionum) Veteranorum./ / L(ucio) Antonio L(uci) f(ilio)/ Gal(eria tribu) Crecenti/filio Iulia C(ai) f(ilia)/ Maxima mater.

That is: C. Iulius Niger was aedile and decurion of the Veterani (one of the two communities that made up the colony); his grandson L. Antonius Crescens was aedile, duovir and flamen. Date: first-second century A.D.

[71] See C. Cid Priego C., "El monumento conocido por "Torre de los Escipiones", en las cercanías de Tarragona", *Ampurias* 9–10, 1947–8, 137–69; T. Hauschild, S. Mariner y H.G. Niemeyer, "Torre de los Escipiones". Ein römischer grabturm bei Tarragona", *MadrM* 7 (1966), 162–88, and G. Alföldy, *Die Römischen Inscriften von Tarraco*, Berlin 1975, no. 921. The inscription, very fragmented, has been reconstructed as: *Ornate ea quae linquit speciose, vitae rebus positis negligens; unum statuit locum iis sepulchrum ubi perpetuo remanet.*

[72] G. Fatas y M. Martin, "Un mausoleo de época imperial en Sofuentes (Zaragoza)", *MadrM* 18, 1977, 232–71.

[73] A.T. Fear (*op. cit.*, 107) hints at the possibility that the Tomb of the Elephant may have belonged to a rich family from *Carmo*, whose most distinguished member might be represented in the worn relief of the niche excavated beside the pool. And also that the nearby graves might be those of the family's slaves or freedmen.

Attis from *Gades*, there were also figures of the god adorning some country *villae* and objects of everyday use.[74] In consequence, perhaps it is not advisable to reduce this varied iconography to the simple stereotypes of *Attis tristis* and *Attis hilaris*.

In fact, this wide-ranging symbolism is what explains the different iconographic versions of Attis, in which there is never any suggestion of his *eviratio*[75] and from which have disappeared, moreover, his most individualising attributes, such as the pine tree, *tympanum*, *pedum*, *syrinx* and, on occasion, even the *anaxyrides*. As a consequence of this iconographic depersonalisation, it is sometimes difficult to distinguish an Attis *tristis* from other divine figures that in the same era also assumed a funerary symbolism, above all Endymion, Ganymedes, Mithras and his two torchbearers Cautes and Cautopates, who were so often represented with the Phrygian cap and in the same melancholy and pensive posture considering life's end.[76] The loss of individualising iconographic features of these deities is closely linked to the

---

[74] Unfortunately, many figures of Attis are of unknown provenance. Nonetheless, we know of one that appeared in the *villa* of "Els Vilars" (Puig de Cebolla, Valencia; see A. Balil, *Esculturas . . .* p. 129) and another in "Villa Fortunatus" (Fraga, Huesca; *CCCA* 206. See J. de C Serra Rafols, "La villa Fortunatus de Fraga", *Ampurias* 5, 1943, pp. 5–35 and P. de Palol, "La conversion de l'Aristocratie de la Péninsule Ibérique au IVᵉ siècle", in *Miscellanea Historiae Ecclesiasticae* VI,1, Brussels 1983, pp. 47–69, esp. 59–60). The reliefs of *Segisama* (Burgos) decorate the bronze handles of a vase (*CCCA* 201). The Attis-figures from *Acinipo* (*CCCA* 157), *Cisimbrium* (*CCCA* 163), *Munda* (*CCCA* 172), Muriel (*CCCA* 200) and another from an unknown origin in *Tarraconensis* (*CCCA* 214) are all appliques. Finally, Graillot (p. 475) mentions a small silver statue of Attis that would be the applique of a vase. This figurine and another two quoted by Graillot are catalogued by Vermaseren in *CCCA* VII, no. 93–95: also of unknown provenance, they are currently in the Archaeological Museum of Madrid.

[75] The two occasions on which Attis reveals his belly and genitals do not refer to his emasculation but to his bisexual or androgynous nature. They are the *Attis hilaris* from Cádiz (*CCCA* 159), which could exceptionally hold *pedum* and *tympanum*, and that from the late Roman sarcophagus of *Emporiae* (*CCCA* 210), which wears *anaxyrides*.

[76] Various monuments of Attis catalogued by Vermaseren may have been representations of other oriental divinities related to the cycle of life and death, and, indeed, Vermaseren himself had already pointed out the frequent uncertainty in differentiating these gods (*The Legend of Attis . . .* p. 54). For instance, G.E. Bonsor believed that the figure of the "Tomb of the Mourner" (Necropolis at Carmona) "represented a Phrygian slave with short tunic in the well-known attitude of the genius of Mithras, guardian of funerary monuments" (*The archaeological sketch-book of the roman necropole of Carmona*, New York 1931, 63); R. Thouvenot considered the standing Attis with a basket of fruit in the Archaeological Museum of Madrid as a genie (*Catalogue des figurines et objets de bronze du Musée archéologique de Madrid. I.* Paris 1957, 12, no. 18 and pl. III = *CCCA* VII, no. 95); and similar interpretations have been made of the figures of the "Torre de los Escipiones" (see C. Cid Priego, *op.*

syncretistic spirituality of this time, which allowed the expression of
the same religious or philosophical sentiment with images of different divinities. What was important is then not the mythology of the
god, but the sentiment which he embodies (often shared with other
gods). In the case of Attis, his evolution from a mythical character
into a symbolic figure might have been facilitated by the numerous
versions of his mythology prevalent in the West, all of them having
in common the tragic death of a young god provoked by the Mother
Goddess herself (or Nature itself), who would later return to him
a new, immortal life. In this sense, Attis may be the winter presag-
ing the spring, as represented on the sarcophagus of *Emporiae* (*CCCA*
210) and, by extension, the god of vegetation or the solar figure
whose decline is always ephemeral. In other words, Attis assumes a
religious symbolism that proceeds from very heterogeneous mythic
accounts.[77]

Therefore, the historian should not lose himself in erudite investigations (ultimately sterile) of the mythological identification of these
funerary representations, nor believe that the Hispano-Roman society was imbued with extensive theological and exegetical knowledge.
Most of the figures catalogued by Vermaseren presumably belong to
Attis, but there can be no doubt that other deities fulfilled a similar
function and—what is most important—that this Attis no longer bore
any relation with the Phrygian god loved by Cybele nor with the
theology of the Great Mother. It is quite clear, in any case, that his
devotees professed religious (or philosophical) beliefs that did not
require rituals or festivities in the manner of Cybele, but which were
expressed in the meditation and the melancholy of the *Attis tristis*.

One final reflection: during the second and third centuries, some
sectors of the middle and upper classes of Hispania made use of the
symbolic iconography of Attis to express, not so much their hope of
resurrection, but their feelings towards death. In the fourth century,

---

cit,. pp. 137–69 and, in general, fig. 4), of some figures of Attis from Valencia (see
Balil, *Esculturas . . .* p. 29), of the Attis from Tarragona (see J. Tulla, P. Beltran y
C. Oliva, "Excavaciones en la necrópolis romano-cristiana de Tarragona", *MJSEA*
88, 1927, p. 66), of the supposed Attis from Granada (A. Garcia y Bellido, *Esculturas . . .*
127–8), and of the bronze figure that Vermaseren catalogued in *CCCA* VII,
no. 93, p. 29 (Madrid, Archaeological Museum) with the following warning: "the
figurine is interpreted by Hübner as a *gallus*, by Graillot as a dancing Attis, by
Touvenot as an "adolescent".
[77] On this point see J. Alvar, "Muerte de amor divino. Atis", III *Coloquio Arys*
1991 (forthcoming), that analyses all the literary sources and provides the fundamental bibliography.

these human and religious concerns would be expressed, with similar iconographic techniques, by means of biblical symbols and characters engraved on some fifty Christian sarcophagi.[78] There is nothing to indicate, however, that the Hispanic Christianity of the fourth century "triumphed" over the cult of Attis, nor do we know of any confrontation, violent or otherwise, among their devotees. On the contrary, Fortunatus (the owner of the villa in Fraga where a mourning Attis was found) was probably a Christian landowner (see note 74); two heads of Attis appeared in the paleo-Christian cemetery of San Fructuoso in *Tarraco* (*CCCA* 203) and others were found in Roman necropolies that must also have been used by Christians,[79] such as that of *Emerita, Corduba* (*CCCA* 178) or *Valentia* (*CCCA* 198). This all leads us to conclude that the most enthusiastic Christians of the third and fourth centuries originated from the same social and political background as the persons interred under the symbolic favour of Attis: both groups belonged to the economic elites of the towns and actively participated in their religious and political life.[80]

Therefore, it may be no sheer chance that the first sculpted Christian sarcophagi should appear precisely in those areas where the imagery of Attis was most developed: the South and East of Hispania. In my opinion, these stylistic, social and geographical coincidences show, at least, that during the fourth century syncretistic feelings regarding man's final fate found a new, unitary expression in the mythology of Christianity. It is perhaps within this historical context that we could understand the well-known assertion of the priest of Attis to Augustine, in defence of his religion: *et ipse pileatus christianus est*. But, unlike Attis, the Christian God does not appeal so much through a philosophical acceptance of death as through His promise of a certain resurrection into eternal life.[81]

---

[78] M. Sotomayor, *Sarcófagos romano-cristianos de España*, Granada 1975.

[79] The letter 67 of Cyprian informs us that already in the middle of the third century, there were Spanish Christians—even bishops—buried in the same cemeteries as were pagans. This custom still persisted in the early fourth century (see J.F. Ubiña, "Ritual y autoridad en el concilio de Elvira", *Homenaje Juliana Cabrera*, Granada 1993, 345–69; *idem*, "Le Concile d'Elvire et l'Esprit du paganisme", DHA 19,1, 1993, 309–318).

[80] J.F. Ubiña, "Doctrine, rituel et hiérarchie dans les premières communautés chrétiennes d'Hispania", DHA 17,1, 1991, 401–422.

[81] *In Iohan.Evang.Tract.*VII,I,6. The same sense might be given to the judgement of Firmicus Maternus referring Attis: *habet ergo diabolus christos suos* (*De Errore prof.rel.*22,3). We must remember, however, that also the symbolism of Attis as hope of resurrection was developed in the Late Empire (cf. H. Hepding, *Attis, seine Mythen und sein Kult*, Giessen 1903 and Vermaseren, 123).

INDEX

(It is always difficult to know what to include and what to exclude in constructing an index. In this case, given the disparity of the articles, I have decided to concentrate on the major ancient proper names, and on the material included in the text. Names of modern authorities, and of persons mentioned only in the footnotes, will therefore not appear here.)

I. *Divine names*

Adonis 99, 303, 392–3, 401
Agdistis 73, 127, 354
Ahura Mazda 5
Al-'Uzza 96–7
Anaeitis 10
Aphrodite, Venus 53, 58, 93–4, 96–99, 105–6, 289, 311, 368, 378, 401, 404
Apollo 9, 12, 93, 151, 179, 240, 245, 279, 282, 332, 344, 402
Ares, Mars 96, 176, 178–80, 277, 368
Aristoboule 278–80
Artemis, Diana 7, 10–13, 79, 106, 148, 159, 279, 282, 323ff.
Asclepius, Asculapius 78, 138–9, 151, 186, 332, 416
Astarte, Ishtar 93, 99, 182, 376, 381
Ataecina 414
Atargatis 93–96, 117
Athena, Minerva 168, 182–85, 245, 281, 414
Attis, *passim*

Bendis 174, 303
Bona Dea 355

Cautes and Cautopates 431
Christ, Christianity 37–50, 381, 393, 416, 421, 423, 427, 433
Cybele, Kybele, Kybebe, etc. *passim*

Danube Riders 114–15
Dea Caelestis, Tanit 174, 182
Demeter, Ceres 72, 106–7, 110, 112–13, 148, 156–7, 159, 172, 182, 197, 240, 245, 282, 284, 286, 289, 291–2, 302, 309ff., 344, 350–53, 356, 359, 364, 380, 388

Dionysus, Bacchus 2, 109, 141, 151, 154, 158, 179, 210–11, 215, 245, 261, 279, 282, 284, 302, 304, 309, 311ff., 346, 351–53, 361, 365, 378, 392
Dioscuri 74–75, 80, 82–85, 197, 114, 154, 351

Enodia 301
Eros, Cupid 106–07, 109–10

Gaia, Ge 228, 247, 257, 262, 274–76.

Hadad 95
Hathor 89
Hecate 72, 75, 106, 110–13, 153, 332, 351–52, 399
Helios, Sol 43, 96, 107, 183, 379, 398
Hera, Juno (including Hera Meilichia, Juno Regina, etc.) 138–41, 158–59, 174, 178, 182, 299, 414
Hermes, Mercury 62, 65, 70, 72–73, 75, 85, 90, 110–14, 153, 158, 172–73, 176–79, 184–85, 281, 311, 349, 390
Hygeia 182

Inanna 89–90, 93–94
Isis 43, 89, 156–57, 202, 358

Kronos, Cronus, Saturn 182, 186, 212, 240ff., 301, 367, 378, 397

Leto 262
Liber 344
Luna, Selene 90, 197, 183, 401
Lunus 90–91

Matronae 179
Men 9, 12, 391
Mens 368
Meter, Matar, Magna Mater, etc.,
  passim
  Meter Kotiane 153
  Meter Plastene 297
  Meter Steunene 62, 327
Mithras 42, 108–09, 115, 180, 392,
  431

Nike, Victory 107, 112, 148, 159,
  173, 179, 349, 374
Ningal 89, 90, 94
Noreia 185
Nymphs 62, 172, 262, 294, 303

Ops 182
Osiris 358, 392

Pan 51, 62, 68, 151, 216, 265, 167,
  351, 353, 365
Persephone, Kore 72, 106, 112,
  156–57, 159, 172, 289, 311ff., 351,
  353
Poseidon 179, 255, 257, 286, 290

Rhea 67, 197, 211, 228, 239, 247,
  253, 255–56, 262–63, 275, 277, 280,
  296, 298, 360, 374
Roma, goddess 184

Sabazius 174, 180, 309–10, 354
Sarapis, Serapis 40, 128, 180, 202,
  416
Sin, moon-god 87ff.

Tammuz 99
Themis 53, 256, 262, 348
Thracian rider 107, 114–15
Tyche, Fortuna 156–57, 168, 171,
  175–79, 184

Uranus 397

Vulcan 180

Zeus, Jupiter (including Zeus
  Meilichios, Jupiter Dolichenus,
  etc.) 2–4, 6, 9, 11–13, 65, 73, 85,
  196, 114, 138–41, 148, 151, 156,
  158–59, 174, 178–80, 183, 240–41,
  245–75 *passim*, 286, 288ff., 340, 344,
  397

II. *Mythological names*

Aeneas 49, 57, 369
Amaltheia 256, 262
Argonauts see Cyzicus, Apollonius of
  Rhodes

Cabiri 74–75, 83–84, 154
Cecrops 275, 277
Charites, Graces 289, 390
Corybantes 69, 81, 84, 85, 140–41,
  152, 154–55, 158, 214, 246, 254,
  261, 269, 288, 292–93, 302, 344,
  353
Curetes 69, 151, 154, 211, 246,
  252–54, 269, 286, 288, 292–95,
  302–03, 344, 351

Dido 49

Endymion 393, 431
Euboulos 157

Ganymede 431

Hector 263–64
Helen (of Troy) 310ff.
Herakles, Hercules 104, 298, 344

Io 89

Marsyas 68, 123, 129–30, 212
Minos 251
Muses 154, 289

Orpheus 37

Pasithea 380
Pelops 288, 295–97, 301
Pentheus 314–16

Sibyl, Sibylline books 345, 367–69,
  374

Tantalus 296–97
Triptolemus 113

III. *Rulers (Roman, unless otherwise noted)*

Agathocles of Syracuse 77
Alexander Severus 37, 176, 375
Alexander the Great of Macedon
   5, 87, 324–25
Antiochus III of Syria 373
Antoninus Pius 131, 157, 175, 418
Artaxerxes II of Persia 5
Attalus I of Pergamum 370ff.
Attalus II of Pergamum 58
Augustus Caesar 276, 327

Caracalla 90
Claudius I 47, 172, 339, 355, 410
Cleopatra VII of Egypt 49
Constantius I 176

Darius III of Persia 333
Dionysius II of Syracuse 76
Domitian 47

Gyges of Lydia 4, 228

Hadrian 175, 276
Hieron I of Syracuse 51, 56, 264–65

Hieron II of Syracuse 57, 76–77

Julia Domna 177
Julian the Apostate 44, 46, 90, 96,
   127, 130, 197, 258, 314, 390, 392ff.
Julius Caesar 153

Marcus Aurelius 108
Maximinus Thrax 418
Midas of Phrygia 228

Nabonidus of Babylon 87, 91, 94
Nerva 175

Philip V of Macedon 368–69
Postumus, emperor in Gaul 176
Ptolemy I of Egypt 42, 128

Septimius Severus 177

Theodosius I 50

Vespasian 175

IV. *Place-names*

Abritus 172, 174, 176, 182, 184, 188
Aegina 69
Aezani 62, 237, 255
Akrai, Sicily 56ff., 150, 155, 260, 262
Almo, river 339, 343
Alpheius, river see Olympia
Amorgos 270, 273
Amphipolis 155
Ancyra 121
Apollonia Maris Euxini 103
Aquileia 392
Arcadia 246, 253ff., 281
Asea 254
Assos 9
Athens 52, 68, 85, 111, 140, 154,
   196–97, 215, 230, 240–42, 246,
   252, 255ff., 270, 272, 279–81, 284,
   290, 299, 305ff. 339, 356–57
Azania 254, 281

Baetica 410ff.
Bithynia 234, 297

Borysthenes river 104
Bospori Regnum 101

Caicus river 1
Caria, Carians 4–5, 9, 12
Callatis 108
Camarina 78
Capua 115
Carmo 407, 430
Carnuntum 186
Carthage 174
Çatal Hüyük 303, 376
Cayster river 1, 2, 7, 13
Calaenae 123, 129–31
Chios 79–80, 85, 230, 279
Civitas Limicorum 413
Colophon 84
Conimbriga 415
Corduba 415, 417–8, 420, 423, 433
Corfu, Kerkyra 139
Corinth 76, 266
Cos 78–79, 81, 85, 138, 239, 280

Crete 185, 241, 246–53, 267–68,
  295, 319
Cyprus 150, 152, 271
Cyzicus 84, 145, 151, 153, 172, 229,
  240, 246, 267ff., 272, 282, 288, 290,
  291, 299–301, 304, 350

Dacia 101
Daskyleion 136–37, 144
Delphi 53, 228, 301, 348, 368, 370
Delos 68, 79, 82–83, 145, 241–42,
  280
Dicte, Mt. 248, 251, 295
Dura Europus 95

Edessa 87, 94–95
Egitania 412, 416
Eleusis 159, 244, 256, 284–84, 290,
  311, 313, 350
Emerita 407, 417, 420–21, 423, 428,
  430, 433
Emesa 97
Emporiae, Ampurias 180, 188, 430
Ephesus 5, 7, 10–11, 13, 62,
  84–85, 114, 150, 157, 260, 288,
  303, 323ff.
Epidaurus 288–290
Eretria 172
Erythrae 288, 290, 299ff.
Eryx 57

Gades 431
Gallaecia 410ff.
Gallus river 123ff, 398
Gela 55, 79
Germany 106
Gordion 83, 149, 224, 227, 229–30
Gortys Arcadiae 253
Gygaean Lake 7, 9

Harran 87ff.
Hatra 95
Hermus river 1, 2, 7, 13, 229
Hierapolis Mabbug 92, 94–95
Hierapolis Phrygiae 401
Hispania 405ff.
  Tarraconensis 407ff.
Hypaipa 7, 10–11, 13

Ida, Mt. (Crete) 247–48, 250ff, 261,
  267, 290, 294, 297–99
Ida, Mt. (Troad) 309, 311–13, 372,
  379, 381
  Idaean Dactyls 295, 298, 303

Imbros 74
Ios 277
Ithome, Mt. 253–54

Kaiseraugst, Augusta Rauricorum 182
Kalymnos 82, 151
Karios, Mt. 3, 12
Knossos, Cnossus 248–50, 252, 290

Laconia 53
Lebadeia 155, 158, 391
Lemnos 74
Lepcis Magna 177
Locri Epizephyrii 53, 228, 240, 303
Lusitania 407ff.
Lycaeus, Mt. 253–54
Lycosura 254
Lyctus, Lyttus 247–48, 250
Lydia, Lydians 1, 4, 5, 12, 107, 153,
  227–8, 246, 281, 283, 295–95, 303,
  309, 313, 332

Magnesia on the Meander 79, 302
Mago 411, 416, 419, 428
Mantineia 255
Meander river 1
Mecca 95–96
Megalopolis 254
Mesembria 110, 113, 155, 172–73,
  185
Messene 302
Metellinum 415, 417
Methydrium 253
Metapontum 54
Miletus 79, 223, 225ff., 240, 267
Moesia 101
Municipium Ficariense 413
Mylasa 4
Myrtilis 416
Mysia, Mysians 4

Naxos 267, 270
Neda river 253
Nisibis 87, 89
Noricum 106

Olbia 103, 106–07, 109, 111, 269,
  282
Olisipo 414–15, 417, 423, 426
Olympia 242, 254, 288, 290, 295–96,
  299, 301
Olynthus 72, 101, 153, 173–74, 349
Ossonaba 415, 417, 426
Ostia 392, 401

Palmyra 96
Pamphylia 79
Paros 242
Patras 152, 155
Pax Iulia 417, 421–23
Pergamum 62, 84–85, 149, 258, 332, 339, 352, 370ff.
Perinthus 270
Pessinus 48, 121, 125, 129–32, 180, 183, 233, 267, 370ff., 382
Philomelion 130–31
Phocaea 122, 260
Phrygia, Phrygians *passim*
  Phrygian highlands 225ff.
Piraeus 27, 108, 154, 197, 261, 280, 394
Potaissa 111
Potidaia 155

Rhodes 77–78, 80–81, 270–71, 279–80, 283
Rome 43, 45, 47, 50, 153, 155, 172, 233, 337ff.

Salmydessus 103
Samos 53, 150, 260, 274, 277
Samothrace 74, 81–83, 85, 154, 214, 353
Sangarius river 124, 130
Sardis 1, 5, 7–8, 84, 148, 274
Segisama 411, 428
Scythia, Scythians 104, 106, 350

Selinus 55
Sestus 122
Serdica 105
Sicily 55ff.
Sinope 229
Siris 53–54
Sipylus, Mt. 296ff.
Smyrna 79, 84, 297
Syracuse 55, 77

Tarraco 430, 433
Tegea 281
Tenos 158
Teos 147
Termessos 332
Thasos 147, 156, 241–42
Thebes 74, 210, 240, 246, 263ff., 277–78, 283
Thera 243, 271, 281
Thessaly 301
Thrace 101
Thugga 177
Tire 5, 7
Tmolus Mt. 1–3, 6–7, 10–13
Tomis 113, 142–43, 158
Torrhebia 3, 12–13
Trapezus 229
Troy 43

Ur 87, 89

Valentia 433
Velia 54

V. *Authors*

Accius 270, 281
Addai, Doctrine of 92, 94, 96
Aelius Aristides 84, 297
Alexander Aetolus 283, 285
Alexander Polyhistor 126, 128–32
Ammianus Marcellinus 90, 130
Antoninus Liberalis 287
Apollonius Rhodius 214, 150, 267–68, 291, 293, 295, 350, 359
Appian 324, 327, 329, 331
Aratus 250, 267
Aristophanes 308, 310
  Scholia in Aristophanem 318
Aristotle 212, 228, 393, 399, 403
Arnobius 126–28, 132, 363–64, 387ff.
Arrian 343

Artemidorus 206
Athenaeus 284, 295
Athenagoras 394
Augustine, St. 37, 41, 46, 48, 358, 390, 422, 433

Bacchylides 297
Biruni 98, 99

Callimachus 120, 125, 131–32, 250, 253, 256, 295, 365
Catullus 46, 357, 361, 375ff.
Celsus 48
Cicero 355–56, 374
Chrysippus 340
Cleanthes 340

Clemens Alexandrinus   284, 357, 388
Cleidemus   274, 293–94
Cornutus philosophus   218, 314, 398

Damascius   399, 401–02
Demetrius of Scepsis   292
Demosthenes   272, 309, 353
Dio Cassius   343
Dio Chrysostom   254
Diodorus Siculus   77, 353
Diogenes tragicus   308–09, 359
Diogenes Laertius   118, 132, 324,
   326, 328–29
Dionysius of Halicarnassus   341ff, 355
Dioscorides   118–120, 132

Ephorus   295
Ephraem Syrus   91–92
Eumelus of Corinth   6
Euripides   206, 211, 215, 217, 255,
   288–93, 308, 310ff., 352, 379
Eusebius   390

Firmicus Maternus   37–38, 125,
   130–31, 357, 388, 392

Hephaestion metricus   121
Heraclitus, commentator on
   Homer   388
Herodian grammaticus   126, 129–30,
   132
Herodian historicus   90, 125, 130
Herodotus   4, 11, 104, 227, 229, 282,
   304, 350
Hesiod   246–47, 249–50, 252, 256
Hesychius   283, 285
Hippolytus of Rome   393, 395–96
Hipponax   227, 239, 303
Homer   214, 277–78
   Homeric Hymns   211, 289ff., 306,
   309, 312
Horace   362

Iamblichus   397, 400, 427
Ibn al-Nadim   98
Isaac of Antioch   92
Isidore of Antioch   96

Jerome, St.   37, 39, 153
Juvenal   46–48

Livy   122, 327, 363, 367ff.
Lucian   94–95, 117, 213, 281,
   324–25, 328, 334, 427

Lucretius   218, 292–93, 339ff.,
   375–7, 379
Lycophron   263
Lydus, Joannes   6, 389

Macrobius   270–71, 281, 285,
   389, 392
Martianus Capella   125, 130, 392
Melanippides   313
Menander   213
"Musaeus"   256ff.

Nicander   203, 289, 283, 285
Nicolaus of Damascus   3, 327

Ovid   123, 125, 130, 221, 253–54,
   341ff, 362, 370

Paulinus of Nola   186
Pausanias   5, 62, 84, 126, 152, 212,
   237, 239, 246, 253–54, 257, 263–64,
   267, 275–76, 286–98, 353
Persius   361
Philo Judaeus   220
Philochorus   270–72, 274, 277, 281
Philodemus of Gadara   52, 347–8,
   360
Photius   314, 318
Pindar   51, 55, 209–210, 218, 240,
   264–67, 278, 298, 306, 313, 353,
   360
Plato   285, 393, 396
Plautus   324, 328–29, 331, 334
Pliny the elder   124–25, 130–31, 175,
   324, 327–29, 331
Plotinus   388, 390
Plutarch   4, 91, 175, 270, 277, 279,
   281, 324, 327–30, 391
Polemo rhetor   284–85
Pollux lexicographus   285
Polybius   42, 122, 350
Porphyry   251–52, 270–71, 278, 280,
   390–91, 385, 398, 401
Proclus Diadochus   40, 44, 392, 399
Promathidas   128
Propertius   362
Prudentius   41, 363–64, 422
pseudo-Heracleitus   324, 327, 328,
   331

Quintilian   117, 132, 324–25, 328,
   332–33

Rhianos of Crete   200ff.

Sallustius philosophus 44, 126, 131, 394
Scholiast on Aeschines 314, 317
Semonides 303
Seneca 48
Simplicius 400
Sophocles 308
"Spartianus" historicus 90
Statius 381
Strabo 2–4, 6, 13, 69, 222, 324, 329–334, 372
Symmachus 44–45
Synesius 400

Tacitus 46

Telestes of Selinus 295–96, 301
Tertullian 39, 48
Theocritus 380
Theodoretus of Cyrus 186
Thucydides 274
Thyillus 353, 356
"Timotheus" 126–27, 132, 387–88, 402

Valerius Messala, M. 389ff, 397
Varro 38, 46, 341, 352, 356, 358, 370–72, 390

Xanthus of Lydia 3, 6
Xenophon 324, 326, 328–330, 334

VI. *Other significant persons and topics*

Abraham 98
Agorakritos sculptor 198, 243, 308
Anacharsis 104, 282, 304, 350
Antony, Marc 49, 324, 327
Apelles pictor 324–35
Apollonius of Tyana 37
Arcesilaus philosophus 118
Attis (priest's name) 122

Bagoas 325, 333
Battakes 122

Cato the elder 50, 115
"Chaldaean oracles" 393, 397ff.
Corpus Hermeticum 396
criobolium 4, 284, 413, 417, 419, 421, 426, 429

Epimenides 251, 267
Essenes, priests 325, 331–32
evocatio 372

Fabius Maximus, Q. 367
Fabius Pictor, Q. 368–69

Galaxia, festival 241ff, 272
galli 46, 47, 49, 109, 117ff., 193ff., 281, 343, 357, 373–374, 378, 382, 390, 394–95
George, patriarch of Alexandria 395–96

Hannibal 345, 367–69
Hilaria, festival 40, 402

kernos, cernus 283ff, 420, 422
Kleisthenes, Athenian reformer 307
Kronia, festival 240, 245, 270ff.

lavatio 339, 343, 345
Livius Salinator, C. 122

Manlius Vulso 122
"megabyzoi" 323ff.
Megalensia, festival 343–45, 370, 374, 382
Montanus, Montanism 38–40
Moses 37, 417
"Museum" hill, Athens 255ff, 290

Naassenians 393ff, 403

Parabiago lanx 155, 215, 218
Peisistratus, tyrant of Athens 276
Pheidias sculptor 243
Pythagoras 251–52

quindecimviri sacris faciundis 374

taurobolium 40–41, 44–45, 50, 212, 284, 339, 378, 391, 406, 413, 417ff.
Themistocles 279
Timoleon 76
Trophonia, festival 283, 286

Vestal Virgins 368
Volteius, M., moneyer 344–45

RELIGIONS IN
THE GRAECO-ROMAN WORLD

Recent publications:

114. GREEN, T.M., *The City of the Moon God.* Religious Traditions of Harran. 1992. ISBN 90 04 09513 6

115. TROMBLEY, F.R., *Hellenic Religion and Christianization c. 370-529.*
Volume 1. Reprint 1995. ISBN 90 04 09624 8
Volume 2. Reprint 1995. ISBN 90 04 09691 4

116. FRIESEN, S.J., *Twice Neokoros.* Ephesus, Asia and the Cult of the Flavian Imperial Family. 1993. ISBN 90 04 09689 2

117. HORNUM, M.B., *Nemesis, the Roman State, and the Games.* 1993. ISBN 90 04 09745 7

118. LIEU, S.N.C., *Manichaeism in Mesopotamia and the Roman East.* 1994. ISBN 90 04 09742 2

119. PIETERSMA, A., *The Apocryphon of Jannes and Jambres the Magicians.* P. Chester Beatty XVI (with New Editions of Papyrus Vindobonensis Greek inv. 29456 + 29828 verso and British Library Cotton Tiberius B. v f. 87). Edited with Introduction, Translation and Commentary. With full facsimile of all three texts. 1994. ISBN 90 04 09938 7

120. BLOK, J.H., *The Early Amazons.* Modern and Ancient Perspectives on a Persistent Myth. 1994. ISBN 90 04 10077 6

121. MEYBOOM, P.G.P., *The Nile Mosaic of Palestrina.* Early Evidence of Egyptian Religion in Italy. 1994. ISBN 90 04 10137 3

122. McKAY, H.A., *Sabbath and Synagogue.* The Question of Sabbath Worship in Ancient Judaism. 1994. ISBN 90 04 10060 1

123. THOM, J.C., *The Pythagorean Golden Verses.* With Introduction and Commentary. 1994. ISBN 90 04 10105 5

124. TAKÁCS, S.A., *Isis and Sarapis in the Roman World.* 1994. ISBN 90 04 10121 7

125. FAUTH, W., *Helios Megistos.* Zur synkretistischen Theologie der Spätantike. 1995. ISBN 90 04 10194 2

126. RUTGERS, L.V., *The Jews in Late Ancient Rome.* Evidence of Cultural Interaction in the Roman Diaspora. 1995. ISBN 90 04 10269 8

127. STRATEN, F.T. VAN, *Hierà kalá*. Images of Animal Sacrifice in Archaic and Classical Greece. 1995. ISBN 90 04 10292 2

128. DIJKSTRA, K., *Life and Loyalty*. A Study in the Socio-Religious Culture of Syria and Mesopotamia in the Graeco-Roman Period Based on Epigraphical Evidence. 1995.
ISBN 90 04 09996 4

129. MEYER M. & MIRECKI P. (eds.). *Ancient Magic and Ritual Power*. 1995. ISBN 90 04 10406 2

130. SMITH, M.; COHEN, S.J.D. (ed.). *Studies in the Cult of Yahweh*. 2 volumes. 1996. ISBN 90 04 10372 4 (set)
Vol. 1: *Studies in Historical Method, Ancient Israel, Ancient Judaism*. 1996. ISBN 90 04 10477 1
Vol. 2: *Studies in New Testament, Early Christianity, and Magic*. 1996. ISBN 90 04 10479 8

131. LANE, E.N. (ed.). *Cybele, Attis and Related Cults*. Essays in Memory of M.J. Vermaseren. 1996. ISBN 90 04 10196 9